The Economics of Missing Markets, Information, and Games

The Economics of Missing Markets, Information, and Games

edited by
FRANK HAHN

CLARENDON PRESS · OXFORD
1990

Oxford University Press, Walton Street, Oxford OX2 6DP
Oxford New York Toronto
Delhi Bombay Calcutta Madras Karachi
Petaling Jaya Singapore Hong Kong Tokyo
Nairobi Dar es Salaam Cape Town
Melbourne Auckland
and associated companies in
Berlin Ibadan

Oxford is a trade mark of Oxford University Press

Published in the United States
by Oxford University Press, New York

First published 1989
Hardback reprinted (with revisions) 1990
Paperback first published 1990

British Library Cataloguing in Publication Data
The Economics of missing markets,
information, and games.
1. Economics
1. Hahn, F. H. (Frank Horace), 1925–
330
ISBN 0–19–828615–5
ISBN 0–19–828321–0 (Pbk)

Library of Congress Cataloging in Publication Data
The Economics of missing markets,
information, and games.
Bibliography: Includes index.
1. Equilibrium (Economics) 2. Game theory.
3. Information theory in economics. I. Hahn, Frank.
HB145.E27 1989 339.5 88–25487
ISBN 0–19–828615–5
ISBN 0–19–828321–0 (Pbk)

Printed and bound in
Great Britain by Biddles Ltd
Guildford and King's Lynn

Preface

For a number of years, economic theorists in Cambridge have been involved in a project entitled 'Information, Risk, and Quantity Signals in Economics'. All the authors in this volume have been members of that project. The aim of this collection is to give some account of the work, both of others and of ourselves, which we consider to be on the right road. Technicalities have been kept low, which, however, does not mean that there aren't any. But readers should have no difficulties with the central points that are being made. More technical papers have appeared in the journals and in our Discussion Paper series.

The project group meets weekly without agenda (which is why, somewhat whimsically, we call them 'Quaker meetings'). These meetings we regard not only as very successful but also as enjoyable. I hope that this will also be found the case with this book.

The Cambridge project has benefited from ESRC support. It is in the nature of theoretical work that one cannot at all accurately predict the questions that will be found most urgent and interesting, let alone the probable answers. The ESRC has shown that it understands this, and it has never pressed us to be more specific in our plans than would be sensible. For this and for their support, I record our gratitude here.

F. H. HAHN

Contents

PART IV

PART V

PART VI

1

Introduction

FRANK HAHN

The unifying element both in the Cambridge project and in the papers that follow has been the conviction that it was urgent to move beyond the Walrasian paradigm without abandoning the commitment to lucid and rigorous theorizing in which Arrow and Debreu have so memorably pointed the way. It is not the case that we consider Walrasian theory to be useless—far from it. But we do regard it as seriously incomplete.

The theory is incomplete in a number of ways. We now know that its formulation can avoid contradiction (between the postulate of rational self-seeking and perfect competition) only when the economy is very large. Since when production is included actual economies do not seem large enough, one cannot sensibly leave matters there. Agents in economies that are not perfectly competitive will often have to act strategically, and to study such action one is naturally led to game theory, which is rather prominently represented in this volume.

But there are other gaps in the traditional theory. In particular, it is now widely recognized that it postulates there to be many more markets (in particular, insurance markets and markets for future delivery) than we can observe. 'Missing markets' lead to reformulations and questions. The economy has to be studied as one in which there is trading at every date. This in turn requires agents to formulate expectations concerning future market signals in different states of the world. One can postulate that these are 'rational', that is, that each agent knows the future price of every good as a function of the state of nature. However, one is then naturally led to ask how such expectations come to be held; that is, one will be interested in the difficult and very open questions of the learning by agents and with the interaction of such learning with what there is to be learned. Some progress (notably by Margaret Bray) has been made here, but a very great deal remains to be done.

However, one also wants to know why particular markets are missing; can the existence or non-existence of markets be itself a matter for a theory to settle rather than to take exogenously? Here one is at once face to face with the problem of information and information transmittal, a subject now studied very actively in many places. Traditional theory, by neglecting to give explicit attention to informational matters (and so incidentally neglecting some very important world phenomena like fiat money), has had very little to say about institutions that are directly related to asymmetric or imperfect information (e.g. the licensing of doctors, banks, and shops). It also had to be silent on the strategic uses of information (e.g. in innovations and in competition between sellers of a good whose quality is only imperfectly known by the customer). Once this was realized, the matter received much attention and very considerable new insights have been gained. We now understand the need for and importance of incentive compatibility in some markets and in some arrangements which are themselves the consequence of missing markets (e.g. labour contracts). We can study institutions like auctions (see Maskin and Riley, Chapter 14), which are governed by the circumstance that the seller does not know the buyers' reserve prices. We have gained greater insights into market revelation of private information.

Many of these informational problems will be discussed in the papers that follow. (See particularly Anderlini's study of asymmetric information and banks—Chapter 13.) But so far neither we nor, as far as I know, anyone else has managed to integrate the new insights into a comprehensive theory of the economy in the manner of Walrasian theory. This may come, but it has not yet done so. Particularly promising are possible 'first-shot' macroeconomic applications. (The contributions of Makowski, Chapter 21, and Thomas, Chapter 19, are in this direction.) For instance, both the credit market and the labour market are now much more realistically understood, but they need to be brought together in at least a simple model of an economy with information that is both imperfect and market-dependent.

However, it is clear already that welfare economics will be much changed. (See the contribution of Newbery who, of all of us, has managed to say most without algebra—Chapter 10.) The relatively simple Pigouvian formulae are insufficient when, in certain directions, the actions of agents are not co-ordinated by any market. Questions such as the relation of industrial structure to the desired rate of R and D, that is information-seeking activity, are relatively new and only now in the process of being answered. (See Dasgupta's contribution and some of his perhaps somewhat surprising conclusions—Chapter 6.) Certainly, the 'fundamental theorems of welfare economics' do not apply to the world that we are beginning to explore. It seems to me that rather fundamental questions concerning the virtues and vices of market economies may now be nearer to receiving realistic theoretical attention than they have been for some time.

There are thus many questions for which the Walrasian theory will not suffice simply because it has been constructed in a manner that does not allow these questions to be asked. But there are also purely 'internal' problems with the theory, and some of our work has concentrated on these.

It has now been realized that the theory lacks determinateness not because 'everything depends on everything else', but because there are too many equilibrium outcomes. (For a general discussion see Hahn's Chapter 5.) Partly this is due to a realization that it does not make sense to give an economy a predetermined (finite) horizon—that is, one for which in principle no terminal date can be postulated. (It should be remarked that if it *is* postulated other unpleasant theoretical consequences may be entailed; e.g., fiat money would be valueless.) In recent years much work has been done on a particular version of an open-ended (Walrasian) economy in the form of a model of overlapping generations. Three of the papers are concerned with this (Kehoe, Burnell, and Kelsey—Chapters 16, 17, and 18). This analysis confirms not only that there are many Walrasian equilibria (often a continuum), but also that some of these are of the 'bootstrap' variety; that is, the economy behaves as it does because agents hold beliefs conditioned on economically irrelevant events. These events (sunspots or, indeed, the money stock) have no relevance to the 'real' opportunities open to the economy. Besides giving an account of the work in this field pioneered by others, some further extensions will be found in the contributions that follow. It is hoped also that Kelsey's exposition of the technicalities of nonlinear difference equations and their rich possibilities will be found helpful. Burnell in particular is explicit in relating this new theory to the standard Walrasian model.

However, the Walrasian theory is not alone in its determinacy troubles; game theory too has had the difficulty of finding far too many equilibria. Kreps and Sabourian discuss this extensively and put forward various proposals in Chapters 2 and 4, respectively. Canning, on the other hand, gives an account of certain bargaining games that avoid these problems—but at a cost (Chapter 8). It is already clear not only that, until some progress is made here, the project of constructing a theory of the economy with strategically acting agents cannot proceed with any confidence, but also that some very 'deep' issues are involved. Thus, Brandenburger and Dekel's account of 'common knowledge' and his proposal for an 'equilibrium of beliefs' (Chapter 3) not only confirm that there may be too many equilibria but also highlight the unsatisfactory nature of a basic hypothesis that game theory, and economic theory generally, share. That is the postulate of the complete rationality and computational ability of economic agents and, in the case of common knowledge, the possession by agents of a great deal of information about each other. There is now much active research designed to find less demanding postulates, but there is a very long way to go. It may well be that paying more explicit attention to learning and to the process by which it takes place will be, as Hahn argues in Chapter 5, of some help in tying down equilibria. But so far this and other proposals are only straws in the wind.

One particular aspect of rationality which is of central importance to the whole line of enquiry is choice under uncertainty, which is discussed (with his own well-known proposals) by Machina (Chapter 12). Here too more work awaits us, for the theory is still far too demanding to be descriptively satisfactory. Brandenburger (1986b) and Bewley (1986, 1987) have taken more radical steps by relaxing one or the other of Savage's axioms. This looks like a very promising start.

What all of this amounts to is the recognition that we are only at a beginning of enlarging the domain of applicability of economic theory. However, there has been progress, much made by others (which is reported on below), some by ourselves. An example is the attempt to explain the international exchange of similar goods which we all observe. Gatsios reports on this and makes his own contribution (Chapter 9). He uses miniature general equilibrium models which, however, allow market power and increasing returns. While this work relies on a number of rather special constructs and is indeed pared down to essentials, I think it is clear that it at least provides the beginning of understanding. The same is surely true of the labour contract literature which is examined by Worrall (Chapter 15) and of Doyle (Chapter 7), who puts the theory of games with asymmetric information to use on a concrete observed phenomenon and allows us to see how it might be explained.

I hope that I have been able to give an account of a common theme of these, at first sight rather disparate, papers. There are many directions in which we must go if we are to understand the many economic phenomena that are out of the range of tradition. Tradition itself must recognize some of its purely internal problems. On the other hand, tradition also matters. While none of us (I believe) has much sympathy for attempts by hook or crook to fit actual economic data into a (vastly simplified) Walrasian framework, it is also the case that we know that framework to have been, and to continue to be, of great importance to economic theory. A genius may arise and make it totally obsolete. But the rest of us must think our way step by step to a richer and more satisfactory construction.

PART I

2

Out-of-equilibrium Beliefs and Out-of-equilibrium Behaviour

DAVID M. KREPS

1. Introduction

The purpose of this chapter is to explore recent work concerning so-called refinements of Nash equilibrium, especially in the context of signalling games. In brief, a refinement of the notion of a Nash equilibrium is a condition added to the basic requirement that each player choose a best response to the choices of others. I concentrate here on refinements that are built from restrictions on the beliefs that players are presumed to hold when they find themselves faced with a situation of zero prior probability, and the restrictions on out-of-equilibrium actions that those out-of-equilibrium beliefs entail. In the course of the essay, I offer a categorization of some of the refinements according to stories about out-of-equilibrium thought processes that various authors tell. Also, I argue that the validity of a particular refinement for the analysis of a particular economic issue may depend on the setting of that issue in ways that go beyond the formal game-theoretic model that is adopted. That is, it is almost tautological to say that the appropriate model of a particular situation is determined by the reality that one is seeking to understand or explain. I argue that the same may be true of the tool employed to analyse the model; certain refinements of Nash equilibrium are more or less appropriate for the analysis of certain situations, based on considerations outside the formal model. More precisely, what is or is not a reasonable refinement to apply can turn on one's hypotheses about the source of out-of-equilibrium conjectures, which may not be captured very well by the formal extensive-form game model.[1]

I attempt to provide readers with a brief introduction to some of the

I have benefited from conversation and correspondence with many people concerning the subject of this essay, and without implicating them, I wish to thank Anat Admati, Adam Brandenburger, In-koo Cho, Drew Fudenberg, John Hillas, David Newbery, Garey Ramey, Hamid Sabourian, Hugo Sonnenschein, and especially Jean-Francois Mertens. The financial support of the National Science Foundation (Grant SES84-08586) and the Alfred P. Sloan Foundation are gratefully acknowledged.

[1] In the concluding remarks, I will discuss briefly the contrary position that, by building a sufficiently detailed and rich model, the formal theory can incorporate the relevant considerations. While I believe this to be so in theory, models sufficiently detailed and rich would tend to be intractible for purposes of analysis of applications.

ideas behind several of the refinements. However, my treatment is very informal and is aimed at readers who have not followed this literature. Accordingly, much space is devoted to background and to motivation; and when the heart of the matter is (finally) reached, only illustrative examples are given. The reader who finds these issues interesting will certainly have to consult the more formal and exact original treatments of these issues, in order to understand some of the subtle issues involved. Even more so, the treatment is incomplete; many important ideas have been omitted.[2] This essay is not meant to be a complete survey of the field or even a precise survey of a part of the field; rather, it is meant as a (rather opinionated) introduction to some of the motivating concepts.

The chapter is organized as follows. In Section 2, I recall what I consider to be an important source of interest in these questions: the model of market signalling, due to Spence (1974) and Rothschild and Stiglitz (1976), and the problem of out-of-equilibrium signals.

Section 3 provides background. The formal models of extensive games that will be used and, in particular, the formal model of a signalling game are introduced. The basic concept of a Nash equilibrium is discussed, and I give a brief selection of possible answers to the question, Why would anyone use the notion of a Nash equilibrium to analyse a non-cooperative game? The first notion of refinement (of the sorts I discuss here), the sequential equilibrium, is presented, and the issue of restrictions on out-of-equilibrium beliefs is posed.

Sections 4, 5, and 6 examine a number of examples of games which introduce a few of the going sorts of refinements. These sections are organized according to the stories that underpin the refinements discussed. In Section 4 deviations from an equilibrium are thought of simply as mistakes; in Section 5 they are explained by the hypothesis that there is some confusion as to what players ought to do; in Section 6 they are thought of as conscious attempts to signal something.

In Section 7 we return to the market signalling application. The power of the 'conscious signals' refinements for that application is shown, and a brief argument is given in favour of that sort of refinement for this particular application, owing to the ability of economic actors in the setting of market signalling to accompany their deviations with explanations of what the deviation may mean. Concluding remarks are given in Section 8.

2. Motivation—Market Signalling

Among the most important models in the economics of information are those in which one party, possessed of superior information, attempts a

---

[2] In particular, very few words are addressed towards refinements that are based on normal form considerations, most especially the *stability* criterion of Kohlberg and Mertens (1986).

transaction with a second party who lacks that information. Akerlof's (1970) model of the market for lemons shows that, in such conditions, the problem of adverse selection can cause a substantial market failure. If a seller of a good knows things about the quality of the good that the buyer does not know, then the buyer may suspect that the good being purchased is possibly of poor quality and will wish to pay accordingly. The seller, then, will tender the good for sale only if a price appropriate for a good of average quality is enough to make the sale worthwhile. In some cases this causes the highest-quality goods to be withdrawn from the market, with a corresponding decrease in the average quality of goods tendered, and a corresponding decrease in the price any buyer is willing to pay. In extreme cases, only the lowest-quality goods will be offered for sale; the informational asymmetry causes the market virtually to collapse. (That is, Gresham's Law rules the market-place.)

Of course, there are market mechanisms that may alleviate this problem. The party possessed of superior information may seek to communicate that information to the other party to the transaction. If I wish to sell a used car, I may go to a reputable garage and have them inspect the car and issue a report concerning the quality of the car. If by some such means the quality of the good can be communicated from one side to the other in reliable and relatively cheap fashion, then the market failure may be avoided.

But suppose that there is no means by which the information privately held by one side to the transaction can reliably and cheaply be made public. The side possessed of the information may then seek some indirect means for signalling what he knows. By an indirect means is meant some signal which *indicates* but does not fully *verify* the precise information. We are especially interested here in signals that *can* be sent by the first party, no matter what is the first party's private information, but which are relatively more or less expensive to send, depending on that private information. Taking the case of used cars, arrayed in terms of quality, if there is a signal that is cheaper for the owner of a good used car to send than it is for the owner of a lemon (e.g. offering the buyer a limited warranty), then we might expect that owners of good used cars will send that signal to prospective buyers, to distinguish themselves from the owners of poor cars, so as to obtain a higher price.

This, of course, is the *market signalling* model of Spence (1974) and Rothschild and Stiglitz (1976). Spence models education as a signal of ability. Rothschild and Stiglitz speaks in terms of a party buying insurance, where the type of policy purchased signals the party's degree of risk. Since those seminal papers, the same idea has been studied in many contexts, among which are: the use of capital structure to indicate an entrepreneur's quality (Ross 1977); the use of warranties to indicate product quality (Grossman 1981b); the use of prices to indicate costs in an oligopoly setting (Milgrom and Roberts 1982); the use of advertising to indicate product quality (Milgrom and Roberts 1986); the use of the willingness to go to court to indicate the strength of one's case in a lawsuit (among others, Reinganum and Wilde 1986); and the use of delay to indicate bargaining strength in bilateral bargaining (among others, Rubinstein 1985a and Admati and Perry 1987).

The nature of an equilibrium in such models invariably involves the following invocation of rational expectations about the market signals. In equilibrium, the signal sent by the party with superior information is given by some function of that party's information: owners of a car of quality x send signal $\mathbf{f}(x)$; workers of ability level y obtain education level $\mathbf{e}(y)$; and so on. This function is assumed to be known to the other party: having seen signal f, the other side infers that the car in question is of a quality x that satisfies $\mathbf{f}(x) = f$. Note that f needn't be one-to-one—there may be many quality levels x, x', x'', all of which use the same signal $f = \mathbf{f}(x) = \mathbf{f}(x') = \mathbf{f}(x'')$ in equilibrium; then the second party infers that the quality is of one of these levels, and not of a level that sends some other signal f'. The second party, seeing the signal, uses knowledge of the signalling function to infer whatever can be inferred about the first party, and deals accordingly. And, what is the basic equilibrium condition, assuming that the second party will act in this fashion, the first party's optimal signal is the signal prescribed by the signalling function. That is, suppose that the cars come in one of three quality levels, x or x' or x''. Suppose that, in equilibrium, the first party is meant to send signal f in the first two cases and f'' in the third. The second party, then, will interpret f as meaning that the car is either of quality x or of quality x', and f'' as meaning that the car has quality x''. Then we ask, *if* the informed party has a car of quality x', would he prefer to signal f'' ('misrepresenting' himself as having a car of quality x''), and being treated accordingly, rather than send f, as he is supposed to do? Only when the answer is no to all such questions do we have an equilibrium.

We will use the following terminology from this literature. When, in equilibrium, the same signal is sent by the informed party no matter what his private information is (when $\mathbf{f}$ is a constant function of x), we have a *pooling* equilibrium. When each piece of private information is accompanied by a different signal (when $\mathbf{f}$ is one-to-one), we have a *separating* or a *screening* equilibrium. Of course, in general, there will be equilibria that exhibit pooling of some types of private information, and screening of others (as in the simple scenario just sketched.)

There are many important questions left open in this basic story. One that is especially important concerns the origination of the signals. Consider, for example, the context of an insurance market (Rothschild and Stiglitz 1976). Here the market signal sent by the informed party (in this case, the insuree) is the particular policy purchased. In many contexts, it is reasonable to suppose that the insuree is limited to selecting from among those policies that the various insurance companies offer. That is, the uninformed side of the market offers a menu of contracts to the informed side: send such and such a signal, and you will be treated in such and such a fashion. The informed side then acts somewhat passively, taking up that contract from among the menu of offered contracts that best suits it. The point is that the menu of contracts originates with the uninformed. The informed party might wish to send some signal not among those that are offered, but in this story that wish goes unfulfilled. (One is led, in this case, to interesting questions concerning the dynamics of how the market bundle of offered contracts arises; the nature of competition among insurance companies becomes the issue.)

Contrast this with a story in which the informed party takes the active role. The insuree, for example, might present to the insurer a particular insurance contract, with all the terms (including the premium) specified, asking the insurer whether it is prepared to undertake this particular contract. A variation would have the insuree propose to several insurers a particular contract lacking only the specification of the premium, inviting those insurers to bid (in, say, a sealed bid tender auction) premia that they will charge for the contract; the insuree will take up the contract with whichever company asks for the smallest premium. In either variation, it is the informed party that takes the initiative, proposing a contract, and it is the uninformed party (or parties) that takes the relatively more passive role.

The distinction concerning which side takes the initiative is important (see, for example, the analysis in Stiglitz and Weiss 1985). Analysis has tended to the conclusion that, when the uninformed party has the active role, pooling equilibria are relatively more likely to occur, while screening is more likely when the informed party has the active role. (We will see an explanation of the second part of this assertion in Section 7.)

In this essay, we will think in terms of situations in which it is the informed party that takes the active role. In this case, another question that arises concerning any purported equilibrium is, What inferences do the uninformed parties make of signals from the informed party that are not sent at all in the equilibrium?

That is, in our description of the equilibrium condition, we have supposed that the uninformed has rational expectations concerning what particular signals mean (in terms of the private information of the informed party), obtained by inverting the equilibrium signalling function f. But what conclusions are drawn when the signal received is some value f that is not in the range of the function f at all—when no sort of private information is supposed to lead to this signal? The inferences that are drawn from such signals (and the responses that thereupon ensue) turn out to be very important to particular equilibria; what keeps the informed party from sending such a signal in equilibrium is precisely the response that he expects it will engender. It turns out (and we will see later) that, if we can suitably restrict the inferences that are drawn from signals that are not sent in equilibrium, we can often say a great deal about the nature of possible equilibria. Accordingly, analysts have looked for suitable restrictions on such inferences—this provides the motivation for the sort of refinements that we discuss here.

We will return, then, to questions of market signalling in Section 7. But first we will follow the tendency of recent literature, which is to consider the inferences made about *out-of-equilibrium* actions in the abstract setting of non-cooperative game theory.

3. Extensive Games, Nash Equilibria, and Sequential Equilibria

3.1. *Extensive games and signalling games*

(Readers who know how to read the games depicted in Figures 2.1 and 2.2 may skip this subsection. A more formal treatment of extensive form games, done in the style used here, is in Kreps and Wilson 1982.)

We investigate extensive form games, such as the game depicted in Figure 2.1. In this particular game, there are two possible initial starting points, or *initial nodes*, depicted by the two open circles. The choice of

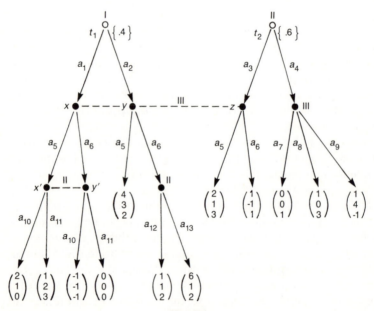

Fig. 2.1

an initial node is made by nature, according to some probability distribution that is part of the data of the game. This probability distribution is denoted by the numbers in curly brackets; in Figure 2.1 we begin at the node t_1 with probability 0.4 and at node t_2 with probability 0.6. (In general, initial nodes will be indexed t_k.) From any initial node, the game can follow a path that moves from node to node along directed arcs, until an endpoint is reached. At each node (open or closed circle), the rules of the game prescribe that a particular player is called upon to move. Players are denoted by Roman numerals I, II, . . . , and in our depictions the Roman numeral next to a node says whose move it is. So, in Figure 2.1, player I has the move at node t_1, player II has the move at t_2, and player III has the move at the node furthest to the right in the second row of nodes. When the player has the move, he chooses from among a list of possible moves or actions at that node, which are depicted by the directed arcs emanating from the node. These moves/arcs will typically be labelled; for example, at the node t_1, player I chooses between actions a_1 and a_2. At the end of each path along these arcs, payoffs are made to the players, given by a vector of numbers—the payoff to player I is listed first, to player II second, to player III third, and so on. So, for example, if the game starts at t_2, player II chooses a_4, and player III (who moves next) chooses a_9; then player I nets 1, player II nets 4, and player III nets -1. Payoffs are in units of cardinal utility—players act in order to maximize their expected payoff.

The one complicating feature in these games concerns what are called *information sets*. Suppose that, in the game described, if the game starts at node t_1 and player I chooses either of his two choices at t_1, or if we begin at t_2 and player II chooses a_3, then it will be player III's turn to move. But player III will not know which of the three sequences of events has led to this choice. That is, player III is called upon to move at the three nodes labelled x, y, and z, but when he does move he doesn't know at which of the three he is. We depict this by joining the three by a dashed line as shown; this says that these three nodes are an information set for the player that is called upon to move. We indicate which player that is by putting the Roman numeral along the dashed line—in Figure 2.1, player III moves at the information set $\{x, y, z\}$. We will always assume that the same player has the move at all nodes in a particular information set (player III has the move at each of x, y, and z) and that the actions the player has available at various nodes in an information set are all the same (player III has available either a_5 or a_6 at each of these three nodes.) Note also the information set consisting of nodes x' and y'—this information set belongs, according to the picture, to player II. At this information set, player II will know that the game began at t_1 and that player I chose a_1, but player II will not know which action player III selected at the information set $\{x, y, z\}$.

In looking at these games, we will always assume that players have *perfect recall*. This means that each player always remembers, if he moves some time after an earlier move that he made, (1) that he did move earlier, (2) how he moved, and (3) anything he might have known when he moved. The casual reader can rest assured that all our examples will have this property; the reader interested in the formal development of these ideas should consult one of the more technical references for a definition (for example, Kreps and Wilson 1982).

Signalling games form a subset of all extensive games that are of particular importance to the subject of refinements. A typical signalling game is depicted in Figure 2.2. There are two players, indexed I and II. Then game begins at one of a set of possible initial nodes, denoted (when finite) by $t_1, t_2, \ldots, t_n$; in the figure, there are three possible starting points. Player I always moves first, and always with knowledge concerning which is the starting point of the game. (Note that none of the initial nodes is joined together in information sets.) It is usual in the literature to refer to player I as being of *type k* when the starting point is t_k. Player I, at each initial node, has a list of possible messages that he can send to player II, denoted by m, m', m'', and so on. After player I sends his message, player II may be called upon to move. (In Figure 2.2 player II does not respond to m''.) Player II always knows which message has been sent, but does not (otherwise) know the type (initial node) of player I. So in Figure 2.2 the nodes that follow message m form one information set of player II, while those following message m' form a second. Note that

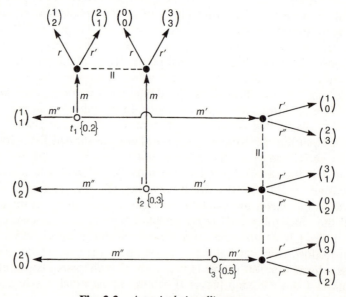

Fig. 2.2 *A typical signalling game.*

message m is not available to player I if he is of type t_3; hence if II hears the message m, II knows that the game began at either t_1 or t_2. At each of player II's information sets, player II has a list of possible responses, labelled r, r', etc. Then payoffs are made. We will use the notation $u(t, m, r)$ and $v(t, m, r)$ to denote payoffs to players I and II, respectively, as a function of the initial node t, message m, and response r.

A signalling game is meant to capture formally the salient aspects of the market signalling situation described in Section 2, when it is the informed party that has the initiative in sending signals. Player I is the party with private information, and the various possible starting nodes or types of the player correspond to the various pieces of private information that the party might have. So we might think of t_1 as representing a situation in which the informed party has a good used car to sell, t_2 a mediocre car, and t_3 a real lemon. The various market signals that the informed party can send are represented by the various messages that can be sent. For example, suppose that the owner of the car can have an inspection performed that will signify that the car is either good or mediocre, without distinguishing between these two, but definitely ruling out the possibility that the car is a lemon. Such an inspection (or, rather, the report of such an inspection) would be represented by a message such as m, which is possible only for types t_1 or t_2. Finally, the responses to the message of the uninformed type are depicted by the responses in the game. Note that it is assumed that .the uninformed player responds knowing what message was sent, but not (otherwise) knowing anything about the private information of the informed player.

Three comments on this formulation of the market signalling situation as a signalling game are in order.

1. In many applications, we will wish there to be an infinite number of possible types, and/or an infinite number of possible signals, and/or an infinite number of possible responses. Most of the formal theory of equilibrium refinements assumes that each of these objects is finite in number. I will describe the formal development assuming a finite number of types, messages, and responses; one must, in the end, make something of a leap of either faith or, at least, interpretation to apply these ideas to contexts of economic interest.
2. In many applications, there is more than one uninformed party involved. (Indeed, in the applications one thinks of both sides of the market being thick, although this has little impact on what follows.) One might wish a for more general model of a signalling game, in which more than one player responds to the signal sent by the first. This, however, turns out not to be crucial to the equilibrium refinements that are put forward in the literature—this will be indicated in Section 7.

3. In some applications, the informed and uninformed parties exchange messages and responses in iterative fashion. The simplest example of this is in back-and-forth bargaining. For such cases, one would prefer a signalling game where the two sides engage in something more complex than the simple one message–one response interaction described. Some of the work in equilibrium refinements has looked at such games; on a first cut, however, it is easier to stay with the simple signalling game outlined above.

3.2. Nash equilibrium

Having posed a game, either in general extensive form or of the restricted class of signalling games, analysis typically moves to finding *Nash equilibria* of the game. A Nash equilibrium consists of a specification of action for every player at every information set such that, given the actions of other players at their information sets, no player can unilaterally deviate at the information sets at which he acts and do strictly better in terms of his overall expected payoff. In specifying actions at information sets, we allow players to randomize—to take one action with probability p and another with probability $1 - p$, if both those actions (together with the others the player takes at other information sets at which he moves) are best responses to the actions of other players.

   In very simple games such as the one in Figure 2.3. It is easy to compute a Nash equilibrium via backwards iteration. Given that player II is given the move in the figure, player II will choose u, that being better than d. Player I, in consequence, does best to choose r; given that II will choose u, r nets 2 for player I, as against the 1 that I nets from l. A slightly more complex game is shown in Figure 2.4. Here we can't be sure which action is better for player II at his information set without knowing what player I is meant to do; if I chooses l, then d is better, while if I chooses r, then u is better for II. But we note that, whatever action II takes, I is better off with r than with l. Hence II, expecting r, chooses u.

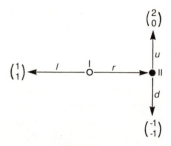

Fig. 2.3

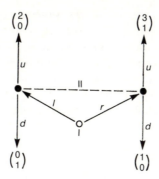

Fig. 2.4

Note well that the assertion that I does better with *r* than with *l* irrespective of the choice of action by II involves implicitly the assumption that II's action at each of the two nodes in his information set must be the same.

These are very easy games to analyse. A more complicated game is shown in Figure 2.5. Here there are two Nash equilibria: if player I chooses *r*, then *u* is a best choice of player II, and if II chooses *u*, then *r* is best for I. But also, the pair of choices *l* and *d* is a Nash equilibrium—each is a best response to the other. (There is a third Nash equilibrium to this game, where each player randomizes in a manner that makes the other player indifferent between his two choices.) What does one do in this case?

Sensible answers to this question are impossible without asking first, For what reason does one compute the Nash equilibria of a game? Put another way, To what question is 'Nash equilibrium' the answer? This question is not so easy to answer as one might think, given the prevalence of Nash equilibrium analysis in non-cooperative game theory. Most

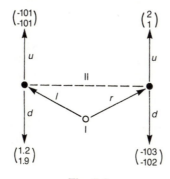

Fig. 2.5

answers to this question run as follows. Suppose that, in the situation that the game models, the players can see, by some means at the moment unspecified, a 'rational way' to play the game. That is, each player sees for himself a clear-cut course of action, and he sees a clear-cut course of action for every other player, which, he believes, all the others see as well. If such a single prescription of actions for all the players does exist, then it is *necessary* that the prescription constitute a Nash equilibrium. Otherwise, some single player, believing that others will carry out their part of the prescribed actions, can deviate and do strictly better for himself.[3]

This does not say that such a 'rational way' prescription does exist in every game, or in any particular game. We do not establish sufficient conditions for such a prescription to exist. We only assert that, if such a prescription does exist, it is necessary that the prescription is a Nash equilibrium. In cases where there is no clear-cut prescription for how to act, then those Nash equilibria that do exist have no particular claim on us. Examples are easy to construct in which, because there is no clear-cut prescription that seems to arise among most players, players will often choose actions that are part of *no* Nash equilibrium. (See, for example, the game in Table 2 of Kreps 1987.)

How might such a prescription arise? At least four sorts of answers are suggested by the literature.

1. In the games of Figures 2.3 and 2.4, we reasoned in terms of *dominance*. More generally, for any game we can ask the question, Which actions by players would make no sense for them, no matter how their opponents act? Which would make no sense, given that their opponents would not take actions identified in the first question? And so on. In some games of interest, one or more iterations of application of the dominance criterion will lead to a single prescription of action for all players. Of course, as one applies this logic iteratively, one puts more and more faith in one's opponents' abilities to answer these questions, so one has perhaps less and less faith in the prescription. But in some games, one can find prescriptions by this means that seem valid in the sense that one expects all the players to see them. The formal programme of finding particular prescriptions by such means as this goes by several names in the literature; studies of *dominance solvability* and the recent literature on *rationalizability* (see Bernheim 1984 and Pearce 1984) form two important parts.

2. Players may be able to engage in explicit preplay negotiation, arriving at some mutually agreeable course of action. In such a case, the necessity that the agreed course of action is a Nash equilibrium can be

---

[3] It should be stressed here that the players' various hypotheses about what each will do must coincide.

rephrased as: the agreed course of action should be self-enforcing. Of course, there is no guarantee that some agreed course of action will emerge. And one becomes interested in the negotiations that precede play of the game.

(When preplay negotiation does take place, correlating devices may enlarge the set of possible self-enforcing agreements (see Aumann 1975, Forges 1986, and Myerson 1986), and explicit binding agreements (backed by some enforcement mechanism) may emerge. Either of these can lead to agreements that are not Nash equilibria, unless one explicitly includes in the model the correlating device and/or the enforcement mechanisms. We take here the position that, when correlating devices or enforcement mechanisms are feasible, they should be included explicitly in the game model.)

3. The game may have some course of action that seems reasonable to all players, based on the type of considerations that Schelling (1960) calls *focal point*. For example, suppose that the game in Figure 2.5 is changed so that the *l* by player I and *d* by II yield payoffs 10.2 and 10.9 to the two players. In this case, it seems likely that each will implicitly understand, without communication, that the other is likely to play *d* and *l*; their mutual interest points uniquely in this direction. In other games, equally strong focal points, based on other considerations, emerge. For example, in the 'split the dollar' bargaining game, even division of the dollar predominates. (See Roth and Schoumaker 1983 for a very provocative experimental study of a case in which even division has two possible interpretations.) If two players are asked to partition, simultaneously and independently, the set $\{A, B, D, E, K, L, N, P, S, T\}$ into two sets, where one set must contain B and the second S, and where payoffs depend on how well they achieve a partition, then the focal point partition $\{A, B, D, E, K\}$ and $\{L, N, P, S, T\}$, based on alphabetical order, predominates. A long discussion of this is contained in Kreps (1987), so I will not go on further, except to say that, while in many situations there do seem to emerge focal points, formal theory is far from giving a useful account of why or when this happens. (Aumann and Sorin 1987 pioneer one possible approach to this issue.)

4. Repeated interactions of the same sort, in which players observe the actions of their fellow players, might lead to 'rational expectations' concerning what each will do. If those rational expectations settle down to a stationary state, and if no one has an interest in 'deviating', then, the story goes, we will be at a Nash equilibrium.

This is an appealing story, but it does have pitfalls. In the first place, if the repeated interactions are with the same group of players, then the very fact that interactions are repeated will make into equilibria strategy prescriptions that are not equilibria in any single interaction. Even if one's opponents change with each interaction, if one carries from an

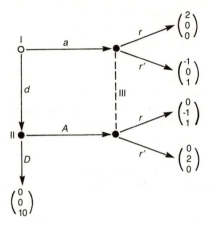

Fig. 2.6

encounter a reputation for play in a particular fashion, then the set of equilibria can enlarge enormously.

Moreover, the story is not very well substantiated in any formal treatment. Some preliminary studies have been made; see, for example, Alger and Huang (1986). They point out the following problem with the story. Consider the game in Figure 2.6 and, in particular, the 'stationary behaviour' in which I plays d and II plays D. This is not Nash behaviour; no matter what action player III is meant to take at his information set, either I or II or both would prefer a or A to d or D. But suppose that I anticipates that III will play r', and II anticipates that III will play r. Then neither would willingly give the move to III. And note that these anticipations could persist in a 'stationary state'. At least, neither I nor II, as long as both continue with d and D, will ever obtain evidence to contravert their (disjoint) hypotheses about III's actions. Player III is never given the move, so no evidence about what III would do is produced. The Nash equilibrium requirement contains within it the requirement that all players hold identical hypotheses as to what each will do and what each *might* do. Stories about stationary states and rational expectations are less convincing when applied to hypotheses about what a player *might* do in a particular circumstance, if that player is never actually called upon to act in that circumstance.[4]

---

[4] A counter-argument to this, put to me by Adam Brandenburger and Drew Fudenberg, is that, with repeated interactions, it is hard to believe that I or II will not sometimes 'try' a or A, either as some sort of experiment or by mistake. Eventually, then, their beliefs as to how III will act, given the move, should become coincident.

3.3. Perfection and sequential equilibrium

Consider again the game in Figure 2.3. It was pointed out before that *r* and *u* constitute a Nash equilibrium. But so do *l* and *d*. It is clear that, if I anticipates that II will select *d*, then *l* is better than *r*. And as long as *l* is the selection of I, II does just as well with the intention (never carried out) of playing *d* as he does with *u*. It is natural, however, to expect that II, called upon to play, would not actually choose *d*: *d* is as good as *u* only as long as I selects *l*, and if II is called on to move, he knows that I *did not* choose *l*. Hence player I, anticipating that II, put on the move, will play *u*, optimally responds with *r*. In a quite intuitive sense, while both (*l, d*) and (*r, u*) are Nash equilibria, the second is a good deal more sensible than the first (and would be the prediction of most who observe this particular game).

There is a clear lesson to be drawn from this example. What constitutes a best choice in a Nash equilibrium is affected by what one supposes will be another's actions *out of equilibrium*—what reactions one expects if one deviates. But out-of-equilibrium reactions by players are not restricted at all by the requirement that actions form a Nash equilibrium: the choice of action out of equilibrium (at an information set that will not be reached if players follow the prescription of the equilibrium) does not affect one's own expected payoff. *If* one can find suitable further restrictions to place on out-of-equilibrium actions, then one may rule out certain Nash equilibria. For example, if we insist that, in the game in Figure 2.3, player II will not be expected by I to play *d*, then we can dismiss the (*l, d*) Nash equilibrium.

This is the basic insight of Selten (1965, 1975), who initiated the study of *perfecting* or *refining* the concept of a Nash equilibrium. The objective is to restrict 'suitably' what players might be expected to do in response to deviations from a given equilibrium, just as the Nash equilibrium notion poses restrictions on what they might be expected to do in equilibrium.

(In fact, the programme for perfecting the notion of a Nash equilibrium has two, seemingly different, motivations. The first is as above: to restrict what players might do following a deviation. The second, which is more naturally posed when the game is put into normal form, is to keep players from choosing strategies that are weakly dominated; that are as good as some other strategy if opponents stick to the equilibrium prescription, but will do worse if someone (simultaneously) deviates. There is, as Selten shows, a very close connection between these two motivations, and the programme of perfecting the notion of a Nash equilibrium has proceeded along both fronts simultaneously. In this essay, I will work within the framework of the first motivation: the restriction of out-of-equilibrium actions. I do not mean to slight the complementary approach, which does indeed yield important complementary insights. But the nature of what I wish to say here is best stated in terms of out-of-equilibrium actions and the like.)

Selten (1965) poses a refinement known as *subgame perfection*, which is suited to examples such as the game in Figure 2.3. Roughly put, if at any point in the play of the game there is some single node, not joined with any other in an information set and all of whose successors (in terms of the possible paths of play) lie in information sets that contain only successors of this single node, then, beginning at that node, we can regard everything that follows as a (sub)game in its own right. To be subgame-perfect, a Nash equilibrium must prescribe, for every such (so-called proper) subgame, actions that constitute a Nash equilibrium in the subgame. The idea is an extension of the basic idea of an equilibrium. If such a node is reached, everyone who moves subsequently will know that it was reached. (This is the import of the requirement that all nodes that share an information set with some successor of the node are also successors of the node.) If the prescription of actions from that node on do not form a Nash equilibrium for the subgame, then some one (or more) player, in that subgame, will have the incentive to deviate from the prescription, given that the player believes that everyone else will follow the prescription. Hence we cannot reliably say that behaviour in the subgame will conform to the prescription. If such unreliable behaviour is important to holding together the equilibrium in the entire game, then the equilibrium in the entire game is equally unreliable.

In some applications, subgame perfection is a very powerful tool, giving strong results (see, for example, Rubinstein 1982). But in many games of economic interest, and in particular in models of market signalling where the informed party takes the initiative, subgame perfection has little bite. Because the informed party takes the initiative in possession of private information that the uninformed, who later responds, will not have, the requirement posed on the information sets of successors of single initial nodes will not generally hold. Accordingly, Selten (1975) develops a stronger condition, known simply as *perfection* (and sometimes referred to as *trembling-hand perfection*). Rather than pursue this (which would follow the chronological development of these ideas), I leave until Section 4 a discussion of perfection.

We turn instead to a somewhat milder refinement, suited to extensive form games, known as *sequential equilibrium* (Kreps and Wilson 1982). Consider the game in Figure 2.7, taken from Selten (1975). In this game, one Nash equilibrium has player I choosing *D*, player II choosing *a*, and player III choosing *l*. Note that II's choice of action lies *off the equilibrium path*—at an information set (in this case, consisting of a single node) that will not be hit so long as player I conforms to the

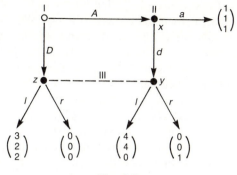

Fig. 2.7

equilibrium prescription of *D*. Hence player II's action is best for him in the trivial sense that it is inconsequential what he does. But this choice is crucial to the equilibrium. If II were to play *d* instead, then I would optimally switch to *A*. (And then III would switch to *r*, which would lead II back to *a*.)

While II's action is inconsequential to his overall expected payoff, we can still ask, If called upon to carry out the action *a*, would II do so, given the supposed (equilibrium) actions of the others? The answer would seem to be no, if II supposes that III will play *l*. For then, given that he is asked to move, II will get 1 by following the dictates of the equilibrium, and 4 if he deviates and chooses *d*. That is to say, II's choice of action is not *sequentially rational*, starting from the point where the choice must be made, under the presumption that III will follow the action prescribed for him. (Subgame perfection does not apply because the node *y* that follows II's node *x* is in an information set with a node, namely *z*, that does not follow *x*.)

Consider next a different Nash equilibrium for this game: I chooses *A*, II chooses *a*, and III chooses *r*. Now it is III whose choice lies off the equilibrium path, and so it is III's choice that is not restricted by the requirements of a Nash equilibrium. Yet III's out-of-equilibrium choice is important to the equilibrium: if III responded with *l*, then I would do better with *D* than with *A*. So we can ask, Is III's choice of action *sequentially rational*?

It is harder to formulate an answer to this question than it was to say that, in the other equilibrium, II's choice was not sequentially rational. This is because II's choice came from a single node; by holding to the hypothesis of no further deviations from the supposed equilibrium, we could evaluate II's expected payoff if he chose *a* against his payoff if he chose *d*, beginning at node *x*. But to evaluate the expected payoffs to III of *l* versus *r*, starting from III's information set, we need to know what are III's beliefs as to which node in his information set pertains. If III believes he is at node z, then l is better; if he believes that he is at node y, then r does best. Since III's information set is off the equilibrium path, we cannot use the supposed equilibrium strategies to deduce for III with what probabilities he is at y and not z; if the equilibrium strategies were followed, he would be at neither.

In a sequential equilibrium, it is required that, at every information set, both on and off the path of equilibrium play, there must some beliefs for the player whose turn it is to move, such that the player's supposed choice of action is sequentially rational if he holds those beliefs as to what has transpired so far together with the hypothesis that the equilibrium prescription will thereafter be followed by others. For example, in Figure 2.7, III's choice of r in the (A, a, r) Nash equilibrium can be rationalized by beliefs that put probability 2/3 or more on the node y.

It is important to note that, whereas a Nash equilibrium consists of a prescription of actions for each player at every information set, a sequential equilibrium consists of both a prescription of the actions of players and the beliefs that those players hold when it is their turn to move. The prescribed actions must be sequentially rational, given those beliefs.

In addition, it is required in a sequential equilibrium that beliefs and the supposed equilibrium actions be *consistent*. The full consistency requirement consists of a technical condition that hides several strong assumptions (see Kreps and Ramey 1987) which may be unpalatable. We will not take up that condition here, except for two remarks that are important for our development.)

1. The consistency of beliefs and actions entails that, at every information set that lies along the equilibrium path (that is reached with positive probability if the actions are followed), beliefs are computed from the actions using Bayes's law. That is, beliefs are fixed by prescribed actions when there have been no obvious deviations from those actions.

2. Within the class of signalling games, point 1 is the full import of the consistency requirement. Thus, a sequential equilibrium for a signalling game takes the following relatively simple form:

(2a) One must prescribe a rule by which player I chooses messages, based on his type. This is given by a family of probability distributions $\rho(\cdot; t_k)$, one for each type t_k, over the set of possible messages, where $\rho(m; t_k)$ is the probability that I sends message m if his type is t_k.

(2b) A response function ϕ must be given for II, specifying for each possible message m the probability $\phi(r; m)$ with which II will take action r.

(2c) Beliefs of II for every message m must be given. We write $\mu(t_k; m)$

for the beliefs of player II that I is of type t_k when message m has been received.

(2d) The beliefs specified in (2c) must be consistent with the prior assessment that II holds concerning I's type (which we denote by $\pi(t_k)$) and the supposed signalling strategy ρ of I. When there is positive probability that the message m will be sent, then Bayes's rule is used. Otherwise, there are no restrictions on beliefs.[5]

(2e) The signalling strategy ρ of I must be optimal for I given the response strategy ϕ of II. And the response strategy ϕ of II must be optimal for II given II's beliefs μ concerning the meaning of each message.

3.4. Restrictions on beliefs

With all the previous development as background, we turn finally to the subject of this essay. Consider the game in Figure 2.8, due to Kohlberg and Mertens (1986). The actions A for I and r for II constitute a Nash equilibrium in this game. The action choice of II is off the equilibrium path, and so we ask whether it is reasonable to suppose that II would indeed choose r given the move. This choice passes the test imposed by sequential equilibrium; if II's beliefs at his information set put probability 1/2 or more at node x', then r is indeed the best choice.

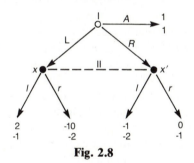

Fig. 2.8

But in the test of sequential equilibrium we allow II to hold *any* beliefs out of equilibrium. We can ask, Are the beliefs needed to support the equilibrium actions as a sequential equilibrium at all reasonable? In this particular example, the answer is no. Even if one thought that (A, r) was a rational way to play the game, one would not mean to say that no other course of play has positive probability. The supposition that (A, r) is the solution is more appropriately a supposition that, with high prior probability, I will choose A and II r, each expecting the other to follow

[5] A compact way to write this is $\mu(t_k; m)(\sum_{t(j)} \pi(t_j)\rho(m; t_j)) = \pi(t_k)\rho(m; t_k)$ for every m and t_k, where the equation reads $0 = 0$ if there is zero prior probability that message m is sent.

this prescription with high prior probability. But if player I somehow did not see this (and act accordingly), we (and, presumably and more importantly, player II) would find it more likely *ex post* that I has played *L* rather than *R*. Reason as follows. Player I, by choosing *A*, can ensure a payoff of 1 for himself. Choosing *R* will obtain 0 *at best*. Choosing *L* might obtain 2; indeed, there is a Nash equilibrium (namely (L, l)) in which I does obtain 2 by choosing *L*. Perhaps, then, I has erred in that he supposed that the two are playing the other equilibrium (see Section 5). In any event, it seems very unlikely that I would choose an action that at best will do worse than what I gets from *A*. Hence we (and, presumably and more importantly, I) might well expect that II, put on the move unexpectedly, will form 'posterior' beliefs that put more weight on the deviation being *L* than *R*. But such beliefs out of equilibrium do not support the equilibrium: if II puts more weight on being at *x* than at *x'* in his 'posterior' beliefs, then the supposed out-of-equilibrium choice of *r* is sequentially irrational. And if II's out-of-equilibrium choice is not *r* but *l*, then I will choose *L* instead of *A*.

Recall that a Nash equilibrium is advanced as a candidate solution for the rational way to play the game, supposing that one such exists. Players are meant to believe, with high prior probability, that each of them understands this. But high prior probability does not mean probability 1; each player surely assesses positive prior probability, however small, of any string of actions from his opponents. The statement that an information set is off the equilibrium path, which means that it has zero prior probability in the model, is translated into reality as: the probability that this information set will be reached is small. But a small probability is not zero, and the thesis being advanced is that, in trying to say what beliefs are held out of equilibrium (hence what actions will be taken, hence what will be reasonable equilibria to look at), one must consider what conclusions players will draw when faced *a posteriori* with the *a priori* small probability event that someone has deviated. There are many sorts of stories that one can imagine the players concocting to explain such deviations, and these different stories may well lead to different sorts of restrictions on beliefs out of equilibrium. In so far as particular concoctions have greater or lesser appeal in particular real situations, one will find greater or lesser appeal in the corresponding refinements.

In the next three sections, three types of stories are sketched that underpin particular types of refinements. Then, in Section 7, we ask: Are any of these stories more or less palatable in the context of market signalling?

4. Simple Mistakes

Perhaps the simplest story that one can tell when faced with a deviation is that the deviation is a mistake on the part of whoever did it. One holds to the hypothesis that all players intend to follow the prescription of the equilibrium, but that they sometimes fail to carry out their intentions—because they are tired, or incorrectly instruct their agents, or somesuch. If one attributes deviations to simple mistakes, then one obtains useful restrictions on out-of-equilibrium beliefs only insofar as one is willing to attribute relative likelihood to particular mistakes, saying that one is twice as likely as a second, or one is much more likely than another.

Suppose that one was willing to say, for example, that no ranking of the likelihood of mistakes at different information sets is possible, but that one holds to the hypothesis that (1) mistakes are very unlikely, but every mistake is possible; (2) conditional on any single mistake, there is no added (or lessened) probability of further mistakes (the chances of mistakes are independent; and (3) the independence in (2) holds not only for mistakes by different players, but also for the occurrence of multiple mistakes by a single player, at various information sets at which the player moves. Then, roughly, one has Selten's definition of a (trembling-hand) perfect equilibrium. Selten's definition, precisely, is that a prescription of behaviour at every information set (or, to use the standard terminology, a strategy profile for the agent normal form of the game) is perfect if there exists some sequence of strictly positive strategy profiles (for the agent normal form) that approach the profile in question, such that the prescription at every information set of the limit profile is a best response to the prescriptions at other information sets for the profiles in the sequence. One may think, roughly, of the difference between the limit strategy profiles and the strictly positive strategy profiles that approach it as the (vanishingly small) chances of mistakes by the player: the limit condition says that the chances of mistakes are vanishingly small; strict positivity says that every mistake is possible; independence of mistakes follows from the independence implicit in any strategy profile; and independence of mistakes at different information sets for the same player follows from the fact that we look at strategies in the agent normal form; and the optimally condition says that what each player intends to do at each information set (the limit prescription) is a best response given what the others will do, taking into account that the others may make mistakes.

Although it is far from obvious, the predictions of sequential equilibrium and perfection so defined are, for most extensive form games, the same.[6] On the one hand, every perfect equilibrium is sequential. Conversely, for almost any game put down at random, any sequential equilibrium outcome is the outcome of a perfect equilibrium.[7] The point

---

[6] This, it should be noted, relies heavily on the consistency condition that is part of the definition of sequential equilibrium.

[7] The outcome of an equilibrium is the probability distribution generated by the strategy prescription on endpoints of the game tree; see Kreps and Wilson (1982) for proofs. It should be noted that all independence restrictions in perfect equilibrium find expression in sequential equilibrium in the precise formulation of consistency of the strategy prescription and beliefs.

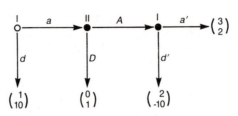

Fig. 2.9

is that, if mistakes are fairly much unrestricted, then any out-of-equilibrium beliefs can be justified. For example, in Figure 2.8, if we assumed that I was ten times more likely to do R by mistake than L, then II would be justified in holding 'posterior' assessments that put weight 10/11 on x' and 1/11 on x, which justifies II's choice of r, which means that both L and R are indeed mistakes. And why might the odds of L by mistake be so much lower than R by mistake? Perhaps because, given II's choice of r, L by mistake nets -10 for I, whereas R by mistake nets 0. Given II's strategy, L is the much more severe mistake, and so I might take special care to avoid it. See the discussion of *properness* to follow.

There are possible weakenings and strengthenings that can be made, depending on what one is willing to say or not about these simple mistakes. Consider first the game in Figure 2.9. This game has no information sets, so we can solve it by backwards iteration: if I is given the move at his second information set, he should choose a'. Hence II, at his node, should choose A. And I, at the start of the game should therefore choose a. But another Nash equilibrium is d, D, and a'. It is player II that is of concern here: II's choice of D at his node is not in violation of the Nash restriction, because this node lies off the equilibrium path. But given that II is put on the move, and given that I is supposed to finish the game (according to the equilibrium) with a', sequential rationality would seem to force II to a choice of A (which in turn will make a better than d at the start of the game).

If, however, II is 'meant' to choose D, then a by I is a mistake. And II will persevere with D in the face of this mistake if he believes that I, having slipped once, is more likely than not to slip again. If we imagine that players make mistakes on the level of entire strategies for the game, we can imagine that I is as likely to deviate from da' with ad' as with aa'. In which case the evidence presented to II that a mistake has been made (being put on the move) will cause II to choose D. Sequential rationality (and, virtually equivalently, Selten's perfection) involve the assumption that a deviation/mistake prior to an information set does not increase the odds (from very small) of subsequent deviations by the same players. But one's image of how mistakes are made (temporary carelessness that may

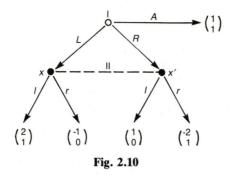

Fig. 2.10

recur in the short run, incorrect instructions to one's agent) may be at variance with this, leading to refinements on Nash equilibrium that are *weaker* than perfection/sequential equilibrium.[8] If mistakes are made on the level of entire strategy prescriptions for players throughout the game (and if one maintains that mistakes by different players are statistically independent), then one is led to the refinement *perfection in the normal form*, which in cases such as Figure 2.9 is weaker than Selten's preferred perfection in the agent normal form (and even subgame perfection).

On the other hand, one may feel that worse mistakes are less likely to be made than those that are less worse—recall our justification for supposing that L by mistake is much less likely than R by mistake in Figure 2.8. A refinement known as *properness*, due to Myerson (1978), is based on such considerations. Myerson supposes that the relative likelihood of a worse mistake is infinitely less than that of a lesser mistake. Consider, in this regard, the game in Figure 2.10, and the Nash equilibrium (A, r). This equilibrium is sequential (and perfect) if one holds that R by mistake is more likely than L by mistake. But given II's equilibrium choice of r, R is a worse mistake than is L. If, accordingly, we supposed that II should think it more likely (out of equilibrium) that he is at x than at x', the equilibrium collapses—II will chose l, and I will chose L. (A, r) is perfect, but it isn't proper. (In this example, one needn't go so far as in properness, which would insist·that, at the equilibrium (A, r), out-of-equilibrium beliefs by II must put weight 1 on x. It suffices in this case that beliefs put more weight on x than x'. But if we changed II's payoff in the event of R and r from 1 to, say, 100, then Myerson's properness would still rule out (A, r), even though (now) the equilibrium can be supported by out-of-equilibrium beliefs that put weight 0·98 on x.)

---

[8] Moreover, there are games in which what comes before and what after a given information set is not so clear-cut as in our simple examples; see Kreps and Ramey (1987).

5. Mistaken theories

A very different story from the one in Section 4 might be called *mistaken theories*. Roughly, it holds that observed deviations from equilibrium play may signify that one (or more) player does not understand what is expected of him. That is, one imagines that the equilibrium prescription is what, with high probability, each player will see to do. But there is small prior probability that a player may not see this; instead, he may have a completely different theory as to how the game is to be played. One would then look for relatively likely alternate theories for how to play the game, to try to see (1) who has defected, (2) what has been the nature of the defection, and/or (3) what might be the consequences of that defection for later play.

The Kohlberg–Mertens example of Figure 2.8 provides a simple example. The Nash equilibria of this game are (A, r) and (L, l). Consider the (A, r) equilibrium. At his information set, if II is put on the move, he might conclude that I has the mistaken impression that (L, l) is what is supposed to happen. There is no similar hypothesis that would support the play of R by I. Hence II, believing that deviations should, when possible, be attributed to players choosing other equilibria, will hold out-of-equilibrium beliefs that put weight 1 on x. This, of course, will kill the (A, r) equilibrium.

A more complex example is shown in the signalling game of Figure 2.11. Consider the equilibrium in which the message sent is m regardless of which initial node is chosen, the response to m is r', and the (out-of-equilibrium) response to m' is r'. Note that the use of r' in response to m' is sequentially rational, where the out-of-equilibrium beliefs are, say, that m' was send by type t_1 with probability 1/2. (That is,

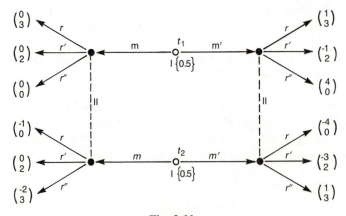

Fig. 2.11

the out-of-equilibrium beliefs are just the prior beliefs.) However:

1. There is an equilibrium in which type t_1 sends m', namely: type t_1 sends m' and the response is r; type t_2 sends m and the response is r''.
2. There is no Nash equilibrium in which type t_2 sends m' with positive probability: for t_2 to send m' with positive probability, it is necessary that the response to m' give expected payoff of at least -2 to this type (so that m is not a better message to send). This requires player II to respond to m' with weight at least $1/4$ on r''. But any such response would cause type t_1 to prefer strictly m' to m; and if t_1 sends m' with probability 1, then every sequentially rational response by II to m' puts no weight on r''.

Hence, II's out-of-equilibrium beliefs in the *both types send m* equilibrium would have to put probability 1 on the node x, if those out-of-equilibrium beliefs were compelled to follow the rule: If there is some alternative equilibrium that hits with positive probability one node in the m' *received* information set, and there is no equilibrium that hits the other node, then weight 1 is put on the node that is hit, according to the hypothesis that player I is mistakenly playing according to the hypothesis that the other equilibrium is correct. This restriction kills the *both types send m* equilibrium — r is the sequentially rational response to beliefs so constrained, which causes type t_1 to send m'.

In the literature, McLennan's (1985) *justifiable beliefs* (which is the first formal study to speak explicitly of restrictions on out-of-equilibrium beliefs) is based on these sorts of considerations ('deviations from the equilibrium path are more probable if they can be explained in terms of some confusion over which sequential equilibrium is "in effect"': McLennan 1985: 891). The details of McLennan's criterion are complex, but he is explicitly thinking along precisely these lines. Recent work by Hillas (1986) also adopts this philosophy. Hillas considers *stable sets* of equilibria; where the out-of-equilibrium beliefs that one holds in any of a stable set of equilibria must (roughly put) be derived from the hypothesis that deviations from the equilibria should be explained in terms of some other of the equilibria in the set whenever possible.

Except for these two studies, this general approach to restricting out-of-equilibrium beliefs has not been much developed. There are, however, two interesting questions that can be posed. First, it is not clear why one would wish to restrict attention to alternative hypotheses that are given by Nash equilibria. That is, one has no guarantee that a given competitive situation has a rational course of action, and there is correspondingly no particular reason to look at Nash equilibria when a rational course of action fails to exist. One might suppose that, in a given situation, there is a candidate prescription of this sort, but that most likely alternative hypotheses are not so *ex post* likely that they themselves must be Nash.

Also, it is not clear that, if one entertains the out-of-equilibrium hypothesis that one of the players has a mistaken theory about the play of the game, why one wouldn't entertain the possibility that the mistake is one's own. (On this point, see also Hillas 1986.) This leads to some very interesting refinements of Nash equilibrium.

Consider again, for example, Figure 2.7, and the (D, a, l) equilibrium. We argued earlier that II's behaviour (which takes place out of equilibrium) is sequentially irrational, given the equilibrium hypothesis that III will play l. But the hypothesis that III will play l is an equilibrium hypothesis, and in this equilibrium I is supposed to play D. The fact that A was played by I might lead II to suspect that he himself has the wrong idea about this game. Now the other equilibrium of this game is (A, a, r). So mightn't II conclude, if he initially thought that (D, a, l) was the solution and he was surprised with A, that r will be the choice of III, and hence that a is correct for himself after all? And (more importantly to support this equilibrium), mightn't I (1) hypothesize that II will think this way, hence play a if shown the out-of-equilibrium move of A, and therefore (2) optimally pick D? And mightn't III, thinking through this all, consider that (when he is given the move) D was chosen by I, and therefore he should choose l?[9] We are not arguing that (D, a, l) is clearly a rational way to play this game. A counterargument is too easy: if I supposes that (D, a, l) is called for, then A by I might be a gambling attempt by I to see if II won't try d. That is, if I thinks that II will interpret the deviation as such an attempt, then it may be worthwhile. And if II does interpret it so, then it is in II's interest to try d. But, in this case, shouln't III see this as well? If so, then III will play r. So II *should* play a, given the move. And then (?) III should interpret being put on the move as . . . what? (There may not be an obvious way to play this game at all.) In any event, if II entertains the out-of-equilibrium hypothesis that he himself has the mistaken theory, then (D, a, l) is not so clearly irrational.

(In comparison, if deviations are manifestations of simple errors, and if simple errors have low and independent probabilities, then one would conclude that (D, a, l) is fairly clearly, irrational. Restating the basic thesis of this essay, what is or is not a reasonable refinement to apply can turn on one's hypotheses about the source of out-of-equilibrium conjectures, which may not be captured very well by the formal extensive-form game model.)

The reader should note well that the thrust of this discussion is more than simply suggesting an interesting refinement in out-of-equilibrium

---

[9] See fn. 15.

beliefs, which should possibly be adjoined to sequential rationality in order to compute sequential equilibria. This is a direct attack on sequential rationality—more specifically, on the maintained hypothesis in sequential rationality that players countenance no further deviations from the equilibrium when evaluating what to do in the face of an apparent deviation. In the previous section we saw how the story of simple mistakes, applied at the level of the strategy of the individual player, would lead to equilibria that are not sequential. We see this again here, but in even more interesting form. If one entertains the hypothesis that the error in theory may be one's own, then a first deviation (from one's own hypothesis) by one player may be taken as evidence that others players are very likely to deviate. Whereas in the previous section we could, at least, rely on perfection in the normal form (mistakes may be at the level of the individual's strategy, but they are, at least, independent between different players), deviations among different players may be reasonably thought to be correlated in stories of 'mistaken theories' when the mistake could be one's own.[10]

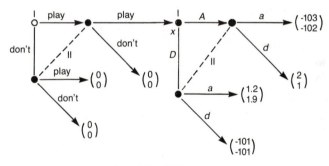

Fig. 2.12

A second example, due to Mertens (private communication 1986), makes a similar point. In order to develop the thesis that the context being modelled matters, I will paint this example a bit more vividly than has been the case so far. The game involves two eminent professors of economics, each an expert in game theory, and a third player (readers should cast themselves in the third role). These two professors are at institutions on opposite sides of the country, and they will not communicate with each other during all the time that this game is explained to them and they play. Refer to Figure 2.12.

We begin by ringing Professor I and explaining the entire game to him. Note that the first move he must make is to signify whether he wishes to

[10] The reader might also look at Fudenburg, Kreps, and Levine (1988), for yet another rationale of correlated trembles at the level of the normal form.

play the game at all. Then we ring Professor II, explain the game to her, and ask whether she wishes to play at all. (She is not informed about the initial decision of Professor I.) If either (or both) professor/s say they do not wish to play, the game is over, and both parties get zero payoff. If both indicate that they wish to play, then they play the game that begins at node *x*. We ring Professor I again, and ask him to choose between *A* and *D*. Then we ring Professor II and, without telling her which choice Professor I made, ask her to choose between *a* and *d*.

The payoffs, the reader will note, are such that both professors make between 1 and 2 if they pick either *A* and *d* or *D* and *a*. (The reader can think of the prizes as being denominated in dollars.) Professor I prefers *A,d,* and Professor II prefers *D,a.* But they both have a strong aversion to the outcomes *A,a* and *D,d*—each will lost at least 100 at these two outcomes.

Now we bring player III (you) into the game. (Your role is not shown in Figure 2.12.) Before ringing the two professors, you are asked to predict how they will respond to the first round of phone calls. Precisely, you are asked to indicate one of the following:

1. Both were willing to play.
2. Professor I was willing to play, but not Professor II.
3. Professor II was willing to play, but not Professor I.
4. Neither was willing to play.

If your prediction is correct, you will be given $1—you get zero otherwise. Next, *if* both are willing to play, before we make the second round of phone calls, you are asked to place a bet on the outcome of this second round. Your choices are:

Bet 1: $9 if the outcome is *D,a,* and zero otherwise.
Bet 2: $9 if the outcome is *A,d,* and zero otherwise.
Bet 3: $9 if the outcome is either *A,a* or *D,d,* and zero otherwise.
Bet 4: $7 if the outcome is either *D,a* or *A,d,* and zero otherwise.

Before reading further, how will you bet concerning the first round of phone calls? And, if called upon to bet on the second round, which bet would you take?

The modal response to the first question has been a bet on neither being willing to play.[11] Indeed, when asked to give a probability assessment over the first round of play, most individuals asked have indicated very high prior probability for this outcome. That is, most people predict that the two professors will play that Nash equilibrium in which neither wants to play. But, at the same time, most respondents to the second question have chosen bet 4. The point is that bet 4, which is

[11] These questions, in slightly altered form, have been addressed to a number of my colleagues, albeit not in well controlled circumstances.

about out-of-equilibrium behavior, is optimal only if you (player III) entertain out-of-equilibrium conjectures of a correlated choice by I and II in the (out-of-equilibrium) second round of phone calls. That is, if one's out-of-equilibrium hypothesis is that the two professors, if called upon to do so, will play in statistically independent fashion, then, no matter what fashion one hypothesizes, one of the first three bets gives higher expected payoff than the fourth.[12] The out-of-equilibrium behaviour of player III is inconsistent with any Nash equilibrium; indeed, it is inconsistent with any hypothesis of independent play by two other distinct players.

Why take the fourth bet, out of equilibrium? Why are out-of-equilibrium conjectures in this game that players I and II will correlate their actions? A typical excuse runs as follows. One expects the two professors to refuse to play the game, because there seems no apparent way to play the subgame that begins at node x for profit. This seems a quite reasonable theory, held with probability close to 1. But, out of equilibrium, one has found that this theory is incorrect. Perhaps one has missed seeing a reasonable way to play the subgame that the two others have found. Perhaps the two professors discussed some similar game in the recent past, or read the same article on a similar game. The game is a variation on a classic simultaneous move game, known as the Battle of the Sexes. Thus it is not *impossible* that the two experts have seen some means of coordinating their actions that you have missed, or that some article appeared on this game in the recent past, or that two experts in game theory recently discussed it, however unlikely these may be *a priori*. When one knows that the two are willing to play the subgame, which entails the risk of substantial losses, it might be thought *a posteriori* that it is quite likely that one of these possibilities or something similar has occurred. The fact that both professors are willing to play the subgame is surely circumstantial evidence in favour of such an *a posteriori* hypothesis. And if player III is unable to see what theory I and II will bring to bear on this game, so that A,d and D,a are both approximately equally likely and have posterior probability summing to close to 1, then bet 4 is optimal.

Nash analysis, which assumes that correlation in diverse players' strategies is not possible (unless the correlating device is modelled explicitly), may be an appropriate tool for analysing situations where the analyst believes that there is little chance that the economic actors being modelled have access to a correlating device. But a small *a priori* chance of this may loom large *a posteriori* when one conditions on being out of equilibrium (or on any event of small prior probability). Indeed—and this is the point of this example—such out-of-equilibrium conjectures may be entirely natural when one explains deviations from the equilibrium using

---

[12] Since payoffs are in dollars, this presumes (close to) risk neutrality in the range of payoffs considered, which is not unreasonable given that the range is from $0 to $9.

a *mistaken theories* story, where the mistake is possibly one's own failure to understand some facet of the situation that others may see. And, of course, one is more willing to credit such an explanation of deviations in certain circumstances—for example, when there is greater reliance on focal points, or when the possibility of preplay communications among some players but not others, while small, is not zero.

6. Conscious Signals

Turn now to Figure 2.13. This game, taken from Cho and Kreps (1987), illustrates a third sort of story one could tell to explain deviations: deviations as a conscious attempt to signal. Accompanying this game is the following story. Player I is one of two types, either a wimp (type t_w) or surly (type t_s), with 90 per cent probability that I is surly. Player I signals to player II by his choice of breakfast, which is either beer or quiche. If I is a wimp, he prefers quiche; if surly, beer. The second player must then decide whether to challenge I to a duel. If I is a wimp, II would prefer to duel. If I is surly, II would prefer to forgo a duel. At the prior probabilities, II will forgo the duel. Whether a wimp or surly, I prefers not to duel. And I's preference to avoid a duel is so strong that I prefers not duelling and his less favourite breakfast to duelling and his more favourite breakfast.

The game has two types of sequential equilibrium.

1. In the first, I has beer for breakfast, regardless of type. Player II, in consequence, holds his prior beliefs if I has beer for breakfast, and doesn't duel. To keep the wimpish type of I from having quiche for breakfast, II must respond to this out-of-equilibrium message by duelling (with probability of 1/2 or more); this is rationalized by out-of-equilibrium beliefs on the part of II that I is, with probability 1/2 or more, a wimp, if he deviates and has quiche for breakfast.

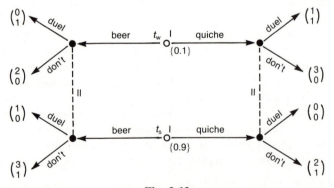

Fig. 2.13

2. In the second type of sequential equilibrium, I has quiche for breakfast, regardless of type, hence II responds to quiche by forgoing the duel. To keep the surly I from having his preferred breakfast of beer, the out-of-equilibrium message *beer* is met with duelling with probability 1/2 or more. This out-of-equilibrium response is rationalized by out-of-equilibrium beliefs that I is a wimp with probability 1/2 or more if he has beer.

Both equilibria are perfect.[13] Both pass tests of the sort posed in the previous section, because there are equilibria in which each type of I sends each message. But still we find the second sort of equilibrium suspicious. In the second sort of equilibrium, player I has expected payoff 3 if he is a wimp and 2 if he is surly. If he sends the out-of-equilibrium message beer and he is a wimp, the best he could hope to do is to get 2—less than he gets in the equilibrium. If, one the other hand, he is surly, then he could get 3, *if* player II recognizes the out-of-equilibrium signal as a signal that he is, indeed, surly. If we were in the second equilibrium and if we imagined that player I could accompany his choice of breakfast with a little speech, we might imagine I saying, between gulps of beer:

You (player II) expected me to have quiche for breakfast, and I am having beer. Having had this breakfast of beer, I cannot possibly do as well as I could have without deviating, if I am a wimp. But I can do better with this breakfast, as long as I can convince you that I am surly, if indeed I am surly. So you see that this message (and deviation) is only conceivably in my interests if I am surly. That should convince that I am, and justify my deviation.

Note well, this speech is very tightly connected to the supposed equilibrium. If it works, it is because, compared with the supposed equilibrium payoffs, only a surly player I could benefit from the deviation. The wimp also will have beer for breakfast, if he thinks that quiche will be met by a duel; beer for breakfast can be ruled out for the wimp *only* if we fix the equilibrium and assume that players believe that they can indeed obtain what the equilibrium promises. Three comments are in order.

1. Note first that the first sort of equilibrium for this game does not fall to such an argument. There, quiche is the out-of-equilibrium message, and out-of-equilibrium beliefs must put substantial weight on the wimp in case of quiche. The equilibrium payoffs to the two types of I are 2 for the wimp and 3 for the surly type, and the surly type has no business at all deviating to quiche (where the best he can do is a payoff of 2)—the wimp would deviate only if he could convince player II that he is surly. One

---

[13] The application of Myerson's properness is a bit suspect, because it involves a comparison of two types of I. But if we are willing to make that comparison, then there are equilibria giving each of the two equilibrium outcomes that are proper.

can't make a good case that this deviation certainly came from the wimp, but the case that deviation came from the surly type is weaker still. Hence the out-of-equilibrium beliefs that support the equilibrium are not so unreasonable as in the second sort of equilibrium.

2. Consider again the game in Figure 2.11, and the *both types send m* equilibrium. Recall that out-of-equilibrium beliefs must put weight on both types to support this equilibrium. It was argued before that no weight should be put on type t_2, because there is no equilibrium in which type t_2 sends m'—only type t_1 might be doing it under the 'mistaken' theory that the other equilibrium is being played. Now consider this equilibrium in light of a conscious attempt by type t_1 to signal that he is type t_1 with the deviation m'. The speech that the surly type makes (given above) does not go quite so smoothly for type t_1 in Figure 2.11; it cannot be argued that t_2 has *no* business sending m' in the *both send m* equilibrium, since this could lead to a payoff of 1 if the response is r''. (However, a speech of the general type indicated might help t_1—he can argue, at least, that type t_2 would *not* wish to claim that he is type t_1 and send m' if II is convinced by this, whereas as type t_1 he would willingly do so. This takes us in the direction of the refinements suggested by Farrell (1985) and Grossman and Perry (1986a); see below.)

3. An argument against the believability of the speech we have put in the mouth of the surly type of player I runs as follows.[14] If the speech is believed, and if player II can work out that the speech should be believed, then the absence of the speech should cause player II to deduce that player I is a wimp. That is, if the speech is believable, then quiche for breakfast should be a sure sign of a wimp, and should be met by a duel. But *then*, we cannot conclude that the wimp would not make the speech—to fail to do so would consign him to a duel (and payoff of 1), compared with the 2 he would get by making the speech. And if we cannot conclude that the speech, if believed, would not be made by the wimp, then we cannot conclude that the speech is believable. Its credibility turns on the fact that the wimp would never make it.[15]

---

[14] I heard this argument first from Joe Stiglitz.

[15] The logic here is similar to that which we applied to Fig. 2.7 above. There, in the (D, a, l) equilibrium, if II is given the move, he might conclude that both I and III are playing their parts of the (A, a, r) equilibrium, which makes a the optimal choice for himself. That is, deviation by one player may indicate a corresponding deviation by another. Here we might imagine II expecting a breakfast of quiche, and reacting to a breakfast of beer with the hypothesis that it could have come from either type of player I—the fact that it came from one means that the hypothesis that *both quiche* is not the equilibrium. But the analogy is not perfect. If II reacts in this fashion to the out-of-equilibrium to *beer*, then should he not continue with the response in the other equilibrium to *beer*, namely no duel? If so, then the surly I would continue to deviate from the *both quiche* equilibrium. Only if II concludes that such a deviation is possible for *either* type of player I, and that it is more probable for the wimp than for the surly type, can we support this equilibrium. On this general line of argument, see Hillas (1986), whose notion of a stable set of equilibria finds, in Fig. 2.13, that both sorts of equilibria, taken as singletons, are stable.

This objection to the speech points out again the critical role played in the speech by the equilibrium that is put forward. The equilibrium payoffs are used quite explicitly, and it is a maintained assumption that players expect that they can get what the equilibrium promises by sticking to the equilibrium. This speech cannot be expected to work if that maintained hypothesis does not hold.

Is the speech credible? That, surely, depends on the strength of the maintained assumption above, which in turn depends on how strongly (and why) one believes in the validity of Nash equilibrium analysis. Is the signal by itself, without the speech, as good as the signal with the speech? That is, can we say that the surly type of player I can have his breakfast of beer, resting easy in the assumption that player II will properly interpret this deviation from the equilibrium as a conscious signal that he (player I) is surly? In any application to a real situation, it seems clear that the signal accompanied by the speech is better than the signal alone. While we might omit from the formal model the opportunity of players to tell each other how to interpret certain actions, we should still note that, in some applications, the opportunity is there, and it affects our willingness to accept the sort of refinement sketched above.

This type of refinement, where a deviation is interpreted as the conscious attempt of a player to signal something to others, and where the credibility of that signal is based on comparisons with the payoffs obtained in the purported equilibrium, has seen the most duty in economic models. The reason for this will been seen in the next section: under certain assumptions, this type of refinement has enormous power in the context of market signalling. The formal development is more recent: Cho and Kreps (1987) develop the criterion we used informally above, called *equilibrium dominance,* which asserts that a type of player I (in a signalling game) will not be believed by player II to have sent an out-of-equilibrium signal if the best response for this type that could reasonably be expected does strictly worse than what the type of player gets in equilibrium. (That is, the out-of-equilibrium message is *dominated by the equilibrium* payoff for this type.) Banks and Sobel (1987) develop stronger criteria, going under the general rubric of *divinity*: roughly, one type of player I is less likely to have deviated in a particular fashion than another type of player I, if any response by player II that makes the first type willing to deviate also makes the second type willing to deviate. For example, in Figure 2.11 and the *both send m* equilibrium, any response by II to m' that would cause t_2 to deviate will cause t_1 to do so as well.[16] The mathematical properties of equilibria that stand up to these restrictions on out-of-equilibrium inferences are easily recovered from properties of *stable equilibria,* a normal form concept due to Kohlberg

---

[16] The reader consulting Banks and Sobel (1987) should note carefully, however, that *divinity* will not suffice for this example; *universal divinity* is required.

and Mertens (1986). (See any of the above three cited papers for connections.) Cho (1986, 1987) develops notions related to equilibrium dominance for games more complex than signalling games.

A somewhat different, but related, approach is taken by Farrell (1985) and Grossman and Perry (1986a). In the previously mentioned studies, a type is thought not to send a particular message if it could not conceivably benefit, relative to the equilibrium payoff, no matter what is concluded from the deviation. Imagine instead that we looked for 'credible explanations' for out-of-equilibrium messages—the explanation is that the message was sent by this or that subset of types, and the explanation is credible if, *given that it is believed,* the subset that explains the message and only that subset would wish to send the message (still comparing with equilibrium payoffs). For example, in Figure 2.11 and the *both send m* equilibrium, m' by t_1 is a credible explanation of m'—II's best reply to m' if it comes from t_1 is r, which would cause t_1 to deviate but not t_2. Note that m' by t_2 is not credible: the best response to this by II is r'', which would indeed cause t_2 to deviate, but also t_1. Farrell studies this sort of credibility when messages are free and freely available; Grossman and Perry work within the context of a game with an exogenously specified set of messages that are relatively more or less costly to particular types.

7. Market Signalling and the Refinements

As noted above, the conscious message story has played a prominent role in studies of market signalling. Grossman (1981b) is perhaps the first paper to use this to argue in favour of a particular equilibrium; many others have adapted the story since. Cho and Kreps (1987) contains a fairly detailed study of the connection between the refinements of this sort and market signalling (in the setting of Spence's model of job market signalling), and I do not wish to repeat all that analysis here. I will, however, sketch out how, in one variation of the basic market signalling story, equilibrium domination breaks any pooling that might go on in an equilibrium.[17] Then I will argue for equilibrium domination as an appropriate tool of analysis in the particular context of market signalling.

The basic market signalling story has a party possessed of private information that is drawn from some distribution on the real line. We denote the realization of this information by x, and we assume that x has bounded support. One can think of x as denoting the skill of the party as a worker, or the quality of a used car that the party wishes to sell, or the level of risk to which the first party is subject. This first party can go to

[17] This variaiton is mentioned in passing in Cho and Kreps (1987), although it is not worked out in the detail I will give here. The idea for it was suggested to me by Anat Admati, and the details of the argument to be given were worked out largely in conversations with In-koo Cho.

any number of uninformed parties (e.g., potential employers, prospective purchasers of the car, insurance companies) and propose a deal. The deal will have two dimensions to it: a one-dimensional signal of the first party's private information (e.g., a level of education, a level of warranty against future repairs, a deductible in the insurance policy); and a (one-dimensional) payoff variable (e.g., a wage rate, a price for the car, the premium paid on the policy). We will denote a typical deal by the two-dimensional vector (e, w) (for education level and wage). The second parties approached with this signal simply indicate whether they are willing to enter into this transaction; if more than one second party says yes, then the transaction is awarded to one at random. Note well that we put almost all initiative in the hands of the informed party in this story. Moreover, we will imagine that the first party can propose any two-dimensional deal at all.[18]

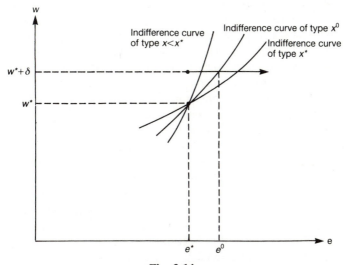

Fig. 2.14

The first, informed, party always strictly prefers higher levels of w and lower levels of e. Moreover, the rate at which the informed party trades one off against the other depends on the party's type x—we make the usual assumption that the indifference curve of type x through a point (e, w) is less steeply sloped than that of type x', if and only if $x > x'$ (see Figure 2.14). That is, a more able worker finds education less distasteful; the

---

[18] Allowing the first party to propose both parts of the deal, and giving the uninformed parties the power only to accept or reject, is what distinguishes this from many treatments of market signalling. It is a consequential distinction, in that it allows the informed party great latitude in out-of-equilibrium signals, hence it gives a great deal of power to refinements that restrict out-of-equilibrium beliefs.

seller of a good used car is more willing to take the risks of an improved warranty than is the owner of a lemon; an insuree who faces less risk is more willing to accept a higher deductible, in the trade-off against a higher wage/sales price/lower premium.

Ceteris paribus, the uninformed parties prefer deals with higher e and lower w. It is necessary to assume that they exhibit strict preference in terms of decreased w. The *ceteris paribus* refers to the beliefs the uninformed hold concerning the quality of the informed party proposing the deal. Fixing the terms of a deal (e, w), the uninformed parties find the deal acceptable if their beliefs as to the quality of the worker/used car/insuree are sufficiently optimistic. The assumption we make is that, if (e, w) is acceptable when beliefs are given by some distribution F on type x, and if F' is a distribution that is strictly higher in the sense of stochastic dominance, then there is some $\delta > 0$ such that $(e, w + \delta)$ is acceptable when beliefs are given by F'. (It is easiest to think of the acceptability of (e, w) as turning on the expected value of x.) We assume further that the acceptability of a deal (e, w) is continuous.[19] We assume that, if the deal is just acceptable, then the uninformed parties do accept. (This assumption can be done without at the cost of minor additional arguments.) We assume that there is some deal (e^0, w^0) that the uninformed parties would accept no matter what their beliefs, which the informed party always finds superior to no deal at all. (This assumption is stronger than usual, but it will simplify later arguments a good deal.)

In an equilibrium, each type of informed party proposes a deal (e, w) to several uninformed parties. (We allow the possibility that type x might actually propose deals according to a randomized strategy.) Each deal proposed is accepted in equilibrium (because of the assumptions that an acceptable deal is always accepted and there is some always acceptable deal that is better than rejection of one's proposal). The uninformed parties have rational expectations about what every deal signifies in equilibrium, just as outlined in Section 2 above.

If thought of as a signalling game, this situation has enormous numbers of sequential equilibria. One can support numerous equilibria by manipulating the out-of-equilibrium beliefs of the uninformed; they may be given pessimistic beliefs about the quality of the sender of any out-of-equilibrium deal, which would cause them to reject such deals, which would keep the informed player from proposing such deals.

But the type of refinement sketched in Section 6 works wonders. In particular, given the assumptions we have made (and one more to come), any pooling of types of the informed party (two different types propose the same deal in equilibrium) is impossible if one restricts beliefs according to equilibrium domination. The argument is not complex. Imagine that we have an equilibrium with some pooling. Let x^* be the

---

[19] Both in the arguments (e, w) and in the uninformed parties' beliefs as to x, the latter is the weak topology on those beliefs.

highest indexed type that is pooled, and let (e^*, w^*) be the specifications of the deal at which this type is pooled. Since some other type is offering this deal with positive probability, we can find some ε sufficiently small so that (e^*, w^*) is proposed with positive probability by types of quality lower than $x^* - \varepsilon$.

Refer to Figure 2.14. By our earlier assumptions, there is some positive δ such that $(e^*, w^* + \delta)$ is strictly acceptable if the uninformed parties believe that it is made by type x^* with probability 1. By the continuity of the acceptability region, then, as we move along the horizontal ray from $(e^*, w^* + \delta)$ in the direction of increasing e, we will come to some level e^0 such that there is a level of quality $x^0 \leqslant x^*$ with (1) $(e^0, w^* + \delta)$ acceptable if beliefs are that the informed party is of type x^0 (or higher); (2) the indifference curve of types $x < z^0$ through the point (e^*, w^*) all lie above and to the left of $(e^0, w^* + \delta)$; and (3) type x^* strictly prefers $(e^0, w^* + \delta)$ if it is accepted to (e^*, w^*). (The technically minded reader will note the importance of our earlier assumption that $(e^*, w^* + \delta)$ is *strictly acceptable*, together with the continuity and monotonicity assumptions, in all this.)

This, virtually, completes the argument. As long as $(e^0, w^* + \delta)$ is an out-of-equilibrium proposal, if type x^* proposes it, then the uninformed parties (applying equilibrium domination) will hold beliefs that put probability 1 on types of quality x^0 or higher, by (2). Thus the deal will be accepted, by (1). And this is better for x^* than the equilibrium, by (3)). If, on the other hand, the deal $(e^0, w^* + \delta)$ is offered in equilibrium, it will be accepted (all deals offered in equilibrium must be accepted), and our original putative equilibrium is not even a Nash equilibrium.

(One implicit assumption may have slipped past the reader, which is certainly worthy of note. It was assumed that, at the pooling point, it was possible to increase both components of the deal. If there is an upper/lower bound on possible signals or payoffs, pooling at the boundary may occur. So, for example, in the bargaining setting of Admati and Perry (1987), one may get pooling, but only at the best possible terms for the informed party.)

We note again the importance in this argument that the informed party take the initiative. If the uninformed party has the initiative, proposing a set of deals from which the informed must select, then there is no guarantee that pools will be broken. Indeed, in some game forms where the uninformed have the initiative, the force of refinements of Nash equilibrium may be in entirely the other direction (Martin Hellwig, 1986, private communication). In circumstances where it is costly for the uninformed to evaluate a deal proposed by the informed party (i.e. in all realistic settings), and where the single informed party is not all that important to the uninformed, it may be quite natural (and, net of transaction costs, optimal) for the uninformed party to refuse to consider every deal that comes its way—pooling, at least at some level, cannot then be ruled out.

We turn at last to the argument that, in the context of market signalling, when the informed parties do indeed have the initiative in proposing deals, the sort of refinement that we have used, based on the conscious signal story, is sensible. The argument is that, of the various sorts of stories we have told, the conscious signals story is one that is best buttressed by the simultaneous free flow of conversation between the parties. Elsewhere (in Cho and Kreps 1987) I have said that, in stating the case for the equilibrium dominance refinement, I would not wish to make too much of the sort of speech used in Section 6. I herewith recant. Such speeches, composed of cheap talk, certainly do take place, and the ability of one party to explain to another why it has taken a deviant action should not be dismissed lightly. We may see such speeches made only rarely, but that is the point: we will not see equilibria persist that are susceptible to deviations as conscious signals, especially if those signals can be accompanied by cheap talk that explains how the deviation is a conscious signal. Others (notably Crawford and Sobel 1982, and Farrell 1985) have pointed out the importance that cheap talk can have in economic situations; I note here another: when it is possible and is not directly modelled, it pushes one away from refinements based solely on 'mistaken theories' stories and towards refinements based on the idea that one party is deviating in a way that has credibility as a conscious attempt to signal, at least when these refinements lead to different conclusions.

8. Concluding Remarks

Game theory, one sometimes hears, is meant to be the study of how perfectly rational individuals will interact in competitive situations. The point of view taken here is that this philosophy is wrongheaded, at least in so far as one wishes to use game theory to analyse and understand real-life situations. If individuals were perfectly rational, and if Nash equilibria are salient in that there is some rational way to play the game, then one couldn't conceive of what inferences would be drawn out of equilibrium; one would not find oneself out of equilibrium.

Instead, the position here is that there are many situations in which one feels there is a clear-cut prescription for what will probably happen, in the sense that the odds *a priori* that various economic factors will follow this prescription are close to 1. If one's model of the situation is a game, and if the model adequately captures the important features of the situation, then the prescription should correspond to a Nash equilibrium in the model.

But in no real situation will one be completely sure that all actors will follow the prescribed course of action. Depending on context, players will interpret out-of-equilibrium actions in various ways; I have tried to suggest a few (by no means all) types of stories that they might reasonably use. And, depending on the story used, one may be led to one or another of the refinements. The connection between the contextual setting and the particular refinement may be via considerations that are omitted from the formal game-theoretic model. For example, 'mistaken theories' stories seem to me to be relatively more sensible when one is depending most heavily on focal points for the salience of Nash equilibrium analysis, and when no explicit communication between players is expected; whereas 'conscious signals' are more sensible in situations where economic actors have the opportunity to engage in cheap talk, and where the purported equilibrium is thought to be well established (by custom, perhaps) in all the actor's minds. One may have to think back from the formal model to the context modelled to select (or reject) a particular refinement.

A quite defensible opposing position is that the stories we have told to explain deviations all really involve details of the situation that ought to be placed into the underlying model of the game. If simple mistakes are consequential, then one should directly model games in which players try to take particular actions but fail to do so. The story of a mistaken theory can be modelled with a game of incomplete information, where a player is 'told' by nature *a priori* what theory he holds about play of the game; correlations built into what theories are held can then be modelled directly. The same is true of conscious attempts to signal. There may remain a need for a good refinement to the notion of Nash equilibrium, but it should apply to all models, if they are properly specified in this sense.

This position is more than defensible; it is possibly the more asthetic position to hold. But for purposes of the modelling of economic situations, it is perhaps not useful. Models that explicitly specify the small probabilities of errors, of differences in theory, and so forth seem likely to prove either intractable or subject to the criticism that the specifications of these things are ad hoc.[20] The selection of a refinement according to the sort of introspection indicated above and its subsequent use in a model with the details left out may prove to be a tractable 'surrogate' for analysis of completely and properly specified models. There is a danger here that we may be misled by simple examples into choosing an inappropriate surrogate, and so the investigation of the existing refinements and the development of new ones is important. But at the current level of the development of the methodology, in order to apply the methodology it seems reasonable to choose one's tools according to the situation, just as one chooses one's model.

---

[20] A good example are the models of reputation based on a little incomplete information, which can be justly criticized on both grounds.

3

The Role of Common Knowledge Assumptions in Game Theory

ADAM BRANDENBURGER AND EDDIE DEKEL

1. Introduction

The notion of common knowledge has been increasingly used in game theory, although usually in an informal, not fully appreciated or articulated, manner. By 'common knowledge' is meant the idea that something is not merely known by all the players in a game, but is also known to be known, known to be known to be known, and so on *ad infinitum*. The concept has been deployed with sufficient frequency to necessitate an assessment of its role. Thus the purpose of this chapter is to examine the common knowledge assumptions that underlie the various solution concepts in non-cooperative game theory.

   Much of the work to be surveyed here is of recent origin in the context of game theory. It represents an attempt to integrate the theory of individual decision-making under uncertainty—often called Bayesian decision theory—with the theory of games. In so doing, the research marks a departure from the conventional view of the function of Bayesian decision theory. Traditionally, Bayesian decision theory has been perceived as appropriate only to 'exogenous' uncertainty, not to uncertainty about the actions of players in a game. For the latter, 'endogenous', variety, it has usually been argued that an equilibrium, or other game-theoretic, concept must be employed. Thus Harsanyi has written: 'every player i . . . will assign a *subjective* probability distribution P_i to all variables unknown to him—or at least to all unknown *independent* variables, i.e. to all variables not depending on the players' own strategy choices' (Harsanyi 1967–8: 167).

   In contrast, the predominant theme of the work to be discussed in this chapter is that the players in a game assign subjective probabilities to *all* uncertainty, including the actions of other players. The distinction between the various game-theoretic solution concepts can then be seen to depend on the common knowledge assumptions respected by the players' subjective probabilities.

   The basic datum for the players in a game is the structure of the game

We would like to thank Ken Binmore, Ben Polak, and Linda Pollock for helpful comments. We are indebted to Bob Aumann for providing detailed comments on an earlier version of this chapter and for sharing some of his thoughts on game theory with us.

itself, that is, the description of the payoff functions, strategy spaces, and so on. At first sight it would seem that, if the structure of a game is not taken to be common knowledge among the players, then any analysis is impossible. This seems to have been the viewpoint, at least implicitly, of early workers in game theory (see e.g. Luce and Raiffa 1957: Ch. 3). Nevertheless, in a seminal series of papers Harsanyi (1967–8) argued that, even if the structure of a game is not common knowledge, there is a well-defined larger game in which Nature first chooses the version of the game to be played, and this larger game *can* be taken to be common knowledge among the players. Harsanyi's arguments have recently been given formal mathematical expression by Böge and Eisele (1979), Mertens and Zamir (1985), and others. This work is described in Section 5 below.

The second crucial piece of common knowledge is that all the players are rational. By rationality is meant the assumption that each player conforms to the axioms of Savage (1954) (or to some related set of axioms), and hence acts to maximize expected utility calculated using some subjective probability distribution over all uncertainty that the player faces—which, as indicated above, will include the actions of the other players. Actually, as will be seen in Section 6, for the purpose of discussing refinements of Nash equilibrium, the theory of subjective expected utility is not sufficiently 'detailed'. At that point a more elaborate theory—subjective expected utility with lexicographic beliefs—will be described and rationality will be taken to mean that the players act in accordance with this modified theory. To sum up, the assumption will be made that the rationality of the players, in one or other sense, is indeed common knowledge.

What does common knowledge of rationality in a game setting amount to? The answer depends on what further *a priori* information there is about the setting. Sections 3 and 4 flesh out this observation. It is shown that, if there is no additional information, then the appropriate solution concept is rationalizability (Bernheim 1984; Pearce 1984); if the players share a common prior, then the correct concept is correlated equilibrium (Aumann 1974, 1987); if the players' beliefs are common knowledge, then common knowledge of rationality is equivalent to Nash equilibrium. Section 6 extends this last characterization to two refinements of Nash equilibrium: perfect equilibrium (Selten 1975) and proper equilibrium (Myerson 1978).

2. Formalizing the Notion of Common Knowledge

An event or proposition is common knowledge among a group of people if it is known to all, known to all that it is known to all, and so on *ad infinitum*. The term 'common knowledge' was used in this context by Lewis (1969), who attributes the basic idea to Schelling (1960). Aumann (1976) proposed the notion independently and offered a precise mathematical formulation in terms of a model of differential information which is by now standard in economics.

There is a finite set Ω of *states of the world*. There are I individuals where each person $i \in I$ has a partition P^i of Ω, representing i's private information about the true state. That is, if $\omega \in \Omega$ is the true state, then i is informed of the element of P^i that contains ω (to be denoted $P^i(\omega)$). P denotes the partition that is the *finest common coarsening* (or meet) of $P^1, \ldots, P^n$. Write $P(\omega)$ for the element of P that contains ω. Aumann's definition of common knowledge can now be stated.

DEFINITION 1 (Aumann 1976). An event $E \subset \Omega$ is common knowledge at a state of the world $\omega \in \Omega$ if $P(\omega) \subset E$.

In order to relate this definition to the intuitive notion of common knowledge, it will be helpful to have the following definitions. Given an event $E \subset \Omega$, say, person i knows E at a state ω if $P^i(\omega) \subset E$. This captures the idea that i is informed that the true state lies in $P^i(\omega)$, and hence also in any set that contains $P^i(\omega)$. The event that i knows E, to be written $K^i E$, is then given by

$$K^i E = \{\omega \in \Omega : P^i(\omega) \subset E\}.$$

It is easy to check that K^i, considered as a function from 2^Ω to 2^Ω (where 2^Ω is the set of all subsets of Ω), has the following properties:

(P1) For any $E \subset \Omega$, $K^i E \subset E$;
(P2) For any $E \subset \Omega$, $K^i E \subset K^i K^i E$
(P3) For any $E, F \subset \Omega$, $K^i(E \cap F) = K^i E \cap K^i F$;
(P4) For any $E \subset \Omega$, $(K^i E)^c \subset K^i(K^i E)^c$ where the superscript c denotes complement.

(P1)–(P4) capture some intuitive (and some *not* so intuitive!) aspects of knowledge formalized in terms of partitions. (P1) says that i can know E only if E happens. (P2) says that if i knows E then i knows that i knows E. (P3) says that i knows E and F if and only if i knows E and i knows F. (P4) says that if i does not know E, then i knows that i does not know E.[1]

Suppose for simplicity that there are just two people, i and j. Using K^i and K^j (the latter being defined analogously to K^i using the partition P^j in place of P^i), it is now easy to write down directly the statement that E is

---

[1] Actually, (P1)–(P4) are characteristic of partition information in the following sense. If a function $K^i : 2^\Omega \to 2^\Omega$ satisfies (P1)–(P4) then there is a partition P^i of Ω such that $K^i E = \{\omega : P^i(\omega) \subset E\}$. To see this, define the class of sets $F^i = \{F \subset \Omega : K^i F = F\}$. F^i is a field. Let P^i be the partition which generates F^i and set $K^i E = U\{\pi \in P^i : \pi \subset E\}$. K^i defined in this way is easily seen to satisfy (P1)–(P4). (See Bacharach 1985).

common knowledge at ω. Let

$$L^i E = K^i E \cap K^i K^j E \cap K^i K^j K^i E \cap \ldots$$

$$L^j E = K^j E \cap K^j K^i E \cap K^j K^i K^j E \cap \ldots$$

Then one would say that E is common knowledge at ω if $\omega \in L^i E \cap L^j E$. It is straightforward to check that this definition is indeed equivalent to Aumann's definition.

PROPOSITION 1. $P(\omega) \subset E$ if and only if $\omega \in L^i E \cap L^j E$.

The proof of this proposition is essentially contained in the discussion of 'reachability' in Aumann (1976: 1237).

A potentially troublesome aspect of this formalization of common knowledge lies in the interpretation of the condition $P(\omega) \subset E$. To interpret this as the statement that E is common knowledge at ω, it must be assumed that the information partitions are themselves common knowledge in an informal sense. Aumann (1976, 1987) has argued that this is not really an extra assumption since, if a state of the world ω is to be *all-inclusive*, it should include lists of those other states ω' that are, for i and j respectively, indistinguishable from ω. That is, ω should describe the manner in which information is imparted to i and j.

The element of self-reference built into this line of argument raises the possibility of some version of the Liar's Paradox being applicable, and hence of a contradiction arising. In fact, problems of self-reference already arise in the single-person case. Properties in the spirit of (P1)–(P4) above, when combined with the axioms necessary for mathematics, lead to the 'Knower's Paradox' (Montague 1974). The nature of Aumann's argument has been much discussed (see e.g. Brandenburger and Dekel 1985; Gilboa 1986; Kaneko 1987; Tan and Werlang 1985).[2] On a related issue, Samet (1987) and Shin (1987) have explored an alternative model of knowledge that satisfies the properties (P1)–(P3) defined earlier, but not the rather less palatable (P4).

3. Common Knowledge of Rationality in Games

This section discusses how to formalize the idea of common knowledge of rationality in the context of games described in normal form. An n-person game in normal form is a $2n$-tuple $\Gamma = \langle A^1, \ldots, A^n; u^1, \ldots u^n \rangle$ where, for each $i = 1, \ldots, n$, A^i is a finite set of pure strategies (henceforth actions) of player i and $u^i : \times_{j=1}^{n} A^j \to R$ is i's payoff function (assigning a von Neumann–Morgenstern utility to each combination of strategies chosen by the players). In games in economics it is typically

---

[2] There are also relevant literatures in computer science, artificial intelligence, linguistics, and philosophy—see Halpern (1986) and the references therein.

assumed that the players' strategy spaces are infinite; for example, player i's strategy space might be taken to be R^+ if i's strategy is to choose a price. But for present purposes it seems preferable to restrict attention to finite games, on the premise that extending many of the results to the infinite case raises technical rather than conceptual questions.

The discussion will also be confined to games in normal form rather than to the more familiar context of games in extensive form, or trees. Although the map from extensive- to normal-form games is many-to-one (see Figure 3.1), and thus an apparent loss of information is entailed in using the normal form, the adequacy of the normal form was the traditional position among game theorists (von Neumann and Morgenstern 1944). Such a stance must be founded, at least implicitly, on an argument of strategic equivalence, for example between the two game trees in the figure. This type of argument can be constructed from the work of Thompson (1952), Dalkey (1953), and Elmes and Reny (1987). These authors demonstrated that, given two game trees with the same normal form (up to duplicated pure strategies), one can be transformed

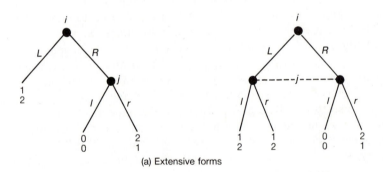

(a) Extensive forms

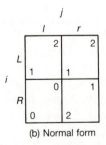

(b) Normal form

Fig. 3.1

into the other by a sequence of elementary and 'inessential' transformations of the game tree. (Kohlberg and Mertens 1986, from whom this
discussion is derived, supply a description of the transformations.) If one
is convinced that the transformations are inessential, then two trees with
the same normal form must be equivalent. From this it follows that a
'good' solution concept should be defined on the normal rather than on
the extensive form, in order to avoid any dependence on the presentation
of the decision problem facing the players. A further point is worth
emphasizing. Despite being defined on the normal form, a 'good' solution
concept may well be required to conform to some notion of extensive-
form rationality (e.g. backwards induction or sequential rationality—see
Kreps and Wilson 1982: 272 and Krep's Chapter 2 above) in any tree with
that normal form. Proper equilibrium (Myerson 1978) is such a solution
concept—see Section 6.

Ultimately, the choice of normal versus extensive form is best viewed
as a choice of axiom. It is of course possible to argue that the
Dalkey/Thompson transformations are *not* inessential, in which case two
trees with the same normal form may well have to be analysed
separately. Chapter 2 above by Kreps surveys the literature on solution
concepts defined on the extensive form. There is a final caveat to this
discussion: the arguments in favour of the normal form certainly rely on
the standard assumption that the players have unlimited computational
power. As soon as one takes explicit account of computational complexity, it may be that a single n-way choice for a player is *not* equivalent
to a sequence of $n - 1$ binary choices (as is implied by a normal-form
approach). Related arguments against a normal-form approach can be
found in Binmore (1987b).

Returning to the objective of this section, the question to be addressed
is, Which normal-form actions $a^i \in A^i$ can a player i choose under the
assumption that the rationality of the players is common knowledge? As
described in the introduction, by 'rationality of player i' is meant that i
chooses an action to maximize expected utility calculated using some
subjective probability distribution over the uncertainty that i faces. This
uncertainty is the choice of actions by the other players. Given sets
$X^1, \ldots, X^n$, let X^{-i} denote the set $X^1 \times \ldots \times X^{i-1} \times X^{i+1} \times \ldots \times X^n$.
For any finite set X, let $\Delta(X)$ denote the set of probability distributions
on X. Rationality requires that i choose an action a^i which solves

$$\max_{\bar{a}^i \in A^i} \sum_{a^{-i} \in A^{-i}} \sigma(a^{-i}) u^i(\bar{a}^i, a^{-i})$$

where $\sigma \in \Delta(A^{-i})$ is a subjective probability distribution over the actions
of the other players. Following standard game-theoretic terminology, a^i
will be called a best reply to σ. So the knowledge that i is a rational
player immediately rules out certain actions of i, in that they are not best

replies to any $\sigma \in \Delta(A^{-i})$. Formally, let $A_0^i = A^i$ and

$$A_1^i = \{a^i \in A_0^i : a^i \text{ is a best reply to some } \sigma \in \Delta(A^{-i})\}.$$

A_1^i is the set of actions that a rational player i can choose. If i knows that each other player j is also rational, then i knows that j can only choose actions a^j in A_1^j (defined in analogous fashion to A_1^i). A probability distribution of i will be inconsistent with this knowledge if it assigns positive probability to an action $a^j \notin A_1^j$. So if i not only is rational, but also knows that every other player j is rational, i should only choose an action $a^i \in A_2^i$ where

$$A_2^i = \{a^i \in A_1^i : a^i \text{ is a best reply to some } \sigma \in \Delta(A_1^{-i})\}.$$

If the rationality of the players is assumed to be common knowledge, then this reasoning can be extended indefinitely. Define inductively

$$A_k^i = \{a^i \in A_{k-1}^i : a^i \text{ is a best reply to some } \sigma \in (A_{k-1}^{-i})\}.$$

By finiteness, there must be a K such that $A_k^i = A_K^i \neq \emptyset$ for all $k \geq K$. The sets $A_K^1, \ldots, A_K^n$ are the sets of actions that the players can choose under the assumption of common knowledge of rationality.

It should be emphasized that the structure of the game $\Gamma = \langle A^1, \ldots, A^n; u^1, \ldots, u^n \rangle$ itself, as well as the rationality of the players, is assumed to be common knowledge in deriving the sets A_K^i. If player i does not know each other player j's utility function u^j, then i cannot calculate the sets A_1^j, and hence cannot restrict him/herself to a probability distribution on A_1^{-i}. Extending this argument shows that the structure of Γ must be taken to be common knowledge.

At first sight, it appears somewhat perverse to be assuming that the utility functions of the players are common knowledge but that their beliefs are not. In Savage (1954), utility functions and subjective probability distributions are derived jointly from preferences over actions. If it is common knowledge of the players' preferences that gives rise to common knowledge of the utility functions, then why are not beliefs also common knowledge? Aumann (1987), Bernheim (1985), and Brandenburger and Dekel (1987) present expanded models with private information in which this objection does not bite. The players' *prior* probability distributions, as well as their utility functions, can be assumed to be common knowledge. But the players' beliefs about other players, which are their *posteriors* calculated using their private information, need not be common knowledge.

The sets $A_K^1, \ldots, A_K^n$ are the sets of actions of the players that remain after iterated deletion of strongly dominated actions. Recall that an action a^i of player i is strongly dominated if there is a $\sigma^i \in \Delta(A^i)$ such that

$$\sum_{\bar{a}^i \in A^i} \sigma^i(\bar{a}^i) u^i(\bar{a}^i, a^{-i}) > u^i(a^i, a^{-i}) \; \forall a^{-i} \in A^{-i}.$$

It is well known (e.g. Ferguson 1967; Pearce 1984: Appendix B) that a^i is strongly dominated if and only if there is no $\sigma \in \Delta(A^{-i})$ to which a^i is a best reply. Hence the sets $A_1^1, \ldots, A_1^n$ are the sets of actions remaining after deletion of strongly dominated actions. Proceeding inductively, $A_k^1, \ldots, A_k^n$ are the sets of actions remaining after k rounds of deletion.

Arguments based on dominance and iterated dominance are nothing new in game theory (see Luce and Raiffa 1957: 108–9), but, rather surprisingly, it is only recently that the foundations have been spelled out in detail by Bernheim (1984, 1985), Pearce (1984), and Tan and Werlang (1988). In fact, the 'rationalizable' actions of Bernheim and Pearce are not quite the same as the sets $A_k^1, \ldots, A_k^n$, the difference being that Bernheim and Pearce require it to be common knowledge that each player's probability distribution on the actions of the other players is stochastically independent. While this makes no difference in the context of two-person games (since a player faces only one opponent), there are three-person games in which the rationalizable actions are proper subsets of $A_K^1, \ldots, A_K^n$. Stochastic independence may be an appropriate assumption in a scenario where each player supposes that his/her opponents are selected independently and play independently. However, in many situations it seems more natural to allow for correlated beliefs.

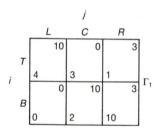

Fig. 3.2

In some games, iterated dominance arguments are successful in the sense of reducing the set of possible actions for each player to a singleton. Consider for example the game Γ_1 of Figure 3.2. R is strongly dominated by the mixed strategy of j which assigns probability 1/2 to L, 1/2 to C. In the reduced game, after deletion of R, T strongly dominates B. Finally, after deletion of B, L strongly dominates C. So iterated dominance leads to i playing T and j playing L. Nevertheless, iterated dominance is often a 'weak' solution concept, placing few or no restrictions on which actions the players can choose. In the game Γ_2 of Figure 3.3 (based on a game in Bernheim 1984), iterated dominance does not eliminate any actions of i or j from consideration.

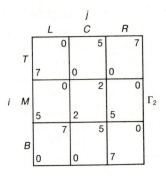

Fig. 3.3

4. Nash Equilibrium

Consider again the game Γ_2. Player i can justify choosing T by the hierarchy of beliefs: i believes j chooses L, i believes j believes i chooses B, i believes j believes i believes j chooses R, and so on in the cycle T-L-B-R-T-.... Notice that i's choice of T can be justified only if i believes that j's belief about i's action is wrong: if j believed that i's choice was T then j would choose R, to which T is not a best reply for i. Although this 'inconsistency' seems to be an accurate reflection of the players' ignorance about each other's beliefs, such a situation can be eliminated by supposing that the players' beliefs are common knowledge. This assumption leads to a characterization of Nash equilibrium (and in the game Γ_2 singles out the unique Nash equilibrium, in which i plays M and j plays C). In order to state the characterization, a preliminary result (Proposition 2 below) will be needed. Write player i's belief over j's choice of action as $\sigma^j \in \Delta(A^j)$, and j's belief over i's choice of action as $\sigma^i \in \Delta(A^i)$.

PROPOSITION 2. Assume that the beliefs $(\sigma^i, \sigma^j) \in \Delta(A^i) \times \Delta(A^j)$ are common knowledge. Then common knowledge of rationality is satisfied if and only if

$$\sigma^i(a^i) > 0 \Rightarrow a^i \text{ is a best reply to } \sigma^j \tag{1}$$

$$\sigma^j(a^j) > 0 \Rightarrow a^j \text{ is a best reply to } \sigma^i. \tag{2}$$

Proof. To prove this proposition, assume first that σ^i, σ^j are common knowledge and that common knowledge of rationality is satisfied. If i assigns positive probability to an action a^j of j, that is, if $\sigma^j(a^j) > 0$, then by common knowledge of rationality a^j must be optimal for j given some belief over A^i. But since beliefs are common knowledge, this belief is just σ^i, so condition (2) is satisfied. A similar argument establishes condition (1). To prove the converse direction, assume that σ^i, σ^j are common knowledge and that conditions (1), (2) hold; i knows that j is rational since, by condition (2), i's belief σ^j assigns positive probability only to actions a^j of j which are optimal for j given the belief σ^i which i knows j to have. Continuing in this fashion establishes that all sentences of the form 'i (or j) knows that j (or i)... is rational' are true. So common knowledge of rationality is satisfied. □

Recall the conventional definition of a Nash equilibrium: it is a pair of *mixed strategies* $(\sigma^i, \sigma^j) \in \Delta(A^i) \times \Delta(A^j)$ such that σ^i is optimal against σ^j and σ^j is optimal against σ^i. It is easy to check that σ^i is optimal against σ^j (resp. σ^j is optimal against σ^i) if and only if condition (1) (resp. (2)) holds. Hence the following result follows immediately from Proposition 2.

COROLLARY 1. Assume that the beliefs $(\sigma^i, \sigma^j) \in \Delta(A^i) \times \Delta(A^j)$ are common knowledge. Then common knowledge of rationality is satisfied if and only if (σ^i, σ^j) is a Nash equilibrium.

The characterization of Nash equilibrium contained in Corollary 1 can be extended to n-person games $(n > 2)$ by supposing that there are commonly known beliefs $(\sigma^1, \ldots, \sigma^n) \in \times_{i=1}^{n} \Delta(A^i)$. In writing the beliefs this way, two assumptions are being made: first, that, for any player i, all players other than i share the same belief σ^i about i's choice of action; second, that (as for rationalizability) each player's probability distribution on the actions of the other players is stochastically independent.

Corollary 1 offers a characterization of Nash equilibrium which seems preferable to the conventional interpretation of Nash equilibrium. According to the orthodox view, player i actually performs a randomization over the set of actions A^i in accordance with the probabilities prescribed by σ^i. Player i is prepared to carry out this randomization provided player j performs the randomization σ^j. But i is indifferent between the precise randomization and any other randomization over the same set of actions, or indeed between σ^i and choosing for sure any action assigned positive probability by σ^i. Why in fact should i perform the randomization σ^i? Yet if i does 'deviate' from σ^i, then j may no longer be prepared to play σ^j. The lack of a clear rationale for a player to randomize is a serious drawback of the conventional view of Nash equilibrium. The view espoused here is to think in terms of an equilibrium of *beliefs* rather than of strategies: σ^i is no longer a randomization of player i but rather reflects the uncertainty of player j over i's choice of action.

An early attempt to advance this viewpoint of equilibrium was made in Harsanyi (1973a). In Harsanyi's formulation a mixed-strategy equilibrium is interpreted as a pure-strategy equilibrium in an augmented game where there is some exogenous uncertainty. The notion of an equilibrium of beliefs is developed in Aumann (1987). Aumann shows that, under the assumption that the players share a common prior (the Common Prior Assumption), his 1974 concept of objective correlated equilibrium can be viewed as a consequence of common knowledge of rationality.

5. Games with Incomplete Information

It was assumed in Sections 3 and 4 that the structure of the game is common knowledge among the players. However, this may not always be the case: players may begin a game with different private information about their possibilities, preferences, and the like. The term 'incomplete information' was introduced by von Neumann and Morgenstern (1944) to describe games of this type, and the key work on these games is that by Harsanyi (1967–8).

Incomplete information about the game may arise in several ways: it may concern how many players there are in the game, the spaces of actions of the players, how the outcome of the game depends on the actions chosen, the players' preferences. Harsanyi (1967–8: 167–8) argued that all these cases can be reduced to uncertainty about the payoff functions by appropriate expansion of the number of players and spaces of actions. So, following Harsanyi, let the (expanded) number of players be n and, for each $i = 1, \ldots, n$, let A^i be i's (expanded) finite set of actions and $v^i : \times_{j=1}^n A^j \times S \to R$ be i's payoff function where S is a space of unknown parameters.

Let us try to analyse this game. Player i's optimal choice of action depends on what i thinks each player $j \neq i$ will do—and this depends on what i thinks each other player j's payoff function is. But what player j will do depends in turn on what j thinks are the payoff functions of the players $k \neq j$. And so on. This argument leads to each player having an infinite hierarchy of beliefs—over S, over the other players' beliefs over S, and so on.

The basic result for games with incomplete information is that a model of infinite hierarchies of beliefs can be closed in the following sense. For each player i there is a well-defined space T^i of all possible infinite hierarchies of beliefs of i such that T^i is homeomorphic to $\Delta(S \times T^{-i})$. That is, it is possible to summarize an infinite hierarchy of beliefs of i in a single object, namely, i's type $t^i \in T^i$, which is associated with a joint probability distribution over the parameter space S and the types of the other players. The proof of this result when S is compact is contained in Mertens and Zamir (1985); for an alternative proof which covers the case when S is a complete separable metric space, see Brandenburger and Dekel (1985). (See also Myerson 1985.) It is worth pointing out that, even if the parameter space S is finite, the type spaces T^i are uncountably

---

[3] The notation $\Delta(X)$ has not been formally defined when X is infinite. $\Delta(S \times T^{-i})$ denotes the set of all probability measures on the Borel field of $S \times T^{-i}$; see Billingsley (1968) for definitions.

infinite.[3] In fact, it is clear that the type spaces T^i could not be finite: $\Delta(S \times T^{-i})$ is uncountably infinite and so could not be homeomorphic to a finite T^i. It is only once the type spaces are uncountable that they can be used to 'encode' the set of probability distributions on themselves.

The tools with which to analyse a game with incomplete information are now assembled. Each type $t^i \in T^i$ of player i induces a belief $q^i(t^i)$ over $S \times T^{-i}$. The parameter s can be integrated out by defining new payoff functions $u^i(a, t)$ and beliefs $p^i(t^i)$ by

$$u^i(a, t) = \int_S v^i(a, s)q^i(t^i)(ds \mid t^{-i})$$

$$p^i(t^i) = \mathrm{marg}_{T^{-i}} q^i(t^i).$$

(Here $\mathrm{marg}_{T^{-i}} q^i(t^i)$ denotes the marginal of $q^i(t^i)$ on T^{-i}.) A game with incomplete information, often called a *Bayesian game,* is then a $4n$-tuple $\Gamma_B = \langle A^1, \ldots, A^n;\ T^1, \ldots, T^n;\ p^1, \ldots, p^n;\ u^1, \ldots, u^n \rangle$ where, for each i and $t^i \in T^i$, $p^i(t^i)$ is a probability distribution over T^{-i} and $u^i : \times_{j=1}^n A^j \times \times_{j=1}^n T^j \to R$. Unlike the game Γ we began with, the structure of Γ_B can be assumed to be common knowledge among the players.

The Bayesian game Γ_B in its full generality is too unwieldy a tool to be useful in practice. In applications it is typically assumed that the players' types lie in a finite 'belief-closed' subset of $T^1 \times \ldots \times T^n$. A finite subset $V^1 \times \ldots \times V^n$ of $T^1 \times \ldots \times T^n$ is said to be belief-closed if, for every i and each $t^i \in V^i$, $p^i(t^i)(V^{-i}) = 1$. That is, each player knows that all the players' types lie in $V^1 \times \ldots \times V^n$, each player knows that all the players know this, and so on. In other words, it is assumed to be common knowledge that the players' types lie in $V^1 \times \ldots \times V^n$.

6. Refinements of Nash Equilibrium

In many games it is agreed that some Nash equilibria are more 'reasonable' than others. There is by now a considerable literature on refinements of Nash equilibrium, which is concerned with formulating criteria for choosing among the set of Nash equilibria. Starting with Selten (1965), one strand of this literature focuses on refinements of the extensive form; the other on refinements on the normal form. This section will be predominantly, though not exclusively, concerned with the second approach, since Chapter 2 above provides a detailed discussion of the first. Some simple examples will be provided to motivate refining the set of Nash equilibria, and some of the proposed solution concepts will be reviewed. Finally, in keeping with aims of this chapter, some recent work will be described revealing how refinements of Nash equilibrium can be understood as a consequence of common knowledge of rationality—albeit of a different type of rationality from that described in Section 3.

The basic idea behind normal-form refinements is to use 'trembles' to

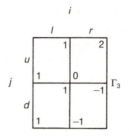

Fig. 3.4

rule out Nash equilibria that are not robust to small perturbations, in particular, equilibria that involve weakly dominated strategies. Consider for example the game Γ_3 of Figure 3.4. (l, d) is a Nash equilibrium but does not seem robust. If j thinks there is any chance of i choosing r, then j would strictly prefer u to d. Expressed differently, d is weakly dominated by u. The only sensible Nash equilibrium of Γ_3 is (r, u). The idea of a (trembling-hand) perfect equilibrium was introduced by Selten (1975) in order to rule out equilibria such as (l, d).[4]

In order to state Selten's definition, some extra notation will be useful. Given a game $\Gamma = \langle A^1, \ldots, A^n; u^1, \ldots, u^n \rangle$, let $v^i(a^i, \sigma^{-i})$ denote i's expected payoff from choosing the action a^i when the other players choose the mixed strategies $\sigma^{-i} \in \times_{j \neq i} \Delta(A^j)$. For any finite set X, let $\Delta^0(X)$ denote the set of all strictly positive probability distributions on X. A mixed strategy of i is called completely mixed if it lies in $\Delta^0(A^i)$.

DEFINITION 2 (Selten 1975). An n-tuple of completely mixed strategies $(\sigma^1, \ldots, \sigma^n) \in \times_{i=1}^n \Delta^0(A^i)$ is an ε-perfect equilibrium (for $\varepsilon > 0$) if, for each i and every $a^i, \bar{a}^i \in A^i$, $v^i(a^i, \sigma^{-i}) < v^i(\bar{a}^i, \sigma^{-i})$ implies $\sigma^i(a^i) < \varepsilon$.

So an ε-perfect equilibrium is an n-tuple of mixed strategies such that every pure strategy receives positive probability, but only best replies get more than ε weight.

DEFINITION 3 (Selten 1975). A perfect equilibrium is a limit (as $\varepsilon \to 0$) of ε-perfect equilibria.

Selten showed that a perfect equilibrium is a Nash equilibrium, and every finite game possesses a perfect equilibrium.

Perfect equilibrium behaves as desired on the game Γ_3: in any ε-perfect equilibrium d must receive weight less than ε so the unique perfect equilibrium is (r, u).

Γ_3 is also the normal form of the game in Figure 2.3 in Kreps's chapter.

---

[4] In fact, most of Selten's paper is concerned with developing a notion of perfection for extensive-form games. The reference is to Section 13 of Selten (1975), which deals with normal-form games.

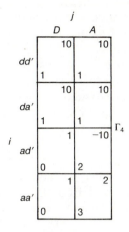

Fig. 3.5

There the Nash equilibrium (l, d) was ruled out by a backwards induction argument. This suggests that there is a close relationship between robustness/weak dominance arguments on the normal form and backwards induction/sequentiality arguments on the extensive form. Indeed, one may ask whether a perfect equilibrium in the normal form always gives rise to backwards induction, or perhaps even sequentially rational, behaviour in the extensive form. The answer is no, as the game Γ_4 of Figure 3.5 shows. (dd', D) is a perfect equilibrium (it is the limit of $((1 - 3\varepsilon, \varepsilon, \varepsilon, \varepsilon), (1 - \varepsilon, \varepsilon))$ strategies). Γ_4 is the normal form of the game in Figure 2.9 in Kreps's chapter, which has the unique backwards induction solution (aa', A). As Kreps discusses, the equilibrium (dd', D) can be ruled out by arguing that a costlier 'mistake' by a player is infinitely less likely than a less costly one. In Γ_4, given j's strategy $(1 - \varepsilon, \varepsilon)$, ad' is a costlier mistake for i than aa'. But, once i puts much less weight on ad' than aa', j will prefer A to D and the equilibrium (dd', D) will collapse. A normal-form refinement that captures this line of reasoning is the notion of proper equilibrium due to Myerson (1978).

DEFINITION 4 (Myerson 1978). $(\sigma^1, \ldots, \sigma^n) \in \times_{i=1}^{n} \Delta^0(A^i)$ is an ε-proper equilibrium (for $\varepsilon > 0$) if for each i and every a^i, $\bar{a}^i \in A^i$, $v^i(a^i, \sigma^{-i}) < v^i(\bar{a}^i, \sigma^{-i})$ implies $\sigma^i(a^i) < \varepsilon \; \sigma^i(\bar{a}^i)$. A proper equilibrium is a limit (as $\varepsilon \to 0$) of ε-proper equilibria.

It is not hard to show that the unique proper equilibrium of Γ_4 is (aa', A). In fact, one can demonstrate: a proper equilibrium of a normal-form game gives rise to a sequential equilibrium in any tree with that normal form. For a precise statement of this relationship and proofs, see van Damme (1982) and Kohlberg and Mertens (1986). The latter paper should also be consulted for a comprehensive discussion of the issue of refinements and for the definitions of further refinements (hyperstable, fully stable, and stable sets of equilibria).

The ideas in this section might appear somewhat removed from the strictly 'decision-theoretic' approach taken in the preceding sections. The emphasis there was on understanding solution concepts in game theory from the perspective of single-person decision theory: players were assumed to be rational in the sense of Savage (1954), and different solution concepts were characterized in terms of varying common knowledge assumptions. But how are the 'trembles' and 'mistakes' of this section to be interpreted within the context of decision theory? Two recent papers (Blume 1986 and Brandenburger and Dekel 1986) have shown that perfect and proper equilibrium can in fact be understood as a consequence of common knowledge of a modified form of rationality *à la* Savage.

In Section 3 rationality of a player i was taken to mean that i has a subjective probability distribution over the actions of the other players, and chooses an action to maximize expected utility calculated using this distribution. This type of behaviour is justified by supposing that player i conforms to the axioms of subjective expected utility in Savage (1954). The papers by Blume and by Brandenburger and Dekel propose a different set of axioms which leads to an alternative theory of decision-making under uncertainty—subjective expected utility with lexicographic beliefs. According to this theory, player i has some finite hierarchy of subjective probability distributions over the actions of the other players, say $(\sigma_1, \ldots, \sigma_K)$, where $\sigma_k \in \Delta(A^{-i})$ for each $k = 1, \ldots, K$, with the property that, for each $a^{-i} \in A^{-i}$, $\sigma_k(a^{-i}) > 0$ for some k. i chooses an action $a^i \in A^i$ over another action $\bar{a}^i \in A^i$ if the first yields a higher subjective expected utility in a lexicographic sense, that is if

$$\left[\sum_{a^{-i} \in A^{-i}} \sigma_k(a^{-i}) u^i(a^i, a^{-i}) \right]_{k=1}^{k} >^L \left[\sum_{a^{-i} \in A^{-i}} \sigma_k(a^{-i}) u^i(\bar{a}^i, a^{-i}) \right]_{k=1}^{K}.$$

Here $>^L$ means that the first vector is lexicographically greater than the second. In other words, player i has a 'primary' belief σ_1 over the actions of the other players and computes expected utilities using σ_1. Only if two actions are deemed indifferent under σ_1 does i then consult his/her 'secondary' belief σ_2 and compute expected utilities using σ_2, and so on.

The connection of these ideas with refinements of Nash equilibrium is apparent from the condition on the hierarchy $(\sigma_1, \ldots, \sigma_K)$ that each $a^{-i} \in A^{-i}$ must be assigned positive probability by some σ_k. This condition says that player i considers all choices of actions by the other players to be possible, although actions assigned positive probability by σ_1 are infinitely more likely than those assigned zero probability by σ_1 but positive probability by σ_2, and so on.

Subjective expected utility with lexicographic beliefs can be used to provide axiomatic characterizations of perfect and proper equilibrium which are analogous to the characterization of Nash equilibrium discussed in Section 4. Both refinements arise from the assumption that the players' lexicographic hierarchies of beliefs are common knowledge—the distinction between perfect and proper equilibrium lies in the precise way in which common knowledge of rationality is formulated. Blume (1986) and Brandenburger and Dekel (1986) should be consulted for further details of the characterizations.

7. Concluding Remarks

The work surveyed in this chapter only analyses certain 'coherent' situations of common knowledge in games and does not explain how the common knowledge itself arises. As in any analysis founded on Bayesian decision theory, the issue of formation of beliefs is side stepped. This deficiency could be remedied by supplementing the formal analysis with either an informal model or a model of learning behaviour by the players. In the first case, the analyst must evaluate the economic or other situation being modelled and judge which common knowledge assumptions seem appropriate. In this respect this chapter complements the one by Kreps, which emphasizes the importance of making a choice, depending on the context, among alternative theories of out-of-equilibrium behaviour in extensive-form games.

The second approach would aim to develop an understanding of how a player learns to predict another player's choice of action. This appears to lead to a new version of the old infinite regress problem: I learn that you learn that I learn . . . . Introducing elements of bounded rationality and computational complexity into the analysis may help to avoid this pitfall.[5] The paper in this volume by Hahn (Chapter 5) contains examples of learning behaviour which highlight the problems in this area. Although this route will probably prove to be the more fruitful, at present there are few results along these lines.

[5] The recent work on applying automata theory to repeated games (Neyman 1985, Rubinstein 1986 and others) marks a first step in bringing complexity theory to bear on game theory.

4

Repeated Games: A Survey

H. SABOURIAN

1. Introduction

In this chapter I shall survey the repeated game (RG) literature. RGs are defined as one-shot games repeated many times (finite or infinite). I shall also briefly discuss more general multi-period games—dynamic games.

In one-shot games, Nash equilibrium (NE), for example Cournot or Bertrand, requires players to choose their best (one-shot) actions, given the action of others. As a result, in many applications of one-shot games, collusive activities cannot be supported as a NE. Moreover, Dubey (1978) has shown that the set of NE of one-shot smooth games with finite number of players is generically (Pareto) inefficient.

In many economic (and social) problems, agents participate in an environment for many periods. In such contexts one often observes some degree of collusion (obeying behavioural norms which are not in the agents' immediate interests) among agents. One explanation of such collusive activities is that agents do not deviate from the norm because of the fear of punishment by other players that the deviation might invoke. (There are of course other explanations of adherence to social norms which are not in terms of 'selfish' utility maximization common in economic theory.) The literature on RGs (the appropriate model if agents participate in an environment for many periods) has tried to model the above explanation of collusive activities in a game-theoretic framework. The result of the research has been that, with the introduction of time, many types of activities (which may at first seem irrational in terms of 'selfish' utility maximization), such as co-operation, altruism, threats, revenge, and so on, can be explained as solutions to some RGs. It can be argued that the RG framework has been too successful; it can explain too many behavioural rules. In fact, in many applications one could go further and argue that the interactions of players over time remove the problem associated with proving the existence of a pure-strategy NE in one-shot games[1] and replace it with a new problem; that of too many equilibria.[2]

I would like to thank L. Anderlini, R. Evans, F. H. Hahn, and E. Maskin for reading the paper and making very helpful comments.
[1] One such application is to monopolistic competition (Roberts and Sonnenschein 1977), where the profit functions, because of the shape of the revenue and/or cost functions , are not concave. Dasgupta and Maskin (1986a) discuss many examples where the existence problem is due to the payoff functions not being continuous.

The existence of a large number of equilibria in RGs is usually demonstrated by construction. For example, the Folk Theorem of RG—that any norm of behaviour that guarantees payoffs to players more than their 'security levels'[3] can be supported as a NE of a RG with no discounting—is proved by constructing RG strategies that punish any deviator from the equilibrium norm. In RGs the possibility of punishment, and therefore the existence of a large number of equilibria, arises because players can choose history-dependent strategies; that is, they can condition their choices of actions upon the history of the game. I shall refer to outcomes of history-dependent equilibrium strategies as 'history-dependent' equilibria. As will become clear, in many history-dependent equilibria, each player chooses a history-dependent strategy because the others condition their actions on the history. Thus, history creates a new bootstrap phenomenon in RGs; it plays a role similar to a correlating device. Since there is a large number of possible histories, one can construct many equilibrium strategies (some of which are highly complicated) in RGs.

There are already two excellent surveys on RGs. Aumann (1981) surveys the early literature, and Fudenberg and Tirole (1983) survey applications of dynamic games to oligopoly models.[4] This paper is complementary to the earlier surveys. Its aim is to provide some intuitions for some of the abstract results in the RG literature. A word of warning: this paper is not a comprehensive survey of RGs and their application. The emphasis has been on the theory of RGs rather than on their applications. Moreover, some theoretical areas such as incomplete-information RGs have been almost entirely omitted. (For incomplete-information RGs see Aumann's survey, recent issues of *International Journal of Game Theory,* and recent papers by Bergin (1986) and Mertens 1986). The above-mentioned omissions reflect partly the fact that these areas have been covered by other surveys, partly my own particular interest, and partly the lack of space. In Section 2 I shall set out the basic RG model which I shall use throughout this survey. In the following six sections I shall consider infinite-horizon RGs with and without discounting, finite-horizon models, continuous-time representation of RGs, static representation of RGs, imperfect monitoring, and 'large' RGs. In the final section I shall briefly examine different possible research strategies (including 'bounded' rationality, learning,

---

[2] The equilibrium notion I will mainly consider is NE and its variant. Chapters 2 and 3 by Kreps and Brandenburger justify NE in terms of rationality and common knowledge (including common knowledge of beliefs). Clearly, these are very strong conditions. In the last section of this paper I shall briefly discuss other equilibrium concepts in the context of RGs.

[3] The security level for player i is the level of payoff below which i cannot be forced by other players.

[4] Two further surveys have recently been carried out by Mertens (1986) and Sorin.

and evolution) for dealing with the multiplicity-of-equilibria problems in RGs.

2. Basic Model

Consider the one-shot game $G = (A_i, \pi_i)_{i=1}^n$ where A_i and π_i are the action space and the payoff function of player i, respectively. Thus, π_i is a mapping from $A \equiv \prod_{i=1}^n A_i$ to R. (Letters with subscript i refer to actions, payoff, etc., of player i and letters without subscript refer to n-tuples of actions, payoffs, etc., of all players.) I shall assume throughout that A_i is compact and π_i is bounded. I define x_{-i} as the vector $x = (x_1, \ldots, x_n)$ without its ith element. I also denote the set of payoffs that Pareto-dominate a NE of G by

$$C(G) = \{\pi \in \pi(A) \mid \pi \geqslant \pi_i(a) \qquad \text{for some } a \in E(G)\} \qquad (1)$$

where $E(G)$ is the set of NE of G.[5] I shall refer to any outcome that generates a payoff vector $m \in C(G)$ as a 'collusive' outcome. Now let

$$\gamma^i \in \arg \min_{a_{-i} \in A_{-i}} \max_{a_i \in A_i} \pi_i(a_i, a_{-i}) \qquad (2)$$

$$v_i = \pi_i(\gamma^i). \qquad (3)$$

Thus v_i is i's security level—the payoff level below which i cannot be forced by other players.

$\bar{a} \in A$ is said to be an individually rational (IR) vector of actions if, for all i, $\pi_i(\bar{a}) > v_i$.[6] I denote the payoffs corresponding to IR actions by $M = \{\pi \in R^n \mid \pi = \pi(a) \text{ for some IR actions } a\}$. Finally, define the set of IR payoffs by $M^* = \{\pi \in \text{convex hull of } \pi(A) \mid \pi_i > v_i, \forall i\}$.

Let us now consider the infinitely RG (supergame), G^∞, generated from G. This is a game where G is repeated infinitely often. (G is called the stage-game of G^∞.) At each stage of G^∞, player i chooses an action in A_i given the information available to him at that stage. In this section, I consider RGs with (almost) perfect information; that is, each player is assumed to observe and remember all the past actions of all the players (including those of his own). Thus, for any player a strategy in a RG, f_i, is a sequence of mappings from the set of histories of the game to the set of actions available to him at each stage, A_i. More formally, let us denote the set of possible histories of actions up to time t by H^t. Therefore $H^0 = \phi$ and, for all $t \geqslant 1$, $H^t = A^t$, where ϕ is the empty set and A^t is the t-fold cartesian product of A. A supergame strategy for i, f_i, is thus a

---

[5] Here I shall only consider the pure-strategy case.

[6] Strictly speaking, $\bar{a}$ is IR if $\pi_i(\bar{a})$ is greater or equal to v_i. I shall only refer to actions $\bar{a} \in A$ such that $\pi_i(\bar{a})$ is strictly greater than v_i as IR because in most RGs one cannot demonstrate that $\bar{a}$ such that $\pi_i(\bar{a}) = v_i$ can be supported as a solution to RGs (e.g. Rubinstein 1979).

sequence of mappings $\{s_i^t( )\}_{t=0}^{\infty}$ where $s_i^t : H^t \to A_i$. Here s_i^t dictates the choice of i at the t-stage of the RG as a function of the choices made by all the players in the proceeding t stages of G^{∞}. I also define $[s_1^t(h^t), \ldots, s_n^t(h^t)] = s^t(h^t)$. The set of RG strategies for i is denoted by F_i. Let $F = \prod_{i=1}^{n} F_i$.

If players choose a vector of RG strategies $f \in F$, the outcome at time t will be denoted by $\sigma^t(f)$ and is defined inductively as follows: $\sigma^0(f) = s^0(h^0)$ and $\forall t \geq 1$, $\sigma^t(f) = s^t[\sigma^0(f), \ldots, \sigma^{t-1}(f)]$. Moreover, I shall denote the sequence $\{\sigma^t(f)\}_{t=0}^{\infty}$ by $\sigma(f)$ and refer to it as the outcome path when f is chosen. A supergame strategy $f \in F$ is said to be stationary if it produces a constant outcome, that is if $\sigma^t(f) = \sigma \ \forall t$.

It remains to define the payoffs of the players in G^{∞}. Given a vector of strategies $f \in F$, player i receives a sequence of payoffs $\{\pi_i[\sigma^t(f)]\}_{t=0}^{\infty}$. Player i is said to prefer $f \in F$ to $g \in F$, $f >_i g$, if he prefers the stream of payoffs $\{\pi_i[\sigma^t(f)]\}_{t=0}^{\infty}$ to $\{\pi_i[\sigma^t(g)]\}_{t=0}^{\infty}$. In the infinite-horizon case one way of comparing streams of payoffs is in terms of the average payoffs. For the no-discounting case the average payoff to player i when strategy f is chosen, $\bar{\Pi}_i(f)$, is defined as

$$\bar{\Pi}_i(f) = \lim_{T \to \infty} \frac{1}{T} \sum_{t=0}^{T-1} \pi_i[\sigma^t(f)]. \tag{4}$$

(If the limit on the RHS of (4) does not exist, lim inf is used). In the case where players discount the future by a factor $\delta < 1$, the average payoff to i when the strategy f is chosen, $\bar{\Pi}_i^{\delta}(f)$, is defined as

$$\bar{\Pi}_i^{\delta}(f) = (1 - \delta) \sum_{t=0}^{\infty} \delta^t \pi_i[\sigma^t(f)]. \tag{5}$$

I shall refer to $\bar{\Pi}_i(f)$ or $\bar{\Pi}_i^{\delta}(f)$ as the long-run payoffs when f is chosen.

Notice that, in the case of average payoffs with no discounting (sometimes referred to as the Limit of the Mean (LM) criterion), any finite sequence of stage payoffs does not contribute to the long-run payoff. This is not the case if the other well-known criterion for comparing infinite streams with no discounting, the overtaking criterion, is used. In this paper I shall deal mainly with the LM case. (See Rubinstein 1979 for RGs with overtaking criterion.)

I can now define the supergame generated from G in normal form (see Chapter 2 above by Kreps) for the case in which players do not discount the future, and for the case in which discount factor is $\delta < 1$, as $G^{\infty} = (F_i, \bar{\Pi}_i)_{i=1}^{n}$ and $G^{\infty}(\delta) = (F_i, \bar{\Pi}_i^{\delta})_{i=1}^{n}$, respectively.

If the one-shot game G is repeated a finite number of times T, the T-period RG can be defined in exactly the same way as in G^{∞}. I shall denote a T-period RG with no discounting by G^T.

DEFINITION 1. For any RG $G^{\infty} = (F_i, >_i)_{i=1}^{n}$ ($>_i$ refers to the criterion for comparing streams of payoffs), f is a NE if $f >_i (f_i', f_{-i}) \ \forall \ f_i' \in F_i$ and $\forall \ i$.

The first thing to note is that equilibria of G, $E(G)$, are also equilibria of the RGs generated by G. Suppose $a^* \in E(G)$; if the supergame strategy for every player $k \neq i$ is to play a_k^* at each stage of the RG independent of the past history, the best policy for player i is to play, at each stage, his static best response to a_{-i}^*, in other words to play a_i^*. It is clear that if $\delta = 0$, $E(G)$ are the only equilibria of $G^T(\delta)$ for any T. If the future is unimportant, then players choose their static best responses. On the other hand, if players care about the future, the optimal policy for each player in a RG may not be his or her static best response. This is because choosing a static best response may lead others to retaliate against the player in the future. As a result, players may follow equilibrium norms that are not in their best short-term (static) interest. The second point to note is that the average payoff to any player i, when a NE strategy in a RG is chosen, is always greater than v_i (i can always guarantee v_i to himself), and thus the set of NE payoffs belongs to the set of IR payoffs.

3. No Discounting Case with an Infinite Horizon

The first result is known as the Folk Theorem:

THEOREM 1. *For any $m \in M$, there exists a NE strategy f in G^∞, where player i's average payoff is m_i, $\forall i$.*

Proof. Let $\bar{a} \in A$ be a vector of actions such that $\pi_i(\bar{a}) = m_i \; \forall i$. For any player i consider the RG strategy f_i, which chooses $\bar{a}_i$ until some player j deviates from $\bar{a}_j$. Thereafter, f_i punishes j by minmaxing him for ever, that is by playing γ_i^j for ever. (If several players deviate from $\bar{a}$ simultaneously, deviations are ignored and $\bar{a}$ is played.) The n-tuple of strategies $f = (f_1, \ldots, f_n)$ is a NE of G^∞, because if a player, say j, deviates from $\bar{a}_j$, he will receive after the deviation a maximum payoff

$$\max_{a_j' \in A_j} \pi_j(a_j', \gamma_j^j) = v_j$$

at each stage of the game. If he does not deviate, his average payoff will be m_j. Since m_j is individually rational, it does not pay j to deviate.   Q.E.D

Remark 1. One could in fact extend Theorem 1 and show that any vector of payoffs $m \in M^*$ could be supported as a NE. This can be achieved in one of the following two ways: (1) by public randomizations: players can choose mixed strategies (and thereby convexify the set of possible payoffs) and the outcome of the randomizations are publicly observed; (2) by allowing non-stationary strategies (f in Theorem 1 is stationary): for any $m \in M^*$ one can find an outcome path $Q =$

$(a^0, a^1, \ldots)$ such that

$$\lim_{T \to \infty} \frac{1}{T} \sum_{t=0}^{T} \pi_i(a^t) = m_i$$

(The LM criterion convexifies the payoff space.) Consider strategies in G^∞ which prescribe playing the sequence $Q = (a^1, a^2, \ldots)$ if no player has deviated from Q. And if player i deviates from Q, then, starting from the next round, the other players minmax i for ever. The payoff to this vector of strategies is m, and, for the same reason as in Theorem 1, the above strategies constitute a NE. The difference is that, if $m \in M^*$ and $m \notin M$, then the sequence of equilibrium actions, Q, which generates an average payoff m will not be stationary, and thus the strategy that will support m will be non-stationary.

In the remainder of this paper I shall mainly consider (pure) stationary strategies and thus all payoffs that are in M. However, by using method (1) or (2), the results in the rest of the paper can be extended in most cases to deal with payoffs in M^*.[7]

Strategies such as those used in the proof of Theorem 1, which punish a player for ever after a single deviation from the (equilibrium) norm, are called 'grim strategies'. However, such strategies may involve threats that are not credible. For example, in Theorem 1 it may not be in player i's interest to minmax j (play γ_i^j) for ever after a single deviation by j from a_j. Selten's (1975) notion of subgame perfect equilibrium (SPE) rules out precisely such empty threats (see Chapter 2 above). A SPE vector of strategies is such that no individual player can make himself better off, given the strategies of others, after any history. More formally, define the strategy induced by $f_i = \{s_i^t(\cdot)\}_{t=0}^\infty$ after any history $h^t = (a^0, \ldots, a^{t-1})$ as $f_i \mid h^t \cdot f_i \mid h^t$ dictates the plans of i after a history h^t, if i follows the strategy f_i. Thus $f_i \mid h^t$ is a sequence of mappings $\{\bar{s}^\tau(\cdot)\}_{\tau=0}^\infty$ such that $\bar{s}_i^\tau(\bar{h}^\tau) = s_i^{t+\tau}(h^t, \bar{h}^\tau)$ for any history $\bar{h}^\tau$.

DEFINITION 2. A vector of strategies $f \in F$ is a SPE if $f \mid h^t = (f_1 \mid h^t, \ldots, f_n \mid h^t) \in F$ is a NE after any history h^t.

The next theorem, due to Aumann and Shapely (1976) and Rubinstein (1976) (A/S–R), shows that the counterpart of Theorem 1 holds for the SPE.

THEOREM 2. For any $m \in M$, there exists a vector of SPE strategies where, for every player i, i's average payoff is m_i.

The idea behind the proof of this theorem is to construct supergame strategies such that it does not pay any player to deviate from them after

---

[7] In some cases private randomization (players can choose mixed strategies and only observe the outcomes of past randomizations) is sufficient to extend the results to M^*.

any history. Consider an IR vector of actions $\bar{a} \in A$ such that $\pi_i(\bar{a}) = m$. The supergame strategy that A/S–R use to support $m \in M$ is to play $\bar{a}$ as long as all players have chosen $\bar{a}$ in the past, leading to the payoff level in G^∞ of $\pi_i(\bar{a}) = m_i$ for i. 'If some player j deviates, he is as before minmaxed but, rather than for ever, only long enough to wipe out any possible gain that he obtained from the initial deviation' (Fudenberg and Maskin 1986). After this punishment, the players go back to playing the IR outcome $\bar{a}$. To induce each punisher $i \neq j$ to minmax j, i is threatened with the prospect that, if he does not minmax j (i.e. does not play γ_i^j for a finite time), he in turn will be minmaxed by others long enough to make such a deviation not worthwhile. 'Thus, there is a potential sequence of successively higher order punishments, where the punishment at each level is carried out for the fear the punishment at the next level will be invoked.'

The crucial thing to notice about A/S–R-type strategies is that, at any stage, if any player deviates from the action prescribed by the RG strategy f_i, he is minmaxed for a finite number of periods. (The length of the punishment period is long enough to offset any initial gain from the deviation.[8]) The strategies of minmaxing a deviant for an infinite number of times will not in general guarantee that all IR outcomes can be supported by a SPE. The problem arises when, for some i and $j \neq i$,

$$v_i = \pi_i(\gamma^i) > \pi_i(\gamma^j). \tag{6}$$

If (6) holds, the threat of minmaxing j for an infinite number of times, after a deviation by j, is not credible: i can always achieve at least v_i, whereas if i minmaxes j he will receive $\pi_i(\gamma^j)$, which is less than v_i by (6). Clearly, if all players prefer minmaxing others to being minmaxed, that is if

$$v_i < \pi_i(\gamma^j) \qquad \forall\, i \neq j, \tag{7}$$

the infinite punishment strategies (IPS) described below can support all $m \in M$. The IPS, which will support $\bar{a}$, prescribes playing $\bar{a}$ if all have followed $\bar{a}$ up to that stage. Minmax i for ever if i has deviated from $\bar{a}$. In a punishment phase, for example when j has to be minmaxed for ever, if a player, say i, deviates (stops punishing j), the strategy vectors prescribe i to be minmaxed for ever.[9] It is precisely to deal with the case in which (7) is violated that A/S–R introduce finite-period punishment strategies

---

[8] The maximum gain that player i makes at any stage from deviating is

$$Q_i = \max_{a_i \in A_i} \pi_i(a_i, \bar{a}_{-i}) - \pi_i(\bar{a}).$$

The loss that i incurs at each stage when minmaxed by others is $m_i - v_i$. Since $m_i > v_i$ and Q_i is bounded, $\exists$ a finite integer T_i such that $T_i(m_i - v_i) > Q_i$. Thus, minmaxing i for at least T_i periods deters i from deviating from the equilibrium path $\bar{a}$.

[9] The difference between grim strategies (defined before) and the IPS is that the latter involves hierarchies of infinite-length punishments whereas the former may not.

(FPS). In the case of FPS, a deviation by any player i is punished (minmaxed) for a finite period T_i and the equilibrium strategy indicates a return to the 'good state' $\bar{a}$ after the punishment phase.[10] The existence of the 'good state' at the end of the punishment phase makes the strategies credible. To demonstrate this, suppose that all players, other than i, choose the FPS strategies f_{-i}; after any history, if player i follows the strategy f_i, he will receive a payoff $m_i = \pi_i(\bar{a})$. (The punishment phase is finite, and all players are to return to $\bar{a}$ after a finite period.) If, after the history, i defects from f_i for a finite number of periods, the point will be reached in a finite time, where all players will play $\bar{a}$ and i's long-run pay-off will be $\pi_i(\bar{a}) = m_i$.[11] Continued defection from f_i, on the other hand, will invoke essentially the infinite punishment strategy by others. In this case the others play γ^i_{-i} or $\bar{a}_{-i}$ depending on whether or not they are punishing i.[12] The maximum payoff i could receive in each case is v_i or

$$\max_{a_i \in A} \pi_i(a_i, \bar{a}_{-i}),$$

respectively. Thus, i may make a gain from deviating only in the second case, when others are playing $\bar{a}_{-i}$. But after each deviation from $\bar{a}_i$, he is minmaxed, and therefore receives v_i for a finite number of periods. By choosing strategies with a long punishment phase, one can wipe out the gain from deviations, when others are choosing $\bar{a}_{-i}$, and thereby make infinite deviations from f_i not profitable.

The set of IR payoffs is obviously extremely large. For example, in the oligopoly models with homogeneous firms and non-decreasing returns to scale, it is equivalent to the set of all prices and quantities that guarantee each firm a non-negative profit: the profit of each firm could be reduced to zero if others produce large quantities of output and/or set low prices.

4. Discounting with an Infinite Horizon

One way of reducing the multiplicity of equilibria in RGs is to introduce discounting. If players do not care for the future as much as they care for the current period, the threat of punishment in the future is not so damaging to players as is the case with no discounting. As a result, in the discounted case there is more incentive to deviate at each period, and thus the number of possible behavioural norms that can be supported as

---

[10] $\bar{a}$ is called a 'good state' because $\pi_i(\bar{a}) > v_i \,\forall\, i$.

[11] With the LM criteria, any finite sequence of payoffs does not contribute to the long-run payoff.

[12] If i defects from f_i at every period, then the others choose γ^i_{-i} at every period and v_i will be the maximum payoff i could obtain in the long run. If, on the other hand, i defects infinitely often but not at every stage, then the other players may stop punishing i and play $\bar{a}_{-i}$ at some stages and revert to γ^i_{-i} immediately after i's next deviation.

an equilibrium will be smaller. The analogue of Theorem 1 for the RG $G^\infty(\delta)$, where $\delta < 1$, is as follows.

THEOREM 3. For any $\bar{a} \in A$, there exists a NE strategy with $\bar{a}$ as its stationary outcome iff

$$\max_{a_i \in A_i} \pi_i(a_i, \bar{a}_{-i}) - \pi_i(\bar{a}) \leq \frac{\delta(\pi_i(\bar{a}) - v_i)}{1 - \delta} \ \forall \ i. \tag{8}$$

A NE strategy that supports $\bar{a}$ is the grim strategy defined in Theorem 1. The LHS of (8) is the maximum one-period gain from deviating (from $\bar{a}_i$), and the RHS of (8) is the loss i will incur, after an initial deviation, if punished (minmaxed) for ever, discounted to the period of deviation. Therefore (8) is a sufficient condition for $\bar{a}$ to be supportable as a NE. Since the RHS of (8) is also the maximum loss i can incur after a deviation, (8) is also a necessary condition.

Notice that the set of payoffs that can be supported as a NE of $G^\infty(\delta)$ increases as δ becomes larger. In the limit, when δ tends to 1, the set of NE payoffs coincides with the set of IR payoffs.

As in the undiscounted case, the above grim strategies may not be credible. Abreu (1983) provides a framework for characterizing the set of SPE of discounted RGs. His analysis is in the spirit of dynamic programming.[13] Here I shall follow a more general (dynamic programming) method for characterizing the set of SPE.[14] Before stating the results, let us denote the set of SPE strategies in $G^\infty(\delta)$ by $\Sigma(\delta)$. Moreover, the set of long-run average payoffs resulting from SPE strategies is written as $P(\delta) = \{\pi \in R^n \mid \pi = \bar{\Pi}^\delta(f) \text{ for some } f \in \Sigma(\delta)\}$. It is clear from the definition of SPE that, if $f \in \Sigma(\delta)$, then $f \mid h^t \in \Sigma(\delta)$ for any h^t. In other words, a SPE strategy must prescribe other 'successor' SPE strategies to follow each history. Now consider any $f \in \Sigma(\delta)$ and its outcome path $(a^0, a^1, \ldots)$. If, at $t = 0$, i chooses an action a_i, he will be faced with the RG strategy $f_{-i} \mid (a_i, a^0_{-i})$ by others in the future. Since $f \mid (a_i, a^0_{-i})$ is a SPE, the maximum average payoff that i will receive, after choosing a_i at $t = 0$, will be the 'successor' SPE payoff $\bar{\Pi}^\delta_i(f \mid a_i, a_{-i})$. It is clear that, if f is a SPE, then

$$\frac{1}{1 - \delta} \bar{\Pi}^\delta_i(f) \geq \pi_i(a_i, a^0_{-i}) + \frac{\delta}{1 - \delta} \bar{\Pi}^\delta_i(f \mid a_i, a^0_{-i}).$$

More generally,

LEMMA 1. For any $\pi^0 \in P(\delta)$, there exists a n-tuple of actions $\bar{a} \in A$ such

---

[13] This should not be surprising, since subgame perfectness is nothing other than a many-player version of the Principle of Optimality in dynamic programming.

[14] The more general method was introduced by Abreu, Pearce, and Stacchetti (1986a,b) and developed by Fudenberg and Maskin (1987a,b) in the context of RGs with imperfect monitoring. My analysis is a non-stochastic version of their works (see Section 7).

that $\forall i$, $\forall a_i$, $\exists \pi^1 \in P(\delta)$ such that

$$\frac{1}{1-\delta} \pi_i^0 \geq \pi_i(a_i, \bar{a}_{-i}) + \frac{\delta}{1-\delta} \pi_i^1 \qquad (9)$$

where π_i^j refers to ith component of π^i, $j = 0, 1$. Moreover, the above inequality holds as an equality if $a_i = \bar{a}_i$.

In the above lemma, if $f \in \Sigma(\delta)$ is a strategy n-tuple that leads to π^0, then $\bar{a}$ refers to the first-period actions when f is chosen ($\sigma^0(f) = \bar{a}$) and π^1 refers to the continuation long-run payoff vector after a deviation by i to a_i ($\pi^1 = \bar{\Pi}^\delta(f \mid a_i, \bar{a}_{-i})$). Lemma 1 says, first, that any $\pi \in P(\delta)$ can be decomposed into a first-period payoff vector and a continuation payoff vector; and, second, that for any single-period deviation from a SPE strategy, there exists a 'successor' vector of SPE payoffs which makes the deviator no better off. The 'successor' payoffs play the role of punishments in the above lemma. The lemma illustrates the recursive nature of the set $P(\delta)$. A converse result can be established using standard dynamic programming techniques.

LEMMA 2. Suppose $\hat{\Pi}$ is a subset of M^*; if, for every element π^0 of $\hat{\Pi}$, $\exists \bar{a} \in A$ such that $\forall i$, $\forall a_i$ (9) is satisfied for some $\pi^1 \in \hat{\Pi}$, then $\hat{\Pi} \subseteq P(\delta)$.

The above lemma says that $\hat{\Pi}$ is a subset of the set of SPE payoffs if all continuation payoffs (π^1 is called a continuation payoff of π^0 if (9) is satisfied) of every element of $\hat{\Pi}$ are contained in $\hat{\Pi}$. Using Abreu–Pearce–Staachetti (1986b) terminology, a set $\hat{\Pi}$ satisfying the hypothesis of Lemma 2 is called 'self-generating'.

Proof of Lemma 2. Suppose $\hat{\Pi}$ is 'self-generating'; then there exist functions $\bar{a}: \hat{\Pi} \to A$ and $L^i: \hat{\Pi} \times A_i \to \hat{\Pi}$ s.t. $\forall \pi^0 \in \hat{\Pi}$, $\forall i$, and $\forall a_i$:

$$\frac{1}{1-\delta} \pi_i^0 \geq \pi_i[a_i, \bar{a}_{-i}(\pi^0)] + \frac{\delta}{1-\delta} L_i^i(\pi^0, a_i). \qquad (10)$$

($\bar{a}_{-i}(\pi^0)$ refers to $\bar{a}(\pi^0)$ without its ith component; $\bar{a}(\pi^0)$ and $L^i(\pi^0, a_i)$ are simply the first-period actions and the continuation payoff, respectively.) The strategy n-tuple f which leads to a payoff $\pi^0 \in \hat{\Pi}$ is constructed as follows. Play $\bar{a}(\pi^0)$ in the first period. Since $L^i(\pi^0, a_i) \in \hat{\Pi}$, $\forall a_i$, the vector of actions corresponding to $L^i(\pi^0, a_i)$, $\bar{a}[L^i(\pi, a_i)]$, is the second-period behaviour for the players if $[a_i, a_{-i}(\pi^0)]$ occurs in the first period. Continuing iteratively in this way, the strategy f that leads to π^0 can be derived. (No conditions need to be imposed on f when more than two players deviate from the equilibrium path.) (10) implies that one-period deviation from $f \mid h^t$, $\forall h^t$, is not profitable given the continuation payoffs. But this implies, using a standard dynamic programming technique, that no finite number of deviations is profitable.

Since players discount the future, the above implies that infinite deviations from f do not pay either.   Q.E.D

There are several points to note concerning the above lemmas. First, π_i^1, the continuation payoff that i receives after any one-period deviation, may be different for different deviations and different times. Second, Lemma 1 implies that $P(\delta)$ is itself 'self-generating'. Thus, it follows from Lemma 2 that $P(\delta)$ is the largest 'self-generating' set. Third, a one-period incentive compatibility condition, such as (9), is all one needs to characterize SPE payoffs in RGs with discounting. Fourth, to show that a given vector of average payoff π can be sustained as a SPE, one needs to construct a self-generating set $\hat{\Pi}$ which (weakly) contains π. I shall use this method to prove J. Friedman's (1971) result for 'collusive' equilibrium and Abreu's characterization of SPE.

PROPOSITION 1. Any $\bar{a} \in A$ can be supported as a SPE $(\pi(\bar{a}) \in P(\delta))$ if, for some $a^N \in E(G)$,

$$\frac{1}{1-\delta}\pi_i(\bar{a}) \geqslant \pi_i(a_i, \bar{a}_{-i}) + \frac{\delta}{1-\delta}\pi_i(a^N), \; \forall\, i \text{ and } \forall\, a_i \in A_i \quad (11)$$

Proof. Consider the set $\hat{\Pi} \equiv \{\pi(\bar{a}), \pi(a^N)\}$; since $\pi(a^N)$ is a NE of the stage-game, it is itself a self-generating set. Therefore it follows from (11) that $\hat{\Pi}$ is self-generating.   Q.E.D

In the above proof, the punishment (the continuation payoff) after any deviation from $\bar{a}$ is to play a NE of the stage-game. (These strategies are sometimes called the 'trigger' strategies.) The punishment is credible because playing NE of the stage-game is a SPE of the RG. Note that the punishment in this case does not depend on the player who deviates, the time, or the type of the deviation. Lemma 1 was first proved by J. Friedman (1971), and it shows that, for δ near 1, all 'collusive' payoffs, $C(G)$, can be supported as SPE of $G^\infty(\delta)$.

In RGs players do not deviate from an equilibrium because they may face a punishment in the future. Thus, the fundamental determinant of the size of the equilibria (and thus the limits of collusions) in these models is the severity of punishment. In the undiscounted case minmaxing is the worst punishment that can be imposed on the player. What are the worst punishments in $G^\infty(\delta)$? It follows from the definition of SPE that, for any strategies to be credible, the punishments that they invoke have to be supportable as SPE. Thus the maximal credible punishment that can be imposed on player i is

$$f^i \in \arg\min_{f \in \Sigma(\delta)} \bar{\Pi}_i^\delta(f).$$

Note that $f^i \in F$, the worse SPE from i's point of view, is in general different from f^j for $j \neq i$.

Abreu [1983] shows that f^i exists for all i in $G^\infty(\delta)$ with continuous payoffs. He defines an 'optimal penal code' as $(f^1, \ldots, f^n)$. Moreover, he argues that, because f^i is the worst credible punishment from i's point of view, $V_i \equiv \bar{\Pi}_i^\delta(f^i)$ is the fundamental determinant of the set of SPE.

PROPOSITION 2. Any path $Q^0 = (a^0, a^1, \ldots)$ can be supported as a SPE iff

$$\forall i;\, \forall a_i \in A_i \text{ and } \forall t,\, \sum_{\tau=t}^{\infty} \delta^{\tau-t} \pi_i(a^\tau) \geqslant \pi_i(a_i, a^t_{-i}) + \frac{\delta}{1-\delta} V_i. \quad (12)$$

Sketch of the proof. To prove that Q^0 can be sustained as a SPE, one needs to construct a self-generating set $\hat{\Pi}$ which contains the payoffs generated when Q^0 is played. $\hat{\Pi}$ is defined as the union of the following two sets: $\{(1-\delta) \sum_{\tau=t}^{\infty} \delta^{\tau-t} \pi(a^\tau),\, \forall t\}$, and $\{\bar{\Pi}^\delta(f^i \mid h^t),\, \forall h^t \text{ and } \forall i\}$. The first set refers to the average payoffs generated by Q^0 and the second refers to the average payoffs generated by the 'optimal penal codes' and their continuation payoffs. Since $f^i \mid h^t$ is a SPE, $\forall i$ and $\forall h^t$, it can be shown, using (12), that $\hat{\Pi}$ is self-generating (a simple exercise). Q.E.D

A RG strategy vector which would support any $Q^0 = (a^0, a^1, \ldots)$ satisfying (12) is, first, to play Q^0 until some player deviates singly from Q^0, and, second, for any j, to play $\sigma(f^j)$[15] if the jth player deviates from Q^k, $k = 0, 1, \ldots, N$, where Q^k is an ongoing previously specified path, and to continue with Q^k if no deviations occur or if two or more players deviate simultaneously.[16] Thus, above Q^0 is supported as a SPE with n possible threats of punishments, $\{\sigma(f^1), \ldots, \sigma(f^n)\}$, one for each player, and each punishment path that may be impaired is only a function of the identity of the deviator and not the entire history of the game.

Since optimal penal codes are also SPE, it follows from Proposition 2 that any outcome path of an optimal penal code, $\sigma(f^i)$, satisfies

$$\sum_{\tau=t}^{\infty} \delta^{\tau-t} \pi_i[\sigma^\tau(f^i)] \geqslant \pi_i[a_i, \sigma^t_{-i}(f^i)]$$

$$+ \sum_{\tau=0}^{\infty} \delta_i^{\tau+1} \pi_i[\sigma^\tau(f^i)] \qquad \forall i, \forall a_i \in A_i, \text{ and } \forall t.$$

Having provided a characterization of the set of SPE outcomes of $G^\infty(\delta)$, let us consider the set of SPE as δ tends to 1. Does the set $p(\delta)$ tend to the set of IR payoffs, M^*? Fudenberg and Maskin (1986) provide an example to show that the result does not hold in general. The problem can arise if (7) is violated. If (7) holds, that is if players prefer to minmax others rather than to be minmaxed, then it can be shown that any IR

---

[15] Note that $\sigma(f^i)$ is the outcome path when players follow f^i.
[16] Abreu calls such a vector of strategies, with at most $(n+1)$ possible outcome paths, $[Q^0, \sigma(f^1), \ldots, \sigma(f^n)]$, the simple strategy profile.

payoffs can be supported as a SPE of a $G^\infty(\delta)$ for δ near 1. The proof of this result requires constructing IPS strategies, described in the previous section, which minmax a deviator for ever.

Many games do not satisfy (7). In these cases, even strategies with finite–period punishment (A/S–R) may not be able to support all IR payoffs, even for δ near 1. To illustrate the problem, consider the A/S–R strategy, f, of the previous section. According to f, players choose an IR vector of actions $\bar{a}(\pi_i(\bar{a}) > v_i, \forall i)$ if all players have played $\bar{a}$, and punish a deviator, say i, by minmaxing him for a finite period T_i and then returning to the 'good state' $\bar{a}$. Any further deviations are similarly punished. Thus there is a potential sequence of successively higher-order punishments. Therefore A/S–R type strategies induce player j to punish a deviator, i, by threatening to punish (minmax) j for a finite number of periods, T_j. If $j \neq i$ prefers to be minmaxed rather than minmax i, that is if (7) is violated, T_j has to be longer than T_i in the discounted RG (as well as in the overtaking criterion case).[17] Thus, with the A/S–R type strategies, the threat of punishment is made credible by the threat of punishments that may last for longer periods. Therefore as the number of deviations increases, the length of punishment periods has to be increased to make the strategies credible. But *for any given $\delta < 1$*, the punishments very far in the future have a very small deterrence effect. Thus, *for any $\delta < 1$*, the strategies that involve punishment phases which become longer as the number of deviations increase are not necessarily credible.

Fudenberg and Maskin (1986) consider strategies that not only punish the last deviator but also, ultimately, reward those who were supposed to punish the last deviator, thereby inducing them to punish. To construct strategies of this type, one needs to be able to reward the latter group (the punishers) without also rewarding the player they punish. This can be achieved if the dimension of IR payoff space, M^*, equals the number of players. (Otherwise one may not be able to increase the payoff of some players without rewarding the others.) Fudenberg and Maskin, by considering strategies just described, show that the set of payoffs that can be supported as SPE of $G^\infty(\delta)$ approximates the set of IR payoffs for δ near 1, if the above 'full-dimensionality' condition holds.[18]

---

[17] If (7) is violated, $T_j \leq T_i$ implies that it may be better for j not to punish i. On the other hand, if $T_j > T_i$, the return to the 'good state' $\bar{a}$ (note that $\pi_j(\bar{a}) > v_j > \pi_j(\gamma^i)$) is postponed further; thus it may pay j to punish i in order to return to the 'good state' sooner.

[18] Fudenberg and Maskin also show that, for the two-player case, the result follows independently of the 'full dimensionality' requirement. In this case they use strategies where players mutually minmax each other after any deviation. With some abuse of terminology, henceforth, a game is said to satisfy the Fudenberg–Maskin full dimensionality 'condition' either if the set of IR payoffs has a full dimension or if the game has only two players.

5. Finite Horizon

In economics, infinite-horizon models are used as an idealization of long, but finite, models. The question that arises, given that agents and markets are finitely lived, is whether infinitely RGs are reasonable idealizations of finitely repeated interactions between players. The first response to this problem is to consider games where at each stage there is a positive probability that the game will continue to the next stage. The formal representation of these games is the same as the infinitely RGs with discounting. In this case the discount factors may be viewed as the probability of the game continuing to the next period, or a measure of impatience, or a combination of the two.

What happens when the game is certain to end in some finite time?[19] It is well known that the solutions for games repeated a finite number of times, no matter how large, can be significantly different from the infinitely RGs; that is, there is a discontinuity at the infinite-horizon limit. Some notable examples are the classic 'Prisoners' Dilemma' (PD) (Figure 4.1), the constant average cost Cournot oligopoly with linear demand (Radner 1980), and the so-called 'chain store paradox' (Selten 1978). In these examples, no outcomes other than the NE of the stage-game can be supported as solutions to finite repetitions of these games. In fact, one can demonstrate the following result.

PROPOSITION 3. For any one-shot game $G = (A_i, \pi_i)_{i=1}^n$ which has a unique NE, $a^N \in A$, and for any finite horizon T, the SPE of G^T, where G^T is the T-period repetition of G, consists of playing a^N at every stage.

Proof. This is given by the following backward induction argument. Clearly, in the last period, T, of any SPE, a^N must be played irrespective of whether deviations have occurred or not. Thus, the decision by one player at $(T-1)$ does not affect the decisions of others at T. Therefore at $(T-1)$ every player must be playing a best response to choices of others at $(T-1)$. Hence a^N is the outcome of any SPE at $(T-1)$. It follows that actions at $(T-2)$ do not influence actions at $(T-1)$ and at T, and so on. Q.E.D

Notice that, although G^T in the above proposition has a unique SPE, playing a^N at every stage, G^T may have other Nash equilibria. In fact, it can be shown that, for any stage-game where NE payoffs and minmax payoffs do not coincide for any player, any IR payoffs can be supported

---

[19] Cremer (1986) and Sabourian (1988) consider overlapping-generation games where players live for a finite time and the game lasts indefinitely. It is shown that 'co-operation' on the part of the young players can be sustained as SPE of such games. In these games, at any stage, players who are to leave the game in the next period always cheat if given the opportunity.

	C_2		D_2	
C_1	2	2	-1	3
D_1	3	-1	0	0

Fig. 4.1

	A_2		B_2		C_2	
A_1	4	4	0	0	0	0
B_1	0	0	2	2	6	0
C_1	0	0	0	6	5	5

Fig. 4.2

as a NE of the game repeated sufficiently often (with no discounting).[20] In the Prisoners' Dilemma case, the NE of the stage-game, (D_1, D_2) in Figure 4.1, coincides with the minmax actions. Moreover, (D_1, D_2) is the only NE outcome of the finitely repeated PD.

The fact that the set of SPE outcomes of games, repeated a large but finite number of times, may be different from that of games repeated infinitely often created a dilemma for game theorists.[21] The result is particularly disturbing because intuition and considerable experimental evidence suggest that some degree of 'co-operation' is plausible even in finitely RGs with unique stage-game NE. Thus, the solutions to infinitely RGs seem to approximate reality better than that of the finitely RGs.

There have been several escape routes from the above dilemma.

(a) Non-uniqueness of the NE set of the stage-game

The discontinuity at the infinite horizon and the lack of any co-operative equilibrium are specific to the games satisfying the hypothesis of Proposition 3. Benoit and Krishna (1985) provide conditions for continuity at the infinite horizon for the SPE of RGs with no discounting. Benoit and Krishna, J. Friedman (1985), and Frayse and Moreaux (1985) show that, if the stage-game has more than one Nash equilibrium, the SPE of the finitely RG may involve co-operative behaviour. To illustrate the point, consider the game G depicted in Figure 4.2. G has two (pure-strategy) NEs, (A_1, A_2) and (B_1, B_2). Note that a co-operative outcome in G is (C_1, C_2), which Pareto-dominates the NEs of G. If G is played twice, the outcomes (C_1, C_2) followed by (A_1, A_2) can be sustained as a SPE of G^2 using the following threat: any deviations in period 1 will be met by playing (B_1, B_2). (B_1, B_2) is a NE of the stage-game; therefore threatening to play (B_1, B_2) is credible. It is trivial to show that deviations from (C_1, C_2) and (A_1, A_2) do not pay, given the above threat.

[20] Any $m \in M^*$ can be sustained as a NE of G^T, for long enough T, by the threat that any deviation will be minmaxed for the rest of the game. These strategies are obviously not credible.

[21] The problem is very similar to that discovered by general equilibrium theorists who tried to introduce money into finite-horizon sequence economies with rational expectations. In these models, money, which acts only as a store of value, has no value in the last period. (The world is to end in the next period.) As a result, the store of value loses its value in the penultimate period. The unravelling continues until the first period, and there will be no demand for money in the first period. With infinite horizon the problem disappears.

In the above example the co-operative outcome (C_1, C_2) in the first period is supported by the threat of playing the worst NE of the stage-game. Such strategies are simple and are basically the trigger strategies. For the no-discounting case, Benoit and Krishna consider more severe punishments than trigger strategies. Following Abreu (see the previous section), they consider the worst credible punishment (SPE) for player i in a T-period repetition of $G = (A_i, \pi_i)_{i=1}^{n}$. They denote it by

$$w_i(T) = \min \left\{ \sum_{t=0}^{T-1} \pi_i(a^t) \mid (a^0, \ldots, a^{T-1}) \in Q(T) \right\},$$

where $Q(T)$ is the set of SPE outcomes of G^T. As in the previous section, $\{w_i(T)\}_{i=1}^{n}$ characterizes the set of $P(T)$.

PROPOSITION 3. The path $(a^0, \ldots, a^{T-1}) \in Q(T)$ iff $\forall i$ and $\forall t < T$:

$$\sum_{\tau=t}^{T-1} \pi_i(a^\tau) \geq \max_{a_i \in A_i} \pi_i(a_i', a_{-i}^t) + w_i(T - t).$$

The proof of the above proposition follows from the definitions of $w_i(T)$ and SPE.[22]

Benoit and Krishna show that, under the same full-dimensionality condition as in Fudenberg and Maskin, $\{w_i(T)\}_{i=1}^{n}$ can be approximately characterized by what they call 'three-phase punishments' for large T. For any player i, the basic idea of a 'three-phase punishment' is to minmax i for a finite number of periods, T_i, in the first phase. The second or reward phase compensates all players $j \neq i$ for their compliance during the first phase without rewarding player i who is to be punished. This phase is needed in order to induce $\forall j \neq i$ to minmax i in the first phase. This requires the 'full dimensionality' of the payoff space.[23] The third phase involves, as it must, playing one or other NE of the stage-game. (Since the game has a finite horizon, the last-period actions of any SPE must be a NE of the stage-game.) The overall duration of these punishment phases is chosen such that i is penalized quite heavily. The important thing to note is that, the longer is the first phase, the closer the payoffs of the above 'three-phase punishment' will be to the minmax payoffs. Benoit and Krishna, using the above 'three-phase punishment', show that, if for each player there are at least two NE payoffs in G and the Fudenberg–Maskin 'full-dimensionality' condition (see the previous section) holds, then any IR payoffs can be approximated by the average payoff of a SPE of G^T for large T. For these types of games the result is proved by constructing, for any n-tuple (SPE) punishments of a $G(T)$, a (SPE) three-phase punishment for $G(T')$ (T' may be different from T) for each player which is more severe in terms of the average payoff (has a

---

[22] Proposition 3 is the analogue of Proposition 2 for the finitely RG.
[23] Note that, if condition (7) holds, the second phase would be redundant.

longer initial phase) than the original punishment. In this way a hierarchy of three–phase punishments is built, 'each derived from the previous one, which in the limit approximate optimal punishments for games with long horizons'. 'Punishments of higher and higher degree are also of longer and longer duration' and also approximate, in the limit, in terms of average payoffs, the minmax payoffs of the stage-game.

(b) Continuous time

This is discussed in the next section.

(c) Incomplete information

In the context of finitely repeated PD (Figure 4.1), Kreps *et al.* (1982) show that co-operation, (C_1, C_2), can be sustained as an equilibrium if each player is not completely certain about the motives of other players (the game is one of ε-incomplete information) and if the horizon is long. More formally, they show that, for any $\varepsilon > 0$, if each player initially believes that with a probability ε the other begins the game by co-operating and subsequently plays tit-for-tat (such a player is called 'crazy'), and if with a probability $(1 - \varepsilon)$ the other does not co-operate (plays 'rationally' if the payoffs are those given by the PD game), the co-operative outcome (C_1, C_2) can be supported as a sequential equilibrium[24] if the number of repetitions is large enough. Fudenberg and Maskin (1986) develop a full Folk Theorem for ε-incomplete-information RGs. By varying the initial beliefs of the complete information game in arbitrary small amounts (i.e. by introducing different types of ε-incomplete information), they show that any IR payoffs can be sustained (approximately) as a sequential equilibrium payoff of an incomplete-information RG if the horizon is long and if the stage-game satisfies the 'full-dimensionality' condition discussed in Section 4. The initial beliefs, one assumes, clearly depend on the IR payoffs one likes to sustain. In these ε-incomplete-information models, players follow rules, which are irrational if the game were complete, in order to build reputations. Reputation models of this type have been extensively surveyed by Wilson (1986a). I shall only give a brief intuition of the results and make some general comments.

Consider a one-shot game $G = (A_i, \pi_i)_{i=1}^n$ with a unique NE, $a^N \in A$, being repeated a finite number of times, T. Let $\bar{a} \in A$ be a 'collusive' outcome ($\bar{a}$ Pareto-dominates a^N). Suppose that every player j believes that, every other player $i \neq j$ with probability $(1 - \varepsilon)$ will play a_i^N (π_i is the payoff of i) and with probability ε is 'crazy' and will play the following trigger strategy: choose $\bar{a}_i$ as long as others have played $\bar{a}_{-i}$; if

---

[24] The equilibrium notion used is the sequential equilibrium because the game is an incomplete-information one.

some player has deviated in the past, i plays a_i^N. What are the optimal strategies in this incomplete-information game? Compare, for any player j (with the payoff function π_j), the policy of deviating in one period versus co-operating (playing $\bar{a}_j$). If j behaves like a 'crazy' player (builds a reputation) and co-operates, his payoff is $\pi_j(\bar{a})$ in each period for the rest of the game if others are all crazy (the probability of this is ε^{n-1}). If one of the other players is not crazy, j receives at least $\min_{a \in A} \pi_j(a)$ in the first period, and in each subsequent period he receives $\pi_j(a^N)$. If j does not co-operate, j receives at most $\max_{a \in A} \pi_j(a)$ in the first period, and in each subsequent period he will receive $\pi_j(a^N)$. Since $\pi_j(\bar{a}) > \pi_j(a^N)$, the expected gain from co-operating lasts for $(T - 1)$ periods, whereas the gain from not co-operating lasts for one period. Therefore for any $\varepsilon > 0$, one can find a large enough T such that co-operating is the optimal policy for j.

There are several points to note concerning the above results. First, they show that a small difference in information may make a large difference in terms of outcomes for games that are repeated a long, but finite, number of times. Second, for finitely RGs, although for any given initial belief the size of the equilibrium set may be much smaller than the set of IR payoffs (i.e., the multiplicity problem may not be so important), by varying the initial beliefs, one can obtain the latter set. Thus, the Fudenberg–Maskin result recasts the multiplicity problem in terms of choosing different initial beliefs rather than in terms of choosing different equilibria. Moreover, it may be argued that not all initial beliefs are equally reasonable, therefore the exercise of choosing the beliefs is a simpler task. Finally, note that in the above games the 'backward-induction' argument is broken by introducing a small uncertainty into the game. Because players are not sure of the type of players they are playing against, optimal responses cannot be worked out simply by looking at the last period and working backwards.

The above demonstrates that in the case where the NE outcome of the stage-game is not unique (case (a)) and in the case of the incomplete information (case (c)), the finite horizon problem (unravelling backwards) does not arise because in both cases at the last stage of the finite RG, there is not a unique optimal behaviour for each player. As a result, the equilibrium behaviour at the last stage, in both cases, may depend on the past. (In the incomplete information case, this occurs throught the beliefs.)

The next two approaches to the problem of discontinuity at the infinite horizon abandon the perfect 'rationality' common in game theory and economic theory.

(d) ε-equilibrium

Radner (1980) introduces the notion of ε-equilibrium: a vector of strategies is a ε-equilibrium if the strategies allow each player to obtain a payoff within ε of his best attainable payoff, given the strategy of others. Thus, for $\varepsilon = 0$, the ε-equilibria coincide with the Nash equilibria of the game. Radner also defines subgame perfect ε-equilibria (ε-SPE): these are simply strategies that are ε-equilibria in every subgame *over the whole horizon.*[25]

Now consider the PD model (Figure 4.1) repeated a finite number of times, T. Suppose that players are concerned with average payoffs. If player j's strategy is to play the grim strategy (co-operate, play C_j, until i plays D_i), player i's best strategy is to co-operate until the last period and then deviate. For player i, the difference between following the above optimal strategy and playing C_i at every stage unless j deviates (the grim strategy) arises at the last stage. Therefore the difference between the above two strategies in terms of the average payoff is simply the difference between the stage payoffs in the two cases at the last period divided by T. Since the payoffs at each stage are bounded, the difference between the two strategies approaches 0 as T increases. In other words, for any ε, one can find a $\bar{T}$ such that $\forall\, T > \bar{T}$, co-operation, (C_1, C_2), is a ε-SPE of PD games repeated T times.

There are several points to note concerning Radner's approach. First, his result depends on one-period gains becoming insignificant as the horizon increases. Second, co-operation satisfies his definition of ε-SPE, because after any history h^t, the grim strategy's payoff is within ε of the optimal strategy payoff if payoffs refer to that over the whole horizon T. If the payoffs over the remaining stages are compared (see fn. 25), $(T - t)$, co-operation will not be ε-credible if $T - t$ is small. Thus, the grim strategies are not ε-SPE in this latter sense. Finally, one should consider the justification for ε-equilibrium. Radner justifies the notion by appealing to the cost of discovering and using alternative strategies— 'bounded rationality' and/or 'satisficing'. He does not specify exactly the type of 'bounded rationality' and/or 'satisficing' he has in mind. I shall later discuss one particular aspect of 'bounded rationality', the cost of storing large number of states in one's mind.

Fudenberg and Levine (1983) generalize Radner's convergence result to a general class of infinitely RGs where long-run payoffs are continuous in strategies at infinity (this means that players do not care much for the future; thus, discounted RGs satisfy this property) and the sets of actions available to players at each stage may depend on past actions. They characterize the set of SPE of these infinitely RGs by considering the ε^T-SPE in the same RG truncated after T periods of play. They show

---

[25] In calculating whether a strategy generates a payoff within ε of the optimal payoff in each subgame, Radner considers the payoff generated by any continuation strategy (after any history) to be the average payoff in all the stages of the game. An alternative definition would be to take the payoff to be the average payoff in the remaining periods after the history.

that the limits of all ε^T-SPE of the above truncated RGs, as $T \to \infty$ and $\varepsilon^T \to 0$, coincide with the set of SPE of the infinite-horizon game.[26] The Fudenberg–Levine results (and that of Harris 1985, which extends their result) imply that, in the above RGs, (1) the SPE of infinitely RGs are good approximations to the ε-SPE (where ε is small) of finitely RGs with long horizon;[27] (2) to characterize the solutions to infinitely RGs one needs to consider the ε-SPE of the finitely RGs with long horizon. The latter may be an easier exercise because backward induction can be applied to the finite case. For example, to study the uniqueness of SPE of infinite-horizon games, one needs to consider the limits of all ε-SPE of truncated games as $\varepsilon \to 0$ and $T \to \infty$. In finite action games, Fudenberg and Levine (1983) use this method to show that the SPE is unique iff changes in strategies at the horizon have no effects on the *equilibrium play* earlier.[28]

Computing machine

Neyman (1985) deals with the lack of co-operation (and thus the discontinuity at the infinite horizon) in the finitely repeated PD by imposing bounds on the complexity of strategies that players may use. Neyman assumes that each player uses a machine (a finite automaton machine called 'Moore machine'—see Hopcroft and Ullman 1979) to implement his strategy. Consider G^∞ generated by the game $G = (A_i, \pi_i)_{i=1}^n$. A (Moore-) machine M_i for player i in this game consists of four elements (Q_i, q_i^0, g_i, r_i), where Q_i is a finite set, $q_i^0 \in Q_i$, $g_i : Q_i \to A_i$ and $r_i : Q_i \times A_{-i} \to Q_i$. Let us now explain intuitively the four elements of machine M_i. Q_i is the set of possible states that the machine can find itself in at any stage. No conditions are imposed on the meaning of the states except that they are finite. q_i^0 is the initial state. g_i is the output function; it specifies a one-shot action for every state. Thus, if M_i is at a certain state $q_i \in Q_i$, it will play the one-shot action $g_i(q_i)$. Finally, r_i is the transition function. It describes the transition from state to state: if at state q_i the other players choose the action a_{-i}, the machine's next state is $r_i(q_i, a_{-i})$. Finally, the size of the finite automaton is the number of states.

Any machine M_i induces a pure strategy for player i in the repeated

---

[26] Denote the set of ε-SPE strategies of the T-period truncated RG by $P(\varepsilon, T)$. The Fudenberg–Levine result amounts to showing that the correspondence $P(\varepsilon, T)$ is continuous at $\varepsilon = 0$ and $T = \infty$ with respect to the topology on the set of strategies they choose.

[27] Benoit and Krishna's result is stronger than above for the games satisfying multiple-stage–Nash equilibria and full dimensionality. In their case the approximation holds for $\varepsilon = 0$.

[28] They call these types of games 'finitely determined'. Using Rubinstein's bargaining game as an example (see Canning's Chapter 8 below), they argue that in continuous-action games, if the effect of changes at the horizon is dampened out as one works backward from the horizon, the SPE of the infinite RG is unique as in Rubinstein's model.

game as follows: for any t and any history of actions $h^t = (a^0, \ldots, a^{t-1})$, player i's action at t is $g_i(q_i^t)$ where

$$\forall t \geq 1, q_i^t \text{ is defined inductively by } q_i^t = r_i(q_i^{t-1}, a_i^{t-1}).$$

Thus one can interpret the machine M_i as a mechanical tool for carrying out a strategy. It is a tool (computer program) for implementing a player's plan.

Modelling human behaviour as a machine obviously does not capture fully the essence of what Simon calls 'procedural rationality'—activities involved in acquiring and processing information and thereby reaching a decision. Nevertheless, in the absence of a satisfactory description of the procedure of human decision-making, modelling players as machines does capture an aspect of 'bounded rationality', namely the complexity of rules of behaviour. For instance, the brain has been modelled as a finite automaton. The latter has also been used for computer operations.

Neyman and others (see Section 9 for further discussion of modelling players as machines) consider as a measure of complexity simply the size of the machine. They do not deal with the complexity of the transition function or with the costs of computing optimal behavioural rules. Neyman defines the machine game $G^T(l_i)_{i=1}^n$ as a T-period RG in which each player i can choose a machine with at most l_i number of states to implement his behaviour. He considers the case where players are concerned with the average payoff over T periods. (His result can be extended to the discounting case.) Thus, if players choose machines $\{M_i\}_{i=1}^n$ to implement their plan, player i's payoff in the machine game will be

$$\frac{1}{T} \sum_{t=0}^{T-1} \pi_i(a^t)$$

where $a_i^t = g_i(q_i^t)$ and $q_i^t = r_i(q_i^{t-1}, a_{-i}^{t-1})$. The NE in $G^T(l_i)_{i=1}^n$ is a vector of machines $(M_i^*)_{i=1}^n$ such that $\forall i$, M_i^* is a best machine for i against M_{-i}^* in the class of all machines with not more than l_i states. For the repeated PD game played by the above machines, Newman shows the following.

PROPOSITION 5. Co-operating, playing (C_1, C_2) in Figure 4.1, at every period can be implemented as a NE of the above machine game iff

$$2 \leq l_i \leq (T-1), \forall i. \tag{13}$$

The intuition behind the necessity part of the above proposition is that, if in equilibrium player j is co-operating at every state, the other player, i, can make himself better off if he deviates, plays D_i, at the last stage (where no reprisal is possible) and co-operates at every other stage. Now if $l_i \geq T$, the above strategy can be implemented by some machine of size l_i. This is because the states of the machine can be used to recognize the stages that are being played. The machine i simply specifies playing D_i at the last stage (corresponding to a particular state) and playing C_i at other stages. The intuition behind the sufficiency part is that, if (13) holds, the machines do not have enough states to recognize the different stages of the game. As a result, if j is playing tit-for-tat (playing C_j if C_i was chosen by $i \neq j$ and D_j otherwise), the best strategy that can be implemented by machines of size l_i is to play tit-for-tat: the only strategy that is better than tit-for-tat is to play D_i at the last stage and C_i at every other stage; but this strategy can be implemented only by a machine with a size of at least T.

The necessity result can obviously be extended to show that, if $l_i \geqslant T \; \forall \, i$, every pure-strategy equilibrium results in the play of (D_1, D_2) at every stage. Thus, co-operation seems to be possible if the sizes of the machines are smaller than the horizon of the game. Neyman, however, obtains a much stronger result with respect to mixed strategy equilibria in $G^T(l_i)_{i=1}^n$. A mixed strategy amounts to a probability distribution over the machines. The players can randomize their choices of machines. Formally, he obtains the following.

PROPOSITION 6. For any integer k, $\exists \, \bar{T}$ such that if $T > \bar{T}$ and $T^{1/k} < \min_i (l_i) < T^K$, there is a mixed strategy equilibrium in a T-period repeated PD (Figure 4.1) in which the average payoff to each player is $2 - 1/k$.

The above proposition implies that there are mixed strategy equilibria that approximate the co-operative outcomes even when machines' sizes are very large relative to T. (They can indeed be chosen to be an arbitrary power of the horizon.) The idea behind the above result is as always by construction: two machines are chosen such that they play the game in a complex pattern of Cs and Ds; as a result, each machine spends a large fraction of its computational resources (states) in determining at each stage what is the next move, and thus has not enough free states to allow for deviating precisely at the last stage (Zemel 1986). Moreover, it does not pay any player to choose a machine that deviates in earlier periods from the above pattern because the other machine is chosen so that it stops following the above pattern and plays D throughout if the other has deviated.

Ben-Porath (1986), Megiddo and Widgerson (1985), and Zemel (1986) pursue this line of research further by looking at zero-sum games, games played by Turing machines, and games that have communication channels.

6. Continuous Time[29]

In discrete RGs players can change their actions once a period length of 1 has elapsed. What about the case in which players can change their

---

[29] Henceforth I shall be concerned with infinitely RGs unless stated otherwise.

actions almost instantaneously? At first glance the question seems naive; it may be argued that a period length of 1 is simply an unimportant normalization. However, it turns out that in RGs the period length does matter, and some behavioural rules that cannot be supported as solutions to discrete RGs can be supported as solutions to games where players can change their actions instantaneously.

To illustrate this point, consider a Bertrand model with a single homogeneous good and two firms. It is easy to see that price-matching behaviour (and thus the kinked demand equilibrium) is not necessarily an equilibrium of the discrete-time RG: if firm j plays the price-matching strategy $p_j^t = \min \{p_i^{t-1}, p_j^{t-1}\}$ when prices are above average cost, it pays player $i \neq j$ to follow a different strategy; for example, i could capture the entire market in every period t by playing the following strategy:

$$p_i^t = \min \{p_i^{t-1}, p_j^{t-1}\} - \varepsilon^t \qquad \text{for small } \varepsilon^t > 0. \qquad (14)$$

The problem is simply that with a discrete-time RG, a player may be able to deviate from a rule of behaviour and make a 'transitory gain' before other players respond. The 'transitory gain' of course is proportional to the length of the periods. The strategy, defined by (14), is preferred to price-matching because i, by following (14), always keeps one step ahead of j, who is price-matching. Intuition tells us that (14) will not be preferred to price-matching if players could respond instantaneously to any deviation. (This intuition turns out to be correct.)

Another example is the finitely repeated PD discussed in the previous section. Co-operation cannot be supported as an equilibrium of this model because with discrete time there is a gain in deviating one period before the other player. (If the other player is playing tit-for-tat, this happens at the last period.) But this gain is proportional to the length of the period. As a result, the gain seems to disappear and co-operation can be supported as an equilibrium if players can respond to each other instantaneously.

The above examples illustrate that the choice of the period length can matter. In some examples one may argue that discrete-time games cause serious conceptual difficulties. One example is the repeated Bertrand model. Here, if at any period t, a firm undercuts the others, it is assumed that it will capture the entire market for that period before the others can respond at $(t+1)$, say. This can be justified if consumers learn about (and act upon) the price cut instantaneously and the earliest the rivals can act is one period later. Thus, in discrete repeated Bertrand models there is an asymmetry problem between the time it takes for consumers and producers to respond to price cuts, which would disappear in a continuous-time model. (See Anderson 1985 for further discussion of this point.)

The natural way of modelling instantaneous changes of actions is to develop continuous-time models. The problem with this approach is that strategies in these games do not necessarily define a unique outcome path for the dynamic game.[30] Consider the following example, due to Simon and Stinchombe (1986). In a game with one player and two choices, l and R, the player follows the strategy f defined by

$$f^t = \begin{cases} \text{play } l \text{ if } t = 0 \text{ or if } l \text{ was chosen at every } s < t \\ \text{play } R \text{ otherwise.} \end{cases} \tag{15}$$

If t is defined over discrete time, the strategy f generates the outcome: play l at every time node. In continuous time any outcome that plays l on $[0, \bar{t}]$ and R thereafter (for any $\bar{t} > 0$) is consistent with the above strategy. The basic problem is that, after any history h^t, time-continuous strategies can define uniquely the actions to be taken at t, but they cannot extend the outcomes in a unique way to any open interval beyond t. With continuous time one constantly has to deal with (half) open intervals.[31]

In some games the above problem does not arise. One notable example is the differential game where players' strategies satisfy the 'state-space' assumption: they are functions of time and the state-variable. (These games are not, strictly speaking, RGs.) The important thing in these models is that state-variables, and thus the value functions, are smooth (as a function of players' actions); as a result, one can overcome the above problem of unique extension of outcomes.[32] But discontinuous changes in the state-variables, as a result of changes in players' actions, are precisely the reason why most co-operative outcomes can be supported as equilibria of RGs.

A natural approach to modelling continuous-time games, particularly for the cases where the above problem of defining a unique outcome to strategies does arise, is to consider the discrete approximation to such games. Anderson (1985) considers the limits of ε-SPE of discrete games as ε and the length of periods approach 0. He justifies the use of ε-SPE (rather than the SPE of discrete games) by appealing to the following result, due to Fudenberg and Levine (1986): for any game where continuous-time formulation is possible (e.g. games of timing), and for any discrete approximations to this game, every SPE of the former game can be approximated by some ε-SPE (though not necessarily by SPE) of the discrete games.

Anderson applies his discrete approximation model to the PD and the oligopoly model. He considers the limits of ε-SPE of discrete models

---

[30] See Anderson (1985) and Simon and Stinchombe (1986) for a more thorough discussion of this point.

[31] Technically, the problem is that continuous time is not well-ordered in the usual ordering.

[32] Starr and Ho (1967a,b) provide a general framework for dealing with non-zero-sum differential games. State-space strategies are discussed in Section 8.

where players incur adjustment costs in changing their actions from one period to the next. He calls the limits of the ε-SPE 'quick response equilibria'. He shows that price-matching policy for oligopolistic firms and thus kinked-demand equilibria can be supported as quick-response equilibria. His model is closely related to Marschak and Selten (1978) on inertia supergames and Sabourian (1984c) on conjectural equilibria (see the next section).

Simon and Stinchombe (1986) develop a general framework for dealing with continuous-time strategies which further justifies the ε-SPE approximation. The problems of continuous time can be resolved if one associates a unique outcome path to each continuous-time strategy. In (15) there is a natural way to resolve the non-uniqueness problems: choose the outcome to be the limit of outcomes generated by playing the strategy on discrete grids (choose l at every t). The problem with this approach is that outcomes generated by playing the strategies on discrete grids may have no sensible limits, or the limit outcomes may be inconsistent with the strategies (see Simon and Stinchombe 1986). Simon and Stinchombe impose conditions on time-continuous strategies (to be interpreted as 'master programs', instructing players how to play the game on every discrete grid) such that there exists an outcome that is the limit of outcomes generated by playing the strategy on *any* sequence of increasingly fine grids. Having defined a unique outcome for each continuous-time strategy, they provide conditions on payoffs (relatively weak) such that the SPE of continuous-time strategies coincide with the limit of ε-SPE of discrete games as $\varepsilon \to 0$ and the discrete time approximates the continuous time (the grids become finer).

7. Static Representations of Repeated Games: Conjectural Models

In conjectural (and reaction function) equilibrium models, each agent calculates his optimal action taking into account the responses of other agents to his action. In these models time is not treated explicitly; however, it is clear that conjectural models have no meaning in static (one-shot) games, where players are simultaneously asked to choose an action once, and there is no opportunity for reactions. Conjectural models should be regarded as static representations of some dynamic (RG) stories. Despite the similarity between these models and RGs, the two subjects have developed independently of each other, though there are a few exceptions. The question that arises is, To what extent can solutions to conjectural models be regarded as solutions to RGs? Sabourian (1984a) considers this question and tries to give a time-explicit story to conjectural models.[33]

---

[33] The lack of any time-explicit stories in conjectural models has prompted some (Makowski 1983) to argue that these models are inconsistent or cannot be understood in terms of non-cooperative games.

Consider the game $G = (A_i, \pi_i)_{i=1,2}$. $c_j(a, a_i') \in A_j$ denotes what i conjectures j to do in response to a deviation by i from a status quo $a \in A$ (and thus the action a_i) to a_i'. Each conjecture in these models is a function of a status quo term and a deviation term. The status quo plays the role of a state-variable and each player believes that the response of the other depends on it. Thus each player's optimal actions depend on the status quo term (commonly observed) and on the conjecture the player has; the best replies of i at status quo a are defined by

$$B_i(a, c_j) = \arg\max_{a_i' \in A_i} \pi_i[a_i', c_j(a, a_i')].$$

A status quo $a^* \in A$ is a conjectural equilibrium if

$$a_i^* \in B_i(a^*, c) \qquad \forall\, i = 1,2. \tag{16}$$

Since best replies are defined for a given vector of conjectures, for simplicity I shall henceforth drop the conjectures c_j from the best-reply mapping $B_i(a, c_j)$ and write the mapping in terms of its first argument only.

There are two points to note about the above definitions. First, players are concerned with payoffs after the others have responded; the transitory profits that players can obtain before the others have responded is unimportant to them in conjectural models. The neglect of the transitory payoff can be justified in a time-explicit setting if one assumes either that players can respond to each other instantaneously or that there are some adjustment costs which offset any transitory gains. Second, agents are myopic and are concerned with payoffs only one period ahead.

In the above definitions, there are no conditions on the conjectures. The natural as well as the most difficult research strategy is to develop a dynamic learning story of how conjectures are formed (see Chapter 5 below by Hahn). The literature has opted for imposing some 'rationality' condition on the conjectures. The most common 'rationality' condition requires each player's conjecture to be 'correct'—to coincide with the optimal responses of the other players. Notice that such requirement is very similar to the subgame perfection requirement in extensive games; the latter also requires the strategy attributed to each player to be the optimal one for that player on any subgame. More formally, a pair of actions and conjectures (a^*, c) is defined to be a rational conjectural equilibrium (RCE) if (16) is satisfied and

$$\forall\, i, j;\, i \neq j \text{ and } \forall\, a_i' \in A_i, \qquad c_j(a^*, a_i') \in B_j[a_i', c_j(a^*, a_i')]. \tag{17}$$

(Notice that the arguments of B_j in the RHS of (17), $[a_i', c_j(a^*, a_i')]$, are elements of A and refer to the status quo after the deviation by i.) The above definition or a variant of it is the most common definition of 'rationality' used in the literature.[34]

In what sense is c_j, satisfying (17), an optimal response for j after a deviation by i to a_i'? From the definition of $B_j[a_i', c_j(a^*, a_i')]$ on the RHS of (17), it is clear that $c_j(a^*, a_i')$ is an optimal response for j if, *after the deviation by i to a_i'*, the following three conditions hold: (1) what is expected of all players to do after i's deviation, $[a_i', c_j(a^*, a_i')]$, is the new status quo; (2) c_i is j's conjecture; and (3) j is concerned with his payoff in the next period after the others have responded. In the light of these three requirements, an appropriate way of looking at (17) would be to regard the conjectural story as an infinitely RG where each player, in choosing an action at any time t, is concerned with the next period payoff (players are myopic) and strategies of the players depend only on what players are expected to do (according to the strategies) and the actions they chose at the last period.

If one extends the 'rationality' requirement to hold at every status quo, that is, if

$$\forall i, j; i \neq j \text{ and } \forall a_i', \qquad c_j(a, a_i') \in B[a_i', c_j(a, a_j')], \qquad (17')$$

then it follows (almost from the definition) that strategies generated by conjectures satisfying (17') are SPE for the game defined above with the two players moving sequentially. The reason for the sequential move is that, in the literature on conjectural equilibrium, it is assumed (implicitly) that after a deviation it is believed (correctly) that the deviator will stick to his action for at least one period. Sabourian (1984a) relaxes this restriction and defines what j conjectures i to do after a deviation to a_i' by $c_i(a, a_i')$. 'Rationality' now requires

$$\forall i, j, \text{ and } \forall a_i' \qquad c_j(a, a_i') \in B[c(a, a_i')] \qquad (18)$$

where $c(a, a_i') = \{c_j(a, a_i')\}_{j=1,2}$. (18) deals with the above myopic game in which players can move simultaneously.

If players are not myopic and are concerned with more than one period ahead, (16) and (18) are not sufficient conditions for (a^*, c) to be a 'rational' conjectural equilibrium (RCE). For example, if players are also concerned with two periods ahead, one may require, for any i,

$$\pi_i(a) \geq \pi_i[c(a, a_i')] \text{ for any conjectural equilibrium } a \in A. \qquad (19)$$

Sabourian shows that (16), (18), and (19) are sufficient conditions for (a^*, c) to be a RCE when players are not myopic. Moreover, it is shown (not surprisingly) that (16), (18), and (19) are sufficient to generate stationary supergame strategies which are SPE of the infinitely RG with adjustment costs (inertia supergame) and no discounting.[35] After any

---

[34] See Sabourian (1984a) for a discussion of different 'rationality' concepts.

[35] Marschak and Selten (1978) introduced the notion of inertia supergame and showed that their 'convolution' concept (a concept similar to RCE) corresponds to what they call 'paraperfect' equilibrium in the inertia supergame. 'Convolution' only requires 'rationality', (17'), with respect to deviations from some status quo, and 'paraperfectness' requires strategies to be NE only in some subgames.

history, these strategies require players to choose actions that other players conjectured them to take in the conjectural model, interpreting the status quo term as what players were expected to do in the previous period. The strategies generated by conjectural models are attractive because they only depend on the previous period's actions and on what players were expected to do in the previous period; that is, the domain on which the strategies are defined remains stationary. The converse result can also be demonstrated—any stationary SPE vector of strategies of an inertia supergame, which depends only on what players were expected to do and on what they did in the last period, can generate a 2-tuple of actions and conjectures satisfying (16), (18), and (19).

The adjustment cost is needed if one is to relate conjectural models to RGs because, as was mentioned earlier, the transitory profit is neglected in the former models. The adjustment costs can be justified on physical, administrative, computational, and/or psychological (inertia) grounds. Such costs become insignificant if the length of periods approaches zero. The limits of ε-SPE of inertia supergame correspond exactly to Anderson's perfect quick-response equilibria. As a result, one can show that strategies generated by conjectures satisfying (16), (18), and (19) are perfect quick-response equilibria.

Conjectural models are easier to deal with than general RGs; the optimization problems in conjectural models are static, whereas one may have to deal with dynamic optimization problems in RGs. (In fact, one could argue that by concentrating on conjectural models, and thus on RG strategies generated by conjectures, one is introducing some kind of 'bounded rationality' into RGs.) For example, in the Bertrand oligopoly model it is fairly easy to show that kinked demand conjectures can be 'rational' and thus can be supported as a SPE of the above RGs: suppose all firms believe that price increases are not followed and price reductions are at least matched; consider firm j's optimum response when $\bar{p}$ is the status quo price and firm i has deviated to p_i'. If $p_i' < \bar{p}$, j conjectures all firms to match p_i'; therefore to obtain some share of the market, j has to match p_i'. If $p_i' > \bar{p}$, j conjectures all firms (including i) to punish i and not to raise their price above $\bar{p}$. Therefore j's optimum policy is not to follow i to p_i'.

There are three further points to note about the conjectural models. First, one can obtain a modified Folk Theorem result with the conjectural models. In fact, if (7) is satisfied (players prefer to minmax others than to being minmaxed), any IR payoffs can be supported as a RCE. The above proposition can be proved by constructing conjectures such that players perceive they will be severely punished (minmaxed) for any deviation from the equilibrium norm. The conjectures are 'rational' because others believe that they will be minmaxed for not punishing. The second point to note is that the 'rationality' conditions in the literature are mainly in terms of correctness. A fruitful approach may be to develop a 'rationa-lity' condition in terms of some learning and/or experimenting. For example, given the costs involved, it does not pay any agents to try to acquire more information (*à la* Wald) concerning the responses of others. (Hahn's Chapter 5 is an example of such an approach.) Finally, note that in this section players' conjectures are required to be correct with respect to actions of every other player. In many conjectural models (especially those in the general equilibrium framework, e.g. Hahn 1978) agents' conjectures are required to be correct with respect to the signals (e.g. some aggregate price) they receive. These conjectural models and the correctness of these conjectures correspond to anonymous RGs and SPE of these games respectively. (See the next section for anonymous games.)

8. Imperfect Monitoring and Large Games

In RGs with little discounting, many norms of behaviour can be supported as equilibria because players observe each other and thereby can (and will) punish a deviator. If players were not observed, there would be every incentive for each player to deviate from a norm that is not in his immediate interest. In the extreme case, where players do not observe any variable that is correlated with past actions of others, only norms that are NE of the stage-game can be NE of the RG. (Here there are no linkages, not even information linkage, between different stages of the RG; as a result, the outcome of RG is the same as that of the stage-game.)

The intermediate case, RG with imperfect monitoring, is where players observe signals that are (partially) correlated to actions taken by others. Obviously if, for each player, there is a one-to-one mapping between the signals observed and the actions taken, one is back to the case of perfect observation, and the Folk Theorem results can be demonstrated. In many interesting economic models the mapping between actions and signals observed is not one-to-one, and in some cases there is randomness in the signals that players observe (moral hazard): in the principal–agent problem the principal (e.g. the capitalist) cannot observe (or finds it very costly to observe) the actions taken by the agent (e.g. the effort level of the worker) and observes only the outcome of the agent's action (e.g. profitability of the firm), which may depend on many other factors. In oligopolistic markets, each firm may not be able to observe (or may find it costly to observe) the quantity or the quality of outputs of other firms and may observe only the price at which it can sell its products. The difficulty, that is the cost of observing other players' actions, clearly increases with the number of players in the games. Thus, imperfect monitoring should be an important aspect of any general equilibrium model of the economy where there are a large number of economic agents. Therefore, if one intends to model the behaviour of the whole economy in terms of RGs, the solutions to games with imperfect monitoring are of fundamental importance.

The problem with enforcing collusion in RGs with imperfect monitoring is that each player can cheat and blame the outcome on the behaviour of others and/or on the (non-observable) state of nature, which may be random. (Imperfect monitoring implies that rivals cannot tell the difference.) The question that arises, Can collusive activities be supported as equilibria of RGs with the above-discussed moral hazard? If the noise is small and discount factors are near 1, Green and Porter (1984) and Porter (1983) show that some collusion can be sustained as a SPE of repeated quantity-setting oligopoly models, even when each firm observes only the market price and not each other's actions. The strategy they use to support a collusive outcome $\bar{a}$, where $\pi(a) \in C(G)$,[36] is that of a 'trigger-price': at every stage firms produce quantities $\bar{a}$, unless the price in the last period falls below a trigger price p^*, in which case a 'punishment phase' begins with firms producing a (Bayesian) Cournot–Nash (non-cooperative) outcome a^N for a finite number of periods, T; the play returns to the co-operative phase, $\bar{a}$, after any T-period punishment phase. Since a^N is a static NE, no firm would wish to deviate from this strategy in the punishment phase. As a result, the strategy can be supported as a SPE if each firm prefers not to cheat in the co-operative state. To decide whether to cheat or not, each firm has to balance the benefit from deviating from $\bar{a}$ against the change in the probability of the price falling below the trigger price p^*. It is clear that, if firms are patient, if T is large, and if the change in output of one firm increases the probability of prices falling below p^*, then some 'collusive' behaviour, $\bar{a}$, can be supported as a SPE.

The point to note concerning the above imperfect monitoring model with stochastic outcomes is that a punishment phase (price war) can occur even if no firm has deviated. This is because with random outcomes the price can fall below the 'trigger-price' even if no firm has cheated. Having observed a price below the 'trigger-price', firm i expects others to produce the punishment output a^N_{-i} and as a result it will produce a^N_i.

The possibility of punishment occurring in equilibrium (i.e. even when no player deviates) is inevitable in games in which players cannot tell the difference between cheating and the occurrence of bad random outcomes. In order to deter cheating, strategies need to be such that punishment can happen if bad random outcomes occur, even when no player has deviated. As a result, in these models the expected payoffs of any player *in equilibrium* will depend on his payoffs in the punishment

---

[36] Here A_i, the action space of i, denotes the set of all quantities of output which firm i can produce.

phase as well as on the payoff in the non-punishment phase. (The higher the probability of the bad random outcome, when no one has deviated, the greater the influence of the punishment phase on the expected equilibrium payoffs.)

Now if the punishment phase involves playing actions that make all players worse off, it is clear that the expected equilibrium payoffs of the players may not be efficient for RGs with discounting. Fudenberg and Maskin (1987a) show that, for suitably 'non-degenerate' two-player RGs with one-sided moral hazard (only one player's action is unobservable), the inefficiency loss required (in equilibrium) to deter players from deviating goes to 0 as the discount factor δ goes to 1. (Radner 1985 first demonstrated the above result in the context of principal–agent RGs, which are examples of one-sided moral hazard; see Radner's paper for other references on principal–agent RGs.) As a result, they show that a full Folk Theorem, like that in Section 3 above, can be demonstrated for such 'non-degenerate' one-sided moral hazard RGs. However, Fudenberg and Maskin (1987b) show that the inefficiency does not disappear as δ goes to 1 if both players' actions are unobservable; as a result, they demonstrate that the SPE outcomes of RGs with two-sided moral hazard are bounded away from the efficient frontier. Very loosely, the intuition for these results is that in the two-sided moral hazard the payoffs that both players receive in the punishment phase are less than those in the non-punishment phase. In the one-sided moral hazard, the player whose actions are unobservable may be punished in such a way that the other player actually gains (relative to the good outcome). This implies that, for the one-sided moral hazard case, if δ is near 1, there may be equilibrium paths which involve actions that are close to the efficient frontier, whereas for the two-player case the equilibrium paths always involve the possibility of inefficient behaviour.[37] The method that Fudenberg and Maskin use to derive their results is dynamic programming applied to RGs. This method was first used by Abreu, Pearce, and Stacchetti (1986a,b) to characterize the set of equilibria of imperfect monitoring RGs with discounting. Their characterization is essentially a stochastic version of Lemmas 1 and 2.

Turning to large games, it has been common to assume that the only reasonable solution for markets with a large number of insignificant agents is the NE of the stage-game, even when players interact for many periods. Putting it differently, in large markets it has been assumed that each player does not take into account the reactions of others to a change in his action. It is clear from the analysis so far that the above assumption is false if players can observe each other's actions. With perfect

---

[37] Radner (1986) shows for repeated partnership games (two-sided moral hazard) efficient outcomes can be enforced as SPE, even with non-negligible noise, if the LM criterion is used.

monitoring, Folk Theorem results can be demonstrated even for games with a continuum of players.[38] A sufficient condition for the set of SPE of RGs to coincide with the NE of the stage-game (history-dependent strategies cannot be sustained as solutions) is for players to be 'informationally insignificant'; that is, each player's action does not affect the signals observed by others. Green (1980) and Kaneko (1982) show that, with a continuum of players, if agents observe a summary statistic representing the action of others (anonymous game), then players are informally insignificant, and as a result the SPE of RGs coincide with the NE of the stage-game. Green (1980) gives an example to show that the above result does not necessarily hold (approximately) for large but finite anonymous games. (See also Lambson 1984 for some replication results for oligopolistic markets with perfect monitoring.) The failure of the approximation result in *some* anonymous RGs is due to there being information about the past behaviour of players which the aggregate signal (e.g. the price) conveys in every anonymous finite game (but not in anonymous games with a continuum of players). This small information reveals to players that some player has deviated, though anonymity implies that the identity of the deviator is not revealed. As a result, collusive behaviour may be sustained as SPE in large, but finite, anonymous RGs by strategies that threaten to punish all players for deviations by any one player.

Green (1980) and Sabourian (1984c) show that the approximation result can be demonstrated if one introduces some randomness into the anonymous RG. More precisely, it is assumed that the distribution of signals, at any period, is a continuous function (with the right topology) of the distribution of players' actions. (The latter paper shows that the approximation result may not hold if the continuity assumption is relaxed.) The assumption used in the above two papers makes each player informationally insignificant as the number of players increases. (In the limit, this is done by making the continuation payoffs continuous functions of player's actions.) A useful application of large anonymous RGs, as mentioned before, is to general equilibrium theory. Marschak and Selten (1974) and Sabourian (1984b) develop a general equilibrium model of the economy in which each agent's action affects the information received by some agents and not that received by others. More precisely, they assume that price-making firms observe and remember past actions of some agents who are 'close' to them (such as their customers, suppliers, and close rivals) and only observe aggregate signals representing the actions of others. Since the economy consists of a large number of agents, the actions of agents who are not 'close' to a firm

---

[38] The proof of the results in Sections 2 and 3 does not depend on the number of players. If a player deviates from the equilibrium norm, he will be punished (minmaxed). The others do punish because otherwise they will in turn be punished. With perfect monitoring the above strategies can be implemented, even for the case of a continuum of players.

do not affect the information received by that firm. As a result, in these papers it is assumed that each agent does not respond to changes of actions of agents who are not 'close'. Such an assumption can be justified by appealing to some of the above results for large anonymous RGs (with noise). On the other hand, it is assumed that players who are 'close' may respond to each other's actions and as a result may follow some collusive norms. In particular, it is assumed that firms in the same industry follow a price-matching strategy. (See Sections 6 and 7 above for conditions under which such a strategy is a SPE.[39])

9. The Multiplicity Problem

The previous sections demonstrated that solutions to RGs are very large, and in the extreme case of the perfect monitoring and little discounting they coincide with the set of IR payoffs. The continuum of equilibria arises because strategies in RGs can be history-dependent; in the case of 'history-dependent equilibria', history matters to each player (i.e. players condition their actions upon the history) because it matters to other players. As a result, history can play a role similar to a correlating device; players do not deviate from any IR outcome because deviations generate histories that force others to punish the deviator. Since there is a large (infinite) number of possible histories, one can construct many equilibrium strategies, some of which are highly non-stationary and extremely complicated.

If the above argument is correct, then one should be able to reduce the size of equilibria in RGs by imposing conditions on the way the strategies depend on the history. One possible justification for restrictions on the strategies is in terms of imperfect monitoring, as in the last section. In Section 9.1 I shall consider other restrictions on the strategies. The second way of dealing with the large number of equilibria is to refine NE (or SPE), or possibly even to consider other equilibrium concepts. This approach is part of a grand project (see chapters by Hahn, Brandenburger, and Kreps, and recent papers of Binmore 1987a concerning the appropriate equilibrium notions in strategic contexts).

Before discussing further the above two approaches for dealing with a large number of SPE in RGs, let us compare the continuum of Nash equilibria of RGs with the result of Dubey (1978). Dubey shows that generically all normal-form games $G = \{F_i, V_i\}_{i=1}^{n}$ have a finite number of Nash equilibria[40] if: (1) F_i has a finite dimension and is compact; (2) V_i is a smooth function of its arguments; (3) n is finite. The RG structure in

---

[39] Sabourian (1984b) shows the existence of a pure-strategy equilibrium price for the economy (given the above strategies for the players), even in the case where firms operate under increasing returns to scale.

[40] Wilson (1971) and Harsanyi (1973) demonstrate (generically) the finiteness of the set of mixed equilibria, for games with finite number of pure strategies.

the normal form, however, differs from games satisfying Dubey's conditions in two respects: (a) the strategy spaces, F_i, no longer have finite dimensions—they are sets of functions defined on histories; and (b) the payoffs are not necessarily continuous (and therefore not smooth) functions of the strategies. Therefore (a), (b), or a combination of the two is the cause of the continuum result in RGs. If Dubey's result could be demonstrated for normal-form games with strategy spaces of infinite dimensions,[41] then it would follow that it is the discontinuities in V_i that are the reason for the continuum of equilibria in RGs.[42] This seems to be a reasonable conjecture in the light of the fact that most 'collusive behaviour' is supported by discontinuous strategies. (Any deviations, however small, are punished severely.)

9.1. Restrictions on RGs strategies

The extreme cases are the 'pre-commitment' and the 'open-loop' equilibria. In the former, players commit themselves to particular actions for the entire time-paths of the RG. In the latter, they do not acquire any information throughout the RG. As a result, in both cases actions taken at any node are independent of the history up to that node and only depend on the time at which the actions are taken. Thus, pre-commitment and open-loop equilibria are really static: decisions are made at the beginning, and strategies are history-independent. The equilibria have the same properties as those of the one-shot game, but with larger strategy spaces. Since strategies are history-independent, the only outcomes of the above equilibria will be NE of the stage-game.

In many applications of game theory to dynamic oligopolies, strategies have been restricted to 'closed-loop' (state-space) ones. At any stage t, these strategies depend on a history $h^t = (a^1, \ldots, a^{t-1})$ only through a state-variable x^t. The state-variables are often generated recursively from the history of outcomes, h^t, according to a function $g: A \times X \rightarrow A$, where X is the space of state-variables. Thus x^t is defined by $x^t = g(a^{t-1}, x^{t-1})$ and the state-variable at time zero is given. It is clear that the size of the closed-loop SPE depends on the amount of information that the state-variables, at any stage, convey about the past. (See Section 8 on imperfect monitoring.) Thus, the choice of the state-variable is crucial to the question of multiplicity. In the literature, the state-variables at any period are usually taken to be variables that are arguments of the payoff

---

[41] Note also that, in Walrasian general equilibrium models, one can show that there is a continuum of equilibria if there is an infinite number of commodities and an infinite number of players (see Kehoe *et al.* 1986b). However, with a finite number of agents and an infinite number of commodities, there is generically a finite number of equilibria. This lends some support to our conjecture that Dubey's result can be extended to smooth games with finite players and strategy spaces with infinite dimensions.

[42] Since strategy spaces have infinite dimensions, continuity (and smoothness) have to be defined with respect to an appropriate topology.

functions at that stage, other than actions taken at that stage. Such variables are sometimes referred to as 'payoff-relevant state-variables' and the strategies that depend only on payoff-relevant state-variables' are called 'Markov strategies'. In RGs discussed so far the 'payoff-relevant' state-space is empty; the past has no *direct* influence on current payoffs. As a result, the Markov equilibria (equilibria generated by Markov strategies) of these games coincide with the Nash equilibria of the stage-games.

The main application of such Markov equilibria has been to more general RGs than the ones discussed so far. In these games, referred to as 'dynamic games' (see Basar and Oldser 1982), the payoffs at stage t depend on the actions taken by players at t and on the state-variable x^t, which in turn depends on the history of the game up to that stage. An example of such dynamic games is the oligopoly model where firms' profit at any stage depends on current decisions and on the level of capital stock (the state-variable) that is determined by past decisions. Fudenberg and Tirole (1983) survey applications of such dynamic games to oligopoly. In many cases 'collusive' outcomes can be supported as solutions to dynamic games even when one restricts strategies to the Markov ones. If one does not impose any restrictions on the strategies in dynamic games, a modified Folk Theorem result can be demonstrated. Since payoffs at each stage depend on the history (through the state-variable at that stage), the security levels in dynamic games are defined as the worse (average) payoff that can be imposed upon a player, over the infinite horizon, by other players. Lockwood (1986) shows, for dynamic games with no discounting, that the set of IR payoffs coincides with the SPE of these games if the security levels and IR payoffs are independent of the initial states. If these conditions are violated, it is possible to construct examples where players are able, by taking certain actions, to move the game to particular absorbing states which are especially advantageous to them. An extreme example where the choice of the state-variable at the beginning of the game affects the long-run payoff is the Benoit–Krishna (1987) duopoly model, where firms choose capacities once and for all at the beginning of the game and pick prices in subsequent stages. Here the capacities chosen at the beginning affect the payoffs in the future. They show that firms, in equilibrium, generally carry excess or idle capacity (the excess capacity is chosen so as to enforce collusion), and as a result are unable to achieve monopoly profit. If firms could adjust their capacity levels quickly, excess capacity would not be necessary to enforce collusion and monopoly profit would be sustained. Benoit and Krishna also show that excess capacity plays an important role even when firms have limited flexibility in changing their capacity levels.

In many applications, further restrictions are imposed on the dynamic games and on the closed-loop strategies—smoothness, sequential moves, linear–quadratic payoffs, and so on. In some of these cases the size of the equilibrium set shrinks dramatically (see Fudenberg and Tirole 1983). One such example is the Rubinstein two-person bargaining problem, where a unique SPE is obtained. Here the structure of the dynamic game, rather than restrictions on strategies, guarantees a unique solution.[43] (Two-person bargaining games have absorbing states i.e. accepting an offer at any stage is an irreversible decision which determines the future payoffs of the players completely.) Another example (surveyed by Fudenberg and Tirole) is the Masking–Tirole (1988) dynamic duopoly models. They assume short-term commitment (inertia) in players' actions (e.g. sequential moves). They also restrict their attentions to Markov strategies. Because of the sequential moves structure, Markov strategies in their models are such that the action taken by any firm at any stage depends only on the action of the other firm (the state-variable) in the previous period; these strategies are called dynamic reaction functions (DRFs). Here the Markov restriction does reduce the size of the equilibria dramatically, and in the linear demand and costs case there is a unique symmetric outcome.

Stanford (1986b) shows that, for the repeated duopoly model where firms choose their actions simultaneously, where payoffs are state-independent (the game is a standard RG), and where there is discounting, the only actions that can be supported by DRF strategies (at any stage the action of any player depends only on the previous period action of the other) are the 'history-independent' ones, that is stage–Nash equilibria. The intuition behind this result is as follows. Consider two histories, h^t, $\bar{h}^t$, which end at $(t-1)$ with actions (a_i, a_j) and (a_i', a_j). The payoffs that j will receive in any SPE in the future depend on h^t and $h^{t'}$ to the extent that i's strategy depends on the two histories. But if i's strategy is a DRF, it will be the same after both histories. Thus i's action at $(t-1)$ has no influence on j's SPE payoffs after that period. This, however, does not mean that i's action at $(t-1)$ does not influence j's SPE actions after that period. (The long-run payoff mapping, $\bar{\Pi}_i^\delta$, from the space of SPE strategies to R is not one-to-one.) By making some further assumptions on the shape of the payoff functions, Stanford shows that the above implies that i's action at $(t-1)$ has no influence on j's SPE strategy after that period, and that therefore no history-dependent strategies can be supported as a SPE when strategies are restricted to DRF ones.[44]

---

[43] The uniqueness result does not generalize to three or more persons' bargaining problem (see Sutton 1986).

[44] Another example where DRF strategies with two players reduce many 'collusive' outcomes is the repeated PD. Here the threat of player i to play D if player $j \neq i$ deviates from C is not necessarily credible when DRF strategies are used: if j has deviated from the collusive outcome and played D, the only reason i has for carrying out his threat (e.g. in tit-for-tat or grim strategy cases) is that j is going to play D. But if j's action is conditioned on i's past actions (no deviations), j may choose to play C.

Stanford (1986a) also shows that the above result does not hold when players do not discount the future and use the LM criterion.

The basic problem with all the above restrictions, including the Markov assumption, is that they need to be justified: why should the strategies depend smoothly on only a small part of the history? Or why are players not able to change all the variables under their control at every stage? One could argue that RGs are too abstract to predict behaviour. By considering the details of real games and/or using concepts such as Shelling's 'focal points' (see Chapter 2 above), one may be able to justify some of the restrictions and thereby to reduce the multiplicity of equilibria.[45]

Continuity of the strategies, and thus the continuity of the payoff functions, may be justified if one introduces some kind of noise into the model. (See the previous section for an example.) One can justify the restriction to 'payoff-relevant state-variables' by arguing that in many applications it is 'the level of tangible variables and not the way in which those levels are achieved that determines subsequent behaviour and performance' (Kreps and Spence 1985). Fudenberg and Tirole (1983) argue that the use of payoff-relevant variables depends on the complexity of the environment: 'In a very complex environment the state-space restriction may be a rational heuristic for firm decisions; in a simple environment firms may be more sensitive to other aspects of history. Similarly, if the state-variables are very "important", the restrictions are more plausible.'

One interpretation of Fudenberg and Tirole's argument—the complexity of the environment—is in terms of limitations of human computational and storage ability. In recent years there have been many formal attempts to introduce 'bounded rationality' into RGs in order to deal with the multiplicity problem. The aim has been to give some formal justification, in terms of 'bounded rationality', for imposing restrictions on the RG strategies. Smale (1980) introduces a bound on the memory of the players. In his model players can retain in their memory some kind of an average of the past payoffs. Sabourian (1986a) characterizes the SPE of RGs with LM criteria when at each stage players can remember only the last M periods of the history. Such equilibria are called M-memory SPE. The first thing to note is that the trigger-strategy can be implemented with one-period memory—play the collusive outcome if the collusive outcome was observed in the last period, play a NE of the stage-game otherwise. Since such trigger-strategies can support all collusive payoffs (see (1)), when the discount factors are near 1, $C(G)$

---

[45] Some examples of such approach are the Rubinstein bargaining problem and oligopoly models where firms, because of the technology, are committed for some time to a choice of capacity.

can be sustained by one-memory SPE strategies. If (7) holds, all IR payoffs can be implemented by one-memory SPE strategies.

In Section 3 it was shown that, in the unbounded memory case, in order to deal with the case where (7) is violated, Aumann and Shapely, and Rubinstein, constructed (A/S–R) strategies that punish (minmax) a deviator for a finite number of times and then return to the 'good' outcome (the reward phase). Thus, to demonstrate a full Folk Theorem result, all that players need to have is the capacity to know when to stop the punishment phase; that is, they need to know the number of times they have punished a particular player. In the case of short-memory strategies, if the punishment phase involves using different vectors of actions, then at any stage the number of times a player has been punished can be decoded from the actions taken in the immediate past. For example, suppose player i has deviated and one wants to minmax i (play $\gamma^i \in A$) for two periods and then return to the 'good' outcome, $\bar{a}$. Suppose also that there exist actions a^1, $a^2 \in A$ such that

$$\forall l = 1, 2 \quad \max_{a_i'} \pi_i(a_i', a_i^l) \leqslant \pi_i(\gamma^i) + \varepsilon.$$

Consider the following strategy vector: (1) play a^1 if i has deviated; (2) play a^2 if a^1 was observed in the last period, and (3) play the 'good' outcome $\bar{a}$ otherwise. It is clear that such strategies require one-period memory, and at the same time they guarantee that in the punishment phase i's payoff is on average ε-close to $\pi_i(\gamma^i)$. By constructing such strategies, Sabourian shows that all IR payoffs can be supported as one-memory SPE if A, the action space at each stage, has 'many' elements (e.g. if it is locally connected). Furthermore, it is shown that, if A does not contain many elements, and if the memories are short, many payoffs below the NE of the stage-game could not be sustained as SPE.

The above Folk Theorem result is not very attractive in terms of 'bounded rationality'. Although bounds are imposed on the memories, the strategies needed to demonstrate a full Folk Theorem may be very complicated—players may have to change their actions many times in the punishment phase. A more interesting result is when players can choose mixed strategies and at each stage they observe only the outcomes of the past randomizations. It can be shown that all IR actions can be supported as a one-memory SPE without imposing any further assumptions on the action set A. This is done by constructing strategies that play the 'good' outcome $\bar{a} \in A$ if $\bar{a}$ was played in the last period. If player i has deviated from $\bar{a}$, or if i was minmaxed in the last period, he is to be minmaxed with probability $p < 1$, and with probability $(1 - p)$, $\bar{a}$ is chosen. By choosing p close to 1, we can deter any deviation from $\bar{a}$. Moreover, since p is less than 1, it is clear that, if a punishment phase starts, with probability 1 the players will return to the 'good' outcome $\bar{a}$ in a finite time. Such a reward at the end of the punishment phases makes the above strategies credible for the no-discounting case.

A theory of 'bounded rationality' needs to compare complexities of different strategies. A natural measure of the complexity of the strategy is through the computer science notice of automaton. In Section 5 I discussed how finite-automata (Moore) machines can implement RG strategies. The points to note concerning these machines are that (1) the transition and output functions are stationary; and (2) there is a finite number of states. The strategies implemented by such machines are similar to closed-loop strategies. In both cases, states summarize the past and the actions depend only on them. The difference is that in the latter the state-variables are usually taken to be some objective variable (influencing the payoffs). In the former case the states have no particular meaning. They can be interpreted as representing the different states of minds and are chosen by players. The important constraint on strategies implemented by machines is that there is a finite number of states. (This constraint is justified on the grounds that the human mind is finite.) Kalai and Stanford (1986) show that all RG strategies can be implemented by machines if infinite states are allowed. They also show that, for any $\varepsilon > 0$, all SPE strategies of discounted RG can be approximated by ε-SPE strategies which are implementable by finite machines. (This is similar to the Fudenberg–Levine approximation results.) Thus, 'finite rationality' restrictions do not reduce the size of the SPE set of RGs.

Rubinstein (1986) and Abreu and Rubinstein (1986) attach costs to the complexity of strategies in two-person repeated machine games. NE in these games involves each player choosing a 'best' (finite-states) machine to implement his strategy, given the other player's machine. A player's preference is assumed to be increasing in the long-run payoff that the player actually receives (given the cost of complexity) and decreasing in costs of complexity (given the long-run payoff). As in other machine game models, the cost of complexity refers to the number of states and not to the complexities of transition or output functions. Abreu and Rubinstein derive several conclusions about the structure of NE machines and outcomes. (1) All the states in the machines will be used during the course of the play (otherwise a player could make himself better off by choosing machines without the unused states). (2) Because machines have finite states and the game is repeated an infinite number of times, the machines must eventually enter a cycle. (3) The number of the states in both machines must be equal; the reason for this is that if player j uses a machine with m states, $i \neq j$ faces a Markovian decision problem with m states; therefore i needs no more than m states to achieve the best long-run payoff. (The same is true for j.) (4) All non-cycle states are used once and appear consecutively at the beginning of the game. (5) A state does not appear twice in the cycle and the number of states that appears

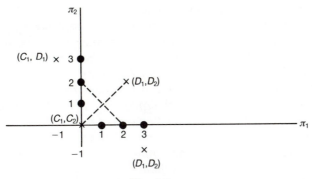

Fig. 4.3

in the cycle (non-cycle) is equal for both players. (6) There is a one-to-one mapping between the two players' actions:[46] if, as in Section 5, g_i refers to the output function of i, in equilibrium

$$\forall t \text{ and } t' \qquad g_1(q_1^t) = g_1(q_1^{t'}) \quad \text{iff} \quad g_2(q_2^t) = g_2(q_2^{t'}). \qquad (20)$$

The intuition behind the above result is that if, for some t and t', $g_1(q_1^t) \neq g_1(q_1^{t'})$ and $g_2(q_2^t) = g_2(q_2^{t'})$, then player 2 can save a state (and thus reduce his cost) by replacing q_2^t and $q_2^{t'}$ by a single state q^* and constructing transition and output functions that leave the sequence of played outcomes the same as before.

The above one-to-one result implies that when one machine changes its action the other must also change its action, and thus the number of distinct actions in any sequence of equilibrium outcomes is bounded above by the minimum number of one-shot actions available to the two players. Thus, in a 2×2 matrix game with four possible outcomes, in any equilibrium of the machine game only two outcomes can be implemented. In the case of repeated PD machine game with no discounting and lexicographic preferences, the above implies that the equilibrium payoffs shrink to the cross in Figure 4.3. This is because the one-to-one result implies that in equilibrium players play either a combination of (C_1, C_2) and (D_1, D_2) or a combination of (C_1, D_2) and (D_1, C_2). Abreu and Rubinstein extend this characterization result to machine games with the discount factor close to 1 and a positive cost per state close enough to zero.

There are several points to note about the Abreu–Rubinstein model. First, the introduction of small implementation costs results in a striking discontinuity in the NE set in terms of strategies, plays, and payoffs. An interesting question to ask is to what extent this result can be extended to

---

[46] This result has to be slightly modified for the no-discounting case.

a more than two-person machine game. Clearly, the number of states in the Markovian problem that each player faces in choosing a machine increases with the number of players. Thus, one would expect that, in equilibrium, the number of states players use increases with the number of players (if the cost of complexity is very small).

Second, the players in the Abreu–Rubinstein model are like 'meta-players' who choose the machines that play the game. These meta-players face no limits on their computational power; in fact, the meta-player may have to solve a more complex problem (choosing the optimal machine) than players in RGs (choosing the optimal strategy). In effect, the above approach transfers the problem of 'bounded rationality' from the players to the meta-players. This may be inevitable in game-theoretic models where bounds on rationality are determined endogenously by players— the complexities of strategies are choice variables.[47] One could, for example, introduce some computational cost in meta-players' decision problems as well. Again, if these costs are to be determined endogenously, one has to introduce 'meta-meta players', who decide, given the costs of complexity, the complexity of the meta-players' strategies and so on. One way out of this hierarchy of meta-players is to reintroduce the exogenous bounds on the complexity at some level of the hierarchy. (Neyman's model, for example, introduces the exogenous bounds at the first level.) Another way out is that of Binmore (1987a), who attaches a metaphorical, rather than real, role to the meta-players (just like the status of the 'auctioneer' in the Walrasian model). Meta-players are seen as a metaphor for an evolutionary process, and the NE in machine games is seen as the equilibrium of this process. Abreu and Rubinstein provide another interpretation for their model. The model considers costs of implementation and not those associated with computing optimal strategies. As a result, they argue that it is applicable to bureaucratic organizations, where each manager, with unlimited computational ability, devises simple rules for others in the organization to implement mechanically in a strategic environment.

Finally, note that in the Abreu–Rubinstein model, once a player chooses a machine he cannot change it. (There is an infinite cost of changing a machine once the play of the game starts.) If one allows for the possibility of changing machines during the course of the game, one has to consider the issues of credibility (perfection). Rubinstein's original paper (1986) allows players to drop states from the machine. As a result, in equilibrium with no discounting, no player wishes to drop states from his machines (given that players pay for states that are held in machines). This implies that the non-cycle states, which appear at the beginning of the game, cannot occur. But the removal of non-cycle states reduces the punishment abilities of the machines (Abreu and Rubinstein interpret the

---

[47] Compare these models with 'bounded rationality' models discussed in Section 4, and the bounded memory models, where the bounds were given exogenously.

non-cycle phase as a demonstration of players' punishment abilities), and as a result many outcomes (e.g. those supported by grim strategies) cannot be implemented as equilibria.[48] Once the assumption that players are committed to a machine is dropped,[49] one could consider other issues related to credibility: for example, one could allow players to change their transition or output functions, or to add states (by incurring large but finite costs).

9.2. *Appropriate equilibrium notion*

The appropriateness of NE (and its variants) has been discussed in other chapters of this book. Here I shall discuss briefly some of the issues in the context of RGs.

In many applications of RGs, the attention has been restricted to Pareto-efficient equilibria. The basic idea is that there is an agreement process (players discuss their strategies without binding themselves) before the game. The outcome of the process has to satisfy certain compelling properties (axioms) such as Pareto efficiency. (See Kurz 1985 for such an approach to a repeated oligopoly problem.) The problem with this approach is that the agreement process, and thus the axioms, are not explained in terms of non-cooperative game. Moreover, if the 'agreement process' is allowed at every stage of the RG, then the Pareto-optimal SPE of RGs cannot be supported by threats that are Pareto-suboptimal. If the threats are not optimal and there is the 'agreement process' after any deviation, the optimal SPE of RGs cannot be credibly sustained. However, if it is possible to threaten to punish the deviator in such a way that another player actually benefits (i.e. if the threat is not Pareto-inferior), then Pareto-optimal SPE may be enforceable.[50] Farrell and Maskin (1987) and others have introduced new equilibrium concepts, renegotiation proof equilibria, which deal precisely with the possibility of negotiation at every stage of the game. They show that their equilibrium concepts do reduce the size of the equilibrium in RGs with two players, if (loosely) there do not exist strategies that threaten to punish any deviator in such a way that the other player actually benefits.

Pareto efficiency basically eliminates equilibria that can be improved upon by the coalition of all players. This leads us to other equilibrium

---

[48] In the case where players can drop states, if one introduces some uncertainty into the machine games (e.g. imperfect monitoring), in equilibrium players may choose machines with non-cycle (punishment) states because the game may enter a punishment phase (in equilibrium) without any player deviating.

[49] In Abreu and Rubinstein's bureaucratic interpretation of the model, changing machines amounts to giving new simple rules to the employees in the organization.

[50] For example in the infinitely repeated PD game, Figure 4.1, the Pareto-optimal SPE, (C_1, C_2), can be sustained by the threat of playing (D_1, C_2) and (C_1, D_2) for a finite time, if players 2 and 1, respectively, deviate. Clearly (D_1, C_2) and (C_1, D_2) are optimal, whereas the threat of playing (D_1, D_2) is not optimal and therefore not credible if negotiation is allowed at every stage.

concepts involving coalitions, such as strong equilibria. Strong equilibrium is defined as an n-tuple of strategies for which no coalition of
players can all do better for themselves by choosing different strategies,
while other players maintain their original strategies. Aumann (1959)
proved that the strong equilibria of the supergame with no discounting
coincide with the B-core[51] of the stage-game. Rubinstein (1980) extends
the result to subgame perfect strong equilibria.

Strong equilibrium is obviously a very stringent concept. It allows
coalitions too much freedom in choosing their joint deviations. Bernheim, Peleg, and Whinston (1987a,b) propose the notion of coalition-
proof NE. For any coalition, this concept considers only deviations that
are self-enforcing—immune to self-enforcing deviations by sub-coalitions.
There are no general results on coalition-proof equilibria. Bernheim *et al.*
also define subgame perfect coalition-proof equilibria for extensive games
and apply them to a simple finitely RG (a variant of the PD). They show
that all such equilibria may involve cyclical co-operation.

Another approach to restricting the number of NE in game theory is to
impose conditions on players' beliefs off the equilibrium path. In a
complete-information RG, SPE requires that each agent's strategy (plan)
be optimal, given the strategies the agent attributes to others, after any
history, including the histories that contradict the strategies attributed to
others. This implies that in any SPE the strategies each player attributes
to others remain unchanged even in the face of what Binmore calls
'counterfactuals'.

Chapters 2 and 3 above by Kreps and Brandenburger discuss refinement of NE in normal- and extensive-form games. One application of
such refinements (in normal form) to infinitely RGs is Sabourian (1986b).
It is shown that many types of 'trembles' (about payoffs or actions) do
not reduce the size of equilibria in RGs with little or no discounting. This
is because in RGs one can construct NE (and SPE) strategies such that a
player is made strictly worse off for any deviation from the equilibrium
outcome. (This is done by punishing the deviator for a very long time.)
Such discontinuities in equilibrium payoffs imply that the equilibrium
strategies remain optimal for players if the game is locally perturbed. On
the other hand, it is shown that, if players are not certain about the RG
strategy of other players ('wrong theory', using Kreps's terminology), the
solutions to the RG may shrink dramatically. This is because, for any NE
$f \in F$ in a RG, there may exist a strategy $f'_i \in F_i$ for player i such that: (1)
(f'_i, f_{-i}) yields the same outcome path as f, and (2) player i prefers f'_i to f_i
if others are following different strategies from f_{-i}.

In RG contexts, uncertainty about the strategies of others (i.e. lack of
common knowledge of beliefs) introduces a new element into the
analysis—learning about other players' strategies. Once learning is

[51] B-core is the set of feasible payoff vectors x such that each coalition can be prevented,
by its complements, from achieving a larger payoff for its members.

introduced, as Hahn argues in Chapter 5 below, the process by which an equilibrium is reached will necessarily determine the nature of the equilibrium.[52] Moreover, in many cases the equilibrium reached will depend on the initial beliefs and thus the history. Binmore (1987a) arrives at similar conclusions in two papers on modelling rational players. He argues that the neglect of 'procedural rationality' in game theory can generate confusions and inconsistencies. He distinguishes between two types of equilibrating environments: the eductive and the evolutive. The former (and the one commonly used in game theory) means that equilibrium is achieved through careful reasoning by players before and during the play of the game. In the evolutive context, on the other hand, the equilibrating process is external to players and visible to an observer as the game is played repeatedly. In the latter case, the environment the players operate in is too complex for players to solve eductively (for example, because of 'bounded rationality'). As a result, players are seen as simple stimulus–response machines which follow rules that have not been eliminated by some form of evolutionary competition. Maynard Smith and others have defined equilibrium concepts such as evolutionary stable strategy (ESS), which are well suited to evolutionary applications in biological sciences. Some of these concepts are closely related to equilibrium concepts of classical game theory.[53] In early biological applications the players were defined by their strategies. (A player is the simplest possible stimulus machine.) As a preliminary approach, this is clearly useful for social scientists. A more satisfactory approach would be to consider more complex stimulus machines—a mixture of mechanical adjustment, short-sighted choices, and learning. For example, one could construct models in which the strategies are 'learning rules'.[54] Harely (1981) has shown, in biological contexts, that learning rules that will evolve are precisely those that will take a population to ESS frequencies. Although in social sciences we do not have a satisfactory evolutionary theory of strategic interactions, the above-mentioned works do indicate that 'bounded rationality' and evolution, in strategic contexts, are extremely fruitful areas where much work remains to be done.

---

[52] Sanghari and Sobel (1976) consider learning in the context of some simple RGs. They conclude that long-run outcomes of such games depend upon decision and updating rules of players. Moreover, they regard the imposition of *a priori* (equilibrium) solution concept as being less fundamental than decision and updating rules.

[53] ESS is a strategy which, when played by most players, cannot be beaten (and therefore invaded) by any rare alternative strategy. Mathematically, ESS strategy looks very similar to NE, which is robust to some small perturbation (similar to trembling-hand perfect equilibrium of Selten—see Kreps' Chapter 2). However, the mechanism by which an outcome is attained is very different in the two cases: NE is arrived at through a personal decision process whereas ESS is the outcome of 'evolutionary decision process'. The former is an example of eductive approach, the latter of evolutive approach. (See Bromze 1986 for a classification of the equilibrium concepts used both in classical game theory and in evolutionary games).

[54] See also Axelrod (1984), who has conducted many simulations along these lines.

5

Information Dynamics and Equilibrium

FRANK HAHN

1. Introduction

I shall want to define the equilibrium of an economy as an economic state such that no agent has an incentive to deviate from the actions he is taking or from his policy of actions. I do not think that this definition will be controversial. It has the following implications.

1. A state of the economy that is singled out as an equilibrium will depend on what is assumed concerning the set of actions that agents perceive to be available and on the agents' beliefs of the consequences of actions (as well as, of course, on the usual description of motives and technology, etc.).
2. The information available to agents and their manner of learning will be important in the characterization of equilibrium states.
3. 1 and 2 will in general imply that equilibrium states are history-dependent.

I am not sure that any of these implications would be widely disputed. But the literature suggests that they have not been taken seriously. For instance, theories like Dreze's (1975) fix-price equilibrium are routinely referred to as 'disequilibrium theories'. It is also a widely held belief that any state that is not a Walrasian general equilibrium state is to be regarded as a disequilibrium. This in turn leads to the view that such states cannot persist—since, on the definition with which I started, agents' actions, etc., persist only in equilibrium. It is this that makes it important both theoretically and practically to avoid slovenly habits of thought and to take the three implications of the definition seriously.

But there is another reason for knowing rather precisely what one is about when engaged in equilibrium analysis. Debreu (1970) has shown that finite Walrasian equilibria are 'almost always' isolated.[1] That still means that there could be infinitely many such equilibria. Recent work (see Woodford 1984) on open-ended (infinite) economies such as arise with overlapping generations has shown that there may be a continuum of equilibria.[2] It has also been shown that the same is true for economies

---

[1] Let E be the set of equilibria (the set of equilibrium allocations to households and activity vectors of firms). Then for any $e \in E$ there is $\varepsilon > 0$ such that e is the only member of $N(e, \varepsilon)$, (e.g. is the ε-neighbourhood of e in E).

[2] That is, for every $\varepsilon > 0$ there is $e' \neq e$ and $e' \in N(e, \varepsilon)$.

that lack a full set of 'Arrow-securities'.[3] This lack of determinateness of equilibrium (until recently ignored for instance by most macro-economists) has led economists (see e.g. Grandmont and Laroque 1987; Evans 1987; Marcet and Sargent 1987; Woodford 1987), to study the behaviour of an economy which, with a given starting point, evolves according to some process along which agents learn about their economic environment. The hope here is to pick the equilibrium among the many that are the outcome of a given historical process. It is early days to judge this work or the examples with the similar message that follow in this essay. But one thing does seem pretty clear: traditional Walrasian equilibrium analysis (which makes special assumptions concerning im-plications 1 and 2) will not suffice—not even for comparative statics or dynamics. The history of an economy will have an influence not only on which equilibrium an economy finds itself in (if it does find itself in one), but also on the properties of such an equilibrium.

In what follows I shall first make these remarks more precise and then proceed to a number of examples. I shall want to show in particular that the characteristics of equilibria may depend on the path of the economy, on the prior beliefs of agents, and on their mode of learning.

2. Some Formalisms

Start with the simplest case as follows. There are n agents labelled $i = 1, \ldots, n$. An agent can take actions (a_i) and these actions have consequence (c_i). I assume that the map from the set of possible actions to the set of consequences is one to one. Let each agent receive a signal $\sigma_i \in \Sigma$, the space of signals, and let $A_i(\sigma_i)$ be the set of actions the agent i who has received the signal *believes* he can choose from. Let C_i be the space of consequences so that

$$C_i \colon A_i(\sigma_i) \Rightarrow C_i \quad \text{or} \quad c_i = \gamma_i[a_i(\sigma_i)]. \tag{1}$$

Each agent has a complete, reflexive, and transitive ordering of C_i represented by $\underset{i}{\geqq}$ (i.e., $c_i \underset{i}{\geqq} c_i'$ reads: c_i is at least as good in preferences as c_i'). Then let

$$\alpha_i(\sigma_i) = \{a_i \mid a_i \in A_i(\sigma_i), \ \gamma_i[a_i(\sigma_i)] \underset{i}{\geqq} \gamma_i[a_i'(\sigma_i)]; \ a_i' \in A_i(\sigma_i)\}. \tag{2}$$

So $\alpha_i(\sigma_i)$ is the set of actions between which agent i, who receives signal σ_i, will be indifferent. (It is the set of preferred actions—it may have only one member.)

---

[3] An 'Arrow security' pays one unit of account in a state of nature s and nothing otherwise. The set of securities is incomplete when there are fewer independent securities than there are states of nature.

Frank Hahn

Now let $a = \{a_1, \ldots, a_n\}$, $\sigma = \{\sigma_1, \ldots, \sigma_n\}$, and let

$$A = \{a \mid a \text{ is feasible for the economy}\} \tag{3}$$

and let us consider the following definition of equilibrium.

An equilibrium of the economy is σ^0, a^0 such that

(i) $a_i^0 \in \alpha_i(\sigma_i^0) \; \forall \, i$
(ii) $a^0 \in A$.

Readers will be able to translate this easily into something familiar: let $\sigma_i = p$ all i where p is a vector of prices, and let a_i be the vector of excess demands of agent i and $A = \{a \mid \Sigma a \geqslant 0\}$. Then our definition yields a Walrasian equilibrium. But there is already one important difference: $\hat{A}_i(\sigma_i)$ is the set of actions from which the agent *believes* he can choose—it need not coincide with the set of choices an informed outside observer would define contingent on the signal. (For example, a firm may believe its production set is Y_i when an outside observer knows it to be Y_i^1.) This makes an important difference to our interpretation of equilibrium, for instance to our judgement of its efficiency. In any case, it is an equilibrium relatively to beliefs (which, as we shall see, depend on information), and it does not seem required for the definition that all beliefs are 'correct'.

But suppose that, when σ^0 is the vector of signals and $a_i^0 \in \alpha_i(\sigma_i^0)$ all i, $a^0 \notin A$. We could argue that none the less there should be an outcome for agent i in the economy. Let $\bar{\gamma}_i(a^0)$ be the outcome for agent i and assume that $\bar{\gamma}_i(a^0) - \gamma_i[a_i^0(\sigma_i^0)]$ all i—the consequence of i's action is what he took it to be. Would we be justified in continuing to designate (σ^0, a^0) as an equilibrium?

Before answering, let us give an interpretation. We now think of a_i as the vector of excess demands signalled by agent i to the market. Agents know that they cannot all meet their excess demands—they will be 'rationed', but they correctly predict what they will in fact get as a function of their signal. Here (ii) in the definition has been replaced by

(ii') $\bar{\gamma}_i(a) = \gamma[a^0(\sigma^0)]$ all i.

We have here an example of a 'rationing equilibrium'.

But is all this satisfactory? In traditional Walrasian theory there is (admittedly in the background) another agent—the 'auctioneer'—who sees to it that when $a \notin A$ the signal is changed. Put more formally, there is a map $s : A_1 \times, \ldots, \times A_n \Rightarrow \Sigma$, write it as $s(a)$, and we now append to the definition of equilibrium the requirement

(iii) $\sigma^0 = s(a^0) = s[a_1(\sigma_1^0), \ldots, a_n(\sigma^0)]$.

The reason why (iii) is in the background is that it is assumed that (iii) holds if and only if (ii) does. None the less, the reason why rationing equilibria are regarded as transitory is that most economists have something like (iii) and the assumption in mind when they think of equilibrium.

But (iii) is something of a *deus ex machina,* and it has not been grounded in a theory of the rational actions of self-interested agents. Of course, there are in the 'real' world markets with auctioneers, and dealers in securities also have this character. There are situations in which information of bids is very good and easily available. Even in such markets, a great many *i*'s have to be dotted and an explicit theory of the auctioneer's behaviour is required. For instance, there are many types of auctions and there typically is a spread between buying and selling price. When it comes to most other markets, including that for labour, the introduction of an auctioneer is simply a 'cop-out' or, even more sinister, *ad hoc.* In particular, it supposes that agents who are responsible for price changes have a great deal of information. If there are a thousand producers of good *i,* it is unlikely that any one of them can know the aggregate excess demand for that good; nor is it at all obvious how an auctioneer in practice would obtain the information (costlessly).

If one takes the natural line that it is the actual agents who change price (or in general the signal), then, as Arrow (1958) noted long ago, one cannot sensibly assume that agents take prices parametrically at all times. For instance, a firm may at least momentarily possess what Arrow called a dynamic monopoly. This occurs for instance when a firm can raise the price of its product in a state where it is in general excess demand; in such a state, the price rise will not induce the loss of all of the firm's custom.

I shall return to the point in the examples. Let us now recapitulate the story so far. The definition of equilibrium without a theory—however rudimentary—of agents' behaviour out of equilibrium is incomplete in that it allows many quite different states to be designated as equilibria. For instance, without (iii) and the assumption concerning it, we have seen that both a situation with rationing and one without meet the definition of equilibrium consisting only of (i) and (ii). Traditional theory has side-stepped all of this by 'the law of demand and supply', which asserts that prices (signals) must change as long as excess demands are not zero and prices are positive. It is a law without theory (which does not of course mean that it needs to be empirically false). My argument is that we must search for the theory in the usual place: the rational actions of agents. I now shall want to argue that, when we do that, the states of the economy that meet the definition of an equilibrium will depend on this theory and in particular on the process that leads to the persistence of actions and plans of actions. In the abstract the argument will be simple; in application it is far harder, and I can only offer simple examples.

It will now be simpler to think of equilibrium as a critical point[4] of a dynamic process. This does no violence to traditional theory. The exact form of such a process is not, at the moment, important. For instance, I shall think of it as taking place in discrete time, but none of the general arguments depend on that. I shall also simplify by assuming away exogenous uncertainty (there is, say, a single possible state of nature), and I shall take the underlying economy to be stationary. By this last I mean that I shall abstract from such things as technical innovation, population change, and so forth. Finally, I want to emphasize that, although I am considering a sequential story, this has nothing to do with incomplete markets. Rather, it arises from the fact that, in the light of their information, agents may make plans and attempt actions that are mutually inconsistent, and I take the market economy as attempting to resolve such inconsistency by a real time process.

I shall now date actions and consequences. The latter, as before, depend on the former. But I shall not now assume that agents know consequences with certainty. For instance, they may not be sure that they can carry out all their desired transactions. I shall also include in the action of an agent at any date the prices at which that agent offers to trade at that date. In this I include accepting to trade at a price offered by some other agent. Let

$$C^t = \{C_{1t}, \ldots, C_{Nt}\} \tag{4}$$

where C_{it} is a consequence for agent i at t of an action taken at t. Also, as before, $a^t = \{a_{1t}, \ldots, a_{Nt}\}$ is the vector of actions taken by agents at t. Then I define the history of the economy up to t by $ht = (a^v, C^v)_0^{t-1}$. An agent i may not be able to observe h_t, and I shall write h_{it} as that part of h observable by agent i^t. I assume that h_{it} always includes $(a_{iv}, C_{iv})_0^{t-1}$, that is, the history of his own actions and his own realized consequences.

Let C_i be the space of consequences for agent i and PC_i a probability space on C_i (with a suitable topology). Let H_t be the space of possible t-histories. Then I write

$$\hat{C}_{it}: A_i(h_{it}) \times H_t - PC_i \tag{5}$$

as the map from i's feasible action set at t (which depends on h_{it}) and H_t to the probability distribution of consequences. Let us write this as

$$\hat{C}_{it} = \hat{\gamma}_i(a_{it}, h_{it}). \tag{6}$$

Notice that, while I now (for reasons of simplicity) assume that the feasible set of actions conditional on history is known for sure, the agents' beliefs concerning the consequences of actions depend on history. In the examples that follow I shall be more specific about this. However,

---

[4] If $Y_{t+1} = F(Y_t)$ is a difference equation where Y and F are either scalars or vectors, then Y^0 is a *critical point* when $Y^0 = F(Y^0)$.

it is important to understand that an agent's action at t is known to affect h_{it+1} since the latter includes both the action and its realized consequence. This gives rise to a somewhat complicated optimization problem, since the agent may take an action in order to learn from its consequence. (I do not include learning in the set of consequences.) Here too, the example will I hope clarify. For the moment I simply suppose than an optimal action plan of an infinitely lived agent can be written as

$$a_{it} = \alpha_i(h_{it}).$$

(I am here assuming that optimum actions are uniquely determined by h_{it}.)

Lastly, we must link actions of all agents at t to realized consequences. I shall here make the simplest assumption concerning realization:

$$C^t = R(a^t).$$

It should be noticed that I am not requiring a^t to be feasible for the economy, and that by actions I mean 'demanding', 'supplying', and so on in the *ex ante* sense.

Since the economy is stationary, we are also interested in a stationary equilibrium. How is that characterized? I write down the description before discussing it.

Let $a^0 = (a_1^0, \ldots, a_N^0)$ be a stationary equilibrium of the economy with the property that, if $h_{it}^0, h_{it+1}^0, \ldots$ is the history generated by a^0, then

$$\alpha_i(h_{it}^0) = a_i^0 \qquad \text{all } t \text{ and all } i.$$

Equilibrium is then a history generated by time-invariant optimizing actions, which, not carrying new information, justifies the time invariance of the actions. Several points are worth noting.

1. It may be that $\hat{\gamma}_i(a_i^0, h_{it}^0)$ is a degenerate distribution with all probability mass concentrated on the ith component of $R(a^0)$. That is, individuals in such an equilibrium are sure of the consequence of a_i^0. Whether that is so or not depends on how agents learn which is embodied in $\alpha i(\cdot)$.

2. It is not the case that $\hat{\gamma}_i(a_i^0, h_{it}^0)$ must degenerate for any $a_i \neq a_i^0$. That is, agents may continue to be uncertain of the consequences of actions that are not stationary equilibrium actions.

3. As already noted, the choice of optimum action by an agent includes, in the considerations that lead to it, the possibility of learning— or, more vividly, the possible benefits of experimentation. The uncertainty of the consequences of non-equilibrium actions is one of the determinants of those actions.

4. The formalism that I have described is dynamically based. Given h_0, $\alpha_i(h_{i0})$ is agent i's chosen action at $t = 0$. Taking all these for all

agents generates through $R(\cdot)$ the realized consequences C_0 and so history h_1. It is clear how to proceed. If this process converges to a stationary equilibrium, there is every reason to suppose that this will not be independent of h_0—the starting point, and so the starting beliefs of agents. (See examples below.)

5. It is important not to misunderstood the process in paragraph 4. The agent i at time 0 looking into the future realizes that he will be learning as history unfolds and may hae a precise rule of how he will learn. That is, he may have a complete contingent plan of actions where actions at each date are functions of history to that date. However, the actual process of realization still depends on the joint, independent, actions of all the agents. Exactly the same arguments would apply in a world in which, at each t, agents communicated their intended actions to a super-auctioneer who, in turn, gave them the consequences that would result. This could be like a *tâtonnement* and need not involve real time. Yet agents would be learning, and, if there is convergence, the convergent point would in general depend on the history of these communications with the auctioneer.

6. It will surprise readers perhaps that I have made no mention of market-clearing. Whatever pertains to this is summed up in $R(\cdot)$ and in the description of optimizing actions. Here is an example. Every year in August it is impossible to find a motel room in the vicinity of Monterrey and Carmel in California. The market does not clear. Motel-keepers know that, at the prices they charge, it will not clear. Yet it seems to their advantage to keep prices where they are. Any one of them may fear, for instance, that if he raised his price his competitors would gain in slack months because of reputation effects. Certainly the consequences of deviation may be highly uncertain. I do not know. But I believe that it is desirable to recognize this as an equilibrium situation since it is precisely what we have always meant by equilibrium.

7. The equilibrium theory that I am putting forward is highly subjective, and one friend has already claimed that it would seem that almost anything could be an equilibrium. Just such an objection as I have already noted can be levied at more conventional constructions. I believe that they are wrong objections. Indeed, if we can invent fictional histories, then to each of these there will correspond a process of belief formation and finally an equilibrium. But what I am here proposing is that, if we want definiteness, we have to put more into our construction: the equilibrium of a real economy will depend on its real history, which we had better know. There could be many histories and so many equilibria an economy could have. It is folly to suppose that from Adam and Eve there must be a unique history to the present, or that, if there is, we could account for it.

3. Some Simple Examples

It will be best to start with very simple cases which avoid strategic behaviour. These cases should help to clarify at least some of the informational problems that will have to be dealt with by a theory of the price mechanism.

Consider a small firm which at the beginning of any 'period' t must make a price–output decision (p, y) to which it is committed until the beginning of period $(t + 1)$. By the firm being small, I mean that it will ignore the effect of its own decision on those taken by other firms. The good that the firm produces is perishable.

Suppose $F_\lambda(p)$ is a family of continuous demand functions parametrized by a vector $\lambda \in \Lambda$. (We may think of λ as the vectors of polynomial coefficients in p.) One assumes that, for all λ and $p > 0$, $F'_\lambda(p) < 0$. At any date t we suppose that the firm has a probability distribution on λ. This distribution is conditioned by the history of the firm's observations of demand, which for the moment we take to be exact. Let $x[p(u)]$ be the demand observed at $t = u$ when price was $p(u)$. Then define

$$h_t = \{x[p(0)], \ldots, x[p(t-1)]\} \tag{7}$$

and refer to it as the history up to date t. If the firm is Bayesian and $\pi(\lambda \mid h_t) =$ probability of λ given h_t, then we have

$$\pi(\lambda \mid h_t) = \frac{\pi(h_t \mid \lambda)\pi(\lambda \mid h_{t-1})}{\displaystyle\int \pi(h_t \mid \lambda)\pi(\lambda \mid h_{t-1}) \, d\lambda}. \tag{8}$$

It is clear that $\pi(h_t \mid \lambda) = 1$ or 0; for, given λ, either $x[p(u)] = F_\lambda[p(u)]$ all $\mu = 0, \ldots, t - 1$, or not. This however is not true of $\pi(\lambda \mid h_{t-1})$, because it is possible that $x[p(u)] = F'_\lambda[p(u)]$, $u = 0, \ldots, t - 2$ for a whole set of $\lambda \in \Lambda$.

I shall now simplify notation by omitting the conditioning history and simply writing $\phi[x(t), p(t)]$ as the probability at t that demand will be $x(t)$ when price $p(t)$ is charged. Also for the moment let us suppose that, because the good is perishable, the firm maximizes expected profits, period by period. (We shall see later that this is not quite correct.) So the firm chooses $p^*(t)$, $y^*(t)$ to maximize

$$p(t) \int_0^{y(t)} \phi(x, p)x \, dx + p(t)y(t) \int_{y(t)}^{\infty} \phi(x, p) \, dx - c(y_t) \tag{9}$$

where I suppose the firm to be risk-neutral. The form of (9) is explained by the fact that the firm's revenue at t is given by $p(t) \min[x(t), y(t)]$. The choice $[p^*(t), y^*(t)]$ is found from the two necessary conditions for the solution of (9):

$$p^*(t) \int_{y^*(t)}^{\infty} \phi[x, p^*(t)]\, dx = c'[y^*(t)] \tag{10}$$

and

$$p^*(t) \int_0^{y^*(t)} \phi_p[x, p^*(t)]x\, dx + p^*(t)y^*(t) \int_{y^*(t)}^{\infty} \phi_p[x, p^*(t)]\, dx$$

$$= -\left\{ \int_0^{y^*(t)} \phi[x, p^*(t)]x\, dx + \int_{y^*(t)}^{\infty} \phi[x, p^*(t)]y^*(t)\, dx \right\}. \tag{11}$$

Both have the obvious interpretation: (10) the expected marginal revenue at the fixed price $p^*(t)$ must equal marginal cost; and (11) the elasticity of expected sales, when output is given, with respect to price must equal -1. (I am here assuming that $\phi_p(\cdot)$ is well defined.)

It is easy to see how the story proceeds. When the firm chooses $p^*(t)$, $y^*(t)$, it will during period t observe $x[p^*(t)]$, the true demand. It will now be able to update its beliefs (over Λ), and with these updated beliefs to solve for $p^*(t+1)$, $y^*(t+1)$. And so on. It is clear that the realizations of excess demand, $z(t) = x[p^*(t)] - y^*(t)$, may differ from zero during this process. The dynamics here is one of learning.

Let us consider what an equilibrium of this process would look like. In doing so it is important to bear in mind that we have implicitly postulated that the firm believes the true demand curve to be non-stochastic and we have explicitly assumed that the firm can observe demanded quantities precisely.

Suppose, at some T, $p^*(t) = p^*(T-1)$. Then it must be that $\phi[x, p^*(T)] = 1$ for $x = x[p^*(T-1)]$, the demand observed at $T-1$. This however does *not* mean that there is no uncertainty concerning λ. The set of λ such that $F_\lambda[p(u)] = x[p(u)]$, all $u = 0, \ldots, T$, will be in the support of the probability distribution of λ. Further, we will not require that $y^*(T-1) = y^*(T)$; for at T condition (10) now reads

$$p^*(T) = c'[y^*(T)] \tag{12}$$

provided $x[p^*(T-1)] \geqslant y_T^*$; that is, one must have $z(T) \geqslant 0$. But at $T-1$ it was not the case that $\phi\{x[p^*(T-1)]\}p^*(T-1) = 1$.

But we also need condition (11) to hold. It is easy to see that under our assumptions this condition can hold only if $z^* = x[p^*(T)] - y^*(T) = 0$; for if $z^* > 0$, the expected elasticity of sales with respect to price is 0.

So if these conditions hold, the firm chooses $p^*(T)$, $y^*(T)$ at T. But then the realization of demand provides no new information. (The firm knows that it will be $x[p^*(T-1)]$.) Hence it will charge the same price and produce the same output at $T+1$. And so on. An equilibrium has been reached. However, we must notice the following features of such an equilibrium.

1. There is nothing to suggest that in equilibrium the firm has discovered the 'true' demand curve (i.e. the true λ). Our construction justifies Negishi's (1960a) idea concerning an equilibrium with a perceived demand curve. In our case, however, it is not a single demand curve that passes through $x(p^*)$ on the true demand curve but a whole set which has not been excluded by past observations.

2. While $z = 0$ is a necessary condition of equilibrium, it is not sufficient. That is, $z(T-1)=0$ does not imply $p^*(T)=p^*(T-1)$. That is sufficiently obvious from the first-order conditions.

3. If Λ is compact, then convergence to equilibrium can be established. But I shall not attempt a demonstration here.

We must now return to the assumption that the firm determines its choice by maximizing single-period profits. As a matter of fact, the assumption that the good is perishable does not suffice as a justification; for the firm knows that by changing price today it will have more information tomorrow, and so an intertemporal connection between expected profits at different dates is established by this route. There is also another reason, which I discuss below.

Let us write (9) as $v[p(t), y(t), h_t]$, that is, the expected profits at t given h_t and the choice $[p(t), y(t)]$. Let $V(h_{t+1})$ be the maximum discounted expected profit over $(t+1, \infty)$ given h_{t+1}. Notice that h_{t+1} depends on the choice of $p(t)$ and so on the expectations concerning the realization $x[p(t)]$. The firm now chooses a strategy or policy $\{p(h_u)\}_0^\infty$, $\{y(h_u)\}_0^\infty$ conditional on its observations such that it satisfies, for all t,

$$V(h_t) = \max_{p(t), y(t)} \{v[p(t), y(t)h_t] + \delta E_{h_t} V(h_{t+1})\} \tag{13}$$

where E_{h_t} is the expectation operator on h_{t+1} conditioned by h_t and δ is a discount factor. This is a more complicated problem than the first one. But it is seen that the firm may rationally sacrifice expected current profits in order to acquire information that raises expected long-run profit.

Let us again suppose that the firm's optimum programme is such that, at some T, $p^*(T)=p^*(T-1)=p^*$, say. Since $y(T)$ has no effect on the second term on that RHS of (13), condition (12) must be satisfied as before. It is also clear that $z^* = x(p^*)-y^*(Y)=0$, else there would be a sure way of increasing both short-run and long-run profit. But condition (11) will be modified to a form which says that there is no profitable way of experimenting with a change in price. That is, the reduction in revenue at T is not compensated by the expectation of the extra information this would generate, and thereby the change in expected long-run profits which it would induce. In spite of this modification, all my remarks concerning the equilibrium of the simpler (one-period maximization) case remain as before. In particular, there is no reason to suppose that the firm will continue changing price until it has learned the 'true' demand curve. (For a closely related analysis see Rothschild 1974.)

But we have not finished yet, for we have not yet paid any close attention to the consumers of the firm's goods.

It is not unreasonable to suppose that a consumer whose planned purchases cannot be carried out incurs a loss in utility. Indeed, if substitutes for that good are imperfect and or substitution takes time, this is obvious. I shall now assume that each of N consumers are identical including in their beliefs. Further, a consumer faces the rationing constraint that if $x \leq r$, then $r = -(y^*/N)$. However, no consumer can observe y^*, the chosen output of the firm. (Of course, they do observe p^*.) Accordingly, I write $f(r, p)$ as the probability the consumer assigns to the ration being r, given that it observes p. I return to this later.

Let X be the consumption vector of all goods other than that supplied by the firm. Then I define $\bar{x}^*$, $\bar{X}^*$ as the solution to

$$\max \int_0^\infty f(r, p)u[\min(x, r)X] \, dr \tag{14}$$

subject to

$$p \cdot x + q \cdot x \leq W$$

where q is the price vector of the goods in X and W is wealth. I shall refer to $\bar{x}^*$, $\bar{X}^*$ as *active attempts* to purchase. Notice that it is assumed that the household is certain that it will not be rationed in any of the goods in X. The first-order condition with respect to x is

$$U_x(\bar{x}^*, \bar{X}^*) \int_{x^*}^\infty f(r, p) \, dr = kp \tag{15}$$

where k is the marginal utility of wealth. It is seen that $(\bar{x}^*, \bar{X}^*)$ coincide with (x^*, X^*), the demand that is not affected by rationing, only if $\int_{x^*}^\infty f(r, p) \, dr = 1$, that is, only if the consumer is certain that he could consume more than $\bar{x}^*$ without running into a rationing constraint.

Now the consumer observes r directly only when he makes a mistake; that is, $\bar{x} > r$. If $\bar{x} \leq r$, then the consumer knows that he can carry out his active attempts to purchase, but he does not know what would be the case if he increased these attempted purchases. Let $v(t) = \max[0, \bar{x}(t) - r(t)]$ and let $H_t = \{v(0), p^*(0), \ldots, v(t+1)p^*(t-1)\}$ stand for the relevant history. $v(t) - 0$ yields the information: attempted purchases were carried out. Then $f[r(t), p(t)]$ will depend on H_t in the usual way. Hence the demand function revealed to the firm, which can only observe active attempts to purchase, will be of the form

$$\bar{x}(t) = g[p^*(t), q(t), H_t]. \tag{16}$$

(We shall take $q(t) = q$ all t, throughout.)

The firm may realize that its own choice at t may affect demand at $t+1$, for example if consumers find that they cannot carry out their purchases at t and update their 'rationing beliefs'. This then will be a further reason for the firm to go beyond short-run expected profit maximization. But the present considerations introduce a kind of strategic element into the picture in that the firm may be interested in affecting the beliefs of its customers. I shall not on this occasion attempt an analysis of this somewhat more difficult problem and shall simply assume that the firm ignores the effect its decisions may have on customer's beliefs and also on their active demand.

I shall say that the firm is in an H_T^*-equilibrium at $(p^*, y^*, \bar{x}^*)$ if

(a) $$p^*(t) = p^* \text{ all } t \geq T$$

(b) $$y^*(t) = y^* \text{ all } t > T$$

(c) $$\int_{x^*}^{\infty} [f(r, p^*) \mid H_{T+t}] \, dr = \text{constant all } t$$

where H_{T+t} is $\{H_T, v_{T+1}, p_{T+1}^*, \ldots, v_{T+t-1}, p_{T+t-1}^*\}$.

(d) $$\bar{x}^* = \frac{y^*}{N}.$$

Notice that by (d) the consumer only gets the information that he needs to fulfil his active demand. Condition (c) then requires this information not to affect the consumer's beliefs concerning the rations he would encounter if he demanded more. Since he gets information about *that* only if he did demand more, and since given his present beliefs it is not worthwhile to try, condition (c) is reasonable. (However as in the case of the firm, to clinch this we should consider a consumer not just interested in instantaneous expected profits. The extension to the intertemporal maximizing case is left to the reader.) Of course, the constant in (c) may be unity, in which case the consumers have their unconstrained demand as active demand. But if the constant is less than unity, then as we know active and unconstrained demands do not coincide.

I do not discuss the existence of H_T^*-equilibrium, but it is sufficiently clear that one can construct one. More importantly, one can construct many by a choice of different priors at the start of the story. The equilibrium is thus history-dependent. For instance, with a degenerate prior on the part of consumers and the firm, we can obtain an H_1^* equilibrium which is that of the textbook. With other priors we can obtain an equilibrium in which active attempts to purchase do not coincide with unconstrained demand.

So far I have taken it for granted that the firm observes z_t. When $z_t < 0$ there is no difficulty—it will find itself with unsold output. But when

$z_t > 0$ matters are less clear. Selling all one has to sell does not self-evidently entail knowledge of what one *could* have sold. One may encounter customers whom one has to turn away without discovering how much they would have bought.

Formally we could proceed as follows. We could think of σ_t as a signal to the firm (e.g. number of customers enquiring) and write $m[\sigma_t(z_t)]$ as the probability of the signal σ_t when $z = z_t$. It can be left to the reader to rewrite the maximand (9) and to show how signals lead to updating of beliefs.

The conditional distribution of σ_t may be degenerate for $z_t < 0$; for example, the signal could simply be z_t in this case. But this will not generally be the case for $z_t \geqslant 0$. A firm may change price and output even though the true $z_t = 0$; for all the probability weight is on being able to sell more at the same price; and so on. The more usual postulate that prices do not change when $z_t = 0$ may thus be false.

It may be objected that here household beliefs are quite arbitrary. This is not altogether correct. What is arbitrary is the prior probability distribution with which households start the story. Thereafter they update their beliefs in a rational—or at least Bayesian—manner. (I have made the strong assumption that they can observe aggregate shortfall of supply at each date—with weaker informational postulates, the case I am making would be stronger.) If the whole process converges to a stationary probability distribution, then it will also be the case that households will have no further incentive to change their active demand. Moreover, if at t one household were to increase its active demand, there would be a positive probability that it will be unsatisfied since output is given. Provided its beliefs attach no lower probability to this event, it will, in not demanding more, have done as well as it can for itself. It is important to recall here that the household is too small to act strategically *vis à vis* the firm.

4. Two Firms

Let us consider the classic Cournot duopoly problem where with one exception we make all the usual assumptions. The exception is that we suppose that the two firms do not, at the start of the game, know the demand function for their product.

To make things simple, we again suppose that at any date a firm's beliefs are given by a probability distribution over downward-sloping demand curves indexed by λ. To stay within the orthodox framework, we assume for now that there is common knowledge of beliefs and rationality. Indeed, we postulate that at each date the firms have the same beliefs and each knows this; and so forth. Further, the firms can observe each other's output. Output is decided upon at the beginning of each period. The price in each period clears the market according to the equation

$$p(t) = g[y_1(t) + y_2(t)] \tag{17}$$

where $y_i(t)$ is the output at t of firm i any $g(\cdot)$ is the true inverse demand function.

Let H_t, as before, be a history $[p(u), y(u)]_{u=0}^{t-1}$ where $y(u) = y_1(u) + y_2(u)$, and where H_0 stands for information available before the game starts. Then a strategy for a firm is s_i, given by

$$s_i = \{y_i(H_0), y_i(H_1), \ldots, \} \tag{18}$$

where $y_1(H_t)$ denotes the firm's output at t given the history H_t. Let s_i^t be the partial strategy

$$s_i^t = \{y_1(H_t), y_i(H_{t+1}), \ldots\}, \ s_i^0 = s_i \tag{19}$$

and let $E_{H_t}\pi_i(s_1^t, s_2^t)$ be the expected profit at t of firm i given that history is H_t.

Given our assumptions, the only possible equilibrium strategies $(\bar{s}_1, \bar{s}_2)$ are those that satisfy

$$E_{H_t}\pi_1(\bar{s}_1^t, \bar{s}_2^t) \geqslant E_{H_t}\pi_1(s_1^t, \bar{s}^t) \qquad \text{all } s_1^t \text{ and all } t \geqslant 0 \tag{20}$$

$$E_{H_t}\pi_2(\bar{s}_1^t, \bar{s}_2^t) \geqslant E_{H_t}\pi_2(\bar{s}_1^t, s_2^t) \qquad \text{all } s_2^t \text{ and all } t \geqslant 0. \tag{21}$$

We assume that such a Nash equilibrium in pure strategies exists and that it is unique.

We now have a story of equilibrium dynamics. The components of the equilibrium strategies, $[\bar{y}_1(H_t), \bar{y}_2(H_t)]$, generate through market-clearing $\bar{p}(t)$, and so H_{t+1}, and so on. Output is changing, but it is an unfolding of an equilibrium contingent production plan. Prices are changing, but markets always clear. The dynamics arises from learning, which however has been allowed for from the beginning. It should be added that customers are passive outsiders because one takes it that there are too many of them to find it worthwhile to act other than as price-takers.

Even game-theorists have difficulties accepting a story such as this, which presupposes common knowledge and computational abilities not to be found in any computer. But apart from this there is another difficulty, which can be illustrated as follows.

Suppose that firms attach a probability 1 to $a = \hat{a}$, $b = \hat{b}$ in the inverse demand function

$$p = a + by. \tag{22}$$

Should they ever observe p not consistent with this, then their beliefs conditioned on this event will be represented by probability distributions over a and b with support in $(0, \infty)$, $(0, -\infty)$. This hierarchy of beliefs can be axiomatically justified.

But now a strategy pair $(\bar{s}_1, \bar{s}_2)$ with constant output each period will be a Nash equilibrium provided the price each period is consistent with their certain belief, say $p(\bar{y})$, that is, if the true demand curve is $\alpha + \beta y$, provided that

$$(a - \alpha) + (b - \beta)\bar{y} = 0. \tag{23}$$

In other words, the true demand curve will never be discovered, nor is it rational for either duopolist to experiment.

This point can be made less extremely. Suppose the firms have beliefs given by probability distributions with support $(\underline{a}, \bar{a})$ and $(\underline{b}, \bar{b})$. Their equilibrium strategies may never lead to prices that could not be made consistent with elements of these distributions. Yet the true demand curve may have coefficients outside this support. Hence even for equilibrium dynamics generated by learning, there is no reason to suppose that agents will learn the truth. In particular, if there is a unique solution when both firms know the true demand function, it need not be the case that the sequence of actions when the demand function is not known will converge on that solution. Moreover, if there is convergence, the outcome may depend on initial beliefs.

In this example output changes as firms learn about their demand conditions. But strategies are given once and for all, and take account of every possible course of history and specify actions for each such history. The assumptions of common knowledge and unbounded computational abilities support this view and justify the Nash equilibrium. But it is plainly all pretty far-fetched. Yet, far-fetched or not, no one is at all clear how to proceed more realistically.

Let us, however, look at an alternative route. We drop the assumption of common knowledge of beliefs. What then would be an acceptable equilibrium notion?

Let firms now have probability distributions over each other's strategies. The support of such a distribution may exclude strategies that are regarded as irrational. As before, the components of a strategy are outputs at each date as a function of the history of observed outputs and prices up to that date. If for this argument we assume that the true demand function is known to both firms, then conditional expectation operators refer to probabilities over the other firm's strategies.

Let us try the following definition: (s_1^*, s_2^*) are equilibrium strategies, and H^* the corresponding history if

$$E_{H_t^*}\pi_1(s_1^{*t}, s_2^t) \geq E_{H_t^*}\pi_1(s_1^t, s_2^t) \qquad \text{all } t \text{ and } s_1^t \tag{24}$$

$$E_{H_t^*}\pi_2(s_1^t, s_2^{*t}) \geq E_{H_t^*}\pi_2(s_1^t, s_2^t) \qquad \text{all } t \text{ and } s_2^t. \tag{25}$$

Compare this with our earlier definition of Nash equilibrium. Here we require that, given the beliefs of a firm concerning the strategy of the other firm, it should have no incentive to deviate from its starred strategy. But notice (1) that beliefs at any date are generated by the history of partial strategies, and (2) that a deviation changes history and so gives information, but since no deviations occur there also is no more information.

As an example suppose $H^* = \{(y_1^*, y_2^*, \ldots)\}$. Then firm 1 will know that $y_2(H_t^*) = y_2^*$ all t when H_t^* is partial history of H^*. But it will not know $y_2(H_t)$ for other histories; that is, it must form beliefs over the strategies of the other firm. If however neither firm finds it profitable to deviate given their beliefs, then neither firm has any reason to change its beliefs. In simple games it may be possible to rule out strategies of the other firm on the hypothesis that it acts rationally and that it forms beliefs rationally—say, that it also assumes rationality on the part of its competitor. But if we reintroduce lack of information concerning the true demand function, and/or if firms do not know each other's cost functions, the lack of common knowledge will still leave us with our formulation.

Game-theorists, however, will not like it at all. For it seems to leave everything hanging in the air—indeed, they will argue, anything could be an equilibrium. If one feels disputationally inclined, one could counter with the observation that, even with common knowledge, super-rationality, and vast computational abilities, game-theorists in very many cases also had to conclude that almost everything could be the outcome. However, *tu quoque* is not a helpful reply. More to the point is the following. Firms (players) bring to the game beliefs based on past experience and observation (history). They cannot do better than to act on these and on what they believe to be actions available to them. As a game progresses, more information is gleaned and beliefs are updated. It is not obvious that the process must converge to some stationary outcome. If it does, it need not be among those outcomes that common knowledge assumptions designate as possible. It is a historical process in that it depends on the starting beliefs and on the process of learning. Of course, it is possible that the latter leads to common knowledge, but as far as I know there is no general proposition to this effect.

Indeed, the above definition of equilibrium strategies is really the definition of a process. Along the history $H_t^*(t-1, \ldots)$ generated by (s_1^*, s_2^*), firms only learn about the other firm's strategy *along that historical path*. What happens off that path is a matter for beliefs, and there is nothing that will allow them to update these.

I can see no way of going beyond this without violently unpalatable postulates. It means that in any concrete instance one needs concrete information on the manner of learning or simply the formation of beliefs.

Even so, the notion that I have been defending is based on uncomfortably strong assumptions. Recall that a strategy is a sequence $(y_1(H_1), y_1(H_2), \ldots, \text{etc.})$, so that I have supposed that a firm's strategy is an output for every history it may possibly observe at each t. (I am still not considering mixed strategies, but that is only for the sake of simplicity.) This is far too demanding. It is likely that the possible histories considered are restricted so that the inequalities in (24) and (25)) hold for $s_1^i \in \bar{S}_1 \subset S_1$ where S_1 is the set of strategies available to firm 1 and where the support of the probabilities of the strategies of firm 2 is similarly restricted to a subset of S_2. One way in which this could be defended is by an appeal to conventions which assume that histories generated by strategies outside the subsets are never observed. Firms then of course are not global maximizers.

All of this does not add up to a theory but rather to a prolegomenon to a theory. By this I mean that it draws attention to the questions that need to be answered: How are beliefs formed and revised? Common knowledge assumptions are a way of telling the questioner to go away. Our discussion however provides further confirmation that the notion of equilibrium is intimately tied to how questions of this sort are answered.

The reader should lastly note that, had we studied the case of two firms producing a similar but not identical good who are uncertain of their demand conditions and who have to announce a price–output pair at the beginning of each period, similar conclusions would emerge. In particular, the equilibrium strategy of a firm consists of actions at each date contingent, among other things, on the history of observable excess demand for its good. I have not been able to prove that for all plausible beliefs and histories a firm's equilibrium strategy must entail raising prices when it observes excess demand in the previous period. One needs to look at many examples before one will be able to determine the useful sufficient conditions for this.

5. Conjectures

In Hahn (1978) I studied what I called 'conjectural equilibria'. The idea was not too dissimilar to that of the previous section except that I thought of small firms who conjectured their demand curve rather than of firms in strategic situations. The firm did not conjecture what other firms would do in response to its own action but rather what it could sell at what price. Certain critics (e.g. Makowski 1983) misinterpreted me and tried to interpret the notion strategically. However, I too was at fault. Since there seemed no restriction on what conjectures could be, I attempted to define 'correct' and 'reasonable' conjectures. It turns out that these notions indeed are best interpreted as perfect equilibria of traditional game theory with all its attendant postulates (Sabourian 1987). But the intention had been to get away from this manner of analysis.

Let us consider an economy with many firms and many goods (say l). Let $p \in R_l^l$ be a price vector. Each firm i can set the price p_i—it is best to suppose that no two goods are perfect substitutes although they may be close substitutes. It will also make for simplicity if we suppose that none of the goods is storable. Lastly, let H_t^i be the history of payoff-relevant events observed by the firm up to but not including date t including its own past actions. Since everything that follows could be translated into the language of probability distributions, and since I am here concerned with a conceptual matter, I shall at the moment take conjectures to be single-valued.

So let $\pi[H_t^i, p_i(t)]$ be the conjectural profit function of the firm at the beginning of period t. It gives the firm's belief of the profits it will receive in period t, given that it sets the price $p_i(t)$ and given the history H_t^i. Let $V_i[H_t^i, p_i(t)]$ be the maximum present value of conjectured profits, given that the firm charges $p_i(t)$ and has history H_t^i. This variable is calculated on the basis of conjectures formed at t. Then the firm chooses $p_i(t)$ to solve

$$\max_{p_i(t)} \{\bar{\pi}_i[H_t^i, p_i(t)] + \delta V_i[H_t^i, p_i(t)]\} \tag{26}$$

an expression which we have met before. (We assume this problem to be well behaved with a unique solution.) The intertemporal aspect of this maximization problem arises from the possibility that the firm may be willing to trade present profits in order to gain more accurate information and thereby increase the maximum profit thereafter. I re-emphasize that the conjectures in question concern an anonymous market condition and are not concerned with the behaviour of any other firm.

So far the model is very similar to that of an earlier section except that we are using single-valued conjectures. However, in general the true demand for that firm's output at any t depends on p and not just on p_i. (We also assume that households never expect to be rationed.) The firm cannot observe the full price vector p. To go to extremes, suppose that it can only observe its own price and the excess demand for its own good; that is,

$$H_t^i = \{[p_i(0), z_i(0)], \ldots, [p_i(t-1), z_i(t-1)]\}.$$

The firm knows that the prices of other firms will affect the demand for its own good, but being small it (1) regards these prices as independent of its own actions, and (2) has the maintained hypothesis that the effects of other price changes on its own demand will on balance cancel out, so that it behaves as if these other prices are constant. Again, (2) is here not because it is essential but because I do not wish to mix expectations (of other prices) with conjectures. So if $\bar{\pi}(t-1)$ is the actual profit earned in $(t-1)$, I suppose that

$$\pi_i[H_t^i, p_i(t-1)] = \bar{\pi}_i(t-1). \tag{27}$$

(This I referred to as the assumption of 'consistent' conjectures (Hahn 1978)— a not altogether happy nomenclature.)

Let us now say that H^* is a stationary conjectural equilibrium for the economy, $H^* = (H^{1^*}, \ldots, H^{l^*})$, there being l firms, if

$$H^{i^*} = [(p_i^*, 0), \ldots] \qquad \text{all } i \qquad (28)$$

and

$$\pi(H_t^{i^*}, p_i^*) + \delta V(H_t^{i^*}, p_i^*) \geq \pi_i(H_t^{i^*}, p_i)$$
$$+ \delta V_i(H_t^{i^*}, p_i^*) \qquad \text{all } i \text{ and } t > 0. \quad (29)$$

Notice that, as before, the history of observations is crucial in the definition. Also, in such an equilibrium firms do not find it profitable to change price in order to get better information. To discuss the existence of such an equilibrium requires assumptions on conjectures and profit functions, and I shall not pursue the matter here.

To make the next point, let us now further simplify and simply assume that the firm will never change price in order to acquire more information. That is, at each t it can do no better than myopically maximize $\pi_i[H_t^i, p_i(t)]$. We can now call conjectures *reasonable* if, for all t,

$$p(t) \neq p_i(t-1) \rightarrow \bar{\pi}_i(t) > \bar{\pi}_i[H_t^i, p_i(t-1)]. \qquad (30)$$

That is, conjectures are reasonable if, when price is changed on their basis, actual profits are increased over those of the previous period. Note that it is not assumed that

$$\pi_i[H^i, p_i(t)] = \bar{\pi}_i(t); \qquad (31)$$

that is, it is not assumed that actual and conjectural profits coincide at t.

Now if all firms have reasonable conjectures at all t, then the actual profits of all firms are increasing. But of course, these profits are bounded above and so profits converge to a limit. (Compare the treatment of Fisher 1983.) That must mean (supposing continuous conjectures) that $p(t) \rightarrow p^*(t)$, where $p^*(t)$ is a limit path. With some technical assumptions on the conjectured profit functions, we can in fact ensure that $p(t) \rightarrow p^*$. Since $p_i(t) \neq p_i(t-1)$ whenever

$$\pi_i[H_t^i, p_i(t)] > \pi_i[H_t^i, p_i(t-1)] = \bar{\pi}_i(t-1), \qquad (32)$$

and since conjectures are reasonable, it must be that

$$\pi_i\left(\lim_{t-\infty} H_t^i, p_i^*\right) = \pi_i\left[\lim_{t-\infty} H_t^i, \lim_{t-\infty} p_i(t-1)\right] \qquad (33)$$

and the economy converges on a stationary conjectural equilibrium. So reasonable conjectures imply that the economy is guided to a stationary conjectural equilibrium. *But* that equilibrium will itself depend on the sort of conjectures there are, and it will not in general be one where all firms know their true demand curve. (Indeed, the equilibrium will be similar to that discussed by Negishi 1960a.)

However, the assumption that conjectures are always reasonable is hardly a persuasive one. Nor are many other aspects of this model. Yet even in spite of the various simplifications, it is clear that the dynamics is complicated, not to say messy. One particular simplification is the assumption that the firm is 'small' in the way described. But a firm may be small relatively to the economy and not relatively to its nearest competitors. In that case game-like elements mingle with those of anonymous markets. One can describe the situation formally, but it seems at present too complicated for analysis.

6. Concluding Remarks

In this paper I have taken a particular bull by the horn, and some readers may feel that it has run away with me. That is not unexpected. But it nevertheless seems clear that this risk had to be taken sometime.

Current economic theory by and large avoids dynamics, at least non-equilibrium dynamics. This has the virtue of allowing orderly argument and conclusion. But such order is bought at too high a price. Moreover, even then, it is not quite as satisfactory as was once thought. Once it was recognized that we must study sequence economies, it also became urgent to include expectations in the description of the agent. To avoid some of the difficulties we have been through, rational expectations were simply postulated, and, with some notable exceptions (Bray 1982, Bray and Savin 1984, Bray and Kreps 1986), were not justified by a learning process. Even so, it was soon found that this postulate is mostly insufficient to yield determinate equilibria. Sunspots are just one case of equilibrium hanging by bootstraps. So even here we need to know something of the process of learning in order to get determinate answers. Also, even here, equilibrium may not reflect 'fundamentals'.

But only economies that are very large in the technical sense allow one to make traditional price-taking assumptions. It seems clear that in the world firms must predict not only prices but also demand. Certainly, as Arrow (1958) argued, this seems to be the case out of Walrasian equilibrium. This has led us to suggest that dynamics should be viewed as a learning process, both about demand conditions and about the strategies of near competitors. Once again, when an equilibrium is defined relatively to such processes, it seems that they are indeterminate unless history—that is information—is explicitly modelled and known. The path of history is the outcome of individual decisions and in turn helps to fix the latter. This is really the main message: the information available to agents at any time is determined by the particular path followed. The economy could have followed a different path and generated quite different information. There is something essentially historical in a proper definition of equilibrium and of course in the dynamics itself.

This lesson I have attempted to illustrate. Obviously a long road stretches ahead. It is a risky and unruly road, but I hope that many more theorists with a bent for rigorous theorizing will embark on it—if for no other reason than that turning the old wheel is now too easy.

PART II

6

The Economics of Parallel Research

PARTHA DASGUPTA

1. Introduction

In selecting investment projects, a decision-maker is confronted simultaneously with three issues: which commodities should be produced, in what quantities, and which techniques of production should be used to produce them. The first two issues concern the mix of products, the third the choice of techniques. They are interrelated, and a vast literature on price theory has explored their relationship. Indeed, cost–benefit analysis is exclusively concerned with these issues.

Research and development projects—or R and D projects, as we will call them here—are also investment projects. They are a special kind of investment projects, possessing features quite different from projects involving the production of conventional goods and services like steel, transistors, and barley. They have been studied far less, but over the past decade or so there has grown an analytical literature around them.[1] In this chapter I will attempt to present an account of the implications of the fact that research and development offer parallel opportunities, or, to be more precise, that there are often several alternative R and D strategies available for solving a given intellectual or technological problem. In short, *parallel* research projects are often available. Now this in itself is no distinguishing feature of research and development as an investment activity. It is merely the counterpart of the fact that there are several ways of manufacturing steel. What makes the economics of parallel research different from the conventional economics of portfolio management and choice of techniques is the fact that the *outcomes* of parallel R and D projects are *valued* differently from those of conventional portfolios (see below). In Section 2 I will formalize the differences. The remainder of the chapter will contain analyses of the implications of parallel research possibilities on market performance of R and D and on socially efficient R and D.

This paper reflects research I have conducted with Paul David, Eric Maskin, and Joseph Stiglitz on various occasions. I am deeply grateful to them for the many stimulating conversations I have had with them over the years. The essay was prepared while I was Visiting Professor at Harvard University and Visiting Fellow at the National Bureau of Economic Research during the spring of 1987. Section 4 was prompted by discussions with Dilip Mookherjee.

[1] For a more complete discussion of this literature, see Dasgupta and Stiglitz (1988).

2. Non-additive Returns from Parallel R and D Projects

I am here thinking of the output of an R and D project as information, and am regarding information as a commodity. An R and D project is thus a (subjective) probability distribution over different kinds of information, or signals. The available set of R and D strategies corresponds to the set of technologies available for the production of conventional goods and services. A decision-maker is therefore faced with a portfolio problem in investment: which problems ought his organization to confront, using which R and D strategies, and how much resource should be devoted to each line?

Since R and D projects have uncertain yields, there may well be a case for *parallel* investigation. By this I mean choosing two or more projects that are aimed at producing the same kind of information, where the information, to give an instance, may be cheaper ways of producing a given commodity. The practice of parallel research and development has been a commonplace. This has been documented by historians of both technology and science. For example, during the Second World War both germanium and silicon appeared promising as semiconductors for use in radar detectors. The US government financed some thirty to forty laboratories to investigate the matter.

We have argued that parallelism does not necessarily imply waste. The decision-maker may well wish to hold an active portfolio of parallel R and D projects on a particular scientific or technological problem. What makes the economics of R and D portfolios different from financial portfolios is in the valuation of outcomes. To illustrate the difference, consider the installation of two manufacturing plants designed to produce the same commodity. As usual, there is some uncertainty in the return from each plant. If the realized rates of return on the plants are 5 and 10 per cent, the aggregate return is some average of the two figures. By way of contrast, consider two R and D projects designed to investigate the same scientific or technological problem. Of their outcomes, *only* the best is worthwhile. For instance, among available methods of manufacturing a commodity, only the best-practice technique ought to be used.[2] To take another example, there is no value added when the same discovery is made a second, a third, or a fourth time. To put it sharply, the winning research team is the sole contributor to social surplus. The point is that the same piece of knowledge can be put to use over and over again without any 'wear and tear'. There is thus little social value to inferior outcomes of parallel research.

---

[2] To be sure, the identity of the best-practice technique depends on relative prices, and societies ought to maintain a record of all discoveries, since currently inferior technologies might turn out to be superior with the passage of time as relative prices change. But this is a different matter altogether.

To formalize this in the context of public expenditure on parallel research and development, suppose there are M parallel R and D projects. Let x_i $(i = 1, \ldots, M)$ be the fund allocated to the ith project. Imagine for simplicity that the 'outcome' of each project can be measured in terms of some scalar quality index. But the outcome is uncertain. So let $h_i(x_i, \tilde{e}_i)$ be the 'outcome' of the ith project, where h_i is a real valued function and $\tilde{e}_i$ is a random variable. Thus h_i is random. To put it another way, if x_i is the investment in the ith project, the 'outcome' h_i is a probabilistic one. Since only the best outcome counts, society will value the realization of the portfolio by the function max $\{h_i(x_i, \tilde{e}_i)\}$.[3] Thus, if the ith project yields the highest 'outcome', h_i measures the social benefit resulting from the project. It is the social surplus. Suppose, for simplicity of exposition, that public R and D expenditure is financed by general taxation. Then the planning problem is:[4]

choose x_i, $i = 1, \ldots, M$ so as to

$$\max E[\max\{h_i(x_i, \tilde{e}_i)\}] - \sum_{i=1}^{M} x_i \qquad (1)$$

subject to the constraints $x_i \geq 0$ for $0 = 1, \ldots, M$.

(In (1), E is the expectation operator.)

The first thing to note about this problem is that, even if $h_i(x_i, \tilde{e}_i)$ is strictly concave in x_i, so long as it is not overly concave, the efficient portfolio consists of complete specialization in one R and D project, even if the project uncertainties are independent of one another. We conclude that, for diversification—that is, parallel research—to be desirable, h_i must be sufficiently concave in x_i, at least for moderate and large values of x_i. In other words, diversification in research and development pays only if diminishing returns set in sufficiently early (see Loury 1979; Dasgupta and Stiglitz 1980b).

These observations concern the manner in which *society* values the outcome of parallel research and development. Turning to the way in which compensation schemes aim to reward research teams in the 'market', we note that they are of the form: 'winner takes all'. The institution of patents obviously aims to mimic this rather ruthless mode of compensation. (If date of success is the quality of the outcome under study, h_i should be thought of as the inverse of development time.) But even in the absence of patents, the first firm to develop a product often makes great inroads into the market, reaping a large share of profits from

---

[3] Contrast this with a financial invesment portfolio, where the aggregate *ex post* value of the M projects would have been $\sum_i h_i(x_i, \tilde{e}_i)$.

[4] We are postulating a risk-neutral decision-maker for simplicity of exposition; that is, it is simplest to regard h_i as monetary payoff. Clearly, one can generalize the formulation in various directions.

the invention. The point is not that inferior inventions earn nothing, merely that they often earn a disproportionately low amount. The winner-takes-all hypothesis is merely an idealization.[5] (See Dasgupta and Maskin 1987 for a more detailed discussion of this.)

These remarks concern the form of compensation to inventors and discoverers in the *market* for knowledge, what one might call technology. But it would seem that the winner-takes-all form of reward is in operation even in non-market social environments, such as academic research. Priority matters greatly in the scientific culture, and this concern is continuously fostered by the community. Academic science encourages the disclosure of inventions and findings. Furthermore, unlike patent rights, there is no proprietory *use* of the finding. It is freely usable by all who need it. The prize to the discoverer is *priority*. Much of the reward is non-pecuniary, in the form of medals, awards, titles, and more generally in peer group esteem. The reason why, in competition among research teams engaged in parallel research, the winner(s) is awarded the entire 'purse'—either with patents or with priority—is not hard to find: it is often impossible to discover subsequently how far behind the winner(s) the unsuccessful contestants were at the time the discovery was made. That is why competition among participants engaged in parallel research assumes the form of a *race*.[6]

There is a great deal of historical evidence of the occurrence of parallel research among competing teams (or firms). For example, the history of the semiconductor industry is replete with cases of parallel research among commercial firms (Braun and Macdonald 1982). Another class of examples is provided by the occurrence of multiple discoveries in science and mathematics, that is, where similar scientific and mathematical advances are made by several individuals and research teams working independently of one another (see e.g. Ogburn and Thomas 1922; Merton 1973.) Indeed, one suspects that parallel research is undertaken more frequently than the data suggest. Historians of science and technology do not usually report on failures: they discuss successes. Data on failures are much harder to come by. Thus, when Merton (1973) talks of 'multiples', he means multiple *discoveries*. But for every recorded success, or achievement, there must have been a great many unrecorded

---

[5] Of one general class of cases, that is. In this paper I am going to ignore spillovers of knowledge among research teams. The 'winner-takes-all' hypothesis is obviously a bad one in those circumstances where informational externalities are strong. For an analysis of R and D competition in the presence of spillovers of knowledge see Reinganum (1981), Katz and Shapiro (1987), and Dasgupta (1988b).

[6] Case histories of important inventions and discoveries have unearthed very many such races. See Dasgupta and David (1987) for a conceptual framework that distinguishes science and technology as social institutions, and priority and patents as compensation schemes in them.

failures, where scientists attempted to solve the same problem but did not succeed, and therefore did not publish. The incidence of multiple discoveries understates the extent of parallel research (see e.g. Kuznets 1962).

In this chapter I shall be much concerned with the characteristics of R and D races. Towards this I shall assume, for ease of exposition, that each potential R and D project is identified with a separate firm, a separate research team. If h_i is the outcome of the R and D project of the ith firm, and if there is some j such that $h_j > h_i$, the ith firm earns nothing. If h_i exceeds h_j for all $j \neq i$, the reward to firm i is $G(h_i)$, where G is an increasing function. (If $G(h_i) = h_i$, the winning firm enjoys the entire social surplus. This would happen, for example, if the winning firm is awarded a patent and the new monopolist practises discriminatory pricing. Usually one would imagine that $0 < G(h_i) \leq h_i$.) These together formalize the winner-takes-all hypothesis.

There remains the question of ties. What does a winning team earn when there are multiple winners? It transpires that nothing of analytical substance depends upon this. In many examples the chance of a tie is nil and so it does not matter what is assumed. In what follows I will be much conscious of Occam's Razor, and so I will make what will be the analytically convenient assumption. For the moment I assume that in the event of a tie rewards are zero.

For simplicity I restrict myself to R and D races under complete information, and in what follows I identify equilibria of such races with Nash equilibria. (See Chapter 3 above by Brandenburger for an identification of conditions under which Nash equilibria are indeed the objects of interest.) Furthermore, I take it that firms are risk-neutral. Thus,

$$\left.\begin{array}{l}\bar{x}_i \ (i = 1, \ldots, M) \text{ is an equilibrium level of R and D investment} \\ \text{for firm } i \text{ if } \bar{x}_i \text{ maximizes} \\ E\{H[h_i(x_i, \tilde{e}_i)] - x_i\} \text{ where } H[h_i(x_i, \tilde{e}_i)] = G[h_i(x_i, \tilde{e}_i)] \text{ if} \\ h_i(x_i, \tilde{e}_i) > h_j(x_j, \tilde{e}_j) \text{ for all } j \neq i \text{ and } H[h_i(x_i, \tilde{e}_i)] = 0 \text{ otherwise.} \end{array}\right\} \quad (2)$$

A central concern in the economics of parallel research is a comparison of the solution of (1) with that of (2).[7] It is useful to know if market portfolios in parallel R and D projects are biased in any way. Furthermore, it is important to seek appropriate public policies in the face of market failure. A general class of public policies consists of suitably altering the reward function, H. Patent policies are an instance of this.

---

[7] The existence of a market equilibrium in (2) needs first of all to be guaranteed. We will confirm its existence in the examples that follow. A general existence theorem can be found in Dasgupta and Maskin (1986a,1986b).

The model I have just presented is prototypical. But is has two weaknesses. The first is that it eschews the time structure of R and D expenditure: R and D investment is perceived as a capital commitment. Even the phasing of this commitment is ignored. We will note subsequently a general insight which can be had if the time sequence of R and D investment is modelled. (Important contributions to this are by Harris and Vickers 1985a, 1985b; Vickers 1986.)

The second weakness concerns the model of the market economy, as formalized in (2). It is a model of R and D competition among firms. But it is just that. The construct does not distinguish entry decisions from decisions on how much to invest in research and development. Entry decisions precede R and D decisions, not to mention more flexible decisions such as advertising, production outlays, and so forth. Entry usually involves costs. In order to provide a ready material for comparison with the theory of contestable markets, I will assume entry to be costless. (See Dasgupta 1988b, and Dasgupta and Stiglitz 1988 for an analysis of the implications of entry costs on R and D activities among firms.) But I will be much concerned with situations where firms *enter* sequentially, even when they make their post-entry decisions simultaneously. Thus, the models that follow will distinguish entry decisions from other decisions.

In Sections 3 and 4 I will study models where entry is costless. I will argue that there is then a dissipation of rents occasioned by R and D competition—in extreme cases, to the point where firms in equilibrium earn no profits (see Dasgupta and Stiglitz, 1980a,1980b). The idea here has surface similarity to the theory of contestable markets developed in Baumol, Panzer, and Willig (1982). But only just. Rent dissipation in the models that follow will be due to *actual* competition, not *potential* competition.

The constructs I will study in the remainder of this chapter will vary also by way of the specification of the R and D technologies, and thus by way of their 'outcomes', h_i. Much of the time I will assume that the uncertainties in R and D projects are independent of one another. This simplifies the matter a great deal. But I will comment on the case where there is a choice of correlation among projects, and will suggest that the market may sustain excessive correlation. In Section 5 I will study the implications of a particular form of entry cost, one where some firms suffer from the disadvantage of having to choose their R and D effort *after* advantaged firms choose theirs. In other words, the model considers sequential moves. The issue of pre-emptive *patenting* (Dasgupta and Stiglitz 1980b) and pre-emptive R and D *leads* (Harris and Vickers 1985a) will be discussed here. I will also discuss competition for *multiple* discoveries and show how strong the conditions are for pre-emptive multiple patenting to occur under competition (see Dasgupta 1986).

3. Rent Dissipation: An Example

Imagine that there is a single invention (of a given quality) in sight. Imagine also that there is a large number of R and D projects available for making the invention. The cost of each project is $\hat{x}$. A project can either be a success or a failure. Project uncertainties are independent of one another. The probability that a project is a *failure* is p, that it is a *success*, $1 - p$.

Suppose first that research and development is in the public sector. The problem before the government decision-maker is to choose the number of R and D teams, or in other words the number of R and D projects. These are all parallel R and D projects, and so I suppose that, if one or more than one chosen project is a success, social benefits amount to V_s. (By normalization, there are no benefits if all fail.) I shall assume that $V_s/\hat{x}$ is 'large', so that the optimal number of projects is 'large'.

Let n be the number of projects chosen. Expected net social benefit, $W(n)$, is then

$$W(n) = (1 - p^n)V_s - n\hat{x}.$$

We wish to find the optimal n. To calculate this, note that the expected net social benefit from having the nth project is

$$(1 - p)p^{(n-1)}V_s - \hat{x}.$$

Since the optimum number is large, $n \simeq n - 1$ and net social benefit from the marginal project is nil. Let n_s be the optimal number of projects. It follows that n_s is the solution of the equation

$$(1 - p)p^n V_s = \hat{x} \tag{3}$$

or, put another way,

$$p^n = \hat{x}/(1 - p)V_s. \tag{4}$$

Since $1 > p > 0$, the larger is $V_s/\hat{x}$, the larger is the desirable number of projects.

Consider now the competitive market mechanism in research and development. I take it that, if there is a single winner, the reward is V_c to the winner. Losers earn nothing. The question arises about the outcome of ties. For ease of exposition, I assume as earlier that profits are nil among winners in case of a tie. One could imagine that the invention in question is a cost-reducing invention, what is often called a *process* invention. If firms compete in prices in the product market, *à la* Bertrand, then, if the invention involves constant unit costs of production, profits will indeed be nil if more than one firm succeeds in making the invention.

I assume that $V_c/\hat{x}$ is large enough to sustain a large number of active firms in equilibrium. I assume as well that entry is free, so that equilibrium involves zero profits even for active firms. In other words, there is complete rent dissipation arising from R and D competition. (For a rigorous discussion of this issue, see Novshek 1980; Dasgupta and Stiglitz 1980a.)

Equilibrium is easy to characterize under such conditions. Recall that I am assuming complete information. If there are n active firms, the representative active firm calculates as follows. The chance that each of the remaining $(n-1)$ projects is a failure is $p^{(n-1)}$. Therefore, the expected private benefit to this firm in undertaking research and development is

$$(1-p)p^{(n-1)}V_c - \hat{x}.$$

But in equilibrium, risk-neutral firms expect to earn no profit in this R and D game. If n_c is the equilibrium number of firms, then it must be the solution of the 'zero profit' condition:[8]

$$(1-p)p^n V_c = \hat{x} \tag{5}$$

or, put another way,

$$p^n = \frac{\hat{x}}{(1-p)V_c}. \tag{6}$$

When we compare equations (4) and (6), we note immediately the following proposition.

PROPOSITION 1. $n_c \gtrless n_s$ as $V_c \gtrless V_s$

Proposition 1 is interesting because it says that in the model economy under study there is full congruence between society and the 'market' if the winner is awarded the entire social benefit from the innovation. The market is efficient. We will see presently that this is an unusually strong conclusion, and that free entry can easily result in the dissipation of rents, leading to an excessive number of competitors.

The model presented in the next section captures this feature sharply. It also assumes that the level of investment in each project is a decision variable. Finally, the model possesses an explicitly intertemporal structure. This enables me to analyse a crucial policy matter, the choice of patent lengths.

4. Optimum Patent Length

The model I will discuss in this section was developed independently by Loury (1979) and Dasgupta and Stiglitz (1980b). A project is characterized by a renewal process, the parameters of the process being dependent on the volume of R and D investment. For the moment, I will interpret the event whose occurrence is described by the renewal process in a loose manner. It may be a single invention, or the beginning of a whole string of them. Subsequently I will confine myself to a single

---

[8] Since by hypothesis $V_c/\hat{x}$ is large, n_c is large. Therefore $n_c - 1 \simeq n_c$.

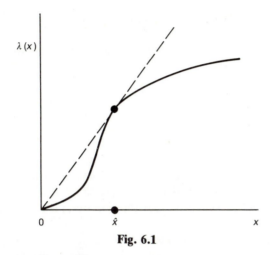

Fig. 6.1

process invention (that is, a cost-reducing invention), and, as earlier, I will not distinguish between invention and innovation.

If x_i is committed at the starting date $(t = 0)$ on the ith project, the probability that the project is successful at or prior to date t is $1 - \exp[-\lambda(x_i)t]$. In other words, the probability that the project is successful during the interval $(t, t + dt)$, conditional on its not having being successful until then, is $\lambda(x_i)dt$. We are therefore confining ourselves to a Poisson discovery process. To have a non-trivial problem, I assume that $\lambda(x_i)$ is characterized by an initial range of increasing returns, followed by decreasing returns, as depicted in Figure 6.1. The *efficient* level of R and D expenditure is $\hat{x}$, the level at which $\lambda'(x) = \lambda(x)/x$.

Project uncertainties are independent of one another. I shall first discuss a nationalized industry. By this I mean, as earlier, not only that production is under government management, but also that the government is directly involved in research and development.

Let V_s denote the capitalized value of (expected) social benefits that flow from the invention. Finally, let $r\ (>0)$ be the social rate of discount. Given the form of R and D technology, $\lambda(\cdot)$, it is clear that it would be inefficient to fund different (active) projects at different rates. Thus, the planning problem is to choose n (the number of active projects) and x (the investment level for each project) which maximize[9]

$$\frac{V_s n\lambda(x)}{[n\lambda(x) + r]} - nx. \tag{7}$$

[9] It should be noted that the expected date of success is $1/n\lambda(x)$. To derive (7), note that $n\lambda(x) \exp[-n\lambda(x)t]$ is the probability rate that the invention will occur at t. Thus the expected discounted flow of social benefit at t is $V_s n\lambda(x) \exp\{-[n\lambda(x) + rt]\}$. Integration of this over the entire future yields the first term in (7).

As before, I assume that n is a continuous variable. (This is justifiable if $\hat{x}$ is small relative to V_s).

Choosing n and x optimally yields the two first-order conditions:

$$\frac{V_s\lambda(x)r}{[n\lambda(x)+r]^2} = x \tag{8}$$

and

$$\frac{V_s\lambda'(x)r}{[n\lambda(x)+r]^2} = 1. \tag{9}$$

From equations (8) and (9) we conclude at once that the optimal level of investment in each active project is $\hat{x}$, the efficient level. The optimum *number* of parallel projects, n_s, can then be obtained from either of the equations.

Consider now competition among private firms for the patent. Firms (or, alternatively, research teams) work independently of another. If x_i $(i=1,\ldots,n)$ is the level of R and D investment chosen by firm i, the probability *rate* that the project will be successfully completed at date t, *and* that it will be firm i that will be successful, is $\lambda(x_i)\exp[-\sum_{j=1}^n \lambda(x_j)t]$. As in Section 2, I assume free entry into the industry. Let V_c be the capitalized value of the flow of rewards (or profits) accruing to the winner. For brevity, let us identify r with the market rate of interest.[10]

Recall (2). Firm i chooses x_i with a view to maximizing

$$\frac{V_c\lambda(x_i)}{[\sum_j \lambda(x_j)+r]} - x_i. \tag{10}$$

Since firms are identical, we look for a symmetric Nash equilibrium. Furthermore, for ease of exposition, I will assume that $\hat{x}$ is 'small' so that in equilibrium the number of active firms is 'large'. But this means that firm i may as well ignore the effect of its R and D expenditure on the expected date of discovery, which is

$$\left[\sum_{j=1}^n \lambda(x_j)\right]^{-1}.$$

I conclude that the condition that a symmetric Nash equilibrium must satisfy is

$$\frac{V_c\lambda'(x)}{[n\lambda(x)+r]} = 1. \tag{11}$$

Entry being costless and the R and D decisions being chosen simultaneously, free entry implies in the present case that expected profits are

---

[10] In other words, I am avoiding distortions arising from an imperfect capital market. This latter introduces a different set of problems from the ones I am discussing here.

nil in equilibrium. Using (10), this means that

$$\frac{V_c\lambda(x)}{[n\lambda(x)+r]}=x. \tag{12}$$

An immediate implication of equations (11) and (12) is that in equilibrium each active firm invests $\hat{x}$ in research and development. As regards individual expenditure, the market is therefore efficient. But not as regards total expenditure. For on using equations (9) and (11), we note that

$$\frac{[n_c\lambda(\hat{x})+r]}{[n_s\lambda(\hat{x})+r]}=\frac{V_c[n_s\lambda(\hat{x})+r]}{V_s r}. \tag{13}$$

And on using equation (8) in the right-hand side of equation (13), we can assert the following proposition.[11]

PROPOSITION 2. $n_c \gtrless n_s$ as $V_c\sqrt{[\lambda'(\hat{x})]} \gtrless \sqrt{V_s}\sqrt{r}$.

Proposition 2 makes precise in a quantitative manner the sense in which large private rewards encourage excessive entry. A special case of considerable importance is $V_c = V_s$. Here, the patent-holder captures all social benefits flowing from the innovation. We are concerned with partial equilibrium analysis in this chapter. If in addition the marginal social value of income to all individuals is the same, we would have $V_c = V_s$ if the patent-holder were to practise fully discriminatory pricing. From equation (13), we may conclude the following.

PROPOSITION 3. If private rewards equal social benefits from innovation, the market sustains an excessive number of competitors, and therefore excessive R and D expenditure. The expected date of innovation under market competition is earlier than is socially desirable.

Proposition 3 displays rent dissipation in a sharp form. The underlying case, where the patent-holder practises discriminatory pricing, is interesting, because by assumption there is no distortion in the market once innovation has occurred. There is distortion only at the stage of R and D competition, or in other words at the level of technological competition. Since $n_c > n_s$ in this case, public policy needs to be directed at reducing private benefits from innovation. One way to do this is to reduce the

---

[11] It should be noted that the arguments in the text imply that total R and D expenditure, nx, times the expected date of innovation, $1/n\lambda(x)$, is independent of market structure. In his well-known study, Schwartzman (1977) has suggested that in the pharmaceutical industry the average cost per new chemical entity is about $17 million per year, and that on average the development period is four to five years. Assuming the upper value and ignoring discounting, this means a total investment of $85 million per new chemical entity. In the context of our model, this means that $\hat{x} = \$85$ million and that $\hat{x}/\lambda(\hat{x}) = 85 \times 5 \times 10^6$ dollar-years. This last is independent of market structure.

length of the patent. (If $V_c = V_s$, the patent is of infinite duration.) I look into this.

Let π_s be the per-period flow of net social benefits from the innovation date, and let $\hat{T}$ be the length of the optimum patent. It follows that $V_s = \pi_s/r$, and, if the optimum patent is enforced,

$$V_c = \frac{\pi_s[1 - \exp(-r\hat{T})]}{r}. \tag{14}$$

(Recall that by hypothesis the patent-holder practises discriminatory pricing.) From equations (13) and (14), or equivalently from Proposition 3 and equation (14), we may infer the following.

PROPOSITION 4. If the patent-holder practises (fully) discriminatory pricing, the optimum patent length, $\hat{T}$, satisfies the relation[12]

$$-r\hat{T} = \log\left\{1 - \frac{r}{[\sqrt{\lambda'(\hat{x})}\sqrt{\pi_s}]}\right\}. \tag{15}$$

From equation (14) we conclude as follows.

PROPOSITION 5. The length of the optimum patent depends on the characteristics of the invention. The more significant an innovation is, the shorter is the duration of the optimum patent.

I find the second part of Proposition 5 interesting. It is interesting because one might have thought that the more significant an innovation is, the more encouragement is needed by the market; that is, that the market needs more help in order to coax it into sustaining the desirable level of R and D activity. Granted, this argument is countered by the fact that the patent-holder practices fully discriminatory pricing, and there is complete rent dissipation. But this merely says that the optimum patent is of finite duration (Proposition 3), not that significant innovations should be protected by short patents.

The assumption that the patent-holder practises fully discriminatory pricing is analytically useful; it is not empirically sound. Derivation of the optimum patent length when the patent-holder charges monopoly price is slightly more involved: there is market distortion during the tenure of the patent-holder. (For an analysis of this, see Dasgupta 1988a; see also Nordhaus 1969.) The question I want to ask instead is this: If patents are of long duration, and if patent-owners charge monopoly price, does the market encourage significant innovations or does it encourage minor innovations?

To answer this I consider a process innovation. The current best-practice technique involves unit cost, c_1, in producing a commodity, the

---

[12] This corrects the analysis in Dasgupta and Stiglitz (1980b: 19), which is valid only when the patent-holder practises fully discriminatory pricing.

market demand for which is iso-elastic, with demand elasticity less than unity. The invention being sought is cost-reducing, and once innovation occurs the best-practice technique will involve unit costs amounting to c_2. I assume that the industry is perfectly competitive prior to the innovation. And for brevity I take it that the patent-holder will have infinite tenure. If Q is total quantity of the commodity in question, I suppose that the market demand curve at each date is given by the function

$$p(Q) = \alpha A Q^{-(1+\alpha)}; \qquad \alpha, A > 0 \tag{16}$$

where A is the 'size' of the market, and $1/(1 + \alpha)$ is the elasticity of demand.

Given the structure of the model, it is immediate that the patent-owner will practise limit pricing. If the flow of profit to the patent-owner is denoted by π_c, it is routine to check that

$$\pi_c = c_1^{\alpha/(1+\alpha)} \left(1 - \frac{c_2}{c_1} \right) (\alpha A)^{1/(1+\alpha)}. \tag{17}$$

Furthermore, if the industry were socially managed, the flow of social benefits would be π_s, where

$$\pi_s = \alpha^{-\alpha/(1+\alpha)} A^{1/(1+\alpha)} c_1^{\alpha/(1+\alpha)} [1 - (c_2/c_1)^{\alpha/(1+\alpha)}]. \tag{18}$$

Now recall Proposition 2. $V_s = \pi_s/r$ and $V_c = \pi_c/r$. From equations (17) and (18) and Proposition 2, we conclude that $n_c > n_s$ if either A is large (the market is large) or c_1 is large (the innovation is significant). We also conclude that $n_c < n_s$ if c_2 is only slightly smaller than c_1 (the innovation is minor). But if $n_c > n_s$, the expected date of innovation under competition is earlier than the socially optimal expected date; and if $n_c < n_s$, it is later. I summarize this by way of the following proposition.

PROPOSITION 6. If patents are of long duration, the market encourages significant innovations and discourages minor innovations, when compared with socially optimum rates of innovation. Furthermore, competition for patents leads to an excessive rate of innovation in markets where the demand for the product is large.

Considerations that yield the optimum length of patents are only slightly more involved than those that led to Propositions 4 and 5. While the patent lasts, the owner earns the flow of profits equal to the amount stated in equation (17). This is less than (18), and so private incentives are less than social incentives. But the consideration leading to Proposition 5 remains valid. Significant innovations are more desirable than minor innovations and so at first blush they may appear to require greater encouragement in the private market. This suggests a longer patent length. But set against it is the opposite consideration: that the longer is the patent, the longer society has to suffer distortions in the product market. In general, Proposition 5 continues to hold.

5. Pre-emptive Patenting of Multiple Patents

The argument that patent-owners have greater incentives than their rivals to undertake process innovations has been much discussed in the literature.[13] In what follows I will present the argument in a way somewhat different from the usual, and I will also argue that an implication, which has often been drawn, that a sitting monopolist will pre-empt his rivals in process innovations is not to be taken seriously. It is based on extreme assumptions, and the evidence belies the claim that monopoly persists *because* of this greater incentive to innovate.[14]

It is useful to think of patent races as bidding games. To get to the essence of the matter, at least to get a sense of the argument I am reviewing, I shall ignore uncertainty in R and D projects. I want to think of patent races in the following way: N players $(N \geqslant 2)$ bid for an indivisible object valued by each at V_c (> 0). All bids are forfeited. (This captures the idea that R and D expenditure is irretrievable.) The highest bidder wins the object. If there are K $(\leqslant N)$ highest bidders, each of the K players wins the object with probability $1/K$.

Let x_i $(i = 1, \ldots, N)$ be i's bid. (This corresponds to i's R and D expenditure.) I may as well then assume that $0 \leqslant x_i \leqslant V_c$. Notice that i's profit function is discontinuous at the set of points $x_i = \max\{x_j; j \neq i\}$. As a preliminary exercise I shall first assume that the players make their bids simultaneously. This corresponds to an assumption I have made so far in this chapter, that firms choose their R and D strategies simultaneously. The difference between the bidding game here and the patent race in Section 4 is that the game here is *discontinuous*. Our earlier games were continuous. They were smooth because of the underlying uncertainty in R and D technologies. Here I am eschewing uncertainty. The highest bidder wins. This is another way of saying that the time–cost curve is deterministic. (In fact, we may think of some decreasing function of x_i as the time required to develop the process innovation as a function of R and D investment. The hypothesis that the reward to the winner, V_c, is independent of the size of the winner's R and D expenditure is merely a simplifying move. It can be relaxed quite easily. See Dasgupta 1988).

So then the bidding game is discontinuous. Therefore we should not be surprised that the game does not possess a Nash equilibrium in pure

[13] The argument was presented originally in Dasgupta and Stiglitz (1980b). See also Reinganum (1984a,b), Salant (1984), and Vickers (1985).
[14] The treatment that follows is based on Dasgupta (1986).

strategies. But there is an equilibrium in mixed strategies.[15] Since the game is symmetric, there must be a symmetric equilibrium. For our bidding game this is easy to compute. At this equilibrium the cumulative distribution function associated with each player's mixed bid is $(x/V_c)^{1/(N-1)}$, for $0 \leqslant x \leqslant V_c$. The characteristics of this equilibrium can be summarized in the following proposition.

PROPOSITION 7. If the number of competitors is more than one, there is complete rent dissipation. Each player expects to bid V_c/N. Thus, the larger is the number of competitors, the more distant is the expected date of innovation.

It is interesting to contrast Proposition 7 with the conclusions we arrived at in Section 4. The fact that the technology of research and development has implicitly been assumed to be deterministic here—in contrast to the continuous probability distribution assumed in Section 4—has much to do with the contrasting nature of the properties of market equilibrium. Research and development is perforce *duplicative* in a model with no spillovers in research technology. Competition is useful only inasmuch as it encourages firms to invest more in research and development than they would in its absence. But beyond $N = 2$, competition is self-defeating: each firm on average reduces its R and D expenditure because the chance of winning the patent is reduced. From Proposition 7, we may conclude that the optimum number of competitors is *two*![16]

In what follows I will study competitive games of this sort, but now I will make the competitor's moves sequential, so as to introduce a crucial asymmetry in the ability of firms to engage in research and development.

Suppose there are two firms, $i = 1, 2$. Firm 1 is the sitting monopolist, the incumbent. One may imagine that the incumbent holds a patent on the existing manufacturing process. The race that we will study is for the next patent, a process innovation. If the incumbent wins, his profit is V_m. But if firm 2 wins, profits to the two players are V_1 and V_2, respectively. Naturally, I assume that $V_m > V_1 + V_2$. (This means that profits earned by the monopolist holding both patents exceeds the sum of duopoly profits.)

The incumbent is the current patent-owner. Thus I allow it an advantage of moving first, that is placing its bid first. The rival is then assumed to follow. The incumbent firm is therefore a Stackelberg leader.

---

[15] It is as well to emphasize that we do not have to see players actually mixing. Equilibrium mixed strategies in games incorporating the full force of the common knowledge assumption are equilibrium beliefs. See Aumann (1986), Binmore and Dasgupta (1986) and Chapter 3 above by Brandenburger.

[16] To see this, note that the expected total bid is V_c. Thus aggregate R and D expenditure is independent of the number of competitors. Since development time is the inverse of a firm's bid, this is minimized when $N = 2$.

If the incumbent firm bids V_2 (plus a tiny bit more, to be exact) it will win the patent. This is because V_2 is the rival's maximum bid. If instead it bids less than V_2, it will lose the race and forfeit the bid. Its choice thus boils down to either bidding V_2 or not bidding at all. If it chooses the former the payoff is $V_m - V_2$; if the latter, it is V_1. It will therefore choose the former. This is the pre-emption result in its simplest form.

Now, one may argue that the result is contrived: the incumbent has an advantage in moving first, in being able to commit itself to its R and D expenditure before its rival can. In fact, the result is in a sense stronger if the rival moves first. So suppose the sequence of bids is reversed. In this case it is immediate that the rival will not place a bid: it knows that it will be outbid by the incumbent. It follows that the incumbent will win the object by bidding a tiny amount. There are then advantages in moving second here. What this result is saying is that, if R and D expenditure has to be committed in advance, and if there is insufficient uncertainty in the R and D technology, an incumbent firm behaves more or less like a pure monopolist, unthreatened by parallel research by rivals. Notice also that the patent the incumbent seeks may be for a technology that is *strictly inferior* to the one that is currently the best-practice one. The pre-emption argument goes through. Plainly, the monopolist will not *use* his new patent: his incentive for winning it is simply to prevent his rival from using it. In this special case the monopolist will pre-empt and hold a sleeping patent.

One can go still further, as have Harris and Vickers (1985a, 1985b) in their interesting work. They make the point that the incumbent may merely wish to take a sufficient *lead* in its research project and then cease investing in the project—the lead being sufficient to deter its rival from entering the race. The argument is a delicate one, requiring an explicit time structure of R and D investment and then using the now familiar backward induction reasoning. But the intuition is clear enough, and the result stronger than the one on sleeping patents. The Harris–Vickers result says that in extreme cases the patent will not in fact be taken out, because the incumbent will not complete its R and D project. Partial investment in it is purely strategic, to prevent the rival from entering the race.

What is the outcome if competitors must commit their expenditures simultaneously, at the initial date? The game is asymmetric, of course, but there is an equilibrium in mixed strategies, where the rival earns zero expected profits.[17] So then this tells us that if the rival has to incur costs to enter the race it will not wish to do so, and the incumbent will be able to pursue its policies unencumbered by threats. The moral is clear.

---

[17] For the rival, the outcome is much like that described in Proposition 1. Expected profit enjoyed by the incumbent is, on the other hand, positive.

Patent races tend to dissipate rents. Firms that face entry costs are therefore deterred from entering. Incumbents face an inbuilt advantage.

How seriously should we take these conclusions? Not very, for there are considerations that work the other way, often decisively; considerations that the foregoing model does not capture. The fact that the incumbent is a specialist, possessing mastery over an existing technology, may itself be the reason why it is relatively inefficient in developing new technologies, based on novel ideas. This is to say that the incumbent may well face a vastly inferior R and D technology. As Rosenberg (1986) has noted, history is replete with evidence of this. Makers of stagecoaches played no role in the development of the steam locomotive. The makers of steam locomotives, in turn, made no contribution to the development of the diesel locomotive. Then again, firms engaged in the production of vacuum tubes failed to transfer their dominance to the semiconductor market. Worst of all, Western Union turned down the opportunity to *purchase* Bell's telephone patent when it was offered to them for a mere $100,000! And here was an invention that had already been made! The incumbent simply misread the significance of the invention.

This is one aspect of the matter. The other is uncertainty—about technological possibilities and about market demand. If there is sufficient uncertainty in either of these, the pre-emptive argument will not go through: there will be some chance that rivals will enter the market with new innovations. This has been argued forcefully by Reinganum (1984a,b).

I want to develop a further argument here, one that does not rely on these considerations. I want to emphasize the fact that there is usually a number of competing process innovations in sight. The race is therefore not for a single patent, but for multiple patents. An incumbent will then persist as a monopolist only if it can acquire all the patents. But will it wish to, even when it suffers from no technological disadvantages? The following argument shows that it will not wish to, unless there are strong increasing returns to scale in the acquisition of patents. The analysis that follows makes this precise. (It is based on Dasgupta 1986.)

For tractability, I assume that the monopolist ($i = 1$) faces a single rival $i = 2$. There are N (≥ 1) patents to be won. They are identical in their economic effects. The payoff for the monopolist in winning $K(0 \leq K \leq N)$ patents is $\bar{V}(K)$ and for the rival is $V^{**}(K)$. By assumption,

$$\bar{V}(K + 1) > \bar{V}(K) > 0 \qquad \text{for } 0 \leq K \leq N - 1,$$

$$V^{**}(K + 1) > V^{**}(K) \qquad \text{for } 0 \leq K \leq N - 1,$$

$$\bar{V}(K) > V^{**}(K) \qquad \text{for } 0 \leq K \leq N$$

and

$$V^{**}(0) = 0.$$

As earlier, I allow the incumbent to bid first. This is followed by bids by the rival.

Consider first the case where the rival's payoff is superadditive:

$$V^{**}(K)/K \geqslant V^{**}(J)/J \qquad \text{for } J < K. \tag{19}$$

If the monopolist intends to win precisely $K(0 \leqslant K \leqslant N)$ patents in such a situation, he should bid nothing for $(N - K)$ and $H(K)$ for *each* of the rest, where

$$H(K) = \frac{[V^{**}(N) - V^{**}(N - K)]}{K}.$$

If he does this, the payoff to him (in obtaining K patents) is

$$M(K) \equiv V(\tilde{K}) - KH(K)$$

or

$$M(K) = \bar{V}(K) - V^{**}(N) + V^{**}(N - K).$$

The monopolist's problem is to choose K so as to maximize $M(K)$. A sufficient condition for complete pre-emption is therefore $M(K + 1) \geqslant M(K)$ for all K; or

$$\bar{V}(K + 1) + V^{**}[N - (K + 1)] \geqslant \bar{V}(K) + V^{**}(N - K) \qquad \text{for all } K. \tag{20}$$

(20) is intuitively appealing, for it says that total industry profits are rising with the number of patents captured by the monopolist. But it does not say directly whether the monopolist enjoys increasing or decreasing returns in the acquisition of patents. However, note that (20) is guaranteed if

$$\bar{V}(K + 1) - \bar{V}(K) > \bar{V}(K) - \bar{V}(K - 1) \qquad \text{for } K \geqslant 1, \tag{21}$$

and

$$\bar{V}(1) - \bar{V}(0) \geqslant V^{**}(N) - V^{**}(N - 1). \tag{22}$$

It follows that (19), (21), and (22) are together sufficient for complete pre-emption.

Suppose instead the other extreme to (19), that is, that the rival's payoff is *subadditive*:

$$V^{**}(K)/K < V^{**}(J)/J \qquad \text{for } J < K. \tag{23}$$

This case does not allow us to obtain as clean a set of sufficient conditions for complete pre-emption on the part of the monopolist.

First, note that, if the monopolist decides to win precisely K patents, then under (23) he will bid nothing for $N - K$ of them and he will bid $L(K)$ for each of the remaining ones, where

$$L(K) = V^{**}(N - K + 1) - V^{**}(N - K).$$

In this event his payoff $M(K)$ is

$$M(K) = \bar{V}(K) - KL(K)$$

or

$$M(K) = \bar{V}(K) + KV^{**}(N - K) - KV^{**}(N - K + 1). \qquad (24)$$

It follows immediately from (24) that a sufficient condition for complete pre-emption $(M(K) \geqslant M(K - 1)$ for $1 \leqslant K \leqslant N)$ is

$$\bar{V}(K) - \bar{V}(K - 1) \geqslant (2K - 1)[V^{**}(N - K + 1) - V^{**}(N - K)]$$
$$\text{for } 1 \leqslant K \leqslant N.$$

The conditions linking the monopolist's payoff and that of the rival that have been stressed here are suggestive of the kind of increasing returns in the profitability of inventions that are sufficient for complete pre-emption. They also suggest that complete pre-emption, and thus the persistence of monopoly, is not to be taken seriously as a possibility.

6. Commentary

Parallel research undertakings occur regularly and quite frequently. In the absence of large-scale knowledge spillovers, the sort of competition that is involved here is that of races: races for patents (as in the market for ideas) and races for priority (as in the scientific culture).[18] In the absence of entry costs of any form, such races lead to a dissipation of rents for the weakest in the race. Therefore, if competitors are of equal ability, all expected rents are dissipated. I am stating matters in bald terms here. The precise additional conditions required to establish these results were stated in earlier sections of this chapter. Rent dissipation by no means implies excessive research and development. This is another matter that I have tried to highlight. But such private races as are occasioned by patent laws and the rule of priority do involve inoptimal allocation of resources. In Section 4 I have explored a possible class of policies that the government would wish to wield to achieve a second-best outcome. Specifically, I have presented some arguments which are relevant for the length of optimum patents.

A central weakness in the models I have reviewed is this: uncertainties among parallel research projects have been assumed either to be independent of one another or to be perfectly (and positively) correlated with one another.[19] But research projects can be based on less or more similar ideas. One may thus ask if patent and priority races encourage

---

[18] If knowledge spillovers are substantial, competition takes the form of waiting games, not races. See, e.g., Katz and Shapiro (1987) and Dasgupta (1988b).

[19] While I did not allude to perfect correlation, the models analysed in Section 5 can accommodate it.

excessive or insufficient correlation. In a recent work Eric Maskin and I have argued that they encourage excessive correlation, (see Dasgupta and Maskin 1987). The point here is simplest to see if the outcome of a research project is either a success or a failure. In this case society plainly does not care who is successful: it cares that at least one project is a success. But to the individual teams the identity of the successful project matters: each team wants to be successful. Thus, in choosing a research project that is less correlated to the chosen project of its rival, a firm contributes a social benefit, often in excess of the private benefit from the choice. It is a simple case of external economy. And there is insufficient amount of it under competition.

Of course, there are all sorts of other imperfections that could be analysed as well, for example those arising from the fact that R and D activity is shot through with moral hazard and adverse selection. They too require policy. Then again, much research and development involves *non*-parallel work.[20] I have ignored all these, precisely so that I could highlight the special features of parallel research and the competition it can engender.

---

[20] For an analysis of this, see Dasgupta and Stiglitz (1980a).

7

Strategy Variables and Theories of Industrial Organization

CHRISTOPHER DOYLE

1. Introduction

Over the recent past there has been a proliferation of papers focusing upon industrial organization, many of which have been formulated within a game-theoretic framework. Visualizing firms in an industry as participating in a game allows for a level of abstraction that captures the principal characteristic of competition among the few, namely, strategic interdependence. Ever since the work of Cournot (1838), economic theorists have regarded firms in oligopolistic industries as institutions that choose strategy variables to maximize some objective function. In this chapter I am going to focus upon the modelling of strategy variables and present several examples of recent research illustrating the role that strategy variables play in shaping industrial organization structures.

In a general sense, strategy variables are chosen by the participants of a game. A firm choosing a variable regards it as strategic if it affects the (expected) payoffs accruing to rival firms in the same industry, or if it affects the (expected) payoffs of customers, or both. At the abstract level, a strategy variable is contained in a firm's strategy set and may represent anything of interest. For example, Cournot constructed a model of duopoly where the strategic variable of interest is the quantity of output chosen by each firm. Bertrand (1883) analysed the same problem by modelling the strategic variable as the price set by each firm. It is well known that the solution to the Cournot duopoly model differs from that of the Bertrand duopoly model. This discrepancy highlights the important role of strategic variables in models depicting industrial organization.[1]

In actual markets, firms are observed to operate a whole host of strategy variables—for example, levels of advertising expenditures, whether to offer free trial periods of consumption, whether to match or undercut rivals' prices, warranty provision, frequent user benefits, introductory offers, research and development, and so on. Typically, strategy variables range from a firm selecting a price to display on a commodity to strategies designed with the intention of signalling infor-

---

[1] Kreps and Scheinkman (1983) discuss this discrepancy and construct a very interesting model reconciling the two approaches to duopoly.

mation to potential customers, or rival firms, or potential rival firms, or all possible participants in an industry. There exists an enormous literature focusing upon theories of industrial organization and strategy variables, and thus I propose to concentrate on a few examples in order to illustrate how we can successfully model a number of different strategy variables.[2]

I will focus upon three particular strategy variables: (1) offers made by firms promising price-matching refunds; (2) firms offering free trial periods of consumption; and (3) advertising expenditures. All the models I will describe are intertemporal and are set in environments where some of the participants are endowed with imperfect information. I will summarize two models that incorporate price-matching refund promises into a firm's strategy set. The first is that of Doyle (1987a), which examines refunds as a device by firms to implement intertemporal price discrimination. The second is a model of refunds in an industry providing an experience good of differential quality where the existence of refund promises, combined with the selling price, signals quality, as described in Doyle (1987b). This latter model also provides an insight as to why firms may offer consumers free trial consumption periods. Finally, I describe a model due to Milgrom and Roberts (1986) which examines how seemingly uninformative advertising expenditures to promote experience goods, when combined with price, act as a signal of quality.

2. Price-matching Refunds as Intertemporal Price Discrimination

Consider a situation where an individual firm may offer a consumer a price-matching promise which takes the form of a refund. The following examples illustrate the type of price-matching refund strategies commonly offered.

In the unlikely event that, at the time you book your package holiday with us, the identical holiday provided by the same tour operator is being offered at a lower price by another travel agent, we will reduce our price accordingly.[3]

We promise to refund the difference if you find you could have bought any of our specially selected Dixon Deal Offers cheaper locally at the time of purchase and call within 7 days.[4]

The insight I offer about such pricing is that it can, in markets where participants do not possess full information, support industry equilibria that display a greater degree of price dispersion than in the comparable case where firms quote the price alone. The intuition is as follows.

---

[2] For further discussion on recent advances in industrial organization theory, see Binmore and Dasgupta (1987b), and Stiglitz and Mathewson (1986).

[3] Thomas Cook Ltd, nationwide advertising campaign in the UK throughout 1985–6.

[4] Dixon Ltd, advert in *The Times*, 20 September 1985.

Suppose a consumer finds it relatively expensive to seek a relatively low price for a good. A consumer of this type may therefore be prepared to pay a relatively high price today and accept a price-matching refund if the expected utility of doing so exceeds that of seeking a lower price and purchasing the good in the future. In other words, a consumer may be aware that there exist firms selling the good at a lower price than that at which he or she has purchased, but the price-match refund allows for the possibility that a consumer may eventually pay a lower price. The maximum price a consumer is prepared to pay for a good is obviously going to be higher when a refund system operates. It is clear that price-matching refunds in this context are a form of intertemporal price discrimination if consumer heterogeneity is a feature of the market.

In Doyle (1987a), I construct a simple model that incorporates price-matching refunds within an oligopolistic market structure. The model may be described as follows. A consumer enters a market seeking to purchase one unit of a commodity for immediate consumption. Each consumer survives for two periods. For convenience, I choose to examine a model where stationarity is assumed and the number of consumers $A > 0$ entering the market is the same each period. Prior to any purchase decision, a consumer is assumed to know the distribution of prices displayed in the market and the proportion of stores offering a refund, but not the price displayed by a specific firm. Therefore, consumers are imperfectly informed about prices. I assume that consumers may acquire full information at a cost and that consumers differ with respect to the costs of acquiring information. For simplicity, I assume only two costs of acquiring information, infinity and zero.[5] All consumers possess an identical reservation price, $R > 0$, and I also assume a common discount factor, $\delta \in [0, 1]$. I assume that an imperfectly informed consumer may observe only a single price by random sampling each period. However, for analytical convenience I assume that an individual can return to the first firm observed (in period 1) in the second period if the first firm offers a refund and the second price observed is below that of the first price observed. Each consumer maximizes discounted expected utility EU.

Every firm is identical with respect to the good produced, and the technology used generates an identical U-shaped average cost curve denoted by the function $AC(\ )$. Let the minimum of this function be $minAC$. Firms seek to maximize discounted expected profits $E\Pi$. An individual firm selects a price p to quote and decides whether to offer a price-matching refund. I assume that, whenever a refund is offered and claimed by a consumer at a particular firm, there is an associated cost $r > 0$. One can think of the cost as representing time spent processing the refund claim. Entry or exit is uninhibited and costless. In Doyle (1987a) I

---

[5] This assumption may be relaxed without affecting the qualitative nature of the result.

outline the conditions that need to be satisfied for a symmetric stationary (Nash) equilibrium in pure strategies. The main conclusions are as follows.

1. At most, two prices $p_1 < p_h$ can be supported in an equilibrium.
2. When a refund system operates, the high price p_h in equilibrium is the reservation price R of consumers. The low price p_1 is equal to minimum average costs.
3. The price refund is offered by firms charging the high price only and is a promise to match the lower price.

The symmetry assumption and stationarity allows a diagrammatic representation as shown in Figure 7.1. The shaded region in the figure represents the expected value of refunds incurred by each high-price store every period. Each store charging a price in excess of p_1 only gets randomizing consumers, where $\zeta = \{(\tau A/l^*) + [(1-\tau)A/N^*]\}$, $\mu = [(1-\tau)A/N^*]$, $\tau \in (0, 1)$ is the proportion of consumers fully informed, l^* is the equilibrium number of stores displaying p_1, N^* is the equilibrium number of stores, and q is the number of units produced each period.

The equilibrium results in zero discounted expected profits for all firms (because of entry and the presence of fully informed consumers). The expected profit each period for a firm offering a refund is (the h subscript denotes high-price firms)

$$E\Pi_h = [(R - AC(\mu)]\mu - (R - \min AC)[l^*/(N^* - 1)]\mu = 0. \qquad (1)$$

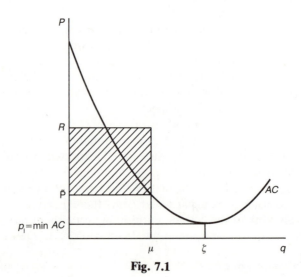

Fig. 7.1

The refund firm obtains profit from selling to a share of randomizing consumers, and loses some revenue to claimants of the refund, that is, to the customers who purchased the good in the previous period and successfully located a lower price this period. Given the stationarity assumption, the probability that the individual consumer who purchases the good in period t locates a lower price in the next period is equal to $l^*/(N^* - 1)$.[6] These assumptions, along with the others, lead to period-by-period profit maximization being equivalent to maximizing expected discounted profits over all time.

A firm not operating a refund offer obtains in equilibrium the following expected profit each period:

$$E\Pi_1 = [\text{min}AC - AC(\zeta)]\zeta = 0. \tag{2}$$

The expected profit is derived from the share of fully informed (who only visit the low-price stores), and the share of randomizing consumers.

High-search-cost customers obtain the following expected utility:

$$\delta(R - \text{min}AC)[l^*/(N - 1)] \tag{3}$$

and low-search-cost customers get for certain $(R - \text{min}AC)$.

I will now sketch the necessary conditions to sustain this equilibrium. For simplicity, assume that $l^* > 1$. If a firm charges the lowest price, it will gain all the fully informed consumers, and if $p_1 > \text{min}AC$, then one firm will always gain by lowering its price infinitesimally. Obviously, a firm will not price below $\text{min}AC$. All we need to show now is that a firm will never increase its price. If an individual firm increases its price, it immediately loses the fully informed consumers and expects to gain profit only from the high-search-cost randomizing consumers. Now suppose p^+ is the highest price at which high-search-cost customers arriving at the firm will be indifferent between purchasing the good this period and randomly choosing a firm from the remaining $N^* - 1$ firms in the next period. The price p^+ is such that the following equality holds:

$$R - p^+ = \delta\{R - [p_1^*(l^* - 1)/(N^* - 1) + p_h^*(N^* - l^*)/(N^* - 1)]\}. \tag{4}$$

If $AC(\mu) \geqslant p^+$, then a low-price firm has no incentive to increase its price. (Thus, in Figure 7.1 $p^+ \in (p_1, \bar{p})$.) If the latter condition holds, then it will always be the case that a high-price firm will not lower its price and withdraw its refund facility. If a high-price firm lowers its price and retains its refund offer, it obviously lowers expected profit. Therefore, it will consider lowering price only if it withdraws its refund offer. It can be shown, by identical reasoning to the above, that the lowest price an individual firm can charge while making imperfectly informed consumers indifferent between immediate purchase and delaying purchase is below

---

[6] Thus, a customer samples without replacement.

p^+; thus, a firm would expect to make a loss if it retains any customers. In Doyle (1987a) I show that firms price-match rather than undercut, and also that no other symmetric stationary Nash equilibrium exists in pure strategies with three or more prices.

It can be seen that price-matching refund offers can act as a device to discriminate against consumers who find it relatively expensive to locate a low price.[7] It is discriminatory because refund offers are made by high-price firms; that is, a firm today can charge a high price if it offers a refund than when it is not allowed to offer a refund. In the next section I shall outline a slightly different model, which illustrates how price-matching refunds may signal quality when combined with the selling price.

3. Refund Promises and Price as a Signal of Quality

The analysis in this section is taken from Doyle (1987b). I will show in a simple model how refund promises like those cited in the previous section when combined with the selling price can signal quality. The model is an illustration of multi-dimensional signalling, which is a situation where a number of variables are used simultaneously to signal the value of an unobservable variable.[8] I will consider an industry equilibrium; for a detailed discussion of a single firm choosing strategies of this nature, see Ramey (1987).

The differences between this model and that of the previous section are as follows. I consider a market where consumers want to purchase a good x that can take on more than one quality type. The quality of x at each individual firm is unobservable to a consumer prior to purchase. Each individual consumer learns for certain the quality of x at an individual firm j if the consumer purchases x at j and consumes the good.[9] Each individual is fully informed about prices and seeks to purchase one unit of the good x. Every consumer knows the possible quality types, and for simplicity I assume that x can be one of two qualities y_l and y_h, referring to low and high quality, respectively.[10]

Assume there are two types of consumers, where $\beta \in (0, 1)$, denoted type l, have two reservation prices, $R_l(y_l)$ and $R_l(y_h)$, and $(1 - \beta)$, denoted type h, have two reservation prices, $R_h(y_h)$ and $R_h(y_l)$. Each price reflects the maximum price a customer of type l or type h is willing to pay for one unit of good x of quality y_l or y_h, respectively. Each

---

[7] A model by Png and Hirshleifer (1987) with some similar features also shows (instantaneous) price-matching to be a price-discriminatory mechanism.

[8] See Engers (1987), Kohlleppel (1983), Quinzii and Rochet (1984), and Wilson (1985).

[9] Thus, x is an experience good in the sense of Nelson (1970). For a model relating experience goods to intertemporal price discrimination, see Doyle (1986).

[10] This assumption may be relaxed to the case of a finite number of quality levels.

consumer maximizes (expected) utility and is risk-neutral. Every consumer therefore maximizes $Ri - p$, where $i = 1$ or h and p is the price at which the good is purchased. If a consumer is indifferent about which firm to purchase from, I assume he or she chooses one of the firms randomly.

A firm can produce either low-quality x or high-quality x, but it can produce x at only one quality level. I assume total costs are given by $c(x, y_l)$ and $c(x, y_h)$ for low- and high-quality producers, respectively. Let $n_l > 1$ and $n_h > 1$ be integers denoting the number of low- and high-quality producers, respectively. The total number of firms of each type in the market is assumed to be fixed and known by consumers. I assume the following inequalities hold:

$$c(x', y_l) < c(x', y_h) \qquad \text{for all } x' > 0. \qquad (5)$$

$$(\partial c / \partial x)\,|_{x', y_l} < (\partial c / \partial x)\,|_{x', y_h} \qquad \text{for all } x' \geq 0. \qquad (6)$$

Therefore, (5) and (6) state that total costs and marginal costs are always greater for a high-quality producer for any given x'. Thus x also refers to the number of units produced. For simplicity, I will assume that fixed costs are zero and marginal costs are constant for all producers.

As quality is not discernible *ex ante*, consumers form a belief B about the quality of each firm j conditional upon the observable choice variable(s) of each firm.[11] The belief B held by an individual is defined as the probability that a firm is selling a high-quality x. Therefore the complement is the probability that a firm is selling a low-quality x. Initially I assume that every firm seeks to maximize profits by choice of price p, which itself is conditioned on quality. Hence, I write $p_j(y)$ to be firm j's choice of p conditional on y. All firms choose p simultaneously and act in a Bertrand–Nash manner. A consumer observing p_j forms beliefs $B(p)$, and then decides whether to purchase the good from the firm type. Every consumer holds beliefs on quality type for every firm. I am only going to focus upon cases where pure strategies are employed. The appropriate equilibrium concept to use is a Bayesian Nash equilibrium (BNE), which is defined as an equilibrium where each firm chooses its strategy as a best response to all other firms' prices and consumers' beliefs, while the equilibrium beliefs of consumers are Bayes's consistent with the strategies employed by every firm.[12]

Of primary interest will be *separating equilibria*, where every consumer can discern each firm's quality type from observation of the choice variable(s). As there are only two firm types, I am interested in the

---

[11] The only beliefs relevant are those of consumers, as these are going to affect purchasing decisions. Each individual firm may be unaware of another firm's product quality, but even if the firm forms beliefs on this these are not going to influence profits.

[12] In this context a BNE is formally identical to a sequential equilibrium.

situation where $B[p(y_l)] = 0 \neq B[p(y_h)] = 1$. In a separating equilibrium, the choice of p_j^* by firm j of type y must satisfy;

$$\Pi_j[p_j^*, B(p_j^*), \mathbf{p}_{-j}^*, y] \geq \Pi_j[p_j, B(p_j), \mathbf{p}_{-j}^*, y] \qquad \text{for all } p_j \text{ and } j \quad (7)$$

$$p_j^*(y_l) \neq p_j^*(y_h) \quad (8)$$

$$B[p_j^*(y_l)] = 0 \quad (9)$$

$$B[p_j^*(y_h)] = 1. \quad (10)$$

As usual, $\mathbf{p}_{-j}$ is a vector of prices excluding p_j. Condition (8) ensures that a separating equilibrium will emerge. Conditions (9) and (10) are the equilibrium beliefs. There is however a problem here: what do we do about off-the-equilibrium-path prices? As such prices will occur with prior probability 0, I am going to assume $B(p_j)$ are formed arbitrarily.[13] An equilibrium profile will therefore be $E^* = E^*(p^*, B^*)$ satisfying (7)–(10).

I will show that a separating BNE does not exist when a firm chooses price only. Therefore, price alone cannot signal quality with certainty. First, suppose the following set of inequalities hold:

$$MC_{yl} \leq R_l(y_l) = R_h(y_l) < R_l(y_h) < MC_{yh} \leq R_h(y_h) \quad (11)$$

$$R_h(y_l) - MC_{yl} \leq R_h(y_h) - MC_{yh} \quad (12)$$

where MC_y refers to the marginal cost of firm type y. In (11) an l-type consumer is willing only to pay an amount for y_h that is less marginal costs.[14] From (12) we can deduce that an h-type consumer will weakly prefer a higher-quality x if both qualities are sold at an identical price.

A possible equilibrium set of strategies p^* is for firms of type y_l to price at MC_{yl} and firms of type y_h to price at MC_{yh}. However, there is clearly an incentive for an individual firm of type y_l to deviate and mimic a firm of type y_h if

$$[n_h/(n_h + 1)]R_h(y_h) + R_h(y_l)/(n_h + 1) - MC_{yh} > R_h(y_l) - MC_{yl} \quad (13)$$

holds, that is, if the expected utility of an h-individual, by purchasing the good at MC_{yh}, exceeds the utility obtained when purchasing at MC_{yl}, as every consumer knows $B(MC_{yl}) = 0$. This latter belief is formed on the basis that every consumer knows that a firm of type y_h will not sell at $p = MC_{yl}$ because it stands to make a loss.[15] Hence, the postulated

---

[13] Some off the equilibrium path prices can be deleted on grounds of economic reasoning. See Chapter 2 above by Kreps on out-of-equilibrium behaviour.

[14] This may be because an l-type consumer cannot afford to pay more than $R_l(y_h)$. Actually, the inequality $R_l(y_l) - MC_{yl} > R_l(y_h) - MC_{yh}$ is enough to sustain the results. This is equivalent to the inequality in (11).

[15] What I am doing here is eliminating all the dominated strategies. Thus, any strategy $p < MC_{yh}$ for a firm of type y_h is dominated by $p \geq MC_{yh}$. Hence, the equilibrium is undominated if a consumer observes $p = MC_{yl}$ and believes a firm of type y_h would play such a strategy with probability 0.

strategies cannot satisfy the equilibrium requirements (7)–(10) if (13) holds.

There does however exist an equilibrium where high quality is not signalled with probability 1. The equilibrium profile is p^* such that some firms of y_l-type price at MC_{yl} and all y_h-type firms price at MC_{yh}. Those y_l firms not pricing at MC_{yl} instead mimic high-quality producers and price at MC_{yh}. Consumers' beliefs are such that $B[p^*(y_h)] = \theta$ and $B[p^*(y_l)] = 0$, where $\theta = [n_h/(n_h + k)]$ and $k \geqslant 1$ is an integer and

$$\theta R_h(y_h) + (1 - \theta)R_h(y_l) - MC_{yh} \geqslant R_h(y_l)$$

$$- MC_{yl} > [n_h/(n_h + k + 1)]R_h(y_h)$$

$$+ \{1 - [n_h/(n_h + k + 1)]\}R_h(y_l) - MC_{yh} \quad (14)$$

holds. Condition (14) states that the expected utility for a h-type consumer is at least as great as the utility obtained from purchasing a low-quality x, but if another individual low-quality producer mimics a high-quality producer this will no longer be the case.

The equilibrium is sustainable because it satisfies the Bayesian Nash requirement. It is obvious l-type consumers will purchase x at price $p = MC_{yl}$ and hold beliefs $B(MC_{yl}) = 0$. It can be seen that $n_h + k$ firms sell x at MC_{yh} while only n_h actually sell high-quality x. The incentive is always for a low-quality producer to mimic a high-quality seller, but in this instance an individual low-quality seller charging $p = MC_{yl}$ contemplating a change in p realizes that customers' beliefs change to cause all h-type consumers to purchase x at MC_{yl}, believed with probability 1 to be a low-quality seller. Hence, a low-quality firm pricing at MC_{yl} is no better off by choosing another p. Price equals marginal cost because of the usual *epsilon* undercutting and capturing the whole market argument if the price lies above marginal cost in each firm type. Any $\theta > [n_h/(n_h + k)]$ would always provide an incentive for an individual low-quality producer considering $p = MC_{yl}$ to deviate to $p = MC_{yh}$.

From the above, it is clear that, if firms are allowed to use only price as a strategy variable, high quality cannot be signalled with certainty. Nevertheless, low quality *is* signalled with certainty. I will now examine several schemes which result in the existence of separating BNE where all quality types are signalled with probability 1 beliefs. Suppose a firm now has the option of offering its customers the following scheme. *If after purchase you the customer observe another firm selling an identical good x at a lower price, and you inform us of its location, we promise to refund the difference.* If such a promise is offered by a firm, it is essentially displaying a commitment. Define $\sigma_j \in \{0, 1\}$ to be the variable indicating whether a firm offers the commitment ($\sigma_j = 1$) or does not offer the commitment ($\sigma_j = 0$).

A separating BNE will now be defined as $E_2^* = E_2^*(p^*, \sigma^*, B^*)$ such that, for firm type y,[16]

$$\Pi_j[p_j^*, B(p_j^*, \sigma_j^*), \mathbf{p}_{-j}^*, q] \geq$$
$$\Pi_j[p_j, B(p_j, \sigma_j), \mathbf{p}_{-j}^*, y] \qquad \text{for all } p_j, \sigma_j \quad (15)$$

$$\{p_j^*(y_l), \sigma_j^*(y_l) \neq \{p_j^*(y_h), \sigma_j^*(y_h)\}] \qquad (16)$$

$$B[p_j^*(y_l), \sigma_j^*(y_l)] = 0 \qquad (17)$$

$$B[p_j^*(y_h), \sigma_j^*(y_h)] = 1. \qquad (18)$$

The principal change is allowing each firm another choice variable, and it is assumed that both p and σ are chosen simultaneously by every firm. Upon observing (p_j, σ_j) of firm j, a consumer forms beliefs B on j's quality type. I will assume that, if a consumer actually claims a refund, there is an associated cost incurred by him or her denoted by $w > 0$. This cost is intended to reflect the time spent by a consumer dealing with the refund claim.

The following demonstrates that a separating BNE exists. Prices p^* are such that firms of type y price at MC_y. Low-quality firms are indifferent between $\sigma^* = 0$ or 1, and high-quality firms all set $\sigma^* = 1$. Customers' beliefs are $B(MC_{yh}, \sigma^* = 1) = 1$ and $B(MC_{yl}, \sigma^* = 0$ or $1) = 0$.

First, suppose an individual y_l-type firm contemplates, mimicking the equilibrium strategy choice of a y_h-type firm. The firm will realize that if it did this consumers would form beliefs $B(MC_{yh}, \sigma = 1) = [n_h/(n_h + 1)] < 1$. Assuming (13) is satisfied, a type-h consumer will still purchase from a firm displaying $p = MC_{yh}$. However, subsequent to purchase, those consumers who buy x at the mimicking store learn that x is in fact low-quality. Furthermore, every consumer believes with certainty that a firm setting $p = MC_{yl}$ will be selling a low-quality x. This enables the customer to claim the refund on prices, as he or she will cite the existence of such a firm to the firm considering mimicking.[17] As the firm realizes that there will always exist at least one firm charging MC_{yl}, and as the firm knows that the customers know this, the firm will therefore be committed to paying a refund.[18] Hence, mimicking results in non-positive profits because of the processing cost r associated with every consumer claiming the refund. Thus, there is no incentive for a y_l-type firm to change its strategy. A y_h-type firm will always set $\sigma = 1$. If an individual y_h firm did not set $\sigma = 1$, then every type-h consumer would prefer to purchase from a firm where $p = MC_{yh}$ and $\sigma = 1$. This is because h-consumers believe such firms to be definitely selling high-quality x,

---

[16] The subscript 2 merely indicates the number of choice variables available to each firm.
[17] A refund equilibrium exists if it pays a consumer to claim a refund if necessary. Therefore, I assume $MC_{yh} - MC_{yl} - w \geq 0$.
[18] In effect, low-quality sellers become common knowledge; see Chapter 3 by Brandenburger.

whereas for the individual y_h-type firm with $\sigma = 0$, beliefs are arbitrarily defined.[19] As the promise involves zero costs, y_h-type firms are better off offering it.

Marginal cost pricing for each firm type is sustained in the equilibrium because of the processing costs r and w. Consider any symmetric equilibrium like the above except that the price at each firm type y_l and y_h may lie in the intervals $[MC_{yl}, R_l(y_l)]$ and $[MC_{yh}, R_h(y_l)]$, respectively. Suppose an individual firm were to increase its price, but otherwise follow the equilibrium given above. Then l- and h-consumers will prefer to purchase at the lower-price firms rather than at the deviating firm so as to avoid incurring the process costs w. In other words, each consumer still believes the deviating firm is a high- or low-quality firm for certain, but the other firms' quality types are also known for certain. Undercutting rivals' prices guarantees that the selling price will be at marginal costs, because consumers of each type will always prefer to visit a lower price firm.

4. Free Trial Periods and Price as a Signal of Quality

Another ploy that firms often use in the market place is offering potential buyers free trial periods of consumption. Offers of this nature are usually accompanied with a statement of the following form: *If you are dissatisfied with the quality of our product you are under no obligation to buy.* Using the same structure as above, I can show that a separating E_2^* exists. The structure of the model needs to be further specified for this case. I assume all h-type consumers initially accept the free trial period made by firms wanting to sell the good at $p = MC_{yh}$. After the trial period consumers simultaneously return and make their purchase decision. If any consumer decides not to buy at the asking price, he or she is allowed the option of immediately purchasing from another firm.

By replacing the price refund promise with the new offer in the above, the equilibrium E_2^* will be exactly as before. Thus, there is no incentive for an individual y_l-type firm to mimic. If an individual y_l-type firm mimics and customers' beliefs are such that (13) is satisfied, then those h-consumers sampling from such a firm would return the good and purchase from one of the other firms setting $p = MC_{yh}$. All consumers would purchase elsewhere because they would update beliefs in such a way that they would know with probability 1 the firms selling a high-quality x. Therefore revenue would be non-positive if any individual low-quality producer mimics the strategies employed by a high-quality producer. In the next section I will outline a model of Milgrom and

[19] All that is necessary to sustain the equilibrium is for $B(MC_{yh}, \sigma = 0) < 1$ to be held by every consumer for the individual firm considering a strategy deviation.

Roberts (1986) that shows how seemingly uninformative advertising and price can signal quality.

5. Seemingly Uninformative Advertising and Price as a Signal of Quality

Milgrom and Roberts also construct a model that features multi-dimensional signalling. They characterize, in a model similar to those outlined in the previous two sections, that uninformative advertising with respect to an experience good where consumers may repeat purchase can act as a signal of quality when combined with the selling price. The authors provide an example of the type of advertising they mean. In the United States a recent advertising campaign on television for Diet Coke featured a large concert hall full of people and a long chorus line with many celebrities present, all of which was accompanied with the announcement that Diet Coke was the reason for this assembly. The idea behind this type of advertising seemed to be to signal a message that the firm had spent a large amount of money on the advert, suggest Milgrom and Roberts. Hence, the level of advertising expenditure can be communicated, and this may therefore be used in conjunction with the selling price to signal something about the unobservable quality of a good.

Their model is of a single firm selling a product perceived to be an experience good by potential customers. The firm produces the good at a single quality level which is chosen at the beginning of period 1 and remains constant for all time. However, consumers are unaware of the quality of the firm's product prior to consumption, and there does not exist any credible way of directly announcing the quality. The problem is that the firm may wish to convince potential customers that the good is of a certain quality to stimulate repeat purchasing. Unfortunately, there may exist an incentive for the firm to *rip off* consumers by selling a low-quality product (which is cheaper to produce) by pretending to be a high-quality producer. As consumers are aware of this, each consumer will believe that the firm produces a high-quality good only if the signalling message is credible. Thus, it should never pay the firm to sell a low-quality product by pretending that the product is of a high quality. I will outline the main points of the model, but will not derive their results.

A single firm introduces a new brand to the market. The firm has to decide upon the price to set and the level of advertising expenditure in the first period and all subsequent periods. Consumers, after observing the values chosen by the firm, decide whether to buy the good. If a consumer purchases the good, the quality is revealed through consumption. Two quality levels are possible, high and low. The profit for a firm of given quality type y_i ($i = 1$ or h) is given by

$$\Pi[p, y_i, B(p, D)] - D \qquad (19)$$

where D is the level of advertising expenditure and $B(p, D)$ is a function representing consumers' beliefs about whether the firm is producing a high-quality product. From (19) it can be seen that advertising only affects beliefs. For the purpose of investigating the signalling properties, the interesting values for $B(p, D)$ are 0 and 1. Following Milgrom and Roberts, I will let $\Pi(p, y_h, h) = \Pi[p, y_h, B(p, D) = 1]$ refer to the profit of a high-quality producer believed by consumers with probability 1 to be selling a high-quality good. A function is similarly defined for a low-quality producer believed to be selling a low-quality good.

A separating sequential equilibrium exists if for some (p, D) the following holds:

$$\Pi(p, y_h, h) - \Pi(p_l, y_h, l) \geq D \geq \Pi(p, y_l, h) - \Pi(p_l, y_l, l). \qquad (20)$$

The left-hand side states that the difference between profits to a high-quality producer signalling the fact that it is a high-quality seller (by making $B(p, D) = 1$) rather than signalling that it is a low-quality seller is at least as great as D. Therefore it pays a high-quality producer to signal that it is a high-quality seller. The right-hand side states that the difference between profits to a low-quality producer signalling that it is a high-quality seller rather than a low-quality seller is no greater than D. Therefore a low-quality firm will set $D = 0$ and thus reveal itself to be a low-quality seller.

If (20) holds in equilibrium, then the choice of (p, D) by a high-quality firm must satisy the following:

$$\max_{\{p,D\}} \Pi(p, y_h, h) - D \qquad (21)$$

$$s.t. \ \Pi(p, y_l, h) - D \leq \Pi(p_l, y_l, l) \qquad (22)$$

$$p, D \geq 0. \qquad (23)$$

This states that the firm maximizes profits while ensuring that it convinces potential customers that a low-quality producer stands to lose if it chooses the same values for the variables, given by the constraint in (22).

Milgrom and Roberts present the model in greater detail and utilize some of the refinements of sequential equilibrium discussed in Chapter 2 above by Kreps. The conclusion to be derived is that a high-quality firm, by choosing a price low enough and a D high enough, can convince customers that it is not a low-quality seller.

6. Conclusion

I have outlined several different models of industrial organization that illustrate the relationship that strategy variables have upon resulting equilibria. The purpose of the exercise is to convey the message that, when economic theorists seek to model industrial structures and comment upon them, the choice of strategy variables is of crucial significance. Ever since the work of Cournot and Bertrand, economic theorists have realized this point. In the recent past economic theorists have also recognized the importance that information has on affecting equilibrium outcomes in models of industrial organization.[20] The majority of models on industrial organization are cast within a game-theoretic framework, and the use of game theory has enabled researchers to work within a formal structure and provide many interesting insights about industrial organizational structures. The theory of industrial organization, the significance of strategy variables and information structures, and the importance of game theory continues to be an exciting area of research, and much work remains to be done, particularly in the area of multi-dimensional signalling.

---

[20] The importance of information was suggested by Stigler (1961) and some of the first formal models explicitly accounting for different informational structures were the contributions of Akerlof (1970), Arrow (1973), and Spence (1974).

8

Bargaining Theory

DAVID CANNING

1. Introduction

The problem of bargaining between two agents to determine the division of the surplus from trade has a long history in economic analysis. The contract curve in the Edgeworth box (Edgeworth 1881) is an early example. The difficulty of the problem is eloquently attested by the widespread use of the assumption of perfect competition in economic theory, an assumption that effectively rules out any surplus over opportunity cost in bilateral exchanges (see Ostroy 1980).

Two different approaches to analysing the division of any surplus from bilateral trade have been adopted. The axiomatic, co-operative, game-theoretic method relies on deriving the result from the basic elements of the problem, without considering the actual bargaining process itself. The contract curve is an example of this line of reasoning; it takes as axiomatic that each agent should get as least as much as without trade and that any agreement reached should be Pareto-efficient. By adding further restrictions the contract curve can be shrunk, eventually to a point.

The alternative approach is to consider an actual bargaining process, in which the actions of the agents—their offers, threats, and counter-offers—are modelled explicitly as a non-cooperative game. We can think of the expected utility-maximizing strategies of agents in such a game as a solution for the bargaining problem being examined. The advantage of this type of approach is that it shows how the outcome depends on the structure of the bargining game, the moves available to the players. The disadvantage is the solutions are model-specific and it is seldom clear how perturbations to the game will affect the results. One interesting area that will be investigated here is the connection between the two approaches: what type of non-cooperative bargaining games give rise to the proposed axiomatic solutions?

In turn, two different types of non-cooperative bargaining games can be envisaged. Agreement can be forced by the use of either terminal or non-terminal threats. Terminal threats are threats to quit bargaining for good, for example by trading with another agent. Non-terminal threats impose some cost, often simply that of delay, but allow bargaining to continue. Quit or fire threats are terminal, a strike threat is non-terminal; the two lead to different models of the bargaining process.

Bargaining games where all information is common knowledge can usually be satisfactorily dealt with using the standard tools of game theory. Finding the solution to such games is frequently complex but involves the use of fairly routine methods. The problem of games with asymmetric information is more open. With asymmetric information, an agent with private knowledge realizes that his actions will, to some extent, signal his private information to his opponent. Taking this into account, the choice of action depends as much on what it signals as what it achieves in concrete terms. The problem is that the choice of what each action signals is often arbitrary and there may be a multiplicity of equilibria depending on this assignment.

An exciting new development in bargaining theory is the modelling of markets as a sequence of bilateral trades between agents, combining bilateral bargaining with a technology for matching agents. While this approach is relatively new, it promises to provide insights into how markets operate and how prices are formed. One of the most interesting questions arises in the study of the robustness of perfect competition: what assumptions are necessary to generate competitive pricing in a model with bilateral bargaining?

2. Axiomatic Bargaining Theory

Axiomatic bargaining theory tries to deduce solutions to the bargaining problem from first principles, without worrying overmuch about the framework of negotiations. Two common axioms are individual rationality, whereby each party will agree to an outcome only if they get as least as much as if they disagree, and Pareto efficiency, whereby the gains from bargaining are exhausted. Nash (1950) also assumes that the agents' utility functions are von Neuman–Morgenstern and so are defined only up to a positive linear transformation, and he adds a symmetry axiom: if the game is symmetrical, the outcome should be the same for both sides. In addition, Nash imposes the 'independence of irrelevant alternatives'; that is, if two agents agree to an outcome x in one game and the set of possible outcomes is then reduced but still includes x, they would continue to choose x in the reduced game. This amounts to the assumption that the removal of alternatives that are not chosen does not affect which alternative is agreed upon. Luce and Raiffa (1957) discuss the reasonableness of this axiom.

Nash shows that, given a game—that is, a set of possible agreements, a utility function for each agent, and threat point—there is a unique function of these data to a solution that satisfies these axioms. If U and V are the utility functions of the two agents, X is the set of individually rational possible agreements, and (u, v) is the threat point (the utility levels of the agents without an agreement), then the Nash bargaining solution is given by

$$\arg \max_{x \in X} [U(x) - u][V(x) - v].$$

Another axiom that can be imposed is monotonicity: if the set of possible agreements is enlarged, neither side becomes strictly worse off. It is easy to construct examples to demonstrate that the Nash bargaining solution does not satisfy monotonicity. Kalai (1977) shows that, if we impose monotonicity, the only solutions that are admissible are those that give fixed proportional gains from trade. Such solutions must involve interpersonal utility comparisons.

For games with more than two players, Harsanyi (1959) generalizes the Nash bargaining solution, while Kalai and Samet (1983) generalize the monotonic solution. If all possible coalitions of the players are allowed, and utility is freely transferable between agents, then the Shapley value (Shapley 1953), in which each agent's payoff is proportional to the sum of their marginal contributions to all possible coalitions, seems the appropriate solution concept. The problem of coalitions in bargaining with three or more players is a difficult one and will not be dealt with here. Binmore (1985) discusses this problem and gives some examples of possible solutions.

For games with uncertainty, Harsanyi and Selten (1972) propose the generalized Nash bargaining solution:

$$\arg \max_{x \in X} [U(x) - u]^{\alpha}[V(x) - v]^{\beta}$$

where α and β can be interpreted as 'bargaining powers'. Myerson (1984) develops an axiomatic generalization of the Nash bargaining solution for games with asymmetric information. A more detailed survey of the axiomatic approach to bargaining can be found in Roth (1979).

3. Non-terminal Threats

Consider an actual bargaining game. Two agents negotiate over the division of a pie of size 1. If a division x is agreed to at time t, the payoffs of the two agents are given by

$$U(x, t) = \delta_1^t x, \qquad V(x, t) = \delta_2^t (1 - x), \qquad 0 < \delta_1, \delta_2 < 1.$$

The game takes place in real time. Offers are made and accepted or rejected in turn. The key point is that the bargaining process takes time, and, as time passes without an agreement, the agents become worse off with a particular agreement x, because of their time preference.

Formally, the game consists of a sequence of decision nodes $k = 0, 1, 2, \ldots, n$. At each node k one agent makes an offer x_k which the other either accepts or rejects. If it is accepted, the game ends and the outcome is $[x_k, t(k)]$ where $t(k)$ is the time elapsed at node k. If it is rejected, we proceed to node $k + 1$ where the other agent makes an offer; that is, agents make offers alternatively. Negotiations continue until an offer is accepted or we reach node n, where, if the offer is rejected, the payoffs of the two sides are assumed to be zero. Suppose $t(k) = sk$ so the nodes are evenly spaced in time at intervals of length s, and let $T = sn$ be the length of the game (the potential duration).

The game can be represented by the tree drawn in Figure 8.1. It is

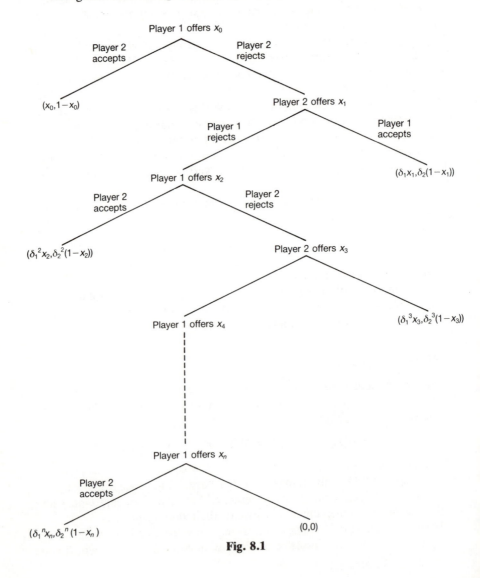

Player 1 offers x_0

Player 2 accepts   Player 2 rejects

$(x_0, 1 - x_0)$

Player 2 offers x_1

Player 1 rejects   Player 1 accepts

$(\delta_1 x_1, \delta_2(1 - x_1))$

Player 1 offers x_2

Player 2 accepts   Player 2 rejects

$(\delta_1^2 x_2, \delta_2^2(1 - x_2))$

Player 2 offers x_3

Player 1 offers x_4

$(\delta_1^3 x_3, \delta_2^3(1 - x_3))$

Player 1 offers x_n

Player 2 accepts

$(\delta_1^n x_n, \delta_2^n(1 - x_n))$ $(0, 0)$

Fig. 8.1

assumed that agents have complete information and perfect recall, and that all information is common knowledge. Complete information means that each side knows the form of the game tree and the payoffs each side gets at the terminal nodes. Perfect recall requires that at each node all previous moves are known. Common knowledge implies that all players have the same information, know that they have the same information, know that each knows that they have the same information, and so on. Formalization of this common knowledge concept is surprisingly difficult, but its effects on the game are easy to see. It allows each agent to predict what the other will do, since each can 'think himself' into the other's position.

The solution concept used will be the subgame perfect equilibrium developed by Selten (1965, 1975), and similar to the idea used by Stahl (1972). Subgame perfection requires that at each node the equilibrium strategies form a Nash equilibrium of the subgame constructed by considering only the node reached and the nodes that can be reached subsequently from that point. (See Chapter 2 above by Kreps for a discussion of this equilibrium concept.)

In the case of the bargaining game set out in this section, this solution concept is easy to apply since the agents move alternately and the game is finite. At the last node the agent with the accept/reject decision has a simple maximization problem: accept the offer, or get zero. Given that the agent making the offer at node $n-1$ can predict this choice, he in turn has a simple problem: to choose an offer to maximize his payoff. At each stage the agent can predict exactly the future actions in the game and so has a simple maximization problem; by backward induction we can solve the game, giving the agents' maximizing choices all the way back to node 0.

Suppose that player 1 makes the initial offer at node 0 and n is even. Let x_k^* be the subgame perfect equilibrium offer at node k (k even) if k is reached, and assume that this offer is accepted.

At node $k-1$ player 1 accepts the offer x_{k-1}, provided that

$$x_{k-1} > x_{k-1}^* = \delta_1^s x_k^*.$$

If player 1 rejects the offer x_{k-1} at node $k-1$, he makes the offer x_k^* at time k, which is accepted; he will be willing to accept any offer at node $k-1$ that gives at least the present discounted value of x_k^*.

Suppose that player 2 offers x_{k-1}^*; this should be accepted, and it is easy to check that $(1-x_{k-1}^*) > \delta_2^s(1-x_k^*)$, so player 2 is better off offering x_{k-1}^* than waiting to get x_k^*. Since x_{k-1}^* is the lowest offer player 1 will accept at $k-1$, it is the subgame perfect equilibrium offer at $k-1$ and is accepted.

Similarly, at node $k-2$ player 2 must be offered x_{k-2}^* such that

$$(1 - x_{k-2}^*) = \delta_2^s(1 - x_{k-1}^*)$$

which player 2 accepts. This gives

$$x^*_{k-2} = 1 - \delta^s_2 + (\delta_1, \delta_2)^s x^*_k$$

and so, by induction,

$$x^*_0 = \left[(1 - \delta^s_2) \sum_{i=0}^{n/2-1} (\delta^s_1 \delta^s_2)^i\right] + (\delta_1 \delta_2)^{T/2} x^*_n.$$

At node n player 1 makes the offer (for n even) and so $x^*_n = 1$, since player 2 cannot do better than 0 by refusing.

Clearly, for $n = 0$ we have $T = 0$ and $x^*_0 = 1$. Player 1 gets the entire surplus, he can make a 'take-it-or-leave it' offer to player 2, whose alternative is 0. In general, the outcome will depend on the number of nodes n, the length of the interval s between offers, and the order of play, that is, who makes the initial offer.

The equation for x^*_0 gives the general solution of the problem for particular values of s, n, and T. To get a clearer picture of the forces at work, it is helpful to consider a number of limiting cases.

Consider what happens as the number of nodes n becomes large, that is, as the potential length of negotiations tend to infinity. We have

$$\lim_{T\to\infty} x^*_0 = \lim_{T\to\infty} (1 - \delta^s_2)[1 + (\delta^s_1 \delta^s_2) + (\delta^s_1 \delta^s_2)^2 + \cdots + (\delta^s_1 \delta^s_2)^{T/2-1}]$$

$$= \lim_{T\to\infty} (1 - \delta^s_2) \frac{(1 - \delta_1 \delta_2)^{T/2}}{1 - \delta^s_1 \delta^s_2} = \frac{1 - \delta^s_2}{1 - \delta^s_1 \delta^s_2}.$$

First, set $s = 1$ so that there is a unit time interval between nodes. This gives us

$$\lim_{T\to\infty} x^*_0(s = 1) = \frac{1 - \delta_2}{1 - \delta_1 \delta_2}.$$

So x^*_0 is increasing in δ_1 but decreasing in δ_2. The limit of our finite game as T becomes large is the same as the subgame perfect solution of the infinite game analysed directly by Rubinstein (1982); he assumes an infinite number of nodes spaced one time unit apart. Fudenburg and Levine (1983) discuss general conditions under which this property, the convergence of the solution of a sequence of finite games to the subgame perfect equilibrium of the infinite game, holds.

Now consider what happens if, in addition to T becoming large, the interval s between offers becomes small. This gives

$$\lim_{s\to 0 \atop T\to\infty} x^*_0 = \lim_{s\to 0} \frac{1 - \delta^s_2}{1 - \delta^s_1 \delta^s_2} = \lim_{s\to 0} \frac{-\delta^s_2 \ln \delta_2}{-\delta^s_1 \delta^s_2 \ln (\delta_1 \delta_2)}$$

by L'Hopital's rule. Taking limits and setting $d_i = \ln (1/\delta_i)$,

$$\lim_{s\to 0 \atop T\to\infty} x^*_0 = \frac{d_2}{d_1 + d_2}.$$

As s gets small and T gets large, the solution tends to become independent of the time between nodes and of the order of play.

Consider the generalized Nash bargaining solution of the game with utility functions $U(x) = x$, $V(x) = 1 - x$, threat point $(0, 0)$, and bargaining powers d_2 and d_1, respectively. The Nash bargaining solution for this game is

$$x^* = \arg\max_{x \in [0, 1]} [x^{d_2}[1 - x]^{d_1}] = d_2/(d_1 + d_2)$$

The non-cooperative game described here implements the Nash bargaining solution of the co-operative game, in the limit, as the potential length of negotiations becomes large and the time interval between offers becomes small. We can think of d_i as a measure of player i's impatience; the greater the rate of time preference by one side, the stronger the bargaining power of the other.

As long as the game is finite, backward induction is relatively easy. In Rubinstein (1982) the game examined is similar to that presented above but with no terminal node and a potentially infinite duration. Backward induction is now more difficult because we have no endpoint from which to begin the process. However, if the discount rates of the two players are constant over time, or if delay imposes a constant cost per unit time, the structure of the infinite game is recursive. If we actually arrive at node $k + 2$, the structure of the game is identical from that point on to the game played from node k; the subgame at any even node is the same as the game itself.

If we can assume that a unique subgame perfect equilibrium exists at $k + 2$, we can use the payoffs associated with this to work back and find the subgame perfect equilibrium strategy at node k. As noted by Shaked and Sutton (1984), if the structure is recursive and the two subgames are identical, we have $x_k^* = x_{k+2}^*$ and can use this fact to solve the game. The real problem is the existence and uniqueness of equilibrium. This Rubinstein proves directly. Binmore (1980) shows that the solution of the infinite game tends to the Nash bargaining solution as the time interval between offers is reduced.

So far we have assumed that the utility functions U and V of the agents are linear in the division: this simplifies the analysis. The point is that at each stage the agent with the offer must calculate $U^{-1}(u^*)$ for his opponent, where u^* is the known utility from refusal and continuing the bargaining process; this calculation gives the smallest offer the opponent will accept. For linear utility functions this is very easy. Hoel (1986) studies a Rubinstein bargaining game where the utility functions of the two agents are nonlinear. Provided U and V are increasing and concave in the share of the division of the surplus which the agent receives it is possible to show that the game gives a unique outcome. If the time between nodes is allowed to decline towards 0, this unique solution converges to the generalized Nash bargaining solution

$$x_0^* = \arg\max_{x \in X} [U(x)^{d_2} V(x)^{d_1}].$$

Hoel shows, however, that for large s and utility functions that are not concave, the perfect equilibrium of the bargaining game may not be unique.

The general result derived from models of this type is that, if the number of bargaining rounds is finite or the interval between offers is large, the actual structure of the game can affect the result. However, if the number of bargaining rounds is potentially infinite, then, allowing the time interval between decision nodes to go to 0 forces the outcome to converge on the Nash bargaining solution. It then depends only on the underlying characteristics of the agents and not on the framework of negotiations. This is an appealing conclusion; for, if we envisage bargaining games where the structure of negotiations, such as the interval between offers and the order of play, affect the result, we should enquire as to why the agents do not use these as strategic variables.

Since Rubinstein's paper, the alternating offer bargaining game with fixed positions for the decision nodes has become the central model in bargaining theory. In these games of perfect and complete information, agreement is always achieved at the first decision node. Each side can predict the eventual outcome if there is a delay (because of full information and common knowledge), and they will always prefer an agreement at the beginning, which gives each side more than they would gain by continuing negotations—if we know we are going to reach a particular agreement in the future, and time is costly, why not make that agreement now?

Extending the negotiation space to many variables, as in Canning (1982), does not affect the general results. Each agent makes offers that give his opponent the same utility level from accepting as from rejecting the offer. Given this constraint, they both make offers that maximize their own utility level, which forces Pareto efficiency. Once again, the Nash bargaining solution can be derived in the limit.

4. Terminal Threats

We now consider a model in which, as well as having a cost of delaying agreement, both sides have the possibility of an outside option. That is, in addition to bargaining with the other agent, each side may get offers from outside the bargaining game while the game is in progress. The possibility of quitting to take up an outside option can be thought of as a terminal threat. Sutton (1986) examines a model in which outside options of the two agents are correlated; at any time, either both sides have an outside option or neither have. Here I consider a similar game where the outside options of the two agents are independent.

Again, the two agents bargain over a pie of size 1. However, now as time passes each has a chance of receiving an offer from outside. For simplicity, we shall assume that this outside offer is 1. We should of course model the meeting with the new agent explicitly, and analyse the bargaining that takes place. For simplicity, we simply assume that the agent gets a take-it-or-leave-it offer.

Suppose agent i searches for a period t; the probability of finding this outside offer is given by the Poisson process

$$P_i(t) = 1 - e^{-\lambda_{it}}$$

so that for small t the probability of finding an outside offer is approximately $P_i(t) = \lambda_{it}$. Taking the discount rates to be i for agent i as before, let u_i be the expected utility from searching until the outside offer is found. The Poisson process implies that the probability of finding the outside offer is independent of the time elapsed, so we can define u_i recursively by

$$u_i = \delta_i^t P_i(t) + \delta_i^t[1 - P_i(t)]u_i.$$

If the agent searches for a time t, either he finds the outside option and gets the payoff 1, or he does not find it and has the same expected payoff as before from the new position. Note than we assume that, if an offer is found during the interval t, it cannot be taken up until the end of the interval. This gives

$$u_i = \delta_i^t P_i(t)/(1 - \delta_i^t[1 - P_i(t)])$$

where t is the search interval, the minimum time required to find and accept an outside offer. Taking the limit as t goes to 0 gives

$$\lim u_i = \lambda_i/(\lambda_i + d_i) \qquad \text{where } d_i = \log(1/\delta_i), \text{ as before.}$$

We shall assume that $u_1 + u_2 < 1$; this is necessary if there are to be any possible gains from trade for the two agents in bargaining. If the sum of the expected payoffs from searching exceeds 1, no agreement is possible; each side will search for his outside offer. If the sum is less than 1, then the two sides can agree to a division of the pie and stop searching. Note that each does worse than if he gets his outside option (1), but the cost of searching is too great to make it worthwhile to quit from the internal agreement.

The problem with outside options is subgame perfection. If the outside options are small, less than the agent gets in the normal equilibrium of the Rubinstein game, then they will not affect the outcome; an agent can never actually quit to take up such an offer, so it does not constitute a threat. Here the outside offers are better than each side can do in bargaining, and the threat that one side will take such an option is real.

The game is similar to the alternative offer game analysed in Section 3 with a potentially infinite duration. The difference here is that, in addition to making offers and accepting or rejecting, each agent can quit the game and take up his outside option if this has appeared. In this case the payoff to the other side is simply the expected utility he derives from searching for his outside option.

As before, suppose that there exists a unique subgame perfect equilibrium offer x_k^* which player 1 makes at nodes 0, 2, 4, 6, and so on, and which player 2 accepts. Given this, an offer by player 2 at node $k-1$ will be accepted only if

$$x_{k-1}^* \geq \delta_1^s \{P_1(s) + [1 - P_1(s)]x_k^*\}$$

where s is the time interval between decision nodes. Player 1 estimates the expected payoff from refusing the offer x_{k-1}: if he rejects, either he finds the outside offer, with probability $P_1(s)$, or he fails to do so, with probability $1 - P_1(s)$, and offers x_k^* at node k which is accepted. Similarly, at node k we require

$$(1 - x_k^*) \geq \delta_2^s \{P_2(s) + [1 - P_2(s)](1 - x_{k+1}^*)\}$$

Assuming each side makes the highest acceptable demand and setting $x_0^* = x_k^* = x_{k+2}^*$ we can derive an expression for x_0^*. Taking the limit of this expression as the time interval between nodes becomes small gives

$$\lim_{s \to 0} x_0^* = \frac{d_2 + \lambda_1}{d_1 + d_2 + \lambda_1 + \lambda_2}.$$

Clearly, for $\lambda_1 = \lambda_2 = 0$ there is no chance for either side to get an outside option and the game reduces to the standard non-terminal threat game with the same result as in Section 3. If δ_1 and δ_2 approach 1 we have d_1 and d_2 approach 0, and players do not discount the future very much. In this case we can think of the outcome as depending only on each side's chance of finding an outside option. What motivates agreement is the risk that the other side will find an outside option if we delay agreement. The probabilities of finding these outside options give each side its bargaining power.

In a labour dispute between a union and a firm it is usually only the cost of delay that motivates agreement; neither side usually has any outside options. Outside options may however be an appropriate model in a more open market; the main subjective cost of delay in such a market may not be the actual time involved but the risk of another buyer appearing who is willing to pay more, or of the prospective purchaser finding a different seller offering a lower price.

Sutton, Shaked, and Binmore (1985) conduct an empirical investigation of player's behaviour in a simple bargaining game with outside options. Their conclusion is that there is more support for the non-cooperative theory presented above than for the Nash bargaining solution, with the threat point given by the reservation values u_1 and u_2. If u_1 and u_2 are small, non-cooperative theory predicts that they will be irrelevant and will not affect the outcome at all, since even if an agent has such an outside option it is never credible to threaten to take it.

These results emphasize the importance of the choice of threat point and bargaining power variables when using the Nash bargaining solution to solve bargaining problems. Threats that are not subgame perfect, that are not credible in the sense that the agent can never rationally choose to carry them out, should not affect the result, and should not be used as the threat point. However, care is needed. Taking a lower paid job is not a credible threat for a worker who is well paid if by taking the job he rules out getting his highly paid job back; that is, if the threat is terminal. However, the availability of such a threat if he goes on strike may be important: it will raise his conflict payoff and enable him to hold out for a higher wage. In this case the key point is that taking the low paid job is a non-terminal threat; negotiations can continue, and the worker hopes to return to his old job on better terms.

5. Bargaining with Asymmetric Information

So far we have assumed that all information is common knowledge. This allows each agent to calculate his or her optimal strategy at any node. Even if the future is uncertain, the agent making the offer can calculate his opponent's subjective expected utility from refusing the offer, and so calculate the minimum offer that will be accepted. If information is asymmetric, the agent making the offer will be unsure of his opponent's subjective expected utility from refusing the offer and continuing to bargain, and the minimum acceptable offer cannot be calculated in a clear-cut way.

The solution concepts used in analysing games with asymmetric information are all extensions of the concept of sequential equilibrium developed by Kreps and Wilson (1982). At each information set agents take the action that maximizes their expected payoffs in the game, given their beliefs; and at each information set beliefs are updated by Bayes rule wherever this is possible. The following simple example demonstrates both the power and weakness of this solution concept.

Consider the two-period bargaining game described in Figure 8.2. Player 1 makes the initial offer at node 0. If this is accepted the game ends with this agreement. If it is refused player 2 makes a counter-offer at node 1. If this is accepted by player 2 the game ends with this agreement. If it is refused the game ends without agreement and the players get payoffs u and v, respectively. The payoffs to the two players if an

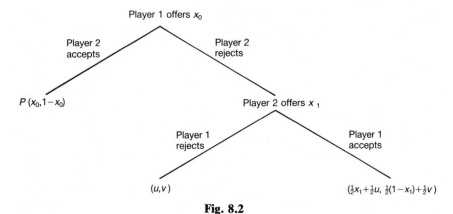

Fig. 8.2

agrement is reached at time t is given by

$$U(x, t) = x(1 - t) + ut$$

$$V(x, t) = (1 - x)(1 - t) + vt$$

and we take $t(0) = 0$ and $t(1) = \frac{1}{2}$. We can think of u and v as being flows of income during a disagreement while x and $1 - x$ give the flows at the agreement x. If all information is common knowledge, it is easy to calculate the subgame perfect equilibrium of this game. It involves player 1 making the offer $x_0^* = \frac{1}{2}(1 + u - v)$ at node 0 and player 2 accepting this offer. This is also the Nash bargaining solution for the game with threat point (u, v).

Now suppose we add some imperfect information to the game. Suppose player 2 has two possible conflict payoffs v and v' with $v' > v$. It is useful to follow Harsanyi (1967–8) and consider a chance move as selecting one of two possible types of player 2, a strong type (high v') or a weak type (low v). This changes the game from one of incomplete information, with player 1 not knowing player 2's payoff, to one of complete but imperfect information, with player 1 knowing the payoffs of all the players but not which type 'nature' has chosen at the beginning of the game. The game is represented by Figure 8.3. The dotted lines represent the fact that player 1 does not know which node in that information set he is at if such a point is reached. Suppose that nature selects v' with probability q and v with probability $1 - q$. This probability is assumed to be common knowledge to the players, but player 2 knows the outcome of this chance move while player 1 does not.

To solve the game we work backwards. At node 1 player 2 will make the offer $x_1^* = u$ which will be accepted. At node 0 player 1 has a choice. Table 8.1 shows the probability of each possible offer being accepted. If player 1 makes a low demand, both types prefer to accept rather than

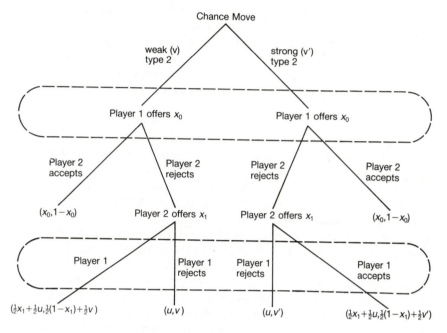

Fig. 8.3

continue bargaining. If he makes a high demand, both types will prefer to continue to node 1 rather than accept. However, there is an intermediate range of demands which the weak type player 2 will accept while the strong type rejects. The point is that the weak type is less willing to reject an offer at node 0 because his payoff while waiting for agreement at node 1 is low, the strong type player 2 is more willing to delay, having a higher income during the disagreement period.

Maximizing player 1's expected utility (given that he only gets u if his offer is rejected and we proceed to node 1), we have

$$x_0^* = \tfrac{1}{2}(1 + u - v') \qquad \text{if } q > (v' - v)/(1 - u - v)$$
$$x_0^* = \tfrac{1}{2}(1 + u - v) \qquad \text{if } q < (v' - v)/(1 - u - v).$$

Table 8.1

Offer x_0	Probability of acceptance
$x_0 < \tfrac{1}{2}(1 + u - v')$	1
$\tfrac{1}{2}(1 + u - v') < x_0 < \tfrac{1}{2}(1 + u - v)$	$1 - q$
$x_0 > \tfrac{1}{2}(1 + u - v)$	0

If $q = (v' - 1)/(1 - u - v)$, player 1 is indifferent between these two demands. If q is large, player 1 acts as if he were playing the strong type for sure and makes a low demand which is sure to be accepted. If q is small, player 1 acts as if his opponent were weak and makes a high demand, taking a chance. If player 2 actually is weak this high demand is accepted, but if player 2 is strong the demand is rejected and we proceed to node 1.

This is the unique sequential equilibrium of the game. The player with the private information reveals it unambiguously in the simple accept/reject decision at node 1. Games where the player with the private information is limited to accept/reject decisions, such as Fudenburg and Levine (1983) and Fudenburg, Levine, and Tirole (1985), usually have this property that the equilibrium is unique.

The result is typically that the agent making the offers starts with a low initial offer and gradually raises it as time passes. The greater the time elapsed, the more weight he must put on the probability that the player with the private information is strong and so does not mind waiting.

Although the game analysed above is very simple, it brings out an important distinction between games of perfect and games of imperfect information. With imperfect information there is no guarantee of efficient outcomes. Agents may delay agreement, or sometimes there may be no agreement at all. Agents take this risk because they are unsure of the strength of their opponent and may make offers that are unlikely to be accepted.

If the player with the private information can make offers, the problem becomes much more difficult to solve. Consider the game set out above but where player 1 has the private information. Figure 8.4 shows the new situation; player 1 has either a low-conflict payoff u or a high one u' while player 2's conflict payoff is fixed at v. The probability that the strong type of player 1 is selected is p, which is common knowledge, but the outcome of this chance move is known only to player 1. Suppose we reach node 1, player 2 having rejected the initial offer at node 0. At node 1 player 2 will have a probability assignment on player 1 being strong, depending on the initial objective probability p of the strong type being chosen, and modified in the light of the offer made at node 0 by player 1. Let p_1 denote this probability assignment at information set 1.

Player 2 will make an offer x_1 at information set 1. The subjective probability he assigns to an offer being accepted is given in Table 8.2. Maximizing player 2's expected utility implies that he chooses

$$x_1^* = u' \qquad \text{if } p_1 > (u' - u)/(1 - u - v)$$

$$x_1^* = u \qquad \text{if } p_1 < (u' - u)/(1 - u - v)$$

and is indifferent between these two offers if $p_1 = (u' - u)/(1 - u - v)$.

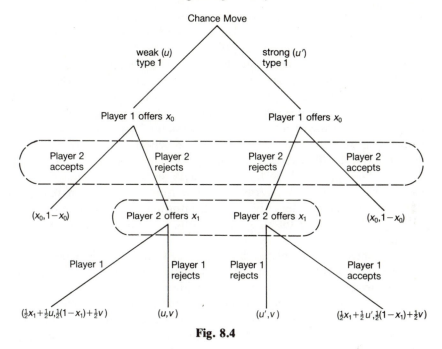

Fig. 8.4

If p_1 is large player 2 makes a high offer which is sure to be accepted, while if p_1 is low he makes a small offer, taking a chance that player 1 is strong and will refuse it.

Now consider player 1's offer at node 0. Define the critical value $p^* = (u' - u)/(1 - u - v)$. Suppose $p > p^*$. Any pure strategy choice x_0^* in the set $[u', \frac{1}{2}(1 + u' - v)]$ is a sequential equilibrium for both types of player 1 provided player 2 adopts the beliefs

$$p_1 = \begin{cases} 0 & \text{if } x_0 \neq x_0^* \\ p & \text{if } x_0 = x_0^* \end{cases}$$

where p_1 is the conditional probability on player 1 being strong given that player 2 observes x_0.

Table 8.2

Offer x_1	Probability of acceptance
$x_1 < u$	0
$u < x_1 < u'$	$1 - p_1$
$x_1 > u'$	1

It is easy to check that this forms a sequential equilibrium for any x_0 in the interval. The updating obeys Bayes's rule where possible; if player 2 observes the equilibrium strategy x_0^* it conveys no information, since both types play this strategy, and the posterior probability is the same as the prior, p. If player 2 observes an offer not equal to the equilibrium strategy his prior gives a probability 0 to this observation, and Bayes's rule cannot be applied. Given that Bayes's rule does not apply, almost any probability assignment satisfies the sequential equilibrium criterion. In this case we have assumed that player 2 believes that only the weak type of player 1 will deviate from the equilibrium strategy.

Given that player 2 is forming beliefs in this way, player 1 is maximizing by playing x_0^*. Any deviation from x_0^* results in player 2 setting $p_1 = 0$ and offering only $x_1^* = u$ at information set 1. Both types of player 1 are better off offering, and getting agreement on, any x_0^* that exceeds u'.

The problem is that player 2 has decided that any deviation from equilibrium signals that player 1 is weak, therefore player 1 never has an incentive to deviate; but this supports a wide range of equilibria.

For p large, these pooling equilibria, equilibria in which both types of player 1 play the same strategy and are not distinguishable, are the only type of equilibrium. For p small, the equilibria are partially separating; sometimes player 1 will identify himself by his offer at node 0.

Consider what would happen if we had $p < p^*$ and both types of player 1 made the same offer. Since the offer gives no information, player 2 has $p_1 = p < p^*$ and his best strategy is to reject the offer and reply with the low offer u at node 1. This cannot be an equilibrium since the weak type of player 1 now has an incentive to make a lower offer (but greater than u), which identifies him as weak but which player 2 will prefer to accept rather than go on to node 1. (Player 2 prefers any offer not greater than $\frac{1}{2}(1 + u - v)$.)

In the case of low p, the equilibria are given by

$$x_0^*(u') \in [u', \tfrac{1}{2}(1 + u' - v)]$$

$$x_0^*(u) = \begin{cases} x_0^*(u') & \text{with probability } y \\ \tfrac{1}{2}(1 + u - v) & \text{with probability } 1 - y. \end{cases}$$

where the offer is written as a function of the agent's type. If $x_0 \leqslant \frac{1}{2}(1 + u - v)$ player 2 accepts. If $x_0 = x_0^*(u')$ player 2 accepts with probability z and rejects with probability $1 - z$. Other x_0 are always rejected. If player 2 rejects x_0 he offers $x_1^* = u$, which the weak type player 1 accepts but the strong type rejects. The probabilities y and z are given by (taking $x_0^* = x_0^*(u')$)

$$y = \frac{p(1 - p')}{p'(1 - p)}$$

where

$$p' = \frac{x_0^* + \frac{1}{2}(1 - u + v)}{\frac{1}{2}(1 - u - v)}$$

and

$$z = \frac{\frac{1}{2}(1 - u - v)}{x_0^* - u}.$$

If player 1 is strong he makes the demand x_0^*. The weak type either copies this demand or plays $\frac{1}{2}(1 + u - v)$. If he does not imitate the strong player he identifies himself as weak and we are back in a game with complete information and common knowledge. If player 2 observes this low offer he accepts it and the game ends.

On the other hand, if player 2 observes x_0^* he still has imperfect information. He will be unsure if he is playing the strong type or a weak type who is bluffing. The subjective probability he assigns to the types is given by Bayes's rule:

$$p_1 = \frac{p}{p + (1 - p)y} = p'$$

which, given our choice of y, reduces to the expression given above. At this subjective probability we have

$$\tfrac{1}{2}(1 - u)(1 - p') + \tfrac{1}{2}p'v + \tfrac{1}{2}v = 1 - x_0^*$$

so player 1 is indifferent between accepting x_0^* and rejecting it to offer u at node 1. (Clearly, $p' < p^*$, so if node 1 is reached player 1 offers u rather than u'.)

The value of y is determined by the fact that it must induce this critical probability p'. If y is set too high, p_1 is less than p'; the weak agent bluffs too often and player 2 always rejects x_0^*. This cannot be an equilibrium because the weak agent now has no incentive to bluff. Similarly, if y is set too low, the weak agent does not bluff often enough, and p_1 is above p'. However, in this case player 2 should always accept the high demand, since he is reasonably sure his opponent is strong. This cannot be an equilibrium, since if player 2 is accepting the high demand the weak type of player 1 should always play it.

Given that player 2 is indifferent between accepting and rejecting x_0^*, we can set his probability of acceptance at z. At this value of z we have

$$x_0^* z + (1 - z)u = \tfrac{1}{2}(1 + u - v)$$

so the weak type of player 1 is indifferent between demanding $\frac{1}{2}(1 + u - v)$, which is accepted, and demanding x_0^*, with only a probability z of acceptance.

This equilibrium is sustained by the same types of beliefs as before:

$$p_1 = \begin{cases} p' & \text{if } x_0 = x_0^* \\ 0 & \text{if } x_0 \neq x_0^* \end{cases}$$

The strong player plays a pure strategy x_0^* while the weak player randomizes between this and $\frac{1}{2}(1 + u - v)$. If either of these demands is observed, player 2 can update his beliefs by Bayes's rule. For other demands Bayes's rule does not apply: they are not equilibrium strategy choices for any agent. The arbitrary belief that player 2 assigns is that $p_1 = 0$ if any of these other demands are seen; that is, he assumes that any deviation from equilibrium is undertaken only by the weak type.

This out-of-equilibrium belief, that it is the weak type who has deviated, tends to support many equilibria; it gives no incentive for any player to deviate since to do signals weakness, and so almost any strategy can be supported as an equilibrium.

This multiplicity of equilibria is typical of bargaining games in which the agent with the private information can make offers. Since the offer is also a signal, the interpretation of offers that lie outside the equilibrium strategy set poses problems. Bayes's rule does not apply because the probability of such offers occurring is 0. A major research topic in game theory is how to limit the set of equilibria in games of asymmetric information by imposing restrictions on the out-of-equilibrium beliefs adopted by agents.

The sequential equilibrium itself imposes some restrictions on the set of beliefs that can be adopted, but these restrictions are weak. They stem from the logical problem, that, if we observe a zero probability event, all our beliefs, even those about completely unconnected things, become arbitrary.

Consider the event B with the prior $p(B) = 0$. For any event A we have

$$p(A \cap B) = p(A \mid B)p(B).$$

For $p(B) = p(A \cap B) = 0$, so $p(A \mid B)$ is undefined, for any event A. For example, suppose we have the event B as an agent choosing a particular strategy and we assign the probability 0 to this event. If this event actually occurs, the posterior probability that we assign to the earth being flat becomes arbitrary. This seems implausible, but it is a logical consequence of the point that the occurrence of an impossible event allows us to deduce anything we please.

What we would like to say is that, if two events are independent, then the probability we assign to one does not depend on the outcome of the other. This is true when both have non-zero priors but it need not hold if the prior probabilities are 0. Kreps and Wilson (1982) force the beliefs adopted when zero probability events occur to be the limit of some sequence of beliefs that are adopted when agents choose a sequence of strategies that can generate the observed event with positive probability, this sequence converging to the equilibrium strategies of the players.

This implies that what players do when they see a zero probability event is to ask, Is there a set of strategy choices, close to the equilibrium set, which could generate this observation? If there is, they then adopt the belief associated with this new strategy choice. By assigning a small probability that one type plays the observed strategy we have a strategy close to our equilibrium. This rules out changing beliefs about unconnected (independent) events.

This consistency restriction in perfect equilibrium is very weak; bargaining games with asymmetric information tend to have many sequential equilibria. Three research strategies have been adopted in an effort to overcome this problem. First, we can simply assign 'plausible' beliefs off the equilibrium path. This is the approach originally suggested by Kreps and Wilson and is used by Rubinstein (1985a) to solve an infinite-horizon bargaining game with incomplete information. Rubinstein (1985b) discusses the effects on the set of equilibria of adopting different 'plausible' beliefs, for example optimistic or pessimistic conjectures.

In our simple asymmetric information bargaining game above, where player 1 has the private information, imposing the condition on beliefs that

$$p_1(x_0') > p_1(x_0) \qquad \text{if } x_0' > x_0$$

gives a unique outcome, the strong type of player 1 always plays $x_0^* = \frac{1}{2}(1 + u' - v)$ and the weak type randomizes between this and $\frac{1}{2}(1 + u - v)$. This restriction sipply says that the probability player 2 assigns to player 1 being strong is increasing in player 1's demand, which seems plausible.

Of course, the problem is that, while plausible, restrictions of this kind are *ad hoc*, different theorists can impose different plausible beliefs giving different results in the same game. While this may be the correct answer—that is, the outcome may indeed be somewhat arbitrary in such games—many theorists are searching for a more formal method of overcoming the problem.

A second approach which sidesteps the problem is to restrict the strategy space of the bargaining game, or increase the number of types of agent, to ensure that every possible action is part of an equilibrium strategy choice. This ensures that every possible action has positive probability in equilibrium and so the problem of out-of-equilibrium beliefs does not arise. Restricting the strategy space is the route chosen by Sobel and Takahashi (1983), who allow only the uninformed player to make offers. In Canning (1982), a sequential bargaining model is presented in which both sides have private information but are restricted to their initial offer once the game has started; once the game is underway they are limited to simply accepting or rejecting their opponent's offer. Since there is a type that always prefers to reject, and acceptance ends the game, no out-of-equilibrium beliefs are necessary. A similar game with fixed offers is analysed in Chatterjee and Samuelson (1987).

Rather than restrict the strategy space, we can enlarge the set of types of agent to make every strategy have positive probability. The easiest way to do this is to allow every agent to have a possibility of making a mistake so that every strategy is chosen with a positive but small probability. If all agents have the same chance of making a mistake, the occurrence of a mistake conveys no information about what type we are playing against. The problem with this approach is that it amounts to much the same thing as the adoption of plausible beliefs, in this case the belief that out-of-equilibrium behaviour conveys no information.

The third approach is to consider *a priori* restrictions on the set of beliefs that agents can adopt off the equilibrium path. Kreps discusses some of these refinements in Chapter 2 above. One possible approach is that adopted by Grossman and Perry (1986a). In their perfect sequential equilibrium, they impose the restriction that updating must be credible. The argument is that, just as some Nash equilibria in the extensive-form game are supported by threats that are not credible, in the sense that if the point is reached they will not be carried out, some sequential equilibria are supported by the 'threat' that an agent will take on an incredible belief if he observes a particular action.

For example, in our two-person bargaining game with $p = 1$, we have a unique subgame perfect equilibrium with $x_0^* = \frac{1}{2}(1 + u' - v)$. However, for any p less than 1, no matter how close, there is an equilibrium in which player 1 is forced to play $x_0^* = u'$, player 2 is committed to the belief $p_1 = 0$ for any observed x_0 different from u'. The question is, If player 2 actually observes such an offer, is such a belief credible?

Grossman and Perry argue that to be credible a belief must satisfy three conditions.

1. The support of player 2's probability distribution over player 1's type is contained in the support of his original prior distribution.
2. If the observed strategy is part of the equilibrium strategy set, player 2 updates by Bayes's rule.
3. Let player 2 observe an out-of-equilibrium strategy. Suppose player 2 can subdivide the types of player 1 into three distinct groups: those who deviate to the observed out-of-equilibrium strategy; those who randomize between deviating and staying at their equilibrium choice; and those who stick at the equilibrium strategy with certainty. Given this division, player 2 can use Bayes's rule to give posterior probabilities on the types he is playing. This out-of-equilibrium belief induces an action for player 2: he can ask, 'Which types of player 1 are

actually better off after deviating than they were staying at equilibrium, given my induced action?' If he finds that the set of types who were postulated to deviate are better off than at the equilibrium, while those who were postulated not to deviate would be worse off than at the equilibrium, and those who were assumed to randomize are indifferent between deviating and staying with their equilibrium strategy, then the beliefs adopted were credible. Player 2 must adopt a credible belief if any such exists. If none exists, his out-of-equilibrium beliefs are restricted only by condition 1.

All that condition 1 says is that the observation of an out-of-equilibrium event does not change the probabilities that agents attach to things they were certain about. For example, they are not permitted to introduce new types to explain the event, types that *ex ante* they were sure did not exist. Condition 2 is the usual application of Bayes's rule for equilibrium beliefs.

The interesting condition is the third one. This restricts the set of beliefs that player 2 can adopt if he observes out-of-equilibrium behaviour. Player 2 conducts a thought experiment. When he observes the deviation he asks the question, 'Which type of player 1 is it possibly in the interests of to make this deviation?' If he can get a consistent answer to this question, that is, an answer that, if he believes it correct, induces actions on his part that justify the deviation of this, and only this, type, then he must adopt this answer as his belief.

Grossman and Perry state their conditions in much more general and rigorous terms; they go on, in Grossman and Perry (1986b), to apply the perfect sequential equilibrium concept to the infinite-horizon alternating offer bargaining game with asymmetric information.

To give a flavour of the argument, we can find the perfect sequential equilibrium of our simple two-stage bargaining game. Consider any sequential equilibrium where the strong type plays $x_0^* < \frac{1}{2}(1 + u' - v)$. Suppose player 2 observes the offer $\frac{1}{2}(1 + u' - v)$; what is his credible updating rule?

If $p > p^*$ it is easy to show that the only credible belief is that both types have deviated. This results in the belief of player 2 being unchanged at p after observing the higher offer, but since p is bigger than p^*, player 2 should accept the high demand, justifying the deviation by both types.

It follows that $x_0^* < \frac{1}{2}(1 + u' - v)$ is not a perfect sequential equilibrium for p greater than p^*. It is easy to check that $x_0^* = \frac{1}{2}(1 + u' - v)$ is a perfect sequential equilibrium. Any higher demand is refused while any lower demand is accepted. However, since x_0^* is accepted, in equilibrium no type of player 1 is better off by deviating; any beliefs are credible and the equilibrium is sustainable.

This gives the same answer as imposing the plausible beliefs that higher demands imply an increase in the probability that the type we are facing is strong. For the case where $p < p^*$, the analysis is a little more difficult but leads to the conclusion that the unique perfect sequential equilibrium is for the strong type to demand $\frac{1}{2}(1 + u' - v)$ and the weak type to randomize between this and $\frac{1}{2}(1 + u - v)$. The technical difficulties arise because the weak agent is often indifferent between deviating and staying at equilibrium, and the plausible beliefs of player 2 involve this weak player randomizing.

This perfect sequential equilibrium of the game seems intuitively correct; for p near 1, player 1 always acts strong and it is never in player 2's interests to refuse the high demand. If p is small, the strong type of player 1 acts strong but the weak type randomizes between bluffing (impersonating the strong type) or making a low demand and conceding the information that he is weak. We rule out those sequential equilibria that force player 1 to make a low offer by not allowing player 2 to arbitrarily interpret high demands as a sign of weakness.

Bargaining games with one-sided asymmetric information have been analysed by Canning (1982), Gul, Sonneschien, and Wilson (1986), and in the numerical simulations of Grossman and Perry (1986b). The common result seems to be that, as the number of nodes becomes large and the time interval between them goes to 0, the equilibrium of the game tends to the case where both weak and strong types act strong and make a high demand, and this demand is accepted. In terms of the simple example described above, the critical value p^*, above which both types act tough, falls as the space between nodes is decreased, going eventually to 0. This implies that in such a game the value of a very small probability of being strong is as great as that of actually being strong; and the agent without the private information can never improve his expected utility by testing to find if he is facing a weak type who is bluffing.

Bargaining with two-sided asymmetric information has not been analysed in detail, mainly because of the increased problem with out-of-equilibrium offers coming from both sides. Canning (1982) and Chatterjee and Samuelson (1987) are able to find unique sequential equilibria for games with two-sided private information, but only at the cost of fixing the demands during the bargaining process. The outcome is that each weak type randomizes between conceding and rejecting the other's offer at each time while the strong type always rejects. There is an upper bound on the length of time both weak types can reject for; eventually they will have conceded with probability 1.

The outcome in this case is inefficient. With positive probability, the two sides will agree to an outcome after a period of bargaining while both would have been better of to agree to this outcome at the beginning. This outcome is not surprising, given the result found in Myerson and Satterthwaite (1980). They use the revelation principle to show that, if both sides have private information about their reservation values, and these reservation values are drawn from a large enough set, then no efficient bargaining mechanism exists.

The problem is that, if the mechanism is to be efficient and both sides must trade freely, then each side must get at least its reservation value from the agreement. This means they have an incentive to overstate their reservation values since this guarantees a higher payoff if trade occurs. However, if both have an incentive to over-report, they may indicate that trade gives no gains when such gains actually exist.

While no efficient mechanism exists, it may well be the case that the standard bargaining game can be improved upon in efficiency terms. We can ask two questions. First, can some arbitration mechanism for information revelation be designed which increases the expected payoffs for both sides; that is, can we find an arbitration mechanism that is voluntary? Second, can we impose an alternative bargaining mechanism which increases efficiency? A candidate for the second approach is the final-offer arbitration mechanism where an independent arbitrator chooses between the demands of the two sides. (He cannot compromise by taking a middle point.)

The ultimate goal would be the design of a mechanism that achieved the limit in efficiency terms in the sense that we could demonstrate that no more efficient mechanism existed. The problem to be faced then is that, as well as being (constrained) efficient, the mechanism will give a division of the surplus. Unless the outcome of the mechanism can be imposed, one side may have an incentive to ignore the agreement and proceed to bargain along conventional lines using terminal or non-terminal threats. We may well wish to constrain the mechanism further to ensure that each side gets at least its expected utility from the underlying bargaining game.

6. Bargaining and General Equilibrium

Bargaining theory can be used to study behaviour in decentralized exchange economies. In markets with centralized price setting, appeal can be made to some kind of *tâtonnement* mechanism to justify the Walrasian market-clearing equilibrium. In markets where trade is bilateral, it is not obvious that even the idea of a 'market price' is appropriate: each exchange may have its own implicit relative price.

If agents meet randomly over time and bargain over bilateral trades, it is easy to show that the outcome need not be Walrasian. Costly bargaining, time preference, or having only a small number of agents, may cause market 'imperfections'. Individual agents' payoffs may be determined by their luck in the search and pairing process, particularly if the cost of searching is high.

Gale (1986a, 1986b) examines a bilateral exchange bargaining model in which the costs of bargaining are zero and there is no time preference. He shows that, if the number of agents is large, every perfect equilibrium of the bargaining game implements a Walrasian allocation and vice versa. This results supports the idea that the Walrasian allocation is the appropriate equilibrium concept in decentralized exchange economies provided there are no 'frictions'.

The argument for the equivalence of the perfect equilibria and the Walrasian allocation has three stages. First, suppose two agents can make a mutually beneficial trade. Neither will stop searching since this is costless and there is a chance of meeting. Hence the perfect equilibrium of the bargaining game is efficient. Second, there will be a Walrasian equilibrium price vector associated with this efficient allocation. Every agent does as well in the bargaining game as by maximizing relative to this price vector; more precisely, for every $\varepsilon > 0$ we can show that the bargaining equilibrium gives the agent a utility within ε of that achieved at the Walrasian equilibrium. Finally, since time is costless, we need to ensure that every agent eventually finds suitable trading partners and attains the equilibrium allocation, rather than just searching indefinitely. This can be achieved by having enough agents (an atomless measure) of sufficiently diverse types (a continuum).

Gale works directly with the limiting case. An interesting question is whether or not the perfect equilibria of a game with frictions, such as time discounting, converge to the Walrasian equilibria as these frictions go to zero. That is, is the Walrasian equilibrium concept robust?

Rubinstein and Wolinsky (1986) show, in a simple model with a finite number of agents, the possibility that identifying agents allows punishment strategies which support a large class of perfect equilibria. These need not be Walrasian. The argument seems similar to that used to prove the Folk Theorem in repeated games: if agents expect to be punished for deviating, almost any individually rational outcome can be supported, and punishing deviators is rational because anyone who fails to do is himself punished. Rubinstein and Wolinsky argue that the crucial (implicit) assumption in Gale's work is that agents are anonymous.

A great deal of work remains to be done in this area. In what ways can the strict assumptions necessary in Gale's work be relaxed while maintaining outcomes that are close to the Walrasian equilibrium? Can we make the search and matching process endogenous? Can we explain why some agents are price-setters while others are price-takers? We have perhaps opened a window into the internal workings of the market mechanism.

The paper by Shaked and Sutton (1984) studies the link between the bargaining structure and the market outcome in a very simple case of one outsider and one insider competing for a job. The time between receiving the offer of the insider and receiving the offer from the outsider is crucial.

If there is a long delay before the outsider can be hired, the insider can exploit this. Also crucial is the gap between the outsider's offer and the insider's new counter-offer. Once it is the outsider's turn to make the offer, he is like the insider, since if his offer is rejected the firm faces further delay. The sensitivity of the outcome to these parameters is striking. The outcome need not converge to the competitive case as the time between offers becomes small, if the ratio of the time between outside offers is large relative to the time between offers by the insider (though both are close to zero).

7. Conclusion

The alternate offer bargaining game is a tractable model which gives plausible results when all information is common knowledge. In particular, the outcome tends to the Nash bargaining solution (for an appropriate choice of threat point and bargaining powers) if the number of potential offers is large and the time interval between offers is small.

The motivating behind quick agreement is either the cost of delay itself (time preference) or the risk, if agreement is delayed, of the other side getting a better offer from another agent—the pressure of competition. With common knowledge and unbounded rationality, the expected value of any agreement after a delay can be calculated and a mutually advantageous initial agreement found.

With asymmetric information, a problem appears in assigning agents' beliefs when they observe out-of-equilibrium behaviour. If these beliefs are not tightly restricted, the set of equilibria can be very large. Imposing 'credible' beliefs can reduce the set, sometimes making it a unique outcome. The correct solution concept for games with asymmetric information, and the calculation of the equilibria in reasonable games, remains an exciting area of research.

The other promising area of research is embedding a bilateral bargaining model in a larger market context. The terminal threat model in Section 4 presupposes such an outside market but does not model it explicitly. The questions to be faced in modelling such markets is the formulation of the bargaining game when agents meet, and the matching technology for bringing agents together.

The sensitivity of the results to the assumptions made about the exact structure of the bargaining and matching processes seems alarming. The answer may require a more fundamental approach to the problem, since even as the time between nodes becomes very small the exact placing of the nodes may have a bearing on the outcome. It may require modelling the endogenous placing of the decision nodes and an endogenous search and matching process to overcome these problems.

9

Imperfect Competition and International Trade

K. GATSIOS

1. Introduction

The growing scepticism and even dissatisfaction among trade theorists about the traditional trade theory can be traced from two sources.

First, international trade statistics reveal that a large proportion of world trade is carried out among the industrialized countries, that is, between countries with more or less similar factor endowments, technologies, and preferences.[1] Yet, according to the traditional theory, trade patterns are based on structural differences between the trading countries, usually on differences in factor endowments or technologies. The more pronounced those differences are, the more trade would take place, according to the predictions of the traditional theory. Second, empirical observations primarily due to Balassa (1967), Kravis (1971), and Grubel and Lloyd (1975) show that in the post Second World War period there has been a tremendous increase in the share of intra-industry trade in world trade, where by 'intra-industry trade' we mean a two-way trade in similar (but not necessarily identical) products. It has, moreover, been observed that this sort of trade is especially predominant among developed countries. Yet, the theory of comparative advantage dictates that each country will export those goods that it can produce relatively more cheaply in comparison with the others; in other words, the theory provides an explanation of *inter*-industry but not *intra*-industry trade.

The above observations made clear to a growing number of economists that new theoretical departures had to be made which would enable us to capture those features of trade that traditional theory could not— departures especially from the assumptions of perfect competition and constant (or decreasing) returns to scale in production on which the bulk of the traditional theory is based.[2]

I am indebted to Frank Hahn and Partha Dasgupta for their useful comments on a previous draft of this paper. Of course, the usual exclusion holds. Financial support from the State Scholarships Foundation of Greece (IKY) is gratefully acknowledged.

[1] According to World Bank reports, it is estimated that something like 70% of the total exports of the developed countries have, as a destination, markets of similarly industrialized countries.

[2] Some notable exceptions are those by Marshall (1879), Ohlin (1933), and Haberler (1936), who were especially interested in the welfare implications of the increasing returns for the trading countries.

The first part of this chapter attempts to offer possible explanations of intra-industry trade. It involves economies of scale in production which result in imperfect markets, the markets being oligopolistic or monopolistically competitive in the Chamberlinian tradition. In contrast with previous formal treatments of increasing returns in the theory of international trade (see, for example, Matthews 1949–50; Melvin 1969; Kemp 1969; Negishi 1969; Chacholiades 1970), this new line of research assumes that the economies of scale are internal to the firms and external to the particular industries, rather than vice versa, so that markets are no longer perfectly competitive.

In the second part of the paper I shall focus on the strategic behaviour and the trade policies that are associated with international markets that are oligopolistic in their structure. It is well known that, in the traditional Walrasian framework, the central proposition related to commercial policy is that interference with trade in the form of, say, tariffs is justified only for large economies seeking to improve their terms of trade. In an environment, though, in which the firms are large enough, so that they are not price-takers any more, and in which every decision-maker unit in setting up its strategy takes into account the actions of the other (rational) decision-makers, the strategic interdependence between firms (as well as governments) is bound to have significant consequences for trade policies. Indeed, it is shown that in oligopolistic markets there is room for strategic interventions by the governments of the trading countries aiming at improving the strategic position of their firms *vis à vis* their rivals. Furthermore, it is shown that, even if the trading countries favour trade liberalization or at least some loosening of protectionist policies, they are none the less unwilling to undertake such policies unilaterally. Indeed, it is observed that policies towards trade liberalization have been rather multilateral in character.

2. Intra-industry Trade

2.1. *Intra-industry trade in identical products*

The group of models that we shall examine here uses the strategic interdependence of oligopolistic firms in order to explain intra-industry trade in identical products.

Take, to start with, the extreme case of two completely identical countries producing a homogeneous product. In the traditional Walrasian framework there would be no reason for trade. However, as we move away from the assumption of perfect competition to an oligopolistic setting, we can show that 'reciprocal dumping' (also referred as 'cross-hauling') can take place; that is to say, there can be a two-way trade in the same product. This line of research was taken by Brander (1981),

Brander and Krugman (1983), and Brander and Spencer (1984a). The model we shall subsequently use to illuminate these ideas is similar to that used by Brander and Krugman (1983).

Assume that the world consists of two countries, the domestic and the foreign. Each country has one firm producing an identical commodity. We index the domestic country and firm by '1' and the foreign country and firm by '2'. Denote the output of firm i which arrives at the market of country j by Q_{ij}, $i, j = 1, 2$. The downward-sloping demand curve that the two firms face in market i is given in its inverted form by $P_i = P_i(Q_{ii} + Q_{ji})$ $i \neq j$, $i, j = 1, 2$.

Both firms operate under the same cost structure, which is characterized by a constant marginal cost c and a decreasing average cost due to some fixed costs F.

There are assumed to be transportation costs which are incurred in exporting the good from one country to the other. These costs are assumed to be of the 'iceberg' type, so that when one unit is exported from i only g reaches the market of j ($0 < g < 1$). Put differently, if Q_{ij} is sold by i to j, then firm i must product Q_{ij}/g. Therefore, the two profit functions can be written as

$$\pi_i = Q_{ii}P_i(Q_{ii} + Q_{ji}) + Q_{ij}P_j(Q_{ij} + Q_{jj}) - c(Q_{ii} + Q_{ij}/g) - F$$
$$i \neq j, \quad i, j = 1, 2.$$

The two firms are assumed to behave in a Cournot–Nash fashion. Therefore firm i, in choosing its output levels Q_{ii} and Q_{ij}, treats the output levels of its rival Q_{ji}, Q_{jj} as parameters; the same goes for j.

The first-order necessary maximization conditions for firm i are:

$$\partial \pi_i / \partial Q_{ii} = P_i'Q_{ii} + P_i - c = 0 \qquad i \neq j, \quad i, j = 1, 2 \qquad (1a)$$

$$\partial \pi_i / \partial Q_{ij} = P_j'Q_{ij} + P_j - c/g = 0. \qquad (1b)$$

They describe in implicit form the 'best-reply' (or reaction) functions of firm i. We assume that each firm's profit function is strictly concave in its own output and, following Hahn (1962), that each firm's marginal revenue is decreasing as its rival increases its own output. As is well known, these assumptions guarantee the uniqueness and stability of the Nash equilibrium.[3]

In calculating the latter, one notices, by inspecting (1a) and (1b), that each market can be separated from the other. This is due to the assumption of constant marginal costs.[4] The two first-order conditions

[3] For an excellent discussion on the comparative statics for oligopolistic markets, see Dixit (1986).

[4] Constant marginal costs are not crucial to the results of the model. If they were not constant they would just make the computations more difficult, since in such a case the four equations would have to be solved simultaneously for the four output levels. Clearly, symmetry in the cost structures is not crucial either.

associated with each market can be solved jointly for the relevant output levels. As long as the (common) equilibrium price in each market exceeds the marginal costs of exports, i.e. $p_i > c/g$ $i = 1, 2$, the equilibrium output levels will be positive, which, of course, implies that at equilibrium there will be a two-way trade in the same product.

It should be clear by now to the careful reader that the model presented is actually based on market segmentation and price discrimination exercised by the duopolists. It is easy to show that, in equilibrium, each firm will capture a larger part of its own market than its rival; this is due to the presence of transportation costs. Therefore, for each firm the perceived marginal revenue will be greater in its export market than in its domestic one. At the same time, the marginal cost of actually delivering a unit of output into the export market is higher than for a unit for domestic sales, owing to transportation costs. Each firm will equate in both markets the perceived marginal revenue with the marginal cost, in this way giving rise to two-way trade. Moreover, the f.o.b. price of exports will be below the price for domestic sales; each firm has a smaller markup over costs in its export market than at home.

Hence, the model just described gives a possible explanation of intra-industry trade. The welfare implications of such trade are interesting. To start with, it is immediate that the equilibrium outcome of our model is not Pareto-efficient. Furthermore, the presence of transportation cost implies that resources are wasted in a pointless transportation of the same product across national borders. Because of this, one may be tempted to conclude that the opening of trade is socially undesirable; but this is not necessarily correct. For the opening of trade increases competition and leads to a lower price by reducing the monopoly distortions; this of course will cause welfare to rise. The final effect on welfare arising from the opening of trade is not therefore clear, as is usually the case in second-best situations like the present one. If the transportation costs are negligible, the reciprocal dumping will result in gains from trade owing to the pro-competitive effect; if they are high, the opening of trade may cause welfare to decline, because in this case the pro-competitive effect will be dominated by the wasting of resources.

Surprisingly enough, if we allow free entry to take place before and after the opening of trade, the cross-hauling will result in welfare improvements. Firms will move down on their average cost curves and the price will fall; free entry strengthens the pro-competitive effect. Since the price falls and profits remain at zero by free entry, consumer surplus and therefore welfare rises.

2.2. *Intra-industry trade in differentiated products*

Empirical observations suggest that, in general, intra-industry trade refers to trade in similar but not identical products. The aim of this section is to provide a framework that can capture this characteristic of intra-industry trade. It is clear that the preliminary requisite for this purpose is a model of demand for differentiated products. In formulating this, basically two approaches have been used. The first is the 'love of variety' approach. This was first introduced for a closed economy by Dixit and Stiglitz (1977) along the lines of the Chamberlinian model of imperfect competition. The basic model developed along these lines for open economies was originally introduced by Krugman (1979). According to this approach, which besides Krugman (1979, 1980, 1982) has also been used by Dixit and Norman (1980), the representative consumer wishes to consume all available differentiated products. The second, so-called 'characteristics', approach was developed by Lancaster (1979, 1980) and bears a considerable degree of similarity to Hotelling's spatial model. According to this approach, each variety of the differentiated product is viewed as a collection of characteristics. Each consumer is assumed to have a most preferred (ideal) variety which he attempts to attain. This model was used in explaining international trade patterns by Helpman (1981, 1984, 1985).

The model I shall sketch next is based on Gatsios (1985) and attempts to capture and present the main results of the literature in this area in an integrated way. The formulation of demand I adopt follows the 'love of variety' approach, but the model is now extended from that of Krugman's (1979) to include a second sector producing a homogeneous product under conditions of perfect competition. In this way our model, besides being a generalization of Krugman's work, also provides some rather interesting results concerning the welfare effects of trade on the trading countries and is able to incorporate the main results of Helpman's (1981) model.

Assume a two-sector economy A, with one factor of production, say labour. One sector, denoted by '0', produces a homogeneous product, say 'food', under decreasing returns to scale[5] and perfect competition.

The other sector, denoted by '1', produces a large number of varieties of a product, say 'manufactures', under increasing returns to scale and monopolistic competition which is Chamberlinian in nature.

Denote by $Q_{0,A}$ and $Q_{1i,A}$ the output of food and of variety i of manufactures respectively, and by $n_{1,A}$ the number of varieties produced in country A. All individuals share the same utility function in which all varieties enter symmetrically. Denoting the individual consumption of food and of variety i by $c_{0,A}$ and $c_{1i,A}$, we assume the utility function to

---

[5] The fact that 'food' is produced under decreasing returns to scale indicates that there is another scarce factor of production, say 'land', which has not been explicitly modelled. We assume throughout this model that 'land' is owned by 'landlords' who consume only food.

take the form of

$$V_A(\mathbf{c}) = c_0^\gamma \sum_{i=1}^{n_{1,A}} u(c_{1i,A}) \tag{2}$$

where $0 < \gamma < 1$, $u' > 0$ and $u'' < 0$.

The homogeneous good is produced under a very simple production function:

$$L_{0,A} = Q_{0,A}^{1/\delta}, \qquad 0 < \delta < 1$$

where $L_{0,A}$ is the labour force employed in the food sector.

In sector 1 all firms produce under the same cost function:

$$l_{1i,A} = \alpha + \beta Q_{1i,A} \qquad \alpha, \beta > 0$$

where $l_{1i,A}$ denotes the labour employed in firm i. Clearly, the increasing returns take the form of a falling average cost and of a constant marginal cost. The total amount of labour employed in the manufacturing sector is $L_{1,A} = \Sigma_i l_{1i,A}$, and by assuming full employment we have $L_A = L_{0,A} + L_{1,A}$, where L_A is the total labour force in country A.

The representative consumer maximizes his utility function (2) subject to his budget constraint given by

$$P_{0,A}c_{0,A} + \sum_i P_{1i,A}c_{1i,A} = W_A \tag{3}$$

where $P_{0,A}$, $P_{1i,A}$, and W_A denote the price of food, of variety i, and the wage rate respectively.

The first-order necessary maximization conditions are

$$\gamma c_{0,A}^{\gamma-1} \sum_i u(c_{1i,A}) = \lambda P_{0,A} \tag{4a}$$

$$c_{0,A}^\gamma u'(c_{1i,A}) = \lambda P_{1i,A} \tag{4b}$$

where the Lagrangian multiplier λ can be interpreted as the marginal utility of income. The symmetry of our model implies that in equilibrium $P_{1i,A} = P_{1,A}$, $Q_{1i,A} = Q_{1,A}$, $c_{1i,A} = c_{1,A}$ for every i, so henceforward we shall delete the subscript i.

Equation (4b) describes the demand facing a particular firm i. Its price elasticiy is given by $\varepsilon(c_{1,A}) = -u'/(u''c_{1,A}) > 0$. In fact, in equilibrium it must be that $\varepsilon(\cdot) > 1$. We shall further assume that $d\varepsilon/dc_{1,A} < 0$, for reasons that will become clear later.

Let us now turn to the production side of our economy. In the perfectly competitive sector the necessary condition for the maximization of profits, $P_{0,A}Q_{0,A} - W_A L_{0,A}$, implies that

$$P_{0,A}/W_A = \delta^{-1}Q_{0,A}^{(1-\delta)/\delta}.$$

In sector 1 firms are assumed to be profit-maximizers but free entry drives their profits to zero (Chamberlinian assumption). The representative firm chooses its price to maximize

$$\pi_{1,A} = P_{1,A}Q_{1,A} - (\alpha + \beta Q_{1,A})W_A.$$

The necessary condition for a maximum is given by

$$P_{1,A}/W_A = \beta\varepsilon(\varepsilon - 1)^{-1}. \tag{5}$$

One can verify that our assumption $d\varepsilon/dc < 0$ guarantees that the second-order condition is satisfied as well; in fact, what is needed is the slightly weaker assumption $d\varepsilon/dc \leqslant 0$. Notice that, since $\varepsilon > 1$ in equilibrium, then $P_{1,A}/W_A > \beta$; also, $d\varepsilon/dc_{1,A} < 0$ implies that $d(P_{1,A}/W_A)/dc_{1,A} > 0$.

Free entry (and exit) means that profits will be zero in equilibrium, which implies that

$$P_{1,A}/W_A = \beta + \alpha/Q_{1,A} = \beta + \alpha/(L_Ac_{1,A}). \tag{6}$$

The equilibrium prices (relative to the wage) and the output levels of the firms in sector 1 will be determined by the joint satisfaction of (5) and (6).

In Figure 9.1, ZZ represents the profit maximization condition whereas the rectangular hyperbola AA represents the zero profit condition. Their intersection determines $P_{1,A}/W_A$, $c_{1,A}$, and therefore $Q_{1,A}$ ($= L_Ac_{1,A}$).

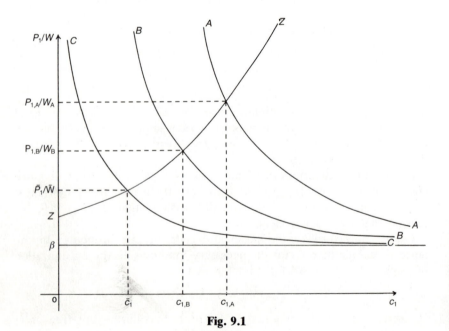

Fig. 9.1

From the consumer's budget constraint (3) and (4a), (4b), one can get that

$$n_{1,A}c_{1,A}P_{1,A}/W_A = \mu(c_{1,A})/[\mu(c_{1,A}) + \gamma] \equiv \sigma(c_{1,A}) \qquad (7)$$

where $\mu(c_{1,A}) = u'c_{1,A}/u > 0$.

Clearly, $0 < \sigma(\cdot) < 1$ and $\sigma(\cdot)$ is the share of the per capita (labour) income devoted to the consumption of manufactured products. Note that μ' (and so σ' as well) can take any sign; we assume throughout that μ' (and σ') is one-signed for all c_1. If $\mu' = 0$, then the consumer spends a fixed share of his income in each sector irrespective of relative prices.[6]

Expression (7) closes our model. It provides the equilibrium number of varieties (firms) and consequently the labour force employed in the manufactures sector. The labour force employed in the food sector, the equilibrium output and price of food, and the landlord's rent can then be computed in a straightforward way.

Consider now another economy B, identical to all respects to A but with a higher population size, so that $L_B > L_A$. The closed economy equilibrium for country B can be calculated along the same lines with that of country A. In Figure 9.1, the line *BB* represents the zero profit condition in the manufacturing sector of country B; it lies throughout below line *AA*, reflecting the fact that $L_B > L_A$; its intersection with *ZZ*, which represents the profit maximization condition, determines the equilibrium output levels and prices in the manufacturing sector.

It turns out that country B will involve, in autarkic equilibrium, larger firms than A; with a higher population, the firms in B can better realize their economies of scale in production. However, the number of firms (varieties) in each country depends on the sign of σ'; if $\sigma' \leq 0$, then country B produces in autarky more varieties than A; if $\sigma' > 0$, we cannot say. The share of each country's labour force employed in each sector, which can be taken as a measure of industrialization, also depends on the sign of σ'; for $\sigma' \lessgtr 0$, the share of the labour force employed in the manufacturing sector in country B will be respectively higher than, equal to, and less than that of country A.

Now suppose that trade opens between the two countries. The discussion will be confined to the case of a symmetrical equilibrium, with no impediments to trade and incomplete specialization, that is with both countries producing both food and manufactured products. A symmetrical equilibrium in our model is one in which all varieties are sold at the same price. It is trivial then to see that both symmetrical equilibrium and incomplete specialization imply that the wages will be uniform across countries. As usual, what is required to make factor price equalization consistent with symmetrical equilibrium and incomplete specialization is

---

[6] A utility function that can give rise to such a result is $V = c_0^{\gamma} \Sigma_i c_{1i}^{\zeta}$, γ, $\zeta < 1$. One can easily check that in this case $\varepsilon = (1 - \zeta)^{-1} > 1$, $\mu = \zeta$, and $\sigma = \zeta/(\zeta + \gamma)$.

that the two countries do not differ 'too much' in the ratio of their factor endowments, that is (in our model) in their labour sizes.[7]

From now on, I indicate with a bar over a variable its value in the trading equilibrium. The latter will be determined in a similar way as in the autarkic ones. In Figure 9.1 the hyperbola *CC*, which represents the zero profit condition for the world economy, lies below *BB* owing to the fact that $L > L_B > L_A$, where L represents the world's population. The intersection of *CC* with *ZZ* will determine as usual the world equilibrium prices and quantities in the manufacturing sector.

As expected, the trading equilibrium will involve larger firms than the autarkic ones. At the same time, since the two countries possess the same aggregate production function for food, they will share the world's production of it. This in turn implies that the labour force employed in the manufacturing sector in country B will be larger than that of country A. Consequently the number of firms (varieties) in country B will be larger than in A.

What in fact we obtain is a version of the Rybczynski Theorem: country B, which is relatively more abundant in labour, used more intensively in the manufacturing sector, will produce a larger number of varieties per capita (as well as in absolute terms) and less food per capita than country A. Notice that this result holds irrespective of the sign of σ'.

Clearly, both intersectoral and intra-industry trade will take place. Since the number of varieties per capita produced in country B is larger than in A, then in trading equilibrium country B will be a net exporter of manufactured products and a net importer of food. This result indicates that the Heckscher–Ohlin Theorem continues to explain the pattern of intersectoral trade; each country will be a net exporter of the good that requires for its production a relatively more intensive use of the factor with which each country is relatively more abundantly endowed with. On the other hand, the intra-industry trade is explained by the increasing returns, monopolistic competition, and product differentiation characteristics of our model. These characteristics ensure that each firm produces a certain variety, and therefore each country a certain range of varieties. At the same time, the 'love of variety' structure of the utility function guarantees that each consumer demands all available varieties produced worldwide. Consequently both countries will export the varieties they produce, giving rise in this way to intra-industry trade.

What does determine the share of intra-industry trade in world trade? By using the standard index introduced by Grubel and Lloyd (1975: 22), it turns out that, the more similar the countries are (that is, the more similar their endowment ratio is), the greater the share of intra-industry

---

[7] For more details on this point see Gatsios (1985). For a general discussion on the factor price equalization region, see for example Dixit and Norman (1980), or Helpman and Krugman (1985).

trade in total trade becomes. In our model, for example, in the limiting case where $L_A = L_B$, all the trade will be intra-industry in nature. The above results fit well with the empirical evidence on trade patterns.

The welfare effects of trade in the context of our model are rather interesting. To start with, we are in a second-best situation arising from the distortions inherent in a departure from perfect competition, and therefore complete and definite assessments about welfare cannot be made. None the less, it turns out that a country will gain from trade if trade allows it to further concentrate its production activities in the sector operating under increasing returns to scale, provided that the total number of varieties produced worldwide is now higher than that produced by each country in autarky. This will certainly be the case for the more intensively populated country B, so long as $\sigma'(\cdot) \leq 0$—that is, for a broad family of utility functions. The gains for country B in this case result from an increased number of varieties consumed ($\bar{n}_1 > n_{1,B}$) and a higher real income ($\bar{P}_1/\bar{W} < P_{1,B}, W_B$ and $\bar{P}_0/\bar{W} < P_{0,B}/W_B$).[8] For country A, the welfare effects of trade are in general dubious; country A may be better off or worse off with trade. Therefore one may say that, loosely speaking, the country that is relatively better endowed in the factor used relatively more intensively in the sector operating under economies of scale (in our model, country B) is more likely to gain from trade.[9,10]

3. Strategic Interactions and Profit-shifting in International Markets

In an oligopolistic setting, the firms are assumed to be sufficiently large so that they act in a strategic way; in choosing their strategies, they take into account their interdependence with their rivals. We have already seen in Section 2.1 that such a framework can provide an explanation of intra-industry trade in a homogeneous product.

In this section we shall be focusing on another aspect of an oligopolistic (international) market: the super-normal profits associated with oligopolies. Since each country stands to gain, other things being equal, by an increase in the profits made by its firms operating in international markets, then each government has an incentive to improve, if possible,

[8] Country B will still be better off with trade in the case where $\sigma'(\cdot) > 0$, provided that the total volume of manufactured products consumed by its residents under trade is greater than that consumed under autarky (i.e. $\bar{n}_1\bar{c}_1 > n_{1,B}c_{1,B}$). However the same is not necessarily true for country A.

[9] It is perhaps of interest to note that similar results concerning the welfare effects of trade were reached by Chacholiades (1978: Ch. 7), in a model where the increasing returns were Marshallian in nature, i.e. external rather than internal to the firms, so that the assumption of perfect competition still holds.

[10] Our welfare remarks are derived by examining the worker-consumer. We can observe that industrialization harms the landlords by reducing the levels of rent for land. There is therefore a 'conflict' in our model between workers and landlords concerning industrialization.

the strategic position of domestic firms *vis à vis* their rivals, so that it can shift excess profits from the latter to the former.

This government intervention can be captured in the context of a game which is sequential in nature. The governments first choose their policies in an irreversible manner, and then the firms set their own strategies at the second stage of the game. In this way, the commitment of the governments to some particular policies alters the equilibrium outcome in a way that the firms could not do on their own.

The essence of profit-shifting was first introduced in the work of Brander and Spencer (1984a, 1984b, 1985); their basic model was extended by Dixit (1984) and Eaton and Grossman (1986).

I shall start by presenting in a compact way a model based on Gatsios (1986). This model includes the basic model of Brander and Spencer (1985) as a particular case; it extends their results and offers some new ones.

Suppose there are two firms, a domestic firm and a foreign one, producing a homogeneous product. The two firms operate under a learning curve and compete for the market of a third importing country. For simplicity, the analysis will take place in two periods. Let x_i, y_i be the output of the domestic and foreign firm respectively in period i, $i = 1, 2$. The market demand is assumed to be independent of time and is given in its inverted form by $P(Q)$, where Q is total output. We assume that $P(\cdot)$ is a time-invariant, decreasing, twice continuously differentiable function with $QP''(Q) + P'(Q) < 0$, so that the instantaneous revenue of each firm in both periods is concave in its own output. We take the discount rate to be nil, so that the profit function of the domestic firm is given by

$$\pi(x_1, y_1, x_2, y_2) = R_1(x_1, y_1) - c_1 x_1 + R_2(x_2, y_2) - c_2(x_1)x_2$$

where $R_i(\cdot)$ denotes the revenue in period i, c_1 is the constant unit cost of production in period 1, and $c_2(x_1)$ is the unit cost in period 2 which depends on the firms' output in period 1.

Similarly, the profit function of the foreign firm is given by

$$\pi^*(x_1, y_1, x_2, y_2) = R_1^*(x_1, y_1) - c_1^* y_1 + R_2^*(x_2, y_2) - c_2^*(y_1)y_2.$$

We assume that $dc_2/dx_1 < 0$, $d^2c_2/dx_1^2 > 0$, and similarly for the foreign firm. This assumption captures the 'learning-by-doing' effect: each firm's unit cost of production in the second period is falling as its own output of the first period increases. There are no spillovers across countries (firms).

In this two-period model the strategic interactions between the firms are best captured by making use of Selten's (1975) concept of subgame perfect Nash equilibrium; each firm's strategy prescribes what would be the best response to all courses of events possible.

First, I shall solve the second-period subgame looking for a Nash equilibrium in x_2 and y_2; x_1 and y_1 are taken as parameters at this stage of the game.

The first-order necessary maximization conditions are

$$\partial \pi / \partial x_2 = \partial R_2 / \partial x_2 - c_2(x_1) = 0 \qquad (8)$$

$$\partial \pi^* / \partial y_2 = \partial R_2^* / \partial y_2 - c_2^*(y_1) = 0. \qquad (8^*)$$

The solutions for x_2 and y_2 are derived by jointly solving (8) and (8^*) and they will depend on x_1 and y_1; so we can write them as $x_2 = x_2(x_1, y_1)$ and $y_2 = y_2(x_1, y_1)$.

To calculate the perfect equilibrium of our model, note that the firms in choosing their strategies take into account the dependence of their second-period output levels on the first-period ones. Therefore, define

$$\hat{\pi}(x_1, y_1) \stackrel{\text{def}}{=} R_1(x_1, y_1) - c_1 x_1 + R_2(x_2, y_2) - c_2(x_1)x_2$$

$$\hat{\pi}^*(x_1, y_1) \stackrel{\text{def}}{=} R_1^*(x_1, y_1) - c_1^* y_1 + R_2^*(x_2, y_2) - c_2^*(y_1)y_2$$

where now $x_2 = x_2(x_1, y_1)$, $y_2 = y_2(x_1, y_1)$ are the solutions to the second stage-game.

The necessary conditions, which we assume to be sufficient, are

$$\partial \hat{\pi} / \partial x_1 = \partial R_1 / \partial x_1 - c_1 + (\partial R_2 / \partial x_2 - c_2)(\partial x_2 / \partial x_1)$$
$$+ (\partial R_2 / \partial y_2)(\partial y_2 / \partial x_1) - (dc_2 / dx_1)x_2$$

(by (8)) $\qquad = \partial R_1 / \partial x_1 - c_1 + (\partial R_2 / \partial y_2)(\partial y_2 / \partial x_1) - (dc_2 / dx_1)x_2 = 0$

and a similar expression holds for $\partial \hat{\pi}^* / \partial y_1 = 0$. They describe, in implicit form, the firms' best-reply functions in the first-period output space.

We can observe that, since $\partial R_2 / \partial y_2 < 0$, $\partial y_2 / \partial x_1 < 0$, and $dc_2 / dx_1 < 0$, then at equilibrium $\partial R_1 / \partial x_1 < c_1$ and similarly for the foreign firm, $\partial R_1^* / dy_1 < c_1^*$. Consequently, we notice that in the first period each firm produces, for any given output level of its rival, at a level at which its (instantaneous) marginal cost exceeds its (instantaneous) marginal revenue, which in turn implies, by the concavity of the (instantaneous) revenue function, that it will produce more output now than it would have produced if faced with a single-period problem. Put differently, the best-reply curves of both firms are shifted outwards in the first-period output space. Therefore in symmetric equilibria both firms (and in asymmetric equilibria at least one of them) will produce in the first period more output than they would in the single-period non-cooperative equilibrium. They are now prepared to make lower instantaneous profits in the first period by producing more because, owing to the 'learning effects', they will be able in this way to make even greater profits in the second period and, as a result, to maximize their total stream of profits.

The solution to $\partial \hat{\pi} / \partial x_1 = 0$ and $\partial \hat{\pi}^* / \partial y_1 = 0$, x_1 and y_1 along with $x_2 = x_2(x_1, y_1)$ and $y_2 = y_2(x_1, y_1)$, is the perfect equilibrium outcome of our model.

One can easily check that

$$dx_2 / dx_1 > 0, \qquad dy_2 / dx_1 < 0, \qquad dx_2 / dy_1 < 0, \qquad dy_2 / dy_1 > 0.$$

K. Gatsios

Therefore an increase in firm 1's (2's) first-period output will increase its second-period output and decrease firm 2's (1's) second-period output. In other words, both market share and output of firm 1(2) will increase in the second period as a result of an increase in firm 1's (2's) first-period output.

This last observation raises the issue of possible government intervention. In particular, I want to ask whether each government will have an incentive to subsidize the first-period output of its domestic firm. This is a well-known policy prescription related to the infant industry argument: by subsidizing output in the first period, more of it will be produced, and therefore the firm will take better advantage of the dynamic increasing returns in the second period.

Assume, for the moment, that the homogeneous good is produced solely for export. This, by removing consumer surplus from welfare calculations, allows us to focus entirely on profits. The interactions between the profit-shifting motive and the concern for domestic consumer surplus are left to be examined at a later stage. To fix ideas, suppose that only one government, say the domestic one, commits itself to subsidize the first-period output of its domestic firm. One can therefore think of the two-stage game being extended to a three-stage one in which the domestic government makes the first move. The subsidy will affect the first-period output levels but not the resolution of the last stage-game, $x_2 = x_2(x_1, y_1)$ and $y_2 = y_2(x_1, y_1)$.

The domestic and the foreign firm will aim respectively to maximize

$$\hat{\pi}(x_1, y_1; s_1) = R_1(x_1, y_1) - c_1 x_1 + R_2(x_2, y_2) - c_2(x_1)x_2 + s_1 x_1$$

$$\hat{\pi}^*(x_1, y_1) = R_1^*(x_1, y_1) - c_1^* x_1 + R_2^*(x_2, y_2) + c_2^*(y_1)y_2$$

where $x_2 = x_2(x_1, y_1)$, $y_2 = y_2(x_1, y_1)$, and s_1 denotes the rate of subsidy.

The first-order necessary maximization conditions $\partial \hat{\pi}/\partial x_1 = 0$ and $\partial \hat{\pi}/\partial y_1 = 0$ can be solved for x_1 and y_1, which will now depend on s_1, so we write $x_1 = x_1(s_1)$ and $y_1 = y_1(s_1)$.

To see the impact of s_1 on the first-period output levels, totally differentiate the first-order conditions with respect to x_1, y_1, and s_1, put in a matrix form, and note that

$$\partial^2 \hat{\pi}/(\partial x_1 \partial s_1) = 1 \quad \text{and} \quad \partial^2 \hat{\pi}^*/(\partial y_1 \partial s_1) = 0$$

to get

$$\begin{bmatrix} \partial^2 \hat{\pi}/\partial x_1^2 & \partial^2 \hat{\pi}/(\partial x_1 \partial y_1) \\ \partial^2 \hat{\pi}^*/(\partial y_1 \partial x_1) & \partial^2 \hat{\pi}^*/\partial y_1^2 \end{bmatrix} \begin{bmatrix} dx_1/ds_1 \\ dy_1/ds_1 \end{bmatrix} = \begin{bmatrix} -1 \\ 0 \end{bmatrix}.$$

By solving, we have $dx_1/ds_1 > 0$ and $dy_1/ds_1 = (dy_1/dx_1)(dx_1/ds_1) < 0$.

But then, the increase in x_1 and decrease in y_1 as a result of the subsidy implies that x_2 will increase and y_2 will decrease. So we conclude that the use of a subsidy by the government for the first-period output of its domestic firm will increase both periods' output of the domestic firm and decrease both periods' output of the rival firm; that is, the domestic firm will increase both its output and its market share in both periods.

It is then a matter of routine calculations to show that, as a result of the subsidy, the stream of profits to the domestic firm will increase (i.e. $d\hat{\pi}/ds_1 > 0$) whereas that of the foreign will decrease (i.e. $d\hat{\pi}^*/ds_1 < 0$). The subsidy has caused a shifting of profits from the foreign to the domestic firm.

The natural question that one wants to ask at this point is, Is the subsidization policy followed by the government a desirable one; in other words, will it increase the country's surplus? Since we have assumed that the product is produced entirely for export, the domestic surplus will consist of the profits of the domestic firm net of the subsidy. Denoting by W_1 the surplus of the domestic country, we have

$$W_1 = \hat{\pi}(x_1, y_1; s_1) - s_1 x_1$$

where $x_1 = x_1(s_1)$ and $y_1 = y_1(s_1)$.

One can check that for $s_1 = 0$, $dW_1/ds_1 > 0$; that is, a marginal increase to a positive subsidy level will increase the domestic surplus. To find the optimal level of the subsidy, we set $dW_1/ds_1 = 0$ and we solve for s_1; it turns out that the optimal subsidy is given by[11]

$$s_1 = (\partial\hat{\pi}/\partial y_1)(dy_1/dx_1) > 0. \tag{9}$$

Therefore, we conclude that the domestic government will have a unilateral incentive to subsidize the first-period output of its domestic firm.

Would this policy continue to be optimal in the case where the domestic firm was a monopolist exporter? It is easy to see that the answer is no. In fact, in such a case the domestic government would have no incentive to subsidize (or tax) because it would experience losses in domestic welfare. The economics of this is rather simple. If the domestic firm were a monopolist, the imposition of a subsidy would increase the firm's marginal profits and therefore the country's marginal gains by x_1 (since in the monopolist, case $d\hat{\pi}/ds_1 = x_1$); on the other hand, the domestic country's marginal losses in subsidy payments would be $d(s_1 x_1)/ds_1 = x_1 + s_1(dx_1/ds_1)$. The net result would be a loss of welfare arising from the amount of subsidy paid for the additional units of output

---

[11] We have that

$$dW_1/ds_1 = (\partial\hat{\pi}/\partial x_1)(dx_1/ds_1) + (\partial\hat{\pi}/\partial y_1)(dy_1/ds_1)$$
$$+ \partial\hat{\pi}/\partial s_1 - s_1(dx_1/ds_1) - x_1.$$

Since $\partial\hat{\pi}/\partial x_1 = 0$ by the first-order maximization conditions, $\partial\hat{\pi}/\partial s_1 = x_1$, and $dy_1/ds_1 = (dy_1/dx_1)(dx_1/ds_1)$, we get that $dW_1/ds_1 = 0 \Rightarrow [(\partial\hat{\pi}/\partial y_1)(dy_1/dx_1) - s_1](dx_1/ds_1) = 0$, which implies (9), since $dx_1/ds_1 > 0$.

that have been produced as a result of the government's commitment to subsidize, namely, a loss in welfare equal to $s_1(dx_1/ds_1)$! A similar argument holds for the case of a tax: $s_1 < 0$.

Therefore it is the rivalry between the two firms that makes the subsidization policy followed by the government meaningful (desirable). The commitment of a government to subsidize alters the industry's equilibrium so that profits shift from the rival firm to the domestic one. In particular, the following result, derived by Brander and Spencer (1985), holds for our model as well. The use of the optimal subsidy by the domestic government for the first-period output of its domestic firm results in an equilibrium in the first-period output space, which is the same as the one that would have resulted if there were no subsidy and the domestic firm were a Stackelberg leader.

In Figure 9.2, we denote the Nash equilibrium by N. The imposition of the subsidy shifts the reaction curve of the domestic firm outwards; the new equilibrium is depicted by S, the Stackelberg equilibrium outcome.

From our analysis up to now, it is apparent that in a non-cooperative equilibrium both governments have an incentive to subsidize the first-period output of their domestic firm. In a similar way as before, we can establish that the non-cooperative equilibrium in subsidies is given by

$$s_1 = (\partial\hat{\pi}/\partial y_1)(dy_1/dx_1) > 0 \qquad (9a)$$

$$s_1^* = (\partial\hat{\pi}^*/\partial x_1)(dx_1/dy_1) > 0 \qquad (9a^*)$$

where by s_1^* we denote the subsidy set by the foreign government.

Although both governments have an incentive in a non-cooperative

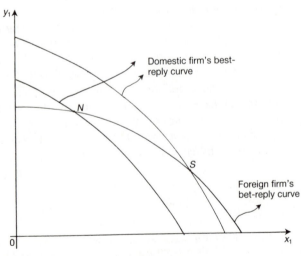

Fig. 9.2

equilibrium to set positive subsidies, the outcome of their behaviour is jointly suboptimal; they could increase their joing surplus by lowering their subsidy levels. Indeed, it turns out that their jointly optimal policy is to tax rather than subsidize the first-period output of their domestic firm; by doing so, they mutually offset the negative effects of an increase in each one's output on the other firm's profits, and the burden of the tax is carried over to the importing country.

How will the results we have up to now concluded be affected in the case where the good is also consumed domestically by the exporting countries?

To address ourselves to this question, let $u(q_i)$ and $u^*(q_i^*)$ denote, respectively, the utility derived in the domestic and foreign exporting country by consuming the good in period i, $i = 1$, 2. For simplicity we assume that any change in income in either country is absorbed by the 'rest' of the respective economy. We furthermore assume that the good is consumed at a common world price and the subsidy applies to all units of production. In this way, in equilibrium, $P_1 = u(q_1) = u^{*\prime}(q_1^*)$ and $P_2 = u'(q_2) = u^{*\prime}(q_2^*)$. The domestic and foreign governments will set their subsidy levels, s_1 and s_1^*, to maximize, respectively,

$$W_1(s_1, s_1^*) = u(q_1) - P_1 q_1 + u(q_2) - P_2 q_2 + \hat{\pi}(x_1, y_1; s_1) - s_1 x_1$$

and

$$W_2(s_1, s_1^*) = u^*(q_1^*) - P_1 q_1^* + u^*(q_2^*) - P_2 q_2^* + \hat{\pi}^*(x_1, y_1; s_1^*) - s_1^* y_1.$$

The first-order necessary maximization conditions, $\partial W_1 / \partial s_1 = 0$ and $\partial W_2 / \partial s_1^* = 0$, can be solved jointly for the optimal levels of s_1 and s_1^*. It turns out that both governments will still have, as before, an incentive in a non-cooperative equilibrium to subsidize the first-period output of their respective firms.

At this point a relevant question to ask is whether the non-cooperative subsidies will be higher or lower now than before, when the good was not consumed domestically by the exporting countries. One may suppose that, since the good is now consumed domestically, a higher subsidy than that given by (9) will be appropriate to increase the domestic welfare. In fact, this is not necessarily so. The optimal subsidies may now be lower than before. Each government in setting its policy has to consider the negative effects of an increase of its subsidy on the output of the rival firm and the possible adverse effects that this may cause to consumer surplus. In the case of symmetrical firms, the equilibrium subsidies will be higher now than before. This is because in this case a marginal increase in a government's subsidy above its level given by equations (9) will decrease both period prices of the homogeneous good and will increase, therefore, both period consumer surpluses. For asymmetrical cases, though, it is possible that the opposite will be true; that is, the non-cooperative equilibrium may involve lower subsidies now than before. This is because in this case, although the first-period price still goes down as a result of a marginal increase of a subsidy, the second-period price may indeed go up, and therefore the consumer surplus in this period may in fact decrease. This will happen if the (negative) cross-effects on the rival's output caused by an increase of a subsidy dominate the (positive) own-effects. Consequently, if the drop in the second-period consumer surplus outweighs its first-period increase, then, for any given subsidy level chosen by its rival, each government will set a lower subsidy now than before. In other words, the two best-reply curves in the subsidy space will move inwards, and the non-cooperative equilibrium may involve lower subsidies now than those described by (9a) and (9a*).

It must also be said that the possibility of lower subsidies just described depends very crucially on both the dynamic returns to scale that have been adopted and the presence of the rival. If for instance we relax the 'learning-by-doing' assumption, so that our model becomes a single-period one, then we notice that each government will set, for any given subsidy level of its rival, a higher subsidy now than before; that is, the best-reply curves will move outwards in the subsidy space. Similarly, if we retain our 'learning-by-doing' assumption but assume that there is no rival, then the optimal subsidy will now be positive and therefore higher than the optimal level of subsidy (nil) in the corresponding case where the good was produced only for export.

When the good was solely produced for export, we saw that the jointly optimal policy for the exporting countries was to tax their first-period output. Now, as one would suspect, things are somehow different. First, it still holds true that the non-cooperative outcome is suboptimal; the two countries would improve their joint welfare if they were to lower their non-cooperative subsidy levels. However, unlike before, it turns out that their jointly optimal policy would be to tax their first-period output only if their joint consumption were less than each country's individual production; in this case their gains from exports would be enough to compensate their losses in consumers' surplus. Otherwise, they would choose to subsidize.

Notice that, as has already been pointed out, in both cases, whether the good is consumed domestically by the exporting countries or not, the non-cooperative equilibrium involves subsidy levels that are higher than the jointly optimal ones. This is due to the competition among firms (and governments) to capture a large share of the third (importing) country's market. The two exporting countries are caught in this way in a Prisoners' Dilemma situation. Although it is true that, by cooperating and possibly setting a mechanism of side-payments, they could both be better off, there is nothing in our model that can make this sort of agreement binding. The non-cooperative equilibrium is the only stable one in our model.

To complete the analysis of the model, the last question I want to address is the response of the importing country: will it tax or subsidize its first-period imports?

Denote by $\bar{u}(M_1)$ and $\bar{u}(M_2)$ the utility derived by the importing country in periods 1 and 2, respectively, where M_i denotes imports at period i. We still take the social discount rate to be nil and we assume away income effects, so that equilibrium $\bar{u}'(M_1) = \bar{P}_1$ and $\bar{u}'(M_2) = P_2$, where $\bar{P}_1$ is the price of the good including the tariff. By interpreting P_1 as the price net of the tariff, that is, $P_1 = \bar{P}_1 - t_1$ where t_1 the tax on imports, our previous results still hold.

The importing country will choose t_1 to maximize its welfare:

$$W_3 = \bar{u}(M_1) - \bar{P}_1(x_1 + y_1)M_1 + t_1 M_1 + \bar{u}(M_2) - P_2(x_2 + y_2)M_2.$$

If the marginal increase in the domestic price of the importing country is higher than the marginal increase in the tariff itself, that is, if $\partial \bar{P}_1 / \partial t_1 > 1$, then the importing country will choose to subsidize its first-period imports. This will be the case as Brander and Spencer (1984a, 1984b) have pointed out for a demand sufficiently convex to the origin (for instance, constant elasticity demand curves).

In the opposite case, $\partial \bar{P}_1 / \partial t_1 < 1$, which will be true for the case of linear demands as well as many other plausible ones, the result is ambiguous. Note that, if our model were a single-period one, then the importing country would, in this case, impose a tariff. Now, owing to the second-period effects caused by the 'learning-by-doing' process, the result can be the reverse. Indeed, it can be shown that, if the learning effects are 'strong' enough, the importing country would still want to subsidize its imports. The same remark would hold for a monopolist exporter, a case that has also been analysed by Dasgupta and Stiglitz (1985).

To conclude, if the marginal increase in the first-period domestic price caused by an increase of the tariff is higher than the marginal increase of the tariff itself, then the importing country will choose to subsidize its first-period imports. In the opposite case, a subsidy on imports will still be appropriate if the learning effects are strong enough and/or the imports constitute a significant part of world's production; otherwise the importing country will impose a tariff on its first-period imports.

Very similar to the model described above is the recent work of Fudenberg and Tirole (1984a) and of Bulow, Geanakopoulos, and Klemperer (1985). These models are two-period ones in which the firms rather than the governments commit themselves to, say, capacity levels. Since these commitments are irreversible, they have the same effects as a tax or a subsidy imposed by a government. The optimal strategies adopted by the firms depend on the nature of the game they play. In the

Cournot case their strategies involve a higher level of capacity than a one-stage-game would entail (recall that in our model we have instead a higher level of first-period output); in the Bertrand case, a lower level is required. In the terminology of Fudenberg and Tirole, in the first case the firms adopt a strategy of a 'fat cat', whereas in the second case they want to be regarded as 'puppy dogs'.

Brander and Spencer (1981) consider the case of a foreign monopolist exporter and a domestic importing country. They assume that the monopolist uses limit-pricing to deter entry of the domestic firms into the market. Then it can be shown that, so long as the foreign monopolist's optimal strategy remains the limit-pricing one, the domestic country can capture part or all of the monopolist's profits by imposing a tariff; the tariff in this case is used as a 'rent-extracting' device.

Krugman (1984) develops a two-country duopoly model similar to one we have already presented, that is, with the two firms operating under a learning curve. The two markets are segmented owing to transportation costs. We know (Section 2.1) that in this case reciprocal dumping will take place; both firms will supply both markets. Therefore there is an interdependence in their marginal costs. Krugman examines the 'open-loop' equilibrium of this model; in particular, he assumes that the foreign firm reacts passively to any trade intervention made by the domestic government. Under this assumption, it is then clear that protection of the domestic market, which excludes the foreign firm from it partly or totally, will raise the output of the domestic firm and lower that of the foreign firm. In turn, this will lower the domestic firm's marginal cost and will raise its rival's one. Therefore, the equilibrium in both the home and the foreign market will shift in favour of the domestic firm, which demonstrates that import protection can also act as export promotion. This is the main message that Krugman wished to deliver. None the less, although Krugman's paper gives useful insights, one needs to observe that the key to the result lies in the assumption concerning the behaviour of the foreign firm. The open-loop equilibrium is not at least in my opinion, a useful one for multi-period strategic games; in fact, it erodes the strategic character of the game.

4. A Concluding Comment

It should by now be clear that the line of research presented above has a distinctly neo-protectionist character. However, one should be careful not to jump prematurely to conclusions; the body of research on imperfectly competitive markets and international trade, although growing rapidly, is still in its infancy. In particular, we are still seeking general principles in a more general equilibrium setting. None the less, it is also evident that, as soon as we depart from the traditional Walrasian environment to an imperfectly competitive one—being oligopolistic or Chamberlinian in nature—a number of conventional beliefs related to trade patterns and/or commercial policies must, in one way or another, be modified or even abandoned. It is not unreasonable, therefore, to suspect that the theoretical challenges of this area of economic theory will generate a considerable volume of literature over the coming years.

PART III

10

Missing Markets: Consequences and Remedies

DAVID M. NEWBERY

1. Introduction

Economists frequently defend the case for government intervention in the economy on the grounds that without such intervention the markets would fail to achieve an efficient allocation of goods. The First Theorem of Welfare Economics states that, if markets are complete, competitive, and in equilibrium, then the allocation is Pareto-efficient.[1] That is, it is impossible to find an alternative feasible production plan and allocation of goods among consumers which makes at least one consumer better off and none worse off. The proof is simple. A competitive equilibrium is one in which each firm maximizes the value of its net output, taking prices as given, and each consumer chooses the best bundle of goods, given the same prices and his budget constraint (i.e. the value of his endowment). At these prices the value of supply must equal the value of demand. If the allocation were not Pareto-efficient, then it would be possible to find an alternative feasible allocation that made one consumer, say Mr Jones, better off and none worse off. The value of Mr Jones's new bundle must be higher than his original bundle, else he would have chosen it, and the values of all other bundles must be at least as high as the original bundles (for the same reason), so the value of the total consumer demand is greater than before. But this is impossible, for it must equal the value of production, which had already been maximized and therefore cannot be increased. Thus it is impossible to make anyone better off without making someone else worse off, and the original allocation must therefore have been efficient.

Of course, efficiency by itself is quite inadequate, as the allocation may be grossly inequitable. The Fundamental Theorem of Welfare Economics claims that, if social welfare is an increasing function of individual

I am grateful to Bob Evans and Herbert Stein for comments on an earlier draft and to Christine Hudson for proofreading.

[1] The proof requires the additional but mild technical assumption that no consumer is satiated; that is, it must be possible to find a small change in each consumer's consumption which he strictly prefers to the original allocation (see, e.g., Koopmans 1957: 47). It also requires that there are no externalities, but this can be interpreted as a market completeness condition, where externalities and public goods are reinterpreted as named private goods. See below.

utilities, and if production and preference sets are convex (i.e. no increasing returns), then the allocation that maximizes social welfare could in principle be supported by a complete set of competitive markets and a suitable redistribution of initial endowments. Efficiency *is* desirable, provided that income can be redistributed by non-distortionary lump-sum transfers. On the face of it, this theorem does not appear to have much practical relevance, as the Benevolent Dictator entrusted with achieving the social optimum would need complete information about tastes in order to determine the appropriate set of lump-sum transfers. This information could not be derived by observations on consumers' choices, for if consumers knew that their liability to taxes depended upon their revealed choices, then they would alter these choices. The taxes would cease to be non-distortionary, and would in fact amount to income and commodity taxes.

The next important development came with the paper of Diamond and Mirrlees (1971). They showed that, if markets were competitive and pure profits were either zero (as they would be under constant returns) or completely taxed, then the best tax structure would preserve production efficiency, and redistribute income by taxes on final consumers—some combination of value added taxes and direct taxes. In the plausible case in which commodity taxes gave no additional leverage over the distribution of income compared with what could be achieved through the system of direct taxes and transfers, indirect taxes would not be needed. Once again, efficiency, or, to be precise, production efficiency, became a desirable objective of public policy. This in turn meant that the standard approach for an economist arguing the need for a policy intervention in the productive sector was first to identify the market failure responsible for the inefficiency, and then to propose a remedy to eliminate the source of the inefficiency (or at least to improve the allocation as far as possible). In this context another powerful organizing principle was that corrective interventions should be directed as closely as feasible to the source of the market failure.

Market failure means that the existing markets fail to achieve the efficient allocation that the idealized, perfectly competitive markets of the First Theorem would ensure. They may fail for a variety of reasons—perhaps most obviously because agents find it profitable to exercise market power. In this chapter I wish to explore a particular type of market failure: that caused by incompleteness of the market structure. The market structure may be incomplete in many ways, as is shown in the next section, but the main emphasis in this chapter will be on missing risk or insurance markets.

2. Types of Market Incompleteness

It is useful to distinguish two senses in which markets may be incomplete. Suppose first of all that there are no externalities or public goods, so that all goods are pure private goods.[2] For the First Theorem to apply, goods must be distinguished by their physical characteristics, by their place and date of delivery, and also by the state of the world. Thus, a taxi to meet the 18.46 train in Cambridge on 1 June 1988, if raining, is distinguished from the same taxi if sunny (and is presumably more valuable). In the idealized world of abstract General Equilibrium Theory (GE), agents have a complete preference ordering over all such goods (and firms have full information about all production possibilities of turning inputs into bundles of outputs of these goods). At the beginning of time, they contract on the complete set of markets at the announced market-clearing set of prices. Thereafter, as time passes and the sequence of actual states of the world unfolds, they deliver and receive the contracted amounts of goods. Obviously, this is an extraordinary notion, and quite impossible. There is a rich set of spot markets at each date, but only some twenty to thirty goods can be traded on futures markets, and the number of insurance markets is similarly very restricted. (Perhaps a more fundamental criticism of the relevance of General Equilibrium Theory is that the kinds of goods needed for the markets to work as postulated are reasonably well approximated only by those small number of goods that can be traded on futures markets. The reason is that futures markets require precisely defined, homogeneous and hence liquid goods which can be traded sight unseen. Even spot markets are unlikely to be perfectly competitive if goods do not satisfy these criteria, although they may be workably competitive for many purposes.)

Arrow (1953) suggested a slight weakening of the number of markets required for completeness by introducing the notion of pure securities which yield one unit of a numeraire good in a specified date–event pair, and zero otherwise. He demonstrated that any allocation achievable as a competitive equilibrium with a complete set of contingent markets (one for each contingent commodity) could also be achieved as a competitive equilibrium with a complete set of markets in pure securities in the initial period and subsequent spot markets. In other words, the securities offer the possibility of transferring purchasing power between states, and hence of obtaining a given bundle of goods in each state, provided the agents know the prices of goods that will rule on the spot markets in each state. For any future date, if there are S states and N goods, only $S + N$ transactions will be required instead of NS. For the present, it is unnecessary to distinguish between market completeness in the sense of a complete set of contingent markets and in the sense of a complete set of securities markets.

Market incompleteness in this first sense simply means that there is not a complete set of futures and contingent (or insurance) markets for each

---

[2] That is, the production or consumption of any good has no direct effect on the production possibilities of any firm, nor on the utility achievable from a given bundle of consumption goods purchased by any consumer.

date–event pair. Agents will typically be able to transfer purchasing power between periods (by holding assets), and may be able to trade a limited range of goods on futures markets. Although some risks are insurable (lives, houses, cars, health, belongings), for most of these the transaction costs are a very high fraction of the price (typically, more than half for such widely insured items as cars). The closest approximation to the contingent markets of GE are the shares issued by firms which give claims on the pattern of output of the firm across states of the world, although these differ from the pure Arrow securities in yielding revenue in each state of the world, not just in one state. Unless there are as many (linearly independent)[3] securities as states of the world, the market structure will remain incomplete.

The second sense in which markets may be incomplete is best appreciated in a static model with no uncertainty, so that futures and contingent markets are irrelevant. Suppose that there are H households, N pure private goods, and one pure public good, which, for concreteness, is a television transmission that can be received by everyone. This economy is equivalent to one in which the television company produces H identical TV signals, one for each household, and each of these is a separately distinguished named good ('TV signal for household h'). The number of goods has been increased from $N + 1$ to $N + H$, but each of them is now a pure private good. Market completeness now means that there is a market for each of the $N + H$ goods, and a competitive equilibrium is defined exactly as before. Supply equalling demand implies that each agent buys no more than the quantity of television produced (and if he buys less, its price falls to zero), and that the *sum* of the prices paid for the last unit of TV signal is equal to the value of production of the last unit, which will be set equal to the marginal cost of production. By constructing an isomorphic economy which satisfies the requirements of the First Theorem, we can identify the efficient equilibrium of an economy with a pure public good as the competitive equilibrium in the isomorphic economy, and hence can characterize the efficient equilibrium. The result is the same as the Samuelson (1954) condition that the *sum* of the marginal rates of substitution be equal to the marginal rate of transformation of the public good for some numeraire good.

3. Missing Markets for Externalities

On this view, externalities and public goods cause market failures because of market incompleteness. If the smoke from my polluting factory were the subject of a market transaction so that you, the owner of a neighbouring laundry, could signal to me the efficient level of smoke to

---

[3] *Pure* securities are necessarily linearly independent.

produce, then the externality would not lead to inefficiency. If there is no such market, and if there is no equivalent institutional arrangement, such as bargaining over relevant property rights in Coase's (1960) formulation, then the outcome is likely to be inefficient. On the face of it, this may seem a remarkably unhelpful way of approaching the general problem of externalities (including public goods), since these markets are most unlikely to exist, and even if they did exist they would not behave competitively, as only two agents would be able to transact on each named market. There are three immediate defences of the approach, as well as a further, rather less obvious one, which links the two senses in which markets may be incomplete.

The first defence has already been given; for by notionally completing the market structure we were able to characterize the efficient allocation with externalities by direct appeal to the First Theorem. The second defence is that markets are but one institutional device to facilitate efficient exchange, and, in the absence of markets, alternative institutional solutions may be sought. Once the problem is interpreted as one of missing markets, then one should be alerted to the possibility that market alternatives may exist. Before concluding that the absence of the market is prima facie evidence of market failure and hence of the need for corrective action, it is important to check that the alternative institutional solution is not already solving the problem better than the proposed intervention, and further, that the intervention will not interact with the existing remedy and make things worse. This principle—of taking account of non-market as well as market responses to market failure—has widespread validity, and will be illustrated further below.

This point is well illustrated by Coase's (1960) argument. Coase claimed that, provided property rights can be defined appropriately, and negotiations are costless, then it would seem sensible for bargaining to continue so long as there are mutually beneficial trades. The bargaining will cease only when an efficient equilibrium is reached. Given convexity, the Fundamental Theorem tells us that any efficient allocation can be supported as a competitive equilibrium together with a suitable redistribution of the initial endowment. Thus the bargaining can be thought of as the combination of two activities—a zero-sum game bargaining over the distribution of the initial endowment, and a beneficial trade at the competitive price. Bargaining, in this case induced by the threat of seeking legal redress, is an exact counterpart to a market transaction, while the definition of property rights corresponds to an allocation of initial endowment. Different allocations of the property rights (the right to clean air, or the right to emit smoke, in the earlier example) are equivalent to different allocations of initial endowment, and one's view of which party is damaging which, will depend on this allocation. Thus, if the laundry exercises its right to clean air, and the factory has to compensate the laundry for damage done, then the pollution harms the factory more than if there had been no laundry to protest.

This interpretation of Coase's bargaining solution immediately throws light on a long-standing controversy over the appropriate remedy for externalities, and provides the third defence for the value of the missing market approach to externalities. Pigou (1938), and more particularly his followers, such as Baumol and Oates (1975), argued that, if a factory emitted smoke which imposed an unrequited cost on the laundry, then the marginal social cost of producing the smoke exceeded the marginal private cost. The appropriate remedy was to impose a tax on smoke equal to the excess of the marginal social cost over the marginal private cost, thereby inducing the factory to choose the efficient level of smoke emission. In Figure 10.1 the appropriate level of tax would be t, according to this argument. Coase (1960) disputed this by arguing that, not only would bargaining lead to efficiency without the tax, but the tax would distort the bargaining outcome away from efficiency—in particular, there would be too little smoke produced. (See Coase 1960; Turvey 1963; or Newbery 1980: 110–25 for fuller details.) In the figure the effect of the tax t would be to shift the marginal benefit schedule down, so that, starting from the level of smoke z^*, both parties would find it advantageous to negotiate a reduction to z'.

If one starts from the missing market approach, though it is clear that the appropriate tax interpretation is a tax on smoke produced *together* with a subsidy on the recipient of the smoke—in short, the tax is transferred to the recipient(s), and thus removes their incentive to

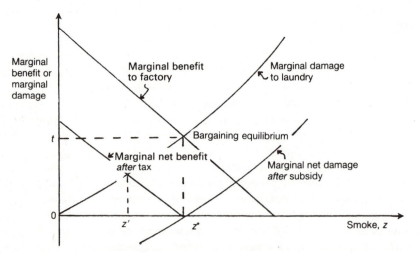

Fig. 10.1 *Effects of taxes and subsidies on two-agent externalities.*

bargain their way to an alternative (inefficient) position. The problem with the Pigouvian tax is that it mimics only one side of the market, while the tax subsidy solution replicates both sides of the transaction. The main reason for the subsidy is not one of equity, but to prevent further bargaining which would lead to inefficiency. If it could be guaranteed that such bargaining would not take place, then the subsidy would not be needed (but would do no harm). In the figure, the subsidy would shift the marginal damage schedule down by t, the two schedules would once again intersect at the efficient level z^*, and there would be no incentive to either party to negotiate any change in pollution levels from this point. Where large sums are at stake (such as the likely changes in property values caused by the location of a noisy airport, a nuclear waste processing plant, etc.), then failing to compensate those who suffer may well lead to political bargaining, even if not to the kind of bilateral financial bargaining envisaged by Coase.

3.1. The inefficiency of equilibria with externalities

The standard conclusion from the theory of public goods and externalities is that there is a presumption that the existing set of competitive markets will fail to ensure allocative efficiency. This view needs qualification in two important respects. The first has already been noted, for with two-person externalities bargaining is relatively simple and may lead, via the Coase argument, to efficiency by non-market means. If many agents are involved in producing and/or receiving the externality (traffic congestion, air pollution), then it becomes less plausible that the affected parties will bargain efficiently on a bilateral basis. The same argument applies to pure (non-excludable) public goods, which would require all beneficiaries to bargain collectively with the supplier.

The second qualification is that, for public goods and many-person externalities, there is an alternative institution to the market and bilateral bargaining—the political process. In Wicksell's (1896) formulation, the whole community assembles and votes on budget proposals, which include the level of supply of public good and the set of individual levies or taxes which together will finance the supply of the public good. Anyone may propose a budget (that is, a set of taxes and level of supply that breaks even) and everyone has a veto. Proposals are put to the vote, and if vetoed are rejected and replaced by the next alternative. Voting continues until there is unanimity, that is until no one exercises a veto, at which point the allocation must be efficient, since any inefficient allocation should be vetoed by those who would gain under the alternative in which at least one person is better off and no one is made worse off. The analogy with Coase's bargaining solution is close, for to work the process must involve no transaction costs. If everyone had complete information about preferences, then anyone could compute an efficient allocation and put it to the vote, and everyone else would know that no other proposal would be better for everyone, so that all alternatives would be vetoed; and they should unanimously accept the proposal. But it is the absence of public information which makes the public good problem intractible, and in its absence the policy would presumably have to try a very large number of alternatives, surely at high cost if only in terms of time.

The compromise is to accept majority voting, which will select the choice of the median voter. If, implausibly, preferences are symmetrically distributed, then this may be a good approximation to the efficient solution (Bowen 1943). If not, or if there are many public goods and preferences are not single-peaked, then the voting process may be less satisfactory (Atkinson and Stiglitz 1980: Lecture 10; Mueller 1976). If the public goods are local, there is yet another mechanism that will yield efficient outcomes under strong assumptions. Tiebout (1956) argued that, if there were enough competing local jurisdictions, each offering a menu of public goods and property taxes, and if consumers were mobile, then the consumers would choose to locate in the local jurisdiction that best matched their preferences. Essentially, the problem of preference revelation is solved by agents voting with their feet, rather than either voting (Wicksell) or buying (for normal private goods).

Although these various political alternatives to the market go some way towards correcting the market failures normally associated with public goods (and many-person externalities), there remain many examples of uncorrected market failures, and in these cases there is a strong presumption of inefficiency, and specifically of an undersupply of public goods, or an oversupply of harmful externalities. The natural question to ask is whether this presumption of inefficiency caused by missing externality markets (where not compensated by alternative institutions) carries over to the case of missing risk markets.

4. Missing Risk and Futures Markets

Before we can address the question of whether a competitive equilibrium with an incomplete set of risk and/or futures markets is efficient, we need an appropriate definition of efficiency. It does not seem reasonable to compare the allocation achievable with a complete set of markets with that achieved with an incomplete set of markets. There are usually good economic reasons why the market structure is incomplete. It may be that the costs of running the markets are too high, or that asymmetric information gives rise to adverse selection, moral hazard, or principal/agent problems. Whatever the form that the transaction costs take, it seems unreasonable to ignore them in choosing a benchmark for assessing the efficiency with which the economy allocates resources. At this point one can ask two rather different questions:

1. Does the economy provide the 'right' set of markets? Would the benefits of creating a new market (say, a futures market in some commodity) outweigh the costs of setting up and running the market?
2. Could the government reallocate resources using the existing set of markets and make everyone better off?

Both questions are relevant in judging the efficiency of an economy, though it is clear that the first question is both harder and more open-ended than the second. Later I shall report on a specific example in which creating a market may make everyone worse off, so that, even if it were costless to create, it would not be desirable to do so. It seems unlikely that we shall be able to proceed much beyond specific examples demonstrating that there is no presumption that the right set of markets will be set up. The second notion of efficiency is more tractable, and most studies of incomplete markets have taken this notion of *constrained efficiency* as the appropriate benchmark by which to judge the performance of an economy with an incomplete set of markets. The idea is that, in contemplating alternative allocations, the government is *constrained* to use the same set of markets.

The next issue raised by market incompleteness is more fundamental. Markets not only provide the opportunity for agents to trade, they also provide information about the terms on which trades may be made. If the market is missing, then agents will have to conjecture the terms on which trade might have taken place. Different conjectures will lead agents to take different actions, and will result in different equilibria (if, indeed, equilibrium is the appropriate description of this process of learning, revising conjectures, and adjusting actions). Consider a concrete example. Suppose a farmer must choose his crop pattern at the start of the agricultural year. The prices of the alternative crops will be determined on competitive markets, which will open after the harvest. Suppose also that the farmer faces no uncertainty in the production possibilities and output levels resulting from given input decisions (perhaps because he grows on irrigated land and is not affected by variations in rainfall). Nevertheless, the market-clearing price varies randomly (perhaps because set on world markets and influenced by randomness in supplies elsewhere). Finally, and to allow us to disentangle the risk-sharing and informational roles of futures markets, suppose that the farmer is risk-neutral.

If there are futures markets in the various crops, then the farmer should rationally use these futures prices as *action-certainty-equivalent* prices in choosing his crop plan—that is, he can ignore the uncertainty about the future market-clearing prices, and *act* as though he knew the future prices with *certainty*. (That is a general result, which does not require risk neutrality, though it does require that the only randomness lies in the future prices of goods that can be traded on futures markets.) In the simplest model, suppose that x is input, price is w, $f(x)$ is output, p is the future market-clearing price (a random variable), p^f is the futures price, and z is the level of sales on the futures market. The income of the farmer, y, then

$$y = pf(x) - wx + z(p^f - p). \tag{1}$$

He chooses x, z to maximize expected utility, $EU(y)$, for which the first-order conditions are

$$EU'pf' = UE'w; \qquad EU'p^f = EU'p \tag{2}$$

where $U' = U'(y)$, the marginal utility of income, and $f' = f(x)$, the marginal product of the input x. Combining the two equations of (2) gives

$$p^f f' = w \tag{3}$$

which implies that the farmer, in choosing the level of input, x, uses the futures price, p^f, and ignores the uncertainty of the future price, p. (The uncertainty about the future price, p, will affect the amount of hedging, z, that the farmer engages in, but not his production decisions.)

If the farmer is risk-neutral, and if he believes that the futures market is unbiased (that is, that $p^f = Ep$, the expected future price in the example above), then he would not wish to hedge his crops on the futures markets, and in this special case the sole function of the futures market would be to provide him with information about the expected future prices (Ep in the single crop example above). In the absence of futures markets, the farmer would need to conjecture, or form expectations, about future prices, and the complexity of his decision-making problems would be greatly increased.

If agents make mistaken forecasts about future prices, and hence choose a production plan that differs from the plan they would have chosen with the information provided by the futures markets, then the outcome will be inefficient. Completing the market structure, in this case providing futures markets, would eliminate these mistakes and the inefficiencies resulting from such mistakes. If we wish to make the strongest case for the constrained efficiency of incomplete markets, then it seems clear that agents should not be mistaken in their forecasts about future market-clearing prices. We are thus led to postulate that agents hold *rational expectations* about future market-clearing prices when testing for the efficiency of economies with incomplete markets. The argument for postulating rational expectations (RE) is not that it is a good description of reality, but that it allows us to distinguish between the various senses in which a competitive but incomplete market structure may be inefficient. Agents may be mistaken about market-clearing prices, in which case providing them with the correct information will eliminate inefficiencies arising from errors. The remaining inefficiencies are those due to market incompleteness alone.

4.1. Rational expectations

In its strong form, agents are said to hold RE if their beliefs about the market-clearing prices that will prevail in each state of the world are correct, and a RE equilibrium is one in which each agent bases his actions on these beliefs, and the resulting equilibrium confirms those beliefs—that is, the prices that actually prevail are those that were expected to prevail in that state. Stated in this strong form, the postulate is quite unreasonable, but it can be substantially modified and made somewhat more palatable. First, notice that the only expectations that are relevant are those that influence choices and actions. The prices of grain and cotton next harvest-time may be of the most direct interest to our farmer, but the prices of non-storable consumer goods may be of no interest, as there is nothing that can be done about them now.[4] Second, it may not be necessary for agents to know the prices that prevail in each state, but only a *sufficient statistic* of the price distribution, that is, a smaller set of pieces of information which summarize the relevant features of the problem. In the example considered above, the action-certainty-equivalent prices served as sufficient statistics of the price distributions, and these in turn were just equal to the expected future prices—a result that follows from the special assumptions of risk neutrality and no supply risk. If one wished to defend the empirical plausibility of RE in this particular model, then one would argue that over time, provided that tastes, technology, and the source of the randomness remained unchanged, farmers would repeatedly observe the market-clearing prices and would gradually improve the precision of their estimates of the mean prices. Of course, as they changed their estimates of the mean price, so their planned (and realized) levels of outputs would change, and the market-clearing prices would change in response to these supply changes. Given enough time, and provided the supply and demand schedules had slopes that ensured stability in the learning process, the learning process would converge and the agents would asymptotically learn the RE expected price.

If production were subject to shocks (if weather affected the yields per acre, for example), then the problem of identifying the action-certainty-

---

[4] If the farmer had to decide how much to save, then the real rate of interest on his savings would be important, and this requires some estimate of the future cost of living. But even this would not affect his choice of crops.

equivalent price becomes harder, for now the correlation between output and the market-clearing price will affect the return per acre—if p is the price and q output, then $Epq = EpEq + \text{cov}(p,q)$. A farmer who observes prices and his own level of output, but who fails to appreciate the correlation between them, may eventually learn Ep and Eq and believe that $Epq = EpEq$, but his expectations will not be rational according to the definition of RE. Put another way, the action-certainty-equivalent price is not equal to the expected price in this case. In general, its calculation will require information about higher moments of the distributions, although in this case it may be derived from estimates of average revenue per acre divided by average output: Epq/eq.

The whole issue of whether rational agents can learn of the rational expectations equilibrium is of the greatest importance in its own right, and is surveyed by Blume, Bray, and Easley (1982).

5. The Constrained Inefficiency of Rational Expectations Equilibria

I argued above that conventional externalities caused inefficiencies because of the absence of markets (or their analogues) on which the affected agents could exhaust the possibilities of beneficial trades. Essentially the same is true for missing risk markets, and the analogy is helpful. But there is one important difference, for there are special cases in which the absence of risk markets causes no inefficiency. More generally, with public goods or beneficial externalities, there is a presumption that the resulting equilibrium will diverge from the efficient equilibrium in a predictable direction—there will be an undersupply of the public good or the externality. With missing risk markets, it may not be at all obvious how the resulting equilibrium diverges from efficiency. Another way of expressing the same point is to say that a risky action gives rise to externalities (non-market-mediated impacts), but it may be hard to tell whether these externalities are beneficial or harmful (that is, whether the action should be further encouraged or discouraged).

I shall begin, therefore, by presenting an important example in which there are no risk or futures markets, but the outcome is not only constrained-efficient, but fully Pareto-efficient. (Nor is this coincidence accidental, as I shall argue below.) Consider an economy in which farmers grow grain which can be stored from one season to the next, and where we are interested in finding the socially optimal level of storage or carry-over. Suppose also that the only source of risk is the weather, which affects the output of grain, but nothing else. Larger levels of carry-over will increase the current demand for grain and drive up its price, while next year the wider availability of grain (from the stock as well as the new harvest) will depress prices. The price changes will affect the supply decisions of the farmers, and the level and variability of the farmers' incomes, as well as the level and variability of the real incomes of consumers. Solving for the optimal buffer stock (or equivalently the optimal degree of price stabilization) will in general be a complex problem.

Now suppose that everyone (farmers, consumers, and the stock-holders) has rational expectations and is risk-neutral, and that the government considers the distribution of income satisfactory. The competitive equilibrium in which the stockholders choose the expected profit-maximizing level of carry-over to buy will be Pareto-efficient, for the following reason. Consider an isomorphic economy which differs only in having a complete set of risk and futures markets for grain. Since it has a complete set of markets, the competitive equilibrium will be Pareto-efficient, and it will also be identical to the equilibrium of the original economy, for the following reasons. The futures and risk markets will reveal the prices in each state of the world, but this information is redundant as the agents are assumed to hold rational expectations. The markets allow trading opportunities, but since the agents are risk-neutral there will be no reason to insure, and hence no trade. Hence closing the markets will have no effect, and the original economy must therefore be Pareto-efficient.

This argument has two direct implications, as Newbery and Stiglitz (1982a) show. First, since commodity markets are usually considered prime examples of competitive markets, the case for a publicly funded price stabilization or buffer stock scheme must rest on the failure of one or more of the above assumptions—either the buffer stock agency has superior forecasting ability, or some of the agents are risk-averse. In the first case, publishing the forecasts is a more direct solution than operating a buffer stock, so only the argument of risk aversion is compelling. The question then resolves into whether risk aversion on the part of farmers, or consumers (or both), indicates that storage should be expanded or contracted.

The second implication is that it is often simpler to characterize and solve for a competitive equilibrium than to attempt to solve the original problem. It is then easy to see that the competitive solution is radically different from most proposed methods of stabilizing prices, and it is not difficult to show that these alternatives are costly as well as vulnerable to speculative attack by private stockholders (Newbery and Stiglitz, 1981). Further, it is also easier to identify the direction of the bias between the competitive and (risk-averse) social optimum than to solve for the social optimum directly. The question of whether to encourage or discourage storage can thus be directly addressed. In the present example, if consumers are risk-neutral (which is plausible if they spend a small fraction of their income on this grain), then storage should be increased if the demand schedule is linear and inelastic, and reduced if demand is isoelastic with elasticity greater than unity in absolute amout (Newbery) and Stiglitz, 1982a: 419). If consumers are risk-averse, which is likely if they are poor, they will want greater availability in periods of low harvests, and hence from their point of view increasing storage is desirable.

This example thus shows that competitive equilibrium may be Pareto-efficient, but that if agents are risk-averse and cannot insure via futures or risk markets, then the rational expectations competitive equilibrium is constrained inefficient. Perhaps not surprisingly, since efficiency is possible, and since price stabilization may reduce or increase *income* risk for producers, the bias (the divergence between the competitive and constrained efficient equilibrium) could be of either sign. The next example illustrates the potential inefficiency of competitive equilibrium more dramatically, and allows us to explore the question of market structure raised above. In it I shall show that it may be Pareto-improving to *reduce* the number of markets, thus casting doubt on the view that, if the market structure is incomplete, then increasing the number of active markets will improve matters.

5.1. Pareto-inferior Free Trade

A perfectly symmetrical island is divided into two identical halves by a mountain range running north–south. Farmers on each side of the island can grow two crops—one risky, the other safe. The risky crop does well if there is rain, poorly if not, while the safe crop always produces the same yield. If the wind blows from the west it rains in the west and is dry in the east, and conversely. With equal probability, the wind blows either from the east or the west, but the sum of the output per acre of the risky crop in the west and the east is always the same. Consumers have unit (price)-elastic demands for the two crops, and constant incomes.

Now compare two market configurations. In the first, there is no trade in the two crops between the two halves of the island, so that for agricultural purposes they are autarkic. The farmers face a unit-elastic demand for each crop, so total consumer expenditure on each crop is always the same, and hence so is revenue and farmers' incomes, regardless of the state of the world (rain or dry). Farmers therefore face no income risk, for although their output varies, so does the price in an exactly offsetting manner. Consumers bear all the risk, for their consumption of the risky crop varies with the weather.

In the alternative market equilibrium, there is free trade in agricultural goods (perhaps a pass through the mountains is opened up). As both halves are identical, there is a symmetrical equilibrium in which farmers on each side plant the same area of risky crops, and the total production is constant. Consequently the price of both crops is now constant, and consumers bear no risk. The output of farmers continues to vary, but since the price is constant, their incomes now fluctuate with the weather and all the risk is borne by the farmers. As the risky crop is now truly risky for the farmers, they reduce the amount of the risky crop planted and increase the amount of the safe crop. This in turn drives up the average price of the risky crop to the consumers.

It is relatively easy to compare the two configurations, and the details are set out in Newbery and Stiglitz (1981: Ch. 23). Free trade is unambiguously worse than agricultural autarky for the farmers, as their average income is unchanged (the unit-elastic demand assumption), but it is now risky instead of constant. If the consumers were risk-neutral, they would also prefer the allocation between the crops chosen by the farmers under autarky to that produced under free trade. If they are risk-averse, then the two factors work in opposite directions. They would prefer the risklessness of free trade and the consumption bundle of autarky, and, depending on the relative magnitudes of their risk aversion and that of farmers (which will determine the size of the reallocation of outputs in going from autarky to free trade), they will prefer either autarky or free trade. In particular, if farmers are sufficiently risk-averse and consumers are sufficiently insensitive to risk, both groups will be better off under autarky than with free trade.

Obviously the example is contrived, but its simplicity makes its various implications much clearer. The first implication is that it may be possible to make everyone better off by closing down a market or markets (in this case the market for the risky good). It is certainly not true that increasing the number of markets improves matters starting from an incomplete set. (Only if all but one market is present could this be deduced.) As an immediate consequence, the free trade competitive equilibrium is constrained-inefficient. In fact, a rather stronger result holds, for reductions in the average level of trade will make both consumers and producers better off provided only that farmers are sufficiently risk-averse.[5] The third lesson that can be drawn is that when the market structure is incomplete, the remaining markets perform multiple tasks, allocating commodities and risk jointly. Agents cannot unbundle the combination of goods and risk offered, but a change in the market structure provides different bundles, which may be better or worse. Thus, the unit-elastic demand schedule facing farmers as a whole offers them income insurance and a market for their risky crop. A move to free trade

---

[5] This follows because a small reduction in trade only exposes consumers to a small amount of risk, which is essentially costless, though it has a first-order effect on the level of risk facing producers. Consequently the allocative effect of changing crop patterns dominates the risk effect for consumers initially, at least if producers are sufficiently risk-averse (see Newbery and Stiglitz 1981: 362.)

eliminates the implicit income insurance offered by the commodity market, and makes farmers worse off.

Another way of making the same point is that, when a farmer chooses his level of output of the risky crop, he acts competitively in taking the pattern of prices and risk as given. His action, however, changes the pattern of risk facing other farmers. (In this example, it affects the income risk of farmers in the other region.) This risk is costly, but the farmer is not penalized for increasing the level of risk—his action thus creates a negative externality of increased riskiness. The risk in the economy can also be thought of as a public good (or bad), collectively produced by the individual actions of a large number of uncoordinated agents. As with normal public goods, there is every reason to expect that the level of supply (in this case the amount and nature of the risk) will be inefficient. There is thus a close analogy between viewing externalities as examples of market incompleteness, and viewing market incompleteness as giving rise to externalities.[6]

One final conclusion can be drawn from this very simple example. If one asks what kind of interventions might be warranted to alleviate the inefficiency of free trade, then two natural instruments suggest themselves. It is relatively easy to show that some trade is preferable to autarky, just as some restriction on trade is preferable to free trade for sufficiently risk-averse producers. Consequently neither extreme is ideal, and some intermediate level of trade will be preferable. Since the object is to reduce the level of trade below the free trade level, but not to eliminate it, the choice would seem to be between tariffs or quotas. In the absence of risk, the two are equivalent (provided the quotas are auctioned, or the tariff revenue is returned to the producers as lump-sum transfers). In the presence of risk the two differ markedly. Tariffs keep the price difference between the two countries at or below the height of the tariff barrier. If outputs are relatively similar in the two regions (so that autarky prices would be similar), the tariffs prevent trade, but for large differences in output trade is only moderately restricted. Quotas act in the opposite way, allowing free trade for small differences in output (when the trade flows are less than the quota limit), but restricting trade relatively more with large discrepancies. Tariffs truncate the price distribution while quotas truncate the trade distribution, and the two have markedly different impacts on the level of risk associated with any

---

[6] One might wonder why creating risk markets would solve the externality problem, for it appears that the farmer whose actions contributes to the risk would not be charged or paid for the effect his actions had on risk. The point is that those affected by risk can insure themselves if there is a complete set of risk markets, and their demand for insurance will affect the price of insurance, which in turn will affect the farmer's supply decisions, and hence the supply of risk. Creating risk markets transforms direct externalities into pecuniary externalities, which affect the distribution of income, but not the efficiency of equilibrium.

average level of trade. The implication is that the choice of optimal policy intervention is now more complex, for it may be desirable to use price interventions such as taxes or tariffs, or it may be preferable to use quantity controls such as quotas, rations, or the like.

6. The Improbability of Constrained Efficiency

The storage example showed that, if agents were risk-neutral and held rational expectations, then the competitive equilibrium was not only constrained-efficient but fully (i.e. Pareto-) efficient. This appears to be a general result. Newbery and Stiglitz (1982b) examined a more general model of production under risk, where outputs affected relative prices. They allowed the government to make lump-sum transfers which did not depend on the state of the world (this ensures that efficiency and social optimality go together), and to control the choice of technique (i.e. the risky production choice) but not to introduce additional markets. The resulting choice, which maximizes social welfare subject to the existing set of markets, can then be compared with the market equilibrium—if they coincide, then the market equilibrium is constrained-efficient. Their basic result has already been used in the storage example; a sufficient condition for the constrained optimality of the market equilibrium is the *redundancy* of risk markets. Markets are said to be redundant if their absence makes no difference to anyone's welfare, for example if there is no trade on them. Further, if risk markets are redundant, then the market equilibrium is a full Pareto optimum. The interesting question is whether the redundancy of risk markets is *necessary* as well as sufficient for constrained (and hence also full) efficiency.

It is possible to find conditions under which risk markets are redundant, but they are very stringent, and amount to conditions under which either there is no risk, or the agents are risk-neutral in the relevant sense. For example, if consumers' demands are unit-elastic and all producers experience perfectly correlated risk, then, as in the autarkic island example, the producers experience no risk as a result of stochastic production. If in addition consumers are *price*-risk-neutral,[7] then they will be indifferent to the resulting price fluctuations. The risk markets would be redundant, as farmers would not experience risk and the consumers would not worry about risk.

---

[7] Income risk neutrality means that agents are indifferent between a gamble involving a risky income receipt and the expected value of the gamble. Price risk neutrality means that an agent is indifferent between the option to buy the commodity at a variable price and the option to buy at a certain price with the same expected value. The two concepts differ, and price risk neutrality is arguably a less restrictive assumption than income risk neutrality. Indeed, in general consumers would prefer to buy at random prices than at the average price, since the indirect utility function defined over prices is normally convex. See Newbery and Stiglitz (1981).

Any slight perturbation of technology (perfect risk correlation) or tastes (unit elasticity of demands, attitudes to risk) will destroy the identity between the market equilibrium and the constrained social optimum, and hence will reveal the market equilibrium to be inefficient. In that sense one can say that *generically* (i.e. almost always) the market equilibrium is constrained-inefficient, and that generically the redundancy of risk markets is necessary (as well as sufficient) for constrained optimality. In this sense constrained efficiency is effectively as stringent a condition as full Pareto efficiency.

Geanakoplos and Polemarchakis (1985) have established essentially the same result for the case of incomplete asset markets, using formal mathematical techniques. They show that the competitive equilibrium allocations are generically constrained-suboptimal when agents have perfect conditional foresight (equivalent to the strong form of rational expectations set out above). They show in one example that, if individuals could have been induced to save different amounts, and hence to hold a different portfolio of assets, they could all have been made better off. Their intuitive explanation parallels that given above, for they point out that any asset reallocation in an economy has two effects: a direct income effect, and an indirect effect caused by price changes. When the asset market is complete, the price changes can be decomposed into a combination of assets that have already been priced by the market. Thus small changes in individual asset holdings keep the agents on their original budget constraints (and hence locally keep them at the same level of well-being). These changes therefore create no opportunities not already presented by the existing set of feasible trades, and there is no way of making anyone better off. When the asset markets are incomplete, however, the resulting price changes of a perturbation will generically cause income redistributions across states which the market itself could not directly offer. As Geanakoplos and Polemarchakis put it, 'In essence, the central planner has access to a wider class of assets than those directly traded.'

They also show that there are special cases in which markets are constrained-efficient. There is an apparent perversity in that, although the examples are in some sense improbable (compared with all the specifications of technology and taste that one might have chosen), they seem likely to be chosen by randomly drawn economists, whose criterion for specifying a model is not so much that it is representative as tractable. We now know that, if there is multiplicative risk which does not affect relative commodity prices (technological risk in a one-commodity world, as in Diamond's 1967 model of the stock market), then, although the stock market is an incomplete asset market (which does not allow one to insure against particular states of the world occurring, only against bundles of states), it nevertheless is sufficient for constrained efficiency.

This result no longer holds once commodity prices vary across states of the world, which in general they will.

The conclusion so far is thus rather pessimistic. Since the market structure is self-evidently incomplete, there is no presumption that the market equilibrium is constrained-efficient, even if firms behave competitively and everyone holds rational expectations. The next question to ask is whether the inefficiencies are large enough to warrant government intervention.

6.1. The costs of competitive inefficiency

If one is to argue that the failures of the competitive market justify government intervention, then a number of subsidiary arguments must be established. First, one would have to argue that the inefficiencies are significant. If the potential improvements in social welfare are trivial, then it is difficult to claim that they should attract pressing attention. Second, before justifying government intervention, one would have to be sure that existing institutional solutions (such as futures markets, long-term contracts between firms, and various privately conducted activities such as commercial storage) are not already achieving essentially the same benefits at lower cost. Put another way, it is important to measure the benefits of intervention relative to the existing set of markets and other institutional arrangements. Third, it must be possible to collect the information needed to identify the required intervention without excessive cost (relative to the potential gains). Finally, one would have to be confident that the proposed intervention would indeed achieve its objective at lower cost than the available benefits. That is, one would have to be confident that government failures are less serious than market failures.

These questions would seem to be very specific, and the answers will presumably depend on the particular market failure under study. The answers will also depend on the type of intervention, bearing in mind the two different ways in which the market may be inefficient. If the concern is with the constrained inefficiency of the existing set of markets, then the problem is to devise a set of taxes or quantity restrictions to introduce into the existing market structure. At a more ambitious level, the aim may be to expand the set of markets or institutions in order to deal with the perceived high cost of their absence. Nevertheless, it would be useful to know whether the gains from intervention are usually small, or sometimes large. I shall argue that the gains from intervention appear to be small if the government is constrained to the existing market structure, and are peculiarly difficult to identify in most cases. The more promising alternative is to create new institutions, but even here it is difficult to find convincing cases of large potential benefits when single market failures are considered, at least if the risks currently being privately borne do not involve asymmetric information. The main reason for this is that there frequently exist a variety of alternative institutional responses which are likely to achieve most of the readily available gains from intervention. This is not to deny that there may be important cases where the costs of market absence may be high; but the conjecture is that this is likely to be because the costs of operating markets or market substitutes are also high, typically because of the difficulty of obtaining the relevant unbiased information. Such cases are discussed later, and there may well be cases where government intervention is highly cost-effective.

6.2. The potential benefits of reducing constrained inefficiencies

The first point to make is that the potential gains from intervening in the existing market structure are bounded above by the gains from completing the market structure, and are likely to be substantially less than such gains. These gains can be roughly quantified for single production activities (such as the risks involved in growing grain, or being a farmer) and likewise for consumption (having to buy grain at variable and uninsurable prices), and some rough attempts are offered below. Of course the cumulative losses involved in not having a complete set of markets for all activities may be very large indeed, but that is hardly a useful benchmark—policies are usually directed to deal with the problems arising in a particular activity, not in the economy as a whole. The gains to be had in single markets do not appear to be very large—less than 5 per cent of average income might be a reasonable estimate for the agricultural examples considered in the next section. It is of course possible that someone could construct a different type of example in which the gains were substantially greater, and to do so would be a valuable contribution.

The other alternative is to model some particular economic activity in which constrained inefficiency is felt to be severe, and compute the numerical value of the difference between the constrained optimum and the market equilibrium. I know of only one such numerical calculation, though others could doubtless be provided. Newbery and Stiglitz (1982b) compare the market and efficient choice of technique in a model in which farmers can choose the pattern of outputs across two states of the world (wet and dry, for example) along a linear transformation schedule. (This is likely to overstate the extent to which agents are able to choose between alternative patterns of output across states of the world, and so should give an upper bound to the benefits.) They calculate the proportional benefit from persuading farmers to choose the optimal choice of technique and hence eliminate the constrained inefficiency, and show it to be extremely small in a special example—perhaps as low as one-sixth of one per cent.[8]

Of course, the example is artificial, and no doubt better examples could be given. One of undoubted practical importance would be to calculate the loss of relying on competitive private storage rather than socially optimal storage, as in the first example, though the problem here is that is is hard to derive analytical expressions for the socially optimal (as opposed to the competitive) storage rule, and techniques such as those employed by Wright and Williams (1984) would be required. Again, it would not be very difficult to calculate the welfare gains from optimal tariff or quota intervention in the island example considered above, though this too is an artificial example devised to dramatize the potential inefficiencies of competitive equilibrium.

Artificial though these examples are, they share one feature which is likely to be robust. In each case the direction of the bias, as well as its magnitude, depends on hard-to-measure parameters such as the degree of relative risk aversion (discussed in the next section), or the elasticity of demand and the relative curvature of the demand schedule (as in the storage example). Thus, these interventions fail to satisfy the third criterion of ease of obtaining the necessary information set out above. Geanakoplos and Polemarchakis (1985) are if anything even more pessimistic about the feasibility of reducing inefficiency, arguing that even a complete knowledge of investors' market demands for assets will not in general be enough (and would in itself be impossible to obtain).

It is interesting to speculate on the circumstances in which the potential gains are likely to be large, and this is done in the next section.

7. The Benefits of Creating New Markets

If there appear to be small gains from reducing inefficiencies within the existing market structure, what about the possibility of addressing the problem of market incompleteness directly, either by creating new markets or by devising new institutions which allow the existing risks to be transferred and shared by those better able to bear them? Apart from

---

[8] The formula for the loss is approximately

$$L \approx \beta^2 (\alpha^m)^2 / [2(l - \beta)]$$

where $\beta = \alpha(1 - R^c)$, α is the expenditure share by consumers on the commodity (presumably small), R^c is the consumer's coefficient of relative risk aversion, and σ^m is the coefficient of variation of output at the market equilibrium. Thus, if $\alpha = 0.2$, $R^c = 2.0$ (see next section for a discussion of the meaning and measurement of the coefficient of relative risk aversion), and $\sigma = 0.3$ (erring if anything on the high side for all parameter values), then $L = 0.0015$, or less than one-sixth of one per cent.

being an interesting question in its own right, estimates of the potential gains should bound above the gains from direct market intervention, as argued in the previous section. For the moment I shall concentrate on cases of risky agricultural production, which has the great advantage that markets seem competitive, agents are numerous, and a wide variety of institutional responses to risk can be observed.

The first obvious question to ask is how costly self-insurance is for farmers, assuming that no alternative insurance possibilities are available. The standard method of measuring the cost of risk is to offer the farmer a choice between the risky wealth from farming, and a perfectly certain wealth whose value is somewhat less than the average or expected value of the risky wealth. The difference between this average value and the level of certain wealth which the farmer considers exactly as valuable is the *risk premium* associated with the risky choice, and the ratio of this premium to the certainty-equivalent wealth is the proportional risk premium—a useful dimensionless measure of the relative cost of bearing the risk. Figure 10.2 shows the risk premium ρ associated with an equal chance of receiving an amount $\bar{W} + h$ or $\bar{W} - h$. If W^* is the certainty-equivalent wealth, then $\rho = \bar{W} - W^*$. If $U(W)$ is the utility produced by receiving W, and $EU(W)$ is the expected utility, then ρ is equivalently defined by the equation

$$U(EW - \rho) = EU(W) = U(W^*). \tag{4}$$

An approximate value for ρ can be found by expanding $U(W)$ as a Taylor expansion about its mean value $\bar{W}$:

$$EU(W) \approx U(\bar{W}) + E(W - \bar{W})U'(\bar{W}) + E(W - \bar{W})^2 U''(\bar{W})/2. \tag{5}$$

(Primes refer to derivatives, and again E is the expectations operator.)

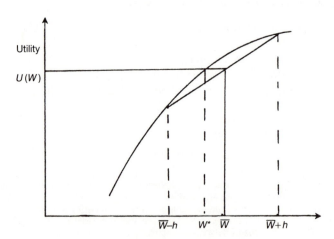

Fig. 10.2   *The value of risky income.*

The left-hand side of (4) can also be expressed as a Taylor expansion about $\bar{W}$:

$$U(\bar{W} - \rho) \approx U(\bar{W}) - \rho U'(\bar{W}). \tag{6}$$

Equate the right-hand sides of (5) and (6) to obtain

$$\rho \approx A \, \text{var}(W)/2, \tag{7}$$

where A is the coefficient of absolute risk aversion:

$$A \equiv -U''(W)/U'(W). \tag{8}$$

The proportional risk premium $\rho/\bar{W}$ can be expressed in terms of the coefficient of relative risk aversion, R, and the coefficient of variation (CV) of W, σ:

$$\rho/\bar{W} \approx R\sigma^2/2, \qquad R \equiv -WU''(W)/U'(W) = AW. \tag{9}$$

As shown, these expressions for the risk premium are approximate, with the accuracy of the approximation depending on the shape of the utility function and the nature of the risk. In certain cases these formulas are completely accurate, for example if W is normally distributed and the utility function exhibits constant absolute risk aversion (see Newbery and Stiglitz 1981: Ch. 6). Equation (9) is the most useful as it is dimensionless.

In principle, to find the cost of risk, all we need are attitudes to risk, measured by R, and a measure of the riskiness of income, σ. In practice, neither is easy to measure, for two closely related reasons. First, what we are really interested in is the variability in real consumption over time. If successive years' incomes were statistically independent, then farmers could consume at a steady rate in real terms and absorb fluctuations in income by saving and dissaving the difference between actual and normal or average income. Second, one is ideally interested in attitudes to variations in *wealth*—that is, in present discounted income, since that is what constrains the time-path of consumption. Observations on attitudes to risk by Binswanger (1981) suggest that individuals appear to treat each lottery independently, rather than calculating the effect of a particular risky choice on the underlying riskiness of total wealth. (See also Quizon, Binswanger, and Machina 1984.) One way of interpreting the evidence is that, although individuals appear to behave in a systematic and predict- able way, it is hard to believe that their behaviour reveals their underlying level of well-being according to the conventional theory of revealed preference (see Newbery and Stiglitz 1981: Ch. 7).

If, despite these reservations, we are prepared to accept the empirical evidence, then a value for R (defined over fluctuations in current income) of between 1 and 2 is defensible. The variability in the export revenue obtained from individual primary commodities by developing countries was typically 20–25 per cent for representative countries for cocoa, coffee, cotton, jute, and rubber for the period 1951–75 (Newbery and Stiglitz 1981: Table 20.5). The variability of an individual farmer's revenue from any one of these crops would typically be higher, since some smoothing takes place in the process of aggregation, but typically farmers receive income from more than one crop, and so their total farm revenue will be less variable than the variability of any one component. Then again, incomes will be more variable than revenue because the production costs will be less variable than revenue, but consumption will be less variable than income for the reasons set out above. As a compromise, suppose that a typical CV of income is 30 per cent. The cost of risk will be 9 per cent, taking a high value of $R = 2$; a farmer would on this argument be indifferent between his original risky income and a certain income 91 per cent of its average value.

Now a cost of risk of 9 per cent of average income is quite large, but it assumes that the farmer has no alternative but to bear all the risk. In practice, there is a whole variety of ways in which this cost can be reduced using existing institutions, and indeed, a large part of the reason for the existence of at least some of these institutions is that their risk-reducing benefits make them cost-effective. The main point to note about the formula for the cost of risk is that the cost goes up as the square of the risk, so quite small reductions in risk have a relatively large impact on the cost. For example, if the risk is shared equally between two parties, so that each bears half the risk, then the cost to each is only one quarter of the original cost (assuming equal degrees of risk aversion) and the total cost of risk has been halved. Share contracts, in which the landlord receives a set fraction (frequently about one-half) of the total harvest, provide just such an example of a risk-sharing and hence cost-reducing action. Futures markets play a similar role, and are particularly relevant in the present context, for they provide a partial response to the problem of market incompleteness, just as the stock exchange also provides a partial response. Both go some way towards completing the market structure, and both can be remarkably effective at reducing the costs of incompleteness, even if they do not eliminate it. They therefore merit further (if brief) attention.

7.1. Futures markets for risk reduction

Futures markets offer price insurance, whereas agents want income insurance. In some cases the two are synonymous, for if the only source of income risk is price risk, then futures markets allow this to be insured. For example, if the only source of risk is the fluctuating demand facing the producer, and his production is completely certain, then he can sell his entire future output by means of a futures contract for a currently known and certain price. A stockholder who buys grain now to sell later in the season can hedge his purchase by an offsetting futures sale now. Farmers, however, typically face production risk as well as price risk and cannot therefore perfectly insure their income. Nevertheless, if they have access to an *unbiased* futures market (that is, one in which the futures price is an unbiased predictor of the future spot price), they may be able to reduce their income risk substantially, the exact amount depending on the elasticity of market demand and the correlation between their own output and the spot price. For example, if the elasticity of market demand is 0.5 and the CV of output is 20 per cent, and if the sole source of risk lies on the supply side, with all farmers experiencing perfectly correlated risk, then an optimal trade on an unbiased futures market will reduce the cost of risk to one-quarter of its unhedged value. (See Newbery and Stiglitz 1981: 187, where the formulas lying behind such calculations are derived and presented.) In more realistic examples, both prices and outputs are risky and imperfectly correlated, so the benefits of futures trading will be lower; but if one takes the five crops mentioned above, and examines the leading producer of each commodity to determine the relevant risk and correlation coefficients (given in Newbery and Stiglitz 1981; 291, Table 20.4), then optimal trades on unbiased futures markets would reduce the cost of risk by between one-half and three-quarters. While there is still considerable dispute as to whether or not futures markets are biased, the consensus appears to be that, if there is a bias, it must be sufficiently small to be ambiguous.

Another way to judge the risk-reducing effectiveness of futures markets is to compare them with a popular alternative form of intervention—that of operating a buffer stock in order to stabilize the price. Again, price stabilization is an imperfect method of reducing income risk, but because it provides price insurance (compulsory rather than optional) it is easy to compare with futures markets. The answer is clear: futures markets offer better income insurance than perfect price stabilization unless the correlation between price and output is very low (typically less than about 20 per cent). (See Newbery and Stiglitz 1981: 187 for the formula and illustrative calculations.) If the correlation is very low, then neither price stabilization nor futures markets is very helpful in reducing risk, and the relative advantage of price stabilization is very small, and almost certainly offset by various disadvantages (Newbery 1983). Intuitively, the reason for the superiority of futures markets over price stabilization is that with a futures market the farmer is free to choose the optimal amount of harvest to hedge, while price stabilization gives him no choice, and may actually increase his income risk (as it did in the island example considered above). It is also worth remarking that perfect costless price stabilization is feasible only within a single country, not at the level of the whole world, where storage costs alone make it infeasible. (Within a single country the government can operate a marketing board offering a guaranteed price, and match local supply to demand by importing or exporting. Effectively the government absorbs all the price risk. See Newbery 1983.)

If the question is whether the government should set up a marketing board to stabilize prices, then the answer appears to be that a futures market would normally achieve larger benefits at lower cost, and in cases where this is disputable the benefits themselves are so small that any operating costs are likely to outweigh them. If the question is whether the government should introduce a futures market when there is currently not one available, the answer is problematic. Certainly futures markets appear to offer attractive insurance opportunities at low cost when they exist, and competition between major futures exchanges is continually generating new contracts for futures trading, many of which fail to attract sufficient volume to warrant continuing. The absence of a futures market for a particular commodity suggests either that there is insufficient demand (i.e. the value of the insurance services it offers are small compared with those currently available through alternative institutions), or that transactions costs are too high (perhaps because the commodity is insufficiently liquid), or that the government has either outlawed futures trading or intervened directly in the commodity markets (e.g. by operating a price stabilization scheme), and hence has eliminated an otherwise effective demand for futures trading. In the last case the remedy is clear, but in the first two cases it is not self-evident that the government would be able to operate a viable futures market whose social benefits exceeded the private benefits by enough to offset the transactions costs.

At this point it might be argued that the main benefit of a futures market is not its price insurance role, but its price discovery role, and this function is a non-appropriable public good (Grossman and Stiglitz 1980). Again, one can calculate the benefits of providing unbiased price information, at least if it is possible to describe the way in which agents make price forecasts in the absence of futures markets. Again, I know of few explicit calculations of the likely magnitude of such gains, though Newbery and Stiglitz (1981: 143–8) calculate their magnitude for an agricultural market in which initially producers make naive forecasts. If prices in such a market are stabilized, then this naive forecasting rule will yield correct decisions, but not if the market is stochastic and output is correlated with price. The results suggest that the gains from improved information are small compared with the gains from price stabilization (which themselves are not large, as argued above). They may be only a few per cent of the stabilization gains, although they have a much larger effect on the distribution of income between producers and consumers. The final point to make is that it may not be necessary to set up a futures market in order to provide better price forecasting services—the US Department of Agriculture disseminates large quantities of information about likely levels of production of major crops, and other institutions perform similar informative roles. Again, the relevant question is, How much additional information is provided, and at what additional value relative to its extra cost?

If futures markets and price stabilization through marketing boards offer small gains for countries in which output is poorly correlated with world price, then why not instruct the marketing board to stabilize revenue, rather than price? Specifically, if the normal or trend level of revenue is $\bar{R}$, and if actual production in a given year is Q, then the marketing board could set the price at $p = \bar{R}/Q$. Provided each farmer's output were reasonably well correlated with total output, this would offer income insurance. Moreover, this system of insurance is evidently attractive since it would still be in the interest of each farmer to produce the efficient level of output, as his own production would not affect the price he received. (Some systems of crop insurance guarantee a minimum return per acre, regardless of the farmer's effort. In such cases the farmer often has no incentive to care for the crop.) This proposal raises two obvious questions: If it is so attractive, why don't private insurance companies offer such contracts? If they don't, why don't governments offer them instead? The answers are that we do observe such contracts offered by the private sector, and there are government schemes of this kind, but the schemes are vulnerable to arbitrage in some cases, and hence would not be viable.

As an example of a privately supplied income insurance scheme similar to that proposed, consider the so-called flexible cash rent contract which is beginning to appear in areas of predominant share-cropping in the United States. Share contracts have already been cited as a risk-sharing and hence cost-reducing response to risk, but they appear to have the disadvantage that, by not rewarding the tenant with the full value of his marginal product, the tenant will be encouraged to slack unless carefully monitored. Share-cropping is very prevalent in the Midwest of the United States, and recently contracts have emerged in which the rent payable is determined by average yields in the local agro-climatic zone (DeBraal and Wunderlich 1983: 138, and refs.). If the weather is bad and yields are low, then rent is low and the tenant keeps a larger amount than under a fixed-rent tenancy, conversely if conditions are good. If on the other hand the tenant is idle or incompetent, then his rent is not thereby reduced, as it would under standard share tenancy contracts. (Although a landlord suspecting such behaviour would be unlikely to renew the contract, so there are incentives for efficiency even under traditional share cropping.) One reason why such schemes are not more prevalent is that they require accurate, timely, public, and credible information on yields for well-defined zones, and this information is likely to be obtained only by public agencies.

As examples of a government response with almost exactly this form, both the European Community's STABEX and the Compensatory Financing Facility of the IMF operate by lending the shortfall on export earnings on favourable terms to commodity exporters. The main problem with the pricing aspect of the proposal is that it may give unreasonable incentives to farmers or others to store commodities when domestic output is high and hence the market board price is low.

8. Other Responses to the Absence of Risk Markets

Two of the main responses have already been mentioned—diversification across current sources of income by choosing a variety of crops to grow, and diversification over time by averaging successive years' incomes. Again, if two crops yield the same average income, are equally risky, but are independent, then the cost of risk of a portfolio of equal amounts of each crop is only one-half that of specializing. Averaging over time is even more effective; for if successive years' incomes are independent, and the farmer can borrow and lend any amount at the same rate of interest, then the cost of risk can, over a long period of time, be reduced to approximately the same fraction as the annual interest rate (Newbery and Stiglitz 1981: 203). Even if farmers operate with a relatively short time-horizon and can only lend and not borrow, the effective cost of risk can still be greatly reduced.

Commodity storage is the standard way in which commodity price stabilization schemes operate, but it will be supplied by competitive agents if the storage costs are not too high relative to the price variability. It will in general provide some income stabilization (though not always), and provide a powerful stimulus to the development of forward and futures markets, which are relatively more effective ways of providing income insurance.

Futures markets operate when commodities are highly liquid—when they have unambiguous and readily replicated attributes, and are able to be traded sight unseen on markets with a large number of participants on both sides of the market. If these conditions are not satisfied, rather less satisfactory substitutes may emerge. Forward contracts differ from futures contracts in that the contract cannot be traded during its life on an organized market, so that its risk-sharing effect is limited to the two original signatories. Other agents not possessing the commodity or wishing to accept delivery cannot therefore use the market to hedge risks that are believed to be correlated with those affecting the commodity, as they can with futures markets. If, for example, I believe that the profitability of my aluminium smelter is positively correlated with the price of copper, then I can insure against low profits by selling copper futures. If there were no copper futures market, I could in principle buy spot copper, store it, and sell it forward, but it would then be more sensible to sell aluminium forward directly. To the extent that forward markets are thinner, they are likely to be less efficient in identifying the agents most willing to accept the risks involved, or in spreading the risks as widely and hence in lowering their total costs as much; but otherwise they have rather similar properties to futures markets.

Moving further down the range of less liquid substitutes for futures markets, long-term contracts are the next step, followed by vertical integration. The oil market offers a fascinating example of the gradual substitution of market-mediated relationships for the original internal transactions within the vertically integrated majors. As the industry evolved and new smaller firms entered at various points in the chain of production, from lifting oil to final sales to consumers, so the demand for more open markets in intermediate products grew. After the oil shocks of the 1970s, uncertainties about availability and price gave further impetus to the development of spot markets, forward markets, and eventually futures markets. (Mabro *et al.* 1986 give a fascinating account of the development of the Brent market for North Sea crude, which rapidly evolved in response to the need to establish a market price for North Sea crude in the face of a government-determined fiscal price used to determine tax liability. Although initially transactions were for specific cargoes of crude oil, they rapidly evolved into paper transactions comparable to those on futures markets.)

Perhaps the best example of long-term contracts are labour contracts in which workers are paid a relatively stable wage in the face of fluctuations in the value of their marginal product, the firm absorbing most of the risk. Such contracts are usually implicit to a considerable degree, if only because of the complexity of the contract and the difficulty of enforcement (see Newbery and Stiglitz 1985). They therefore encounter a variety of problems of enforcement which will be discussed below, but there is no doubt that they are a more plausible response to individual risk than the creation of a set of income insurance markets.

Gas is typically sold under long-term contracts by the producer to the distributor, in this case because it is usually difficult to reroute supplies to an alternative destination once the well has been drilled and the various pipeline connections made. For all long-term contracts, one of the key problems is how to ensure efficient short-run decisions in the absence of a short-run market-responsive price to guide decision makers. Indeed, it becomes necessary to distinguish between the long-run contract price and the short-run efficient price, the difference between the two being best seen as the insurance transfers between the signatories to the contract. Thus, a labour contract can be seen as the sum of a variable wage (equal to the short-run marginal product of the worker) and an insurance payment, equal to the difference between the insured wage (the contract wage) and the marginal product. At various times the worker will be paying in premiums (when his marginal product is high) and receiving compensation (when his marginal product is low). The employer should decide whether or not to employ or lay off the worker by comparing his marginal product with his reservation wage, not by comparing his contract wage with the marginal product, in which case (contract) wage rigidities should not lead to (inefficient) unemployment (though, as remarked above, there are problems with the enforcement of such contracts).

In the case of arm's-length long-term contracts, the same problem of making efficient decisions arises, and has prompted many economists to argue that the inflexibility of the contract price may make up for some missing futures or risk markets, but at the expense of suppressing the more important spot market. The problem is, of course, that spot transactions may be costly to organize, and the resulting markets may be very thin (just the original supplier and several potential distributors of gas, for example). Wilson (1986) has shown that rationing via priority service may be almost as efficient as a spot market, while economizing on these transaction costs. Customers can bid for different priorities, paying more for higher priority. In the event of a shortage, all high-priority customers are allocated their predetermined ration, then the next-highest-priority customers are served, until the supply is exhausted. Thus priority rations are rather like options to buy in certain states of the world at a predetermined (favourable) price, and they go some way to completing the market structure.

Finally, of course, firms making these and other contracts and thus accepting risk can in turn spread the risks by issuing equities, and the stock market itself is the most obvious evidence of an attempt to create risk markets. If the securities issued *span* the space of states of the world that is, if one treats a security as a vector of pay-offs with the *s*th element representing a pay-off in the *s*th state of the world, and there are as many linearly independent vectors as states of the world), then these securities act as a perfect substitute for a complete set of risk markets. It is hard to believe that securities offer much practical insurance against adverse states of the world, though their liquidity means that they can be widely held and the cost of the risks they represent greatly reduced.

It is hard to escape the conclusion that a wide variety of alternative methods exist for reducing the cost of risk, only some of which explicitly involve the use of insurance or futures markets. Given that the risk itself may not be so costly even if it is not diversified, it follows that the residual cost remaining to be further reduced by the government creating a new institution is likely to be even smaller, and not such as to give large comfort to one arguing against the admittedly imperfect market solution. One possible exception has already been noted, and that is where income insurance schemes for producers facing similar correlated risk would be attractive, but which need government support in collecting the necessary information on which the contracts would be written.

8.1. Moral hazard and adverse selection

At this point it is worth asking under what conditions is it likely to be difficult to shift risk, to better understand when the potential gains from institutional reform may be appreciable. This essentially reduces to asking when agents are likely to be denied insurance or loans (which would allow them to spread risks over time). Two standard problems, both arising from asymmetric information, may make insurance contracts unattractive: moral hazard, and adverse selection. The first arises because the insured person has less incentive to take care, or to continue to work as diligently as when uninsured. If the insurer could observe effort or care levels, this would not be a problem, and even if he cannot, it may be possible to devise incentive schemes that effectively deter such behaviour. In many cases, however, the moral hazard will remain, unless, as in the income scheme proposed above, it is possible to make the payments to an agent depend on the outcomes produced by other agents. The fact that moral hazard prevents otherwise desirable insurance contracts from emerging on sufficiently favourable terms does not mean that government intervention would solve the problem, for exactly the same problem would confront a government-run insurance scheme.

Adverse selection occurs when the insurance company cannot distinguish finely enough between different risk classes, although the agents themselves know in which class they fall. If forced to offer a standard contract to cover the average risk, agents facing higher risks will find the contract relatively more attractive, while those facing lower risks may find it sufficiently unattractive that they decline the insurance. The remaining pool of those seeking cover has thus been adversely selected to contain those of above-average risk. In such circumstances there may be no competitive equilibrium in the market for insurance, or there may be an equilibrium in which agents select from a range of contracts, thereby sorting themselves out into risk classes. If self-selection is feasible, the low-risk prospects will always receive less than complete insurance, for otherwise the high-risk agents would wish to choose the same contract and the contracts would not have served their purpose of sorting the risk classes (see Rothschild and Stiglitz 1976). Evidently, such market failures could result in considerable risk costs being borne by the un- or under-insured individuals. Furthermore, in these cases the adverse selection may be avoidable by the requirement that all agents must be compulsorily insured, perhaps by a state insurance scheme. The British national health service has this feature, and unemployment insurance is similarly typically compulsory and state supplied.

9. Conclusions

If the market structure is incomplete, the resulting market equilibrium is likely to be constrained-inefficient, even under the most favourable assumptions that agents are competitive and hold rational expectations. On the face of it, this suggests that government intervention, either within the existing market structure or, more radically, by expanding the set of markets or institutions available, might be able to improve matters. The argument advanced here is that the prospects for such intervention are poor, except in a small number of circumstances. Two cases where intervention might be effective were identified. The first arises where the information needed to provide appropriate contracts is potentially available, but has the nature of a pure public good. In such cases, the government has a natural role to play in collecting or arranging for the collection of this information. This step is likely to be sufficient for the emergence of privately organized remedies that are at least as effective as public ones. In the second example, adverse selection made non-coercive insurance schemes unprofitable, but the coercive power of the state offered a remedy.

In other cases it appeared that the benefits from government intervention within the existing market structure were likely to be extremely small, and required subtle information about the shapes of demand schedules and attitudes to risk which are almost impossible to identify. When it comes to creating new institutions, the government does not have a monopoly on institutional innovation, and the evidence from at least some parts of the economy is one of considerable ingenuity in meeting expressed needs for new types of contract. In fact, casual observation suggests that this inventiveness surpasses that of public sector bodies, which, if anything, since they are often created to deal with other kinds of market failure, have an even greater need for such innovation.

None of this is to deny that there may be desirable interventions, although my belief is that they will be associated with other forms of market failure than missing risk and futures markets. If markets are uncompetitive, if economies of scale are important, if externalities or public goods are at issue, then the conventional cases for public intervention survive. The aim here has been the more modest one of examining competitive but incomplete market structures, to see how far their inefficiencies warrant remedial intervention.

11

Rational Expectations, Information, and Asset Markets

MARGARET BRAY

1. Introduction

Financial markets are a subject of perpetual fascination to economists and others. There are very large sums of money to be gained and lost on them. They are obviously crucially important not only to the people and institutions who invest directly, but also to the many others who invest indirectly through holding unit trusts (mutual funds), pension or life assurance policies. Moreover, the financial markets do not operate in isolation; they affect and are affected by the rest of the economy.

One important economic function of such markets is the spreading and sharing of risk. An entrepreneur can reduce the risks that he carries by selling shares in his firm. Investors may be willing to carry some of the risk because they are less risk-averse than the entrepreneur. They may also be willing to invest even if they are more risk-averse because the market allows them to hold a diversified portfolio which reduces risk. Investing £10,000 in ten different firms whose profits are imperfectly correlated is very much less risky than investing £10,000 in one of the firms. The view that such markets perform a socially important function in spreading risk reasonably well is widely held. (See Arrow 1964 and Diamond 1967 for theoretical models.) But there are distinguished dissidents; in Chapter 12 of the *General Theory,* Keynes argues forcefully that the markets increasingly provide a casino for speculators, rather than a guide for investors, and may be socially useless or even positively dangerous.

Recent theoretical work on asset markets, based on the rational expectations hypothesis, has argued that they may have an additional informational role. Traders have information which affects their evaluation of the value of assets, the demand for the assets, and thus prices. Other traders may attempt to infer the information from prices. The major achievement of recent work has been to develop a coherent description of this phenomenon, and to use it to ask how well the markets transmit and aggregate the information.

I am grateful to Craig Alexander, Jeremy Edwards, Anna Lemessany, Peter Sinclair, and Martin Weale for comments on an earlier version of this paper.

Much of this literature is hlghly technical, and inaccessible without a considerable mathematical apparatus. Yet the basic issues can be understood with much less background, as this paper seeks to demonstrate. It is written as an introduction to recent work on information in asset markets, assuming intermediate microeconomics, enough calculus to differentiate a quadratic, a little manipulation of linear equations, and enough probability theory to know about means, variances, and conditional distributions. I use expected utility theory, but anyone who does not know the theory, and is willing to take on trust my assertion that it is a sensible way to model choice under uncertainty, should be able to follow the argument.

Much of the paper is concerned with elaborating a simple model. The model introduced in Section 2 is the standard deterministic partial equilibrium model of supply and demand in a spot market, modified by the assumption that production decisions must be made before the market operates on the basis of price expectations. I use this model to introduce a perfect foresight equilibrium, the deterministic version of a rational expectations equilibrium. In Section 3 I introduce a futures market, operating at the date when production decisions are made. A futures contract is a financial asset, whose gross return is the spot price. I argue that arbitrage implies that in this deterministic model, if expectations are held with certainty, the futures price must be equal to the present discounted value of the expected spot price. Section 4 introduces briefly the expected utility theory of choice under uncertainty. Section 5 applies this theory to a stochastic version of the model on the assumption that dealers are risk-neutral, using an arbitrage argument to establish that the futures price is equal to the present discounted value of the expected spot price. Section 6 shows how the simple arbitrage argument breaks down when risk-neutral dealers have diverse information, introducing the informational role of asset prices. The formal definition of a rational expectations equilibrium in an asset market with asymmetric information is introduced in Section 7. Section 8 introduces risk aversion, simplifying matters mathematically by working with exponential utility functions and normal random variables. The joint equilibrium of the spot and futures market when dealers are risk-averse is calculated, on the assumption that no one has any private information about the spot price when trading on the futures market. Information is introduced in Section 9, first on the assumption that all dealers have the same information, second on the assumption that there are informed and uninformed traders, but the informed traders all have the same information, and third on the assumption that dealers have diverse information. In this model the futures market is remarkably informationally efficient; it aggregates information perfectly. Section 10 is concerned with the implications and robustness of the informational efficiency result in this and related models. In the models I use, calculating the rational expectations equilibrium is relatively straightforward, but in Section 11 I introduce a version of the spot and futures market model which has no rational expectations equilibrium. I discuss the nature and significance of the problems associated with the existence of rational expectations equilibrium, and the literature on the subject. Section 12 attempts an evaluation of the models, discussing the assumptions, concentrating largely on the rational expectations assumption, and referring briefly to the empirical and experimental evidence. Section 13 discusses some open questions prompted by these models.

The results that I establish have no claims to originality. The first model that I develop has its origins in the cobweb model (Kaldor 1934), and in Muth's paper on rational expectations (1961). The futures market model is based on Danthine (1978), and is related to Grossman (1976, 1977) and Bray (1981). The non-existence example in Section 11 is new in detail, but is similar to that of Kreps (1977). I give references to other, related literature, where appropriate. A more technical introduction to this and many other topics can be found in Radner's (1982) survey of 'Equilibrium under Uncertainty' and in the symposium issue (April 1982) of the *Journal of Economic Theory* on 'Rational Expectations in Microeconomic Models', in particular the introduction by Jordan and Radner. Stiglitz (1982) discusses a range of issues concerned with information and capital markets.

2. Supply and Demand with a Production Lag: Perfect Foresight Equliibrium

In the standard model of supply and demand, production and consumption decisions are taken simultaneously, based on the price. If production takes time, production decisions have to be based on the expected price. For example, a farmer plants a crop in January which will be harvested and sold in June. To begin with, assume that there is no uncertainty, an assumption that will be relaxed in Section 4. Demand $D(p_s)$ is a deterministic function of p_s, the spot price of wheat in June. Supply $S(p_s^e)$ is a deterministic function of p_s^e, the farmers' point expectation belief in January about what the spot price will be in June. For now assume that all farmers are subjectively certain about what the price will be, and all have the same beliefs. If the market in June clears, supply equals demand: $D(p_s) = S(p_s^e)$. The expected price determines production which in turn determines the actual price. In fact, the price p_s is a function of the expected price.

In Figure 11.1, when the price is p_s^e, $Q = S(p_s^e)$ is produced. When Q is put on the spot market in June the price is p_s. If $p_s \neq p_s^e$, the farmers, despite their subjective certainty, are wrong. Beliefs are wrong unless

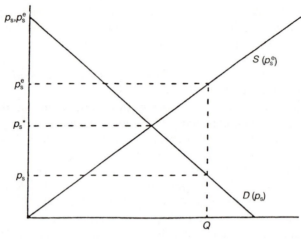

Fig. 11.1

$p_s^e = p_s^*$, the price at which the supply and demand curves intersect so that $S(p_s^*) = D(p_s^*)$. This could well be described as a self-fulfilling belief. However, the standard terminology is a perfect foresight equilibrium or, more recently (following Muth 1961), a rational expectations equilibrium.

A rational expectations equilibrium can be defined as a situation in which people do not make systematic mistakes in forecasting. In this case, where beliefs are point expectations held with certainty, rational expectations equilibrium requires that beliefs be correct, that is, that people have perfect foresight. The rational expectations assumption is now used very widely, but it remains controversial. The assumption avoids many of the difficult dynamic problems apparently associated with expectation formation, making it possible to proceed with other questions. For the time being I will simply assume rational expectations without further discussion, returning to the matter in Section 12.

3. Financing Production: Futures Markets and Arbitrage

The revenue from selling the crop arrives some time after most of the production costs are incurred. This leaves a farmer with the problem of finding funds to cover the investment in planting the crop. He may have sufficient wealth to finance this from his own resources. If not, he will have to borrow.

Assume that everyone knows that the price in June will be p_s. There are perfect capital markets; that is, the farmer can borrow or lend as much as he wishes at the same interest rate. £1 borrowed in January must be repaid with £$(1+r)$ in June. Suppose that a farmer has wealth W_0 in January, and incurs the costs of producing output y, which have a present discounted value in January of $C(y)$. He invests the remainder of his wealth $W_0 - C(y)$ at interest rate r until June. His wealth in June is the sum of his revenue from output $p_s y$ and the return on his other investment:

$$W = p_s y + [W_0 - C(y)](1+r) = p_s y - C(y)(1+r) + W_0(1+r).$$

The value of profits from production in June is $p_s y - C(y)(1+r)$. Note that $W_0 - C(y)$ may be negative, in which case the farmer is borrowing to cover some of his costs. The farmer maximizes his June wealth by maximizing profits. If C is a convex function of y and $p_s > C'(0)(1+r)$, this is done by setting $p_s = C'(y)(1+r)$. The value of y is independent of his initial wealth, which simply determines how much, if anything, he has to borrow.

The farmer may also finance his production by selling on the futures market. A futures market is an institution on which money is exchanged for promises to deliver goods in the future. For example, a farmer may sell wheat in January for delivery in June. As before, suppose the farmer has wealth W_0 in January, produces y, incurring costs $C(y)$, and sells z on the futures market at price p_f. This leaves him $W_0 - C(y) + p_f z$ to invest at interest r. In June he sells the remainder of his output $(y - z)$ on the spot market. His wealth in June is

$$W = p_s(y - z) + [W_0 - C(y) + p_f z](1+r)$$
$$= p_s y - C(y)(1+r) + [p_f(1+r) - p_s]z + W_0(1+r). \qquad (1)$$

The farmer maximizes his wealth, as before, by choosing output y so that $p_s = C'(y)(1+r)$. If $p_f > p_s/(1+r)$, so that the futures price exceeds the present discounted value of the spot price, he can make arbitrarily large profits by selling on the futures market. He will increase z indefinitely, and will wish to set $z > y$, selling more on the futures market than he produces, meeting the shortfall $(z - y)$ by buying on the spot market. However, he is unlikely to find a willing buyer at this price. There are two possible classes of buyers, consumers and speculators. Consumers (e.g. food manufacturers and wholesalers) may choose to buy futures in January rather than buying on the spot market in June, thus hedging against uncertainty about the June spot price. For the sake of simplicity, I will assume that consumers do not participate in the futures market; if they did, it would complicate the models without substantially affecting the conclusions. Speculators buy futures contracts, which they sell on the spot market, never actually taking delivery of the goods, in the hope of making a profit on the difference between the futures price and the present value of the spot price. Suppose a speculator with wealth W_0 in January buys x futures contracts in January, sells x on the spot market in June, and invests the rest of his wealth in the safe asset paying interest r. His wealth will be

$$W = p_s x + (W_0 - p_f x)(1 + r)$$

$$= [p_s - p_f(1 + r)]x + W_0(1 + r). \tag{2}$$

If $p_f > p_s/(1 + r)$, both speculators and farmers will wish to sell futures. With no willing buyers, the market cannot clear. If $p_f < p_s/(1 + r)$, both speculators and farmers will want to buy futures. Thus, the only price at which the futures market can clear is when $p_f = p_s/(1 + r)$. This is an example of an arbitrage argument—these arguments are based on the premise that in equilibrium it cannot be possible for anyone to make arbitrarily large certain profits. If the market is perfectly arbitraged, $p_s = p_f(1 + r)$. The wealth in June of farmers and speculators does not depend on the size of their future trades. In this deterministic model with perfect foresight, a futures contract is a safe asset paying interest r. There is no reason for anyone to use the futures market in preference to borrowing or lending at rate r elsewhere. If the futures market ceased to exist, no one would be any better or worse off.

In fact, under certainty there seems little reason for the futures market to exist. Any understanding of futures markets, and other asset markets such as the stock market, depends upon introducing uncertainty.

4. Choice under Uncertainty

The farmer faces risks in both the quantity and the price of output. A futures market allows the farmer to shift the price risks to speculators. If his output y is certain he can completely eliminate the risk by setting $z = y$, selling his entire output on the futures market. But why will the speculator be willing to assume the risk, and at what price? The currently available answers to this, and many other questions about economics under uncertainty, are derived from a widely accepted model of choice under uncertainty: the theory of expected utility. An introduction to the theory can be found in, among other places, Deaton and Muellbauer (1980), in a survey by Schoemaker (1982), or in a valuable collection of readings by Diamond and Rothschild (1978).

Assume that an investor has decided to invest a certain amount W_0 for a period. He has a number of different assets to choose between, and a definite set of beliefs about the joint probability distribution of the returns on the different assets. He cares only about the probability distribution of his wealth $\tilde{W}$ at the end of the period, which depends upon the way he allocates his initial wealth W_0 between the different assets. The theory of expected utility shows that, if his preferences over the probability distribution of $\tilde{W}$ satisfy some plausible assumptions, he will choose a portfolio that maximizes the mathematical expectation $EU(\bar{W})$ of a function $U(\bar{W})$, given his beliefs about the probabilities. For a discrete probability distribution, $EU(\bar{W}) = \sum_i U(W_i)p_i$ where W_i is wealth in state i and p_i the probability of state i. For a continuous probability distribution,

$$EU(\bar{W}) = \int_{-\infty}^{\infty} U(W)f(W)\, dW$$

where f is the probability density function. In both cases, the probability distribution depends upon the investor's beliefs, and his choice of portfolio.

The theory has two essential elements: the utility function, and the probability distribution which determines the mathematical expectation. The functional form of the utility function U describes attitudes to risk. U is increasing provided investors prefer more to less wealth. If $U(\bar{W}) = \bar{W}$ the investor is risk-neutral, caring only about expected wealth, and not at all about its riskiness. If $U(\bar{W})$ is strictly concave the investor is risk-averse, strictly preferring investments yielding the expectation of $\bar{W}$ for sure, to random $\bar{W}$. Risk aversion in investment choices for an individual seems highly plausible, and is often assumed.

The assumption that uncertainty can be described in terms of probability distributions is widely made today, but historically it has not commanded universal acceptance. Keynes was a notable dissenter. There is very little controversy about applying the mathematical theory of probability to assess the probabilities associated with a series of similar events, where after a time there are enough data to construct probabilities from frequency distributions (for example weather or life expectancy data), situations described by Knight (1921) as risk. The argument is rather whether meaningful probabilities can be assigned to unique events where there are no objective frequency data to rely on, situations described by Knight as uncertainty. The subjectivist or Bayesian viewpoint on probability is that Knight's distinction is invalid. It is always possible to elicit probabilities by forcing people to make bets (see Raiffa 1968). There is however no guarantee in subjectivist theory that different people will form the same probability distributions, unless there are frequency data to base them on, which brings us back to Knight's risk. For some purposes, it is enough to assume that people act as if they had subjective beliefs expressible as probability distributions. However, many models postulate that people have the same correct beliefs about probability distributions (rational expectations). These models do not seem to be applicable to situations that Knight would describe as uncertain.

I am now in a position to use the theory of expected utility to extend the theory of asset pricing under certainty to uncertainty. Initially I will assume risk neutrality, and will then proceed to consider risk aversion.

5. Risk Neutrality: Arbitrage Again

Returning to the futures market example, suppose that, once farmers have chosen their level of inputs, their output y is certain. The June spot price is uncertain because spot demand is uncertain. A risk-neutral farmer will choose his output y and futures sales z to maximize the expected value of his wealth; from (1), this is

$$E\tilde{W} = E\tilde{p}_s y - C(y)(1+r) + [p_f(1+r) - E\tilde{p}_s]z + W_0(1+r).$$

(Throughout this paper, a tilde above a variable indicates that it is random.) A speculator will choose his futures purchases x to maximize the expected value of his wealth; from (2), this is

$$E\tilde{W} = [E\tilde{p}_s - p_f(1+r)]x + W_0(1+r).$$

Decisions depend upon the mathematical expectation $E\tilde{p}_s$ of $\tilde{p}_s$, its average value. The risk-neutral dealers do not care about any other characteristics of the probability distribution. $E\tilde{p}_s$ is not a point expectation held with certainty; the dealers are aware that there is uncertainty and would expect to observe that usually $E\tilde{p}_s \neq \tilde{p}_s$.

Precisely the same arbitrage argument as before implies that, unless $p_f = E\tilde{p}_s/(1+r)$, there are unlimited positive expected profits to be made and the market cannot clear. The argument is less compelling than under certainty. Although a speculator may wish to exploit opportunities for making positive expected profits, he may not be able to do so. Suppose that $E\tilde{p}_s > p_f(1+r)$, so buying futures contracts generates a positive expected return. A risk-neutral speculator will choose to spend his entire wealth on futures contracts; he will also wish to borrow without limit to exploit further the opportunity for profit. There is a chance that the spot price will be so low that he cannot repay his debts; lending to the speculator becomes risky. Speculators may face either a higher interest rate than r, or limits on credit, limiting their ability to arbitrage the market.

6. Diverse Information

The simple arbitrage argument also breaks down if different dealers (farmers and speculators) have different beliefs about the expected spot price. This is not incompatible with the dealers having rational expectations, if they have access to different information. Suppose for example that $\tilde{p}_s = \tilde{I} + \tilde{e}$ where $\tilde{I}$ and $\tilde{e}$ are independent random variables; $E\tilde{e} = 0$, and so $E\tilde{p}_s = E\tilde{I}$. There are two types of dealers. The informed dealers observe $\tilde{I}$ before the futures market opens; their expectation of $\tilde{p}_s$ is conditional upon $\tilde{I}$, $E(\tilde{p}_s \mid \tilde{I}) = \tilde{I}$. The uninformed dealers observe nothing; their expectation of $\tilde{p}_s$ is $E\tilde{p}_s = E\tilde{I}$. If both types of dealers are risk-neutral, face no borrowing constraints, and stick to their beliefs, the informed will want to buy or sell an unlimited amount unless $p_f = E(\bar{p}_s \mid \bar{I})/(1+r) = \bar{I}/(1+r)$, and the uninformed dealers will want to buy or sell an unlimited amount unless $\bar{p}_f = E\bar{p}_s/(1+r)$. Unless by coincidence $E(\bar{p}_s \mid \bar{I}) = E\bar{p}_s$ (i.e. if $\bar{I} = E\bar{I}$), the market apparently cannot clear.

It is however most unlikely that the uninformed dealers will stick to their beliefs. Knowing that there are informed dealers in the market whose trading affects the futures price, they will try to make inferences from the futures price about the spot price. They are using the price of a financial asset, a futures contract, to make judgements about its quality. Judging quality from price is not confined to financial markets. Consumers may also do so, assuming that cheap goods are also cheap and nasty. One of the major successes of recent economic theory has been the development of models that take this into account.

In these models prices have two roles: their conventional role in determining budget sets for consumers and profit opportunities for firms, and an additional role in transmitting information. Hayek (1945), in a discussion of decentralization and planning, argues that the conventional role of prices must also be understood as an informational one. In standard Walrasian competitive equilibrium models, once households and firms know current prices, they have no use for any further information about the plans, characteristics, and opportunities of others in the economy; they need make no attempt to infer this information from prices. As Grossman (1981a) argues, recent models of asymmetric information move beyond this; some agents want some information held by others, in this case information about the spot price in the future. They try to infer as much information as they can from current prices. In some cases the price system may be entirely efficient at transmitting information; prices are so informative that there is no additional information currently known to anyone in the economy which would be helpful. In other cases prices may be less informationally efficient, conveying some information, but still leaving a frustrated desire to see the current contents of someone else's mind or computer file. In either case, agents are trying to look beyond prices, to solve an inference problem, which is unnecessary in standard Walrasian models. The central question addressed by the models that I am about to discuss is, How informationally efficient are prices? These models make use of the idea of a rational expectations equilibrium. I will now show how this equilibrium is defined, and explain how it yields an equilibrium price for this example.

7. Rational Expectations Equilibrium and Risk Neutrality

The definition of a rational expectations equilibrium for the spot and futures markets has four parts. A very similar definition can be formulated for any asset market model. The first part describes how dealers form their beliefs.

PART 1. Each dealer (farmer or speculator) observes some private information I_i and the futures price $\bar{p}_f$. Given this information, he has beliefs about the spot price $\bar{p}_s$ which can be expressed as a conditional probability distribution.

For example, dealer i might believe that, given the futures price $\bar{p}_f$ and private information $\bar{I}_i$, the conditional distribution of $\bar{p}_s$ was normal, with mean $E(\bar{p}_s \mid \bar{p}_f, \bar{I}_i) = \frac{1}{2}\bar{p}_f + \frac{1}{4}\bar{I}_i$ and variance $\frac{1}{8}$. At this stage I have not required that the beliefs be correct, only that they exist.

The second part of the definition states that, given their beliefs, dealers choose their portfolio in accordance with expected utility theory.

PART 2. Each dealer chooses the holding of futures contracts, and (for farmers) output which maximizes his expected utility, given his beliefs about the spot price, conditional upon his private information and the futures price.

Parts 1 and 2 of the definition give the supply and demand for futures. Note that supply and demand are affected both by the numerical value of the futures price and information, and by beliefs. If a risk-neutral dealer believes that $E(\bar{p}_s \mid \bar{p}_f, \bar{I}_i) = \frac{1}{2}\bar{p}_f + \frac{1}{4}\bar{I}_i$, he will buy or sell an unlimited amount depending on whether $\bar{p}_f - (\frac{1}{2}\bar{p}_f + \frac{1}{4}\bar{I}_i)/(1+r)$ is positive or negative. To emphasize this point, I will write $d_i(\bar{p}_f, \bar{I}_i; B_i)$ for dealer i's demand for futures, where B_i is shorthand for beliefs.

The next part of the definition is

PART 3. The spot and futures prices are at levels where both markets clear.

In different years the information will be different, so if the markets are to clear, prices must be a function of the information. Demand and the market-clearing prices also depend upon beliefs, so I will write

$$\bar{p}_f = f(\bar{I}_1, \bar{I}_2, \ldots, \bar{I}_n; B_1, B_2, \ldots, B_n)$$
$$\bar{p}_s = g(\bar{I}_1, \bar{I}_2, \ldots, \bar{I}_n; B_1, B_2, \ldots, B_n).$$

An omniscient economist could calculate the function f. Knowing the joint distribution of $(\bar{I}_1, \bar{I}_2, \ldots, \bar{I}_n)$, the economist could then calculate the joint distribution of $(\bar{p}_f, \bar{p}_s, \bar{I}_1, \bar{I}_2, \ldots, \bar{I}_n)$, and so the conditional distribution of $\bar{p}_s$ given $\bar{p}_f$ and $\bar{I}_i$ for each i. This would tell the economist what the correct beliefs for each dealer would be, call them $\hat{B}_i$. As the joint distributions depend upon the original beliefs, $(B_1, B_2, \ldots, B_n)$, the correct beliefs $(\hat{B}_1, \hat{B}_2, \ldots, \hat{B}_n)$ also depend upon the original beliefs. A more formal way of saying the same thing is that $(\hat{B}_1, \hat{B}_2, \ldots, \hat{B}_n)$ is a function of $(B_1, B_2, \ldots, B_n)$.

The last part of the definition is

PART 4. Each agent has rational expectations. They have correct beliefs about the joint probability distribution of the futures price, spot price, and private information; so

$$B_i = \hat{B}_i \qquad i = 1, 2, \ldots, n.$$

Note that this states that beliefs about the entire conditional probability distribution are correct. Much of the macroeconomic literature works with models where only the conditional mean is relevant, but the rational expectations hypothesis is not confined to such models.

This definition may appear unnecessarily long-winded. Stating that the beliefs are correct in Part 1 would make for greater brevity, but stating the definition in this way gives more insight. It is helpful in calculating the rational expectations equilibrium in simple models, where making a guess about the functional form of beliefs, calculating supply and demand, and then checking to see if there is indeed a set of beliefs that generates rational expectations often works. This approach is also very helpful in understanding issues associated with the existence and stability of rational expectations equilibrium.

I have stated the definition in terms of a spot and futures market, but very similar definitions can be formulated for any set of financial asset markets. I have not been specific about the information $\tilde{I}_i$. All that is required is that it be a random variable, but it may be continuous or discrete, a scalar or a vector. It may always the same value, $\tilde{I}_i = 0$, in which case it is effectively no information.

I will now calculate the rational expectations equilibrium for the futures market example with risk-neutral dealers. Here the informed agents observe $\tilde{I}$ and the uninformed agents observe nothing. Recall that $\tilde{p}_s = \tilde{I} + \tilde{e}$, $\tilde{I}$ and $\tilde{e}$ are independent, and $E\tilde{e} = 0$. In accordance with Part 1 of the definition, suppose that the informed dealers believe that $E(\tilde{p}_s \mid \tilde{I}, \tilde{p}_f) = \tilde{I}$, and the uninformed dealers believe that $E(\tilde{p}_s \mid \tilde{p}_f) = \lambda \tilde{p}_f$ where λ is a constant. Utility maximization (Part 2 of the definition) for risk-neutral dealers implies that the informed dealers will want to buy or sell an unlimited amount unless $E(\tilde{p}_s \mid \tilde{I}, \tilde{p}_f) = \tilde{p}_f(1 + r)$, and the uninformed dealers will want to buy or sell an unlimited amount unless $E(\tilde{p}_s \mid \tilde{p}_f) = \tilde{p}_f(1 + r)$. Thus, market-clearing (Part 3 of the definition) implies that

$$E(\tilde{p}_s \mid \tilde{I}, \tilde{p}_f) = \tilde{I} = \tilde{p}_f(1 + r)$$

and

$$E(\tilde{p}_s \mid \tilde{p}_f) = \lambda \tilde{p}_f = \tilde{p}_f(1 + r).$$

That is impossible unless $\lambda = 1 + r$, and $\tilde{p}_f = \tilde{I}/(1 + r)$. It remains to check that Part 4 of the definition holds. If $\tilde{p}_f = \tilde{I}/(1 + r)$, knowing $\tilde{p}_f$ tells the informed dealers nothing about $\tilde{I}$ and $\tilde{p}_s$ which they did not know already from observing $\tilde{I}$ directly. As $\tilde{p}_s = \tilde{I} + \tilde{e}$, the correct conditional expectation for the informed dealers is $E(\tilde{p}_s \mid \tilde{I}) = (\tilde{p}_s \mid \tilde{I}, \tilde{p}_f) = \tilde{I}$. The uninformed dealers observe $\tilde{p}_f = \tilde{I}/(1+r)$, so can infer $\tilde{I}$ from $\tilde{p}_f$, knowing that $E(\tilde{p}_s \mid \tilde{I}) = \tilde{I}$; their correct conditional expectation is $E(\tilde{p}_s \mid \tilde{I}) = E(\tilde{p}_s \mid \tilde{p}_f) = \tilde{I} = (1+r)\tilde{p}_f$, which is the form assumed with $\lambda = 1 + r$. This is a rational expectations equilibrium.

This is a very striking result, indicating that the market is completely efficient as a transmitter of information from the informed to the uninformed. Much of the recent theoretical work on asset markets has been concerned with investigating the circumstances under which a rational expectations equilibrium exists, and is informationally efficient.

This example has a number of peculiar features. The assumption of risk neutrality is special, and I have argued that, even with risk neutrality, the market may not be perfectly arbitraged. In equilibrium neither farmers nor speculators have any reason to trade futures. The expected profits from trade are always zero. It seems possible that the futures market will die away. But without a futures market, the informational differences will persist, so there will be a motive for trade. These peculiarities stem from the risk neutrality assumption.

8. Rational Expectations Equilibrium under Risk Aversion

I will now introduce risk aversion into the model. This can generate considerable mathematical complexities, which I will minimize by assuming that both farmers and speculators have utility functions of the form

$$U_i(\tilde{W}) = -e^{-k_i \tilde{W}} \equiv -\exp(-k_i \tilde{W})$$

where k_i is a positive constant. I will use the second form of notation, which avoids the need for superscripts. Remember that 'exp' is an abbreviation for 'exponential' and not for 'expectation'.

This utility function is widely used and has some attractive properties. Its first derivative is positive ($U' > 0$), implying that utility is increasing in wealth. The second derivative is negative ($U' < 0$), implying risk aversion. The constant $k_i = -U''/U'$ is the coefficient of absolute risk aversion; higher values of k_i imply greater risk aversion. Above all, there is the very useful result that, if $\tilde{W}$ is normal with mean $E\tilde{W}$ and variance var $\tilde{W}$

$$E[-\exp(-k\tilde{W})] = -\exp[-k(E\tilde{W} - \tfrac{1}{2}k \text{ var } \tilde{W})]. \tag{3}$$

This result implies that the expected utility-maximizing portfolio is one that maximizes $E\tilde{W} - \tfrac{1}{2}k$ var $\tilde{W}$. As I will demonstrate, this makes for a very tractable model of asset demand, which is linear in expected asset return and prices. The major unattractive feature of the utility function, which I will also demonstrate, is that asset demand is independent of wealth.[1]

I will now use (3) to analyse the behaviour of the spot and futures market model under risk aversion. The first step in defining and calculating the rational expectations equilibrium is a description of the information and beliefs. The first case I will look at is where dealers have no private information; each farmer and speculator has the same belief that

$$\tilde{p}_s \sim N(\mu, \sigma^2). \tag{4}$$

Later I will look at a version of the model where each agent has the same piece of information, and then at versions with diverse private information. Once the mathematics has been done for the first case, the others follow very simply.

Equation (4) gives the beliefs described in Part 1 of the definitions of a rational expectations equilibrium. I will use this to derive the utility-maximizing speculators' demand for futures, and the farmers' demand for futures and spot supply (Part 2 of the definition). I will then make an assumption about spot demand which enables me to write down market-clearing conditions for the spot and futures markets (Part 3 of the definition). These conditions will generate a 'correct distribution' for the spot price which will depend upon the parameters of the model, including μ and σ^2. I will show that there are values of μ and σ^2 which generate correct beliefs (Part 4 of the definition), thus deriving the rational expectations equilibrium.

There are n dealers, m farmers, and $n - m$ speculators. Farmers are indexed by $i = 1, 2, \ldots, m$, and speculators by $i = m + 1, \ldots, n$.

8.1. Speculators

Speculator i has a utility function $-\exp(-k_i \tilde{W}_i)$. If he buys x_i futures at price p_f, sells them on the spot market at price $\tilde{p}_s$, gets interest r on a safe asset, and has initial wealth W_{i0}, his final wealth $\tilde{W}_i$ is from (2) a random variable:

$$\tilde{W}_i = [\tilde{p}_s - p_f(1 + r)]x_i + W_{i0}(1 + r).$$

As speculators believe that $\tilde{p}_s \sim N(\mu, \sigma^2)$, they believe that $\tilde{W}_i$ is normal, and

$$E\tilde{W}_i = [\mu - p_f(1 + r)]x_i + W_{i0}(1 + r)$$

$$\text{var } \tilde{W}_i = \sigma^2 x_i^2.$$

[1] $E[\exp(-k\tilde{W})]$ is the moment-generating function of the random variable $\tilde{W}$, an object that mathematicians find interesting. The result is proved in most texts on probability, e.g. Meyer (1970).

From (3), the speculator will choose x_i to maximize

$$E\bar{W}_i - \tfrac{1}{2}k_i \operatorname{var} \bar{W}_i = [\mu - p_f(1+r)]x_i + W_{i0}(1+r) - \tfrac{1}{2}k_i\sigma^2 x_i^2.$$

Thus

$$x_i = \frac{1}{k_i\sigma^2}[\mu - p_f(1+r)] \qquad (i = 1, \ldots, n). \tag{5}$$

The speculator buys futures if $\mu > p_f(1+r)$ (there is a positive expected profit to be made on holding futures) and sells futures if $\mu < p_f(1+r)$ (there is an expected loss to be made on holding futures). His trades are inversely proportional to σ^2, the variance of the spot price, and to k_i, which measures risk aversion. Note that x_i does not depend on initial wealth W_{i0}, owing to the special utility function, for which the coefficient of absolute risk aversion $k_i = -U''/U'$ does not depend on wealth.

8.2. Farmers

The speculators choose to take on risk by entering the futures market. If the farmers' output is certain, they can entirely avoid risk by hedging, selling their entire output on the futures market. If they sell more or less than this, they are assuming risk which they could avoid, in pursuit of profits, effectively acting as speculators. If y_i is farmer i's output and z_i his future sales, $x_i = y_i - z_i$ can be thought of as speculative purchases of futures. The farmer's wealth is from (1) a random variable:

$$\bar{W}_i = [p_f y_i - C(y_i)](1+r) + [\bar{p}_s - p_f(1+r)]x_i + W_{i0}(1+r).$$

The first term represents profits from production if all output is sold on the futures market. The second term is profits from speculation. The third term is the future value of initial wealth. As he believes that $\bar{p}_s \sim N(\mu, \sigma)$, he believes that $\bar{W}_i$ is normal, with mean and variance

$$E\bar{W}_i = [p_f y_i - C(y_i)](1+r) + [\mu - p_f(1+r)]x_i + W_{i0}(1+r)$$

$$\operatorname{var} \bar{W}_i = \sigma^2 x_i^2.$$

If the farmer has a utility function $-\exp(-k_i\bar{W}_i)$, from (3) he chooses (x_i, y_i) to maximize

$$E\bar{W}_i - \tfrac{1}{2}k_i \operatorname{var} \bar{W}_i = [p_f y_i - C(y_i)](1+r) + [\mu - p_f(1+r)]x_i$$
$$+ W_{i0}(1+r) - \tfrac{1}{2}k_i\sigma_i^2 x_i^2.$$

I will assume that the farmer's costs are

$$C(y_i) = \tfrac{1}{2}c y_i^2$$

where c is a positive constant. Thus the farmer will maximize

$$(p_f y_i - \tfrac{1}{2}c y_i^2)(1+r) + [\mu - p_f(1+r)]x_i + W_{i0}(1+r) - \tfrac{1}{2}k_i\sigma_i^2 x_i^2$$

The first-order condition for y_i implies that $p_f = cy_i$. The futures price determines the level of output, which is set so that the futures price is equal to the marginal cost of production. This result is valid for arbitrary utility functions. In this case it implies that

$$y_i = c^{-1}p_f \qquad (i = 1, \ldots, m). \tag{6}$$

The first order condition for x_i implies that

$$x_i = \frac{1}{k_i \sigma^2}[\mu - p_f(1+r)] \qquad (i = 1, \ldots, m). \tag{7}$$

The farmer's speculative demand for futures is precisely the same as if he were a pure speculator. This result is not valid if output is uncertain, but it is convenient (see Bray 1981).

8.3. The futures market

The futures market-clearing condition is

$$\sum_{i=1}^{n} x_i = \sum_{i=1}^{m} y_i. \tag{8}$$

The sum of speculative demand for futures from farmers and speculators is equal to farmers' output, sold forward to hedge against uncertainty. Using the expressions for x_i, and y_i, (5)–(7)

$$\sum_{i=1}^{n} \frac{1}{k_i \sigma^2}[\mu - p_f(1+r)] = \sum_{i=1}^{m} c^{-1}p_f = mc^{-1}p_f. \tag{9}$$

Thus, the futures price depends upon the distribution of the spot price μ and σ^2. However, the spot price depends upon the physical quantity produced, $\sum_{i=1}^{m} y_i$, which in turns depends upon the futures price. The equilibria of the spot and futures markets have to be considered simultaneously.

8.4. The spot market

ASSUMPTION: Spot demand is

$$D(\bar{p}_s) = \bar{a} - b\bar{p}_s$$

where $\bar{a}$ is a normal random variable with mean $E\bar{a}$ and variance var $\bar{a}$, and b is a positive constant.

Thus, spot demand is subject to random variation as $\bar{a}$ varies. Spot supply comes from two sources. Farmers sell any output which they have not already sold on the futures market, so farmer i sells spot $x_i = y_i - z_i$. Speculator i sells spot everything which he bought on the futures market from farmers, x_i. Total spot sales $\sum_{i=1}^{n} x_i$ are thus equal to farmers' total output $\sum_{i=1}^{m} y_i$. (This is implied by the futures market clearing condition (8).) As (6) implies that $\sum_{i=1}^{m} y_i = mc^{-1}p_f$, the spot market clears when

$$\bar{a} - b\bar{p}_s = mc^{-1}p_f. \tag{10}$$

8.5. Rational expectations equilibrium

Eliminating p_f from the market-clearing conditions (9) and (10) implies that

$$\bar{p}_s = b^{-1}\bar{a} - b^{-1}mc^{-1}\phi^{-1}\mu \tag{11}$$

where

$$\phi = 1 + r + mc^{-1}\sigma^2 \left(\sum_{i=1}^{n} k_i^{-1} \right)^{-1}. \tag{12}$$

As $\bar{a}$ is normal and all the other terms on the right-hand side of (11) are constants, $\bar{p}_s$ is normal. The dealers' beliefs about the form of the distribution of $\bar{p}_s$ is correct. From (4), they believe that $\bar{p}_s \sim N(\mu, \sigma^2)$. Equation (11) implies that

$$E\bar{p}_s = b^{-1}E\bar{a} - b^{-1}mc^{-1}\phi^{-1}\mu \tag{13}$$

and

$$\text{var } \bar{p}_s = b^{-2} \text{ var } \bar{a}. \tag{14}$$

Beliefs about the mean and variance are correct if $E\bar{p}_s = \mu$ and $\text{var } \bar{p}_s = \sigma^2$. In this case (13) and (14) imply that the beliefs are correct if and only if

$$\sigma^2 = b^{-2} \text{ var } \bar{a} \tag{15}$$

$$E\bar{p}_s = \theta^{-1}\phi E\bar{a} \tag{16}$$

where, substituting for σ^2 in (12),

$$\phi = 1 + r + mc^{-1}b^{-2} \text{ var } \bar{a} \left(\sum_{i=1}^{n} k_i^{-1} \right)^{-1} \tag{17}$$

and

$$\theta = b\phi + mc^{-1}. \tag{18}$$

Thus, from (11), (16), and (18), as $\mu = E\bar{p}_s$,

$$\bar{p}_s = \theta^{-1}\phi E\bar{a} + b^{-1}(\bar{a} - E\bar{a}) \tag{19}$$

and from (10) and (19),

$$p_f = \theta^{-1}E\bar{a}. \tag{20}$$

If the futures price is given by (20) and dealers' beliefs about the expected spot price by (15)–(18) the futures market clears. The futures price determines output. Output determines the distribution of the spot price. At this futures price, and this expected spot price, dealers' beliefs about the distribution of the spot price are correct. This is a rational expectations equilibrium.

Introducing risk aversion changes the model in several respects. If all dealers are risk-neutral, arbitrage implies that $(1 + r)p_f = E\bar{p}_s$: the expected return on risky futures is the same as the return on the safe asset. Dealers are indifferent about how many futures they hold, and have no positive reason to trade on the futures market. In this model with risk aversion, (16) and (20) imply that $\phi p_f = E\bar{p}_s$, and from (17), $\phi > 1 + r$. The risk premium $\phi - (1 + r)$ is an increasing function of the variance of the spot price, $b^{-2} \operatorname{var} \bar{a}$, and each dealer's risk aversion parameter k_i. Speculators are willing to take on some of the farmer's risk in order to earn a positive expected return. This model in fact overemphasizes the riskiness of speculative portfolios, because it considers only a single risky asset. In practice, speculators can diminish, but not eliminate, risk by holding a portfolio of several risky assets whose returns are imperfectly correlated.

Both speculators and farmers wish to hold definite amounts of futures, and the market will trade actively. As $\mu = E\bar{p}_s > p_f(1 + r)$, (5) and (7) imply that demand from speculators, and the speculative element of farmer's demand, will be strictly positive in equilibrium. Farmers as a whole must be net sellers of futures, to meet the demand from speculators. But an unusually risk-tolerant farmer might be a net purchaser.

9. Rational Expectations Equilibrium and Information

In the model that I have just analysed, the spot price is stochastic and differs from year to year, but the futures price is a constant, a function of the parameters of the model, including the mean and variance of $\bar{a}$, the stochastic intercept in the spot demand function, which is by assumption the source of all the uncertainty.

I am now going to modify the model by assuming that dealers have information about $\bar{a}$ in January when the futures market operates. I will look at three different information structures of increasing complexity, asking in each case how well the futures price reflects the information.

Example 1: Symmetric information. Assume that

$$\bar{a} = \tilde{I} + \tilde{e} \tag{21}$$

where $\tilde{I}$ and $\tilde{e}$ are independent scalar normal variables, $E\tilde{I} = E\bar{a}$, and $E\tilde{e} = 0$. As the sum of normal variables is normal, $\bar{a}$ is still normal; $\operatorname{var} \bar{a} = \operatorname{var} \tilde{I} + \operatorname{var} \tilde{e}$. Assume also that all dealers, farmers, and speculators observe $\tilde{I}$ each January. Conditional upon the information $\tilde{I}$, each dealer believes correctly that $\tilde{a}$ is a normal random variable whose mean $E(\tilde{a} \mid \tilde{I}) = \tilde{I}$ is random, whereas $\text{var}(\tilde{a} \mid \tilde{I}) = \text{var}\,\tilde{e}$ is not random. The model is unchanged, apart from the fact that beliefs about the mean of $\tilde{a}$ change from year to year. The rational expectations equilibrium can be calculated as before. Paralleling (14) and (16)–(20),

$$\text{var}(\tilde{p}_s \mid \tilde{I}) = b^{-2} \text{var}(\tilde{a} \mid \tilde{I}) = b^{-2} \text{var}\,\tilde{e} \tag{22}$$

$$E(\tilde{p}_s \mid \tilde{I}) = \theta^{*-1}\phi^* E(\tilde{a} \mid \tilde{I}) = \theta^{*-1}\phi^* \tilde{I} \tag{23}$$

where

$$\phi^* = 1 + r + mc^{-1}b^{-2}\,\text{var}(\tilde{a} \mid \tilde{I})\Big(\sum_{i=1}^{n} k_i^{-1}\Big)^{-1} \tag{24}$$

$$\theta^* = b\phi^* + mc^{-1} \tag{25}$$

$$\tilde{p}_s = \theta^{*-1}\phi^* E(\tilde{a} \mid \tilde{I}) + b^{-1}[\tilde{a} - E(\tilde{a} \mid \tilde{I})] = \theta^{*-1}\phi^* \tilde{I} - b^{-1}\tilde{e} \tag{26}$$

and

$$\tilde{p}_f = \theta^{*-1}E(\tilde{a} \mid \tilde{I}) = \theta^{*-1}\tilde{I}. \tag{27}$$

These equations differ from (14) and (16)–(20) in two ways. First, the terms relating to the unconditional distribution of $\tilde{a}$, $E\tilde{a}$, and $\text{var}\,\tilde{a}$ in the previous equations have been replaced by the corresponding terms for the distributional conditional upon the information $E(\tilde{a} \mid \tilde{I})$ and $\text{var}\,(\tilde{a} \mid \tilde{I})$. Second, the futures price $\tilde{p}_f$ is now a random variable rather than a constant.

The expressions θ^* and ϕ^* are not random because $\text{var}(\tilde{a} \mid \tilde{I})$ is not random. Thus, provided the numerical values of θ^* and ϕ^* are known, it is possible to infer $\tilde{I}$ and $E(\tilde{p}_s \mid \tilde{I})$ from $\tilde{p}_f$:

$$E(\tilde{p}_s \mid \tilde{I}) = \theta^{*-1}\phi^* \tilde{I} = \phi^* \tilde{p}_f,$$

and so the conditional distribution of $\tilde{p}_s$ given $\tilde{p}_f$ is normal:

$$E(\tilde{p}_s \mid \tilde{p}_f) = E(\tilde{p}_s \mid \tilde{I}) = \phi^* \tilde{p}_f \tag{28}$$

and

$$\text{var}(\tilde{p}_s \mid \tilde{p}_f) = \text{var}(\tilde{p}_s \mid \tilde{I}) = b^{-2}\text{var}(\tilde{a} \mid \tilde{I}) = b^{-2}\text{var}\,\tilde{e}. \tag{29}$$

Anyone knowing the numerical value of ϕ^* would form the same conditional expectation of the spot price $\tilde{p}_s$ from the futures price $\tilde{p}_f$ as if he knew the information $\tilde{I}$. This observation is perhaps not very interesting in the context of this example, in which, by assumption, all the dealers know $\tilde{I}$, but it is helpful in analysing the next two examples.

Example 2. As in the previous example,

$$\tilde{a} = \tilde{I} + \tilde{e}$$

where $\tilde{I}$ and $\tilde{e}$ are independent, and normal, $E\tilde{a} = E\tilde{I}$, and $E\tilde{e} = 0$. However, now only some of the dealers observe $\tilde{I}$. The others have no private information. In the rational expectations equilibrium the uninformed dealers will infer what information they can about the spot price from the futures price. If the futures price is completely efficient as an information transmitter, the uninformed traders will trade as if they had the information.

This observation suggested to Radner (1979) and Grossman (1978) that models with asymmetric information could be analysed by considering the corresponding model in which the information is pooled and made available to all dealers (called a 'full communications equilibrium' by Radner, an 'artificial economy' by Grossman). If the futures price is a perfect transmitter of information in the rational expectations equilibrium of the original model, dealers' beliefs about the distribution of the spot price given the futures price in the original model will be the same as if they had the information available to them in the full communications equilibrium. Thus supply, demand, and prices will be the same in the full communications equilibrium as in the rational expectations equilibrium of the original model.

Observing this point, Radner and Grossman argued that the first step in analysing this type of model should be to examine the full communications equilibrium. This is much easier than looking at the rational expectations equilibrium with asymmetric information directly, because if dealers know all the information that could possibly be reflected in prices already, they have no motive for using prices as information, so prices do not affect beliefs in the full communications equilibrium. Having characterized prices in the full communications equilibrium, ask what dealers' correct beliefs would be conditional on the full communications equilibrium prices. In particular, ask whether the beliefs are the same as they would be if dealers know all the information. If they are, it has been established that a rational expectations equilibrium exists in which beliefs, prices, supply, and demand are the same as in the full communications equilibrium.

Consider the four-part definition of a rational expectations equilibrium in an asset market with asymmetric information. The first part refers to beliefs, the second to utility maximization given beliefs, the third to market-clearing, and the fourth to correct beliefs. If the full communications equilibrium prices allow dealers to form precisely the same beliefs as if they had all the information, utility maximization leads to the same trades as in the full communications equilibrium. As the trades are the same, the market clears at the same prices. The beliefs generating the trades are correct. This is a rational expectations equilibrium. This argument breaks down if beliefs given the full communications equilibrium prices are not the same as beliefs given all the information. In this case, if a rational expectations equilibrium exists, prices transmit some, but not all, information.

In this example the full communications equilibrium is one in which all dealers observe $\tilde{I}$. This is precisely example 1, where I have already argued that conditioning on the futures price alone leads dealers to the same beliefs as if they knew the information $\tilde{I}$. Thus, the full communications equilibrium prices of example 1 are also rational expectations equilibrium prices for example 2. In this rational expectations equilibrium the futures price transmits all the information from the informed to the uninformed dealers.

Example 3: Diverse information. I now generalize the information structure considerably. Suppose that each dealer observes a random information variable $\tilde{I}_i$. This may be a scalar or a vector; it may be constant, in which case it is effectively no information. The only restriction is that $(\tilde{a}, \tilde{I}_1, \tilde{I}_2, \ldots, \tilde{I}_n)$ has a joint normal distribution. It seems an impossible task to ask a single price to aggregate all this diverse information, so that in the rational expectations equilibrium dealers can trade as if they had all the information. Yet this is in fact so, owing to the following properties of normal random variables.

LEMMA: *Conditional distributions of normal random variables.* If $(\tilde{a}, \tilde{I}_1, \tilde{I}_2, \ldots, \tilde{I}_n)$ has a joint normal distribution,

$$\tilde{I} = E(\tilde{a} \mid \tilde{I}_1, \tilde{I}_2, \ldots, \tilde{I}_n),$$

and

$$\tilde{e} = \tilde{a} - \tilde{I},$$

then $\tilde{I}$ and $\tilde{e}$ are independent normal random variables, $E\tilde{a} = E\tilde{I}$, $E\tilde{e} = 0$, var $\tilde{a} = $ var $\tilde{I} + $ var $\tilde{e}$. The conditional distribution of $\tilde{a}$ given $\tilde{I}$ is the same as the conditional distribution of $\tilde{a}$ given $\tilde{I}_1, \tilde{I}_2, \ldots, \tilde{I}_n$. Both conditional distributions are normal, with mean

$$E(\tilde{a} \mid \tilde{I}) = E(\tilde{a} \mid \tilde{I}_1, \tilde{I}_2, \ldots, \tilde{I}_n) = \tilde{I}$$

and variance

$$\mathrm{var}(\tilde{a} \mid \tilde{I}) = \mathrm{var}(\tilde{a} \mid \tilde{I}_1, \tilde{I}_2, \ldots, \tilde{I}_n) = \mathrm{var}\ \tilde{a} - \mathrm{var}\ \tilde{I} = \mathrm{var}\ \tilde{e}.$$

Proof. See appendix.

This result shows that, for the purposes of forming beliefs about $\tilde{a}$, knowing $\tilde{I} = E(\tilde{a} \mid \tilde{I}_1, \tilde{I}_2, \ldots, \tilde{I}_n)$ gives the same information as knowing $\tilde{I}_1, \tilde{I}_2, \ldots, \tilde{I}_n$. The conditional mean $\tilde{I}$, a single number, aggregates perfectly all the diverse information. (It is a sufficient statistic for the information.)

This result can be used to compare two full communications equilibria, for the spot and futures market model. In the first equilibrium dealers observe the vector of random variables $\tilde{I}_1, \tilde{I}_2, \ldots, \tilde{I}_n$. In the second they observe $\tilde{I} = E(\tilde{a} \mid \tilde{I}_1, \tilde{I}_2, \ldots, \tilde{I}_n)$. In both equilibria the conditional distribution of $\tilde{a}$ is normal, with the same mean and variance. Thus, the equilibrium prices are the same. The equilibrium in which all dealers observe $\tilde{I}$ is the equilibrium of the first model studied in this section. The prices in both equilibria are given by (22)–(27). In these equilibria, from (27),

$$\bar{p}_f = \theta^{*-1}\tilde{I} = \theta^{*-1}E(\tilde{a} \mid \tilde{I}_1, \tilde{I}_2, \ldots, \tilde{I}_n) \tag{30}$$

and from (22) and (23),

$$\text{var}(\bar{p}_s \mid \bar{p}_f) = \text{var}(\bar{p}_s \mid \tilde{I}) = \text{var}(\bar{p}_s \mid \tilde{I}_1, \tilde{I}_2, \ldots, \tilde{I}_n) = b^{-2}\,\text{var}\,\tilde{e} \tag{31}$$

$$E(\bar{p}_s \mid \bar{p}_f) = E(\bar{p}_s \mid \tilde{I}) = E(\bar{p}_s \mid \tilde{I}_1, \tilde{I}_2, \ldots, \tilde{I}_n) = \theta^{*-1}\phi^*\tilde{I} = \phi^*\bar{p}_f \tag{32}$$

and

$$\bar{p}_f = \theta^{*-1}\tilde{I} = \theta^{*-1}E(\tilde{a} \mid \tilde{I}_1, \tilde{I}_2, \ldots, \tilde{I}_n). \tag{33}$$

Conditioning only on the futures price, dealers form the same beliefs about the spot price as they would if they know either $\tilde{I} = E(\tilde{a} \mid \tilde{I}_1, \tilde{I}_2, \ldots, \tilde{I}_n)$, or the entire information vector $\tilde{I}_1, \tilde{I}_2, \ldots, \tilde{I}_n$. By the same argument as before, these must also be rational expectations equilibrium prices for the model in which dealer i observes information $\tilde{I}_i$.

This is a much stronger result than before. It argues that a market price not only can transmit a single piece of information from one set of dealers to another, but also can aggregate a large and diverse set of information perfectly.

10. The Robustness of the Informational Efficiency Result

In the previous section I showed that in a simple futures market model the market price can aggregate diverse information so efficiently that each dealer's beliefs about the return on holding an asset (the spot price) given only its price are the same as if he had access to all the information to the market. He finds his own private information completely redundant.

This surprising result is not limited to futures markets. From a speculator's point of view, a futures contract is one of many financial assets; others include shares and bonds issued by firms, and government securities. The original version of this model (Grossman 1976) considered a stock market. The stock lasts for one period, and pays a random gross return $\tilde{R}$. An investor with wealth W_{i0}, who buys x_i units of the stock at price p and invests $W_{i0} - px_i$ in a safe asset paying interest r, has final wealth

$$\bar{W}_i = [\tilde{R} - p(1+r)]x_i + W_{i0}(1+r).$$

The gross return $\tilde{R}$ pays a role precisely analogous to the spot price in the futures market. If $\tilde{R}$ is normally distributed and the investor has an exponential utility function $-\exp(-k_i \tilde{W}_i)$, the argument used to derive the speculator's demand for futures yields the investor's demand for the stock:

$$x_i = \frac{1}{k_i \operatorname{var} \tilde{R}} [E\tilde{R} - p(1+r)]. \tag{34}$$

If there are n investors and a fixed supply of the stock S, market-clearing requires that

$$\sum_{i=1}^{n} \frac{1}{k_i \operatorname{var} \tilde{R}} [E\tilde{R} - p(1+r)] = S. \tag{35}$$

The stock and futures markets models are mathematically very similar, apart from the fact that the supply of the asset in the stock market is taken as exogenous.

Now suppose the investors have diverse information, $\tilde{I}_1, \tilde{I}_2, \ldots, \tilde{I}_n$, and that $(\tilde{R}, \tilde{I}_1, \tilde{I}_2, \ldots, \tilde{I}_n)$ is joint normal. Experience with the futures market model suggests looking at the full communications equilibria, in which market-clearing implies that

$$\sum_{i=1}^{n} \frac{1}{k_i \sigma^2} [E(\tilde{R} \mid \tilde{I}_1, \tilde{I}_2, \ldots, \tilde{I}_n) - (1+r)\tilde{p}] = S$$

where $\sigma^2 = \operatorname{var}(\tilde{R} \mid \tilde{I}_1, \tilde{I}_2, \ldots, \tilde{I}_n)$; so

$$E(\tilde{R} \mid \tilde{I}_1, \tilde{I}_2, \ldots, \tilde{I}_n) = \sigma^2 \left(\sum_{i=1}^{n} k_i^{-1} \right)^{-1} S + (1+r)\tilde{p}. \tag{36}$$

Anyone knowing the numerical value of $\sigma^2 (\sum_{i=1}^{n} k_i^{-1})^{-1} S$ and $(1+r)$ could infer $E(\tilde{R} \mid \tilde{I}_1, \tilde{I}_2, \ldots, \tilde{I}_n)$ from the price $\tilde{p}$, and would form the same beliefs about $\tilde{R}$ as if he knew $\tilde{I}_1, \tilde{I}_2, \ldots, \tilde{I}_n$. By a now familiar argument, this implies that the full communications equilibrium is also a rational expectations equilibrium: the rational expectations equilibrium price aggregates the information perfectly.

Grossman wrote the paper embodying this result before he had the idea of using an artificial economy, or full communications equilibrium, to analyse the model. He had to use more complex arguments and was not able to prove such a general result. The paper was important first because it was the first satisfactory asset market model embracing risk aversion and asymmetric information, and second because Grossman pointed out a most important paradox. In Grossman's model, just as in the spot and futures market model, knowing the asset price renders dealers' private information. redundant. If this information is costly, no dealer has any incentive to gather the information, particularly if he knows that another dealer is using the same information. Yet if no one gathers the information it cannot be reflected in the price, which generates incentives to gather the information.

Grossman and Stiglitz (1980) resolve this paradox by modifying the model slightly. Suppose now that the asset supply is a normal random variable $\tilde{S}$. The relationship between the full communications equilibrium price $\bar{p}$, $E(\tilde{R} \mid \tilde{I}_1, \tilde{I}_2, \ldots, \tilde{I}_n)$, and $\tilde{S}$ is given by (36), modified only by replacing the constant S by random $\tilde{S}$:

$$E(\tilde{R} \mid \tilde{I}_1, \tilde{I}_2, \ldots, \tilde{I}_n) = \sigma^2 \left(\sum_{i=1}^{n} k_i^{-1} \right)^{-1} \tilde{S} + (1 + r)\bar{p}. \tag{37}$$

Even if the numerical values of $\sigma^2 (\sum_{i=1}^{n} k_i^{-1})^{-1}$ and $(1 + r)$ are known, it is impossible to infer $E(\tilde{R} \mid \tilde{I}_1, \tilde{I}_2, \ldots, \tilde{I}_n)$ from $\bar{p}$ because $\tilde{S}$ is different each time the market operates. Conditioning on $\bar{p}$ does not yield the same information as conditioning on $\tilde{I}_1, \tilde{I}_2, \ldots, \tilde{I}_n$. The full communications equilibrium is not a rational expectations equilibrium. (This is also true in the spot and futures market model, if farmers' output is uncertain and dealers have information about both spot demand and output: (Bray 1981).

Grossman and Stiglitz calculate the rational expectations equilibrium for a version of the stock market model in which there are two groups of dealers. The informed dealers all observe the same information, on which they base their expectations. The uninformed dealers form their expectations on the basis of the price. The informativeness of the price increases as the proportion of informed dealers increases. In the absence of information costs, the informed dealers have higher expected utility than the uninformed, because they are less uncertain of the asset return. (Its conditional variance is lower for the informed than the uninformed.) If information is costly, informed dealers may be better or worse off. If the proportion of informed dealers is large and the price conveys much of the information to the uninformed dealers, they are likely to be worse off. If the proportion of informed dealers is small and the price conveys little information to the uninformed, they are likely to be better off. Grossman and Stiglitz show that for each level of information costs there is an equilibrium proportion of informed dealers, so that the benefits of the information just balance the costs, and dealers are indifferent between being informed and uninformed. They derive a variety of interesting comparative-static results from this model.

11. Existence of Rational Expectations Equilibrium

Expectations play a crucial role in all the models that I have presented, as in many others. Whenever I have needed to close models by specifying expectations, I have followed standard practice in postulating rational expectations. In each case I have been able to show that a rational expectations equilibrium exists by solving explicitly for the equilibrium. This is not always possible. Indeed, in some examples, such as the one that follows, it can be shown that there is no set of prices and beliefs that satisfies Parts 3 and 4 of the definition. There is no rational expectations equilibrium.

The example is similar in form to that of Kreps (1977). It is a somewhat modified version of the spot and futures market model. For mathematical simplicity, assume that there is one farmer and one speculator. Each maximizes the expectation of a utility function $-\exp(-\tilde{W})$. The speculator believes the spot price $\tilde{p}_s \sim N(\mu, \sigma^2)$. The interest rate $r = 0$. Arguing as before, the speculators' excess demand for futures is

$$x_s = \frac{1}{\sigma^2}(\mu - p_f). \tag{38}$$

The farmer has a cost function for output $C(y) = sy + \frac{1}{2}y^2$. He also believes that $\tilde{p}_s \sim N(\mu, \sigma^2)$. Utility maximization for the farmer implies that he sets output so $C'(y) = p_f$ or

$$y = p_f - s. \tag{39}$$

He hedges by selling y on the futures market, and in addition speculates by buying futures:

$$x_f = \frac{1}{\sigma^2}(\mu - p_f). \tag{40}$$

Futures market-clearing implies that $x_s + x_f = y$, or, from (38)–(40),

$$\frac{2}{\sigma^2}(\mu - p_f) = p_f - s. \tag{41}$$

Spot demand is

$$D(p_s) = \tilde{a} - \tilde{p}_s$$

where $\tilde{a}$ is a normal random variable, and var $\tilde{a} = 1$. Spot market-clearing implies that $D(\tilde{p}_s) = y$; that is,

$$\tilde{a} - \tilde{p}_s = p_f - s. \tag{42}$$

Equation (42) implies that

$$E\tilde{p}_s = E\tilde{a} - p_f + s \tag{43}$$

and

$$\text{var } \tilde{p}_s = \text{var } \tilde{a} = 1. \tag{44}$$

If the farmer and speculator are to form rational expectations, $\mu = E\tilde{p}_s = E\tilde{a} - p_f + s$, and $\sigma^2 = \text{var } \tilde{p}_s = 1$. The futures market-clearing condition

(41) becomes

$$2(E\tilde{a} - p_f + s - p_f) = p_f - s$$

so

$$p_f = \tfrac{1}{5}(2E\tilde{a} + 3s). \tag{45}$$

Spot market-clearing and rational expectations imply (43), which with (45) implies that

$$E\tilde{p}_s = \tfrac{1}{5}(3E\tilde{a} + 2s). \tag{46}$$

So far I have had no difficulty in calculating the rational expectations equilibrium, but introducing asymmetric information can cause complications. Suppose that there are only two sorts of weather, good and bad. The farmer observes the weather; the speculator does not. If the weather is good, $E\tilde{a} = \tfrac{5}{4}$ and $s = \tfrac{1}{6}$. If it is bad, $E\tilde{a} = 1$ and $s = \tfrac{1}{3}$.

There are only two possibilities: either the futures price is different in different weather or it is not. If the futures price is different, the speculator can infer the weather from the price. Trades and prices will be the same as if both farmer and speculator knew the weather. In this case in good weather $E\tilde{a} = \tfrac{5}{4}$, $s = \tfrac{1}{6}$, from (45) $p_f = \tfrac{3}{5}$, and from (46) $E\tilde{p}_s = \tfrac{49}{60}$. In bad weather $E\tilde{a} = 1$, $s = \tfrac{1}{3}$, from (45) $p_f = \tfrac{3}{5}$, and from (46) $E\tilde{p}_s = \tfrac{44}{60}$. Thus the futures price is the same in both weathers, contradicting the supposition that it was different.

The alternative supposition is that the futures price is the same whatever the weather, in which case the speculator's demand will be the same. If the farmer has rational expectations, his excess demand for futures will be using (39), (40), (43), and, recalling that $\sigma^2 = 1$ and $\mu = E\tilde{p}_s$,

$$\begin{aligned} x_f - y &= (E\tilde{p}_s - p_f) - (p_f - s) = E\tilde{p}_s + s - 2p_f \\ &= E\tilde{a} + 2s - 3p_f. \end{aligned}$$

In good weather $E\tilde{a} + 2s = \tfrac{19}{12}$; in bad weather $E\tilde{a} + 2s = \tfrac{5}{3}$. If p_f is independent of the weather, the speculator's demand for futures is independent of the weather but the farmer's is not. The futures market cannot clear at the same price in both weathers. This exhausts the possibilities. In this example the assumptions of market-clearing and rational expectations are logically inconsistent. There is no rational expectations equilibrium.

In defining a rational expectations equilibrium for an asset market model in Section 3, I argued that the market-clearing condition induces a mapping from the beliefs people hold to the correct beliefs. This is an almost universal feature of models with expectations; it crops up for example in equation (13), which gives the correct expected spot price, $E\tilde{p}_s$, as a function of the subjectively held expectation μ. A rational expectations equilibrium is a fixed point of this mapping. Fixed-point theorems give conditions under which mappings have fixed points, notably, continuity. The non-existence problems for rational expectations models with asymmetric information stem from discontinuities in the mapping, where a small change in prices can induce a large change in the information that can be inferred from them. In the example, if prices are identical in both weathers the speculator cannot infer the weather, but if they are very slightly different he can.

Checking that an equilibrium exists is an essential preliminary to using a model; assuming that an equilibrium exists, and arguing from there, can yield no valid conclusions if in fact no equilibrium exists. Knowing the circumstances under which a model has an equilibrium puts logical limits on the range of applicability.

Existence problems are attacked from two directions: existence theorems and non-existence examples. Existence theorems establish that under certain conditions, typically conditions on preferences, technology, and the structure of transactions and information, an equilibrium exists. For some special models equilibrium can be shown to exist by calculating the equilibrium, but in general the problem is attacked indirectly, often using fixed-point theorems which establish that a set of equations has a solution, but not what the solution is. Non-existence examples show that in certain cases no equilibrium exists. These examples are helpful because they show that certain conjectured general existence results cannot be valid; a claim that *all* models of a certain type have an equilibrium is wrong if a single such model has no equilibrium, just as a single black swan is enough to invalidate the claim that all swans are white.

The non-existence example that I demonstrated earlier is not robust; a small change in the parameters of the model would allow an equilibrium to exist; non-existence is a freak eventuality. Radner (1979) studies a much more general asset market model which shares two features with this example. In both models there is only a finite number of different possible information signals. In the example there are two: good weather or bad weather. In Radner's model there may be a large but finite number of different signals received by a finite number of individuals. The vector of joint signals can only take a finite number of different values. In Radner's model, as in my example, there may be no rational expectations equilibrium. Radner shows rigorously that equilibrium exists generically. Generic existence is defined precisely in the paper; the idea it captures is that, while equilibrium may fail to exist in some special cases, almost any perturbation of the model will restore existence. Radner's proof proceeds by considering the full communications equilibrium, in which dealers pool all their information signals before trading. The price vector in the full communications equilibrium $\bar{p}$ is a function of the joint signal $\bar{s}$, $\bar{p} = p(\bar{s})$. If the price vector is different whenever any element in the signal is different, the price reveals the signal; the full communications equilibrium is a rational expectations equilibrium, in which prices fully reveal the information.

The crucial question is whether the map from the signals into prices is invertible. There is a finite number, m, of signals, whereas prices can be any vector in R^{n+}, so there is an infinity (indeed, a continuum) of different possible prices. Radner's result confirms the intuition that, if the utility functions generating demand are reasonably well behaved, the map from signals to prices fails to be invertible only in special circumstances, in which case a small perturbation of the model restores invertibility.

The assumption that there is a finite number of different possible signals plays a crucial role in this invertibility argument. If there is a continuum of different possible signals, the argument may break down. Jordan and Radner (1982) devise an example with informed and uninformed dealers and one relative price. The informed dealer observes a signal $\bar{s}$ in $[0, 1]$. Given the price, the informed dealer's demand changes with the signal; if there are two different signals, $s_1 \neq s_2$, with $p(s_1) = p(s_2)$, the informed dealer's demand is different for the two signals, but the uninformed dealer, who observes only the price, has the same demand. The market cannot clear at the same price for both s_1 and s_2. On the other hand, if the function is invertible, the uninformed dealer can infer s from p; the prices are the same as in the full communications equilibrium. But Jordan and Radner show that the full communications equilibrium price function has the form shown in Figure 11.2, and is not

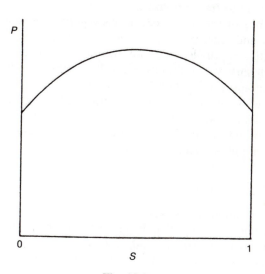

Fig. 11.2

invertible. This is a robust example; changing the parameters of the model changes the price function a little, but does not make it invertible.

The importance of invertibility for the existence of rational expectations equilibria in which prices reveal all the information suggests that the relative dimensions of the signal space and the price space may be important. This is confirmed by Allen (1982), who shows that, if the dimension of the signal space is less than the dimension of the price space, a fully revealing rational expectations equilibrium exists generically. Jordan (1983) shows that, if the dimension of the price space is higher than the dimension of the signal space, rational expectations equilibrium exists generically, but is not fully revealing.

The literature on fully revealing equilibria is concerned with equilibria in which dealers can infer the entire information signal from the prices. This is sufficient to enable them to form the same expectations as if they saw the signal. But it is not necessary; dealers want to know about a vector of asset returns $\tilde{R}$. If $\tilde{R}$ and the information $\tilde{I}$ are joint-normal, knowing $E(\tilde{R} \mid \tilde{I})$ tells them as much as knowing $\tilde{I}$. The vector $E(\tilde{R} \mid \tilde{I})$ has the same dimension as $\tilde{R}$, the number of risky assets. This may be much lower than the dimension of $\tilde{I}$. Grossman (1978) uses this result to analyse a stock market model in which returns are normal, and dealers care only about the mean and variance of return. By applying the captial asset pricing model, Grossman shows that, provided the market portfolio is not a Giffen good, dealers can infer $E(\tilde{R} \mid \tilde{I})$ from the information, and so a rational expectations equilibrium exists in which dealers trade as if they had all the information. Grossman also exploits the properties of normal random variables in his paper on futures markets (1977), showing how they can act to transmit information.

The existence of rational expectations equilibrium in asset markets is an attractive and challenging problem for mathematical economists. A more sophisticated discussion, and further references, are in Radner (1982), which surveys the literature on 'Equilibrium under Uncertainty', and in Jordan and Radner (1982) which introduces a symposium issue of the *Journal of Economic Theory* on 'Rational Expectations in Micro-economic Models', which includes a number of related papers. More recent work on the matter includes Jordan (1982a, 1982b), Allen (1983), and Anderson and Sonnenschein (1985).

12. Evaluating the Models

A model is a simplified, stylized description of certain aspects of the economy. It omits many details in order to concentrate on certain features and their interrelationships. One of the major objectives of modelling is often to show that the description is logically consistent by demonstrating that an equilibrium exists, an issue which I have discussed at some length. If a model is to be used as a basis for saying something about real economies, logical consistency is essential; even grossly unrealistic models may be useful in establishing logical limits to rhetoric. But it is obviously desirable that a model be a correct, as well as a consistent, description.

Unfortunately, there is no clear and universally applicable criterion for the correctness of models. Any model omits details, abstracts and simplifies. Reality is too complicated to be thought about in totality. Assumptions in economic models are most unlikely to be completely adequate descriptions of behaviour. The question to ask is whether they are plausible enough to generate implications which say something about the aspects of reality with which the model is concerned. This is inevitably a matter of judgement, and must often depend upon the use to which a model is being put.

The three major assumptions made in the financial market models that I described are that markets clear, that agents are price-takers, and that agents have rational expectations. These assumptions are very widely made; they are also central to the 'new classical' macroeconomics (Begg 1982a). Market-clearing and price-taking seem in general quite plausible for financial markets; where prices move readily, there is little evidence of sustained excess supply and demand, and a large number of traders.

The rational expectations hypothesis can be stated loosely as follows: people do not make systematic mistakes in forecasting; more precisely, people's subjective beliefs about probability distributions correspond to the objective probability distributions. Employing the rational expectations hypothesis imposes two logical requirements: that objective probability distributions exist, and that a rational expectations equilibrium exists. In constructing a model, an economist creates the objective probability distributions, but these models can only be applied to situations where the distributions could, in principle at least, be derived from data. This requires that the structure and parameters of the economy are in some way constant through time. Rational expectations models describe long-run stationary equilibria.

One important criticism of the rational expectations hypothesis is that it assumes that agents know too much. Consider the spot and futures market model with asymmetric information. In rational equilibrium the uninformed dealers believe correctly that the conditional distribution of the spot price given the futures price is normal, has conditional mean given by (28), $E(\bar{p}_s \mid \bar{p}_f) = \phi^* \bar{p}_f$, and a constant conditional variance. All they need to know is the fact of normality, and the numerical values of ϕ^* and $\text{var}(\bar{p}_s \mid \bar{p}_f)$. The uninformed dealers do not have to know the structure of the model, just two parameters of the reduced form. Further, by observing the markets operating in rational expectations equilibrium for a number of years, the numbers ϕ^* and $\text{var}(\bar{p}_s \mid \bar{p}_f)$ could be estimated by standard statistical techniques. Apparently it is quite easy to learn how to form rational expectations.

In financial markets there are very large amounts of money at stake; and there is every incentive to apply the considerable abilities and resources of professional investors to make the best possible forecasts. However, the argument that it is easy or even possible to learn how to form rational expectations by applying standard statistical techniques is misleading. Economists are interested in expectations because they believe that expectations affect what happens. This belief is reflected in the models; if agents in these models do not have rational expectations, the model behaves differently from the rational expectations equilibrium. In Section 7 I defined a rational expectations equilibrium as a fixed point of the mapping from subjectively held beliefs into 'correct beliefs' induced by the market-clearing condition. Outside rational expectations equilibrium, subjective beliefs differ from both correct beliefs and the rational expectations equilibrium beliefs. For example, in the spot and futures market model in rational expectations equilibrium, dealers believe that $E(\bar{p}_s | \bar{p}_f) = \phi^* \bar{p}_f$. If dealers believe that $E(\bar{p}_s | \bar{p}_f) = \phi \bar{p}_f$ where $\phi \neq \phi^*$, the correct conditional expectation will be of the form $E(\bar{p}_s | \bar{p}_f) = \hat{\phi} \bar{p}_f$ where $\hat{\phi} \neq \phi$. This expectation is incorrect, and $\hat{\phi} \neq \phi^*$, the correct expectation, is not the same as in the rational expectations equilibrium. Changing to the 'correct' expectation formation rule, $E(\bar{p}_s | \bar{p}_f) = \hat{\phi} \bar{p}_f$, changes the behaviour of the model, and this rule becomes incorrect. The obvious question to ask is whether repeated changes of the expectation formation rule ultimately lead to a rational expectations equilibrium. Is it possible to describe a plausible learning process which ultimately yields rational expectations? The answer depends upon how 'plausible' is understood. One possibility is to insist that agents learn using correctly specified Bayesian models. David Kreps and I argue elsewhere (Bray and Kreps 1986) that it is in fact not plausible, because it in effect assumes a more elaborate and informationally demanding form of rational expectations equilibrium. However, if agents do learn in this way, and if the model has suitable continuity properties, expectations eventually become rational in the conventional sense.

Another possible way to model-learning is to assume that agents estimate the model as if it were in rational expectations equilibrium; for example, in the spot and futures market model they regress $\bar{p}_s$ on $\bar{p}_f$ using ordinary least squares, and use the estimated regression coefficients in forecasting $\bar{p}_s$ from $\bar{p}_f$. In Bray (1982) I studied this procedure for the model of example 2 where there are uninformed dealers and informed dealers, all of whom have the same information. I found that, provided the uninformed dealers did not form too large a proportion of the market, the model would eventually converge to its rational expectations equilibrium. Bray (1983)[2] and Bray and Savin (1986) study similar econometric learning processes for a simple macroeconomic model and a version of the cobweb model. In both these models, if the parameters of the supply and demand functions have the usual signs, agents eventually learn how to form rational expectations. In all these examples, agents are estimating misspecified economic models, so convergence to rational expectations equilibrium is not based on standard theorems on the asymptotic properties of estimators; this is somewhat surprising, and is hard to prove. Convergence to rational expectations equilibrium may be slow, and take place only if the parameters of the model lies in a certain range. Although many of the examples that have been studied converge in economically plausible circumstances, there is no general theory that establishes that convergence will always take place.

Expectations are important for economics; they crop up unavoidably in considering a vast range of issues. The enormous virtue of the rational expectations hypothesis is that it gives a simple, general, and plausible way of handling expectations. It makes it possible to formulate and answer questions, for example, on the efficiency of markets as transmitters of information which would otherwise be utterly intractable. All recent progress on the economics of information is built on the rational expectations hypothesis.

Consider for a moment the alternative hypotheses. One possibility is that agents use a simple forecasting rule which generates systematic mistakes. In any application it is necessary to specify the rule, for example adaptive expectations. If there is good evidence that people do forecast in this way, this is attractive, but it seems implausible that in the long run in a stable environment they will fail to notice their mistakes and modify the rule. Another alternative is to try to model the dynamics of the learning process. At present this seems to make for models that are too complicated and mathematically difficult to use for addressing most questions. Rational expectations equilibrium is a way of avoiding many difficult dynamic issues; if an issue is intractable in the current state of knowledge, circumventing it is probably the most fruitful research strategy.

Another alternative is to rely on survey data for expectations. Where possible this may be valuable in empirical work, if not very helpful for theorists.

---

[2] Bray (1983) is much the shortest and simplest of these papers on learning, and the best introduction to the issues as I see them. Bray and Savin (1986) contains computer simulations which shed light on the rates of convergence and divergence, and discusses the relationship between this work and time-varying parameter models in econometrics. Related literature is surveyed briefly in Blume, Bray, and Easley (1986). Bray and Savin (1986) contains more recent references.

A further alternative is to follow Keynes and argue that expectations cannot be described as probability distributions; they are volatile, and are not susceptible to formal description. This makes it impossible to incorporate expectations explicitly into formal models, except by treating them as exogenous. Begg (1982b) argues that this is Keynes's strategy in the General Theory and is followed in traditional textbook treatments of Keynesian theory. In some cases I think this is an entirely defensible, indeed attractive, strategy for modelling short-term events. The danger is that, if expectations are unobservable, inexplicable, exogenous, and volatile, it leaves the model with no predictive and very little explanatory power, as anything can be attributed to a shift in expectations. The rational expectations hypothesis also postulates unobservable expectations, but otherwise, in total opposition to Keynes, treats expectations as explicable, exogenous, and stable (unless the underlying model changes, in which case expectations change appropriately). In medium- to long-term models the extreme rational expectations hypothesis is more attractive than the extreme exogenous expectations hypothesis. There is currently no generally acceptable intermediate hypothesis. Note that, although Keynes himself would probably shudder if he knew, there is no reason why rational expectations should not be incorporated into 'Keynesian' models, which would have quite different properties from the 'new classical' rational expectations models (see Begg 1982b).

The rational expectations hypothesis seems at present much the most satisfactory generally applicable hypothesis on expectations formation. But it must be remembered that rational expectations models describe long-run equilibria, on the assumption that the dynamics induced by learning eventually converge to rational expectations equilibrium. We have no good reason to believe that this assumption is always, or even often, valid.

I have discussed the assumptions of the financial market models at some length. The other criterion for the correctness of the models as descriptions is to look at implications of the models, and compare them with data. There are two sources of data: experimental data from laboratory situations, and empirical data from real markets. Ultimately the objective is to understand real markets, but laboratory data, generated by setting up a market with groups of students, enable the experimenter to control and design the experiment, eliminating the host of extraneous factors that affect real market data.

Plott and Sunder (1982) set up a series of asset markets with informed and uninformed traders. The return on the asset depended on which of two or three states of the world occurred. The informed traders all had the same piece of information, in most cases telling them with state of the world had occurred. Plott and Sunder calculated two prices for each market: first, the rational expectations equilibrium price in which the uninformed dealers inferred as much as possible from the price, and second, the prior information price in which the uninformed dealers traded only on the basis of their prior information. Although the rational expectations model was not a perfect fit, prices did show a tendency to move towards their rational expectations equilibrium level. Plott and Sunder interpret the data as supporting the rational expectations rather than the prior information model.

Real market data have been used to test the efficient markets hypothesis, that using information in addition to the current price of an asset does not make for better predictions, as the market price efficiently aggregates all the information. Three different forms of the hypothesis have been considered; the weak form, considering the information in past prices; the semi-strong form, considering more general publicly available information; and the strong form, considering private information. The empirical literature is vast; Brealey (1983) provides a very readable introduction, and numerous references. Broadly, the literature supports the weak and semi-strong forms of the efficient markets hypothesis, but private information does seem to give some advantage. The efforts of numerous academic investigators have failed to uncover a rule for forecasting market prices in order to manage a portfolio that does significantly better than holding a fixed, well diversified portfolio. These results are consistent with the theoretical models that I have been describing and can be taken as support for the application of the rational expectations hypothesis to financial markets.

13. Further Questions

These models answer some questions, but provoke others. Many of the models consider asset markets in isolation, taking the return generated by the asset as exogenous. (The spot and futures market model is an exception.) But financial markets are part of a larger system. One of their major functions is to enable enterprises to spread, and share risk, with consequences for output, investment, and employment. It now appears that the markets may also have a role as transmitters of information. The ramifications of this role are not understood, but may be investigated using techniques similar to those I have described.

Another set of open questions concerns the mechanism of price formation. In these models price is a function of information, for example in the spot and futures market model where dealers have diverse information the futures price $\bar{p}_f = \theta^{*-1}E(\bar{a} \mid \bar{I}_1, \bar{I}_2, \ldots, \bar{I}_n)$, (30), where θ^* is a parameter, and $\bar{I}_i$ agent i's information, a normal random variable. As the information varies from year to year, the price varies. If the dealers have diverse information, no individual dealer can check that the price is at the correct level given all the information. If a dealer thinks that the futures price is high or low given his private information, he can only conclude that others dealers have different information which leads them to expect a high or low spot price. Any numerical value of $\bar{p}_f$ can clear the market; it is far from clear what pushes $\bar{p}_f$ to its correct value. (This point is originally due to Beja 1976.)

Universal price-taking is of course a convenient fiction. People set prices, unilaterally, by auction procedures, or by haggling. If there is a very limited range of prices at which goods can be sold, price-taking is a good approximation. It may be necessary to consider the detailed mechanics of price-making, the activities of brokers, jobbers, and market-makers, to understand some aspects of the determination of prices in asset markets. In discussing their experimental results, Plott and Sunder suggest that some of the information is transmitted by the oral auction process which they use, including unaccepted bids and offers. If this is so, it provides an additional reason for looking at the institutional details of market structure.

The models have a very stark, simple, time structure; things happen at only two dates. In practice, many financial markets operate repeatedly and the same asset is traded at a large number of dates; indeed, trade may best be modelled as a continuous-time process. There is a literature on continuous-time models of financial markets (e.g. Black and Scholes 1973, and Merton 1973), but this literature takes no account of informational asymmetries. Continuous-time models with asymmetric information are attractive means of investigating the rate at which markets disseminate information, although they may pose formidable technical difficulties. There is certainly a case for looking at a richer temporal structure than has been considered up to now.

APPENDIX: PROOF OF LEMMA (CONDITIONAL DISTRIBUTIONS OF NORMAL RANDOM VARIABLES)

Anderson (1958) shows that

$$\bar{I} = E(\bar{a} \mid \bar{I}_1, \bar{I}_2, \ldots, \bar{I}_n) = E\bar{a} + \Sigma_{ay}\Sigma_{yy}^{-1}(\bar{y} - E\bar{y}) \tag{A1}$$

where $\bar{y}$ is notation for the vector $(\bar{I}_1, \bar{I}_2, \ldots, \bar{I}_n)$. $\Sigma_{ay} = \text{cov}(\bar{a}, \bar{y})$, $\Sigma_{yy} = \text{var}(\bar{y})$. Equation (A1) implies that $\bar{I}$ is a linear function of $(\bar{I}_1, \bar{I}_2, \ldots, \bar{I}_n)$. As linear functions of normal random variables are normal, $\bar{I}$ and $\bar{e} = \bar{a} - \bar{I}$

$$\text{cov}(\bar{e}, \bar{y}) = \text{cov}[\bar{a} - E\bar{a} - \Sigma_{ay}\Sigma_{yy}^{-1}(\bar{y} - E\bar{y}), \bar{y}] = \Sigma_{ay} - \Sigma_{ay}\Sigma_{yy}^{-1}\Sigma_{yy} = 0.$$

Thus $\bar{e}$ and $\bar{y}$ are uncorrelated and, since they are normal, independent. Since $\bar{I}$ is a linear function of $\bar{y}$, $\bar{I}$ and $\bar{e}$ are uncorrelated; that is,

$$\text{cov}(\bar{I}, \bar{e}) = \text{cov}(\bar{I}, \bar{a} - \bar{I}) = 0 \tag{A2}$$

and so $\bar{I}$ and $\bar{e}$ are independent.

From (A1),

$$E\bar{a} = E\bar{I} \tag{A3}$$

and so $E\bar{e} = E\bar{a} - E\bar{I} = 0$. As $\bar{I}$ and $\bar{e}$ are independent,

$$\text{var } \bar{a} = \text{var}(\bar{I} + \bar{e}) = \text{var } \bar{I} + \text{var } \bar{e}.$$

As $\bar{I}$ is a function of $\bar{I}_1, \ldots, \bar{I}_n$ and $\bar{e}$ is independent of $\bar{I}_1, \bar{I}_2, \ldots, \bar{I}_n$, the conditional distribution of $\bar{a} = \bar{I} + \bar{E}$ given $\bar{I}_1, \bar{I}_2, \ldots, \bar{I}_n$ is normal (as $\bar{e}$ is normal), with mean

$$E(\bar{a} \mid \bar{I}_1, \bar{I}_2, \ldots, \bar{I}_n) = E(\bar{I} \mid \bar{I}_1, \bar{I}_2, \ldots, \bar{I}_n) + E(\bar{e} \mid \bar{I}_1, \bar{I}_2, \ldots, \bar{I}_n)$$
$$= \bar{I} + E\bar{e} = \bar{I} = E(\bar{a} \mid \bar{I})$$

and

$$\text{var}(\bar{a} \mid \bar{I}_1, \bar{I}_2, \ldots, \bar{I}_n) = \text{var}(\bar{e} \mid \bar{I}_1, \bar{I}_2, \ldots, \bar{I}_n) = \text{var } \bar{e} = \text{var}(\bar{a} \mid \bar{I}).$$

It can be shown that the conditional expectation of $\bar{a}$, given $\bar{I}_1, \bar{I}_2, \ldots, \bar{I}_n$, is the unique linear function of $\bar{I}$ of $\bar{I}_1, \bar{I}_2, \ldots, \bar{I}_n$ satisfying (A2) and (A3). These equations characterize the conditional expectation of one normal random variable given another. (See Bray 1981 for an application of this fact.)

12

Decision-making in the Presence of Risk

MARK J. MACHINA

1. Introduction

Virtually all social, economic, or technological decisions involve some degree of risk or uncertainty. In some cases, such as games of chance, the probabilities of the alternative consequences can be accurately determined. In other cases, actuarial or engineering data must be used to construct estimates of these likelihoods. To the extent that these probabilities can be quantified, however, individuals' attitudes towards risk can be subjected to theoretical analysis and empirical testing.

The seventeenth-century founders of modern probability theory such as Pascal and Fermat assumed that individuals would evaluate alternative monetary gambles on the basis of their *expected values,* so that a lottery offering the payoffs $(x_1, \ldots, x_n)$ with respect probabilities $(p_1, \ldots, p_n)$ would yield as much satisfaction as a sure payment equal to its expected value $\bar{x} = \sum x_i p_i$. Such an approach could be justified by appealing to the *law of large numbers,* which states that, if a gamble is indefinitely and independently repeated, its long-run average payoff will necessarily converge to its expected value.

However, in a one-shot choice situation which cannot be replicated or averaged, individuals may well base their decisions on more than just the expected values of the alternative prospects. This point was dramatically illustrated by an example offered by Nicholas Bernoulli in 1728 and now known as the 'St Petersburg Paradox':

Suppose someone offers to toss a fair coin repeatedly until it lands heads, and to pay you $1 if this occurs on the first toss, $2 if it takes two tosses to land a head, $4 if it takes three tosses, $8 if it takes four tosses, etc. What is the largest sure payment you would be willing to forgo in order to undertake a single play of this game?

Since this game offers a 1/2 chance of winning $1, a 1/4 chance of winning $2, and so on, its expected payoff is $(1/2)\$1 + (1/4)\$2 + (1/8)\$4 + \cdots = \$1/2 + \$1/2 + \$1/2 + \cdots = \$\infty$. However, even if such a well-backed offer could be made, it was felt that few individuals would

Reprinted with permission from *Science* (1 May 1987, vol. 236, pp. 537–43) © AAAS. I am grateful to the National Science Foundation (Grant SES 83-08165) and the Alfred P. Sloan Foundation for financial support, and to J. Sobel and M. Rothschild for helpful remarks on this material.

forgo more than, say, $20 for a one-shot play—a far cry from its (infinite) expected value.[1] The resolution of this paradox, proposed independently by Gabriel Cramer and Daniel Bernoulli (Nicholas's cousin), would form the basis for the modern theory of decision-making under risk.[2]

Arguing that a gain of $1000 was not necessarily valued ten times as much as a gain of $100, Cramer and Bernoulli hypothesized that individuals possess a *utility of wealth* function $U(x)$, and that they would value a lottery on the basis of its *expected utility* $\bar{u} = \sum U(x_i)p_i$ rather than its expected value $\bar{x} = \sum x_i p_i$. If utility took the logarithmic form, $U(x) \equiv \ln(x)$ for example, the sure monetary gain ξ which would yield the same level of satisfaction as the St Petersburg gamble would be given by the solution to

$$\ln(w + \xi) = (1/2)\ln(w + 1) + (1/4)\ln(w + 2) + (1/8)\ln(w + 4) + \cdots \quad (1)$$

where w denotes the individual's initial wealth. If $w = \$1000$, the individual would be indifferent between taking this gamble or receiving a sure gain of about $6; if $w = \$50,000$, this amount is about $9. Of course, someone with a different utility function $U^*(\cdot)$ would assign a different sure monetary equivalent.

Two centuries later, this approach was formally axiomatized by Frank Ramsey (1931) in his treatise on the philosophy of belief, by John von Neumann and Oskar Morgenstern (1944) in their development of the theory of games, and by Leonard Savage (1954) in his work on the foundations of statistical inference. The simplicity and intuitive appeal of its axioms, the elegance of its representation of risk attitudes in terms of properties of the utility function, and the tremendous number of theoretical results it has produced have led the expected utility model to become the dominant, and indeed almost exclusive, model of decision-making under risk in economics, operations research, philosophy, and statistical decision theory (see Hey 1979; Hillier and Lieberman 1986; Ells 1982; De Groot 1970).

However, these theoretical advances have been accompanied by an accumulating body of empirical evidence which suggests that individuals systematically violate the predictions of the expected utility model. The largest and most systematic class of these violations concerns the key behavioural assumption of the model, the so-called *independence axiom*. This has led to a growing tension in the field of decision theory, with

---

[1] The infinite expectation in this example is not really necessary to make the point: agreeing to limit the game to at most one million tosses will still lead to a striking discrepancy between most individuals' valuations of the modified gamble and its expected payoff of $500,000.
[2] G. Cramer, correspondence to N. Bernoulli, 1728, and Bernoulli (1738). For historical discussions of the St Petersburg Paradox and its impact, see Todhunter (1949) and Samuelson (1977).

defenders of the expected utility approach stressing the 'rationality' of this axiom and the theoretical power of the model, and others emphasizing the importance of the empirical evidence and developing alternatives to the expected utility model.

My purpose in this chapter is to give an overview of these developments in the field of decision-making under risk. The following sections provide a description of the expected utility model both as a theoretical tool and as a behavioural hypothesis, a summary of the evidence on systematic violations of the independence axiom, and a report on the newer non-expected utility models of decision-making currently being developed. This latter work has shown that the basic results of expected utility analysis are in fact quite robust to violations of the independence axiom. However, separate evidence suggests that some of the other standard assumptions in the theory of choice under uncertainty may also be suspect.

2. The Expected Utility Model

The expected utility model follows standard economic theory by specifying a set of objects of choice and assuming that the individual's preferences can be represented by a real-valued function over this choice set. Since it is a model of decision-making under risk, the objects of choice are not the ultimate outcomes that might obtain (for example, alternative wealth levels,) but rather *probability distributions* over these outcomes. Given a set $\{x_1, \ldots, x_n\}$ of potential outcomes, the choice set thus consists of all probability distributions $P = (p_1, \ldots, p_n)$ over $\{x_1, \ldots, x_n\}$, where p_i denotes the probability of obtaining x_i and $\Sigma p_i = 1$.

The model then assumes that the individual's preferences can be represented by a real-valued maximand or *preference function* $V(\cdot)$ over probability distributions, in the sense that the distribution $P^* = (p_1^*, \ldots, p_n^*)$ is preferred to $P = (p_1, \ldots, p_n)$ if and only if $V(P^*) > V(P)$, and is indifferent to P if and only if $V(P^*) = V(P)$. The essence of the expected utility approach is that $V(\cdot)$ takes the *linear* form $V(P) \equiv \Sigma U(x_i)p_i$ for some set of coefficients $\{U(x_i)\}$, so that expected utility preferences can be described as being *linear in the probabilities*. When the outcome set is a continuum such as the interval $[0, M]$, the probability distribution of a random variable $\tilde{x}$ over $[0, M]$ can be represented by its density function $f(\cdot)$, or, more generally, by its cumulative distribution function $F(\cdot)$ (where $F(x) \equiv \Pr(\tilde{x} \leq x)$), and preferences over such distributions are assumed to be representable by linear preference functionals of the form $V(f) \equiv \int U(x)f(x)\, dx$ or $V(F) \equiv \int U(x)\, dF(x)$, which can again be interpreted as the expectation

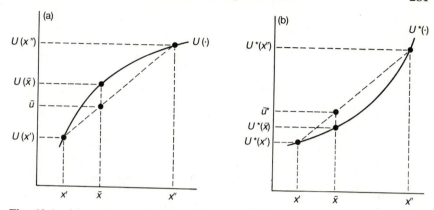

Fig. 12.1 (a) *Concave utility function of a risk-averse individual.* (b) *Convex utility function of a risk-preferring individual.*

of $U(\cdot)$.[3] Since it is clear that the transformed utility function $aU(\cdot) + b$ ($a > 0$) will generate the same ranking over distributions as $U(\cdot)$, utility functions are often normalized so that $U(0) = 0$ and $U(M) = 1$.

Figure 12.1 illustrates how this model can be used to represent various attitudes towards risk. The monotonicity of the utility functions $U(\cdot)$ and $U^*(\cdot)$ in the figures reflects the property of stochastic dominance preference, where one probability distribution is said to *stochastically dominate* another if it can be obtained from the latter by a sequence of rightward shifts of probability mass. Since such shifts raise the probability of obtaining at least x for all values of x, stochastic dominance preference is the probabilistic analogue of the view that 'more is better'.

The points $\bar{x} = (2/3)x' + (1/3)x''$ in the figures denote the expected value of the gamble offering a $2/3:1/3$ chance of the outcomes x' or x''; and $\bar{u} = (2/3)U(x') + (1/3)U(x'')$ and $\bar{u}^* = (2/3)U^*(x') + (1/3)U^*(x'')$ give the expected *utilities* of this gamble for $U(\cdot)$ and $U^*(\cdot)$. For the concave (that is, bowed upward) utility function $U(\cdot)$, we have $\bar{u} < U(\bar{x})$, implying that the individual would rather receive a sure payment equal to the expected value of the gamble than actually take the gamble itself. For the convex (bowed downward) utility function $U^*(\cdot)$, we have $\bar{u}^* > U^*(\bar{x})$, so that this individual would prefer to bear the risk rather than receive a sure payment of $\bar{x}$. Since Jensen's inequality[4] implies that these

---

[3] The *Riemann–Stieltjes integral* $\int U(x)\,dF(x)$ denotes the integral of $U(\cdot)$ with respect to the probability measure associated with the cumulative distribution function $F(\cdot)$ (Bartle 1976: Sec. 29).

[4] This result from probability theory states that the expectations $\Sigma U(x_i)p_i$, $\int U(x)f(x)\,dx$, or $\int U(x)\,dF(x)$ will be no greater (no less) than $U(\bar{x})$ whenever $U(\cdot)$ is a concave (convex) function (Feller 1971).

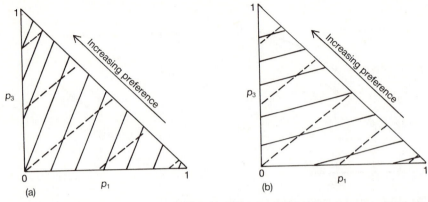

Fig. 12.2 (a) *Relatively steep indifference curves of a risk-averse individual.*
(b) *Relatively flat indifference curves of a risk-preferring individual.*

respective attitudes will extend to *all* risky gambles, $U(\cdot)$ is referred to as *risk-averse* and $U^*(\cdot)$ as *risk-preferring*.[5]

Researchers such as Arrow (1974) and Pratt (1964) have shown how the *relative* concavity or convexity of a utility function, as measured by the curvature index $-U''(x)/U'(x)$, can lead to theoretical predictions of how risk attitudes, and hence behaviour, will vary with wealth or across individuals in a variety of different risky situations.

Although these figures illustrate the flexibility of the expected utility model compared with the Pascal–Fermat expected value model, an alternative graphical approach can be used to highlight the *behavioural restrictions* implied by the hypothesis of linearity in the probabilities. Consider the set of all distributions $\{p_1, p_2, p_3\}$ over the fixed outcome levels $\{x_1, x_2, x_3\}$, where $x_1 < x_2 < x_3$. Since $p_2 \equiv 1 - p_1 - p_3$, we can represent this set of distributions by the points in the unit triangle in the (p_1, p_3) plane in Figure 12.2. Since upward movements in the triangle increase p_3 at the expense of p_2 (i.e. shift probability mass from the outcome x_2 up to x_3) and leftward movements reduce p_1 to the benefit of p_2 (shift probability from x_1 up to x_2), these movements (and, more generally, all north-west movements) result in stochastically dominating distributions and would accordingly be preferred. Since the individual's *indifference curves* or iso-expected utility loci in this diagram are given by the solutions to

$$U(x_1)p_1 + U(x_2)(1 - p_1 - p_3) + U(x_3)p_3 = \text{constant}, \qquad (2)$$

---

[5] More generally, a concave (convex) utility function will be averse to (will prefer) all increases in risk, where a pair of shifts of probability mass is said to constitute an *increase in risk* if it moves mass away from the centre of a probability distribution out towards its tails in a manner that preserves the expected value of the distribution (Rothschild and Stiglitz 1970).

they will consist of parallel straight lines (the solid lines in the figures), with more preferred indifference curves lying to the north-west. This implies that knowledge of an individual's indifference curves over any small region is sufficient to know their preferences over the entire set of distributions.

The dashed lines in Figure 12.2 are not indifference curves but rather *iso-expected value lines,* that is, solutions to

$$x_1 p_1 + x_2(1 - p_1 - p_3) + x_3 p_3 = \text{constant}. \tag{3}$$

Since north-east movements along these lines do not change the expected value of the distribution but do increase the probabilities of the tail outcomes x_1 and x_3 at the expense of the middle outcome x_2, they represent the set of *increases in risk* in this diagram.[6] When the utility function $U(\cdot)$ is concave (risk-averse), its indifference curves can be shown to be steeper than the iso-expected value lines (Figure 12.2(a)) and increases in risk will lead to lower indifference curves. When $U(\cdot)$ is ·convex (risk-preferring), its indifference curves will be flatter than the iso-expected value lines (Figure 12.2(b)), and increases in risk will lead to higher indifference curves. If we compare two different utility functions, the one that is more risk-averse (more concave) will possess the steeper indifference curves.

The property of linearity in the probabilities can also be represented as a restriction on the individual's attitudes towards *probability mixtures* of distributions. Given an outcome set $\{x_1, \ldots, x_n\}$, the $\alpha:(1 - \alpha)$ probability mixture of the distributions $P^* = (p_1^*, \ldots, p_n^*)$ and $P = (p_1, \ldots, p_n)$ is defined as the distribution $\alpha P^* + (1 - \alpha)P = [\alpha p_1^* + (1 - \alpha)p_1, \ldots, \alpha p_n^* + (1 - \alpha)p_n]$. This may be thought of as that single-stage distribution which yields the same ultimate probabilities over $\{x_1, \ldots, x_n\}$ as a two-stage lottery that offers an $\alpha:(1 - \alpha)$ chance of winning the distributions P^* or P.[7] Since linearity of $V(\cdot)$ implies that $V[\alpha P^* + (1 - \alpha)P] \equiv \alpha V(P^*) + (1 - \alpha)V(P)$, expected utility preferences will exhibit the following property:[8]

INDEPENDENCE AXIOM. If P^* is preferred (indifferent) to P, then the mixture $\alpha P^* + (1 - \alpha)P^{**}$ will be preferred (indifferent) to $\alpha P + (1 - \alpha)P^{**}$ for all $\alpha > 0$ and P^{**}.

---

[6] See n. 5 above.

[7] The $\alpha:(1 - \alpha)$ probability mixtures of the density functions $f^*(\cdot)$ and $f(\cdot)$ and the cumulative distribution functions $F^*(\cdot)$ and $F(\cdot)$ are given by $\alpha f^*(\cdot) + (1 - \alpha)f(\cdot)$ and $\alpha F^*(\cdot) + (1 - \alpha)F(\cdot)$, and possess similar interpretations.

[8] This follows since $V(P^*) > (=)V(P)$ implies $V[\alpha P^* + (1 - \alpha)P^{**}] = \alpha V(P^*) + (1 - \alpha)V(P^{**}) > (=)\alpha V(P) + (1 - \alpha)V(P^{**}) = V[\alpha P + (1 - \alpha)P^{**}]$. Early statements of this axiom may be found in Marschak (1950) and Samuelson (1952).

This condition, which is in fact *equivalent to* the property of linearity in the probabilities, can be interpreted as follows:

In terms of the ultimate probability of obtaining each outcome, the choice between the mixtures $\alpha P^* + (1 - \alpha)P^{**}$ and $\alpha P + (1 - \alpha)P^{**}$ is equivalent to being offered a coin with a $(1 - \alpha)$ chance of landing tails, in which case you will receive the lottery P^{**}, and being asked *before the flip* whether you would rather receive the lottery P^* or P in the event of a head. Now either tails will come up, in which case your choice won't have mattered, or else heads will come up, in which case you are 'in effect' back to a choice between P^* or P, and you 'should' have the same preferences over them as you had before.

Even though its conclusion is *prescriptive,* this argument has played a large role in the widespread adoption of expected utility maximization as a *descriptive* model of choice under risk. However, with a few exceptions in the early 1950s, it is only recently that the expected utility hypothesis has undergone the type of empirical testing that such a widely used behavioural hypothesis might be expected to receive.

3. Systematic Violations of the Independence Axiom

The earliest example of systematic violation of the independence axiom (or, equivalently, of linearity in the probabilities) is known as the *Allais Paradox* (Allais 1953; see also Allais 1979). This example involves obtaining individuals' preference rankings over each of the following pairs of gambles:

$$a_1: \{1.00 \text{ chance of } \$1{,}000{,}000 \quad \text{versus} \quad a_2: \begin{cases} 0.10 \text{ chance of } \$5{,}000{,}000 \\ 0.89 \text{ chance of } \$1{,}000{,}000 \\ 0.01 \text{ chance of } \$0 \end{cases}$$

and

$$a_3: \begin{cases} 0.10 \text{ chance of } \$5{,}000{,}000 \\ 0.90 \text{ chance of } \$0 \end{cases} \quad \text{versus} \quad a_4: \begin{cases} 0.11 \text{ chance of } \$1{,}000{,}000 \\ 0.89 \text{ chance of } \$0 \end{cases}$$

Setting $\{x_1, x_2, x_3\} = \{\$0, \$1{,}000{,}000, \$5{,}000{,}000\}$, these four gambles form a parallelogram in the (p_1, p_3) triangle of Figure 12.3(a). Under the expected utility hypothesis, a preference for a_1 in the first pair would indicate relatively steep indifference curves (as in the figure), and hence a preference for a_4 in the second pair. In the alternative case of relatively flat indifference curves, the gambles a_2 and a_3 would be preferred.[9] However, experimenters have repeatedly found that the modal, if not majority, preference of subjects has been for a_1 in the first pair and a_3 in the second,[10] suggesting that indifference curves are not parallel but rather *fan out* (Figure 12.3(b)).

---

[9] Algebraically, these cases are equivalent to the cases where $0.10U(5{,}000{,}000) - 0.11U(1{,}000{,}000) + 0.01U(0)$ is negative or positive, respectively.

[10] Morrison (1967); Raiffa (1968); Slovic and Tversky (1974); Moskowitz (1974).

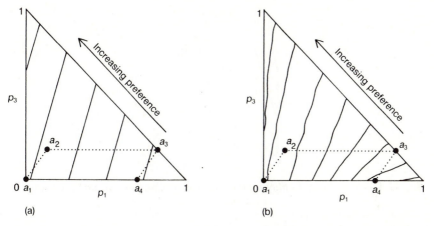

Fig. 12.3 (a) *Expected utility indifference curves and the Allais Paradox:* (b) *Non-expected utility indifference curves that fan out, and the Allais Paradox.*

Although initially dismissed as an isolated example, the Allais Paradox is now known to be a special case of a general empirical phenomenon termed the *common consequence effect.* This effect involves pairs of probability mixtures of the form:

$$b_1: \alpha\delta_x + (1-\alpha)P^{**} \qquad \text{versus} \qquad b_2: \alpha P + (1-\alpha)P^{**}$$

and

$$b_3: \alpha\delta_x + (1-\alpha)P^* \qquad \text{versus} \qquad b_4: \alpha P + (1-\alpha)P^*$$

where δ_x is the degenerate distribution yielding the outcome x with certainty, P involves outcomes both greater and less than x, and P^{**} stochastically dominates P^*.[11] Although the independence axiom clearly implies choices of either b_1 and b_3 or else b_2 and b_4, researchers have again found a tendency for subjects to prefer b_1 in the first pair and b_4 in the second.[12] When the component distributions δ_x, P, P^*, and P^{**} are each over a common outcome set $\{x_1, x_2, x_3\}$, the prospects b_1, b_2, b_3, and b_4 will again form a parallelogram in the (p_1, p_3) triangle, and a preference for b_1 and b_4 again implies indifference curves that fan out (see Figure 12.4). It is important to note that it is not merely the high degree of such violations (ranging from 20 to 80 per cent) that is important, but rather the *systematic* nature of these departures from linearity in the probabilities: although a preference for b_2 and b_3 would

---

[11] The Allais Paradox choices a_1, a_2, a_3, and a_4 correspond tó b_1, b_2, b_4, and b_3, where $\alpha = 11/100$, $x = \$1,000,000$, P is a $(10/11):(1/11)$ chance of $\$5,000,000$ or $\$0$, $P^* = \delta_{\$0}$, and $P^{**} = \delta_{\$1,000,000}$.

[12] See MacCrimmon (1968); MacCrimmon and Larsson (1979); Kahneman and Tversky (1979); Chew and Waller (1986).

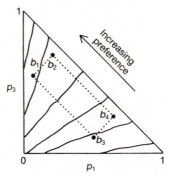

Fig. 12.4 *Non-expected utility indifference curves that fan out, and the Common Consequence Effect.*

also violate the expected utility hypothesis (implying indifference curves that fan *in*), such choices account for a very small proportion of the total violations of expected utility in these studies.

A second class of systematic violations, stemming from another early example of Allais (1953, 1979) is known as the *common ratio effect*. This phenomenon involves pairs of gambles of the form:

$$c_1: \begin{cases} p \text{ chance of } \$X \\ 1-p \text{ chance of } \$0 \end{cases} \quad \text{versus} \quad c_2: \begin{cases} q \text{ chance of } \$Y \\ 1-q \text{ chance of } \$0, \end{cases}$$

and

$$c_3: \begin{cases} rp \text{ chance of } \$X \\ 1-rp \text{ chance of } \$0 \end{cases} \quad \text{versus} \quad c_4: \begin{cases} rq \text{ chance of } \$Y \\ 1-rq \text{ chance of } \$0, \end{cases}$$

where $p > q$, $0 < X < Y$, and $r \in (0, 1)$, and includes the 'certainty effect' of Kahneman and Tversky (1979) and the 'Bergen Paradox' of Hagen (1979) as special cases.[13] Setting $\{x_1, x_2, x_3\} = \{0, X, Y\}$ and plotting these gambles in the (p_1, p_3) triangle, the line segments $\overline{c_1 c_2}$ and $\overline{c_3 c_4}$ are seen to be parallel, as in Figure 12.5(a), so that the expected utility model again predicts choices of c_1 and c_3 (if indifference curves are steep) or c_2 and c_4 (if they are flat). However, investigators have found a systematic tendency to depart from these predictions in the direction of preferring c_1 and c_4,[14] which again suggests that indifference curves fan out (Figure 12.5(a)). In a variation on this approach, Kahneman and

---

[13] Thus, for example, Kahneman and Tversky found that 80 per cent of their subjects preferred a sure gain of 3000 Israeli pounds to an 80 per cent chance of winning 4000, but 65 per cent preferred a 20 per cent chance of winning 4000 to a 25 per cent chance of winning 3000.

[14] See MacCrimmon and Larsson (1979); Chew and Waller (1986); Tversky (1975).

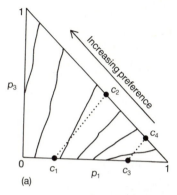

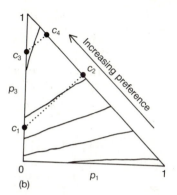

Fig. 12.5 (a) *Non-expected utility indifference curves that fan out, and the Common Ratio Effect.* (b) *Non-expected utility indifference curves that fan out, and Common Ratio Effect with negative payoffs.*

Tversky (1979) replaced the gains of X and Y in the above gambles with losses of these magnitudes and found a tendency to depart from expected utility in the direction of c_2 and c_3. Defining $\{x_1, x_2, x_3\}$ as $\{-Y, -X, 0\}$ (to maintain the ordering $x_1 < x_2 < x_3$) and plotting these gambles (Figure 12.5(b)), a choice of c_2 and c_3 is again seen to reflect the property of fanning out.

A third type of systematic departure from the expected utility model involves the elicitation or *assessment* of subjects' utility functions, and hence has important implications for the use of such procedures in applied decision analysis. A standard assessment procedure, termed the *fractile method*, begins by adopting the normalization $U(0) = 0$ and $U(M) = 1$ for some positive M and then picking a fixed mixture probability, say 1/2. The next step involves determining the individual's sure monetary equivalent ξ_1 of a $1/2:1/2$ chance of M or 0, which implies that $U(\xi_1) = (1/2)U(M) + (1/2)U(0) = 1/2$. Finding the sure monetary equivalents of the $1/2:1/2$ chances of ξ_1 or 0 and of M or ξ_1 yields the values ξ_2 and ξ_3, which solve $U(\xi_2) = 1/4$ and $U(\xi_3) = 3/4$. By repeated application of this procedure, the utility function can in the limit be completely assessed. However, there is no reason why the mixture probability must be 1/2. Picking any other $\alpha \in (0, 1)$ and defining ξ_1^*, ξ_2^*, and ξ_3^* as the sure monetary equivalents of the $\alpha:(1 - \alpha)$ chances of M or 0, ξ_1^* or 0, and M or ξ_1^*, yield the equations $U(\xi_1^*) = \alpha$, $U(\xi_2^*) = \alpha^2$, and $U(\xi_3^*) = \alpha + (1 - \alpha)\alpha$, and such a procedure can also be used to recover $U(\cdot)$.

Although this assessment procedure ought to recover the same (normalized) utility function for any mixture probability α, researchers have found a systematic tendency for higher values of α to lead to the 'recovery' of higher-valued utility functions, as in Figure 12.6(a) (see

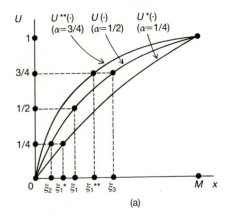

(a)

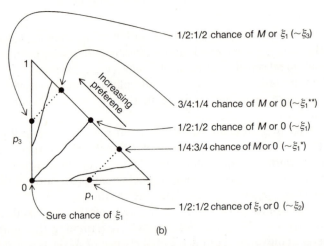

(b)

Fig. 12.6 (a) *'Recovered' utility functions for mixture probabilities 1/4, 1/2, and 3/4.* (b) *Preferences that would generate the responses of Figure 6(a)* (~ *denotes indifference*).

Karmarkar 1978, 1974; McCord and de Neufville 1983, 1984). By illustrating the probability distributions used to obtain the responses ξ_1, ξ_2, and ξ_3 for $\alpha = 1/2$, ξ_1^* for $\alpha = 1/4$, and ξ_1^{**} for $\alpha = 3/4$, Figure 12.6(b) shows that, as with the common consequence and common ratio effects, this *utility evaluation effect* is precisely what would be expected from an individual whose indifference curves departed from expected utility by fanning out.[15]

---

[15] Set $\{x_1, x_2, x_3\} = \{0, \xi_1, M\}$. Then the ordering of the values ξ_1, ξ_2, ξ_3, ξ_1^* and ξ_1^{**} in Figure 12.6(a) is derived from the individual's preference ordering over the five distributions in Figure 12.6(b) for which they are the respective sure monetary equivalents.

Some proponents of the expected utility model have criticized the above findings on grounds such as 'the experimental subjects were not experienced at making decisions under uncertainty'; 'once subjects were made aware of their violations of the independence axiom they would correct their choices'; and 'the experiments did not involve real money payments and hence do not reflect real-world behaviour'. To the extent that these claims have been examined by the appropriate experimental modifications, however, they have not been supported (Slovic and Tversky 1974; Moskowitz 1974; MacCrimmon 1968). In an interesting extension of these studies, Battalio, Kagel, and MacDonald (1985) have shown that laboratory rats choosing among gambles involving substantial variations in their actual daily food intake also exhibit fanning-out behaviour.

4. Non-expected Utility Models

The extent and systematic nature of these observed departures from expected utility have led several researchers to generalize this model by positing *non*linear functional forms for the preference function $V(\cdot)$. Examples of these include the functional forms $V(P) \equiv \Sigma v(x_i) \pi(p_i)$, $V(P) \equiv \Sigma v(x_i) \pi(p_i) / \Sigma \pi(p_j)$, $V(P) \equiv \Sigma v(x_i) p_i + [\Sigma \tau(x_j) p_j]^2$, $V(P) \equiv \Sigma v(x_i) p_i / \Sigma \tau(x_j) p_j$, and $V(P) \equiv \Sigma v(x_i) [g(p_1 + \cdots + p_i) - g(p_1 + \cdots + p_{i-1})]$, as well as their extensions to density functions $f(\cdot)$ or cumulative distribution functions $F(\cdot)$.[16] Many (though not all) of these forms are flexible enough to exhibit the properties of stochastic dominance preference and risk aversion/risk preference in a non-expected utility framework and have proven to be both theoretically and empirically useful. As in the expected utility case, these preference functions can be empirically assessed and then used to predict the individual's behaviour in other situations.

However, while such forms allow for the modelling and analysis of preferences that are more general than those allowed by the expected utility hypothesis, they possess two limitations.

1. Each requires a different set of conditions on its component functions $v(\cdot)$, $\pi(\cdot)$, $\tau(\cdot)$, $g(\cdot)$, ... for the properties of stochastic dominance preference, risk aversion/risk preference, comparative risk aversion, and so on, so that expected utility theorems linking properties of the function $U(\cdot)$ to such aspects of behaviour will typically *not* extend, for example, to the corresponding properties of the function $v(\cdot)$ in these models.

---

[16] Kahneman and Tversky (1979); Chew and Waller (1986); Karmarkar (1978); Edwards (1955); Quiggin (1982); Fishburn (1983); Yaari (1987); Machina (1982, 1983); Chew (1983); Fishburn (1984).

2. Each replaces the independence axiom by some other (albeit more general) global restriction on preferences, possibly subject to similar types of systematic empirical violations.

An alternative approach to the study of non-expected utility preferences proceeds not by specifying a *particular* nonlinear form for the preference function, but rather by considering nonlinear functions *in general,* and using calculus to extend results from expected utility theory in the same manner in which is it typically used to extend results involving linear functions (Machina 1982, 1983). Specifically, taking the first-order Taylor expansion of a differentiable ('smooth') preference function $V(\cdot)$ about the distribution P yields

$$V(P^*) - V(P) = \Sigma U(x_i; P)(p_i^* - p_i) + o(\|P^* - P\|) \qquad (4)$$

where P^* is any other distribution, $U(x_i; P) \equiv \partial V(P)/\partial \operatorname{prob}(x_i) = \partial V(p_1, \ldots, p_n)/\partial p_i$, $\|P^* - P\| = [\Sigma(p_i^* - p_i)^2]^{1/2}$ is the Euclidean norm, and $o(\cdot)$ denotes a function that is zero at zero and of higher order than its argument. In the case of a preference *functional* $V(\cdot)$ over cumulative distribution functions, this expansion can be shown to take the form

$$V(F^*) - V(F) = \int U(x; F)[dF^*(x) - dF(x)] + o(\|F^* - F\|) \qquad (5)$$

where $\int U(x; F)[dF^*(x) - dF(x)]$ is the classical variational derivative of the functional $V(\cdot)$ and $\|F^* - F\| \equiv \int |F^*(x) - F(x)|\, dx$ is the standard L^1 norm.

In each of these cases, it follows that the individual's evaluation of *differential* shifts from the distributions P or $F(\cdot)$ will be determined by the first-order (i.e. linear) terms $\Sigma U(x_i; P)(p_i^* - p_i)$ or $\int U(x; F)[dF^*(x) - dF(x)]$. However, since these may be written as $\Sigma U(x_i; P)p_i^* - \Sigma U(x_i; P)p_i$ or $\int U(x; F)\, dF^*(x) - \int U(x; F)\, dF(x)$, it follows that an individual with smooth preferences will evaluate alternative differential shifts from either P or $F(\cdot)$ *precisely as would an expected utility maximizer* with 'local utility function' $U(x_i; P)$ or $U(x; F)$. Thus, for example, an individual would prefer all first-order stochastically dominating differential shifts from P or $F(\cdot)$ if and only if $U(x_i; P)$ or $U(x; F)$ were increasing in x, and would be averse to (prefer) all differential increases in risk,[17] if and only if $U(x_i; P)$ or $U(x; F)$ were concave (convex) in x. Intuitively, this result follows immediately from (multivariate or variational) calculus: since smooth preferences are 'locally linear' in the probabilities, and linearity in the probabilities is equivalent to expected utility maximization, smooth preferences will be 'locally expected utility-maximizing'.

---

[17] See no. 5 above.

Of course, the above results will hold exactly only in a vanishingly small neighbourhood of any probability distribution. However, we can exploit another result from standard calculus to show how 'expected utility' theory may be applied to the exact *global* analysis of smooth preferences over probability distributions. Recall that in many instances a differentiable function will exhibit a particular qualitative property if and only if this property is exhibited by its linear approximations at every point: for example, a differentiable function will be non-decreasing if and only if its linear approximations are non-decreasing (i.e. its partial derivatives are non-negative) at each point. Most of the fundamental aspects of attitudes towards risk and their expected utility characterizations turn out to be of this type. In particular, it can be shown that

1. a smooth preference functional $V(F)$ will prefer all local or global first-order stochastically dominating shifts if and only if its local utility functions $U(x; F)$ are increasing in x for all $F(\cdot)$;
2. a smooth preference functional $V(F)$ will be averse to (prefer) all local or global increases in risk if and only if its local utility functions $U(x; F)$ are concave (convex) in x for all $F(\cdot)$; and
3. the smooth preference functional $V_a(F)$ will be *more* risk-averse (in the appropriately defined senses) than $V_b(F)$ if and only if the Arrow–Pratt curvature indices $-U_a''(x; F)/U_a'(x; F)$ of its local utility functions $U_a(x; F)$ are greater than $-U_b''(x; F)/U_b'(x; F)$ for all x and $F(\cdot)$.

with analogous results holding for the preference function $V(P)$ and its local utility functions $U(x_i; P)$ in the case of a finite outcome set $\{x_1, \ldots, x_n\}$.

Figure 12.7 illustrates this second result for the outcome set $\{x_1, x_2, x_3\}$. The solid curves are the indifference curves of a smooth non-expected utility preference function $V(P)$. The solid parallel lines

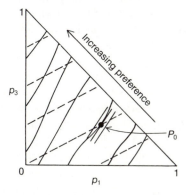

Fig. 12.7 *Concave local utility functions are equivalent to global risk aversion.*

near the point P_0 denote the expected utility preference field that approximates these preferences in the neighbourhood of P_0, or in other words the indifference curves generated by the local utility function $U(x_i; P_0)$. Since these lines are tangent to the actual indifference curve at P_0, a differential shift from this distribution will be preferred (will lead to a higher indifference curve) if and only if it is preferred by the local expected utility approximation (leads to a higher tangent line). Since increases in risk consist of north-east movements along the dashed iso-expected value lines, *global* risk aversion is equivalent to the condition that the indifference curves are everywhere steeper than these lines. However, this is equivalent to the condition that all of the tangent approximations are steeper than these lines, which is in turn equivalent to the condition that all of the local expected utility approximations are risk-averse, or in other words that all of the local utility function $U(x_i; P)$ are concave in x_i (Machina 1983).

This approach may also be used to obtain a uniform characterization of the type of departures from linearity in the probabilities described in the previous section. In particular, it can be shown that an individual's indifference curves will fan out in the (p_1, p_3) triangle for every triple $\{x_1, x_2, x_3\}$ if and only if the local utility function becomes more concave (in the sense of Arrow and Pratt) when evaluated at stochastically dominating distributions. Although the refutable predictions and public policy implications of this characterization (see Machina 1983) are of course weaker than those of the expected utility model, they are at least more closely tied to what we have actually observed about preferences.

My fellow researchers and I have shown how this and similar techniques can be applied to the analysis of both general and specific non-expected utility preference functionals in a manner that simultaneously exploits and demonstrates the robustness of the large body of theoretical results derived in the expected utility framework.[18] It is hoped that the development and successful application of such an approach will tempt the mainstream of expected utility-trained researchers to examine the empirical nature and theoretical implications of behaviour that departs from this standard model.

5. Unresolved Issues

Although the departures from linearity in the probabilities cited above constitute the best documented and most systematic body of evidence on the validity of the expected utility hypothesis, investigators have uncovered additional empirical phenomena which call into question even

---

[18] Machina (1982, 1983); Chew (1983); Fishburn (1984); Machina (1984); Dekel (1986); Allen (1987); Epstein (1985); Karni and Safra (1987).

more fundamental aspects of the model.[19] One such class of examples is known as the *preference reversal phenomenon*. Here, individuals are presented with three questions, typically embedded in a random order among a group of several other questions. One asks their preferences over of a pair of prospects of the form

$$\text{P-bet:} \begin{cases} p \text{ chance of } \$X \\ 1 - p \text{ chance of } \$x \end{cases} \quad \text{versus} \quad \text{\$-bet:} \begin{cases} q \text{ chance of } \$Y \\ 1 - q \text{ chance of } \$y \end{cases}$$

where X and Y are respectively greater than x and y, p is greater than q, and Y is greater than X. (The names 'P-bet' and '$-bet' come from the greater probability of winning in the first gamble and greater possible gain in the second.) In some cases, x and y took on small negative values. The second and third questions involve obtaining the individuals' sure monetary equivalents, ξ_P and $\xi_\$$, of these two prospects.

When the probabilities and outcomes are such that the expected values of the gambles are similar, experimenters have found a tendency for the majority of subjects to prefer the P-bet to the $-bet in a direct comparison. However, when asked for their sure monetary equivalents, a majority will assign a higher sure monetary equivalent to the $-bet than to the P-bet.[20] On the assumption that individuals will always prefer greater *sure* amounts to smaller ones, this implies that the $-bet is indifferent to the amount $\xi_\$$, which is preferred to the (smaller) amount ξ_P, which is indifferent to the P-bet, which is preferred to the $-bet, so that preferences are cyclic or *intransitive*. Since such intransitivity is incompatible with the existence of any real-valued maximand or preference function (expected utility or otherwise), it constitutes evidence against both the expected utility model and each of the *non*-expected utility models described above. It is worth noting that this phenomenon has proven to be remarkably robust, having withstood testing by (initially) sceptical experimenters, the use of real-money gambles, and the use of subjects presumably well versed in making decisions under uncertainty (professional gamblers).[21]

Another class of empirical phenomena, termed *framing effects*, consists of examples in which alternative, but probabilistically equivalent, statements of a decision problem yield different expressed choices. Early examples of this phenomenon involved different ways of generating the same probability distributions out of compound gambles or additive pairs of gambles, and resulted in reversals of choice (Slovic 1969; Payne and

---

[19] For a more complete discussion of the following evidence and how researchers have responded to it, see Machina (1987).

[20] Lindman (1971); Lichtenstein and Slovic (1971, 1973); Grether and Plott (1979); Pommerehne, Schneider, Zweifel (1982); Reilly (1982); Mowen and Gentry (1980).

[21] Lichtenstein and Slovic (1973); Grether and Plott (1979); Pommerehne, Schneider, and Zweifel (1982); Reilly (1982); Mowen and Gentry (1980).

Braunstein 1971). More recent studies have found, for example, that the preferred choice will depend upon whether an otherwise identical problem is phrased as a decision about whether or not to 'gamble' versus whether or not to 'insure', whether the effects of a preventive vaccine programme are specified in terms of 'lives saved' or 'lives lost', and so on.[22]

In addition to this evidence that probabilistically equivalent restatements of a problem may affect decisions, there is also evidence that, when experimenters do not explicitly state probabilities, subjects may not formulate uncertain choice problems in *any* probabilistically coherent manner. In the simplest of a class of examples, due to Daniel Ellsberg,[23] subjects were presented with a pair of urns, the first containing 50 red balls and 50 black balls and the second containing 100 red and black balls but in an unknown proportion. When faced with the choice of staking a prize on drawing a red ball from either urn, a majority of subjects strictly preferred to draw from the first urn. However, a majority *also* strictly preferred drawing from the first urn when the prize was staked on drawing a black ball. It is clear that there exists no subjectively assigned pair of probabilities $p : (1 - p)$ of drawing a red versus a black ball from the second urn (even $1/2 : 1/2$) which can simultaneously generate *both* of these strict preferences.

Researchers have attempted to extend the non-expected utility models of the previous section to address each of these types of empirical phenomena. Models of non-transitive preference rankings have been developed which are able to accommodate the preference reversal phenomenon as well as many of the observed violations of linearity in the probabilities.[24] Although there is as yet no single uniform principle (analogous to fanning out) known to underlie the diverse group of framing examples, some progress has none the less been made in this area as well.[25] Finally, Ellsberg-type phenomena have inspired generalizations of expected utility theory where individuals' probabilistic beliefs are represented by non-additive probability measures which do not satisfy the standard laws of probability theory (Schmeidler 1989). As with the non-expected utility models described earlier, the long-run success of these endeavours will depend upon the extent to which they can usefully address the tremendous number of issues in the theory of individual and group choice under uncertainty to which the expected utility model has been applied.

---

[22] Schoemaker and Kunreuther (1979); Hershey and Schoemaker (1980); Tversky and Kahneman (1981); Kahneman and Tversky (1982); Hershey, Kunreuther, and Schoemaker (1982).

[23] See Slovic and Tversky (1974); MacCrimmon and Larsson (1979); Ellsberg (1961) and MacCrimmon (1965).

[24] Bell (1982); Fishburn (1982); Loomes and Sugden (1982).

[25] Fischhoff (1983); Kahneman and Tversky (1984); Tversky and Kahneman (1986).

PART IV

13

Theoretical Modelling of Banks and Bank Runs

LUCA ANDERLINI

1. Introduction

There are at least two major reasons why the theoretical understanding of the existence and working of financial intermediaries should be important to economists. The first is the sheer scale of the institutions involved. The amount of resources channelled through them in advanced capitalist economies is enormous. This makes their influence on the economy far-reaching.

The second reason concerns our understanding of monetary phenomena at large. More importantly, the very existence of a financial sector is neglected by most analyses of the effects of monetary policy. However, the presence of financial intermediaries undeniably reduces the degree of direct control that the authorities have over monetary aggregates. A good theory of financial intermediaries is an obvious prerequisite to understanding fully the effects of monetary policies and how these are transmitted, through the financial system, from the central bank to the rest of the economy.

Our theoretical understanding of financial institutions has advanced rapidly during the extremely fast development of the economics of imperfect information over the last ten years. I shall mention three main approaches that have emerged in the literature. These are not mutually exclusive, as will be evident below. My intention here is not so much to provide a complete survey of the literature, but rather to supply a more general framework for the liquidity transformation model analysed in Sections 2–5 below.

A particular version of the principal (bank)–agent (borrower) model has been used in the *credit rationing models*. This literature owes its name to the main result obtained in this class of models by various authors (e.g. Jaffee and Russel 1976; Stiglitz and Weiss 1981); in *equilibrium*, a loan market may be characterized by credit rationing. In a pool of indistinguishable (by the bank) loan applicants, some are rejected and would not receive a loan even if they offered to pay a higher interest rate. The key to this result lies in imperfect information about the riskiness of borrowers and/or in the limited control over their actions that the bank has. Two separate effects can be identified.

Suppose that the bank cannot distinguish between good risks and bad risks. The interest rate may then become a sorting device among borrowers. Bad risks will be willing to pay higher interest rates because they perceive their probability of repaying the loan to be low. As a result, average riskiness of a pool of loan applicants may become an increasing function of the interest rate charged by the bank. This is known as the *adverse selection effect*.

Similarly, suppose that the bank has no control over the riskiness of the project undertaken by borrowers. It can be shown (Stiglitz and Weiss 1981) that under suitable conditions higher interest rates induce firms to undertake projects yielding higher returns when successful but also entailing a higher probability of default. This is known as the *incentive effect*.

Both the adverse selection effect and the incentive effect may make the bank's *expected* return on loans a function that is first increasing and then decreasing in the interest rate charged. In other words, the bank's expected return on loans as a function of the interest rate charged may have an interior maximum. If at this 'optimal' interest rate the demand for loans exceeds the supply of funds, a rationing equilibrium is obtained. The bank will not be willing to lend to applicants offering to pay a higher rate than the 'optimal' one. This is because, by declaring their willingness to pay more, the applicants 'reveal' themselves as wanting to undertake projects that are either too risky or as bad risks, or both.

A second, more recent, line of research is concerned with the form of *debt contracts* (Gale and Hellwig 1985), which is taken as given in all credit rationing models. A particular information structure gives rise very naturally to the standard debt contract with costly bankruptcy. The setup used is, again, a version of the principal (borrower or entrepreneur)–agent (bank or investor) model.[1] Entrepreneurs have access to a risky technology. The outcome of the technology (the state) is costlessly observable to the entrepreneur. The investor incurs a cost in order to observe the state. Before the state is realized, the investor and entrepreneur get together to write a debt contract. It can be shown (cf. Gale and Hellwig 1985) that under suitable conditions the contract that maximizes the entrepreneurs' return subject to the investor receiving a return sufficient to cover his opportunity cost is the standard debt contract with a bankruptcy clause.

Because the observation of the state by the investor is costly, the optimal contract does not stipulate that such observation should always happen. When the state is not observed by the investor, the entrepreneur pays back a *fixed amount* irrespective of the state that is realized. This is because facing the entrepreneur with a non-constant repayment schedule would simply induce him to 'declare' the state to which the lowest

---

[1] One interpretation of this is that of a perfectly competitive bankers' market.

repayment is associated. Any non-constant repayment schedule would thus not be incentive-compatible. When the return from the technology is too low to cover the fixed repayment, the investor observes the state and gets the entire output. Thus, the costly observation of the state by the investor is identified with bankruptcy.

A model and information structure similar to the one just described has also been used by Diamond (1984) to provide a rationale for the existence of financial intermediaries. The function of financial intermediaries in this model is that of *delegated monitoring*. Suppose that either indivisibilities or diversification advantages make it desirable that many investors finance any one project. Then it becomes efficient to delegate the observation of the state to one or more agents. Compared with the case in which all investors observe the state, a smaller amount of resources will be used up by the observation procedure.

Providing a rationale for the existence of financial intermediaries is also one of the goals of the *liquidity transformation models* (Anderlini 1986a; Diamond and Dybvig 1983; Smith 1984). This class of models—to which the one below belongs—focuses on the depositors' side of the banking system. The need for financial intermediaries in these models arises from the combination of two main ingredients: consumers who are unsure as to when they want to consume, and a production technology which is illiquid in the sense that 'production takes time'. Because early disinvestment is penalized, the amount that each individual agent is willing to invest in the technology is limited by the risk of wanting to consume early. The financial intermediaries offer a partial solution to this problem; by pooling resources they are able to smooth out the returns for lenders on their investment. This is possible because the law of large numbers ensures that the proportion of lenders who want to back out of their investment early will be stable in the aggregate.

The liquidity transformation approach has also proved extremely fruitful in analysing issues concerning the 'stability' of the financial system. If the return to early disinvestors is low enough (or, in some models of this kind (Diamond and Dybvig 1983), if lenders (depositors) are sufficiently risk-averse), bank runs are possible in the liquidity transformation models. A bank run is a 'bad' Nash equilibrium in which all depositors panic about the bank and attempt to withdraw as much as possible. Because of the illiquidity in the technology, this does indeed make the bank go bankrupt. This supports the initial panic as a Nash equilibrium of the appropriate game.

Crucial to this result is the form of the contract between the bank and the depositors. It is assumed that the bank is constrained to service in full those depositors attempting to withdraw until all its assets have been liquidated. This is known as *sequential service constraint* (Diamond and Dybvig 1983), and its form is taken as exogenously given.

The possibility of bank runs raises the issue of the regulation of the banking system (Diamond and Dybvig 1983; Friedman 1960; Anderlini 1986c). Two types of devices seem to be available in order to prevent runs in this class of models. These are the suspension of convertibility (of deposits into 'cash'), or an automatic bail-out mechanism supported by either deposit insurance or a lender of last resort. An automatic bail-out mechanism, in turn, induces a moral hazard problem for the bankers (Anderlini 1986c). They may intentionally rely on the bail-out mechanism in order to compete for depositors with other banks. I discuss some of these issues in the concluding section of the paper.

The rest of the chapter is organized as follows. In Section 2, I set up the liquidity transformation model. Section 3 reviews the equilibrium of the economy without a banking sector. In Section 4 I show that there is room in the model for a banking sector, and I characterize the bank deposit contract. Section 5 analyses the depositors' banking game and shows that, provided the production technology is illiquid enough, a bank run is an equilibrium of such game. Section 6 contains some concluding remarks.

2. A Liquidity Transformation Model

The model below is a much simplified version of the one contained in Anderlini (1986a). I believe it to represent a good compromise between the deceptive simplicity of the model used in the pioneering paper by Diamond and Dybvig (1983) and the notational and technical complication entailed by any further generalization.

2.1. Technology

There are three time periods ($T = 0$, 1, 2) and a single homogeneous good in the model. All agents in the model have access to a linear production technology. Investment in the technology is illiquid. To model this crucial feature I make a distinction between the beginning of each time period, which is also the end of the previous one, and its midpoint. Three assumptions about the technology are made.

ASSUMPTION 1. *Timing.* Inputs for the technology have to be provided at the beginning of each period. Consumption takes place at the midpoint.

ASSUMPTION 2. *Linearity.* An amount $x \geq 0$ invested in the technology at T yields a 'high' return Rx ($R > 1$) at the beginning of $T + 1$. If output is collected at the midpoint between T and $T + 1$, a 'low' return Lx ($L < 1$) is obtained.

ASSUMPTION 3. *No storage.* The good cannot be stored from the beginning of T period to the beginning of $T + 1$. Short-term storage, between the beginning and the midpoint of a time period, is allowed at no cost.

This is a crude but convenient way to model the illiquidity of physical investment. Assumption 2 can be thought of as the stipulation that 'production takes time'.

2.2. Consumers

There is a continuum of *ex ante* $(T = 0)$ identical consumers who live for three periods. Consumers are endowed with one unit of the good at the beginning of $T = 0$ and none thereafter.[2] At the beginning of $T = 1$, consumers are realized as being of type 1 or 2. Type $i = 1$, 2 consumers have a utility function of the form

$$U(c_1) + \theta_i U(c_2) \tag{1}$$

where c_1 and c_2 are non-negative scalars representing consumption at $T = 1$ and $T = 2$, respectively, and $U(\cdot): R_+ \to R$ is strictly increasing and concave; it is bounded below, twice differentiable, and satisfies $U' \to +\infty$ as $x \to 0$. Throughout the paper I assume $\theta_1 > \theta_2 \geq 0$.[3] Each consumer faces an equal and independent chance of turning into type 1 or 2 at the beginning of $T = 1$. The probabilities of these events are π_1 and $\pi_2 = 1 - \pi_1$, respectively. Because of the continuum hypothesis, π_1 and π_2 are also the proportions of consumers turning into types 1 and 2, respectively. At $T = 0$, subject to appropriate constraints set out below, consumers maximize

$$\sum_{i=1;2} \pi_i [U(c_1^i) + \theta_i U(c_2^i)] \tag{2}$$

where c_K^i is consumption in period K for a type i consumer. Lastly, no agent can observe the type of any other agent. Each consumer observes his own type at the beginning of $T = 1$. Types are *private information*. This informational asymmetry is crucial in many respects.

3. Equilibrium without a Banking Sector

The equilibrium of the model when only spot and forward competitive markets are allowed is not difficult to characterize. It is impossible for consumers to write contracts for delivery of the good contingent upon types. This is so simply because types are not observable. The information available to consumers at the beginning and at the midpoint of each period is the same. This is trivially true for $T = 0$ and $T = 2$. By assumption, it is also true for $T = 1$. An important consequence of this

---

[2] This assumption is simply designed to ensure that agents will want to transfer wealth forward rather than borrow against future endowments.

[3] The realization of 'types' should be thought of as a state of nature in the proper sense. For instance, a low θ could be interpreted as 'poor health' at $T = 1$.

remark is that the facility for early collection of 'low' output is never used since it is dominated by short-term storage. Hence there is no loss of generality in assuming that markets open at the beginning of each period only. Given the linear technology, this implies that prices on the futures markets are uniquely determined by arbitrage conditions. A familiar result will then hold: prices on the futures markets are such that agents will always be indifferent between trading consumption ahead and operating the technology. Hence there is also no loss of generality in assuming that the competitive equilibrium of the model entails no trade at all.

The equilibrium of the model, without a banking sector can be characterized analysing the optimization problem that each agent faces given his endowment and the technology. At the beginning of $T = 0$ the entire endowment will be invested in the technology. This yields an output of R units of the good at the beginning of $T = 1$. At the beginning of $T = 1$ each agent also knows his type. A type $i = 1; 2$ agent will solve

$$V_i = \max U(c_1^i) + \theta_i U(c_2^i)$$

(Problem 1)

$$\text{s.t.} \quad c_1^i + c_2^i R^{-1} \leq R$$

$$c_1^i \geq 0 \qquad c_2^i \geq 0.$$

The solutions to these problems entirely characterize the competitive equilibrium of the model without a banking sector.

4. Equilibrium with a Banking Sector

Because of the unobservability of consumers' types, there is an incomplete set of markets in the model. The simple competitive markets equilibrium of Section 3 does not allow any trade across states of nature. It does not provide consumers with any insurance against the future fluctuations of their discount rates. However, a particular 'insurance' contract can be constructed which induces consumers to reveal truthfully the realization of their types. In the model there is room for incentive-compatible insurance against the fluctuations of consumers' discount rates. Such an insurance contract is like a bank demand deposit contract is a sense that will shortly become apparent.

Throughout the paper I assume that there is only one institution providing bank deposit contracts and that its objective is that of maximizing *ex ante* consumers' welfare. In the case of *ex ante* identical agents, this can be shown to be equivalent to the assumption of a perfectly competitive bankers' market.[4]

---

[4] Of course, agents are indeed *ex ante* identical in the present model. For an extended version of the model presented here, a discussion of this point can be found in Anderlini (1986a).

Imagine initially that the bank can observe agent's types and that consumers are required to deposit their endowment at the bank. Let q_K^i be the bank's payout to a type i agent at $T = K$. Because of the continuum hypothesis, the bank's resource constraint is

$$\pi_1 q_1^1 + \pi_2 q_1^2 + (\pi_1 q_2^1 + \pi_2 q_2^2)R^{-1} \leqslant R. \tag{3}$$

However, the bank is not able to observe consumers' types. Hence at $T = 1$ the bank must leave its depositors free to choose among the two pairs $(q_1^1; q_2^1)$ and $(q_1^2; q_2^2)$. The quantities q_1^1 and q_1^2 should be interpreted as possible withdrawals at $T = 1$, and the quantities q_2^1 and q_2^2 as the resulting balances at $T = 2$. Depositors are left free to withdraw either q_1^1 or q_1^2. For the bank's resource constraint (3) to make sense, one then has to ensure that type 1 agents will choose to withdraw q_1^1 and type 2 will choose to withdraw q_1^2.

As is generally the case in problems of incentive compatibility, there is no loss of generality in assuming that depositors 'declare' their type to the bank rather than choose between q_1^1 and q_1^2. Depositors will not have an incentive to lie only if the following incentive compatibility constraints hold:

For all $i = 1, 2$ and $j = 1, 2$, $\quad U(q_1^i) + \theta_i U(q_2^i) \geqslant U(q_1^j) + \theta_i U(q_2^j)$. (4)

The bank's aim is that of maximizing welfare. Hence it faces the following problem:

$$V_B = \max \sum_{i=1;2} \pi_i [U(q_1^i) + \theta_i U(q_2^i)]$$

(Problem 2)

$$\text{s.t.} \quad U(q_1^i) + \theta_i U(q_2^i) \geqslant U(q_1^j) + \theta_i U(q_2^j) \qquad \forall i; j$$
$$\pi_1 q_1^1 + \pi_2 q_1^2 + (\pi_1 q_2^1 + \pi_2 q_2^2)R^{-1} \leqslant R$$
$$q_1^1 \geqslant 0 \qquad q_1^2 \geqslant 0 \qquad q_2^1 \geqslant 0 \qquad q_2^2 \geqslant 0.$$

It now remains to check that the temporary assumption that agents are required to deposit their endowment is redundant. This is the case if *ex ante* consumers prefer the consumption stream offered by the bank to the one that they can obtain operating the technology individually. Formally, I prove Theorem 1.

THEOREM 1. The following inequality holds:

$$V_B > \pi_1 V_1 + \pi_2 V_2 \tag{5}$$

and hence there is room for a banking sector in the model.

Proof. Let $(\bar{c}_1^1, \bar{c}_2^2, \bar{c}_2^1, \bar{c}_2^2)$ and $(\bar{q}_1^1, \bar{q}_1^2, \bar{q}_2^1, \bar{q}_2^2)$ be the solutions to problems 1 and 2, respectively. It is straightforward to check that $(\bar{c}_1^1, \bar{c}_1^2, \bar{c}_2^1, \bar{c}_2^2)$ belongs to the opportunity set of Problem 2. Hence it is enough to prove that $(\bar{c}_1^1, \bar{c}_2^2, \bar{c}_2^1, \bar{c}_2^2)$ does not solve Problem 2. From first-order conditions, it is obvious that (since $\theta^1 > \theta^2$),

$$\bar{c}_1^1 < \bar{c}_1^2 \quad \text{and} \quad \bar{c}_2^1 > \bar{c}_2^2. \tag{6}$$

By strict concavity of $U(\cdot)$ and hence uniqueness of $(\bar{c}_1^1, \bar{c}_2^2, \bar{c}_2^1, \bar{c}_2^2)$, it follows that

$$U(\bar{c}_1^i) + \theta_i U(\bar{c}_2^i) > U(c_1^j) + \theta_i U(c_2^j) \qquad \text{for all } i \text{ and } j. \tag{7}$$

Suppose now that the theorem is false and hence that $(\bar{c}_1^1, \bar{c}_1^2, \bar{c}_2^1, \bar{c}_2^2)$ solves Problem 2. Choose then two *small* real numbers $\delta_1 > 0$ and $\delta_2 < 0$ such that

$$\pi_1 \delta_1 + \pi_2 \delta_2 = 0 \tag{8}$$

and

$$\bar{c}_1^1 + \delta_1 < \bar{c}_1^2 + \delta_2. \tag{9}$$

Define also

$$\Delta U_i = U(\bar{c}_1^i + \delta_i) - U(\bar{c}_1^i) \qquad i = 1, 2. \tag{10}$$

Applying the mean value theorem, one knows that there exist $f_1 \in (\bar{c}_1^1; \bar{c}_1^1 + \delta_1)$ and $f_2 \in (\bar{c}_1^2 + \delta_2; \bar{c}_1^2)$ such that

$$\pi_1 \Delta U_1 + \pi_2 \Delta U_2 = \pi_1 \delta_1 U'(f_1) + \pi_2 \delta_2 U'(f_2). \tag{11}$$

From (9), and strict concavity of $U(\cdot)$, one has

$$U'(f_1) > U'(f_2) \tag{12}$$

and hence from (11) and the choice of δ_1 and δ_2,

$$\pi_1 \Delta U_1 + \pi_2 \Delta U_2 > U'(f_1)(\pi_1 \delta_1 + \pi_2 \delta_2) = 0. \tag{13}$$

By (13), the array $(\bar{c}_1^1 + \delta_1; \bar{c}_2^2 + \delta_2; \bar{c}_2^1; c_2^2)$ yields higher expected utility than $(\bar{c}_1^1, \bar{c}_1^2, \bar{c}_2^1, \bar{c}_2^2)$. By (7) and the choice of δ_1 and δ_2, such array is also feasible for Problem 2. Hence $(\bar{c}_1^1, \bar{c}_1^2; \bar{c}_2^1; \bar{c}_2^2)$ cannot solve Problem 2, and this proves the theorem.

Theorem 1 says that a new equilibrium is possible for the model. Imagine the bank offering the contract $(\bar{q}_1^1; \bar{q}_1^2; \bar{q}_2^1; \bar{q}_2^2)$ at the beginning of $T = 0$ and make the following four assumptions.

ASSUMPTION 4. *Mid-point.* Bank contracts can allow withdrawals only at the midpoint of any time period.

ASSUMPTION 5. *No post-dated cheques.* Futures markets in bank withdrawals are prohibited.

ASSUMPTION 6. *Expectations.* Depositors expect the bank to honour its commitments with probability 1.

ASSUMPTION 7. *Willingness to be truthful.* When a depositor is indifferent between lying and reporting his true type, the true type is reported.

Because of the timing assumption 1, the midpoint Assumption 4 does not prevent depositors from enjoying the consumption of the good they withdraw. Assumptions 4 and 5, together with the no-storage assumption 3, are designed to prevent the reopening of markets after withdrawals at $T = 1$ have taken place. This is necessary since the deposit contract $(\bar{q}_1^1, \bar{q}_1^2, \bar{q}_2^1, \bar{q}_2^2)$ involves nonlinear pricing in terms of interest rates which is the subject of Theorem 3 below. Assumptions 6 and 7 ensure that, when an incentive-compatible and resource-feasible contract is offered, all depositors report their true types to the bank. I discuss Assumption 6 in the next section.

Theorem 1 says that, if the contract $(\bar{q}_1^1, \bar{q}_1^2, \bar{q}_2^1, \bar{q}_2^2)$ is offered at the beginning of $T = 0$, all consumers will be willing to deposit their endowment at the bank. The above assumptions ensure that the contract itself constitutes a complete description of a new, *ex ante*, Pareto-superior equilibrium of the model.

The contract that the bank offers to depositors is like a demand deposit contract in the sense that depositors are free to choose how much to withdraw at $T = 1$ and the consequences of their actions can be interpreted as a balance for the following period. This can be generalized to a model with $N \geq 3$ periods and $M \geq 2$ types (cf. Anderlini 1986a).

There are two additional features of the contract $(\bar{q}_1^1, \bar{q}_1^2, \bar{q}_2^1, \bar{q}_2^2)$ which correspond to observed features of bank deposit contracts. The first is simply that a higher withdrawal at $T = 1$ entails a lower balance at $T = 2$. This is a trivial consequence of the incentive compatibility constraint which the contract satisfies. For the sake of completeness, however, I prove the following theorem.

THEOREM 2

$$\bar{q}_1^1 < \bar{q}_1^2 \quad \text{and} \quad \bar{q}_2^1 > \bar{q}_2^2.$$

Proof. By construction, the optimal contract satisfies

$$U(\bar{q}_1^1) + \theta_1 U(\bar{q}_2^1) \geq U(\bar{q}_1^2) + \theta_1 U(\bar{q}_2^2)$$
$$U(\bar{q}_1^2) + \theta_2 U(\bar{q}_2^2) \geq U(\bar{q}_1^1) + \theta_2 U(\bar{q}_2^1). \tag{14}$$

Adding up these two inequalities and rearranging some terms, we get

$$(\theta_1 - \theta_2)[U(\bar{q}_2^1) - U(\bar{q}_2^2)] \geq 0 \tag{15}$$

where the inequality is weak only if both inequalities in (14) are weak as well. But if both inequalities in (14) are weak, it must be that

$$\bar{q}_1^1 = \bar{q}_1^2 \quad \text{and} \quad \bar{q}_2^1 = \bar{q}_2^2. \tag{16}$$

These last two equalities contradict Theorem 1 since they imply that $(\bar{q}_1^1, \bar{q}_1^2, \bar{q}_2^1, \bar{q}_2^2)$ is feasible for Problem 1. Hence the inequality in (15) is strict, and since $\theta_1 > \theta_2$, this implies, by monotonicity of $U(\cdot)$, that $\bar{q}_2^1 > \bar{q}_2^2$. Suppose now that $\bar{q}_1^1 \geq \bar{q}_1^2$. Then, since $\bar{q}_2^2 > \bar{q}_2^1$, the second inequality in (14) must be reversed. This contradiction establishes the theorem.

The second interesting property of the bank contract is that it entails an interest rate that is increasing in the balance left in the account after withdrawal of $T = 1$. Since it is type 1 agents who have the higher balance (cf. theorem 2) after withdrawal at $T = 1$, I prove the following theorem.

THEOREM 3. Let

$$z_i = \bar{q}_2^i (R - \bar{q}_1^i)^{-1}. \tag{17}$$

(Henze z_i can be interpreted as the return earned between $T = 1$ and $T = 2$ when q_1^i is the $T = 1$ withdrawal.) Then $z_1 > z_2$.

Proof. I start by proving that the bank contract satisfies

$$\begin{aligned} U(\bar{q}_1^1) + \theta_1 U(\bar{q}_2^1) &> U(\bar{q}_1^2) + \theta_1 U(\bar{q}_2^2) \\ U(\bar{q}_1^2) + \theta_2 U(\bar{q}_2^2) &= U(\bar{q}_1^1) + \theta_2 U(\bar{q}_2^1). \end{aligned} \tag{18}$$

Indeed, suppose that (18) were false. Recall that the optimal contract by construction satisfies (14). As noted in the proof of Theorem 2, it cannot be that both relations in (18) hold as equalities. Also, if both the left-hand sides in (18) were strictly greater than the right-hand sides, one could contradict the fact that the contract solves Problem 2 exactly as in the proof of Theorem 1. Hence if (18) is false, we have

$$U(\bar{q}_1^1) + \theta_1 U(\bar{q}_2^1) = U(\bar{q}_1^2) + \theta_1 U(\bar{q}_2^2)$$

$$U(\bar{q}_1^2) + \theta_2 U(\bar{q}_2^2) > U(\bar{q}_1^1) + \theta_2 U(\bar{q}_2^1).$$

But then we can pick two small real numbers $\delta_1 > 0$ and $\delta_2 < 0$ satisfying $\pi_1 \delta_1 + \pi_2 \delta_2 = 0$, and by letting $\bar{q}_1^1 = \bar{q}_1^1 + \delta_1$ and $\bar{q}_1^2 = \bar{q}_1^2 + \delta_2$, we can contradict the optimality of $(\bar{q}_1^1, \bar{q}_1^2, \bar{q}_2^1, \bar{q}_2^2)$ exactly as in the proof of Theorem 1. Hence I have proved that (18) holds. Let now

$$\begin{aligned} w_1 &= \bar{q}_1^1 + \bar{q}_2^1 R^{-1} \\ w_2 &= \bar{q}_1^2 + \bar{q}_2^2 R^{-1}. \end{aligned} \tag{19}$$

Evidently it cannot be that $w_1 = w_2$, otherwise $(\bar{q}_1^1, \bar{q}_1^1, \bar{q}_2^2, \bar{q}_2^2)$ would be feasible for Problem 1, contradicting Theorem 1. I now prove that $w_1 > w_2$. If this were not the case, since it cannot be that $w_1 = w_2$, it must be that $w_1 < w_2$. Consider now the following contract:

$$(\bar{q}_1^1, \bar{q}_1^2, \bar{q}_2^1, \bar{q}_2^2) \tag{20}$$

where $\tilde{q}_1^2$ has been set equal to $\tilde{q}_1^1$ and $\tilde{q}_2^2$ has been set equal to $\tilde{q}_2^1$. The contract in (20) also trivially satisfies the incentive compatibility constraints of Problem 2. Since (18) holds, we can check that the level of expected utility yielded by the contract in (20) is precisely V_B. So the contract in (20) must be a solution to Problem 2. Also, since $w_1 < w_2$, it must be that

$$\pi_1 \tilde{q}_1^1 + \pi_2 \tilde{q}_1^2 + (\pi_1 \tilde{q}_2^1 + \pi_2 \tilde{q}_2^2)R^{-1} < R \tag{21}$$

so that the contract in (20) is also resource-feasible for Problem 2. Hence it must solve Problem 2. On the other hand, because of (21) it is possible to increase $\tilde{q}_1^1$ and $\tilde{q}_1^2$ by a small amount without violating any constraints in Problem 2 and obviously increasing expected utility. Hence the contract in (20) cannot solve Problem 2. This contradiction proves that it must necessarily be that $w_1 > w_2$. Notice now that, since the bank's resoure contraint must hold as an equality, $w_1 > w_2$ implies that $w_1 > R$ and $w_2 < R$, and this directly implies that $z_1 > R$ and $z_2 < R$, which proves the theorem.

Figures 13.1 and 13.2 depict the contracts solving Problems 1 and 2 respectively and may be of help in following the above proofs. The budget constraint in both figures is given by the production technology. In Figure 13.1 both consumption points have to lie on the budget constraint, while in Figure 13.2 the two consumption points only have to satisfy the budget constraint 'on average'. Indifference curves for type 1 and 2 depositors are denoted by U_1 and U_2, respectively.

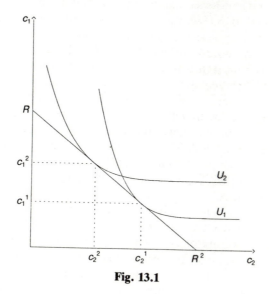

Fig. 13.1

Luca Anderlini

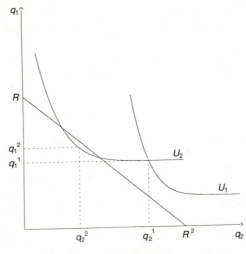

Fig. 13.2

5. Multiple Nash Equilibria: Bank Runs

The expectations assumption 6 above is not a good one. Suppose that a fraction of depositors, of positive measure, deviates from truthfully reporting their types. If this causes the bank not to have enough resources to keep its promises, it may ruin the incentive compatibility of the bank contract and hence justify the deviation from truth-telling.

What is needed to analyse the problem is a proper game setting where the strategic variables are depositors' declarations, given the bank contract. The bankruptcy rule which the bank has to follow when it is short of funds is crucial in determining the set of equilibria of this game. In what follows, I shall assume that the bank has to obey what has been called Sequential Service Constraint (Diamond and Dybvig 1983). Informally, this can be thought of as the stipulation that the bank is constrained to service withdrawal requests in full, at random, until all its assets have been liquidated. The randomness of servicing can be thought of as the result of potential withdrawers joining a queue at the bank in random order, and then being serviced sequentially.

Consider the model of Section 4 at the beginning of $T = 1$. All consumers have deposited their endowment at the bank and have to decide whether to declare that they are type 1 or 2. Let λ_{ij} be the proportion of depositors of type i who declare that they are of type j (clearly, $\lambda_{i1} + \lambda_{i2} = 1$, $i = 1, 2$). The payoffs to the players are a function of their declarations, of the bank contract, and of λ_{ij}. To formalize the Sequential Service Constraint, one needs a definition of the liquidation value of the bank's assets at the midpoint of $T = 1$ (cf. the midpoint assumption 4). At the beginning of $T = 1$ the bank will store an amount $\pi_1 \bar{q}_1^1 + \pi_2 \bar{q}_1^2$ to cover withdrawals and will reinvest $R - \pi_1 \bar{q}_1^1 - \pi_2 \bar{q}_1^2$ to cover its $T = 2$ commitments. Hence, using the linearity assumption 2, the liquidation value of the bank's assets at the midpoint of $T = 1$ is

$$A = \pi_1 \bar{q}_1^1 + \pi_2 \bar{q}_1^2 + L(R - \pi_1 \bar{q}_1^1 - \pi_2 \bar{q}_1^2). \tag{22}$$

The Sequential Service Constraint can then be formalized as follows.

ASSUMPTION 8. *Sequential service constraint.* Let $\lambda = (\lambda_{11}, \lambda_{12}, \lambda_{21}, \lambda_{22})$ and $\bar{q} = (\pi_1 \lambda_{11} + \pi_2 \lambda_{21}) \bar{q}_1^1 + (\pi_1 \lambda_{12} + \pi_2 \lambda_{22}) \bar{q}_1^2$. ($\bar{q}$ should be thought of as attempted withdrawals at $T = 1$.) The payoff at $T = 1$ to depositors declaring type i is

$$\hat{q}_1^i(\lambda) = \begin{cases} \bar{q}_1^i \text{ with Pr. } \zeta = \min(1; A/\bar{q}) \\ 0 \text{ with Pr. } 1 - \zeta. \end{cases} \tag{23}$$

The payoff at $T = 2$ to depositors declaring type i is

$$\hat{q}_2^i(\lambda) = \begin{cases} 0 & \text{if } \zeta < 1 \\ \bar{q}_2^i & \text{if } \bar{q} \leqslant \pi_1 \bar{q}_1^1 + \pi_2 q_1^2 \\ \text{any non-negative random variable } \mu^i \text{ such that} \\ \quad E(\mu^i) \leqslant \bar{q}_2^i \text{ if } \zeta = 1 \text{ and } \bar{q} > \pi_1 \bar{q}_1^1 + \pi_2 \bar{q}_1^2. \end{cases} \tag{24}$$

The payoffs at $T = 1$ are a straightforward formalization of the Sequential Service Constraint. The payoffs stipulated for $T = 2$ can be interpreted as follows. If $\zeta < 1$, it must be that withdrawal requests at $T = 1$ exceed A. Hence the bank collects no output at $T = 2$ and so it cannot pay out anything. If attempted withdrawals are no greater than their normal level $\pi_1 \bar{q}_1^1 + \pi_2 \bar{q}_1^2$, each depositor is given the payout corresponding to his $T = 1$ declaration. If withdrawal requests are between A and their normal level, the bank can be imagined to adopt any payout policy that does not pay, on average, more than $\bar{q}_2^i$.

Thus, the bankruptcy rule specified in Assumption 8 is incomplete. It is however enough to obtain two results about the Nash equilibria of the depositors' game. The first result is a consequence of incentive compatibility of the bank contract (Hurwicz 1972). It states that truth-telling is always a Nash equilibrium for the banking game. The second result states that, provided the low return from the technology, L, is 'low' enough, another equilibrium for the game is given by all agents declaring that they are type 2. The latter is equivalent to all agents attempting to withdraw as much as possible at $T = 1$ because they expect the bank to be bankrupt at $T = 2$. For this reason it is called a bank run.

DEFINITION 1. A Nash equilibrium for the depositors' game is an array $(\lambda_{11}, \lambda_{12}, \lambda_{21}, \lambda_{22})$ of real numbers, all lying in $[0, 1]$ and such that

$\lambda_{i1} + \lambda_{i2} = 1$ $(i = 1; 2)$ and

$$\lambda_{ij} > 0 \Rightarrow E\{U[\hat{q}_1^i(\lambda)]\} + \theta_i U[\hat{q}_2^i(\lambda)]$$
$$\geq E\{U[\hat{q}_1^h(\lambda)]\} + \theta_i U[\hat{q}_2^h(\lambda)] \text{ for } h = 1, 2. \tag{25}$$

The two results on the Nash equilibria of the depositors' game can now be stated and proved.

THEOREM 4. Suppose that Assumption 8 holds. Then truth-telling is a Nash equilibrium for the depositors' game. In other words,

$$\lambda_{11} = 1; \quad \lambda_{12} = 0; \quad \lambda_{21} = 0; \quad \lambda_{22} = 1$$

constitute a Nash equilibrium for the game.

Proof. It is enough to show that (25) holds when $\lambda_{11} = 1$, $\lambda_{12} = 0$, $\lambda_{21} = 0$, $\lambda_{22} = 1$ are substituted into (23) and (24). Indeed, since

$$A > \pi_1 \bar{q}_1^1 + \pi_2 \bar{q}_1^2,$$

these values guarantee that $\zeta = 1$. Also, substitution into (24) immediately yields that the $T = 2$ payoff to agents declaring that their type is i is $\bar{q}_2^i$ with probability 1. Hence the incentive compatibility constraints which the bank contract satisfies by construction are the same as the inequalities in (25) for $i = j$. This is clearly enough to prove the theorem.

The next theorem formalizes the claim that the depositors' game also has a run equilibrium if L is small.

THEOREM 5. Suppose that Assumption 8 holds. Then there exists an $L > 0$ such that

$$\lambda_{11} = 0; \quad \lambda_{21} = 0; \quad \lambda_{12} = 1; \quad \lambda_{22} = 1$$

constitute a Nash equilibrium for the depositors' game.

Proof. For L small, A can be made close to $\pi_1 \bar{q}_1^1 + \pi_2 \bar{q}_1^2$. By Theorem 2, $\bar{q}_1^2 > \pi_1 \bar{q}_1^1 + \pi_2 \bar{q}_1^2$. this implies that if $\lambda_{12} = \lambda_{22} = 1$, for L small it must be

$$\zeta < 1 \quad \text{and} \quad \hat{q}_2^i(0, 0, 1, 1) = 0 \quad \text{for } i = 1, 2.$$

This directly implies that $\lambda_{12} = \lambda_{22} = 1$ satisfies the definition of equilibrium, and hence it proves the theorem.

Theorem 5 says that, provided L is low, a run is always an equilibrium for the depositors' game. It must be noticed that this is true independently of the state of the bank. Perfectly healthy banks can be hit by runs caused by purely expectational disturbances. A bank run can, in principle, be caused by bad 'sunspots' (Azariadis 1981; Anderlini 1986b).[5]

---

[5] See Chapter 17 by Burnell and Chapter 16 by Kehoe on this topic. Sunspots have acquired the meaning of extrinsic uncertainty which actually changes the set of equilibria of a model. Here they are merely a 'selection mechanism' between different equilibria.

6. Concluding Remarks

In the equilibrium of the economy without banks, there are missing markets because of the unobservability of types. The truthful equilibrium with a banking system provides an allocation that is better for all agents than the one achieved without a banking system. It does not, however, allow the implementation of the fully optimal allocation that would be achieved if types were observable (i.e. if there were no missing markets). The incentive compatibility constraint imposed on the bank contract 'bites'. This is in contrast with the model used by Diamond and Dybvig (1983) in their pioneering paper.

The possibility of bank runs in this class of models yields at least two further questions. The first concerns the effects of the anticipation of bank runs by depositors. In a model with a simpler structure than the present one (Anderlini 1986b), I have proved that runs can still happen even when they are properly anticipated. What is required is that their anticipated probability is small in some appropriate sense.[6]

Which instruments are available to prevent runs is the second obvious question raised by this class of models. A suspension-of-convertibility clause is enough to prevent runs in a model like the Diamond and Dybvig (1983) one, and in the present one. In a more general setting this is not always true (Anderlini 1986a) in a straightforward manner. Moreover, if the model is modified so as to leave some aggregate uncertainty, suspension of convertibility will occur in equilibrium. This makes this instrument less attractive than it may appear to be in this simple setting. A bail-out mechanism supported by either deposit insurance or a lender of last resort is also effective in preventing runs in some models in this class (Anderlini 1986c; Diamond and Dybvig 1983). This, however, as I have mentioned, creates a moral hazard problem in the bankers' market. The bankers may intentionally rely on the bail-out mechanism in order to compete for depositors. In very simple models this moral hazard problem can be solved using a simple interest rate ceiling regulation. In general, it seems that models of a run-vulnerable banking system represent an obvious starting point to analyse the scope for regulation of the financial system.

---

[6] See also Diamond and Dybvig (1983) and Postelwaite and Vives (1987) on the 'anticipation' of bank runs.

14

Optimal Multi-unit Auctions

ERIC MASKIN AND JOHN RILEY

1. Introduction

Recently, a large literature has examined alternative methods for auctioning off an indivisible good. (See McAfee and McMillan 1987; Milgrom 1986; and Wilson 1987 for surveys.) Particular attention has been paid to two auctions used frequently in practice: the open, ascending-bid auction (also called the English auction), and the sealed, high-bid auction. A theoretical benchmark is provided by the Revenue Equivalence Theorem (Vickrey 1961b; Myerson 1981, and Riley and Samuelson 1981). This theorem asserts that, when each bidder's reservation price for the good is an independent draw from the same distribution and bidders are risk-neutral, the two common auctions give rise to exactly the same expected revenue for the seller.[1]

A good deal of research has considered the implications of relaxing one or more of the underlying hypotheses. Thus, Holt (1980) substitutes risk-averse for risk-neutral buyers and shows that, in this case, the sealed-bid auction generates greater expected revenue than its open counterpart.

In contrast, Milgrom and Weber (1982) show that, when reservation prices are not independent but are positively correlated, the additional informational about other buyers emerging in the open auction raises revenue on average relative to that in the sealed-bid auction.

A third strand of this research (Maskin and Riley 1986) relaxes symmetry. That is, buyers' reservation values are no longer postulated to be identically distributed. In this case, the ranking of the two auctions depends on how the distributions vary across buyers.

Rather than simply compare the expected revenue from specific auction schemes, one may wish to characterize *optimal* selling procedures, that is, selling procedures that maximize the seller's expected revenue. Under the hypotheses of the Revenue Equivalence Theorem, and provided that the distribution of reservation prices is sufficiently

The helpful comments of David Kreps, David Levine, Steven Matthews, Rober Myerson, and Barry Nalebuff are gratefully acknowledged. This research was supported by the National Science Foundation and the UK Social Science Research Council.

[1] For a formal statement of this result, generalized to the case of multiple units, see Section 2.

regular (see Section 3 for a precise definition of regularity), the open- and sealed-bid auctions are both optimal if the seller sets an appropriate minimum allowable bid (called a reserve price). Myerson (1981) characterizes optimal auctions when regularity fails and also when the symmetry assumption is dropped. Matthews (1983), Maskin and Riley (1984b), and Moore (1984) study the case of risk-averse buyers, whereas Myerson (1981), Maskin and Riley (1981), and Cremer and McLean (1985) consider correlated reservation prices. Finally, Harris and Raviv (1981) relax the assumption that only a single good is to be sold.

This last paper is the starting point of our analysis here. For the special case of a uniform distribution of reservation prices, Harris and Raviv show that the Revenue Equivalence Theorem continues to hold if there are multiple units for sale and each buyer wishes to purchase at most a single unit. Here we establish equivalence for all distributions, and also show that, as long as the regularity assumption mentioned above is satisfied, the standard auctions with appropriate reserve prices are optimal for the seller. In addition, we characterize the optimal auction when this restriction is violated.

We then relax the restriction to unit demand and instead assume simply that each buyer has a downward-sloping demand curve. We observe that, in general, the standard auctions are no longer optimal. Instead, an optimal procedure is to set a payment schedule $T(q)$ and ask each buyer to submit an order q; a buyer who demands q pays $T(q)$. If aggregate demand is less than supply, the auctioneer fills each order. If, however, orders exceed supply, the auctioneer scales down each buyer's demand, in a predetermined way, until the capacity constraint is met.

The optimal procedure is thus a nonlinear pricing scheme modified to take account of the supply constraint. Not surprisingly, therefore, the methods of analysis build on earlier work on nonlinear pricing, in particular that of Mussa and Rosen (1978) and Maskin and Riley (1984a).

2. Formulation of the Seller's Optimization Problem

The seller has q_0 units of a good for sale. There are n buyers, each of whose 'type' v is drawn independently from the same distribution $F(v)$. A buyer of type v has preferences represented by the utility function

$$U(q, R, v) \equiv \int_0^q p(x, v)\, dx - R \equiv N(q, v) - R \qquad (1)$$

where q is the number of units purchased from the seller and R is total spending on these units. The seller and other buyers do not observe a buyer's v but know that it is drawn from $F(v)$. Throughout, we shall assume that higher levels of v are associated with higher demand.

Moreover, we suppose that buyers' demand curves are never positively sloped and that demand is finite for all $p \geq 0$.

To be precise, we impose the following restrictions.

ASSUMPTION A1. For all v, the demand price function $p(q, v)$ is finite, twice continuously differentiable, strictly decreasing in q, and strictly increasing in v whenever p is greater than zero.

Since it is of independent interest, we shall sometimes make the alternative assumption of unit demand, as follows.

ASSUMPTION A1*. *Unit Demand.* Preferences are given by the demand price function

$$p(q, v) = \begin{cases} v, & q \leq 1 \\ 0, & q > 1, \end{cases}$$

so that v is the buyer's reservation price.

We also assume that the unobservable parameter v is continuously distributed and that the cumulative distribution function $F(\cdot)$ satisfies the following assumption.

ASSUMPTION A2. The cumulative distribution function $F(v)$ is strictly increasing and continuously differentiable on the interval $[0, \bar{v}]$, with $F(0) = 0$ and $F(\bar{v}) = 1$.

Although, in general, it is not possible to rule out gains to randomized selling procedures, we show in Section 5 that, under a fairly weak restriction on the distribution of types, the following assumption is sufficient for the optimal selling scheme to be deterministic (if we interpret (1) to be a buyer's von Neumann–Morgerstern utility function).

ASSUMPTION B1. *Non-decreasing Price Elasticity.* Demand elasticity is non-decreasing in the demand price. That is,

$$\frac{\partial}{\partial v} \left(-\frac{q}{p} \frac{\partial p}{\partial q} \right) \leq 0.$$

For a buyer of type v, formula (1) gives us

$$\frac{\partial}{\partial v} \left(-\frac{\partial^2 U}{\partial q^2} \Big/ \frac{\partial U}{\partial q} \right) = \frac{1}{q} \frac{\partial}{\partial v} \left(-\frac{q}{p} \frac{\partial p}{\partial q} \right).$$

Assumption B1 implies, therefore, that absolute risk aversion with respect to consumption is non-decreasing in v.

Readers should note that we have a great deal of flexibility of our choice of a parameterization. In particular, if $p(q, v)$ represents a family of inverse demand curves satisfying Assumptions A1, A2, and B1, then $p[q, \omega(v)]$ represents the same family and also satisfies these three assumptions if $\omega(\cdot)$ is strictly increasing and twice continuously differentiable. For convenience, we shall henceforth choose, without loss of generality, a parametrization for which the increases in demand price are non-decreasing as v rises.

ASSUMPTION B2. $p_{22}(q, v) \leq 0$.

Elsewhere (Maskin and Riley 1984a) we have shown that there are large classes of preferences satisfying these four assumptions.

The seller cannot force buyers to purchase his goods; his sales depend on their behaviour. Hence, a *selling procedure* is a rule that assigns buyers quantities and charges them prices on the basis of their actions. Depending on the procedure, an action might consist of making a bid, submitting a demand function, or, in principle, anything else that a buyer might do to signal his demand. Formally, a procedure is a schedule of pairs, one for each buyer:

$$[\bar{q}_i(s_1, \ldots, s_n), \bar{R}_i(s_1, \ldots, s_n)], \qquad i = 1, \ldots, n \tag{2}$$

where s_i is buyer i's strategy, lying in strategy space S_i, and $\bar{R}_i$ and $\bar{q}_i$ are, respectively, his payment and allocation of the good. Allocations must satisfy the aggregate supply constraint

$$\sum_{i-1}^{n} \bar{q}_i(s) \leq q_0 \tag{3}$$

where $s \equiv (s_1, \ldots, s_n)$. The tildes reflect the possibility that payments and allocations may be random. Initially, however, we restrict attention to deterministic procedures, so that (2) can be rewritten in deterministic form as

$$[\hat{q}_i(s_i, s_{-i}), \hat{R}_i(s_i, s_{-i})] \tag{4}$$

where $s_{-i} \equiv (s_1, \ldots, s_{i-1}, s_{i+1}, \ldots, s_n)$.

We suppose that the seller can select any selling procedure it desires and makes its selection to maximize expected revenue. The key to solving its optimization problem is the incorporation of the constraints implied by the buyers' choice of strategies. We assume that buyers choose their strategies without collusion. Thus, they play a game of incomplete information. A natural non-cooperative solution concept for such a game is the Bayesian equilibrium of Harsanyi (1967–8), an extension of ordinary Nash equilibrium.

To define a Bayesian equilibrium, we introduce the notion of a strategy rule for buyer i, a function $s_i^*(\cdot)$ that, for each possible type v_i, assigns a strategy $s_i^*(v_i)$. With buyers behaving non-cooperatively, the vector of strategy rules $(s_1^*(\cdot), \ldots, s_n^*(\cdot))$ is an equilibrium if, when conformed to by all others, each buyer's best option (in the sense of maximizing his expected utility) is to conform to it also. Of course, there is no reason, in general, why equilibrium should be unique. (But see Maskin and Riley 1982 for a treatment of uniqueness in sealed-bid and open auctions.) Thus, when we speak of a procedure that maximizes expected revenue, we really mean that there is *an* equilibrium of that procedure that maximizes expected revenue.

Consider the expected surplus of buyer i if, when his parameter value is v_i, he chooses the strategy $s_i = s_i^*(x)$ instead of $s_i^*(v_i)$. With other buyers adopting the strategy rules

$$s_{-i}^*(\cdot) \equiv [s_i^*(\cdot), \ldots, s_{i-1}^*(\cdot), s_{i+1}^*(\cdot), \ldots, s_n^*(\cdot)],$$

buyer i has an expected surplus of

$$\Pi_i(x, v_i) = E_{v_{-i}}[N(\hat{q}_i(s_i^*(x), s_{-i}^*(v_{-i})), v_i) - \hat{R}_i(s_i^*(x), s_{-i}^*(v_{-i}))] \quad (5)$$

where $N(q, v_i) \equiv \int_0^q p(z, v_i)\, dz$ and where the expectation is taken with respect to the distribution $F(\cdot)$. Let us suppress the functions $s_i^*(\cdot)$ and define

$$\begin{aligned} q_i(x, v_{-i}) &= \hat{q}_i(s_i^*(x), s_{-i}^*(v_{-i})) \\ R_i(x) &= E_{v_{-i}} \hat{R}_i(s_i^*(x), s_{-i}^*(v_{-i})). \end{aligned} \Bigg\} \quad (6)$$

Then (5) can be rewritten as

$$\Pi_i(x, v_i) = E_{v_{-i}} N(q_i(x, v_{-i}), v_i) - R_i(x). \quad (7)$$

Since we have defined $s_i^*(v_i)$ to be buyer i's optimal strategy, if his parameter value is v_i, it follows that $\Pi_i(x, v_i)$ must take its maximum at $x = v_i$; that is, for all i and v_i,

$$\Pi_i(v_i, v_i) = \max_x \Pi_i(x, v_i). \quad (8)$$

We now show that, given (6)–(8), we can express maximized surplus $\Pi_i(v_i, v_i)$ solely in terms of the allocation rule $q_i(v_i, v_{-i})$.

PROPOSITION 1. *Necessary Condition for Self-selection, i.e., Incentive Compatibility.* Under Assumptions A1 (or A1*) and A2, the maximized expected surplus of buyer i with parameter value v_i can be written as

$$\Pi_i(v_i, v_i) = \Pi_i(0, 0) + E_{v_{-i}} \int_0^{v_i} N_2(q_i(z, v_{-i}), z)\, dz. \quad (9)$$

Remark. We have derived $[q_i(\cdot), R_i(\cdot)]$ from $[\hat{q}_i(\cdot), \hat{R}_i(\cdot)]$ through (6). However we can think of $[q_i(\cdot), R_i(\cdot)]$, $i = 1, \ldots, n$, as a selling procedure itself in which buyers announce parameter values as strategies; in other words, it is a *direct revelation mechanism*. Condition (8), moreover, ensures that buyers announce their *true* values in equilibrium. Of course, if instead we confront a buyer with *arbitrary* functions $q_i(\cdot)$ and $R_i(\cdot)$, it may not be in his interest to reveal truthfully. Proposition 1 implies that, if $\Pi_i(x, v_i)$ is defined by (7), a necessary condition for truthful revelation is (9). That is why we have attached the label 'incentive compatibility' to the proposition.

Proof.[2] Because $\Pi_i(v_i, v_i) \geq \Pi_i(x, v_i)$ (from (8)), and if $(v_i > x)$ $\Pi_i(x, v_i) \geq \Pi_i(x, x)$,

$$\Pi_i(v_i, v_i) - \Pi_i(x, x) \geq 0, \quad \text{for} \quad v_i > x. \tag{10}$$

Also, from (7),

$$\Pi_i(v_i, v_i) - \Pi_i(v_i, x) = E_{v_{-i}}(N(q_i(v_i, v_{-i}), v_i) - N(q_i(v_i, v_{-i}), x))$$

$$= E_{v_{-i}} \int_0^{q_i(v_i, v_{-i})} \int_x^{v_i} p_2(z, y) \, dy \, dz$$

$$\leq E_{v_{-i}} \int_0^{q_i(v_i, v_{-i})} \int_x^{v_i} p_2(z, x) \, dy \, dz, \tag{11}$$

where the inequality follows from Assumption B2 (which, without loss of generality, we can assume holds). Hence, for all $v_i \geq x$,

$$0 \leq \Pi_i(v_i, v_i) - \Pi_i(x, x) \leq (v_i - x) E_{v_{-i}} \int_0^{q_i(v_i, v_{-i})} p_2(z, x) \, dz. \tag{12}$$

Therefore, $\Pi_i(v_i, v_i)$ is continuous. In fact, since $0 \leq q_i \leq q_0$, the expectation in (12) is bounded and so $\Pi_i(v_i, v_i)$ is an absolutely continuous function.

From (8), for all x and v_i,

$$v_i \in \arg\min_x [\Pi_i(x, x) - \Pi_i(v_i, x)]. \tag{13}$$

From (7), $\Pi_i(v_i, x)$ is a differentiable function of x. Moreover, as we have just argued, $\Pi_i(x, x)$ is continuous and non-decreasing, hence differentiable almost everywhere. Thus, almost everywhere we can write the first-order condition for (13) as

$$\frac{d\Pi_i}{dx}(x, x) - \frac{\partial \Pi_i}{\partial x}(v_i, x) = 0 \quad \text{at} \quad x = v_i.$$

From (7),

$$\frac{\partial \Pi_i}{\partial x}(v_i, x)\bigg|_{x=v_i} = E_{v_{-i}} N_2[q_i(v_i, v_{-i}), v_i].$$

A necessary condition for (8) to hold, therefore, is

$$\frac{d}{dv_i} \Pi_i(v_i, v_i) = E_{v_{-i}} N_2(q_i(v_i, v_{-i}), v_i) \text{ almost everywhere.} \tag{14}$$

Moreover, since $\Pi_i(v_i, v_i)$ is absolutely continuous, we can rewrite (14) in the more convenient integral form (9).   Q.E.D

---

[2] For the proof presented here we acknowledge the helpful suggestions of Steven Matthews.

Because the seller cannot force any buyer to participate, the expected surplus of every buyer must be non-negative. Since $\Pi_i(v_i, v_i)$ is a non-decreasing function, this 'voluntary participation' constraint can be expressed simply as

$$\Pi_i(0, 0) \geqslant 0. \tag{15}$$

Propositions 1 showed that (9) is a necessary condition for arbitrary functions $[q_i(\cdot), R_i(\cdot)]$, $i = 1, \ldots, n$, to constitute a direct revelation mechanism in which truth-telling is an equilibrium. We next show that, if the function $q_i(\cdot)$ is suitably monotonic, then conditions (9) and (15) are sufficient conditions.

LEMMA 1. Suppose that preferences satisfy Assumption A1 or A1*. Assume that $q_i(v_i, v_{-i})$ is a non-decreasing function of v_i, and *define* Π_i by (9). Then if Π_i satisfies (15), we have

(i) $\Pi_i(v_i, v_i) \geqslant \Pi_i(x, v_i)$

and

(ii) $\Pi_i(v_i, v_i) \geqslant 0$

for all x and v_i.

Proof. If $\Pi_i(v_i, v_i)$ satisfies (9), then for any $y \geqslant x$

$$\Pi_i(y, y) - \Pi_i(x, x) = E_{v_{-i}} \int_x^y N_2(q_i(z, v_{-i}), z)\, dz$$

$$\geqslant E_{v_{-i}} \int_x^y N_2(q_i(x, v_{-i}), z)\, dz \tag{16}$$

since, by hypothesis, $q_i(z, v_{-i})$ is non-decreasing in z, and, by Assumption A1 (or A1*), $p_2 = N_{12}$ is non-negative and N_2 is positive. Hence, from (15), (ii) holds. But, from (7),

$$\Pi_i(x, y) - \Pi_i(x, x) = E_{v_{-i}} \int_x^y N_2(q_i(x, v_{-i}), z)\, dz. \tag{17}$$

Thus, combining (16) and (17), we obtain

$$\Pi_i(y, y) \geqslant \Pi_i(x, y), \quad y > x.$$

Hence, (i) holds for all $x < v_i$. An almost identical argument establishes that it holds for all $x > v_i$ as well. Q.E.D

A selling procedure can be extremely complicated, and therefore, in principle, so can be maximizing expected revenue over the class of all procedures. As we have seen, however, any selling procedure is equivalent (in allocation and expected payments) to a direct revelation mechanism. (This equivalence is sometimes called the Revelation Principle.) Thus, the optimization can be restricted to the much smaller class of such mechanisms. Lemma 1 helps simplify this optimization by establishing that, if the functions $[q_i(v_i, v_{-i})]$ are non-decreasing, then there exist corresponding payment functions $[R_i(\cdot)]$ such that $[q_i(\cdot), R_i(\cdot)]$, $i = 1, \ldots, n$ is a direct revelation mechanism in which truth-telling is an equilibrium. Indeed, from (7) and (9), the expected payment by buyer i with valuation v_{-i} is

$$R_i(v_i) = E_{v_{-i}}\left[N(q_i(v_i, v_{-i}), v_i) - \int_0^{v_i} N_2(q_i(z, v_{-i}), z)\,dz\right] - \Pi_i(0, 0). \quad (18)$$

Thus, the seller's problem boils down to maximizing over functions $q_i(\cdot)$. Specifically, the expected revenue from buyer i can be written as

$$\bar{R}_i = E_{v_i, v_{-i}}\left[N(q_i(v_i, v_{-i}), v_i) - \int_0^{v_i} N_2(q_i(z, v_{-i}), z)\,dz\right] - \Pi_i(0, 0).$$

Integrating the second term on the right by parts, we obtain

$$\bar{R}_i = E_{v_i, v_{-i}}[N(q_i(v_i, v_{-i}), v_i) - N_2(q_i(v_i, v_{-i}), v_i)/\rho(v_i)] - \Pi_i(0, 0) \quad (19)$$

where $\rho(v_i) = (dF(v_i)/dv)/[1 - F(v_i)]$ is the hazard rate for F.

Because the expression in (19) enclosed in braces is independent of $\Pi_i(0, 0)$, and because the latter must satisfy (15), maximization of expected revenue clearly implies setting $\Pi_i(0, 0) = 0$. Summing over n, we obtain the following proposition.

PROPOSITION 2. *Expected Seller Revenue.* Consider a selling procedure $[\hat{q}_i(s), \hat{R}_i(s)]_{s_i \in S_i}$ in which a buyer with parameter value zero has zero expected surplus in equilibrium. Under Assumptions A1 or A1* and A2, expected revenue equals

$$E_{v_i, v_{-i}}\left[\sum_{i=1}^n I(q_i(v_i, v_{-i}), v_i) \,\middle|\, \sum_{i=1}^n q_i(v_i, v_{-i}) \leq q_0\right] \quad (20)$$

where

$$I(q_i, v_i) \equiv N(q_i, v_i) - N_2(q_i, v_i)/\rho(v_i) \quad (21)$$

and $[q_i(\cdot), R_i(\cdot)]$ is the direct revelation mechanism corresponding to $[\hat{q}_i(\cdot), \hat{R}_i(\cdot)]$.

As a direct implication of Proposition 2, we can demonstrate that two standard selling procedures—the open and sealed-bid auctions—generate the same expected revenue when buyers have unit demand. In the open auction, the auctioneer raises the asking price continuously until all but q_0 bidders have dropped out (assuming that there are q_0 units for sale). Each remaining bidder receives one item and pays the final price. In the sealed-bid auction, buyers all submit secret bids. The winners are the q_0 highest bidders, and they pay their bids.

PROPOSITION 3. *Revenue Equivalence.* If Assumptions A1* and A2 hold, expected seller revenue is the same under the sealed-bid and the open auctions.

Remark. Harris and Raviv (1981) and Vickrey (1961a) establish this result for the case of a uniform distribution.

Proof. It is clear, first, that in both types of auctions $\Pi_i(0, 0) = 0$. In the open auction, each buyer's dominant strategy is to remain in the auction until the asking price equals his parameter value. The items for sale are thus sold to those with the q_0 highest values; that is,

$$q_i(v_i, v_{-i}) = \begin{cases} 1, & \text{if } v_i \text{ is among the } q_0 \text{ highest values} \\ 0, & \text{otherwise.} \end{cases} \tag{22}$$

In view of Proposition 2, it remains only to show that (22) holds as well in the sealed-bid auction. To do so, it suffices to show that there exists an equilibrium in which buyers all use the same, strictly increasing, bidding strategy $b_i = B(v_i)$. In such an equilibrium, the goods are clearly sold to those with the highest values. The methods of Maskin and Riley (1982) can, moreover, be applied to establish that this is the unique equilibrium. Define

$$P(x) = \Pr\{\text{fewer than } q_0 \text{ of } n - 1 \text{ buyers have valuations greater than } x\}$$

$$= \sum_{k=0}^{q_0-1} \binom{n-1}{k} F(x)^{n-1-k}[1 - F(x)]^k.$$

Suppose $B(x)$ is the solution to the differential equation

$$\frac{d}{dx}[P(x)B(x)] = x \frac{dP(x)}{dx}, \qquad B(0) = 0. \tag{23}$$

Rewriting (23) in integral form, we obtain

$$P(v_i)B(v_i) = \int_0^{v_i} x \frac{dP}{dx}(x)\, dx. \tag{24}$$

Because $dP(x)/dx > 0$,

$$\int_0^{v_i} x \frac{dP}{dx}(x)\, dx < \int_0^{v_i} v_i \frac{dP}{dx}(x)\, dx = v_i P(v_i), \qquad v_i > 0.$$

From (24) it thus follows that, for $v_i > 0$, $B(v_i) < v_i$. From (23),

$$P(v_i)\frac{dB(v_i)}{dv} = \frac{dP}{dv}(v_i)[v_i - B(v_i)].$$

Because $B(v_i) < v_i$, it follows that $B(v_i)$ is strictly increasing.

Suppose that all buyers but i bid according to $B(\cdot)$ and that buyer i bids $b_i = B(x)$ for some x not necessarily equal to v_i. His expected surplus is then

$$\Pi_i(x, v_i) = \Pr\{x \text{ is among the } q_0 \text{ highest valuations}\}(v_i - b_i)$$
$$= P(x)[v_i - B(x)].$$

Differentiating by x, we obtain

$$\frac{\partial \Pi_i}{\partial x}(x, v_i) = v_i \frac{dP(x)}{dx} - \frac{d}{dx}[P(x)B(x)].$$

Substituting from (23), we can rewrite this as

$$\frac{\partial \Pi_i}{\partial x}(x, v_i) = (v_i - x)\frac{dP(x)}{dx}.$$

Because $P(x)$ is strictly increasing, it follows immediately that buyer i's optimal choice is $x = v_i$, that is, to bid $B(v_i)$. Thus, $B(\cdot)$ is indeed an equilibrium bidding strategy. Because it is strictly increasing, we conclude that (22) holds for the sealed-bid auction. Q.E.D

Remark 1. An almost identical argument can be used to establish the equivalence of the open and sealed-bid auctions when the seller sets a non-zero reserve price.

Remark 2. We have concentrated in Proposition 3 on the open and sealed-bid auctions, but it is clear that there are many other auctions as well that satisfy $\Pi_i(0, 0) = 0$ and (22) and so generate the same expected revenue. For example, the (admittedly peculiar) auction in which buyers submit sealed bids and the q_0 highest are winners, but only *losers* pay their bids satisfies these conditions.

3. Solving For the Revenue-maximizing Selling Procedure: the Regular Case

To solve for the optimal (deterministic) selling procedure, we begin by choosing $q(\cdot) = [q_1(\cdot), \dots, q_n(\cdot)]$ to maximize (20). We then show that the solution to this problem $q^*(\cdot) = [q_1^*(\cdot), \dots, q_n^*(\cdot)]$ is monotonic as required by Lemma 1 if the distribution is 'regular' in the sense defined below. Thus, $q^*(\cdot)$ solves the seller's optimization problem. The regularity assumption, which we will invoke throughout this section, is as follows.

ASSUMPTION C. *Regularity of the Distribution Function*[3]

$$J(v) \equiv v - \frac{1}{\rho(v)} \tag{25a}$$

---

[3] See Maskin and Riley (1984a) for a discussion of this assumption. Clearly, it is satisfied if the hazard rate $\rho(v)$ either increases or does not decline too rapidly with v. We noted earlier that we can always choose our parametrization so that Assumption B2 is satisfied. The choice, however, may affect whether or not Assumption C holds.

is increasing or

$$\frac{1}{p_2(\bar{q}(v), v)} \frac{\partial}{\partial v} \left[\frac{p_2(\bar{q}(v), v)}{\rho(v)} \right] < 1 \qquad (25b)$$

where $\bar{q}(v)$ solves $(\partial I / \partial q)(q, v) = 0$.

We first consider the case of unit demand, Assumption A1*. Although units are themselves indivisible, the optimization problem is not so constrained, since we can give q_i a probabilistic interpretation. That is, q_i between zero and unity should be thought of as the probability that buyer i receives a unit. Given Assumption A1*,

$$I(q_i, v_i) = J(v_i) \min\{q_i, 1\} \qquad (26)$$

where $J(\cdot)$ is given by (25a). Substituting (26) into (20), we seek the solution to

$$\max_{q(v)} \left[E_{v_i, v_{-i}} \sum_{i=1}^{n} J(v_i) q_i \,\middle|\, 0 \leqslant q_i \leqslant 1, \sum_{i=1}^{n} q_i \leqslant q_0 \right]. \qquad (27)$$

Define

$$v^0 = \max\{v \mid J(v) = 0\}. \qquad (28)$$

If Assumption C holds, so that $J(v)$ is increasing,[4] then $J(v)$ is positive if and only if $v > v^0$. It follows immediately that the solution to (27), $q^*(\cdot)$, satisfies

$$q_i^*(v_i, v_{-i}) = 0, \quad v_i < v^0.$$

We now establish the following proposition.

PROPOSITION 4. *Optimal Selling Procedure for Unit Demand: the Regular Case.* If buyers' preferences satisfy A1* and $F(v)$ satisfies Assumption C (so that $J(v)$ is increasing), expected seller revenue is maximized by selling up to q_0 units to those buyers with the highest reservation prices in excess of v^0 (defined by (28)).

Remark. There are clearly many selling procedures that satisfy the conditions of Proposition 4 and are therefore optimal. Indeed, the open and sealed-bid auctions described above are optimal as long as the auctioneer sets a minimum price of v^0.

Proof. Suppose there are m buyers for whom $J(v_i) > 0$, that is, m buyers with reservation values exceeding v^0. If $m \leqslant q_0$, the term in braces in (27) is maximized by setting $q_i = 1$ if $v_i > v^0$ and $q_i = 0$ otherwise. If $m > q^0$, the term in braces is maximized by setting $q_i = 1$ for those q_0 buyers with the highest values of J, that is, with the q_0 highest reservation

---

[4] For the unit demand case, condition (25b) reduces to (25a).

values. To summarize, (27) is solved by choosing

$$q_i^*(v_i, v_{-i})$$

$$= \begin{cases} 1, & \text{if } v_i \geqslant v^0 \text{ and } v_i \text{ is among the } q_0 \text{ highest reservation values} \\ 0, & \text{otherwise.} \end{cases}$$

$$(28a)$$

Since $q_i^*(v_i, v_{-i})$ is a non-decreasing function of v_i, it satisfies the hypotheses of Lemma 1. Thus, $q_i^*(v_i, v_{-i})$, $i = 1, \ldots, n$, is the expected revenue-maximizing allocation rule.   Q.E.D

We now consider the problem of general downward-sloping demand curves. Perhaps the best-known selling procedure for demand curves of this type is the US Treasury bill auction. Buyers may submit orders at one or more prices. Thus, in principle, a buyer can approximate any demand curve arbitrarily closely. Current practice is for the Treasury to fill orders at the prices submitted until orders filled equal the size of the offering. However, the Treasury has also experimented with a sealed bid auction in which all buyers pay the price of the highest unsuccessful bidder.[5]

As we will see, neither of these auctions is optimal even with a reserve price. Moreover, expected revenue from the two auctions is not in general the same.

Suppose that Assumptions A1, A2, B1, B2, and C hold. Consider the problem of maximizing (20). If, for all i, the solution $q_i^*(v_i, v_{-i})$ is non-decreasing in v_i, then once again the hypotheses of Lemma 1 are satisfied. Thus, if $q_i^*(v_i, v_{-i})$ satisfies this monotonicity property, it is the solution to the seller's optimization problem. The following lemma is helpful.

LEMMA 2. If Assumptions A1, A2, B1, B2, and C hold, then

(a) $I(q, v)$ is a strictly quasi-concave function of q (that is, its second derivative with respect to q is negative whenever its first derivative is non-negative); and
(b) $\partial I / \partial q$ is strictly increasing in v.

Proof. We first establish that Assumptions A1, A2, and B1 together imply (a). From (21),

$$\frac{\partial I}{\partial q} = p(q, v) - p_2(q, v)/\rho(v). \tag{29}$$

---

[5] The Treasury has not yet announced the results of its experiment with the one-price auction. In future work we plan to use the results of this paper to compare the two forms of Treasury bill auctions with the theoretical optimum. For a discussion of the one-price auction when buyers bid for a share of a divisible good, see Wilson (1979) and Maxwell (1982).

Hence,

$$\frac{\partial I}{\partial q} > 0 \text{ if and only if } 1/\rho < p/p_2. \tag{30}$$

Note that

$$\frac{\partial^2 I}{\partial q^2} = p_1 - p_{12}/\rho.$$

If p_{12} is non-negative, $\partial^2 I/\partial q^2$ is negative, since, by Assumption A1, $p_1 < 0$ for $p > 0$. If p_{12} is negative, then by (30),

$$\frac{\partial I}{\partial q} > 0 \to \frac{\partial^2 I}{\partial q^2} < p_1 - \frac{p_{12}p}{p_2} = \frac{p_1^2}{qp_2} \frac{\partial}{\partial v} \left(\frac{-qp_1}{p} \right).$$

By Assumption B1, the final expression is non-positive. Thus, $I(q, v)$ is indeed strictly quasi-concave. Furthermore,

$$\frac{\partial^2 I}{\partial q \partial v} = p_2 \left[1 - \frac{1}{p_2} \frac{\partial}{\partial v} \left(\frac{p_2}{\rho} \right) \right]$$

$$= p_2 \left(1 + \frac{d\rho/dv}{\rho^2} \right) - \frac{p_{22}}{\rho}$$

$$= p_2 \frac{dJ}{dv} (v) - \frac{p_{22}}{\rho},$$

since $dJ(v)/dv = 1 + (d\rho/dy)/\rho^2$. Thus, by Assumptions B2 and C, $\partial^2 I/\partial q \, \partial v$ is strictly positive Q.E.D

Form the Lagrangean for the maximization of (27); that is,

$$L = E_{v_i, v_{-i}} \left[\sum_{i=1}^{n} I(q_i, v_i) + \mu(v_i, v_{-i}) \left(q_0 - \sum_{i=1}^{n} q_i \right) \right].$$

The solution $q_1^*(\cdot), \ldots, q_n^*(\cdot)$ satisfies

$q_i^*(v_i, v_{-i}) \geq 0$ and $\mu(v_i, v_{-i})$ non-negative

$$\left.
\begin{aligned}
&\mu(v_i, v_{-i}) \left[\sum_{i=1}^{n} q_i^*(v_i, v_{-i}) - q_0 \right] = 0 \\[2mm]
&q_i^*(v_i, v_{-i}) \left[\frac{\partial I}{\partial q} (q_i^*(v_i, v_{-i}), v_i) - \mu(v_i, v_{-i}) \right] = 0 \\[2mm]
&q_i^*(v_i, v_{-i}) = 0 \to \frac{\partial I}{\partial q} (0, v_i) \leq \mu(v_i, v_{-i}).
\end{aligned}
\right\} \tag{31}$$

Given the hypotheses of Lemma 2, $I(q_i, v_i)$ is strictly quasi-concave in q; hence the necessary conditions (31) are also sufficient. To show that $q_1^*(\cdot), \ldots, q_n^*(\cdot)$ solves the seller's maximization problem, it remains to argue that $q_i^*(v_i, v_{-i})$ is non-decreasing in v_i, so that we can apply

Lemma 1. For given (v_i, v_{-i}), either $q_i^*(v_i, v_{-i}) = 0$, in which case $(\partial q_i^*/\partial v_i)(v_i, v_{-i})$ is trivially non-negative, or else $q_i^*(v_i, v_{-i}) > 0$. In the latter case, (31) implies that

$$\frac{\partial I}{\partial q}(q_i^*(v_i, v_{-i}), v_i) = \mu(v_i, v_{-i}).$$

Moreover, the equality holds in a neighbourhood of (v_i, v_{-i}). Differentiating this last equation with respect to v_i, we obtain

$$\frac{\partial^2 I}{\partial q^2}\frac{\partial q_i^*}{\partial v_i} + \frac{\partial^2 I}{\partial q\, dv} = \frac{\partial \mu}{\partial v_i}. \qquad (31a)$$

Suppose that $\partial \mu/\partial v_i$ is non-positive. Because $\partial^2 I/\partial q\, \partial v$ is positive and (thanks to strict quasi-concavity) $\partial^2 I/\partial q^2$ is negative. (31a) implies that $\partial q_i^*/\partial v_i$ is positive. Assume, therefore, that $\partial \mu/\partial v_i$ is positive; this implies, in particular, that $\mu > 0$. If, for $j \neq i$, $\partial I(q_j^*(v_i, v_{-i}), v_j)/\partial q < \mu$, then $\partial q_j^*/\partial v_i = 0$. Moreover, if $\partial I(q_j^*(v_i, v_{-i}), v_j)/\partial q = \mu$, then $(\partial^2 I/\partial q^2)(\partial q_j^*/\partial v_i) = \partial \mu/\partial v_i$, implying that $\partial q_j^*/\partial v_i \leq 0$. In either case, therefore $\partial q_j^*/\partial v_i$ is non-positive for $j \neq i$. But because

$$\sum_{k=1}^{n} \frac{\partial q_k^*}{\partial v_i}(v_i, v_{-i}) = 0$$

(since $\mu > 0$), we can deduce again that $\partial q_i^*/\partial v_i$ is non-negative. Hence $q_1^*(\cdot), \dots, q_n^*(\cdot)$ solves the seller's problem.

Define $\bar{q}(v_i)$ so that $(\partial I/\partial q)(\bar{q}(v_i), v_i) = 0$ for all v_i, and let $\phi(\cdot)$ be the inverse of $\bar{q}(v_i)$. Take

$$\bar{R}(q_i) = R_i^*(\phi(q_i)) \qquad (32)$$

where $R_i^*(v_i)$ satisfies (18) with $q_i(\cdot) = q_i^*(\cdot)$ and $\Pi_i(0, 0) = 0$. Given the preceding analysis, the following result describes an optimal selling procedure.

PROPOSITION 5. *Optimal Selling Procedure for General Demand: the Regular Case.* If Assumptions A1, A2, B1, B2, and C hold, expected revenue from the sale of q_0 units is maximized if the seller sets the payment schedule $\bar{R}(q_i)$ defined by (32). Each buyer i submits an order q_i and pays $\bar{R}(q_i)$. If total orders exceed supply, final allocations are reduced according to the rationing scheme:

$$q_i^*\left[\frac{\partial I}{\partial q_i}(q_i^*, \phi(q_i)) - \mu\right] = 0$$

$$\sum_{i=1}^{n} q_i^* \leq q_0 \qquad (33)$$

$$q_i^* = 0 \to \frac{\partial I}{\partial q_i}(0, \phi(q_i)) \leq \mu.$$

For the special case in which demand curves have the simple form

$$p(q_i, v_i) = v_i - \gamma q_i,$$

the allocation rule is especially straightforward. From (33), we obtain

$$q_i^* > 0 \rightarrow \gamma(q_i - q_i^*) - \mu = 0 \rightarrow q_i^* = q_i - \mu/\gamma.$$

Thus, the seller simply reduces each buyer's order by the same amount (subject to its remaining non-negative) if demand exceeds supply.

It is easy to see that the open and sealed-bid auctions,[6] as well as the two Treasury bill procedures, cannot be optimal in general. Suppose, for example, that q_0 is so large that the supply constraint is never binding. Then all these auctions have the property that the equilibrium price is just the seller reserve price, at which buyers can buy all they want. In the optimal selling procedure, however, pricing is nonlinear: a buyer with value v_i buys $\bar{q}(v)$, solving $I(\bar{q}(v), v) = 0$, and pays

$$R(v) = N(\bar{q}(v), v) - N_2(\bar{q}(v), v)/\rho(v).$$

4. Optimal Selling Procedures: the General Case

We next study revenue-maximizing procedures when Assumption C is not imposed. To simplify matters, we consider only the case of unit demand.

In addition to the necessary conditions (9) and (15) derived in Section 2, we first note that the allocation rule must satisfy a monotonicity conditoon. (Earlier we noted that monotonicity was a *sufficient* hypothesis for Lemma 1.) For unit demand, (7) becomes

$$\Pi_i(x, v_i) = E_{v_{-i}} v_i q_i(x, v_{-i}) - R_i(x).$$

Thus,

$$\Pi_i(x, x) - \Pi_i(x, v_i) = (x - v_i) E_{v_{-i}} q_i(x, v_{-i}). \tag{34}$$

From (8),

$$\Pi_i(x, x) - \Pi_i(v_i, x) \geq 0 \text{ and } \Pi_i(v_i, v_i) - \Pi_i(x, v_i) \geq 0.$$

Adding these two inequalities and substituting from (34), we obtain

$$(v_i - x) E_{v_{-i}} [q_i(v_i, v_{-i}) - q_i(x, v_{-i})] \geq 0.$$

Thus, the allocation rule $q_i(v_i, v_{-i})$ must satisfy the condition that

$$E_{v_{-i}} q_i(v_i, v_{-i}) \text{ is non-decreasing in } v_i. \tag{35}$$

---

[6] When buyers may want more than one unit, these auctions must be modified slightly. In the open auction the auctioneer continuously raises the price, and at each level buyers indicate how many units they would want to buy. The actual price is determined when the level is raised high enough so that supply equals demand. In the sealed-bid auction, buyers submit demand curves, and the auctioneer uses these to compute the market-clearing price and allocations.

Adding this constraint to programme (27), we obtain the maximization problem

$$\max_{\{q_i(\cdot)\}} \left\{ E_{v_i, v_{-i}} \sum_{i=1} J(v_i) q_i \; \middle| \; E_{v_{-i}} q_i(v_i, v_{-i}) \text{ is non-decreasing,} \right.$$

$$\left. 0 \leqslant q_i \leqslant 1, \sum_{i=1}^{n} q_i \leqslant q_0 \right\}. \quad (36)$$

In general, the function $J(v) = v - 1/\rho(v)$ is non-monotonic, and so the earlier argument does not generalize immediately. Instead we begin by defining a modified function $J^*(v)$ that *is* monotonic, and solve for the optimal $\{q_i^*(\cdot)\}$ with J^* replacing J. We then show that this allocation rule also solves the original problem. Finally, we interpret the optimal selling procedure as an auction.

MODIFIED J FUNCTION. Let $\{[x^\omega, y^\omega] \mid y^\omega < x^{\omega+1}\}_{\omega \in \Omega}$ be a collection of subintervals of $[0, \bar{v}]$ such that (a) the function

$$J^*(v) = \begin{cases} J(v), & \text{if } v \in \bigcup_{\omega \in \Omega} [x^\omega, y^\omega] \\ J(y^\omega), & \text{if } v \in [x^\omega, y^\omega] \quad \text{for some } \omega \end{cases}$$

is non-decreasing, and (b) the function

$$K^\omega(v) = \int_v^{y^\omega} [J(z) - J(y^\omega)] \, dF(z)$$

satisfies

$$K^\omega(v) \begin{cases} \leqslant 0, & \text{for all } v \leqslant y^\omega \\ = 0, & v = x^\omega. \end{cases}$$

A proof that the collection $\{[x^\omega, y^\omega]\}$ exists can be constructed along the following geometrical lines. Consider Figure 14.1. Starting at $v = \bar{v}$ and moving to the left, we define $J^*(v) = J(v)$ until a point y^1 is reached at which, for some $x < y^1$,

$$\int_x^{y^1} [J(z) - J(y^1)] \, dF(z) \geqslant 0. \quad (**)$$

Since $J(v) \leqslant v_i \leqslant \bar{v} = J(\bar{v})$, y^1, if it exists, is less than $\bar{v}$. Define x^1 to be the smallest such x satisfying inequality (**) and define $J^*(v) = J(y^1)$ over $[x^1, y^1]$. This process is continued until $v = 0$.

PROPOSITION 6. *Optimal Allocation Rule.* For any (v_i, v_{-i}), choose $\hat{J}$ so that the number, M, of buyers with parameter values v_i for which $J^*(v_i) \geqslant \hat{J}$ is at least q_0, and the number, m, for which $J^*(v_i) > \hat{J}$ is at most $q_0 - 1$. Then expected seller revenue is maximized by

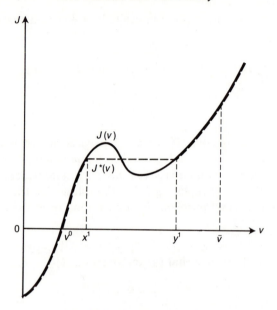

Fig. 14.1   *Derivation of J*.*

$q_i^*(\cdot), \ldots, q_n^*(\cdot)$ satisfying

$$q_i^*(v_i, v_i) = \begin{cases} 1, & \text{if } J^*(v_i) > \hat{J} > 0 \\ \dfrac{q_0 - m}{M - m}, & \text{if } J^*(v_i) = \hat{J} \geqslant 0 \\ 0, & \text{otherwise.} \end{cases} \tag{37}$$

Proof. Because $J^*(\cdot)$ is non-decreasing, $q_i^*(v_i, v_{-i})$ is non-decreasing in v_i. Hence, (35) is satisfied. The proof is completed in three steps. First, we show that, for any $q_1(\cdot), \ldots, q_n(\cdot)$ satisfying the constraints of (36),

$$E_{v_i,v_{-i}} \sum_{i=1}^{n} J(v_i)q_i(v_i, v_{-i}) \leqslant E_{v_i,v_{-i}} \sum_{i=1}^{n} J^*(v_i)q_i(v_i, v_{-i}). \tag{38}$$

Next, we show that $q_1^*(\cdot), \ldots, q_n^*(\cdot)$ defined by (37) solves the modified optimization problem in which $J(\cdot)$ in (36) is replaced by $J^*(\cdot)$. Finally, we confirm that, for $q_i(\cdot) = q_i^*(\cdot)$, (38) holds with equality.

To prove the first step, we define

$$\mathring{q}_i(v_i) = E_{v_{-i}} q_i(v_i, v_{-i})$$

for any allocation $\{q_i(\cdot)\}$ satisfying the constraints of (36). Then,

$$E_{v_i, v_{-i}}[J(v_i) - J^*(v_i)]q_i(v_i, v_{-i}) = \int_0^{\bar{v}} [J(v) - J^*(v)]\mathring{q}_i(v) \, dF(v)$$

$$= \sum_{\omega \in \Omega} \int_{x^\omega}^{y^\omega} [J(v) - J^*(v)] \frac{dF}{dv}(v)\mathring{q}_i(v) \, dv$$

$$= \sum_{\omega \in \Omega} - \int_{x^\omega}^{y^\omega} \frac{dK^\omega}{dv}(v)\mathring{q}_i(v) \, dv \qquad (39)$$

where the last two equations follow directly from the definitions of J^* and K^ω. By construction, $K^\omega(v)$ is non-positive and $\mathring{q}_i(v)$ is non-decreasing. Thus, integrating by parts, we obtain

$$- \int_{x^\omega}^{y^\omega} \frac{dK^\omega}{dv}(v)\mathring{q}_i(v) \, dv \leq K^\omega(x^\omega)\mathring{q}_i(x^\omega) - K^\omega(y^\omega)\mathring{q}_i(y^\omega) \leq 0 \qquad (40)$$

from the definition of K^ω. Inequality (38) follows from (39) and (40).

Next, consider the maximization problem

$$\max_{\{q_i(\cdot)\}} \left\{ E_{v_i, v_{-i}} \sum_{i=1}^n J^*(v_i)q_i(v_i, v_{-i}) \,\middle|\, 0 \leq q_i \leq 1, \sum_{i=1}^n q_i \leq q_0 \right\}. \qquad (41)$$

Because J^* is non-decreasing, the solution, from the argument in Section 3, is to set $q_i^* = 1$ for the (up to) q_0 buyers with the highest non-negative values of J^*. Since J^* is not strictly increasing, ties occur with positive probability. These can be broken by randomizing—that is, by giving all buyers with $J^* = \hat{J}$ a chance $(q_0 - M)/(M - m)$ of winning—thereby obtaining exactly q_0 'winners'. Thus, $\{q_i^*(\cdot)\}$ given by (37) solves the maximization problem (41).

By definition, $q_i^*(v_i, v_{-i})$ is a constant as a function of v_i on any interval $[x^\omega, y^\omega]$, $\omega \in \Omega$. Hence,

$$\int_{x^\omega}^{y^\omega} \frac{dK^\omega}{dv}(v)\mathring{q}_i^*(v) \, dv = [K^\omega(y^\omega) - K^\omega(x^\omega)]\mathring{q}_i^*(y^\omega) = 0$$

where

$$\mathring{q}_i^*(v) = E_{v_{-i}}q_i^*(v, v_{-i}).$$

Thus, (39) implies that (38) holds with equality.

Finally, note that, because $q_i^*(v_i, v_{-i})$ is non-decreasing in v_i, Lemma 1 implies that, because it solves (36), it solves the seller's optimization problem. Q.E.D

Combining (18) and (37), we can readily compute the expected payment $R_i^*(v_i)$ made by buyer i with parameter value v_i in the optimal selling procedure. Thus, the seller can maximize expected revenue through a direct revelation mechanism in which, if the n buyers 'announce' parameter values $(x_1, \ldots, x_n)$, the allocation and expected payments are

$$[q_i^*(x_1, \ldots, x_n), R_i^*(x_i)], \qquad i = 1, \ldots, n.$$

We next show that, alternatively, the seller can use a modification of the open-bid auction.

PROPOSITION 7. *Optimal Multi-unit Auctions with Unit Demand.* Let $\{[x^\omega, y^\omega]\}_{\omega \in \Omega}$ be the collection of intervals in the definition of J^*. For each ω, there exists $z^\omega \in (x^\omega, y^\omega)$ such that if, in an open auction, the asking price is started at $v^0 = \max[v \mid J^*(v) = 0]$, and is raised discontinuously from x^ω to z^ω whenever it reaches x^ω, then that auction is optimal.

Remark. When the price rises from x^ω to z^ω, buyers' decisions about whether to continue bidding must be revealed simultaneously (since, with positive probability, several will drop out at the same time). One way of achieving this is for the auctioneer to confer (privately) with each buyer to determine whether more than q_0 wish to continue bidding. If not, those remaining in the auction pay z^ω and receive one unit. The winners among those dropping out are selected at random and pay x^ω.

Proof. It suffices to show that we can choose z^ω such that the corresponding allocation rule is defined by (37). For each ω, choose z^ω so that

$$E_{v_{-i}}[q_i^*(x^\omega, v_{-i}) \mid \#_i(x^\omega, v_{-i}) > q_0 - 1](y^\omega - x^\omega)$$
$$= E_{v_{-i}}[q_i^*(y^\omega, v_{-i}) \mid \#_i(x^\omega, v_{-i}) > q_0 - 1](y^\omega - z^\omega), \quad (42)$$

where $\#_i(v_i, v_{-i})$ is defined to be the number of buyers (other than i) whose parameter value is at least v_i. In (42), z^ω is chosen so that a buyer with reservation value y^ω is indifferent between staying in and dropping out when the price reaches x^ω. Hence all buyers with values less than y^ω drop out when (or before) the price rises to x^ω but stay in if their reservation values exceed y^ω. The induced allocation rule of this modified open auction thus equals that of (37). Q.E.D

We should point out that in the auction of Proposition 7 all buyers with reservation values in an interval $[x^\omega, y^\omega]$ have an equal chance of winning. This means that there is a positive probability that a buyer who does not have one of the q_0 highest reservation values will be assigned a unit. The proposition therefore assumes implicitly that the seller can enforce a no-resale provision. In the absence of such a provision, the prospect of resale changes buyers' behaviour, and expected seller revenue declines. None the less, we show in Maskin and Riley (1980) that the conditions under which it is optimal for the seller to raise the asking price discontinuously are the same with and without resale.

We conclude this section by illustrating the seller's potential gain from using the optimal rather than the sealed-bid or open auctions. Suppose that the distribution $F(\cdot)$ can be approximated by the following two-point distribution:

$$F(v) \approx \begin{cases} 0, & v < 32 \\ 3/4, & 32 \leqslant v < 80 \\ 1, & v \geqslant 80. \end{cases}$$

Suppose there are two buyers and one unit for sale. Clearly, if the ordinary open auction with reserve price is to be used, the seller is best off setting the reserve price equal to 32 or 80. If the former, the item sells for 32 unless both buyers have a valuation of 80. Since the latter occurs with probability 1/16, expected seller revenue is

$$\left(\frac{15}{16}\right)32 + \left(\frac{1}{16}\right)80 = 35.$$

If the reserve price is 80, there are no bids with probability $(3/4)(3/4) = 9/16$. Expected seller revenue is therefore

$$\left(\frac{7}{16}\right)80 = 35.$$

Thus, in this example a reserve price of either 32 or 80 is optimal for the seller in an open auction.

Alternatively, suppose that the seller uses an auction like that of Proposition 7 and opens the bidding at 32 but then jumps the bid to (just less than) 56. Suppose that buyer 2 stays in the auction only if his reservation value is 80. Then buyer 1 gains from staying in himself only if buyer 2 has a low reservation value. (If both stay in, all consumer surplus is bid away.) His expected gain is therefore slightly greater than

$$\frac{3}{4}(80 - 56) = 18.$$

If buyer 1 chooses not to stay in the auction, he wins (with probability 1/2) only if buyer 2 has a low valuation. Thus his expected gain is

$$\frac{3}{8}(80 - 32) = 18.$$

Buyer 1 therefore has an incentive to use the same strategy as buyer 2, so that this is the equilibrium bidding strategy. Expected seller revenue is therefore

$$\left(\frac{9}{16}\right)32 + \left(\frac{1}{16}\right)80 + \left(\frac{6}{16}\right)56 = 44.$$

By jumping the bid, the seller can thus increase its expected revenue by 9, a gain over 25 per cent.

5. Randomized Selling Schemes

At the outset, we noted that the seller could in principle use a selling procedure in which the outcome is a random schedule

$$[\tilde{q}_i(v_i, v_{-i}), \tilde{R}_i(v_i, v_{-i})]_{i=1,\ldots,n}.[7]$$

We restricted attention however, to deterministic selling procedures. In this section we investigate the desirability of randomness.

Because preferences take the form

$$U_i(q, R, v) = \int_0^q p(x, v)\,dy - R,$$

so that buyers are neutral towards income risk, i.e., they are indifferent between the random payment $\tilde{R}_i(v_i, v_{-i})$ and its mean (given v_i). Thus, we may assume that the optimal selling procedure is of the form

$$[\tilde{q}_i(v_i, v_{-i}), R_i(v_i)].$$

Moreover, for the special case of unit demand, it is clear that there is no loss in generality in assuming that each realization of $\tilde{q}_i(v_i, v_{-i})$ is no greater than unity. Thus,

$$U_i(\tilde{q}_i, R_i) = v_i\tilde{q}_i - R_i$$

is linear in $\tilde{q}_i$, and so buyers are again indifferent to risk. Hence, in the case of unit demand, the seller gains nothing by using random selling procedures. We next show that the same principle applies to a broad class of smooth demand curves.

PROPOSITION 8. *Under Assumptions A1, A2, B1, B2, and C, the optimal deterministic selling procedure generates at least as much expected revenue as any random one.*

Proof. Let $[\tilde{q}_i(\cdot), R_i(\cdot)]$ be a random selling procedure. Although $\tilde{q}_i(v_i, v_{-i})$ is now a random variable, we can still argue as in Section 2 to establish the following counterpart of (9):

$$\Pi_i(v_i, v_{-i}) - \Pi_i(0, 0) = E_{v_{-i}}\left[E\int_0^{v_i} N_2(\tilde{q}_i(z, v_{-i}), z)\,dz\right] \qquad (43)$$

where the inner expectation is over the possible realizations of $\tilde{q}_i(z, v_{-i})$. It follows immediately that the counterpart of (18) holds, namely,

$$R_i(v_i) = E_{v_{-i}}\left\{E\left[N(\tilde{q}_i(v_i, v_{-i})) - \int_0^{v_i} \tilde{N}_2(\tilde{q}_i(z, v_{-i}), z)\,dz\right]\right\} - \Pi_i(0, 0).$$

$$(44)$$

[7] We are expressing all selling procedures in this section as direct revelation mechanisms, which, by the Revelation Principle, we are entitled to do.

Since there can be no gain to supplying the buyer with more than $q^0(v_i)$, the amount he would purchase at a zero price, we can assume that each realization of $\bar{q}_i$ satisfies $\bar{q}_i \leq q^0(v_i)$. Thus, $N(q_i, v_i)$ is strictly increasing over the domain of q_i, and we can define the inverse function

$$q_i = N^{-1}(n, v_i). \tag{45}$$

For any random variable $\bar{q}_i$ and $\bar{n} = N(\bar{q}_i, v_i)$, we can then choose $\bar{q}_i = N^{-1}(\bar{n}, v_i)$ where $\bar{n} \equiv E(\bar{n})$. That is,

$$EN(\bar{q}_i, v_i) = N(\bar{q}_i, v_i) = \bar{n}. \tag{46}$$

Consider the function

$$G(n) = N_2(N^{-1}(n, v_i), v_i). \tag{47}$$

We shall suppose that $G(\cdot)$ is convex. (We will later confirm that this is the case.) Thus

$$EG(\bar{n}) = EN_2(\bar{q}_i, v_i) \geq G(\bar{n}) = N_2(\bar{q}_i, v_i). \tag{48}$$

Next, define

$$\bar{\Pi}_i(v_i, v_i) = E_{v_{-i}} \int_0^{v_i} N_2(\bar{q}_i(z, v_{-i}), z)\, dz, \tag{49}$$

where $N(\bar{q}_i(v_i, v_{-i}), v_i) = EN(\bar{q}_i(v_i, v_{-i}), v_i)$. Then $\bar{q}_i$ satisfies the necessary condition (9). Arguing exactly as in Section 2, we deduce that the expected payment schedule for buyer i is

$$\bar{R}_i(v_i) = E_{v_{-i}}\left[N(\bar{q}_i(v_i, v_{-i}), v_i) - \int_0^{v_i} N_2(\bar{q}_i(z, v_{-i}), z)\, dz \right] - \Pi_i(0, 0). \tag{50}$$

From (46), the first terms on the right-hand side of (44) and (50) are equal. From (48), the second term in (44) is no greater than the second term in (50). Thus

$$\bar{R}_i(v_i) \geq R_i(v_i). \tag{51}$$

We now show that the procedure $[\bar{q}_i(\cdot), \bar{R}_i(\cdot)]$ satisfies the aggregate feasibility condition

$$\sum_{i=1}^n \bar{q}_i(v_i, v_{-i}) \leq q_0.$$

By Assumption A1, N is an increasing, concave function of q. Therefore, from Jensen's Inequality,

$$EN(\bar{q}_i(v_i, v_{-i}), v_i) \leq N(E\bar{q}_i(v_i, v_{-i}), v_i),$$

and so

$$\bar{q}_i(v_i, v_{-i}) \leq E\bar{q}_i(v_i, v_{-i}).$$

But

$$\sum_{i=1}^n \bar{q}_i(v_i, v_{-i}) \leq q_0,$$

establishing feasibility.

Because we are imposing regularity (Assumption C), the optimal deterministic selling procedure $[q_i^*(\cdot), R_i^*(\cdot)]_{i=1,\ldots,n}$ solves the problem of maximizing expected revenue subject *only* to feasibility, (9), and (15). In particular, we need not impose monotonicity; thanks to the proof of Proposition 4, it is satisfied automatically. Now, $[\bar{q}_i(\cdot), \bar{R}_i(\cdot)]$ satisfies (9) and (15) by construction, and as we have seen it satisfies feasibility. Hence $E\Sigma R_i^*(v_i) \geqslant E\Sigma \bar{R}_i(v_i)$. Thus, in view of (51), $E\Sigma R_i^*(v_i) \geqslant E\Sigma R_i(v_i)$; that is, the optimal deterministic selling procedure generates at least as much expected revenue as the random one.

It remains to establish that, as hypothesized, $G(n)$ is convex. From (45) and (47),

$$G(N(q_i, v_i)) = N_2(q_i, v_i).$$

Thus, differentiating by q_i and rearranging, we obtain

$$\frac{dG}{dn}(N(q_i, v_i)) = N_{12}/N_1 = p_2/p.$$

Differentiating again by q_i, we obtain

$$\frac{d^2G}{dn^2}[N(q_i, v_i)]p(q_i, v_i) = \frac{\partial}{\partial q}\left(\frac{p_2}{p}\right)$$

$$= \frac{p_{12}p - p_1 p_2}{p^2}$$

$$= \frac{\partial}{\partial v}\left(\frac{p_1}{p}\right)$$

$$\geqslant 0 \text{ by Assumption B1.}$$

6. Concluding Remarks

In this paper we have shown how the earlier analysis of optimal auctions by Harris and Raviv (1981), Myerson (1981), and Riley and Samuelson (1981) can be generalized to multiple units. We conclude with some comments on the crucial assumptions.

First of all, we have assumed agents to be neutral towards income risk. With risk-averse buyers, the analysis is considerably more complicated. With only a single, indivisible unit for sale, it is relatively easy to show that the sealed high-bid auction generates greater expected revenue than the second-bid auction. However, the expected profit-maximizing selling scheme is no longer a simple auction. Instead, as Matthews (1983) and Maskin and Riley (1984a) establish, the seller can exploit buyer risk aversion still further by making losers as well as winners pay in a sealed-bid auction.

A second important assumption is that parameter values are drawn independently. This implies that any pair of buyers, with possibly very different parameter values, has the same beliefs about the parameter value of a third buyer. Although this is the natural first approximation, there are situations in which it is clearly deficient. For example, suppose that, as in the auctioning of mineral rights, the true value of the item is unknown. Each buyer has an estimate based on his research. In this case it is natural to assume that a buyer with a low estimate will have more conservative beliefs about the estimates of other buyers than a buyer with a high estimate. Milgrom and Weber (1982) apply the concept of 'affiliatedness' (implying positive correlation of parameter values) to formalize this idea to compare the sealed-bid and open auctions. A central result is that the information revealed as the open auction progresses raises the expected selling price. With risk-neutral buyers, there is no equivalent effect in the sealed-bid auction, and so the open auction dominates in terms of expected revenue.[8]

This conclusion suggests that the seller might be able to exploit the correlation of buyer's reservation values with a selling procedure very different from either of the usual auctions. Indeed, work by Myerson (1981), Cremer and McLean (1985), and Maskin and Riley (1981) shows that, when buyers are risk-neutral and their parameter values are correlated and discretely distributed, the seller can extract *all* surplus.

Finally, agents' parameter values are assumed to have been drawn from the same distribution. Although symmetry is a commonly invoked theoretical simplification, it is certainly a strong restriction. To illustrate, suppose that several contractors bid for the right to resurface a section of roadway. If one contractor is much busier than the others, he will have to hire workers overtime, reduce maintenance, and so on. If, moreover, the other bidders know about this, symmetry is violated. As we show in Maskin and Riley (1986), either the sealed-bid or the open auction can dominate the other (in terms of expected revenues), depending on the nature of the asymmetry.

---

[8] Because risk aversion has the effect of improving the sealed bid auction relative to the open auction, there is no simple ranking of the two except given risk-neutral buyers.

15

Labour Contract Theory

TIM WORRALL

1. Introduction

Almost every economic transaction is governed by a contract. Buying a newspaper from a news-stand involves a trivial contract: the vendor contracts to supply you with a newspaper in exchange for the specified price. But there are much more complicated contracts. Joskow (1985) examines a contract between a coal supplier and an electricity generator. The coal supplier can, by giving six months' notice, choose between a price indexed to demand factors and a price equal to cost plus a markup. Kawazaki and McMillan (1985) look at contracts between Japanese car manufacturers and their component suppliers. The chosen component supplier is usually guaranteed a monopoly over the lifetime of the car with prices determined by cost, revisions being made every six months. Any specific investment the component supplier has to make is usually financed by the manufacturer.

Formal contracts are especially common in the labour market. In the footwear industry wages are determined by a piece-rate system but with a guaranteed minimum of seven-eighths of average earnings from the previous year (see White 1981). In the early part of this century the wages of coal miners were indexed by a sliding scale to the retail price of coal. This was a major cause of the bitter mining disputes of the 1920s when the retail price of coal fell.

This chapter concentrates on contracts in the labour market, but the arguments and analysis could equally well be applied to other markets. The labour market has however, always been thought to have some special features which make it less amenable to Walrasian analysis than other markets. It is worth quoting Hicks (1932) at some length:

the labour market is . . . by nature . . . a very special kind of market that is likely to develop 'social' as well as purely economic aspects. The conditions for this to happen are: (1) that the workers should be free to change his employer . . . (2) that employment should be regular, i.e. non-casual, so that there is a presumption that the relation between the employer and . . . his employees will be a continuing relation . . . For the purely economic correspondence between the

Financial support from the Economic and Social Research Council is gratefully acknowledged.

wage paid to a particular worker and his value to the employer is not a sufficient condition of efficiency; it is also necessary that there should be no strong feelings of injustice about the relative treatment of different employees and there should be some confidence about fair treatment over time . . . Compromise is necessary, with the result that wage rates are more uniform both between workers and over time than they would be if the labour market worked like a commodity market.

Hicks emphasizes the importance of continuity of employment. Continuity is conducive to the establishment of a contract between employer and employee. And contracts might bring some of the so-called social aspects into economic perspective. Fairness and compromise are likely to be achieved only if there is some sort of contractual commitment.

On the other hand, suppose for the moment that real wages are determined by the equation of demand and supply. Then if, as seems reasonable, the supply of labour is fairly stable and inelastic, and if the demand for labour is much more erratic, shifting with shocks to technology, resources, world prices, and so on, it is to be expected that real wages and employment will move together. Real wages will be pro-cyclical; they will vary a lot and employment will vary little. But there has been a long-held view that real wages are, if anything counter-cyclical. For example, Henry Thornton (1802) wrote:

A fall (in price) arising from temporary distress will be attended probably by no correspondent fall in the rate of wages; for the fall in price, and the distress, will be understood to be temporary, and the rate of wages, we know, is not so variable as the price of goods.

This view was maintained by Keynes in the *General Theory*, probably from casual empiricism rather than any theoretical considerations. Keynes's counter-cyclical assumption was challenged by Dunlop (1938) and Tarshis (1939). Recent evidence is equally contradictory. Kuh (1966) and Bodkin (1969) could find no relationship between real wages and employment. Neftci (1978) and Sargent (1978) concluded that there was indeed a negative relationship. Most of this evidence is based on aggregate data, but there may be severe problems with aggregation bias. If the unemployed are predominantly the low-skilled with low wages, then there will be a counter-cyclical bias, and if risky industries have higher wages or overtime is paid at a premium, then there will be a pro-cyclical bias. More recent evidence by Bils (1985) using postwar panel data suggests that real wages are pro-cyclical but not for all groups. So the evidence is inconclusive: it is not clear if the variability in real wages is consistent with the equation of demand supply. Nevertheless, contracts do exist and it is necessary to have some theoretical explanation.

Analytically, the notion of a labour contract is simple to formalize. Suppose there are just two time-periods, $t = 0, 1$, and suppose at time

$t = 1$ there are S possible states of nature, $s = 1, 2, \ldots, S$. These states
may represent shocks to demand or changes in the workers' opportunity
cost or whatever. If an employer and employee wish to trade labour at
date $t = 1$, and if they differ in risk aversion,[1] it will be in their interest to
negotiate a labour contract at date $t = 0$. The contract will specify how
much labour the employee is to supply in each state of nature, $l(s)$, and
the wage to be received in each state, $\omega(s)$. To be slightly more specific,
suppose the employee supplies labour inelastically and derives utility
from a wage ω, according to a strictly concave utility function $u(\omega)$.
Then if the employer is risk-neutral, the best contract will offer a fixed
wage $\bar{\omega}$ independently of the state of nature. For such a contract the
marginal product equals the marginal disutility of labour but the real
wage need equal neither. As Hicks suggests, the equation of the real
wage and the marginal product has been replaced by another condition
that real wages be uniform or independent of the state.

The study of contracts is an example of non-Walrasian analysis. To see
why, suppose labour could be sold forward at date $t = 0$ contingent upon
the state s at time $t = 1$. Then the contract would be irrelevant; it could
do nothing to allocate the gains from trade the market could not do. But
labour is the most obvious example of a commodity that can be sold
forward only with difficulty. Anyone who has tried to borrow against his
or her future labour income will know this to be true. That is to say,
there is an incomplete set of futures markets. Contracts are negotiated in
response to this incompleteness. Agents have become active participants
in making the market work, rather than simply passive actors. But
precisely the same set of factors that makes the set of markets incomplete
is likely to make contingent contracts difficult to negotiate. These factors
include informational asymmetries, the difficulty of enforcement, and the
bounded rationality of the agents themselves. They determine the nature
of the contract.

In a Walrasian market, exchange can take place contingent only on
information that is common to the trading partners. A contract, by
contrast, has greater flexibility. It may be possible, by propitious design,
to elicit information that is private to one of the agents and to condition
the contract upon it. Such a contract is called 'incentive-compatible' and
examples are examined in Section 3. In practice, many contracts do
specify performance contingent upon endogenous events; the piece-rate
contract mentioned above is an example. In a Walrasian market, the
wage is the return to labour. But labour or effort may not be easily
observable, so a piece-rate contract where the wage is contingent upon
output, which is endogenous but observable, may give the worker the
right incentives.

---

[1] In this chapter firms and workers contract to share risks. Training costs, job specific
skills, mobility costs, etc., are complementary reasons.

A contract may in principle be made contingent upon any event, endogenous or exogenous, which is observable by one of the contractors. But the contract can be enforced at law only if the contingency is also verifiable by the courts. For example, even if a firm can monitor a worker's effort at very little cost, a contract contingent upon effort cannot be easily enforced, since, unless the court can directly monitor effort, the firm will always have an incentive to say that the monitored effort was low and to pay a low wage. Therefore contracts enforceable at law will in general be incomplete; they will be contingent only upon verifiable events. Incomplete contracts are discussed in Section 4.1 below.

Even for events that are verifiable, legal costs may be so high as to make enforcement infeasible. If contractors trade repeatedly, it may be possible to design a contract that is self-enforcing. In a self-enforcing contract no one ever has an incentive to renege; that is, the long-term benefits from adhering to the contract always exceed any short-term gain that might be had from reneging. Indeed, if self-enforcing contracts do exist, they may provide a reason why agents wish to trade with other designated agents rather than with an amorphous market. Trading with one particular agent leads to some degree of trust and mutual confidence. There is an assurance that contractors will behave reasonably now so as to procure the gains from the contract in the future. Self-enforcing contracts are examined in Section 4.2 below.

The third issue is the bounded rationality of the individual contractors. If it can be enforced, a contract can be made contingent upon any event that impinges on the contractors. So a labour contract may have provisions depending upon the prices of other inputs, commodity prices, the profits of rival firms, the rate of interest, money supply, and so forth. The list seems endless, and optimal contracts might be exceedingly complex. In contrast, real-world contracts appear relatively simple. They may be simple because some information is sufficiently summarized by a single statistic, or because the costs of additional complexity outweigh the benefits. Simple rules or rules of thumb may be good enough. But one of the major costs of writing contracts may be the calculation of the costs and benefits of additional complexity. Then the problem becomes circular and there is no optimal level of complexity. Section 5 discusses bounded rationality.

Informational asymmetries, the degree of enforceability, and bounded rationality all affect the design of the contract and hence how efficiently the gains from trade are allocated. From the point of view of the individual agent, they cannot be made worse off by agreeing to a contract simply because there was always the option not to agree. Actually, if the contractors are good negotiators, the contract ought to be *ex ante* efficient. However, *ex ante* efficiency need not imply *ex post* efficiency. The incentive-compatible contract of Section 3.1 is not *ex post* efficient. Contracts may also create negative externalities. As mentioned above, the gains from contracting may encourage agents to trade with the same partner repeatedly. This can lead to a reduction in competition *ex post* which may be detrimental. An example is given in the Appendix, where contracts reduce the mobility of labour and hence everyone's utility *ex ante*.

The outline of this chapter is as follows. Section 2 presents the basic model. The spot market equilibrium and the equilibrium with labour contracts is compared and contrasted. Section 3 examines asymmetric information both in the context of a short-term contract (Section 3.1) and a long-term contract (Section 3.2). In Section 4 incomplete and self-enforcing contracts are examined. Section 5 discusses the problem of bounded rationality, Section 6 discusses macroeconomics, and Section 7 contains some brief bibliographical notes.

2. The Basic Model

This section examines the differences between two situations, one where the labour market is equilibrated by supply and demand (the spot or auction market equilibrium), and the other where the labour market is equilibrated by contracts. The model is deliberately simple. It is the basis for subsequent discussion.

Consider an economy with two dates, $t = 0$, 1, and two states, $s = 1$, 2, at date $t = 1$. There are two types of agents, firms and workers, and two goods, consumption and leisure. All trade takes place at date $t = 1$ once state s is known. There are no forward markets in consumption or labour.

There are m identical firms, each endowed with one unit of capital. Capital can be thought of as entrepreneurial ability; it is non-transferable. At date $t = 0$ firms make an initial investment of capital. It enables them to combine with labour l, at date $t = 1$, to produce some output y. The production function $y = sf(l)$ is subject to a random technological shock s. The two states, s_1 and s_2 ($s_1 > s_2$), occur with probability p and $(1-p)$. The function $f(l)$ is assumed to be strictly increasing and strictly concave; there are diminishing returns to labour. Capitalists consume profits and are assumed to be risk-neutral.

There are n identical workers, each endowed with one unit of labour. Labour is supplied perfectly inelastically: one unit is supplied or nothing. Since there are no forward markets, the price of the consumption good in both states can be set equal to 1. Therefore if the real wage paid to the worker in state s is w_s, his utility is $u = u(w_s)$ if he is working and $u = u(w_s + R)$ if he is not. R is the reservation wage of labour. If w_s is less than R the worker will not wish to supply labour. The worker is assumed to be risk-averse: $u(\cdot)$ is strictly increasing and strictly concave.

The following assumption is made to contrast the spot market with the market mediated by a contract.

ASSUMPTION. $s_1 f'(n/m) > R > s_2 f'(n/m)$.

This means that full employment will be efficient in state $s = 1$ but not in state $s = 2$. Note that n/m is the average number of workers per firm. Any integer problems will be ignored.

2.1. The spot market equilibrium

Since there are no futures markets, the labour market is equilibrated by supply and demand in each state s. There are just two wage rates $\{w_s\}$, $s = 1, 2$ which clear the market. All agents are assumed to act competitively and treat w_s parametrically. The demand for labour in state s, l_s, is determined by firms maximizing profits, $sf(l_s) - w_s l_s$. Workers will choose to supply labour if $w_s \geqslant R$ but not otherwise. The outcome (A_1, A_2) is drawn in (w, l)-space in Figure 15.1(a). In state s_1 there is full employment; each firm employs n/m workers at a wage w_1 equal to the marginal 'product, $s_1 f'(n/m)$. In state s_2 total employment is $mf'^{-1}(R/s_2)$, which is less than n by assumption. Employment levels are efficient in both states, but wages are variable. Variable wages are disliked by workers because the workers are risk-averse.

2.2. The contract market equilibrium

As spot market wages are variable, a risk-neutral employer may be able to offer a contract at date $t = 0$ which reduces wage variability in return, say, for a reduction in their average level. A contract will specify the wages and employment levels in both states at date $t = 1$. It can be quite general; the contract may specify different wages in different states and different wages to workers who are employed or who may be laid off.

Consider a firm that hires l^* workers at date $t = 0$. Each worker will be offered a contract δ which specifies a job retention probability r_s, the wage w_s^c to be paid to a retained worker and the wage w_s^u to be paid to a laid-off worker all in each state s. Suppose workers are retained at random (there is nothing in the model to distinguish one from another); then if l_s workers are employed in state s the retention probability is l_s/l^*. The expected utility of a worker with contract δ is $Eu = E_s[r_s u(\omega_s^c) + (1 - r_s)u(\omega_s^u + R)]$. The expected wage bill per worker is $W_s = r_s \omega_s^c + (1 - r_s)\omega_s^u$. The firm's expected profits are $E\pi = E_s[sf(l_s) - W_s l^*]$. Workers will accept a contract only if there are none better available. So the expected utility Eu must exceed some minimum level $\bar{u}$, where $\bar{u}$ is determined by competition among firms at date $t = 0$. The set of feasible contracts is

$$\Lambda(\bar{u}) = \{\delta \mid Eu \geqslant \bar{u}; 1 \geqslant r_s \geqslant 0; s = 1, 2\}.$$

Firms will choose the feasible contract that maximizes expected profits.

The best contract is easy to describe. First, notice $\omega_s^e = \omega_s^u + R$ for each state $s = 1, 2$, so within each state the worker is perfectly insured against layoff. This might be taken to mean that there is no involuntary unemployment. This is quite a robust result and holds for all models considered in this chapter.[2] To see why it holds, suppose it did not. If, for example, $\omega_s^e > \omega_s^u + R$, then, given any retention probability r_s, it is possible to reduce ω_s^e by a small amount and increase ω_s^u so as to leave the expected wage bill per worker, W_s, unaffected. Profits in state s are unchanged, but since the variability in utility is decreased, the expected utility in state s, $r_s u(\omega_s^e) + (1 - r_s)u(\omega_s^u + R)$, is increased. A similar argument can be made for $\omega_s^e < \omega_s^u + R$. So a contract δ is a 4-tuple $\{\omega_s, r_s\}$ $s = 1, 2$ where ω_s is ω_s^e, the wage paid to a retained worker, and the laid-off worker is understood to receive $\omega_s - R$. The wage bill per worker is $W_s = \omega_s - (1 - r_s)R$.

By similar reasoning, it is possible to argue that the contract will pay a constant wage ω is independent of the state s. If this was not so, the firm could pay just the expected value in each state without reducing expected profits but increasing expected utility.

Since all firms are identical, they will hire the same number of workers $l^* = n/m$. The employment level in each state will be efficient: $l_2 = f'^{-1}(R/s_2)$ and $l_1 = l^*$. Employment levels are exactly what they are in the spot market equilibrium. Again, if it were not true, it would be possible to change the labour input and increase profits or utility *ex post* and therefore to increase expected profits or utility *ex ante*.

The equilibrium contract wage ω is equal to the expected spot market wage $E_s w_s$. The reason $\omega = Ew_s$ is that, to equilibrate the labour market at date $t = 0$, the labour demand must be the same as it was in the spot market. Therefore, the firm's expected wage bill must be the same under both systems. Firms are indifferent between the spot and contract market equilibria, but workers are strictly better off with contracts because, by Jensen's inequality,

$$\bar{u} = u(\omega) = u(E_s w_s) > E_{su(ws)}.$$

The labour contract equilibrium (C_1, C_2) is drawn in Figure 15.1(b). The model is highly stylized, yet there are a number of important points to be made by comparing Figures 15.1(a) and (b). First, the equilibrium (C_1, C_2) is Pareto-efficient. A contract that produces this outcome is therefore first-best. The outcome is Pareto-efficient because there are no externalities. In the Appendix a new wrinkle is introduced: two firms

---

[2] It holds when there is asymmetric information and when the firm is risk-averse. For cases where it does not hold, see Hahn (1984) and Malcolmson (1985).

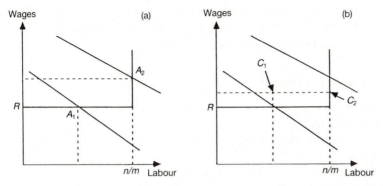

Fig. 15.1 *The basic model*: (a) *spot market solution*; (b) *contract solution*.

each produce a different good; random preferences mean that more of good 1 is demanded in state 1 and more of good 2 is demanded in state 2. Firms and workers would still like to contract to reduce the variability of real wages, but by doing so the mobility of labour is restricted and consequently so is the responsiveness of supply to demand. A contract in one firm reduces the availability of labour to another firm at date 1. This externality means that, for certain parameter values, the spot market equilibrium can Pareto-dominate the labour contract equilibrium.

Second, the outcome (C_1, C_2) has employment at the efficient levels. Contrary to what some of the initial literature suggested, contracts of this type do not account for suboptimal levels of employment. Third, the model assumes that both firms and workers are perfectly and symmetrically informed. The firm knows the worker's utility function and the worker knows the production technology and the technological shock. It is a major criticism of the contract equilibrium that it assumes that agents know too much. In the spot market equilibrium firms do not need to know the worker's utility function and workers do not need to know the firm's technology. An attempt to relax the assumption of perfect information is made in the next section, where it is supposed that the worker cannot observe the technological shock.

Fourth, at the outcome C_1 the employees would rather trade at the spot market wage if this were available and at C_2 the firm would prefer to hire at the spot market wage. Equally, at C_1, given the wage, the firm is retaining more workers than it would wish to if it had discretion over labour input. Both these points suggest that the contract may be quite difficult to enforce. An issue taken up in Section 4.

Fifth, at C_2 the firm is making losses, though they are balanced by the profits made at C_1. At C_2 the firm may prefer to declare itself bankrupt. No bankruptcy constraints could be imposed on the design of the contract, but the issue is not discussed here.

Finally, the shock to technology may be multi-dimensional or difficult
to specify. The best contract may be very complicated. The cost of
complexity will be touched upon in Section 5.

3. Asymmetric Information

In this section we examine labour contracts when the employees cannot
observe the technological shock s. Two additional assumptions are
needed to make the analysis work: first, the firm is assumed to be
risk-averse; second, we examine only a partial equilibrium. Macroeconomic implications are discussed in Section 6.

3.1. One-period contracts

Figure 15.2(a) reproduces the contract (C_1, C_2) in (W, r)-space, where W
is the expected wage bill per worker and r is the probability that a worker

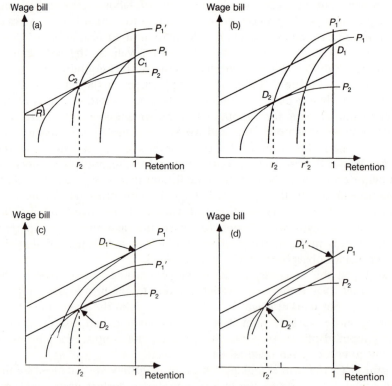

Fig. 15.2 *One-period contracts*: (a) *risk-neutral firm*; (b) *risk-averse firm,
first-best contract implementable*; (c) *risk-averse firm, first-best not implementable*;
(d) *risk-averse firm, second-best contract.*

is retained. The concave lines marked P are the firm's iso-profit curves. Their slope is equal to the marginal product $sf'(\cdot)$ since in state s profits are $\pi_s = sf(r_s l^*) - W_s l^*$. They are concave because the marginal product is decreasing. Profits increase to the south-east.

It has already been argued that $\omega_s^e = \omega_s^u + R = \omega_s$, and this is true whether or not the workers observe the shock s. So the workers' utility in state s, $r_s u(\omega_s^e) + (1 - r_s)u(\omega_s^u + R) = u[W_s + (1 + r_s)R]$, and their indifference curves in (W, r)-space are straight lines of slope R. Intuitively, it costs the firm R to move one worker from unemployment to employment if expected utility is unchanged. C_1 and C_2 are on the same indifference curve because the optimal contract gives the workers the same level of utility independent of the state, and the iso-profit line, P_2, through C_2 is tangential to the indifference curve because $R = s_2 f'(r_2 l^*)$.

The important point is that if the firm is risk-neutral it does not matter whether or not the worker observes the state of technology. If the worker cannot observe the state of technology, the firm can choose either C_1 or C_2, but given (C_1, C_2) it will never have an incentive to lie about the true state. In jargon, the contract is implementable under asymmetric information. Or the contract (C_1, C_2) is incentive-compatible.

In state 1 the iso-profit line through C_1 is P_1 and the iso-profit line through C_2 is P_1'. Since P_1' is to the north-west of P_1 it represents lower profits, and the firms will never choose C_2 in preference to C_1 when state 1 is the true state. Profits are lower at C_2 than C_1 in state 1 because $R < s_1 f'(l^*)$ at C_1 so P_1 always lies below the indifference curve through C_1. Similarly, in state 2 the iso-profit line P_2, through C_2, always lies below the indifference curve because $R = s_2 f'(r_2 l^*)$: there is a loss to the firm in choosing C_1 over C_2 when the true state is state 2.

If the firm as well as the worker is risk-averse, matters are more difficult. Suppose the firm has a concave utility function v defined over profits. The firm will not offer complete insurance to the workers between states, though there will still be complete insurance within each state; $\omega_s^e = \omega_s^u + R$. It seems reasonable that the wage should be higher in the good state. So it will be assumed that $\omega_1 > \omega_2$.[3] A first-best contract, say (D_1, D_2), must equate the ratio of marginal utilities between states for the firm and the worker:

$$v'(\pi_1)/v'(\pi_2) = u'(\omega_1)/u'(\omega_2); \tag{1}$$

otherwise reallocating wages across states could lead to an increase in expected utility for everyone. What needs to be shown is whether the contract (D_1, D_2) is implementable when the worker cannot observe the

[3] $\omega_1 > \omega_2$ if $s_1 f(l^*) > s_2 f(r_2 l^*) + (1 - r_2)Rl^*$

state of technology and what happens if the contract (D_1, D_2) is not implementable.

Figures 15.2(b) and (c) illustrate when (D_1, D_2) is implementable and when it is not. In part (b) employment is still determined at r_2 and 1, but D_1 is on a higher indifference curve than D_2 because it is assumed that $\omega_1 > \omega_2$. However, the contract is implementable. The iso-profit curve P_1' through D_2 lies to the north-west of the line P_1 through D_1 and so represents lower profits: the firm will not choose D_2 in state 1. Similarly, because P_2 is tangential to the indifference curve through D_2 the firm will never choose D_1 in state 2.

In part (c) of the figure by contrast, the iso-profit line, P_1' through D_2 is to the south-east of P_1, so the firm will choose the point D_2 whatever the true state. There is clearly a trade-off here; the point D_2 represents decreased output since $r_2 < 1$ but also decreased costs because $\omega_1 > \omega_2$. If the reduction in wage costs is sufficiently great the contract (D_1, D_2) cannot be implemented.

If (D_1, D_2) is not implementable it may be possible to modify the contract to make it implementable. Figure 15.2(c) shows that, if the new contract is to be implementable, it is necessary to move (D_1, D_2) so that P_1' no longer lies below P_1. This can be done by reducing ω_1, increasing ω_2, or reducing r_2, or by some combination of the three.

In fact, if the new contract is implementable, it must involve some reduction in r_2 below the efficient level of employment (see part (d) of the figure). Suppose D_2 is changed to D_2' without any reduction in r_2. Then the new contract must raise ω_2 relative to ω_1 so that $u'(\omega_1)/u'(\omega_2) > v'(\pi_1)/v'(\pi_2)$. A small reduction in r_2 along the iso-profit line reduces ω_2 and increases π_2. As π_2 is increased and ω_2 reduced, $u'(\omega_1)/u'(\omega_2)$ and $v'(\pi_1)/v'(\pi_2)$ are brought closer together. As $u'(\omega_1)/u'(\omega_2)$ and $v'(\pi_2)/v'(\pi_2)$ are more nearly equalized, there is a first-order gain in risk-sharing whereas there is only a second-order loss in the reduction in r_2 because $R = s_2 f'(r_2 l^*)$. Therefore any implementable contract will involve a reduction in employment in state 2 below the first-best level. This implementable or second-best contract, (D_1', D_2'), is drawn in Figure 15.2(d).

3.2. Long-term contracts

Most labour contracts last for more than one period. Hicks suggested that the continuing relationship between employer and employee was an important factor explaining the existence and the structure of labour contracts. Casual labour is likely to be contracted on a different basis from more permanent labour.

To examine how a long-term contract differs from the one-period contract, we will extend and simplify the basic model. The model is extended by assuming that there are two dates at which labour is traded, $t = 1, 2$, and that states are identically and independently distributed at each date. (We continue to assume the firm is risk-averse.) The model is simplified by assuming that $s_2 f'(l^*)$ is sufficiently greater than R so that full employment is always optimal. Since full employment is always optimal, only the wage structure of the long-term contract can be examined; but even this is quite difficult. Units can be chosen so that l^* and $f(l^*)$ equal 1.

In the simplified model a one-period contract pays a wage that is independent of the state. (If the wage did depend on the state, the firm would choose to declare whichever state had the lowest wage.) But a constant wage contract does not share risk very well when the firm is risk-averse. The firm would prefer to lower the wage in state 2 and increase it in state 1 so as to equalize profits between the two states.

Equalizing profits between states may be possible with a two-period contract. In a two-period contract the wage in the second period can be conditioned on the state in the first period. So a higher wage may be paid in state 1 in the first period if it is offset by relatively lower wages in the second period.

Let s be the state at date 1 and ω the wage paid. Equally, let z be the state at date 2 and σ the wage paid. In the second period (the last period) the firm will declare whichever z guarantees the lowest σ. So (just like the one-period contract) σ cannot be conditioned on z. But both ω and σ may be conditioned on s. This two-period contract can be illustrated in (ω, σ)-space.

Let $V = v(s - \omega) + \alpha E_v v(z - \sigma)$, the firms expected discounted utility in the first period, where α is the discount factor. Let $U = u(\omega) + \alpha u(\sigma)$ be the workers' discounted utility in the first period. The level curve for V, in (ω, σ)-space, is downward-sloping and concave to the origin. The level curve for U is downward-sloping and convex to the origin. At any point in (ω, σ)-space the level curve for V in state 1 is more steeply sloping than the level curve in state 2. Just for the moment, suppose workers can observe state s (but not z). Wages will be chosen so the level curves for U and V are tangential to each other in both states and σ is independent of s. Let (C^1, C^2) be the outcome. (Superscripts represent time periods.) It is drawn in Figure 15.3(a) where $\omega_1 > \omega_2$ because $u'(\omega_1)/u'(\omega_2) = v(s_1 - \omega_1)/v'(s_2 - \omega_2)$.

Now suppose workers cannot observe s. The contract (C^1, C^2) is not implementable. The firm will always declare state 2 because the wage bill is lower in state 2. An implementable outcome (D^1, D^2) is drawn in Figure 15.3(b). With the contract (D^1, D^2) the firm gets the same utility in state 1 whichever state he declares. (V_1 passes through D^1 and D^2.)

With the contract (D^1, D^2), wages are pro-cyclical and negatively serially correlated. Wages are pro-cyclical because $\omega_1 > \omega_2$ and σ is

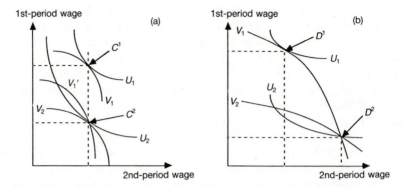

Fig. 15.3 *Two-period contracts*: (a) *risk-averse firm: workers observe s but not z*; (b) *risk-averse firm: workers observe neither s nor z.*

independent of current productivity. They are negatively serially correlated because if current wages are high future wages will be low and if current wages are low future wages will be high. Neither property depends on there being just two states or just two time-periods.

Like the one-period asymmetric information contract (Figure 15.2(d)), (D^1, D^2) is *ex post* inefficient. In Figure 15.3(b) at D^2 the slope of V_2 is steeper than that of U_2.[4] *Ex post* in state 2 both profits and utility could be increased by raising ω_2 and reducing σ_2. But raising ω_2 and reducing σ_2 would not be incentive-compatible. The firm would have an incentive to lie in state 1. Given the information asymmetry, the contract (D^1, D^2) is the best that can be done.

4. Contract Enforcement

This section examines how contracts might be enforced when the legal system is imperfect. In Section 4.1 it is assumed that the state of technology is not verifiable by the courts and therefore that contracts

---

[4] It is clear from Figure 15.2(d) that the curve U_1 must be tangential to V_1 at D^1. By drawing similar diagrams, it is easy to show that U_2 cannot be more steeply sloped than V_2 at D^2. It remains to show that they are not tangential. If they were,

$$\frac{u'(\omega_1)}{v'(s_1 - \omega_1)} = \frac{u'(\sigma_1)}{E_z v'(z - \sigma_1)} > \frac{u'(\sigma_2)}{E_z v'(z - \sigma_2)} = \frac{u'(\omega_2)}{v'(s_2 - \omega_2)}.$$

With σ_2 fixed, increase σ_1 and ω_1 and reduce ω_2 so that $v(s_1 - \omega_1) - v(s_1 - \omega_2) - \alpha\{E_2[v(z - \sigma_2) - v(z - \sigma_1)]\}$ is unchanged. This leads to a first-order gain by reducing the middle inequality but only a second-order loss, so we can conclude

$$\frac{u'(\sigma_2)}{u'(\omega_2)} < \frac{E_z v'(z - \sigma_2)}{v'(s_2 - \omega_2)}$$

and $\sigma_2 > \omega_2$, $\omega_1 > \sigma_1$.

contingent upon state s cannot be enforced. It is shown that there is some similarity between non-contingent or incomplete contracts and the incentive-compatible contracts examined in Section 3.1. In Section 4.2 there is no legal system, but since trade takes place over time it is possible to design self-enforcing contracts in which the short-term benefits from defaulting are always exceeded by the long-term benefits of adhering to the contract.

4.1. Incomplete contracts

Incomplete contracts arise because there are some events or contingencies to which the contractors would like to index their trading arrangements but which are just not verifiable by the courts. There might be a number of reasons for this. The description of the contingency may be quite complicated or difficult to define, or it may involve some information that is private to one or more of the contractors. An example of the latter might be the effort level of a worker as monitored by a supervisor. Then the only contract that can be enforced at law is a contract contingent only upon verifiable events.

To keep matters as simple as possible, it will be assumed that *ex post* the mobility costs of the firm and workers are extremely high, so that at date $t = 1$ there are no outside opportunities for the firm or worker. That is to say, there is some specific investment, training costs, hiring costs, and so on at date $t = 0$ which commit the contractors *ex post*. The opposite is assumed in the next section. It will also be assumed that agents are legally bound to honour their contractual commitments; so the courts can impose and enforce a suitably large fine. Also, the defaulter must have the ability to pay. The assumption is probably unwarranted for the worker whose capital is likely to be mostly human capital and not easily appropriated.

It will be shown that there is a close relationship between incomplete contracts and contracts under asymmetric information. First, consider the contract (C_1, C_2) in Figure 15.2(a). The contract can be legally enforced even if the courts cannot verify which state s has occurred. Obviously, there are no problems with the wage payment since this is state-independent. Employment, however, does depend on the state. But as the contract is *ex post* efficient, given that $\omega^e = \omega^u + R$, the employer is retaining exactly the number of workers he/she would wish to in state 2 and is constrained by the labour pool l^* in state 1. Similarly, workers are indifferent between working and being laid off, so employment can be left to be determined by the firm.

If however the firm is risk-averse, then the wage payment is state-dependent, and this suggests there may be some problems enforcing the contract if the state s is not verifiable by the courts. In Figure 15.2(b) the contract (D_1, D_2) is implementable even if there is asymmetric information. It is also enforceable without state verification. If, as might reasonably be supposed, total employment is observable by the courts, the wage paid can be made contingent upon employment in the firm. Suppose that the iso-profit line for state 1 through point C_2' cuts the ω_2 indifference curve at r^*. Then a wage schedule that pays ω_2 if $r < r^*$ and ω_1 if $r \geq r^*$ implements the contract without the courts having to observe the state of technology. Simply, if state 1 occurs the firm would like to reduce the wage to ω_2 but keep employment at l^*. However, with the new rule the wage ω_2 can be paid only if employment is reduced below r^*. But then the firm would lose profits. The contract can be enforced by making wages contingent upon employment.

In Figure 15.2(c) the first-best contract cannot be implemented under asymmetric information as the firm has higher profits in state 1 at the point D_2 than at the point D_1. Neither can the contract be enforced if s is not verifiable, irrespective of whether the worker observes s or not. The wage payments cannot be conditioned upon the employment level so as to implement the contract. For example, if the wage payment was ω_2 if $r \leq r_2$ and ω_1 if $r > r_2$, then the firm would choose employment to be r_2 in both states. *Ex post* workers are powerless to stop this. Of course, reputation could matter and is discussed in the next section.

The second-best contract (D_1', D_2') in Figure 15.2(d), however, can be enforced by a non-state-contingent contract. If the employment level in state 2 is r_2' and the employment wage is ω_1' in state 1 and ω_2' in state 2, then a wage schedule that pays ω_2' if $r \leq r_2'$ and ω_1 otherwise implements the contract. In fact, (D_1', D_2') must be the best that can be done if s is not verifiable independent of whether there is symmetric or asymmetric information between the worker and firm. Notice that, assuming workers behave non-cooperatively, *ex post* renegotiation will always set $\omega^e = \omega^u + R$. Therefore a non-contingent contract will simply specify a wage $\omega = \omega^e$ contingent upon employment. Since $\omega^e = \omega^u + R$, the employment decision can be left to the firm. The best contract that can be achieved is (D_1', D_2'). The outcome is the same if there is asymmetric information and state-contingent enforcement or if there is symmetric information and enforcement only of non-contingent contracts. Only the interpretation is different.[5]

4.2. Self-enforcing contracts

A possible mechanism of enforcement is reputation. Reputation will be important if, once an agent reneges, this influences the type of contract he/she can sign in the future. To examine the role of reputation, consider

---

[5] What happens when works act collectively is an interesting and open question.

again the model of Section 2.2 above with risk-neutral firms and symmetric information but with an infinite sequence of dates $t = 0, 1, 2, \ldots, \infty$. Suppose the two states are identically and independently distributed over time and each agent discounts the future by a common factor α. Firms and workers are allowed to sign contingent contracts and to renege on these contracts when it is to their advantage. That is to say, there are no courts to enforce contracts and no mobility or 'lock-in' costs. It is assumed that if a worker reneges he or she can find work at the spot market wage. Similarly, if a firm reneges it is assumed it can hire however many workers it would like at the spot market rate. This may be motivated as follows. Suppose there are, in addition to the n infinitely lived workers and m infinitly lived firms, at each date m workers and n firms who live for only one period. Since there is no enforcement mechanism and no mobility costs, the one-period-lived agents trade at the spot market outcome (A_1, A_2) drawn in Figure 15.1(a). The infinitely lived agents are competitive and thus treat these spot market wages as given.

To discuss the effect of reputation, some strong assumptions will have to be made. If an agent can renege without being observed by anyone and therefore can sign a contract with someone else next period, then reputation has no role to play. But suppose the opposite is true: when an agent reneges it is observed by everyone else, and once he has reneged he has proved himself unreliable and no one will sign a contract with him again. A more complete model of reputation would generate this assumption as a result, but for the moment analysis will be confined to examining the effect of this assumption on the type of contracts that are signed. In particular, can the first-best contract be enforced by this reputation effect, and if not what contracts are feasible, or self-enforcing?

Let $h^t = (s^1, s^2, \ldots, s^t)$ be the history of states up to date t. It is assumed that history is common knowledge so there is complete and symmetric information. Since information is complete and symmetric, employment will be determined efficiently at each date and workers will be perfectly insured against unemployment; $\omega_s = \omega_s^e = \omega_s^u + R$. With employment determined at the efficient levels, a contract will simply specify a sequence of wage payments $\omega(h^t)$ conditional upon the history of states. A contract signed at date $t = 0$ therefore is written $\delta_0 = [\omega(h^t)]_{t=1}^{\infty}$.

The contract δ_0 will be feasible if no agent ever has an incentive to renege. No agent will have an incentive to renege if, at every date and for every possible history, the long-run gain from adhering to the contract exceeds any short-term gain that might be had by reneging. Consider the worker; if the history is h^t and the state at time t is s, then the short-term benefit from reneging on the contract is

$$u[\omega(h^t)] - u(w_s).$$

There is obviously a short-term benfient from reneging if $w_s > \omega(h')$. If the contract is to be feasible, this must be offset by the expected long-term benefit from adhering to the contract:

$$E\Big\langle \sum_{\tau=t+1}^{\infty} \alpha^{\tau+t}\{u[\omega(h^{\tau})] - u(w_s)\} \mid h' \Big\rangle$$

where $E\langle \cdot \mid h' \rangle$ is the expectation conditional upon h'. Let $U_s^t(h')$ be the sum of these two terms; it is the total gains to the employee from adhering to the contract at date t in state s when the history is h'. If the employee is not to renege, $U_t^s(h')$ should be non-negative. Since these constraints are forward-looking, the notational dependence on h' can be dropped and U_s^t can be defined recursively:

$$U_s^t = u(\omega_s) - u(w_s) + \alpha E_q U_q^{t+1}$$

where E_q is the expectation taken over all possible states at date $t+1$.

Similarly, the gain to the employee from adhering to the contract can be defined recursively as

$$V_s^t = l^*(w_s - \omega_s) + \alpha E_q V_q^{t+1}$$

where $l^*(w_s - \omega_s)$ is the short-term gain or loss to the employer of reneging on the contract.

It can now be seen why an infinite time-horizon is necessary. If there is a last date T, there is no future to offset the short-term benefits from reneging. So either the firm or the worker will have an incentive to renege unless $\omega_s^T = w_s$. But if $\omega_s^T = w_s$ for each state, there are no future benefits to adhering to the contract at date $T-1$. Hence $\omega_s^{t-1} = w_s$ for each state. Working backwards, there is no feasible self-enforcing contract which does not pay the spot market wage in every state. When $T = \infty$ there are always future benefits from adhering to the contract. The discount factor α can be interpreted as the probability the firm and worker will trade with each other next period. So what is really important is not that $T = \infty$ but that both firm and worker should always believe they will trade again next period.

An optimal contract will maximize V^0 subject to $U^0 \geqslant \bar{U}$ and the self-enforcing constraints $U_s^t \geqslant 0$, $V_s^t \geqslant 0$ for all s, t. The optimal contract can be found by dynamic programming (see Thomas and Worrall 1984). The solution depends on the discount factor α. As an example, suppose $u(\omega) = \sqrt{\omega}$ and $w_1 = 4$, $w_2 = 1$ with $p = \frac{1}{2}$. In Figure 15.4 wages are plotted against the discount factor α. Two lines are drawn. One line, marked $\bar{\omega}_2$, is equal to 1 for low α but starts to rise when $\alpha = 2\sqrt{2} - 2$, reaching the average spot market wage, 5/2, when $\alpha = 1$. The other line, marked ω_1, is 4 at low α but falls when $\alpha = 2\sqrt{2} - 2$ until it reaches the certainty equivalent wage 9/4 at $\alpha = 1$. The two lines cross at $\alpha = 7 - \sqrt{37}$.

As might be suspected, $\wp_1$ is the lowest wage the contract can offer the employee in state 1 without tempting him to renege and $\bar{\omega}_2$ is the highest wage the contract can pay in state 2 without causing the employer to hire from the spot market. (So $\bar{\omega}_2$ rises with the discount factor because the less the future is discounted, the better the short-term incentive to renege can be counteracted. Similarly, $\wp_1$ falls as α rises.) Of course, it is never optimal to pay a wage greater than 4 or less than 1, so the maximum feasible wage in state 1 is $\bar{\omega}_1 = w_1$ and the lowest feasible wage in state 2 is $\wp_2 = w_2$.

There is a simple rule whereby contract wages are updated from one period to the next: Keep the wage constant if possible, and if not adjust it by the smallest possible amount. This accords well with intuition. Since the firm is risk-neutral and the worker risk-averse, it is desirable to keep wages as constant as possible while not violating any of the self-enforcing constraints.

Then for $\alpha < 2\sqrt{2} - 2$ there is no non-trivial self-enforcing contract. The only contract that is self-enforcing replicates the spot market outcome (A_1, A_2). To calculate the contract for $\alpha > 2\sqrt{2} - 2$ it is necessary to know the initial contract wage. It was shown in Section 2.2 that the gain from the contract to the employer was zero in equilibrium; that is, $V^0 = 0$. So V_1^0 and V_2^0 are both zero and the initial contract wage is $\bar{\omega}_1$ if state 1 occurs and $\bar{\omega}_2$ if state 2 occurs. So for $\alpha \in [2\sqrt{(2-2}, 7 - \sqrt{37}]$ the contract wage is $\bar{\omega}_1$ if state 2 has not occurred in the past, $\wp_1$ if the current state is 1 and state 2 has occurred in the past, or $\bar{\omega}_2$ if the current state is 2. For $\alpha > 7 - \sqrt{37}$ the contract wage is $\bar{\omega}_1$ if state 2 has not occurred in the past and $\bar{\omega}_2$ otherwise.

Given the updating rule, it is possible to determine $\wp_1$ and $\bar{\omega}_2$ precisely. For example, suppose the intervals are disjoint and let $V(\omega_s)$ be the total gain to the firm from adhering to the contract in state s when the current wage paid is ω_s. From the recursive definition of V_s,

$$V_2(\bar{\omega}_2) = l^*(w_2 - \bar{\omega}_2) + \alpha p V_1(\wp_1) + \alpha(1 - p)V_2(\bar{\omega}_2).$$

But $V_2(\bar{\omega}_2) = 0$, so $V_1(\wp_1) = l^*(w_2 - \bar{\omega}_2)/\alpha p$. Also,

$$V_1(\wp_1) = l^*(w_1 - \wp_1) + \alpha p V_1(\wp_1) + \alpha(1 - p)V_2(\bar{\omega}_2)$$

or $V_1(\wp_1) = l^*(w_1 - \wp_1)/(1 - \alpha p)$. Therefore

$$\alpha[p\wp_1 + (1 - p)\bar{\omega}_2] + (1 - \alpha)\bar{\omega}_2 = \alpha[pw_1 + (1 - p)w_2] + (1 - \alpha)w_2.$$

Following the same procedure of calculating total gains for the worker,

$$\alpha[pu(\wp_1) + (1 - p)u(\bar{\omega}_2)] + (1 - \alpha)u(\bar{\omega}_2)$$
$$= \alpha[pu(w_1) + (1 - p)u(w_2)] + (1 - \alpha)u(w_2).$$

These two equations can be solved simultaneously for $\bar{\omega}_2$ and $\wp_1$.

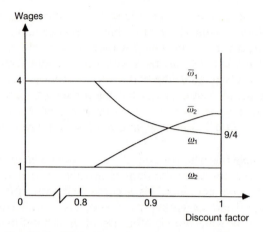

Fig. 15.4 *Wage intervals against discount factor.*

Similarly, if the intervals overlap,

$$\bar{\omega}_2 = [pw_1 + (1-p)w_2] + (1-\alpha)w_2$$

$$u(\underline{\omega}_1) = \alpha[pu(w_1) + (1-p)u(w_2)] + (1-\alpha)u(w_2).$$

Figure 15.4 was drawn by substituting $w_1 = 4$, $w_2 = 1$, $p = \frac{1}{2}$ into these equations.

5. Bounded Rationality

Bounded rationality means either limited information or limited computational ability, or both. Information is limited in two ways. First, it may be difficult to give objects or events a precise, unequivocable meaning. For example, the firm may not know the worker's utility function exactly, or it may be able to describe the state of the economy only in vague terms like 'healthy' or 'poor'. Second, even if an unequivocable meaning can be given to an event, its occurrence may still be uncertain.

Computational ability is limited both practically and theoretically. To compute any function effectively requires an algorithm (a finite set of instructions) which works in finite time. Theoretically, it is not possible to tell if any algorithm will always work in finite time.[6] The problem is undecidable. Practically, time and computer technology are constraints on effectively computing any function. For example, in chess, whatever

---

[6] Take for example the algorithm that computes the function of algorithms, which is defined if and only if the algorithm never terminates. Since the original algorithm is in the domain of the function it computes, we always have a contradiction.

the position is, there is an optimal strategy, but computationally it is too difficult to work out.

Nevertheless, even in complex situations decisions have to be taken, so there has to be a way to decide which decisions to take. Limited information may be represented by subjective degrees of belief or subjective probabilities, but this usually makes the problem computationally more difficult if not intractable. It might be thought possible to specify a cost for computation and equate marginal benefits to marginal cost. Unfortunately, if computation is costly, the benefits and costs of extra computation can be worked out only after the fact, once the calculations are already done. since every situation is different, there appears to be no optimal level of computation.[7]

There are two ways out of this dilemma (see Simon 1976). The first is to treat optimal solutions as guides rather than blueprints for rationality; to examine models whose solutions will make for good decisions, not necessarily best decisions in the real world. The second is to give up searching for an optimum and simply seek a satisfactory solution instead.[8] The latter has the disadvantage that it is really only a re-specification of goals which are usually subjective anyway, but it may be useful in some situations.

As an example of the former approach consider the model of Section 4.2. Once the wage intervals are worked out, the rule or algorithm for computing the optimal contract is trivial. Computing the wage intervals involves solving a number of simultaneous equations. If the number of states is small this is not too difficult. but if the number of states is large it may be computationally costly. A possible good decision would be to estimate wage intervals but follow the same rule for updating wages. It is not optimal, but a complex decision has been reduced to manageable proportions.

6. Macroeconomics

The models of Section 3 and 4 provide some strong implications for the pattern of wages and employment with only minimal assumptions. For example, in the self-enforcing contract of Section 4.2 current wages depend on past history: the wage today will be lower if yesterday was 'bad' rather than 'good'. In the long-run contract of Section 3.2, wages are both pro-cyclical and negatively serially correlated.

---

[7] The Blum speed-up theorem in complexity theory says something similar: for any algorithm, there is always another algorithm that computes the same function faster for finitely many inputs.

[8] This is usually the case in policy analysis. Targets are specified and searches carried out for a satisfactory policy. Also, at a social level, Pareto optimality is a satisfactory rather than an 'optimal' outcome.

However, some care is needed to interpret these results at an aggregate or macroeconomic level. For example, in Section 3 it was assumed that the workers could not observe the shock to technology. If the shock is perfectly correlated across firms, this assumption is unreasonable because all firms would be cutting back on employment at the same time and the wage could be conditioned upon aggregate employment. Conditioning wages on aggregate employment would be equivalent to conditioning wages directly on the shock to technology. And if shocks are uncorrelated across firms it is unreasonable to assume firms are risk-averse: they could eliminate risk through the stock market.

A natural approach is to assume that the shock consists both of an economy-wide and a firm-specific component. If firms are unable to distinguish between the two components (because aggregate data are published with a lag), a risk-averse firm will tend to reduce employment below the first-best level whenever it is adversely affected. But a firm that has a favourable shock cannot increase employment beyond l^* so employment fluctuations will tend to be exacerbated.

Another approach is to suppose that an aggregate shock affects the variance of the firm-specific shock (see Grossman, Hart, and Maskin 1983). Then, even if the aggregate shock is publicly observable, the asymmetry of information will cause increased employment fluctuations: in the low-variance state employment will not be changed much, but in the high-variance state badly affected firms will cut back on employment.

Another possibility is that the aggregate shock affects the firm's cost, for example by changing the real rate of interest (see Farmer 1984). If firms have decreasing absolute risk aversion, as profits fall, risk aversion increases. Since employment reductions are greater if the firm is more risk-averse, the aggregate shock increases employment fluctuations.

Labour contract theory offers some important insights into the behaviour of wages and employment. The model of Section 4.2 is probably most applicable to the UK where the majority of collective agreements are not legally enforceable. The asymmetric information models of Section 3 are very sensitive to parameter values and are therefore difficult to validate or disprove empirically. However, there are a number of deficiencies with the theory. First, all employees are identical and join the firm at the same time. So it is reasonable to assume they are laid off at random. In fact, most contracts reduce employment by voluntary retirement and by an inverse seniority rule—last in, first out.[9] This is an important fact which needs explaining. So too is the fact that employment reductions are sometimes made by reducing hours and sometimes by lay-offs. An amalgamation of contract theory with search theories and

---

[9] I am grateful to Andrew Oswald for some pertinent comments about real-world contracts. For an excellent summary, see Oswald and Turnbull (1985).

adverse selection and screening models might prove useful if difficult. The conclusion is that contract theory allows deeper insight into how markets work than that 'they are cleared by prices', but it has some way to go to explain the institutional details of real-world contracts.

7. Bibliographic Notes

There is a large literature dealing with labour contract theory. An excellent overview is contained in Hart and Holmstrom (1986). The following notes are indicative rather than exhaustive.

The basic model follows Azariadis (1975). Baily (1974) and Gordon (1974) independently examined similar models. Sargent (1980) and Akerlof and Miyazaki (1980) introduced lay-off pay.

Asymmetric information was introduced by Barro (1977) and Calvo and Phelps (1977). The model of Section 3.1 is similar to Grossman and Hart (1981, 1983). See also Hart (1983), Worrall (1983), and the 1983 supplement to the *Quarterly Journal of Economics*. Long-term contracts are examined by Roberts (1982). A more general treatment along the lines of Section 3.2 is found in Thomas and Worrall (1985).

Incomplete contracts are investigated in Hart and Moore (1985). Section 4.1 owes a greater debt to Younes (1984). Section 4.2 is based on Thomas and Worrall (1984). Holmstrom (1983) examined the case where only the employee can costlessly renege.

On bounded rationality, see Simon (1976) and Williamson, Wachter, and Harris (1975).

APPENDIX

This appendix presents a slightly modified version of the example given in Section 2. It is shown that the spot market equilibrium (weakly) Pareto-dominates the labour contract equilibrium.

Example. Suppose there are just two firms, $m = 2$, but they each produce different goods. Assume that

$$y_1^1(s) = \sqrt{L^1(s)}, \qquad y_2^2(s) = \sqrt{L^2(s)} \qquad s = 1, 2$$

where $y_g^e(s)$ is the output of good g by employer e in state s, and $L^e(s)$ is the total amount of labour employed by firm e in state s. Both employers are risk-neutral and consume only the good they produce. Suppose that both states are equi-probable; then the utility of each employer is

$$V^e = \tfrac{1}{2} \sum_{s=1}^{2} Z^e(s)$$

where $Z^e(s)$ is the consumption of good e by the employer e in state s. For convenience, suppose there is a continuum of workers with unit mass. Their preferences are represented by

$$u = 2 + \tfrac{1}{2}[a \log x_1(1) + (1 - a) \log x_2(1) + (1 - a) \log x_1(s) + a \log x_2(2)$$
$$- (1 - b)l(1) - (1 + b)l(2)]$$

where $x_g(s)$ is the consumption by the worker of good $g = 1, 2$ in state s and $l(s)$ is the supply of labour in state s. Notice that labour supply is no longer restricted to 0/1 and the randomness in preferences affects both consumption and leisure. Technology is not state-dependent.

Labour Contract Equilibrium Consider the labour contract equilibrium. In equilibrium each employer will hire exactly one-half of the total labour force at date $t = 0$. This must be so by the symmetry of the problem. A contract offered by firm e $\delta^e = [W^e(s), l^e(s)]$ $s = 1, 2$ specifies the remuneration paid to each worker in state s, $W^e(s)$, and the labour supply expected $l^e(s)$. Note $L^e(s) = \tfrac{1}{2}l^e(s)$. Since there are no assets in the model, the price of good $g = 1$ may be normalized to unity in both states. Therefore, using the employee's budget constraints, $\qquad x_1^e(s) + p(s)x_2^e(s) = W^e(s) \qquad e = 1, 2, \quad s = 1, 2,$

the indirect utility function for a worker employed by firm e with a contract δ^e is

$$\hat{U} = 2 + a \log a + (1 - a) \log(1 - a) + \tfrac{1}{2}[\log W^e(1) + \log W^e(2)$$
$$- (1 - a) \log p(1) - a \log p(2) - (1 - b)l^e(1) - (1 + b)l^e(2)].$$

The contract δ^e will be chosen to maximize the profits or utility of firm e subject to offering each employee a contract at least as good as they could get elsewhere. Then, in equilibrium,

$$l^e(1) = (1 + b)/(1 - b) \qquad l^e(2) = (1 - b)/(1 + b) \qquad e = 1, 2$$
$$W^1(s) = \sqrt{2}/2(1 - b^2) \qquad W^2(s) = p(s)\sqrt{2}/\sqrt{(1 - b^2)} \qquad s = 1, 2$$
$$p(1) = (1 - a)/a \qquad p(2) = a/(1 - a)$$
$$\hat{U}^c = \tfrac{1}{2}[\log a + \log(1 - a) - \log(1 - b) - \log(1 + b)] - \tfrac{3}{2} \log 2$$
$$\hat{V}^c = \sqrt{2}/4\sqrt{(1 - b^2)}.$$

Auction Market Equilibrium In the auction market equilibrium there is no way of trading across states, so each state may be treated separately. In state $s = 1$ the worker's demands are

$$x_1(1) = aw(1)/(1 - b), \qquad x_2(1) = (1 - a)w(1)/(1 - b)p(1) \qquad l(1) = 1/(1 - b).$$

where $w(1)$ is the wage at state $s = 1$. The profit-maximiizing labour demands of each employer are

$$L^1(1) = 1/4[w(1)]^2 \qquad L^2(1) = [p(1)]^2/4[w(1)]^2$$

so in equilibrium

$$w(1) = \sqrt{(1 + b)}/2\sqrt{a} \qquad p(1) = \sqrt{(1 - a)}/\sqrt{a}$$

and by symmetry

$$w(2) = \sqrt{(1 + b)}/2\sqrt{(1 - a)} \qquad p(2) = \sqrt{a}/\sqrt{(1 - a)}$$

so

$$\hat{U}^a = \tfrac{1}{2}[a\log a + (1-a)\log(1-a) - \tfrac{1}{2}\log(1-b) - \tfrac{1}{2}\log(1+b)] - \log 2$$

$$\hat{V}^a = \tfrac{1}{4}\{[\sqrt{(1+b)}\sqrt{a} + \sqrt{(1-b)}\sqrt{(1-a)}]/\sqrt{(1-b^2)}\}.$$

Suppose $a = 0.6$ and $b = 0.2$; then each employer is indifferent between the spot market equilibrium and the labour contract equilibrium, since

$$\sqrt{(1.2)}\sqrt{(0.6)} + \sqrt{(0.8)}\sqrt{(0.4)} = (0.6)\sqrt{2} + (0.4)\sqrt{2} = \sqrt{2}.$$

However, each worker actually strictly prefers the spot market equilibrium

$$\hat{U}^c - \hat{U}^a = \tfrac{1}{2}[a\log(1-a) + (1-a)\log a - \tfrac{1}{2}\log(1-b) + \tfrac{1}{2}\log(1+b) - \log 2]$$

$$= -0.46.$$

This is the opposite conclusion to that reached from the simple model outlined above. The reason is simple. In the spot market equilibrium labour can be concentrated in the industry with high demand, and this raises both profits and utility. In the contract market equilibrium wages are stabilized, but at the cost of a misallocation of labour. Interestingly, given the spot market prices, firms and workers would like to contract—although if everyone did prices would change and the resulting equilibria would be Pareto-inferior. For a similar example see Polemarhakis and Weiss (1978).

PART V

16

Intertemporal General Equilibrium Models

TIMOTHY J. KEHOE

1. Introduction

In this chapter we shall explore the properties of two simple intertemporal general equilibrium models, a model with a finite number of infinitely lived consumers, and an overlapping generations model with an infinite number of finitely lived consumers. Both models contain a complete set of markets. The Arrow–Debreu formulation of the Walrasian equilibrium model can, of course, be given a dynamic interpretation in which goods are indexed by date. The models that we study differ from the standard Arrow–Debreu model in that we allow an infinite number of goods. As we shall see, models with infinite numbers of goods can possess very different properties from models with finite numbers of goods. Such models are best regarded as idealizations, however: their properties are interesting in so far as they provide insights into models with large, but finite, numbers of goods.

The model with a finite number of infinitely lived consumers shares three important properties with the standard Arrow–Debreu model: first, all equilibria are Pareto-efficient; second, there is no role to be played by outside money, unbacked nominal debt; and, third, there are, in general, a finite number of locally unique equilibria. In contrast, the overlapping generations model may violate each of these three properties: it may have equilibria that are not Pareto-efficient; it may have equilibria in which outside money plays an important role; and it may have a robust continuum of equilibria. We shall see that there is a close relationship between the possibility of inefficiency of equilibria and the role for outside money. The possibility of indeterminacy of equilibria is a relatively separate issue, however, except in models in which consumers live for only two periods and there is only one good in each period.

Intertemporal general equilibrium models are becoming increasingly important in economic theory, particularly in macroeconomics. The trend

The research presented in this paper has been funded by Grant no. SES-8509484 from the National Science Foundation. My thinking on the issues discussed in this paper has been heavily influenced by interaction with other researchers working in the same area. In particular, I would like to thank David Backus, Jonathan Burke, Stephen Burnell, John Geanakoplos, Frank Hahn, Patrick Kehoe, Andreu Mas-Colell, Walter Muller, Heraklis Polemarchakis, Paul Romer, Michael Woodford, William Zame, and especially David Levine.

there has been to use small general equilibrium models to analyze macroeconomic issues (see, for example, Lucas 1981, and Kydland and Prescott 1982). Not all macroeconomists have been caught up in this trend, however, and the use of explicit general equilibrium models in macroeconomics has been the subject of much controversy, in which one side accuses the other of using *ad hoc* and unrealistic models. Many commentators have interpreted this controversy as an idealogical debate between monetarists and Keynesians. This interpretation is probably unfortunate. An explicit general equilibrium framework imposes a discipline and assures internal consistency. This makes it easy for us to organize our thinking about economic phenomena and to communicate this thinking to others, mostly because the assumptions of the model have well understood implications in this framework. The phrase *ad hoc* is much misused in economics. It has become a synonym for 'yours' and 'bad' and an antonym for 'mine' and 'good'. Most good economic models are *ad hoc* in the strict sense that they are designed for a particular purpose and produce results that follow closely from a particular set of assumptions. The advantage of using explicit general equilibrium models is that they provide a framework in which sets of assumptions are easily understood and compared.

The potential disadvantage is, of course, that the general equilibrium framework can become an intellectual straightjacket. Fortunately, however, this framework is rich enough to allow a wide variety of results. To illustrate this, we employ both of our models to answer Barro's (1974) question of whether government bonds are net wealth. Different models can produce very different answers to this question. There is a close relationship between these answers and the sets of assumptions that distinguish these models.

The models that we study in this paper are both pure-exchange models with no production or storage. Time is discrete and there is no uncertainty. Furthermore, both models are stationary in that the structure of preferences and endowments is constant over time. These models are the simplest to analyse. We indicate, however, how our results extend to more complicated models. We also compare the structures of the two models. On one hand, the overlapping generations model has similar properties to a model with a finite number of infinitely lived consumers who face borrowing and lending constraints. On the other, a model with a finite number of infinitely lived consumers has similar properties to an overlapping generations model in which parents leave bequests to their children.

2. An Infinitely Lived Consumer Model

We begin by analysing an economy with a finite number of agents who consumer over an infinite number of time-periods. There are n goods, which cannot be stored, in each period and h consumers. Consumer j is characterized by a utility function

$$\sum_{t=1}^{\infty} \gamma_j^{t-1} u_j(c_{1t}^j, \dots, c_{nt}^j) \tag{1}$$

and an endowment vector $w^j = (w_1^j, \dots, w_n^j)$, which he has claim to in each period. Here the discount factor γ_j satisfies $1 > \gamma_j > 0$; the momentary utility function u_j is continuously differentiable of the second order for all positive consumption vectors, strictly concave, and monotonically increasing; and the endowment vector w^j is strictly positive.

There are two interpretations of this model. The first is the traditional Walrasian interpretation in which all trades, including those that involve future delivery of goods, take place in the first period. In this interpretation time plays no explicit role and t can be thought of as merely another index on commodities. The consumer's budget constraint is

$$\sum_{t=1}^{\infty} p_t' c_t^j \le \sum_{t=1}^{\infty} p_t' w^j. \tag{2}$$

Here $p_t = (p_{1t}, \dots, p_{nt})$ is the vector of futures prices in period t and $p_t' c_t^j$ is the inner product $\sum_{i=1}^{n} p_{it} c_{it}^j$.

In the second interpretation trades take place over time, but there are perfect capital markets and rational expectations. In this simple model the assumption of perfect capital markets means only that consumers can borrow and lend as much as they want at a competitively determined interest rate, and the assumption of rational expectations means that consumers have perfect foresight. Let $q_t = (q_{1t}, \dots, q_{nt})$ be the vector of spot prices in period t; let r_t be the interest rate between t and $t+1$; and let m_t^j be the net lending done by consumer j between t and $t+1$. We can interpret m_t^j as inside money. Consumer j faces a sequence of budget constraints

$$q_1' c_1^j + m_1^j \le q_1' w^j$$
$$q_2' c_2^j + m_2^j \le q_2' w^j + (1 + r_1) m_1^j \tag{3}$$
$$\vdots$$
$$q_t' c_t^j + m_t^j \le q_t' w^j + (1 + r_{t-1}) m_t^j$$

Dividing the budget constraint in period t by $(1+r_1)(1+r_2) \cdots (1+r_{t-1})$, $t = 2, \dots, T$, and adding up, we obtain

$$\sum_{t=1}^{T} p_t' c_t^j + m_T^j/(1+r_1)(1+r_2) \cdots (1+r_{T-1}) \le \sum_{t=1}^{T} p_t' w^j \tag{4}$$

where $p_t = q_t/(1+r_1)(1+r_2) \cdots (1+r_{t-1})$. In the limit this produces the same budget constraint as does the first interpretation as long as

$$\lim_{T \to \infty} m_T^j/(1+r_1)(1+r_2) \cdots (1+r_{T-1}) = 0. \tag{5}$$

To ensure that this condition holds, we need to put some constraint on the real level of debt that we allow consumer j to incur. We shall see that, with such a constraint, (5) must hold in any equilibrium.

Let us return to the first interpretation of the model. An equilibrium is a sequence of price vectors $(\hat{p}_1, \hat{p}_2, \ldots)$ and a sequence of consumption vectors $(\hat{c}_1^j, \hat{c}_2^j, \ldots)$ for each consumer, $j = 1, \ldots, h$, such that each consumer maximizes utility subject to his budget constraint (2) and demand is equal to supply:

$$\sum_{j=1}^{h} \hat{c}_t^j = \sum_{j=1}^{h} w^j, \qquad t = 1, 2, \ldots \tag{6}$$

Notice that any equilibrium must be such that $\sum_{t=1}^{\infty} \hat{p}_t' w^j$ converges; otherwise the consumer would have infinite income, and his utility maximization problem would have no solution. Because u_j is monotonically increasing, he would want to consume infinite amounts of at least one good, which would make equilibrium impossible.

Since every consumer has finite income, the value of the aggregate endowment must also be finite:

$$\sum_{t=1}^{\infty} \hat{p}_t' \left(\sum_{j=1}^{h} w^j \right) = \sum_{j=1}^{h} \left(\sum_{t=1}^{\infty} \hat{p}_t' w^j \right). \tag{7}$$

This implies that any equilibrium must be Pareto-efficient. The argument is due to Debreu (1954). Suppose, to the contrary, that there is a Pareto-superior allocation plan $(\bar{c}_1^j, \bar{c}_2^j, \ldots)$:

$$\sum_{t=1}^{\infty} \gamma_j^{t-1} u_j(\bar{c}_t^j) \geq \sum_{t=1}^{\infty} \gamma_j^{t-1} u_j(\hat{c}_t^j), \qquad j = 1, \ldots, h, \tag{8}$$

with strict inequality for some j, that is feasible:

$$\sum_{j=1}^{h} \bar{c}_t^j \leq \sum_{j=1}^{h} w^j, \qquad t = 1, 2, \ldots \tag{9}$$

Then the consumption sequence $(\bar{c}_1^j, \bar{c}_2^j, \ldots)$ must cost at least as much as the consumer's income, and strictly more for some consumer; otherwise $(\hat{c}_1^j, \hat{c}_2^j, \ldots)$ would not be utility-maximizing. Consequently,

$$\sum_{j=1}^{h} \left(\sum_{t=1}^{\infty} \hat{p}_t' \bar{c}_t^j \right) > \sum_{j=1}^{h} \left(\sum_{t=1}^{\infty} \hat{p}_t' w^j \right) = \sum_{t=1}^{\infty} \hat{p}_t' \left(\sum_{j=1}^{h} w^j \right). \tag{10}$$

Since the Pareto-superior allocation is feasible, however,

$$\sum_{j=1}^{h} \left(\sum_{t=1}^{\infty} \hat{p}_t' \bar{c}_t^j \right) = \sum_{t=1}^{\infty} \hat{p}_t' \left(\sum_{j=1}^{h} \bar{c}_t^j \right) \leq \sum_{t=1}^{\infty} \hat{p}_t' \left(\sum_{j=1}^{h} w^j \right). \tag{11}$$

This contradiction establishes that there can be no allocation that is Pareto-superior to the competitive allocation and is also feasible.

That the value of the aggregate endowment is finite also implies that there can be no equilibrium with outside money, unbacked debt. Suppose, to the contrary, that there is an allocation that is feasible in which each consumer satisfies the budget constraint

$$\sum_{t=1}^{\infty} \hat{p}_t' \hat{c}_t^j = \sum_{t=1}^{\infty} \hat{p}_t' w^j + m^j, \qquad j = 1, \ldots, h \tag{12}$$

where

$$m = \sum_{j=1}^{h} m^j \neq 0. \tag{13}$$

(If $m = 0$ but $m^j \neq 0$, this is just an equilibrium with transfer payments.) Here m is the stock of outside, or fiat, money, which can be positive or negative. Summing these budget constraints over consumers, we obtain

$$\sum_{j=1}^{h} \left(\sum_{t=1}^{\infty} \hat{p}_t' \hat{c}_t^j \right) = \sum_{j=1}^{h} \left(\sum_{t=1}^{\infty} \hat{p}_t' w^j \right) + m. \tag{14}$$

Multiplying the feasibility conditions (6) by prices and summing, however, we obtain

$$\sum_{t=1}^{\infty} \hat{p}_t' \left(\sum_{j=1}^{h} \hat{c}_t^j \right) = \sum_{t=1}^{\infty} p_t' \left(\sum_{j=1}^{h} w^j \right). \tag{15}$$

Consequently, $m = 0$, which contradicts the assumption that there is an equilibrium with outside money.

This same argument can be used to show that the sequence of budget constraints (3) are equivalent to the single intertemporal budget constraint (2). For consumer j to have a well defined maximization problem, and for the concept of equilibrium to make any sense, the limit in (5) would have to exist. Here, unlike the outside money case that we have just examined, the variables m_t^j are chosen by the consumers. Since utility is monotonically increasing, every consumer would want to choose $(m_1^j, m_2^j, \ldots)$ so that the limit in (5) is negative. The same argument that precludes an equilibrium with outside money also precludes this possibility.

For an equilibrium to exist, however, we must impose a constraint on the real level of debt that we allow consumer j to incur:

$$m_t^j / \| p_t \| \geq b, \qquad t = 1, 2, \ldots \tag{16}$$

for some $b < 0$. Otherwise, the consumer would try to run a Ponzi scheme, rolling over an exponentially increasing amount of debt and making the limit in (5) as negative as possible. In such a case, as was argued above, no equilibrium can exist. Any sort of bound on the real level of debt, no matter how large in absolute value, precludes this possibility.

In general, this model has a finite number of locally unique equilibria. To see this, we transform the equilibrium conditions using an approach developed by Negishi (1960b) and applied to intertemporal models by Bewley (1982). To simplify the exposition, we ignore the possibility of corner solutions to the consumer's utility maximization problem. This can be justified by imposing an additional restriction on u_j (see Kehoe and Levine 1985a). The solution to the consumer's utility maximization problem is characterized by the conditions

$$\gamma_j^{t-1} Du_j(c_t^j) = \lambda_j p_t' \tag{17}$$

for some Lagrange multiplier $\lambda_j > 0$, and the budget constraints (2). (Here $Du_j(c_t^j)$ is the $1 \times n$ vector of partial derivatives of u_j.) An equilibrium is, therefore, characterized by (2) and (17), which are the utility maximization conditions, and (6), which are the market-clearing conditions that demand be equal to supply. This is a system with an infinite number of equations and unknowns.

Consider now the Pareto problem of maximizing a weighted sum of individual utility functions subject to feasibility constraints:

$$\max \sum_{j=1}^{h} \alpha_j \sum_{t=1}^{\infty} \gamma_j^{t-1} u_j(c_t^j) \tag{18}$$

$$\text{s.t.} \sum_{j=1}^{h} c_t^j = \sum_{j=1}^{h} w^j, \qquad t = 1, 2, \ldots$$

Here $\alpha_1, \ldots, \alpha_h$ are positive utility weights. A solution to this problem is characterized by the conditions

$$\alpha_j \gamma_j^{t-1} Du_j(c_t^j) = \pi_t, \qquad j = 1, \ldots, h, \quad t = 1, 2, \ldots \tag{19}$$

for some sequence of vectors of Lagrange multipliers $\pi_t = (\pi_{1t}, \ldots, \pi_{nt}) > 0$, and the feasibility constraints (6). Notice that, if we divide (19) by α_j, then it becomes the same as (17). This is an alternative way of seeing that any competitive equilibrium is Pareto-efficient, that the First Theorem of Welfare Economics holds.

The Second Theorem holds as well: any solution to the Pareto problem (18) satisfies all of the conditions for a competitive equilibrium except the individual budget constraints (2). Such a solution can, therefore, be viewed as competitive equilibrium with transfer payments. The competitive prices are, of course, the Lagrange multipliers π_t. We can compute the transfer payments needed to implement as a competitive equilibrium the Pareto-efficient allocation associated with the welfare weights $\alpha = (\alpha_1, \ldots, \alpha_h)$:

$$t_j(\alpha) = \sum_{t=1}^{\infty} \pi_t(\alpha)'[c_t^j(\alpha) - w^j], \qquad j = 1, \ldots, h. \tag{20}$$

Setting these transfers payments equal to 0 produces a characterization of equilibria in a finite number of equations and unknowns.

Using the strict concavity of u_j, we can demonstrate that transfer functions t_j are continuous. Also, t_j is homogeneous of degree 1 in α because π_t is homogeneous of degree 1 and c_t^i is homogeneous of degree 0; if we double α, for example, the sequences of consumption vectors that solve the problem do not change, but the Lagrange multipliers double. Furthermore, the transfer functions satisfy

$$\sum_{j=1}^{h} t_j(\alpha) \equiv 0 \tag{21}$$

because any solution to the Pareto problem satisfies the feasibility constraints.

The conditions that characterize the equilibria of this model are formally equivalent to those that characterize the equilibria of a static, pure-exchange model with h goods. Indeed, the functions $f_j(\alpha) = -t_j(\alpha)/\alpha_j$ have all of the properties of the excess demand functions of a pure-exchange model: they are continuous; they are homogeneous of degree 0; and they obey Walras's Law, $\sum_{j=1}^{h} \alpha_j f_j(\alpha) \equiv 0$. Debreu (1970) has demonstrated that, if the excess demand functions f_j are continuously differentiable, then almost all economies have a finite number of locally unique equilibria. The phrase 'almost all' is, of course, given a precise mathematical meaning. We can use either the transfer functions t_j or the demand functions f_j to characterize the equilibria of the intertemporal model that we are considering here. Kehoe and Levine (1985a) have shown that Debreu's reasoning extends to this model. Furthermore, by imposing another, fairly weak, condition on u_j, they are able to demonstrate that t_j is indeed continuously differentiable.

The proof of Debreu's result relies on fairly complex mathematical machinery. The intuition behind it is very simple, however. It is, in fact, the same intuition as Walras had when he counted equations and unknowns: There are h equations, $t_j(\alpha) = 0$, in h unknowns, α_j. Because of homogeneity, one of the weights α_j is redundant. Because of the adding-up restriction (21), however, one of the equations is also redundant. Consequently, the equilibrium conditions can be viewed as a syetem of $h-1$ equations in $h-1$ unknowns. Suppose that these equations are independent in the sense that $t_j(\hat{\alpha}) = 0$, $j = 1, \ldots, h-1$, and the $(h-1) \times (h-1)$ matrix of partial derivatives

$$J = \begin{bmatrix} \dfrac{\partial t_1}{\partial \alpha_1}(\hat{\alpha}) & \cdots & \dfrac{\partial t_1}{\partial \alpha_{h-1}}(\hat{\alpha}) \\ \vdots & & \vdots \\ \dfrac{\partial t_{h-1}}{\partial \alpha_1}(\hat{\alpha}) & \cdots & \dfrac{\partial t_{h-1}}{\partial \alpha_{h-1}}(\hat{\alpha}) \end{bmatrix} \tag{22}$$

is non-singular. (We have imposed the normalization $\alpha_h = 1$ and dropped the equation $t_h(\alpha) = 0$.) Then the inverse function theorem of elementary calculus says that, in some open neighbourhood of $\hat{\alpha}$, it is the only solution to the equilibrium conditions; that is, $t^{-1}(0) = \hat{\alpha}$. Using the compactness of the set of possible equilibria and the continuity of the equilibrium conditions, we can easily prove that there is a finite number of equilibria if J is non-singular at every equilibrium.

If J is singular at some equilibrium, then the intuition says that the slightest perturbation in the functions t_j either make it non-singular or else make it impossible for there to be a solution near $\hat{\alpha}$. Figure 16.1 illustrates some possibilities in an economy with two consumers.

To make some of the concepts that we have discussed in this section more concrete, let us consider a simple model with one good in each period and two consumers. Suppose that $u_1(c_t) = u_2(c_t) = \log c_t$ and that $w^1 = w^2 = 1$. The only difference between the two consumers is that $\gamma_1 < \gamma_2$. A solution to the utility maximization is characterized by the conditions

$$\gamma_j^{t-1}/c_t^j = \lambda_j p_t \tag{23}$$

$$\sum_{t=1}^{\infty} p_t c_t^j = \sum_{t=1}^{\infty} p_t. \tag{24}$$

An equilibrium satisfies these conditions and the condition that demand

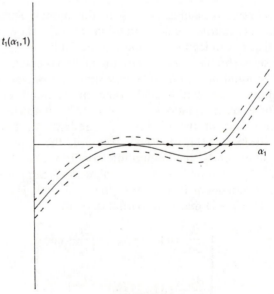

Fig. 16.1

equals supply:

$$c_t^1 + c_t^2 + 2, \qquad t = 1, 2, \ldots \tag{25}$$

The Pareto problem is

$$\max \alpha_1 \sum_{t=1}^{\infty} \gamma_1^{t-1} \log c_t^1 + \alpha_2 \sum_{t=1}^{\infty} \gamma_2^{t-1} \log c_t^2 \tag{26}$$

$$\text{s.t. } c_t^1 + c_t^2 = 2, \qquad t = 1, 2, \ldots$$

A solution to this problem is characterized by the conditions

$$\alpha_j \gamma_j^{t-1}/c_t^j = \pi_t, \qquad j = 1, 2, \tag{27}$$

and (25). These equations can easily be solved to yield

$$c_t^j = \frac{2\alpha_j \gamma_j^{t-1}}{\alpha_1 \gamma_1^{t-1} + \alpha_2 \gamma_2^{t-1}}, \qquad j = 1, 2, \tag{28}$$

$$\pi_t = (\alpha_1 \gamma_1^{t-1} + \alpha_2 \gamma_2^{t-2})/2. \tag{29}$$

The transfer payments needed to implement as a competitive equilibrium the allocation associated with the weights α_1 and α_2 are therefore

$$t_1(\alpha_1, \alpha_2) = \sum_{t=1}^{\infty} \pi_t(c_t^1 - 1) = \frac{\alpha_1}{1 - \gamma_1} - \frac{\alpha_2}{1 - \gamma_2}$$

$$\tag{30}$$

$$t_2(\alpha_1, \alpha_2) = \sum_{t=1}^{\infty} \pi_t(c_t^2 - 1) = \frac{\alpha_2}{1 - \gamma_2} - \frac{\alpha_1}{1 - \gamma_1}.$$

Notice that these functions are continuously differentiable, are homogeneous of degree 1, and sum to 0.

The unique equilibrium of this model is found by setting these transfer payments equal to 0. It is $\alpha_1 = (1 - \gamma_1)/(1 - \gamma_2)$, $\alpha_2 = 1$. Notice that the value of the aggregate endowment is finite since

$$\sum_{t=1}^{\infty} \pi_t(1 + 1) = 2 \sum_{t=1}^{\infty} \left(\frac{1 - \gamma_1}{1 - \gamma_2} \gamma_1^{t-1} + \gamma_2^{t-1} \right) \bigg/ 2$$

$$= \frac{2}{1 - \gamma_2}. \tag{31}$$

There is, of course, no outside money in this model. There is, however, inside money: consumer 1, who is more impatient than consumer 2, spends more than his endowment early in his life. Later he consumes less, paying back his debt. In the limit, his consumption in each period approaches 0 and consumer 2's consumption approaches 2.

3. An Overlapping Generations Model

In this section we consider an overlapping generations model in which there is a single good in each period and a single consumer, who lives for two periods, in each generation. This is the model originally developed by Samuelson (1958) and analyzed extensively by Gale (1973). In the next section we discuss more general models.

The consumer born in period t, $t = 1, 2, \ldots$, solves the utility maximization problem

$$\max u(c_t^t, c_{t+1}^t)$$
$$\text{s.t. } p_t c_t^t + p_{t+1} c_{t+1}^t = p_t w_1 + p_{t+1} w_2. \tag{32}$$

We make the same sort of assumptions on u and (w_1, w_2) as in the previous section. As in the previous model, we can also think of this consumer as facing two budget constraints:

$$\left.\begin{aligned} q_t c_t^t + m^t &= q_t w_1 \\ q_{t+1} c_{t+1}^t &= q_{t+1} w_2 + (1 + r_t) m^t. \end{aligned}\right\} \tag{33}$$

If we normalize the spot prices so that $q_{t+1} = q_t = 1$, divide the second constraint by $(1 + r_t)$, and add both together, we can produce a single budget constraint in which $p_t/p_{t+1} = (1 + r_t)$.

The solution to this problem is characterized by the conditions

$$\left.\begin{aligned} \frac{\partial u}{\partial c_t^t}(c_t^t, c_{t+1}^t) &= \lambda_t p_t \\[2mm] \frac{\partial u}{\partial c_{t+1}^t}(c_t^t, c_{t+1}^t) &= \lambda_t p_{t+1} \end{aligned}\right\} \tag{34}$$

and the budget constraint in (32). Given the strict concavity of u, this consumer has continuous excess demand functions $y(p_t, p_{t+1}) = c_t^t - w_1$ when young and $z(p_t, p_{t+1}) = c_{t+1}^t - w_2$ when old. The form of the budget constraint implies that these functions are homogeneous of degree 0 in (p_t, p_{t+1}) and obey Walras's law:

$$p_t y(p_t, p_{t+1}) + p_t z(p_t, p_{t+1}) \equiv 0. \tag{35}$$

Consider, for example, the case where $u(c_t^t, c_{t+1}^t) = \log c_t^t + \gamma \log c_{t+1}^t$. The excess demand functions can easily be computed using (32) and (34). They are

$$\left.\begin{aligned} y(p_t, p_{t+1}) &= \frac{p_t w_1 + p_{t+1} w_2}{(1 + \gamma) p_t} - w_1 = \frac{-\gamma p_t w_1 + p_{t+1} w_2}{(1 + \gamma) p_t} \\[2mm] z(p_t, p_{t+1}) &= \frac{\gamma(p_t w_1 + p_{t+1} w_2)}{(1 + \gamma) p_{t+1}} - w_2 = \frac{\gamma p_t w_1 - p_{t+1} w_2}{(1 + \gamma) p_{t+1}}. \end{aligned}\right\} \tag{36}$$

Notice that these functions do indeed satisfy continuity, homogeneity, and Walras's Law.

In addition to the consumers born in periods 1, 2, ..., there is a consumer who is alive only in period 1 and who solves the problem

$$\max u_0(c_1^0)$$
$$\text{s.t. } p_1 c_1^0 = p_1 w_2^0 + m. \tag{37}$$

Here m, which can be positive, negative, or zero, is the stock of outside money held by generation 0. If m is non-negative, then it is easily interpreted as fiat money. Even if it is negative, however, there are institutional stories to go with it. Think of an institution that makes loans to consumers when they are young. The institution collects the repayments of these loans when the consumers are old and uses them to make loans to the young consumers in the next generation. There are, of course, many other interpretations.

Since this consumer has preferences for, and endowment of, only the first good, we need not be careful about specifying u_0 or w_2^0. The excess demand function for this consumer is

$$z_0(p_1, m) = \frac{m}{p_1}. \tag{38}$$

An equilibrium of this model is a stock of outside money $\hat{m}$ and a price sequence $(\hat{p}_1, \hat{p}_2, \ldots)$ that satisfies the conditions that excess demand be equal to 0 in every period:

$$z_0(\hat{p}_1, \hat{m}) + y(\hat{p}_1, \hat{p}_2) = 0 \tag{39}$$

in period 1 and

$$z(\hat{p}_{t-1}, \hat{p}_t) + y(\hat{p}_t, \hat{p}_{t+1}) = 0 \tag{40}$$

in period t, $t = 2, 3, \ldots$.

One way to compute the equilibria of this model, developed by Gale (1973) and Cass, Okuno, and Zilcha (1979), is to use the offer curve, the image of $[y(p_t, p_{t+1}), z(p_t, p_{t+1})]$. This curve passes through the origin, stays always in the second and fourth quadrants, and intersects rays through the origin only once (except at the origin itself). In fact, Walras's Law (35) tells us that

$$z(p_t, p_{t+1})/y(p_t, p_{t+1}) = -p_t/p_{t+1}; \tag{41}$$

that is, the point where it intersects the ray with slope $-p_t/p_{t+1}$ has as its coordinates excess demands at (p_t, p_{t+1}). In addition, the offer curve always satisfies $y > -w_1$ and $z > -w_2$.

For example, in our simple log-linear example, we can use the formula for $y(p_t, p_{t+1})$ in (36) to solve for p_t/p_{t+1} in terms of y and substitute the result into the formula for $z(p_t, p_{t+1})$ to obtain the offer curve:

$$z = \frac{\gamma w_1 w_2}{(1+\gamma)^2 y + (1+\gamma)\gamma w_1} - \frac{w_2}{1+\gamma}. \tag{42}$$

The result is pictured in Figure 16.2.

In general, there are two steady states, inflation factors $\beta > 0$, such that the price sequence $p_t = \beta^t$ satisfies

$$z(\beta^{t-1}, \beta^t) + y(\beta^t, \beta^{t+1}) = z(1, \beta) + y(1, \beta) = 0. \tag{43}$$

These are given by the two intersections of the offer curve with the line through the origin with slope -1, $z = -y$. There is only one steady state in the degenerate case where the slope of the offer curve is -1 at the origin.

The steady state where $\beta = 1$ Pareto-dominates the steady state at the origin. One way to see this is to show that the consumption plan found by solving the representative consumer's maximization problem when $p_t = p_{t+1}$ also solves the problem of maximizing the utility of a steady-state consumption plan:

$$\max u(c_1, c_2) \tag{44}$$
$$\text{s.t. } c_1 + c_2 = w_1 + w_2.$$

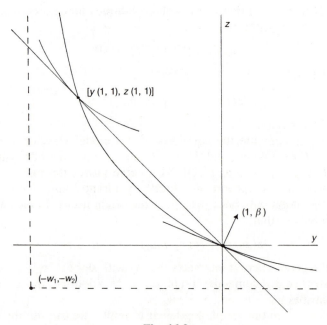

Fig. 16.2

Alternatively, notice that, since no trade is always feasible, the consumer can only be better off if he chooses to trade. Indeed, a simple revealed preference argument implies that the consumer prefers the net trade $[y(1, 1), z(1, 1)]$ to any point that lies on or to the left of the line with slope -1. (Look at Figure 16.2 again.)

To compute equilibria besides the two steady states, we start with $z_0 = \hat{m}/\hat{p}_1$ and read horizontally to the line with slope -1 to find the value of y for which $y(\hat{p}_1, \hat{p}_2) = -z_0$. We then read vertically to the offer curve to find the point $[y(\hat{p}_1, \hat{p}_2), z(\hat{p}_1, \hat{p}_2)]$. We now continue by reading horizontally to the ray with slope -1 to find the value of y for which $y(\hat{p}_2, \hat{p}_3) = -z(\hat{p}_1, \hat{p}_2)$. This process is illustrated in Figure 16.3. The offer curve in the figure corresponds to the case where $\gamma w_1 > w_2$. Notice that, for any value of z_0 such that $z_0 = \hat{m}/\hat{p}_1 < z(1, 1)$, there is an equilibrium that converges to the autarkic steady state in which there is no trade. (There is a natural lower bound on $\hat{m}/\hat{p}_1$ provided by $-w_2^0$, but this is independent of the offer curve of (y, z).) The price sequence is computed by normalizing $\hat{p}_1 = 1$, then using the slope of the line through the origin passing through the offer curve at $[y(\hat{p}_1, \hat{p}_2), z(\hat{p}_1, \hat{p}_2)]$ to find $\hat{p}_2$, using the slope of the line through the origin passing through the offer curve at $[y(\hat{p}_2, \hat{p}_3), z(\hat{p}_2, \hat{p}_3)]$ to find $\hat{p}_3$, and so on. Notice that every equilibrium of this model, except for the one that starts at $\hat{m}/\hat{p}_1 = z(1, 1)$, involves inflation. At the autarkic steady state β, which is the

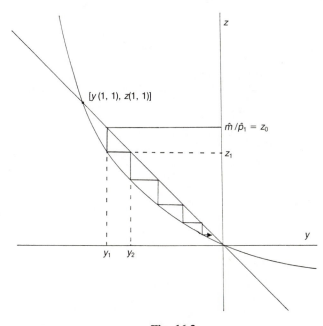

Fig. 16.3

negative of the reciprocal of the slope of the offer curve at the origin, is $\gamma w_1/w_2 > 1$.

Not only is there a continuum of equilibria in this example, but outside money plays a crucial role and equilibria are not necessarily Pareto-efficient. Observe that any equilibria that starts with $0 < \hat{m}/\hat{p}_1 < z(1, 1)$ is Pareto-dominated by the equilibrium with $\hat{m}/\hat{p}_1 = z(1, 1)$: the first generation prefers the highest z_0 possible, and subsequent generations are worse off the further they are from $[y(1, 1), z(1, 1)]$ and the closer they are to autarky. In fact, equilibria with higher $\hat{m}/\hat{p}_1$ Pareto-dominate those with lower starting-points. In the next section we shall see that the equilibria with $\hat{m}/\hat{p}_1 < 0$, although not necessarily Pareto-dominated by equilibria with $\hat{m}/\hat{p}_1 = z(1, 1)$, are not Pareto-efficient. As Shell (1971) has indicated, this failure of the First Welfare Theorem depends on the double infinity of consumers and goods. Although it is possible to mimic this failure of the First Welfare Theorem in a model with incomplete markets, as done, for example, by Cass and Yaari (1966), it should be stressed that it occurs even if all markets are complete.

Figure 16.4 depicts the offer curve for the log-linear model where $\gamma w_1 < w_2$. Notice that, for any values of $\hat{m}/\hat{p}_1$ such that $\hat{m}/\hat{p}_1 < 0$, there is an equilibrium that converges to the steady state where $\beta = 1$. There is also an equilibrium that starts with $\hat{m}/\hat{p}_1 = 0$ and stays at the autarkic steady state. Here $\beta = \gamma w_1/w_2 < 1$. This equilibrium is Pareto-efficient

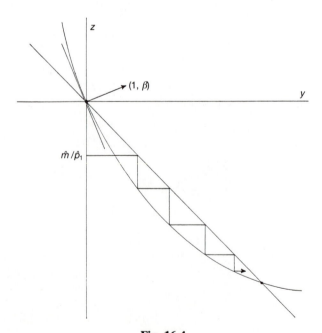

Fig. 16.4

since the value of the aggregate endowment is finite:

$$w_2^0 + w_1 + \sum_{t=2}^{\infty} \beta^{t-1}(w_1 + w_2) = w_2^0 + w_1 + \frac{\beta}{1-\beta}(w_1 + w_2). \qquad (45)$$

As we shall see in the next section, all of the equilibria of this model are Pareto-efficient.

These two examples suggest three hypotheses. First, any indeterminacy of equilibrium is connected to inflation if there is positive outside money. Second, all equilibrium price paths converge to some steady state. Third, any indeterminacy of equilibrium is associated with a non-zero stock of outside money. We now study counter-examples to the first two propositions. In the next section we shall see that the third, although true in any model with one good in each period and consumers who live for two periods, fails in more general models.

The log-linerar examples that we have analysed have the property that, as the price ratio p_t/p_{t+1} increases, $y(p_t, p_{t+1})$ decreases and $z(p_t, p_{t+1})$ increases. This means that the demand functions y and z exhibit gross substitutability. Consider the offer curve depicted in Figure 16.5. Here gross substitutability fails in the backwards-bending section of the offer curve. Notice that, for any value of $\hat{m}/\hat{p}_1$ sufficiently close to $z(1, 1)$, there is an equilibrium that converges to the steady state where $\beta = 1$. The crucial feature of this offer curve is that the slope of the offer curve

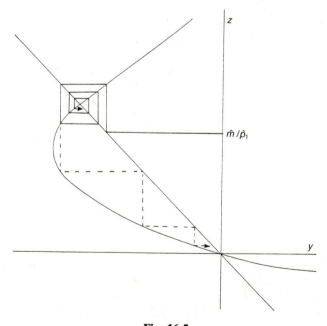

Fig. 16.5

at $[y(1, 1), z(1, 1)]$ is positive and less than one. There are also equilibria that start with $\hat{m}/\hat{p}_1$ near, or even equal to, $z(1, 1)$ and converge to the autarkic steady state: whenever there are two values of z that correspond to a single y, we have a choice of two ways to read from the line with slope -1 to the offer curve.

This example also has equilibria that do not converge to any steady state. Consider the offer curves in Figure 16.6. Here there is a two-period cycle $z_0, z_1, z_0, z_1, \ldots$. The second offer curve is the reflection of the first across the line with slope -1. Cycles are points where these two

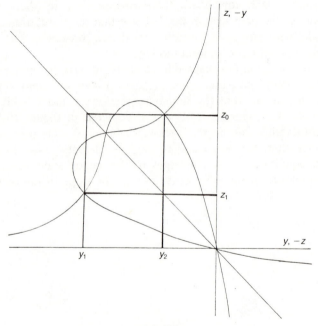

Fig. 16.6

curves intersect, where

$$[y(\hat{p}_1, \hat{p}_2), z(\hat{p}_1, \hat{p}_2)] = [-z(\hat{p}_2, \hat{p}_1), -y(\hat{p}_2, \hat{p}_1)]. \qquad (46)$$

This implies that $\hat{m}$ and $(\hat{p}_1, \hat{p}_2, \hat{p}_1, \hat{p}_2, \ldots)$ are an equilibrium of this model. The possibility cycles in this sort of model was first pointed out by Gale (1973). Benhabib and Day (1982) have shown that there are also examples with equilibria that do not converge to any steady state or to a cycle of any length. The possibility of such strange behaviour, often referred to as chaotic dynamics, has been analyzed extensively by Grandmont (1985).

4. General Overlapping Generations Models

We now turn our attention to overlapping generations models with many goods in each period and many consumers in each generation. If we allow many goods and many consumers, the assumption of two periods of life is completely general: Balasko, Cass, and Shell (1980) present a simple procedure for redefining periods and generations that converts a model in which consumers live for any finite number of periods into one in which they live for only two. Suppose that consumers live for k periods. Then redefine generations so that generations $-k+2, -k+3, \ldots, 0$ become generation 0, generations $1, 2, \ldots, k-1$ become generation 1, and so on. Redefine periods in the same way. Figure 16.7 illustrates this procedure for the case $k = 4$. Notice that each generation lives for just two redefined periods. If there are n goods in each original period, there are $(k-1)n$ goods, indexed by date, in each redefined period. If there are h consumers in each original generation, there are $(k-1)h$ consumers in each redefined generation.

The model with many consumers and many goods has the same potential for equilibria that are Pareto-inefficient and equilibria with unbacked nominal debt as does the simple model of the previous section.

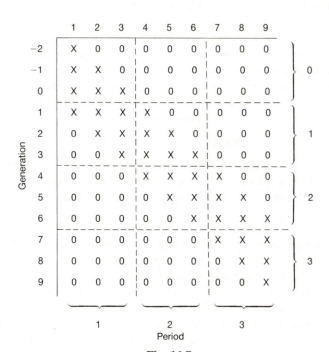

Fig. 16.7

It has even more potential for indeterminacy of equilibria. Consumer j in generation t solves the problem

$$\max u_j(y_t^j + w_1, z_t^j + w_2)$$
$$\text{s.t. } p_t' y_t^j + p_{t+1}' z_t^j = 0. \tag{47}$$

Here y_t^j, z_t^j, w_1, w_2, p_t, and p_{t+1} are all n-dimensional vectors. If his excess demand functions are $y^j(p_t, p_{t+1})$ and $z^j(p_t, p_{t+1})$, then the aggregate excess demand functions for generation t are $y(p_t, p_{t+1})$ and $z(p_t, p_{t+1})$ where, for example,

$$y(p_t, p_{t+1}) = \sum_{j=1}^{h} y^j(p_t, p_{t+1}). \tag{48}$$

We assume that y and z are continuously differentiable for all strictly positive price vectors (p_t, p_{t+1}), are homogeneous of degree 0 in (p_t, p_{t+1}), and obey Walras's law,

$$p_t' y(p_t, p_{t+1}) + p_{t+1}' z(p_t, p_{t+1}) \equiv 0. \tag{49}$$

In addition, there is an old generation, alive only in the first period, that has the aggregate excess demand function $z_0(p_1, m)$. We assume that z_0 is continuously differentiable for all strictly positive price vectors p_1 and an open interval of money stocks m that includes 0, is homogeneous of degree 0 in (p_1, m), and obeys Walras's law,

$$p_1' z_0(p_1, m) \equiv m. \tag{50}$$

An equilibrium of this model again is a stock of outside money $\hat{m}$ and a sequence of price vectors $(\hat{p}_1, \hat{p}_2, \ldots)$ that satisfies (39) and (40) where the variables are reinterpreted as vectors. To see the possibility of indeterminacy, let us count equations and unknowns in the equilibrium conditions. The equilibrium condition in the first period,

$$z_0(\hat{p}_1, \hat{m}) + y(\hat{p}_1, \hat{p}_2) = 0, \tag{51}$$

contains n equations in $2n + 1$ unknowns. Since the equations are all homogeneous, we can impose a normalization to reduce this to $2n$ unknowns. The equilibrium conditions in subsequent periods,

$$z(\hat{p}_{t-1}, \hat{p}_t) + y(\hat{p}_t, \hat{p}_{t+1}) = 0, \qquad t = 2, 3, \ldots, \tag{52}$$

each add n equations and n unknowns. The entire system therefore has n degrees of freedom. If we set $\hat{m} = 0$ *a priori*, there is one fewer unknown, and this reduces the degrees of freedom to $n - 1$. The idea is that we choose $\hat{m}$, $\hat{p}_1$, and $\hat{p}_2$ to satisfy (51) and then use (52) as a nonlinear difference equation to determine $\hat{p}_3, \hat{p}_4, \ldots$.

The problem with simply counting equations and unknowns is that we do not always know whether we can use (52) to continue an equilibrium price sequence for arbitrary $(\hat{p}_1, \hat{p}_2)$. In Figure 16.3, for example, if we start with any value of $\hat{m}/\hat{p}_1$ above $z(1, 1)$, we can continue the equilibrium for a few periods but eventually we reach a situation where we cannot continue because z exceeds w_1 and there is no offer curve to read to vertically! In general, we want to avoid situations where we cannot use (52) to compute a positive value of $\hat{p}_{t+1}$ as a function of $\hat{p}_{t-1}$ and $\hat{p}_t$. One way to do this is to require that the equilibrium price sequence converge to a steady state at which the matrix of partial derivatives of $y(p_t, p_{t+1})$ with respect to p_{t+1} is non-singular. This implies that in some open neighbourhood of the steady state, for fixed $(\hat{p}_{t-1}, \hat{p}_t)$, the function $z(\hat{p}_{t-1}, \hat{p}_t) + y(\hat{p}_t, \cdot)$ is invertible. The implicit function theorem tells us that in this neighbourhood $\hat{p}_{t+1}$ can be computed uniquely as a function of $(\hat{p}_{t+1}, \hat{p}_t)$. Restricting our attention to this neighbourhood of the steady state, we can avoid the problem illustrated in Figure 16.5, where there may be more than one $\hat{p}_{t+1}$ that satisfies the equilibrium conditions. This restriction may force us, however, to ignore some equilibria.

A steady state of this model is a vector of relative prices p and an inflation factor β such that $\hat{p}_t = \beta^{t-1}p$ satisfies (52). There are two types of steady states: nominal steady states, in which there is a non-zero amount of nominal debt transferred from generation to generation, and real steady states, in which there is no such transfer. Notice that in any equilibrium the amount of nominal debt transferred from generation to generation stays constant over time: (50) and (51) imply that $-\hat{p}_1'y(\hat{p}_1, \hat{p}_2) = \hat{p}_1'z_0(\hat{p}_1, \hat{m})$; Walras's law implies that $\hat{p}_2'z(\hat{p}_1, \hat{p}_{21}) = -\hat{p}_1'y(\hat{p}_1, \hat{p}_2)$; (51) implies that $-\hat{p}_2'y(\hat{p}_2, \hat{p}_3) = \hat{p}_2'z(\hat{p}_1, \hat{p}_2)$; and so on. The steady-state condition is

$$z(\beta^{t-1}p, \beta^t p) + y(\beta^t p, \beta^{t+1}p) = z(p, \beta p) + y(p, \beta p) = 0. \qquad (53)$$

This implies that $p'z(p, \beta p) + p'y(p, \beta p) = 0$. Walras's Law implies that $p'y(p, \beta p) + \beta p'z(p, \beta p) = 0$. Subtracting one from another, we obtain $(1 - \beta)p'z(p, \beta p) = 0$. This says that $\beta = 1$ at any nominal steady state. Kehoe and Levine (1984b) prove that almost all economies are such that $\beta \neq 1$ at every real steady state.

Balasko and Shell (1980) and Burke (1987) have shown that a necessary and sufficient condition for Pareto efficiency of an equilibrium is that

$$\sum_{t=1}^{\infty} \|p_t\|^{-1} = \infty. \qquad (54)$$

Here $\|p_t\| = (p_t'p_t)^{1/2}$, the standard Euclidean norm. They impose a uniform curvature condition on indifference surfaces that is natural in a stationary environment. Notice that any equilibrium that converges to a steady state where $\beta > 1$, an inflationary steady state, is Pareto-inefficient since the sum in (54) converges. Any equilibrium that converges to a steady state where $\beta \leq 1$, however, is Pareto-efficient since the sum in

(54) diverges. In fact it is easy to show that if $\beta = 1$ the equilibrium allocation maximizes a weighted sum of utilities of the consumers in a representative generation subject to steady-state consumption constraints.

When there are many goods in each period and many consumers in each generation, there is no need for there to be a unique nominal steady state and a unique real steady state as there are in the example of the previous section. Even with one good in each period, but more than one consumer in each generation, there can be multiple real steady states, although there is a unique nominal steady state. Consider, for example, a static two-person exchange model with multiple equilibria. Such a model is easy to construct in an Edgeworth box; see Shapley and Shubik (1977) for an example. Now convert this into an overlapping generations model in which there are two consumers in each generation with the same preferences for and endowments of the two goods in the two periods of their lives. The multiple equilibria of the static model are real steady states of the overlapping generations model in which each consumer trades only with the other consumer in the same generation. This illustrates the point that real steady states are not, in general, autarkic, as they are in the simple model. With many goods in each period, not even nominal steady states need be unique. Kehoe and Levine (1984b) prove, however, that in general every economy has an odd—in particular, a non-zero—number of nominal steady states and an odd number of real steady states. Furthermore, the matrix of partial derivatives of y with respect to its second vector of arguments is almost always non-singular at every steady state.

To analyse the behaviour of equilibrium price sequences that converge to a steady state, Kehoe and Levine (1985a) linearize the equilibrium conditions (51) and (52). The local stable manifold theorem of dynamical systems theory says that the behaviour of the nonlinear system near the steady state is qualitatively the same as that of the linear system (see Irwin 1980). They consider the set of price pairs $(\hat{p}_1, \hat{p}_2)$ that satisfy the equilibrium condition in the first period and lead to convergence to the steady state when employed as starting conditions for the nonlinear difference equation (52). This set is a manifold, a set of points that is locally equivalent to an open subset of a Euclidean space of dimension smaller than $2n$. (The prototypical manifold is a linear subspace.) Kehoe and Levine demonstrate that this manifold can have dimension as large as n if there is outside money and as large as $n - 1$ if there is no money. This manifold can also have dimension as small as 0, in which case it consists of isolated points. (The best linear approximation to this manifold near the steady state is the intersection of the stable subspace of the linearized version of (52) with the set of vectors that satisfy the linearized version of (51).) Almost all economies are such that any small perturbation produces an economy with the same qualitative properties. Kehoe and Levine also prove that there are robust examples of steady states with no equilibria at all that converge to them. This cannot happen with only one good in each period because Walras's Law implies that m and p can be chosen so that the steady-state price vector $(p, \beta p)$ satisfies $z_0(p, m) + y(p, \beta p) = 0$. Consequently, the steady state itself is an equilibrium.

Notice that we can use a similar trick to that used to convert economies with consumers who live for k periods into economies in which they live for two to convert the study of equilibria that converge to cycles of any finite length into the study of equilibria that converge to steady states. Suppose that an economy has a k-period cycle in the sense that $(p_{t+1}, \ldots, p_{t+k}) = (\beta^t p_1, \ldots, \beta^t p_k)$ satisfies (52). Redefine generations so that, for example, generations $1, 2, \ldots, k$ become generation 1. Similarly, redefine goods. A k-period cycle is now a steady state of the redefined model.

5. The Ricardian Equivalence Theorem

In 1817 Ricardo asked the question, Does it make any difference whether a government finances an increase in expenditure by raising taxes or by selling bonds? (See Ricardo 1951: 244–9.) The simple answer that he came up with, although he realized that there were complications, was that it makes no difference, because consumers anticipate that they have to pay more taxes in the future if there is a bond sale so that the government can make interest payments. This is at odds to Keynes's answer to the same question, that a bond-financed increase in government expenditure has the full multiplier effect, but that a tax-financed increase has a much smaller balanced multiplier effect. The crucial distinction between the two analyses is that in one consumers' savings behaviour is altered by the bond issue and in the other it is not. It reduces to, as Barro (1974) puts it, Are government bonds net wealth?

Let us first answer this question using our model with infinitely lived consumers. We introduce into that model a government that purchases goods $g_t = (g_{1t}, \ldots, g_{nt})$ in period t, $t = 1, 2, \ldots$. We require that this expenditure pattern be feasible in that

$$0 \leqslant g_t \leqslant \sum_{j=1}^{h} w^j, \qquad t = 1, 2, \ldots \tag{55}$$

Suppose first that these purchases are financed by lump-sum taxes $\tau_t^1, \ldots, \tau_t^h$ so that the government budget balances in every period:

$$\sum_{j=1}^{h} \tau_t^j = p_t' g_t, \qquad t = 1, 2, \ldots. \tag{56}$$

Then the budget constraint faced by consumer j is

$$\sum_{t=1}^{\infty} p'_t c^j_t = \sum_{t=1}^{\infty} (p'_t w^j - \tau^j_t). \tag{57}$$

Suppose, on the other hand, that the government issue bonds b_t, $t = 1, 2, \ldots$, that pay interest at the competitively determined interest rate. It finances these interest payments by lump-sum taxes θ^j_t. The government must balance its budget in the sense that the present discounted value of its expenditures is equal to the present discounted value of its revenues:

$$\sum_{t=1}^{\infty} p'_t g_t + \sum_{t=1}^{\infty} b_t = \sum_{t=1}^{\infty} \left(\sum_{j=1}^{h} \theta^j_t + b_t \right)$$

$$\sum_{t=1}^{\infty} p'_t g_t = \sum_{t=1}^{\infty} \sum_{j=1}^{h} \theta^j_t. \tag{58}$$

$\sum_{t=1}^{\infty} b_t$ shows up on both sides of the budget constraint since the present discounted value of a bond is equal to sum of the interest payments on it. The consumer's budget constraint becomes

$$\sum_{t=1}^{\infty} (p'_t c_t + b^j_t) = \sum_{t=1}^{\infty} (p'_t w^j - \theta^j_t) + \sum_{t=1}^{\infty} b^j_t$$

$$\sum_{t=1}^{\infty} p'_t c_t = \sum_{t=1}^{\infty} (p'_t w^j - \theta^j_t). \tag{59}$$

Here b^j_t is the net purchase of bonds by consumer j in period t and

$$\sum_{j=1}^{h} b^j_t = b_t. \tag{60}$$

Notice that, if

$$\sum_{t=1}^{\infty} \tau^j_t = \sum_{t=1}^{\infty} \theta^j_t, \tag{61}$$

these two models are identical in their essentials. In particular, the agents face the same budget constraints. This is the Ricardian Equivalence Theorem. There are a number of important maintained hypotheses. First, there are perfect capital markets. This implies that each consumer faces a single budget constraint. Second, all taxes are lump-sum; otherwise, relative prices would be distorted in different ways by different taxation schemes. Third, taxes are not redistributional. In other words consumers face the same total tax bill under the two taxation scheme; otherwise, relative prices would change because of income effects.

We are not claiming that the equilibrium is the same as if $g_t = 0$, $t = 1$, $2, \ldots$ Since the government is consuming some of the goods that would otherwise have gone to consumers, this cannot be the case. Government fiscal policy always has real effects. It is the way it is financed that is irrelevant.

It is difficult to give the Ricardian Equivalence Theorem an interpretation in an overlapping generations model: alternative tax schemes that time tax collections differently necessarily have redistributional effects because consumers are alive at different times. There are very special situations in which different tax schemes do not affect the equilibria. It does not matter, for example, in which period of life consumers pay taxes as long as each consumer faces a single budget constraint, all taxes are lump-sum, and each consumer faces the same total tax bill under the different schemes. Rather than say that the Ricardian Equivalence Theorem does not hold in an overlapping generations model, we should say that the range of tax schemes that do not affect the equilibria is much more limited in an overlapping generations model than it is in an infinitely lived consumer model.

Another problem with interpreting the Ricardian Equivalence Theorem in a model with infinite numbers of consumers and goods is, as we have seen, that there is no reason for $\sum_{t=1}^{\infty} p_t' g_t$ to converge. The government can therefore issue bonds that it need never pay back. These bonds act like injections of outside money and are, therefore, net wealth. Figure 16.8 depicts an example with a steady state in which $g_t = g > 0$ every period. Here inflation erodes the value of the initial stock of outside money at the same rate as that at which the value of the total

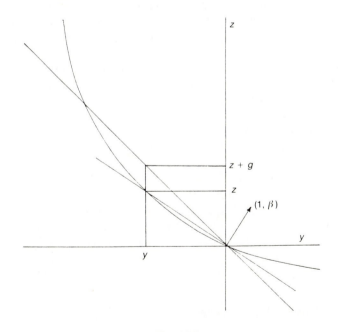

Fig. 16.8

stock of government bonds increases. The total real stock of nominal
debt, outside money and bonds, remains constant at $z + g$. The steady
state interest rate is $r = 1/\beta \; -1 < 0$. Notice that, even though the
government is consuming $g > 0$ of the single good in every period, this
equilibrium Pareto dominates the autarkic equilibrium where it consumes
nothing. Examples of this sort are discussed by Sargent (1987: Ch. 7).

Barro (1974) has argued that the Ricardian Equivalence Theorem
holds for overlapping generations models in which consumers include
their offspring's utility in their own utility functions. Since their offspring
similarly value the utility of their own offspring, this can make a
consumer's utility maximization problem into the problem of maximizing
the utility of an infinitely lived family. The problem with this story is that,
in general, we have to allow some consumers to pass on debts, as well as
bequests, to their offspring. In this case we would want consumers to
include their progenitors' utility in their own utility functions. Think of
our example of the two infinitely lived consumers with log-linear utility
functions as a model of such families. One family of consumers
asymptotically consumes nothing. They use almost all of their income to
service their family debt, which they inherit from their progenitors and
pass on to their offspring. This sort of problem always occurs if different
families have different discount factors in their reduced-form utility
functions. Institutional arrangements in modern societies make this
feature of the bequest story very unrealistic. As Barro himself points out,
if a family is at a corner solution because of a non-negativity constraint
on bequests, the family faces a sequence of budget constraints that
cannot be aggregated into one.

Similarly, a model with infinitely lived consumers who face liquidity
constraints can have similar characteristics to an overlapping generations
model (see Woodford 1986a, for example.) If we cannot reduce the
consumer's utility maximization problem to one with a finite number of
budget constraints, then we cannot prove that the value of the aggregate
endowment is finite. Consequently, equilibria need not be Pareto-
efficient, and there may be equilibria in which outside money plays a
role. Even our argument that there is a finite number of equilibria falls
apart. The essential feature of that argument is that each consumer is
characterized by a single Lagrange multiplier $\lambda_j = 1/\alpha_j$. If the consumer
cannot equate his marginal utility of income in different periods, then he
acts, to some extent, like a sequence of different consumers. There may
be a robust continuum of equilibria, and the Ricardian Equivalence
Theorem need not hold.

6. Implications for Finite Models

What does our analysis of the overlapping generations model tell us
about the properties of models with large, but finite, number of

consumers and goods? Suppose that we truncate the model at some period T using a terminal young generation $y_T(p_T, m)$ analogous to the initial old generation $z_0(p_1, m)$. Outside money now corresponds to a transfer from the terminal young generation to the initial old. There is now a finite number of equilibrium conditions:

$$z_0(\hat{p}_1, \hat{m}) + y(\hat{p}_1, \hat{p}_2) = 0$$

$$z(\hat{p}_1, \hat{p}_2) + y(\hat{p}_2, \hat{p}_3) = 0 \qquad (62)$$

$$\vdots$$

$$z(\hat{p}_{T-1}, \hat{p}_T) + y_T(\hat{p}_T, \hat{m}) = 0.$$

All of the equilibria of this model are Pareto-efficient. In general, there is a one-dimensional continuum of equilibria indexed by the real transfer payment $\hat{m}/\|\hat{p}_1\|$.

This method of truncating this model is often equivalent to specifying expectations of prices in periods after the model ends. For example, we could specify $y_T(p_T, m)$ as $y_T(p_T, \|p_T\| \beta p)$ where (p, β) is a steady state. Here, of course, $m = \|p_T\| \beta p' z(p_T, \|p_T\| \beta p)$. (See Auerbach, Kotlikoff, and Skinner 1983 for an application of this approach.)

Consider a situation where one equilibrium Pareto-dominates another in the infinite horizon model. Each of these can be made an equilibrium of the truncated model with a suitable choice of y_T. Since both of the equilibria of the truncated model are Pareto-efficient, the equilibrium that dominates in the infinite horizon model must assign some members of the terminal generation lower utility than does the inferior equilibrium. Notice that the functions y_T do not necessarily bear any relationship to utility maximization by generation T in the infinite-horizon model. If T is large enough, the model is clear: by sacrificing the welfare of one generation, all others are made better off, and society as a whole is made better off from a utilitarian viewpoint.

In an infinite horizon model there can be n dimensions of indeterminacy if there is outside money and $n - 1$ dimensions if there is not. The single dimension of indeterminacy that shows up because of fiat money corresponds to the indeterminacy parametrized by the real transfer payment. What about the other dimensions? To answer this question, let us suppose that we have two equilibrium price sequences, $(\hat{p}_1, \hat{p}_2, \ldots)$ and $(\bar{p}_1, \bar{p}_2, \ldots)$, which both converge to the same steady state. Suppose too that both involve the same real stock of outside money,

$$\frac{\hat{m}}{\|\hat{p}_1\|} = \frac{\bar{m}}{\|\bar{p}_1\|}.$$

If we truncate using a terminal young generation

$$\hat{y}_T(p_T, m) = y_T(p_T, \hat{p}_{T+1}), \qquad (63)$$

$m = \hat{m}$, then $(\hat{p}_1, \hat{p}_2, \ldots, \hat{p}_T)$ is an equilibrium. If we truncate with the

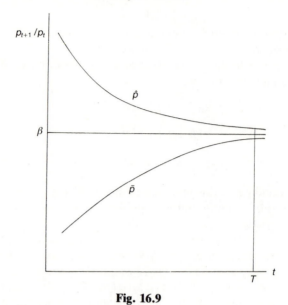

Fig. 16.9

analogous choice of $\bar{y}_T$, then $(\bar{p}_1, \bar{p}_2, \ldots, \bar{p}_T)$ is an equilibrium. Figure 16.9 depicts this sort of situation. For large enough T, $(\hat{p}_T, \hat{p}_{T+1})$ is going to be arbitrarily close to $(\bar{p}_T, \bar{p}_{T+1})$ no matter how far apart are $\hat{p}_1$ and $\bar{p}_1$. Indeterminacy of equilibrium therefore corresponds to sensitivity to terminal conditions, sensitivity of initial prices that becomes more acute as the time horizon T becomes larger. See Kehoe and Levine (1986) for numerical simulations of an example with this propery.

We should point out one other way of reducing an overlapping generations model to a model with a finite time horizon. Suppose that in every period the probability that the world ends before the next period is ρ, $0 < \rho < 1$. It is then natural to assume that consumer j in generation t solves the expected utility maximization problem

$$\left.\begin{array}{l} \max \rho u_j(y_t^i + w_1) + (1 - \rho)v_j(y_t^j + w_1, z_t^j + w_2) \\ \text{s.t. } p_t' y_t^j + p_{t+1}' z_t^j = 0. \end{array}\right\} \tag{64}$$

Here u_j is his utility function if the world ends before the second period of his life and v_j is his utility function if it does not. Even though the world ends in finite time with probability 1, this model is identical to an overlapping with an infinite horizon. It may have equilibria that are not Pareto-efficient, equilibria in which outside money plays a role, and equilibria with one or more dimensions of indeterminacy.

7. Extensions and Conclusions

The results presented in this paper can be extended to more general models. Kehoe *et al.* (1988) have extended this analysis of the model with a finite number of infinitely lived agents to similar models that allow production and capital accumulation. The only difficulty is in ensuring that the transfer functions used in the equilibrium conditions are continuously differentiable. Muller and Woodford (1985) have extended this analysis of the overlapping generations model to models that include infinitely lived consumers, assets, and production. They find that the presence of infinitely lived consumers or infinitely lived assets can force the value of the aggregate endowment to be finite. This rules out Pareto inefficiency of equilibria and outside money. It does not rule out indeterminacy of equilibria, however.

Do Pareto inefficiency of equilibria and outside money depend on there being an infinite number of consumers or on some consumers having finite life-spans? Kehoe (1986) considers a simple pure-exchange model in which there is an infinite number of consumers who all live for ever. This model has equilibria that are Pareto-inefficient and equilibria with outside money. It also has equilibria with several dimensions of indeterminacy.

As we have seen, indeterminacy is a relatively separate issue from Pareto inefficiency and outside money, Kehoe *et al.* (1986b) consider an abstract model with infinite numbers of consumers and goods. The only prices that are allowed assign finite value to the aggregate endowment. This rules out Pareto inefficiency and outside money. Even so, there are robust examples with any dimension of indeterminacy. The reason for this indeterminacy is that we cannot reduce the equilibrium conditions to a finite number of equations and unknowns. These authors also find that there is a finite number of locally unique equilibria if consumers are similar enough. This generalizes our results on economies with a finite number of consumers.

Santos and Bona (1986) and Geanakoplos and Brown (1985) have extended the results of Kehoe and Levine (1985a) for stationary, pure-exchange, overlapping generations models to models with non-stationary structures. Like Kehoe and Levine, these authors need to restrict their attention to equilibria that remain close to each other in some sense. They find that, even in a non-stationary environment, there are n dimensions of potential indeterminacy if there is outside money and $n - 1$ dimensions if there is not.

One disturbing aspect to the potential indeterminacy of equilibria is that it occurs for some values of the parameters of a model but not for others. We would like to somehow classify the parameter values for which indeterminacy does not occur. A first step in this direction has been taken by Balasko and Shell (1981), who consider a model with many goods in each period but a single two-period-lived consumer with a Cobb–Douglas utility function in each generation. They prove that there is no indeterminacy without outside money and only one dimension of indeterminacy with it. Geanakoplos and Polemarchakis (1984) have shown that the essential feature of this analysis is that the single two-period-lived consumer has intertemporally separable preferences. Kehoe and Levine (1984a) have shown further that any small perturbation to a model with a single two-period-lived consumer with intertemporally separable preferences, even if it introduces small heterogeneities among consumers or small interdependencies in consumption over time, results in a model with these same features.

A more significant finding is that of Kehoe *et al.* (1986a), who consider general pure-exchange, overlapping generations economies with many goods in each period and many consumers in each generation, in which all demand functions exhibit gross substitutability. They prove that there is a unique equilibrium if there is no money; although there may be a one-dimensional indeterminacy with outside money, there is at most one equilibrium for each level of real outside money in the first period. Furthermore, their analysis is global rather than local. If the economy is stationary, then there is a unique nominal steady state and there is a unique real steady state, and every equilibrium converges to one of them. Unfortunately, there are plausible examples that violate gross substitutability. Kehoe and Levine (1986) consider a model with a single good in each period and a single three-period-lived consumer in each generation. They give this consumer a constant elasticity of substitution utility function and show that, for plausible parameter values, this model can exhibit indeterminacy without outside money and more than one dimension of indeterminacy with it. Moreover, they choose the crucial parameter, the elasticity of substitution in consumption over time, to agree with empirical evidence.

The present analysis has focused on the differences between models with a finite number of infinitely lived consumers and overlapping generations models. Yet these two types of models have important properties in common. In both, for example, equilibria always exist. Since the equilibrium conditions for a model with a finite number of infinitely lived consumers can be transformed using Negishi's (1960b) approach into those of a model with a finite number of goods, it is straightforward to prove the existence of equilibria in such models. This is done, for example, by Kehoe *et al.* (1988). Proving the existence of equilibria in overlapping generations models involves more subtle issues. Considering the limit of a sequence of truncated economies, Balasko *et al.* (1980) prove the existence of an equilibrium with $\hat{m} = 0$ in a pure-exchange, overlapping generations model. For general models with countably many consumers and goods, Burke (1986, 1988) and Wilson (1981) have proven the existence of equilibria. The presence of outside money may be necessary, however, for an equilibrium to exist.

Another property that these two types of models have in common is that the Second Welfare Theorem holds: any Pareto-efficient allocation can be supported as a competitive equilibrium with transfers. This is proven for the overlapping generations model by Balasko and Shell (1980). The role that outside money plays in supporting a Pareto-efficient allocation can be interpreted as such a transfer. Unfortunately, Cass *et al.* (1979) and Millan (1981) have examples in which no Pareto-efficient allocation can be supported as a competitive equilibrium by giving a transfer only to the first generation. Burke (1987), however, shows that a transfer to the first generation does support efficiency if it is followed by a sequence of taxes on subsequent generations. Furthermore, the sum of real tax payments can be made arbitrarily small.

How much of this analysis extends to intertemporal models with uncertainty? If all markets are complete, then the analysis of the model with a finite number of infinitely lived consumers remains the same. In particular, all equilibria are Pareto-efficient, there is no role for outside money, and there is generically a finite number of equilibria. Goods are indexed by histories of states of nature as well by date. (See Kehoe and Levine 1985b for an analysis of a model of this sort.) In a stochastic overlapping generations model the assumption of complete markets is unnatural, however. In a deterministic setting we have argued that it makes no difference whether all trade takes place in the first period or takes place sequentially; in a stochastic setting setting this is no longer the case. Consumers would want to make trades in periods before they are born to insure themselves against being born into unfavourable circumstances. Dutta and Polemarchakis (1985) present an analysis of a simple stochastic overlapping generations model and show the difference between equilibria with complete markets and equilibria where consumers are allowed to trade only during their own lifetimes.

As we have seen, models with infinitely lived consumers who face incomplete markets have similar properties to overlapping generations models. Bewley (1980, 1983), Scheinkman and Weiss (1986), and Levine (1986) analyse simple stochastic models in which there are infinitely lived consumers who are constrained in their borrowing and lending decisions. Not surprisingly, they find that such models have equilibria that are Pareto-inefficient and equilibria in which outside money plays an important role. Presumably, these models also have indeterminate equilibria, but this property has not received much attention.

The most worrying property of the overlapping generations model is probably its potential for indeterminate equilibria even if there is no outside money. There are two reasons for this. First, indeterminacy makes the model unsuitable for comparative statics analysis. Second, it makes the concept of perfect foresight problematical. Multiplicity of equilibria of any sort presents difficulties for an economist interested in using a model to do a comparative-statics analysis of the impact of a change in parameters. Suppose, however, that a model has a finite number of locally unique equilibria that vary continuously with its parameter values. (Almost all static general equilibrium models possess these properties.) Then the economist could hope that, by appealing to history to justify focusing on one particular equilibrium, and to a (usually unspecified) dynamic adjustment process to justify focusing on the displacement of that equilibrium after a change in parameter values, comparative statics still makes some sense. Even these hopes vanish if there is a continuum of equilibria.

The idea underlying perfect foresight in a model with no uncertainty is the same as that underlying the rational expectations hypothesis in a model with uncertainty: the agents know the structure of the model and use it to predict the relevant values of future variables. If the model does not make determinate prediction, then hypothesis of perfect foresight becomes less attractive. If there is a continuum of perfect foresight paths, the theory is incomplete. Geanakoplos and Polemarchakis (1986) argue that indeterminacy leaves room for factors like fixed nominal wages and animal spirits of investors. As we have seen in our discussion of the Ricardian Equivalence Theorem, if there is a continuum of equilibria, some may have Keynesian features and some may not.

One way to try to make the theory complete would be to fix the values of some variables in the first period, for example the real money stock or a relative price. Even this approach fails if $y(p_t, p_{t+1})$ is not always an invertible function of p_{t+1}. With the backwards-bending offer curve in Figure 16.5, for example, there is an infinite number of equilibria even if we fix the value of $\hat{m}/\hat{p}_1$: at every point where there are two values of $\hat{p}_{t+1}$ such that $z(\hat{p}_{t-1}, \hat{p}_t) + y(\hat{p}_t, \hat{p}_{t+1}) = 0$, we have a choice of a different price path to follow.

Modelling expectations has long been a difficulty in economic theory. Keynes (1973/1936), for example, realized the importance of expectations formation, but claimed to work with a model in which the time period was short enough so that expectations could be taken as exogenous. The simplest way of making expectations endogenous is to make them adaptive as done by, for example, Friedman (1968) and Phelps (1967). The equilibria of the overlapping generations models would be generically determinate if we specified expectations as either exogenous or adaptive: since values of past variables can be taken as exogenous in any period, the equilibrium conditions reduce to a system of a finite number of equations in the same finite number of unknowns.

Computing the equilibria of such a model would reduce to computing the equilibria of a sequence of models that look like static models.

The indeterminacy of equilibria in the overlapping generations models is all the more worrying because it can be associated with the existence of self-fulfilling prophecies. Even though the preferences, endowments, and technology of an economy are deterministic, a random variable can affect the equilibria merely because agents expect it to. This phenomenon is referred to as a 'sunspot', although actual sunspots may actually affect the technology of an economy (see, Mirowski 1984), and may not be themselves stochastic (see, Weiss 1985). There is a large and growing literature on sunspots. A very incomplete list of references includes: Azariadis (1981), Azariadis and Guesnerie (1986), Cass and Shell (1983), and Farmer and Woodford (1984). Woodford (1986b) presents an example in which agents employ a simple learning rule and the economy converges to a perfect-foresight sunspot equilibrium.

Just as worrying as indeterminacy of equilibria is the possibility that an economy may have no equilibrium that converges to a steady state. If the path followed by equilibrium prices is chaotic or periodic of a very long length, the perfect-foresight hypothesis is unattractive for a different reason: it requires too much computational power of the agents of the model. Any theory of expectations formation that is designed to cope with the problem of indeterminacy of equilibrium must also be able to relax the requirement of perfect foresight when equilibrium price dynamics are chaotic or periodic of very long length. Unfortunately, as Benhabib and Nishimura (1985) and Boldrin and Montrucchio (1986) have shown, even the model with a finite number of infinitely lived agents can have equilibria that exhibit periodic or chaotic dynamics.

The above analysis of intertemporal general equilibrium models has provided us with a clear understanding of why Pareto inefficiency and outisde money occur in the overlapping generations model but not in the model with a finite number of infinitely lived consumers. It is also clear how these properties manifest themselves in a truncated version of the model. Although we have attained some understanding of the possibility of indeterminacy, we are still faced with the dilemma that indeterminacy is symptomatic of an incompleteness of the model. What is needed is a serious theory of expectations formation.

17

Sunspots

STEPHEN BURNELL

1. Introduction

The purpose of this chapter is to extend the language of rational expectations so as to consider the possibility of self-fulfilling prophecies. Starting with a simple deterministic overlapping generations model, without production, I introduce the concept of sunspots. A 'sunspot' is to be thought of as a state of nature that does not affect the 'real' parameters of the model; its sole impact is upon the beliefs held by agents concerning prices next period. By focusing upon models in which every state is a sunspot, I can examine the characteristics of equilibria that emerge solely from the introduction of expectations about the future.

The importance of sunspots is that there are certain markets with characteristics that make it plausible for agents to believe that sunspots matter. Consider an asset market where trades today are dominated by agents who are concerned solely about the price of the asset tomorrow. Further, suppose that either the supply of the asset is fixed or the marginal cost of the asset is unrelated to its price. In such a market the price of the asset today will be determined by the expectations—by traders—of its price tomorrow, which, in turn, will be determined by expectations of its price for the day after tomorrow, and so on. Examples of such markets include the share market, the foreign exchange market, and possibly even commodity futures markets. Now, in such markets a rational agent will recognize that the price tomorrow will depend upon the actions of all other agents tomorrow, and hence upon their theories of price formation. The potential then exists for a rational agent to believe that certain events will affect the price of the asset simply because (he believes) other agents believe these events matter. In this way, a theory of price formation can be thought of as a social convention that may have no 'intrinsic' economic justification—the theory simply justifies itself (see Keynes 1973: 152-8). For example, suppose the President of the United States has recently undergone an operation. Further, suppose I believe that if he rides a horse tomorrow then all other agents will be more optimistic about the price of the US dollar relative to the UK pound—for the day after tomorrow—than if he doesn't ride. Even though I may see no obvious economic rationale for their expectations, it is still rational for me to believe that the price of the dollar—tomorrow— will be higher if the President does ride a horse than if he doesn't.

The role of expectations in any model depends upon the nature of markets available to agents. I may believe that the price of the dollar will be higher tomorrow if the President does ride a horse, but if I cannot act upon this belief its inclusion in the model will not matter. In this chapter I consider three types of market structures with sunspots: the first is simply a generalization of the Arrow–Debreu model; the second is a world where agents face complete contingent markets after they have been born into a particular history of states; while third is a world where the only asset or liability is money. With very special assumptions, I am able to discuss the relationships between the sets of equilibria in these three sunspot worlds and also the set of equilibria in the deterministic world. An equilibrium in a sunspot world that is not merely a simple rewriting of a deterministic equilibrium is called a 'sunspot equilibrium'.

Given that every agent has an intertemporally separable utility function, I show there are no sunspot equilibria in the Arrow–Debreu world. If there is only one agent per generation, I then show that every sunspot equilibrium in the money world can be transformed into a sunspot equilibrium in the contingent markets world (in the sense that there are prices yielding the same allocation). A simple example is then constructed that yields a sunspot equilibrium in the money world. Further, the example yields a sunspot equilibrium in the contingent markets world that cannot be transformed into a sunspot equilibrium in the money world.

Finally, the concept of stationary sunspot equilibrium is introduced and sufficient conditions for its existence, in the money world, are stated. Using a particular definition of stationarity, it is easy to see that, if there is more than one good, a stationary sunspot equilibrium in the money world will not, in general, exist. This could be taken to mean that the concept of a sunspot equilibrium is vacuous in models with more than one good. It is my contention, however, that it is the particular definition of stationarity that is vacuous.

2. The Model

Consider the pure consumption, deterministic, overlapping generations model discussed in the last chapter. Suppose that every agent lives two periods and the characteristics (endowments and utility functions) of agents are constant over generations. For reasons that will become clearer later, I initially assume there is only one (perishable) commodity and one agent per generation. Distorting the notation of Kehoe, take $w_1(w_2)$ to be the endowment of each agent when young (old), y_t to be the consumption, when young, of the agent born at t, and z_t to be the consumption, when old, of the agent born at $t - 1$. The utility function of every agent, $U(y, z)$, is assumed to be intertemporally separable; that is, $U(y, z) = u(y) + v(z)$. Further, $u(\cdot)$ and $v(\cdot)$ are both twice continuously differentiable, strictly monotonically increasing, and strictly concave. Taking p_t to be the price of the commodity at t, relative to the good at period 1, the consumption problem of the agent, born at t, can be written as

$$\max u(y_t) + v\left[\frac{p_t(w_1 - y_t)}{p_{t+1}} + w_2\right]. \tag{1}$$

Now, this consumption problem can emerge from at least three types of market structures. First, suppose at period 1 all the agents who will ever receive an endowment (at any date) gather together. They face a complete set of contingent (or future, as there is no uncertainty) markets, and they know that markets will not reopen after period 1. The agent, born at t, wishes to trade in only two markets: those for goods dated at t and at $t + 1$. Hence his consumption problem is given by (1). Such a situation shall be called a world with Arrow–Debreu markets. Second, suppose that at every period, $t \geqslant 1$, there exists a spot market for the commodity (at t) and a contingent (future) market for the commodity at $t + 1$. If there was more than one commodity, perfect foresight would imply that relative contingent prices, announced at t, equal the relative spot prices at $t + 1$. As a consequence, there is no harm in assuming that the agent, born at t, does all his trading at t. Hence his consumption problem is also given by (1). Such a situation shall be called a *world with contingent markets*. Finally, suppose that at every period, $t \geqslant 1$, there exists a spot market for the commodity and a market for 'money'. Agents can either buy or sell money when young, so long as they leave no debts when they die. Perfect foresight implies that the agent, born at t, knows what the spot price of the commodity will be at $t + 1$—relative to, say, the unit of money. Hence, as before, his consumption problem is given by (1). Such a situation will be called a *world with money*.

Now, for all three market structures there exists an agent who is old at period 1. This agent will be called generation 0. He arrives at period 1 with an endowment, w_2, and an initial intergenerational debt, m. His problem is to maximize $v(z_1)$, subject to the budget constraint, $p_1(w_2 - z_1) + m \geqslant 0$. As there is only one good, and as I have normalized prices so that $p_1 = 1$, it follows automatically that $z_1 = w_2 + m$. Clearly, this result holds for all three market structures. As the consumption problem of every agent is the same for all three market structures, it is obvious that they will all have the same set of deterministic equilibria. A deterministic equilibrium can be defined as price sequence, $\{p_t\}$, an initial debt, m, and a consumption stream, $\{(y_t, z_t)\}$, such that

(i) $\forall t \geqslant 1, y_t + z_t = w_1 + w_2$
(ii) $z_1 = w_2 + m$
(iii) $\forall t \geqslant 1, (y_t, z_{t+1})$ solves (1)
(iv) $\forall t \geqslant 1, y_t \geqslant 0, z_t \geqslant 0$.

For the money world, m is simply the constant money stock (which may be negative). It is easy to show that, in equilibrium, $p_t(w_1 - y_t) = m$, for all three market structures. That is, the intergenerational debt is constant over time.

I now wish to relax the deterministic nature of the model and look at the simplest possible case of uncertainty, where there are two possible states of nature each period—call them a and b—and where everyone who is alive at t observes the realized state. At t there is a history of states, given by $r_t = (s_1, \ldots, s_t)$, where $s_i \in \{a, b\}$, $i = 1, \ldots, t$. The (objective) probability of $s_{t+1} = a$ is assumed to depend only upon s_t. It does not depend upon the history before t (r_{t-1}), nor does it depend upon the period, $t + 1$. The probability of the state next period being a, given that the state this period is a, will be written as π_{aa} (the first a represents the state now, while the second a represents the state next period). The probability π_{bb} is similarly defined, and so $\pi_{ab} = 1 - \pi_{aa}$, $\pi_{ba} = 1 - \pi_{bb}$. The two numbers, π_{aa} and π_{bb}, can be thought of as the true theory concerning the realization of states, and it is supposed that every agent knows this theory.

Now, if the endowments or utility functions of agents alive at t depend upon the history, r_t, then the world exhibits intrinsic uncertainty. That is, the real parameters of the model are functions of the history of states. If, on the other hand, neither endowments nor utility functions at t depend upon r_t, then the world exhibits extrinsic uncertainty (see Cass and Shell 1983: 196). The states of nature associated with extrinsic uncertainty have been nicknamed 'sunspots' in the literature, in a somewhat mocking reference to Jevon's work (see e.g. Jevons 1884: 194–243). It should be noted that extrinsic uncertainty can be thought of as a special, or limiting, case of intrinsic uncertainty.

The seeds of extrinsic uncertainty have existed since at least the time of Savage's (1954) theory of rational choice under uncertainty. Savage's reference to any finite sequence of heads and tails, resulting from the repeated tossing of a coin, as a set of events, can now be interpreted as the construction of a subset of sunspots (see Savage 1954: 33, 38–9).

Until recently, the conventional wisdom was to ignore such 'irrelevant' states, presumably because, as they don't change any of the real parameters of the model, it was inferred that they couldn't possibly matter. However, Cass and Shell (1983), and others since, have constructed models in which sunspots do matter. Conditional probability distributions over sunspots are not sufficient, by themselves, to make sunspots matter. It is also necessary for agents to believe that things (for example, prices) will be different for different histories of states. The particular market structure will then determine the set of feasible actions available to agents. Each agent then chooses the action that maximizes his expected utility—and it is here that the probability distributions enter the analysis. A rational expectations equilibrium will then require that the actions of agents are consistent (markets clear) and that their beliefs—about what will happen (to prices) at different histories—are correct. In order to formalize this conception of an equilibrium, I shall now investigate the three market structures discussed above in a world with sunspots.

3. Sunspots and Market Structures

3.1. The Arrow–Debreu world

At $t = 1$, a price for every possible history, r_t, is called, written as $p(r_t)$. As all prices are relative, I shall normalize by taking $p(a) = 1$. For convenience, I suppose that there is no uncertainty at $t = 1$ and that $s_1 = a$, in order to take all prices as relative.

At history, r_t, the consumption of the young (old) agent is written as $y(r_t)[z(r_t)]$. The probability of r_t occurring (conditional upon $s_1 = a$) is $\pi(r_t) = \pi_{as_2}\pi_{s_2s_3} \dots, \pi_{s_{t-1}s_t}$. Given t, the set of possible histories, r_t, is given by R_t. Clearly, as $s_1 = a$, R_t has 2^{t-1} elements. The consumption problem of the agent, who will be born at t, is given by

$$\left. \begin{aligned} \max \sum_{r_{t+1}\in R_{t+1}} \pi(r_{t+1})\{u[y(r_t)] + v[z(r_{t+1})]\} \\[2mm] \text{s.t.} \sum_{r_t\in R_t} p(r_t)[w_1 - y(r_t)] + \sum_{r_{t+1}\in R_{t+1}} p(r_{t+1})[w_2 - z(r_{r+1})] \geqslant 0 \end{aligned} \right\} \tag{2}$$

where, for instance, $p(r_t)$ is the price announced at $t = 1$ for the good, contingent upon the history, r_t, occurring.

The problem for generation 0 is given by

$$\max v[z(a)] \text{ s.t. } [w_2 - z(a)] + m \geqslant 0. \tag{3}$$

(Remember, $p(a) = 1$.)

A rational expectations equilibrium (REE) in the Arrow–Debreu world is then defined to be a price sequence, $\{p(r_t)\}$, an initial debt, m, and a consumption stream, $\{[y(r_t), z(r_t)]\}$, such that

(i) $\forall r_t(t \geqslant 1, s_1 = a), y(r_t) + z(r_t) = w_1 + w_2$
(ii) $z(a) = w_2 + m$

(iii) $\forall\, t \geqslant 1$, $\{y(r_t), z(r_t, a), z(r_t, b)\}(r_t \in R_t)$ solves (2)
(iv) $\forall\, r_t(t \geqslant 1, s_1 = a)y(r_t) \geqslant 0$, $z(r_t) \geqslant 0$.

3.2. The contingent markets world

In the Arrow–Debreu world agents can make contracts contingent upon any possible history they could be born in. Clearly, such a market structure does not capture the sad fact of the human condition; agents can act only after they have been thrown into the world, at a particular history. The contingent markets world takes this observation into account by allowing agents to participate in markets only after they have been born. The agent born at r_t faces a spot market, at r_t, and contingent markets for the two possible histories, (r_t, a) and (r_t, b). As this is the case for every history, r_t, markets reopen every period. However, there is no loss in generality to suppose that every agent carries out all his trades when young. If there is more than one good, it is necessary to suppose that agents have perfect foresight concerning relative spot prices at future histories. The agent, born at r_t, knows that the relative spot prices at (r_t, a) will equal the relative contingent prices, at r_t, for goods available at (r_t, a). He is therefore quite happy to carry out all his trades when young.

Now, it may be wondered who the young agent trades with on the contingent markets—for the agent who will be young next period has yet to be born. One possible story is that there exists an infinitely lived auctioneer, who calls prices and passively trades with agents. At the history, r_t, the young agent trades with the auctioneer—on both the spot and the contingent markets—while the old agent merely fulfils his part of the contract (with the auctioneer) from last period. Hence the old and young do not trade with each other directly, but rather through the auctioneer. The budget constraint of the agent born at r_t implies that the net receipts of the auctioneer at r_t will be zero. In equilibrium the passive auctioneer is required to take from (give to) the old exactly that which he is required to give to (take from) the young.

The consumption problem of the agent born at r_t is therefore given by

$$\left.\begin{aligned}
&\max u[y(r_t) + \pi_{s,a}v[z(r_t, a)] + \pi_{s,b}v[z(r_t, b)]] \\[4pt]
&\text{s.t. } p(r_t)[w_1 - y(r_t)] + p(r_t, a)[w_2 - z(r_t, a)] \\[4pt]
&\qquad\qquad + p(r_t, b)[w_2 - z(r_t, b)] \geqslant 0.
\end{aligned}\right\} \tag{4}$$

The problem of generation 0 is given by (3).

A REE in the contingent markets world is therefore given by a price sequence, $\{p(r_t)\}$, an initial debt, m, and a consumption stream,

$\{[y(r_t), z(r_t)]\}$, such that

(i) $\forall r_t (t \geq 1, s_1 = a), y(r_t) + z(r_t) = w_1 + w_2$
(ii) $z(a) = w_2 + m$
(iii) $\forall r_t (t \geq 1, s_1 = a), [y(r_t), z(r_t, a), z(r_t, b)]$ solves (4)
(iv) $\forall r_t (t \geq 1, s_1 = a), y(r_t) \geq 0, z(r_t) \geq 0$.

3.3. The money world

In the money world, as with the contingent markets world, agents can trade only after they have been born into a particular history of states. At any history, r_t, there exists a spot market for the commodity and a market for money. It is assumed that the agent who is young at r_t knows what the spot prices, at histories (r_t, a) and (r_t, b) will be—relative to the unit of money. Defining $m(r_t)$ to be the amount of money (either positive or negative) the agent, born at r_t, desires to hold from period t to $t + 1$ the consumption problem of the agent is given by

$$\left.\begin{aligned}
\max u[y(r_t)] &+ \pi_{s,a}v[z(r_t, a)] + \pi_{s,b}v[z(r_t, b)] \\
\text{s.t. } p(r_t)[w_1 - y(r_t)] &- m(r_t) \geq 0 \\
p(r_t, a)[w_2 - z(r_t, a)] &+ m(r_t) \geq 0 \\
p(r_t, b)[w_2 - z(r_t, b)] &+ m(r_t) \geq 0.
\end{aligned}\right\} \tag{5}$$

Non-satiation and the fact that $m(r_t)$ can be positive or negative imply that the three inequalities above can be written as two equalities:

$$\left.\begin{aligned}
p(r_t)[w_1 - y(r_t)] + p(r_t, a)[w_2 - z(r_t, a)] = 0 \\
p(r_t)[w_1 - y(r_t)] + p(r_t, b)[w_2 - z(r_t, b)] = 0.
\end{aligned}\right\} \tag{5a}$$

For this agent, the value of a unit of money (relative to, say, $p(r_t)$) is irrelevant. The only relative prices that matter are $p(r_t, a)/p(r_t)$ and $p(r_t, b)/p(r_t)$. Further, while money enables the agent to transfer income across time (either from young to old or from old to young), it does not enable him to transfer income across states when old. Hence there are two budget constraints instead of one. The problem of generation 0 is again given by (3).

A REE in the money world is given by a price sequence, $\{p(r_t)\}$, an initial debt, m, and a consumption stream, $\{[y(r_t), z(r_t)]\}$, such that

(i) $\forall r_t (t \geq 1, s_1 = a), y(r_t) + z(r_t) = w_1 + w_2$
(ii) $z(a) = w_2 + m$
(iii) $\forall r_t (t \geq 1, s_1 = a), [y(r_t), z(r_t, a), z(r_t, b)]$ solves (5)
(iv) $\forall r_t (t \geq 1, s_1 = a), y(r_t) \geq 0, z(r_t) \geq 0$.

It is easy to see from the budget constraints and market-clearing conditions that, in equilibrium, $m(r_t) = m, \forall r_t (t \geq 1, s_1 = a)$. That is, the money stock is constant for every possible history and equals the initial debt. This result is also true for n commodities, h agents per generation with non-separable utility functions, and k states.

Some readers may have difficulty associating the word 'money' with $m < 0$. In fact, several articles on sunspots focus solely upon equilibria with a positive money stock (see e.g. Azariadis 1981; Azariadis and Guesnerie 1986; Grandmont 1986; Guesnerie 1986; and Spear 1984). I am quite happy to drop the word 'money' and speak of 'intergenerational debt' instead. At the back of my mind I have a story involving an infinitely lived banker. When $m < 0$, the young desire to borrow from the banker and pay back this debt (or overdraft) when old. When $m > 0$, the young desire to lend to the banker and be paid back when old. In equilibrium, the net receipts of the banker (at any possible history, r_t) are zero.

Now, it might be argued that when $m > 0$ the banker is superfluous. Instead, the old have a piece of paper which they give to the young in exchange for the commodity. But why do the young accept this piece of paper? If they believe the next generation will accept a piece of paper, is it not rational to refuse to take the piece of paper from the old and create their own (intrinsically worthless) piece of paper to pass on to the next generation? If there is more than one agent per generation, this scheme requires co-ordination, but it still seems to me to be rational, in some sense. As every generation has an incentive to do this, money becomes worthless. I therefore claim (but have by no means proved) that an infinitely lived agent, like my banker, is necessary to generate equilibria with a positive money stock.

4. Some Properties of Rational Expectations Equilibria

PROPOSITION 1. (i) For each of the three sunspot worlds, every deterministic equilibrium can be transformed into a REE.

(ii) Consider a REE in the Arrow–Debreu or contingent markets world and its associated price sequence, $\{p(r_t)\}$. If there exists a deterministic price sequence, $\{p_t\}$, such that $p(r_t) = \pi(r_t)p_t$, $\forall r_t(t \geq 1, s_1 = a)$, then the REE is a transformed deterministic equilibrium.

(iii) Similarly, in the money world, consider a REE and its associated price sequence, $\{p(r_t)\}$. If there exists a deterministic price sequence, $\{p_t\}$, such that $p(r_t) = p_t$, $\forall r_t(t \geq 1, s_1 = a)$, then the REE is a transformed deterministic equilibrium.

Proof. (i) For the Arrow–Debreu and contingent markets worlds, let $p(r_t) = \pi(r_t)p_t$, the initial debt be the same as the deterministic equilibrium, and $[y(r_t), z(r_t)] = (y_t, z_t)$. This is a REE for both worlds. For the money world, let $p(r_t) = p_t$, the initial debt be the same as the deterministic equilibrium, and $[y(r_t), z(r_t)] = (y_t, z_t)$. This is a REE in the money world.

(ii) In the Arrow–Debreu world, it is easy to show that the optimal action of the agent born at t yields $y(r_t^1) = y(r_t^2)(\forall r_t^1, r_t^2 \in R_t)$ and $z(r_{t+1}^1) = z(r_{t+1}^2)(\forall r_{t+1}^1, r_{t+1}^2 \in R_{t+1})$. Define $y_t = y(r_t)$ and $z_t = z(r_t)$. Hence $[\{p_t\}, m, (y_t, z_t)]$ is a deterministic equilibrium.

In the contingent markets world, the optimal action for the agent born at r_t yields $z(r_t, a) = z(r_t, b)$. Further, the consumption problem of the agent born at r_t is identical, $\forall r_t \in R_t$. Therefore define $(y_t, z_t) = [y(r_t), z(r_t)]$. Hence $[\{p_t\}, m, (y_t, z_t)]$ is a deterministic equilibrium.

(iii) The proof is identical to the second part of (ii).   Q.E.D

This proposition continues to hold even when there are n goods, h agents with non-separable utility functions, and k states.

For each of the three sunspot worlds, the set of REE can be split into two distinct subsets: those equilibria that are transformed deterministic equilibria, and those that are not. Those that are not I shall call 'sunspot equilibria'. The question that can now be asked, for each of the three sunspot worlds, is whether the set of sunspot equilibria is non-empty.

In the Arrow–Debreu world, if there is a finite number of time periods (and hence a finite number of agents and commodities), every REE is Pareto-efficient. With an infinite number of agents and goods, this result is no longer true. It can be shown, however, that every REE is weakly Pareto-efficient. A consumption stream, $\{[y(r_t), z(r_t)]\}$, is weakly Pareto-efficient if $y(r_t) + z(r_t) \leq w_1 + w_2(\forall r_t, t \geq 1, s_1 = a)$ and there does not exist a consumption streams $\{[y^1(r_t), z^1(r_t)]\}$, such that

(i) $y^1(r_t) + z^1(r_t) \leq w_1 + w_2 (\forall r_t)$

(ii) $[y^1(r_t), z^1(r_t)] = [y(r_t), z(r_t)]$, except for a finite number of histories

(iii) $\forall t \geq 1, \sum_{r_t \in R_t} \pi(r_t)u[y^1(r_t)] + \sum_{r_{t+1} \in R_{t+1}} \pi(r_{t+1})v[z^1(r_{t+1})]$

$$\geq \sum_{r_t \in R_t} \pi(r_t)u[y(r_t)] + \sum_{r_{t+1} \in R_{t+1}} \pi(r_{t+1})v[z(r_{t+1})],$$

with at least one strict inequality.

The method of proving every REE in the Arrow–Debreu world is weakly Pareto-efficient is identical to that used by Balasko and Shell (1980) for the deterministic world.

PROPOSITION 2. Every REE in the Arrow–Debreu world is a transformed deterministic equilibrium. That is, there are no sunspot equilibria.

Proof. Suppose there exists a sunspot equilibrium. I shall show that it is not weakly Pareto-efficient and hence cannot be a REE, which is a contradiction.

A sunspot equilibrium $(\{p(r_t)\}, m, \{[y(r_t), z(r_t)]\})$, implies that there is a period, $T \geq 1$, and at least two histories, r_T^1, r_T^2, $\in R_T$, such that $y(r_T^1) \neq y(r_T^2)$. Now, construct a new consumption stream, $\{[y^1(r_t), z^1(r_t)]\}$, defined by

$$y^1(r_t) = \sum_{r_t \in R_t} \pi(r_t) y(r_t), \qquad \forall \, r_t \in R_t, \qquad t \leq T$$

$$y^1(r_t) = y(r_t), \qquad \forall \, r_t \in R_t, \qquad t > T$$

$$z^1(r_t) = \sum_{r_t \in R_t} \pi(r_t) z(r_t), \qquad \forall \, r_t \in R_t, \qquad t \leq T$$

$$z^1(r_t) = z(r_t), \qquad \forall \, r_t \in R_t, \qquad t > T.$$

For the first T periods the new allocation is history- (though not necessarily time-) independent and is found by averaging the sunspot consumption over R_t. Strict concavity of the utility function ensures that this new allocation is at least as high in preferences as the sunspot allocation by generations 0 to $T-2$ and is strictly preferred by generation $T-1$. Intertemporal separability, together with the strict concavity of $u(\cdot)$, ensures that the new allocation is also strictly preferred by generation T. Hence the sunspot allocation is not weakly Pareto-efficient and so a sunspot equilibrium cannot exist. Q.E.D

Notice that, without intertemporally separable utility, the new allocation may make generation T worse off. I have therefore been unable to say anything about the existence of sunspot equilibria in the Arrow–Debreu world without the separability assumption. However, the proposition can be extended to include n goods, k states, and h agents with intertemporally separable utility functions.

PROPOSITION 3. Every REE in the money world can be transformed into a REE in the contingent markets world.

Proof. Consider the agent in the money world, born at r_t, facing money prices $[p(r_t), p(r_t, a), p(r_t, b)]$. To maximize expected utility, he chooses the action $[y(r_t), z(r_t, a), z(r_t, b)]$. Consider now the agent in the contingent markets world born at the same history, r_t, facing contingent prices, $[p_1(r_t), p_1(r_t, a), p_1(r_t, b)]$. If

$$p_1(r_t, a) = \frac{\pi_{s+a} v'[z(r_t, a)] p_1(r_t)}{u'[y(r_t)]} \tag{6}$$

and

$$p_1(r_t, b) = \frac{\pi_{s,b} v'[z(r_t, b)] p_1(r_t)}{u'[y(r_t)]} \tag{7}$$

(where $[y(r_t), z(r_t, a), z(r_t, b)]$ is the action chosen in the money world), then the optimizing action of this agent is also $[y(r_t), z(r_t, a), z(r_t, b)]$.

Consider now a REE in the money world, $[\{p(r_t)\}, m, \{y(r_t), z(r_t)\}]$. From (6) and (7), it is possible to construct a price sequence in the contingent markets world such that $[\{p_1(r_t)\}, m, \{[y(r_t), z(r_t)]\}]$ is a REE. Hence every REE in the money world can be transformed into a REE in the contingent markets world. Q.E.D

This proposition can also be generalized to n goods and k states. Further, the assumption of an intertemporally separable utility function is not necessary. The method of proof, however, requires that there is only one agent per generation and that his utility function is strictly concave.

Given the special assumptions outlined earlier in the chapter (one good and one agent with a strictly concave, separable utility function), I have shown that a sunspot equilibrium cannot exist in the Arrow–Debreu world and, further, that every sunspot equilibrium in the money world can be transformed into a sunspot equilibrium in the contingent markets world. I now wish to consider whether there exist economies with a sunspot equilibrium in the money world and, further, whether there exists a sunspot equilibrium in the contingent markets world that cannot be transformed into a sunspot equilibrium in the money world. To investigate these two problems, it will be sufficient to focus upon the set of stationary equilibria.

5. Stationary Sunspot Equilibria

Intuitively, a stationary rational expectations equilibrium (SREE) is a REE where every agent born at state $a(b)$ faces the same consumption problem, irrespective of the period, t, and the history of states before t. More formally, a SREE is a REE with the additional property that there exist four numbers, β_{aa}, β_{ab}, β_{ba}, β_{bb}, such that $p(r_t) = \beta_{as_2} \cdots \beta_{s_{t-1}s_t}$. (Remember, $s_1 = a$, $p(a) = 1$.) Ignoring the Arrow–Debreu world (for which a sunspot equilibrium does not exist), at equilibrium prices the consumption problem of an agent born at r_t with, say, $s_t = a$, is given by

$$\left. \begin{array}{l} \max u[y(r_t)] + \pi_{aa}v[z(r_t, a)] + (1 - \pi_{aa})v[z(r_t, b)] \\[2mm] \text{s.t. the budget constraint} \\[2mm] w_1 - y(r_t) + \beta_{aa}[w_2 - z(r_t, a)] + \beta_{ab}[w_2 - z(r_t, b)] \geqslant 0 \end{array} \right\} \quad (8)$$

for the contingent markets world and

$$\left. \begin{array}{l} w_1 - y(r_t) + \beta_{aa}[w_2 - z(r_t, a)] \geqslant 0 \\[2mm] w_1 - y(r_t) + \beta_{ab}[w_2 - z(r_t, a)] \geqslant 0 \end{array} \right\} \quad (9)$$

for the money world. (Of course the numbers, β_{aa} and β_{ab} will be different for the two worlds.) Clearly, these consumption problems do not depend upon t or r_{t-1}. Hence, in a SREE, the optimizing action of every agent born at r_t, such that $s_t = a_1$, can be written as $[y(r_t), z(r_t, a), z(r_t, b)] = (y_a, z_{aa}, z_{ab})$. Similarly, the optimal action of every agent born at b can be written as $[y(r_t), z(r_t, a), z(r_t, b)] = (y_b, z_{ba}, z_{bb})$.

Now, if $s_t = a$, the consumption of the young agent is y_a while the consumption of the old agent is z_{aa} if $s_{t-1} = a$, or z_{ba} if $s_{t-1} = b$. The market-clearing conditions of a SREE therefore require that

$$\left.\begin{aligned} y_a + z_{aa} = y_a + z_{ba} = w_1 + w_2 \\ y_b + z_{ab} = y_b + z_{bb} = w_1 + w_2 \end{aligned}\right\} \tag{10}$$

That is, in equilibrium, the action of the old agent at a is independent of the state when he was young. A SREE is therefore characterized by four equations and four unknowns. Generation 0 can be ignored by letting $z(a) = z_{aa}$ and $m = z_{aa} - w_2$. The technical advantage of examining SREE is now obvious; instead of having to solve a problem with an infinite number of equations and unknowns, I can simply examine a finite number of market-clearing equations and a finite number of prices.

Now, a stationary deterministic equilibrium, or steady state, is a deterministic equilibrium where the consumption problem of every agent is identical. Hence $(y_t, z_t) = (y, z)$. The price sequence, $\{P_t\}$, is given by $p_t = \beta^{t-1}$, for some number, $\beta > 0$. If $m \neq 0$ then $\beta = 1$, while if $m = 0$, $\beta = v'(w_2)/u'(w_1)$ and $(y, z) = (w_1, w_2)$. Assuming that $u'(w_1) \neq v'(w_2)$, there are two steady states in the one-good case, one yielding autarky and the other associated with $\beta = 1$. (See Chapter 16 above, by Kehoe, for a more detailed discussion.) Clearly, both of these steady states can be transformed into a SREE for both the money and the contingent markets worlds. A stationary sunspot equilibrium (SSE) is therefore defined to be a SREE that is not a transformed steady state. If $m = 0$, it can be shown, for both the money and the contingent markets worlds, that the autarky steady state is the only SREE. Hence a SSE with $m = 0$ does not exist. Of course, if there is more than one good this result need not hold. If $m \neq 0$, a SREE in the money world must have the property that $\beta_{aa} = \beta_{bb} = 1$ and $\beta_{ba} = \beta_{ab}^{-1}$. The budget constraints then imply that $y_a + z_{aa} = y_b + z_{bb} = w_1 + w_2$. Further, if, say, $y_a + z_{ba} = w_1 + w_2$, the two remaining budget constraints imply that $y_b + z_{ab} = w_1 + w_2$. Hence, in the one-good case, if $m \neq 0$, a SREE in the money world is characterized by one equation and one unknown (see Spear 1984). From Proposition 1 it therefore follows that a SSE in the contingent markets world is a SREE with $m \neq 0$ and at least one of the four contingent prices does not equal the associated probability (e.g. $\beta_{11} \neq \pi_{11}$). Similarly, a SSE in the money world is a SREE with $m \neq 0$ and $\beta_{ab} \neq 1$. I am now in a position to construct a simple example of a SSE.

Suppose the utility function of every agent has the form $U(y, z) = \log(y) + \log(z)$. Further, suppose the endowments of every agent are $(w_1, w_2) = (1, 4)$ and the (objective) conditional probabilities are $\pi_{aa} = \pi_{bb} = 7/8$. In the money world, if $\beta_{aa} = \beta_{bb} = 1$ and $\beta_{ab} = \beta_{ba}^{-1} = 12.263$ (approximately), it is easy to check that the expected utility maximizing actions are $(y_a, z_{aa}, z_{ab}) = (2.66, 2.34, 3.87)$ and $(y_b, z_{ba}, z_{bb}) = (1.33, 2.34, 3.87)$. Clearly, this is a SSE in the money world. For the contingent markets world let the prices be (approximately) $\beta_{aa} = 0.993$, $\beta_{ab} = 0.086$, $\beta_{ba} = 0.061$ and $\beta_{bb} = 0.257$. The optimal actions of agents, at these prices, are the same as in the money world. Hence the SSE in the money world has been transformed into a SSE in the contingent markets world.

Now consider another example with the same utility function and probabilities but let $(w_1, w_2) = (4, 1)$. For the world of contingent markets suppose prices are (approximately) $\beta_{aa} = 3.972$, $\beta_{ab} = 0.223$, $\beta_{ba} = 0.374$ and $\beta_{bb} = 1.028$. The optimizing actions are $(y_a, z_{aa}, z_{ab}) = (4.10, 0.90, 2.30)$ and $(y_b, z_{ba}, z_{bb}) = (2.70, 0.90, 2.30)$. Hence I have constructed a SSE in the contingent markets world. Further, this equilibrium cannot be transformed into a SSE in the money world. To see this, remember that for a REE in the money world the money stock is constant over time and so $p(r_t)[y(r_t) - w_1] = m$, $\forall\, r_t(t \geq 1, a_1 = a)$. As there is assumed to be only one physical good, a SSE in the money world has the property that $y_a > w_1$ if, and only if, $y_b > w_1$. In the SSE constructed above, $y_a > w_1$ while $y_b < w_1$. Hence it cannot be transformed into a SSE in the money world. In fact, for this particular utility function, if $w_1 > w_2$—and so the money stock, associated with the nominal (non-autarky) steady state, is positive—a SSE in the money world does not exist. In the contingent markets world, however, if $\pi_{aa} + \pi_{bb}$ is 'close enough' to 2, a SSE will exist. Further, if $w_1 < w_2$—and so the money stock, associated with the nominal steady state, is negative—the result for the contingent markets world still holds and every SSE in the contingent markets world can be transformed into a SSE in the money world. Hence there would appear to be, from this example anyway, a strong link between the indeterminacy of the nominal steady state and the existence of a SSE in the money world (see Gale 1973; Kehoe, Chapter 16 above, and Woodford 1984).

6. Stationary Sunspot Equilibria in the Money World

In this section I shall focus solely upon the money world. The justification for this is twofold: first, the literature on sunspots has concentrated almost entirely upon SSE in the money world, and, second, I do not have the mathematical skills to consider the existence of a sunspot equilibrium in the contingent markets or Arrow–Debreu worlds.

I now wish to remove the assumption of an intertemporally separate utility function but maintain all the other assumptions listed earlier. Consider the steady state associated with $\beta = 1$. Let m^* be the money stock at this state, (y^*, z^*) the consumption stream, and $U_1, U_2, U_{11}, U_{12}, U_{22}$, the first- and second-order derivatives of utility at this consumption level.

PROPOSITION 4. If $m^* < 0$ ($m^* > 0$), then every SSE in the money world yields $m < 0$ ($m > 0$), no matter what the values of the probabilities, π_{aa}, and π_{bb}, are.

Proof. As β_{ab} tends to zero, $y_a < w_1$, and as β_{ab} tends to infinity, $y_b < w_1$ (although in the limit it may be that y_a tends to w_1 and/or y_b tends to w_1). Further, there is, at most, one value of β_{ab} (for $\beta_{ab} \in (0; \infty)$) at which $y_a = w_1$ and, at most, one value of β_{ab} at which $y_b = w_1$. Therefore, if $y_a < w_1$ when $\beta_{ab} = 1$, $y_a < w_1$, $\forall \, 0 < \beta_{ab} < 1$. If $y_a > w_1$ when $\beta_{ab} = 1$, $y_a > w_1$, $\forall \, \beta_{ab} > 1$. Similarly, if $y_b < w_1$ when $\beta_{ab} = 1$, $y_b < w_1$, $\forall \, \beta_{ab} > 1$. If $y_b > w_1$ when $\beta_{ab} = 1$, $y_b > w_1$, $\forall \, 0 < \beta_{ab} < 1$.

Now, if $m^* < 0$, then $y_a = y_b > w_1$ when $\beta_{ab} = 1$, so $y_a > w_1$, $\forall \, \beta_{ab} > 1$ and $y_b > w_1$, $\forall \, 0 < \beta_{ab} < 1$. Hence every SSE yields $m < 0$. Similarly, if $m^* > 0$ then $y_a = y_b < w_1$ when $\beta_{ab} = 1$, so $y_a < w_1$, $\forall \, 0 < \beta_{ab} < 1$ and $y_b < w_1$, $\forall \, \beta_{ab} > 1$. Hence every SSE yields $m > 0$. Q.E.D

PROPOSITION 5. (i) If $m^* < 0$, there exists $\alpha \in [0; 2)$, such that if $\pi_{aa} + \pi_{bb} > \alpha$, a SSE in the money world exists (with a negative money stock).

(ii) If $m^* > 2U_2(U_{11} - U_{22})^{-1} > 0$, there exists $\alpha \in (0; 2]$, such that, if $\pi_{aa} + \pi_{bb} < \alpha$, a SSE in the money world exists (with a positive money stock).

Proof. The proposition follows immediately from the sufficient conditions for a SSE in the money world derived by Spear (1984: 366). Q.E.D

Given the strong relationship between $m^* < 0$ and the existence of a SSE, it seems surprising that almost every article on sunspots has assumed a positive money stock. Azariadis (1981) assumes a separable utility function, which is then relaxed to allow non-separable functions in Azariadis and Guesnerie (1986). The sufficient conditions for a SSE in both articles can be derived from Proposition (5)(ii). The justification for focusing solely upon a positive money stock comes from the assumptions they make about endowments and consumption. In their models (Azariadis 1981; Azariadis and Guesnerie 1986), agents are endowed with, and consume, leisure only when young. Leisure not consumed is thought of as labour used to produce the physical commodity. As the young cannot consume the commodity, they sell it to the old. Hence the young spend nothing and sell the product of their labour. The money stock must therefore be non-negative.

By focusing upon this very special model, Azariadis and Guesnerie (1986) are able to establish that a SSE in the money world exists if, and only if, a 2-cycle exists. A 2-cycle can be thought of as a SSE associated with $\pi_{aa} = \pi_{bb} = 0$. Even for the one-good world, however, if $m^* < 0$ it is possible for a SSE to exist without a 2-cycle also existing. For example, with the log-linear utility function discussed earlier a 2-cycle will never exist, although a SSE in the money world exists if $m^* < 0$. Guesnerie (1986) extends the model of Azariadis and Guesnerie to a world with one agent (with an intertemporally separable utility function) and n commodities. He establishes a sufficient condition for both a SSE in the money world and a 2-cycle to exist. Grandmont (1986) extends the model of Azariadis to include k states and then investigates the existence of SSE near 2-cycles. It seems unlikely, however, that any of these results will hold in more general models.

Spear (1985) investigates the more general case of n goods and non-separable utility functions. He shows that, in general, a SSE in the money world will not exist. The intuition behind this result is very simple. With n goods and two states of nature, a SSE has $4n$ markets that must be cleared (n for each pair, (s_i, s_j), where s_i, $s_j \in \{a, b\}$). The budget constraints then reduce this to $4n - 3$ independent equations. There are, however, only $2n$ prices (n for each state). Normalization then reduces this to $2n - 1$ unknowns. If $n > 1$, there are simply too many equations. Put another way, in a SSE, the total consumption of the old agents at state $a(b)$ must be independent of the state they are young in. This requirement yields $2n - 2$ extra equations. To put it crudely, it is this condition that generates the excess of equations.

Now, it might be argued that this non-existence result makes the concept of extrinsic uncertainty useless for models with more than one good or one agent with separable utility. However, it is my belief that this result merely makes the particular definition of stationarity useless. For, as I indicated above, it is the stationarity requirement that generates too many equations. By either abandoning stationarity altogether or redefining it in some other way, it is possible to construct models with n goods in which a sunspot equilibrium exists. Woodford (1986) takes the second approach and redefines stationarity using histories of infinite length. (Time goes back to $-\infty$.) He then shows that a SSE in the money world exists, near a transformed deterministic steady state, if and only if there exists a continuum of (deterministic) non-stationary perfect foresight equilibria converging to that particular steady state. Clearly, this result can be seen as a verification of his (1984) conjecture that there is a strong link between the existence of sunspot equilibria and the indeterminacy of a steady state. Hence the existence of a sunspot equilibrium can be established in the general case of n goods and h agents.

7. Concluding Remarks

For the one-good case, stationary sunspot equilibria in the money world have been thoroughly analysed. Almost no attention, however, has been paid to other market structures or to non-stationary sunspot equilibria. For the n-good case, only the seeds of understanding exist. Hopefully, with time, the seeds will flower, yielding a deeper comprehension of the role of expectations in general stochastic models. In particular, I hope that it will be possible to construct models with both intrinsic and extrinsic uncertainty. This would then make any model of uncertainty open-ended. The set of relevant states of nature would be what society decides is relevant. Such models, I believe, could take general equilibrium theory very close to Keynes's world of beauty contests and bootstraps.

18

An Introduction to Nonlinear Dynamics and its Application to Economics

DAVID KELSEY

1. Introduction

Economics and weather forecasting have a lot in common. When people are not talking about the weather they talk about the economy. Both weather forecasters and economic forecasters have a bad name with the public. The similarities go further. Both are trying to predict the outcomes of very large systems, the components of which mutually interact in complex ways. The output of both systems has a seemingly random appearance, even though there are certain other regularities (for example, weather is hotter in summer than winter; also, there is higher employment).

In recent years some mathematics known popularly as the 'theory of chaos' has been studied. This deals with systems of equations that are able to produce motions so complex that they appear completely random. It is thought that chaos might be applied within both fluid mechanics (which is the body of theoretical knowledge on which weather forecasting depends) and economic theory.

Anyone who has watched the flow of liquid will realize how complex fluid motion can be. Suppose that water is flowing down a straight channel with smooth sides. The motion will break into a series of swirls which have a somewhat random appearance. Despite the fact that the initial conditions are symmetric in both space and time, the flow will be symmetric in neither. Such fluid flows are described as being *turbulent*. Turbulence is caused by viscosity or friction within the fluid. Viscosity introduces nonlinear terms into the equations of motion which allow complex turbulent solutions to be possible. Because of the random character of turbulent motion, it has been suggested that the mathematics of chaos can be applied in this area. Similar arguments suggest that it

This is a revised version of a paper that appeared in *Oxford Economic Papers*, March 1988. Financial support from the ESRC post-doctoral fellowship is gratefully acknowledged. I would like to thank Colin Sparrow, whose excellent lectures greatly encouraged an interest in this subject, and Jim Crutchfield and the North-Holland Publishing Co. for permission to reproduce Figures 18.5 and 18.6. I am also grateful for comments from Margaret Bray, David Canning, Partha Dasgupta, Jairong Fu, Tim Kehoe, Joy Read, Peter Read, Gene Savin, the referees and editor of *Oxford Economic Papers*.

could be of use to economists. This chapter aims to give an introduction to the applications of chaos in economics.

The models in this chapter are very simple. The reason for this is that a detailed mathematical theory has been constructed only for one-dimensional dynamical systems. (That is, there is only one dependent variable and the system of equations is of the first order in that variable.) In higher dimensions there is no general theory. There have been theories developed of particular equations; two commonly studied examples are the Lorenz equations (Sparrow 1982, Guckenheimer and Holmes 1983) and the Henon map (see Henon 1976). Higher-dimension systems have also been studied by means of computer simulations. These systems can display all the kinds of behaviour discussed in this paper and other forms of complex behaviour as well. These systems studied to date have been motivated largely by applications of dynamic systems theory in the physical sciences.

Thus, economic models involving chaos are not always particularly realistic. The reason is that, as explained above, our research is as yet in its early stages. The simple models studied here are interesting for the following reasons. Most important is that they tell us the ways in which an economic system is capable of behaving. Before this literature, it was largely assumed that, in the long run, an economy would be in a stationary state (or balanced growth). Cycles were considered, but were underemphasized, given the considerable amount of empirical evidence to support the view that the economy is cyclic. Aperiodic motion was not widely considered. Economic data is clearly aperiodic. This, however, was put down to the superposition of random shocks on to an essentially stationary economic system. Nonlinearities in economic systems cannot be denied; little attention, however, was paid to them. (A notable exception, however; can be found in Samuelson 1947: 336–40.) Here I give an account of some aspects of the behaviour of nonlinear systems.

2. Some Results from Nonlinear Dynamics

2.1. Linear and nonlinear difference equations

The simplest difference equation is linear and first-order:

$$x_{t+1} = ax_t \tag{1}$$

to which the solution is $x_t = x_0 a^t$. This grows exponentially if $|a| > 1$. When $0 \leq a < 1$, the solution decays exponentially towards zero in a monotonic fashion. Finally, if $-1 < a \leq 0$, the solution exponentially decays towards zero in an oscillatory manner. If $|a| < 1$, the system converges to a stationary state. In the case where $a = -1$ there is a 2-cycle; i.e. for all t, $x_t = x_{t+2} \neq x_{t+1}$. Thus the only cyclic solution of (1) is a cycle of period 2, and this occurs only for a single value of the parameter a.

If on the other hand we consider difference equations, which are still first-order but are nonlinear, then the behaviour we find is very different. Equation (2), like (1), is a first-order difference equation:

$$x_{t+1} = f_r(x_t) \tag{2}$$

where $f_r(x) = rx(1-x)$, $0 \le r \le 4$. Equation (2) is often known as the *logistic* equation. While (2) is also of the first order, it is quadratic, and hence nonlinear. Quadratic behaviour is the most simple kind of nonlinearity. Hence one might expect (2) to behave in a fairly simple manner as (1) does. In fact, as we shall see, the solution to (2) can be extremely complex. As shown in Figure 18.1 f_r has the following properties: $f_r(0) = f_r(1) = 0$. f_r has a unique maximum at $x = \frac{1}{2}$.

A *stationarity solution* of equation (2) is a sequence $\{x_t\}$ which is a solution of (2) and is such that $\forall t$, $x_t = \bar{x}$ for some $\bar{x}$ such that $0 \le \bar{x} \le 1$. Graphically, a stationary solution occurs at a point where the graph of f_r crosses the 45° line (e.g. at y_r in Figure 18.2). It is easily seen that 0 is a stationarity solution for all values of r.

Figure 18.1 can also be used to illustrate the dynamics of the system. Suppose we start at x_0. The height of $f(x_0) = x_1$ gives the second state of the system. We can find the point corresponding to x_1 on the horizontal axis by reflecting in the 45° line. A similar process of going up to the function and reflecting in the 45° line gives the next state of the system x_2. Further points in the evolution of the system can be found in a similar

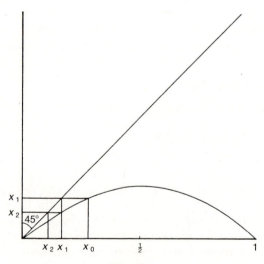

Fig. 18.1

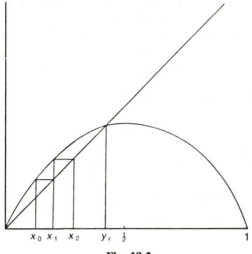

Fig. 18.2

manner. The successive points in the solution path x_0, x_1, x_2, ... are getting closer and closer to the origin. This will happen for any starting point. In Figure 18.1 the unique stationary state at the origin is (globally) stable.

Now imagine that we are gradually increasing the parameter r, and we wish to observe how this affects the properties of the solution. The function f_r has a single hump. As r is increased, the height of this hump increases. When r is greater than 1, the diagram will look like Figure 18.2. The graph of f_r crosses the 45° line at two points: the origin, and $y_r = (r-1)/r$. In fact, for $1 \leqslant r \leqslant 4$, these are the only two stationary solutions of the equation. A change in the dynamics of the system has occurred. Starting from a typical point x_0, subsequent values of x no longer tend to the origin but instead converge on the stationary point at y_r. For $1 \leqslant r \leqslant 3$ the origin is unstable and y_r is stable. Indeed, it can be shown that, from almost every initial value, the path will converge to $(r-1)/r$. The exceptions are the origin, which is also a stationary point, and 1, which is mapped to the stationary point at the origin ($f_r(1) = 0$).

Thus, if $0 \leqslant r \leqslant 3$, the solutions of (2) are not unlike the solutions of a linear difference equation. There is a stationary state to which the system converges from almost all initial values.

2.2. Existence of cycles

A major area of research in economic theory has been to explain economic phenomenon that appear cyclic, particularly business cycles. One reason why economists are interested in nonlinear dynamics is that cyclic solutions are very common. It is thought that this might be useful in theories that try to explain business cycles.

A k-cycle is a set of k distinct points, $x_1, x_2, \ldots, x_k$, such that, for all i, $1 \le i < k - 1$, $f_r(x_i) = x_{i+1}$ and $f_r(x_k) = x_1$. For $r > 3$ there are cyclic solutions to the logistic equation (2). Unlike the linear difference equation (1), there can be cycles of many different periods.

Sarkovskii's Theorem is very informative about the structure of cyclic solutions to nonlinear difference equations. It is a very fascinating result, describing under what circumstances we can get cycles of different periods coexisting.

We define Sarkovskii's ordering $<$ of the positive integers as follows:

$$1 < 2 < 4 \cdots < 2^k < 2^{k+1} <$$
$$\cdots < 2^{k+1}(2m + 1) < 2^{k+1}(2m - 1) < \cdots < 2^{k+1} \times 5 < 2^{k+1} \times 3 <$$
$$\cdots < 2^k(2m + 1) < 2^k(2m - 1) < \cdots < 2^k \times 5 < 2^k \times 3 <$$
$$\cdots < 2(2m + 1) < 2(2m - 1) < \cdots < 2 \times 5 < 2 \times 3 <$$
$$\cdots < (2m + 1) < (2m - 1) < \cdots < 5 < 3.$$

That is, greatest are the odd numbers greater than 3, then the powers of 2 times these odd integers, . . . , and then the powers of 2 backwards.

SARKOVSKII'S THEOREM. If f is a continuous map of an interval into itself with a p-cycle and $q < p$ in Sarkovskii's ordering, then f has a q-cycle.

It is clear from this that first-order nonlinear difference equations can admit a much richer kind of cyclic solution than the corresponding linear difference equations. Consider the mth-order linear difference equation

$$a_m x_{t+m} + a_{m-1} x_{t+m-1} + \cdots + a_1 x_t = f(t). \tag{3}$$

This is not essentially more complicated to solve than (1). The only new difficulties that arise are that it is possible to have multiple or complex roots.[1] Complex roots can give rise to cyclic solutions. But even (2) has a less complex structure than the nonlinear equation. With the mth-order linear equation it is only possible to have a finite number of cyclic solutions. It can be seen from Sarkovskii's Theorem that in the nonlinear case it is possible to get an infinite number of cycles of different periods even with a first-order difference equation. Indeed, this will be true provided that there is a cycle of odd period.

2.3. Stability of cycles

By Sarkovskii's Theorem, there is a large number of cyclic solutions to the logistic equation. Thus, the set of cycles appears very complex. In practice, solutions that are not stable will not be observed. Fortunately,

---

[1] The theory of such equations is explained in many places. A good reference for economists is Sargent (1979).

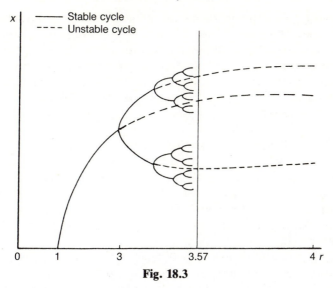

Fig. 18.3

the set of stable cycles is much simpler. Provided that an appropriate convexity condition is satisfied,[2] there will be at most one stable cycle, and trajectories from a typical starting position will converge to a stable cycle if it exists. Thus, for parameter values where a stable cycle exists, in the long run the cycle is all that will be observed. This does not, however, imply that a stable cycle will exist.

Consider the logistic equation (2). While, for any given value of the parameter, r, there is at most one stable cycle, the cycle that is stable changes as r increases. For $0 \leqslant r \leqslant 1$, the stationary solution at the origin is stable. (A stationary solution is a cycle of period 1.) If $1 \leqslant r \leqslant 3$, the stationary solution $y_r = (r - 1)/r$ is stable. By setting $x_t = (r - 1)/r$ in equation (3), one can see that, for all r, $1 \leqslant r \leqslant 4$, y_r is a fixed point of f_r. At $r = 3$, however, the system undergoes a bifurcation. That is, there is a change in the structure of the set of solutions. After $r = 3$, y_r is no longer stable. There is however a 2-cycle which is stable. In this region for an arbitrary starting value the system will eventually settle down into a cycle of period 2.

Figure 18.3 shows a highly simplified account of how the structure of the set of stable solutions to (2) changes as the parameter r varies. At a somewhat higher value of r, there occurs essentially a repeat of what happened at $r = 3$. The 2-cycle becomes unstable, and a stable 4-cycle appears. This process is known as a period-doubling bifurcation. The

[2] What is required here is that f_r have a negative Schwartzian derivative if differentiable, or that f_r should satisfy the cross-ratio property if not differentiable. See Preston (1983) for details. This result was originally proved in Singer (1978).

system now goes through an infinite number of such period-doublings. Stable cycles of length 8, 16, 32, ..., 2^n, ... successively appear and become unstable. This all occurs before a limit point r_∞, which is approximately equal to 3.57. In fact, all of the cycles in this sequence would look to a casual observer like noisy 2-cycles. At r_∞ the system behaves in a very complex manner which is different to that at neighbouring parameter values. Since r_∞ is a single point in the parameter space, I think that such behaviour is unlikely to arise in an economic model. Hence I shall not discuss it further.

The order in which cycles appear bears a close relation to Sarkovskii's ordering of the natural numbers. Thus, Sarkovskii's ordering starts $1 < 2 < 4 \cdots < 2^k <$. First we get a fixed point, then an orbit of period 2, followed by an orbit of period 4. The cycles whose periods are powers of 2 appear first. In particular, if there is a cycle of period 3, there are cycles of all other periods.

Since all the cycles before r_∞ had been obtained from period-doubling bifurcations, they all had periods that were powers of 2 (i.e., for some n the period was equal to 2^n). In fact, between $r = 3$ and $r = 4$ stable cycles of all periods can be seen. The behaviour of the cycle of period 3 is fairly typical.

Below the r-values for which a stable 3-cycle can be observed, the system is chaotic. (See Section 2.4 for a description of chaos.) As r approaches the value at which a 3-cycle appears, a phenomenon known as *intermittent chaos* occurs. In this, the system essentially alternates between following an approximate 3-cycle and chaotic behaviour. It has been suggested that intermittent chaos may be important during the onset of turbulent motion in fluids. Then, as r is increased, a stable 3-cycle appears. Like our fixed point, the 3-cycle undergoes a chain of period-doubling bifurcations. It is successively replaced by stable cycles of period 6, 12, 24, ..., $2^n \times 3$, ... These bifurcations accumulate at a limit point where the behaviour is similar to that at r_∞ (the limit point of the period-doubling sequence following the 2-cycle). After the limit point, the system returns to chaotic behavior. The set of r values from the beginning of the 3-cycle to the limit point of the sequence of bifurcations is known as a *period-doubling window*.

Between $r = 3$ and $r = 4$, there are, in theory, period-doubling windows contianing cycles of all possible lengths. Clearly, most of these period-doubling windows occupy a very small interval in the parameter space. In numerical simulations, the only period-doubling windows that can be seen are those starting with cycles of relatively short periods such as 3, 5, or 7.

Let y_r be the fixed point (stationary equilibrium) of f_r. A necessary and sufficient condition for y_r to be stable is that the absolute value of the derivative of f_r at y_r be less than 1; i.e., $|df_r/dx_0| < 1$. This means that, in a neighbourhood of y_r, the map f_r contracts lengths.

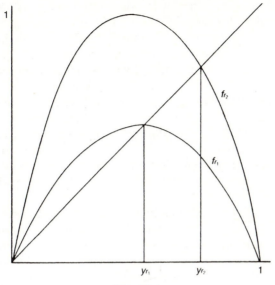

Fig. 18.4

As the value of r increases, the hump of f_r becomes higher. This has the effect of progressively moving the fixed point y_r down the hump into regions where the slope is greater. Thus the fixed point becomes unstable. This is illustrated in Figure 18.4. (In the figure, $r_2 > r_1$.) Similar considerations apply to cycles. If $x_1, x_2, \ldots, x_k$ is a k-cycle, then x_i is a fixed point of f_r^k for $1 \leqslant i \leqslant k$. Here f_r^k denotes f_r iterated with itself k times, e.g., $f_r^2(x) = f_r[f_r(x)]$.) A k-cycle is stable if the absolute value of the derivative of f^k is less than one at a point on the cycle. By the chain rule,

$$\frac{df_r^k}{dx}(x_1) = \frac{df_r}{dx}(x_1)\frac{df_r}{dx}(x_2)\frac{df_r}{dx}(x_3)\cdots\frac{df_r}{dx}(x_k). \tag{4}$$

Hence the absolute value of the derivative is the same at any point on the cycle. Thus our definition of stability does not depend on which point on the cycle we consider. At the maximum x^* of f_r the value of the derivative is zero. Thus the product in (4) is zero. We have an established the simple proposition that any cycle that contains the maximum of f_r will be stable. In fact, as r increases for any cycle, there is an r-value for which x^* will be on that cycle. Hence the cycle will be stable for some r-value. Further, by continuity, the cycle will be stable on a neighbourhood of that r-value. Thus, for any k, there is an interval of r-values for which the system has a stable k-cycle.

2.4. Chaos

Consider the logistic equation (2) when $r = 4$. In this case an analytic solution can be found. Substitute $x_0 = \frac{1}{2}[1 - \cos(u)]$ (where as before x_0 is the initial value of x). Then with some simple algebra, and using the addition formulae for trigonometric functions, one can find that the solution is: $x_t = \frac{1}{2}[1 - \cos(2^t u)]$. It can be seen that the solution is periodic if $u/2\pi$ is rational. Further, by choosing u appropriately, a cycle of any desired length can be found. If $u/2\pi$ is irrational, then the solution is aperiodic.

In addition, the motion has a property known as *sensitive dependence on initial conditions*. Suppose $x_0 = \frac{1}{2}[1 - \cos(u)]$ and $y_0 = \frac{1}{2}[1 - \cos(u + \varepsilon)]$; then the solutions of (2) starting from initial values x_0 and y_0 are $x_t = \frac{1}{2}[1 - \cos(2^t u)]$ and $y_t = \frac{1}{2}[1 - \cos(2^t u + 2^t \varepsilon)]$, respectively. The term $2^t \varepsilon$ becomes large very rapidly indeed. Thus, no matter how small ε is, x_t and y_t will diverge rapidly. (But the time take to diverge will in general depend on ε.)

Although the difference equation (2) is completely deterministic, the behaviour of the system appears random. Practical attempts to observe the system will involve errors in initial measurement and rounding errors in computation. Because of sensitive dependence on initial conditions, these errors will be important and will introduce significant and unpredictable errors into the forecasts made by the system. It is this kind of behaviour that has been called *chaotic*. The term 'chaos' may be misleading, since there is much that can be said about the structure of such a system. Indeed, in this case we have an explicit analytic formula for the solution.

We have given the behaviour for $r = 4$. Between r_∞ and $r = 4$ many complicated changes occur in the system. For a set of values of r having positive measure, this system behaves chaotically.[3] (Somewhat similar to what happens at $r = 4$.) For other values of r cycles can be observed. The set of parameter values that gives rise to cycles also has positive measure.

So far I have analysed the solutions to the dynamic systems generated by a particular family of functions $= \{f_r\}$. One of the more surprising conclusions produced by mathematical theory is that similar results can be obtained for a wide class of families of functions. If a family $\{g_r\}$ of functions is single-peaked, satisfies a convexity condition,[4] and is increasing in r, then our results will go through. In other words, our conclusion is largely independent of the particular family of functions $\{f_r\}$. The reason for this appears to be that, after sufficiently many iterations, the

---

[3] This is proved in Jakobson (1981). Further, it appears that the set of parameter values for which there is sensitive dependence on initial conditions has quite a complex structure; in particular, it contains no intervals. For details see Collet and Eckman (1980: p. 31).

These qualifications might suggest that parameter values for which complex behaviour occurs are quite rare. This impression may be false, since (1) cycles of very long periods are empirically difficult to distinguish from aperiodic motion; (2) in the presence of noise, which is almost inevitable in an economic system, the range of parameter values that give rise to chaos is considerably enlarged.

[4] Technically, the functions g_r should have negative Schwartzian derivative (see also fn. 2).

behaviour of the system depends only on the local properties of f, near its maximum value.

I shall not give a precise definition of 'chaos' here. It is not possible to define it without using a large number of technical terms. Second, there is a number of different definitions of chaos in use (positive topological entropy, positive Liapunov exponents, existence of a strange attractor, etc.). Informally, chaos occurs when, for a typical initial value, there is both sensitive dependence on initial conditions and aperiodic motion. Note that it is possible to have aperiodic motion without sensitive dependence on initial conditions, and sensitive dependence on initial conditions without aperiodic motion. (An example of the latter is given in the conclusion.) Sensitive dependence on initial conditions is the more problematic, since it implies that the system is essentially impossible to predict.

In practice, the difference between aperiodic motion and a cycle of very large period (e.g., 10^{100}) is very small. Both of these may be seen as chaotic by agents in the economy.

In some ways, the behaviour of differential equations is unlike that of difference equations. In this section I have shown that the solution of a one-dimensional difference equation with fairly simple nonlinearities could be extremely complex. This is not true for one-dimensional systems of differential equations, or even for two-dimensional systems. In these cases chaos cannot arise because of the Poincare–Bendixson Theorem (see Hirsch and Smale 1974), which says that any limit of a two-dimensional system of differential equations is either a fixed point or a cycle. In three dimensions this is no longer true. The Lorenz equations are an example of a chaotic three-dimensional system of differential equations.

I think it is clear that this theory has a potential for explaining economic phenomena. Two of the most striking feature of any macro-economic data are their random-like appearance and their seemingly cyclical character. Cycles in economic data have often been noticed, from short-run business cycles to fifty-year Kondratiev waves. There have been many attempts to explain them, including Lucas (1975), who argues that random shocks combined with various lags can give rise to phenomena that have the appearance of cycles, and Samuelson (1939), who uses the familiar multiplier–accelerator model. Despite these and other pieces of research, we are still under the impression that something further could be said about business cycles. Dynamic models of the sort we have been examining here are able to generate cyclic behaviour; therefore there is a good case that they will be able to help us understand business cycles.

2.5. Random disturbances

One interesting question raised by this research is whether there are any truly random events. In the previous section we saw how it was possible for a system which is in fact deterministic to behave in a way that appears random. It could be the case that there are no random events. All of the apparently random phenomena we observe in the universe could be the products of very complex but non-random systems. This is an accurate description of so-called 'random number generators'. In economics, however, it seems inevitable that we will have random terms in our equations. If for no other reason, this will be because economic activity is affected by biological and meteorological phenomena. These systems will almost certainly be chaotic in nature. As far as economics is concerned, they will appear as random terms in our equations. Further, when we are modelling only part of the economy, we have to include random terms to represent chaotic processes in other sectors of the economy.

Having noticed that random terms are inevitable in purely economic systems of equations, we proceed to examine the consequence of such random influences. Suppose that we add a random error term to the logistic equation (2). There are two ways in which we could do this. We could consider an additive error term of the form

$$x_{t+1} = f_r(x_t) + \varepsilon_t = rx_t(1 - x_t) + \varepsilon_t. \tag{5}$$

Alternatively, we could consider the case where the parameter r is itself subject to random perturbations:

$$x_{t+1} = f_{r+\eta_t}(x_t) = (r + \eta_t)x_t(1 - x_t). \tag{6}$$

Here ε_t and η_t are random variables with mean 0. Perhaps surprisingly, it has been found that the systems (5) and (6) behave in similar ways. In fact, Crutchfield, Farmer, and Huberman (1982) explain that there is an equivalence between the two systems. Further, the behaviour of the systems changes little with changes in the distributions of the error terms ε_t and η_t. In all cases, the system behaves at r as a mixture of the behaviour of the deterministic system at neighbouring r values.

This sort of system is studied in Crutchfield, Farmer, and Huberman (1982). As one would expect when (5) is following a stable cycle, it will be perturbed from that cycle by the noise term. Thus, this cyclic orbit will consist of broad bands rather than points. Chaotic behaviour becomes more common. Since the system follows a mixture of the behaviour at adjacent parameter values, many cyclic orbits disappear as they are averaged with chaotic attractors. For instance, if the noise is sufficiently large, the system will have a stable fixed point, then a 2-cycle, then a 4-cycle, and then will pass directly to chaos. Thus, the full period-doubling sequence no longer occurs. As an added complication, there are no longer clear points of bifurcation. These points have become somewhat blurred.

This agrees with what has been observed in experiments on fluid motion. In these, only a finite number of period-doubling bifurcations are

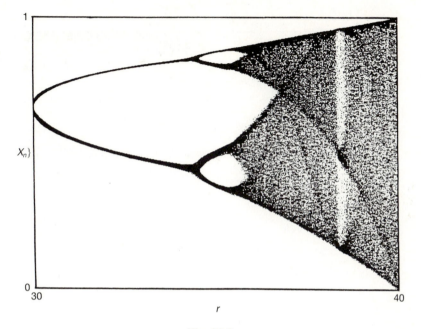

Fig. 18.5

seen before turbulent flow commences. This number is usually low, typically less than 6. (See Citanovic 1984a for further details.) Figure 18.5 shows the results of a computer simulation of this system.[5]

Compared with the system with no random errors, chaos will appear in equation (5) at a lower value of the parameter r. This follows from the fact that in the noisy system the behaviour is essentially a mixture of the behaviour at neighbouring parameter values. As the noise level is increased, this averaging occurs over a wider range of parameters. Hence successively lower r's get averaged with chaotic orbits.

Within the chaotic region, the presence of random errors eliminates most of the periodic windows. In numerical experiments only the period 3 orbit is visible. A curious fact is that the influence of noise on the period 3 orbit is different to its effect on the period 4 orbit. In the deterministic case, the probability density for the period 4 orbit consists of four-point masses. In the presence of random errors, these broaden into four bands with essentially zero density between them. In the case of the period 3 orbit, as well as the three points thickening into bands, a broad background fills in between the peaks. As noise increases, this

[5] I would like to thank Jim Crutchfield and the North Holland Publishing Company for permission to reproduce Figures 18.5 and 18.6, which previously appeared in Crutchfield, Farmer, and Huberman (1982).

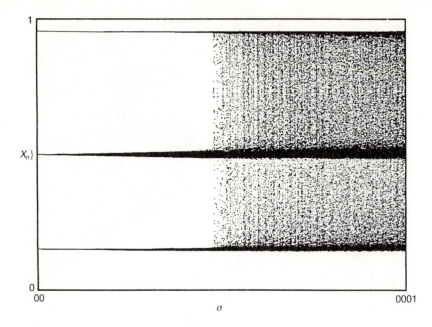

Fig. 18.6

background increases until the peaks are washed out. This arises because the period 3 cycle is much closer to a chaotic orbit than the period 4 cycle. Figure 18.6 shows the effect on the period 3 orbit of raising the level of noise.

Chaotic behaviour is less sensitive to noise than periodic orbits. Many of the periodic orbits with shorter ranges of stability will not be visible. Indeed, it seems that only a finite number of periodic orbits will be visible at any given noise level. Hence an infinite number of orbits are lost. In contrast, chaotic behaviour, if anything, becomes more common as the noise level is raised. Because of this relatively greater sensitivity of cycles to random disturbances, a case can be made for paying more attention to chaotic solutions than to cyclic solutions.

3. Chaos in Economic Theory

3.1. *The overlapping generations model*

Conditions under which chaos can arise in the overlapping generations model have been investigated by Benhabib and Day (1982) and by Grandmont (1985). In this section I will consider a simplified version of Grandmont's model. I present this principally as an example of how an economic system can behave chaotically. We shall then consider some other uses of dynamical systems theory in economics.

Consider an overlapping generations model where each generation lives for two periods. We shall look at a pure distribution economy with one consumption good and a fiat money. We need only consider a representative member of each generation. The representative consumer is assumed to have an additively separable utility function.

$$u(c_1, c_2) = v_1(c_1) + v_2(c_2).$$

Although most of our results are true for more general v-functions, we shall postulate specific forms for v_1 and v_2:

$$v_1(c_1) = \ln(c_1) \qquad v_2(c_2) = \frac{c_2^{1-\alpha}}{1-\alpha}$$

where c_1 and c_2 denote consumption in the first and second periods of life, respectively, and α is a parameter. The consumer is assumed to have positive endowments e_1, e_2 of the consumption good in the two periods. He maximizes utility subject to the budget constraints

$$\left. \begin{array}{c} p_1c_1 + m_1 = p_1e_1 \\ p_2c_2 = m_1 + p_2e_2 \end{array} \right\} \tag{7}$$

where m_1 is the money balance the consumers hold from the first period to the second. The consumption good cannot be stored. Thus, the only way the consumer can transfer consumption from one date to another is by holding money. It is still possible that consumers will choose not to trade or hold money, simply consuming their own endowments in each period. This possibility is usually referred to as an *autarkic equilibrium*. We assume that this does not occur. In all the equilibria we consider, the consumers hold positive money balances. (Technically, this can be ensured by choosing the endowments appropriately.)

Examining the constraints (7), we see that the consumer's consumption in the two periods only depends upon $\theta = p_1/p_2$. That is, demand is homogeneous of degree 0 in prices. Note that p_2 here is the expected price in the second period. In this example we are assuming perfect foresight (which is the same as rational expectations in a deterministic model). People's expectations of prices in the second period are the actual equilibrium prices in that period. Thus, we may write a typical consumer's excess demands as $z_1(\theta)$ and $z_2(\theta)$, where

$$z_i(\theta) = c_i(\theta) - e_i \qquad i = 1, 2.$$

We now consider an infinite sequence of market-clearing prices which gives us the corresponding sequence of relative prices $\{\theta_t\}$. The consumers' budget constraint says

$$\theta_t z_1(\theta_t) + z_2(\theta_t) = 0. \tag{8}$$

For the consumer to maximize utility, the first-order condition is

$$\frac{v_1'[c_1(\theta_t)]}{v_2'[c_2(\theta_t)]} = \frac{p_t}{p_{t+1}} = \theta_t. \tag{9}$$

Substituting (9) into (8), we obtain

$$\frac{v_1'[e_1 + z_1(\theta_t)]}{v_2'[e_2 + z_2(\theta_t)]} z_1(\theta_t) = -z_2(\theta_t). \tag{10}$$

We also have the market equilibrium condition

$$z_1(\theta_t) + z_2(\theta_{t-1}) = 0. \tag{11}$$

Using this, (10) may be rewritten as

$$v_1'[e_1 - z_2(\theta_{t-1})]z_2(\theta_{t-1}) = v_2'[e_2 + z_2(\theta_t)]z_2(\theta_t). \tag{12}$$

Define $\mu_t = z_2(\theta_{t-1})$. It happens that μ_t is the most convenient variable with which to work. We can interpret μ_t as the level of real balances held by a representative consumer. If we rewrite (12) in terms of μ, we obtain

$$v_1'(e_1 - \mu_t)\mu_t = v_2'(e_2 + \mu_{t+1})\mu_{t+1}. \tag{13}$$

This implicitly defines a nonlinear difference equation in μ. If we write $u_1(\mu) = \mu v_1'(e_1 - \mu)$ and $u_2(\mu) = \mu v_2'(e_2 + \mu)$, then (13) becomes

$$\mu_t = u_1^{-1} \circ u_2(\mu_{t+1}) \tag{14}$$

(if f and g are functions $f \circ g(x) = f[g(x)]$.) Let $\chi = u_1^{-1} \circ u_2$; then our basic difference equation becomes

$$\mu_t = \chi(\mu_{t+1}). \tag{15}$$

The first thing we would like to ask about this model is, What are the steady states? This is answered in the following lemma.

LEMMA 1. The only steady states are constant prices $\theta = 1$ or the no-trade (autarkic) equilibrium $\theta = 0$.

   Proof. For proof of this lemma and the following propositions, see Kelsey (1988).

   The next proposition relates this overlapping generations model to the theory of Section 2.

PROPOSITION 1. The function χ is single-peaked, its maximum value occurring at $\mu^* = e_2/(\alpha - 1)$. As $\alpha \to \infty$, $\mu^* \to 0$ and $\chi(\mu^*) \to e_1$.

   The main message of Proposition 1 is that we are now in a position to apply the theory of one-dimensional mappings outlined in Section 2. We have a single-peaked function χ. The size of the peak increases as α increases. Since e_1 is the effective maximum possible value of μ, the limiting case where α tends to infinity corresponds to the case of the logistic map (2) where $r = 4$. In both cases, the map takes the entire interval on to itself. In light of Sarkovskii's Theorem, it is interesting to check whether the system is capable of generating a 3-cycle. If so, there will be cycles of all other periods. Hence we are well into the chaotic region. The following proposition shows that 3-cycles do in fact occur, provided that α is sufficiently large.

PROPOSITION 2. For all sufficiently large α, a 3-cycle exists provided $e_2 < 1$ and $e_1 + e_2 > 1/e_2$.

Thus, our overlapping generations model is capable of generating both cycles and chaotic behaviour. In my opinion, the main message of these results is that nonlinear dynamics is a possible cause of the irregular cycles that we see in macroeconomic data. The particular structure of this model should not be taken too seriously. For instance, the average life of a generation is about 25 years. If we take the division into generations very literally, then the shortest cycle that this model can produce lasts about 50 years. This would make it a sort of Kondratiev wave. We are however much more interested in explaining short-term fluctuations in employment and output. Grandmont goes on to argue that there is a possible counter-cyclic policy, which will smooth out the fluctuations he discovers. It is indeed possible that there may be a government policy which will be able to smooth out Kondratiev waves. But this is a different issue from what is usually meant by a counter-cyclical policy.

3.2. Other economic models involving chaos

Below I give a summary of some of the other economic models that find chaotic behavior. Most of these are based on the same theory of one-dimensional difference equations examined in Section 2 above. Thus, mathematically the papers tend to be rather similar, although they make important contributions to different areas of economic theory.

Day (1983) considers classical economic growth. This is a 'Malthusian'-type model where the level of output determines the rate of population growth. Output in turn depends on the size of the labour force. The interaction of these two effects can produce cycles or chaos.

Benhabib and Day (1981) analyse consumer choice. In this model, actual consumption can influence tastes in future periods (e.g. by addiction). They reach the interesting conclusion that increasing wealth can cause more complicated dynamics to emerge. Thus, the choices of a poor consumer may be quite constant, while the choices of a richer consumer can be cyclical or chaotic. Gaertner (1984, 1986) analyses a similar model. In his theory however, nonlinearities arise not only because current choices affect future tastes, but also because an individual's tastes are affected by the choices of others in society.

There is a problem in consumer theory. It does not seem irrational if a woman eats pork one day and beef the next. This is however difficult to model within conventional consumer theory. If the prices do not change from one day to the next, it would seem that she is violating the axioms of revealed preference. This could be explained as a change in preferences. Such an approach is unsatisfactory, since consumer theory should be able to explain a whole range of choices with one framework. Having different preferences to explain the choices of beef and pork fails to do this.

A second approach would be to model a consumer as choosing all consumption for a long period, say a month, at one time. Then the fact that both pork and beef are consumed, rather than just pork, can be explained by concavity of the utility function. This approach has the disadvantage that certain goods are consumed only once a year, such as when on holiday. Thus, our basic time-period would have to be at least a year. For empirical observations we would need data from several years. Could we be sure that preferences would remain constant over such a long period of time? (This issue is also considered in Sen 1979: 14–16.)

Benhabib and Day's model gives a third explanation. Alternating choices of beef and pork are a cyclic solution of a dynamical system. This is driven by the assumption that what is acutally consumed on one day affects preferences for the next. In the Benhabib–Day framework, it may be better to think of preferences as defined over a much shorter time-period. For instance, alternating choices of beef and pork would be explained by postulating preferences that covered only a single day's consumption. Thus, the consumption of pork one day actually causes the consumer's preferences to change, in such a way that the next day pork is ranked lower *vis à vis* beef—'I couldn't face pork two days in a row.'

Benhabib and Day have abandoned stable preferences and put in their place preferences that change in a stable way. This has the disadvantage that such preferences are much harder to work with—very difficult indeed to apply to actual data. Also, it is not very easy to talk of a consumer having a taste for variety.

One may ask whether chaos will emerge for plausible values of the parameters. The answer is uncertain. Grandmont reports some computer simulations on an overlapping generations model similar to that described in this section. For cycles to appear, it is necessary for the relative risk aversion (α) to rise from $\frac{1}{2}$ to 4 between the first and last periods of a consumer's life. To obtain chaos, relative risk aversion in the second period of a consumer's life must be 8. These both represent marked changes in an individual's behaviour, and it is not easy to believe that they are realistic. Similarly, in Day's (1983) model of economic growth, the emergence of chaotic behaviour depends on a very steep hump in the function relating one period's population to that of the next period. While it is hard to dispute that this relationship is nonlinear, it is doubtful whether it possesses sufficiently sharp curvature to generate chaos.

Montrucchio (1984) and Boldrin and Montrucchio (1985, 1986) discuss circumstances in which optimal growth paths may be chaotic. This is different from most of the other economic papers in this area, which show that not necessarily co-ordinated systems can give rise to chaos. The discovery that optimal behaviour of a single agent is chaotic is in some senses more worrying. Given the difficulty of following chaotic paths, in these circumstances actual behaviour will almost inevitably be suboptimal. Simon (1979) has argued that, owing to the difficulties of calculating an optimal strategy, economic agents will not behave in an optimizing way, but will instead aim for a satisfactory outcome. This sort of behaviour is referred to as *bounded rationality,* or *satisficing.* The possibility that the optimal strategy might be chaotic strongly reinforces Simon's argument. Given the immense difficulties in following a chaotic path, agents might well opt for a suboptimal but less complex strategy.

4. Chaos and Rational Expectations

4.1. Rational expectations models of the business cycle

Time-series of many economic variables have the appearance of being noisy cycles. The traditional explanation of this is that the economy is subject to random shocks. These may be due to the weather, earthquakes, or any similar exogenous phenomena which could influence economic activity. An important example of this approach can be found in the work of Lucas (1975).

In this paper Lucas has a macroeconomic model which is based on a set of linear difference equations with stochastic error terms. The economy is subdivided into 'islands'. Information flows between different islands are imperfect. Because of this, when agents see that prices are rising, they are not able to tell whether prices are rising only on the island on which they are situated or whether they are witnessing a general rise in the price level. Hence purely nominal shocks that cause prices to rise can induce people to invest, even though they make no difference in real profit opportunities. The capital thus invested will remain in place even after the nominal shock has passed. Hence real effects will be felt for some time after a disturbance. (Similarly, shocks that cause the price level to fall will have effects that will persist.)

In particular, Lucas shows that his model will generate pro-cyclical movements in both prices and the share of output devoted to investment.

These, he argues, are a possible explanation of the autocorrelations seen in macroeconomic data. He further argues that, when the economy is subject to a sequence of random shocks, it will behave in a way that resembles a real-life business cycle. (For a survey of business cycle theory, see Zarnowitz 1985).

An alternative explanation of the business cycle would be to use a model involving nonlinear difference (or differential) equations. If a model of this sort exhibited chaotic or cyclic behaviour, then it could provide an explanation of the business cycle. Such an approach would have the advantage of not relying on exogenous random shocks.[6] A second contrast to the results of Lucas is that monetary policy may be effective even if agents have rational expectations. The policy ineffectiveness result does rely very heavily on the assumption that economic relations are log-linear. Grandmont (1985) shows that monetary policy can be highly effective within his overlapping generations model. Snower (1984) also shows that nonlinearities can cause monetary policy to be effective. While this is true, in a chaotic model it might be very difficult in practice to calculate the optimal policy.

The question arises, Which approach is correct? Does Lucas or Grandmont have the true model of the business cycle? First, the question should be reformulated as, Which model is better? Both are extremely drastic simplifications of actual economic processes. Neither even pretends to be realistic or true. As Friedman (1953) argues, realism in economic models is not a desirable end in itself. It should be incorporated in models only to the extent that it tells us something useful about the economy. Nevertheless, a good economic theory should indicate the essential mechanisms that cause economic phenomena. If business cycles are caused by nonlinear dynamics, it is not helpful to explain them by random shocks, trading on islands, and linear relationships.

It is still the mainstream view that economic fluctuations are caused primarily by random shocks. Relatively few people would regard the main cause as being nonlinear dynamics. The reason for this is not clear. it is certainly not the case that there is significant empirical evidence supporting the random shock viewpoint. Indeed, at present there is very little evidence at all that could be used to discriminate between the two theories. Probably the reason why the random shock theory has become established is simply that it was proposed first, and that it is based on statistical techniques commonly taught to graduate students. In fluid mechanics, in contrast, the view is that the seemingly random character

---

[6] It should perhaps be pointed out that business cycles can also be modelled as 'sunspot equilibria'. In this case fluctuations arise because people condition their expectations on some Markov process, which does not directly affect the economy. This approach is connected with nonlinear dynamics, since the existence of a 2-cycle implies the existence of a sunspot equilibrium (see Azariadis and Guesnerie 1986).

of turbulent motion is due to chaotic dynamics. The idea that exogenous random shocks may be responsible is given little consideration.

This is not to deny that the economy is not subject to random shocks. The impact of shocks is however determined by the system. In a strongly stable system, which returns to equilibrium quickly, the impact of an external shock will be small. In a nonlinear system with sensitive dependence on initial conditions, the impact of even a very small shock can be large, and the economy will show no tendency to return to its original time-path.

It must be admitted that information flows in the economy are not perfect, and that some sections of the economy operate more or less independently of one another. Despite this, Lucas's model of an economy situated on different 'islands' seems very arbitrary and unrealistic. Also, the assumption of linearity in fundamental economic relationships does not appear plausible. In summary, chaotic economic models can explain the fact that macroeconomic data have the appearance of being at the same time erratic and containing cycles. They have the advantage over the model of Lucas (1975) in that they avoid certain rather *ad hoc* assumptions.

It is clear that rational expectations is a difficult hypothesis to maintain in chaotic models. It should be pointed out that, even in non-chaotic models, there are several problems with rational expectations. To be consistent, one should really be able to describe a process by which expectations are acquired. It should be known that such a process will lead to a rational expectations equilibrium.[7] This is difficult to analyse. The learning process will affect the behaviour of economic variables, but this will feed-back on the learning process itself. (Indeed, it could be the case that the learning process could cause chaos in an otherwise non-chaotic model, a feedback loop of this kind being one of the common features of chaotic systems.) In any event, this kind of feedback has made describing the learning process very problematic. To date, only very simple cases have been analysed, for example where agents know the basic structure of the economy apart from a single unknown parameter. Agents then use ordinary least squares to estimate this parameter. More complicated cases have not yet been analysed.

Suppose agents attempt to learn about the economy using econometric techniques that are based on a correct specification of rational expectations equilibria. Bray (1982) states:

In doing so they fail to take account of the dependence of outcomes on beliefs. Their estimation technique is based on a misspecification of the situation. For

---

[7] Although this is not particularly a criticism of rational expectations. To be consistent, any alternative theory of expectations should be able to describe a learning process whereby expectations are acquired.

example, in the rational expectations equilibrium of the asset market model studied in this paper, the price and return on the asset at different dates form an independent identically distributed sequence of normal random variables. In this situation, ordinary least squares (OLS) is an appropriate statistical procedure for learning about the price return relationship. However, suppose that the agents in the model use OLS (or any other statistical procedure) to estimate the price return relationship outside the rational expectations equilibrium, and use their estimate in forecasting returns. The stochastic process of price and return is then neither stationary nor independent. The use of OLS estimation is inappropriate.

Despite this mis-specification, Bray shows that the use of OLS can, in certain simple cases, cause the system to converge to rational expectations equilibrium.

In chaotic models, all these problems are still present. Chaos does cause some additional problems. Even if the functional relations are known completely, errors in measurement and computing will eventually make forecasts unreliable. Traditionally, in a deterministic model rational expectations would be assumed to imply perfect foresight. In this model, this view is difficult to maintain if the equilibrium path is chaotic. Perfect foresight must rely on agents observing and learning about their environment. With aperiodic motion, there is no scope for them to observe regularities in the environment. Moreover, if they understand the sensitive dependence on initial conditions, they will realize that it is impossible for them to make forecasts about anything but the immediate future.

4.2. Invariant measures

Thus, in a model with chaotic dynamics, perfect foresight is not a good way to formulate rational expectations. No one has been able to suggest any learning process by which an individual might acquire perfect foresight in a chaotic economy. (The learning process suggested by Grandmont 1985 has only been shown to converge to perfect foresight in a cyclic regime.) It seems very unlikely that such a learning process does in fact exist.

Fortunately, there does exist an alternative way of formulating rational expectations. In some circumstances is is possible to find statistical descriptions of aperiodic motion. Suppose f is a map of an interval into itself. Then sometimes it is possible to find a probability distribution (or measure) that describes the likelihood of the system taking a particular value after a large number of iterations. Let μ denote a measure on the interal concerned, say I. To describe the motion under f, μ must be invariant and ergodic (see Grandmont 1983).

The distribution μ is said to be *invariant* under f if $\mu[f^{-1}(A)] = \mu(A)$ for all sets A, on which μ is defined. This says that the probability is preserved by the map f. It should be clear why it is necessary for the measure to have this property.

The measure μ is *ergodic* for f if, for any μ-integrable function g,

$$\lim_{n\to\infty}\frac{1}{n}\sum_{j=1}^{n}g[f^{j-1}(x)]=\int g\,d\mu$$

for every x (except possibly in a set of μ-measure zero). This is a mathematically precise way of saying that, from a typical starting-point, the points on the future path of x are distributed like randomly chosen points from the probability distribution μ.

This implies in particular that if one considers, for given x, the distribution that assigns probability $1/n$ to each $f^i(x)$ for $i = 0, 1, \ldots, n-1$, then this sequence of distributions will approximate μ unless x is in a set of μ measure zero. Hence the ultimate distribution is the same for all typical starting values. Notice that, after the system has been running for some time, values of the variable x in a set of μ-measure zero will not be observed in practice.

In such circumstances it may be reasonable to assume that an individual with rational expectations would use the probability μ. Given the complexity of nonlinear dynamics, it is not reasonable to suppose that an individual would actually be able to calculate μ. Indeed, pure mathematicians have been able to calculate invariant measures in only a few special cases. It is, however, possible that, by observing the outcome of the system a large number of times, an individual would be able to get a close approximation to the true distribution. A very interesting piece of research would be to construct an actual learning process that could model this. It may be possible to base such a process on our observation above that, when there is an ergodic measure, giving equal probability to all observations will converge to the true distribution.

The best-known example of an invariant measure is the case of the logistic map (equation (2)) when $r = 4$, $x_{t+1} = 4x_t(1-x_t)$. Recall that we have found an analytic solution for this equation in Section 2.4. This system has an invariant measure with density function $1/\pi\sqrt{[x(1-x)]}$. Just as a general probability distribution does not always have a density function (for instance, a discrete distribution would not have a density function), so a density function cannot always be found for an invariant measure. There may be point masses in the distribution. Other complicating factors are also possible. Hence we are especially fortunate in the case of $r = 4$.

For an individual who is interested in the long-run behaviour of the system, a sensible interpretation of rational expectations would be to use the invariant measure as his expected distribution of the variable. There are known examples where there is no invariant measure. In such cases it is not at all clear what a rational expectation would be. This is a difficult problem for those who advocate rational expectations. Most other suggested expectations rules, such as adaptive expectations, will continue to work in chaotic regimes. A qualification should be introduced here. It is not the case that the invariant measure would give a good estimate of next period's value of a particular variable conditional on the current observation: it might, however, be the case that such a measure would provide a reasonable long-run expectation of a chaotic variable.

5. Conclusion

In this chapter I have shown that mathematical solutions of nonlinear differential or difference equations are capable of generating either cyclic or random-like behaviour. These ideas have already begun to be applied in economics, as was described in Section 3. Traditionally, economic theory has been concerned primarily with finding steady states and to a lesser extent with finding cycles. Perhaps one of the greatest services dynamic systems theory has done is to make economists aware that other types of solutions are possible.

As mentioned before, dynamic systems theory has been successfully employed in the study of fluid mechanics. Many of the phenomena (e.g. period-doubling sequences) described in Section 2 have been observed in experiments on fluid motion. (See Citanovic 1984a for further details.) Barnett and Chen (1986) have empirical evidence of chaotic behaviour in monetary aggregates. This confirms the usefulness of these theories. The theory has also been applied in biology to the dynamic behaviour of populations of certain species.

Fluid mechanics has one advantage over economics. The basic equations of motion are known. (These are the Navier–Stokes equations.) It is true that they are capable of generating extremely complicated behaviour, and that in many cases they are unsolvable. Economic theory has all these disadvantages, and the additional problem that we are not really sure of the economic equations of motion. This is the major difference between problems of economic prediction and those of weather forecasting.

Economics contains the following paradox. In microeconomics all economic variables are seen as produced by the rational decisions of maximizing agents. Hence in microeconomics variables are completely deterministic. In macroeconomics, however, economic variables are frequently viewed as being random. How can the same variables be random and deterministic at the same time? This paradox may be explained if the economic system is chaotic.

With nonlinear systems of the sort described in this chapter, adjusting a parameter can move the model from a stable steady state or cycle into the chaotic region. It is possible that such a transition occurred in the macroeconomy around 1967. At that time many industrialized countries switched from conditions of steady growth with some cyclic fluctuations into a period in which economic activity was much more erratic. Since about 1967 the behaviour of many economic variables, such as the price level or exchange rates, have become much less predictable. It is not certain that what we are observing is chaotic dynamics. There are many independent sources of noise which affect economic data. It is, however, possible that some of the observed noise is not extrinsic noise independent of the economic system but is intrinsic noise generated by chaotic dynamics of the system itself.[8]

Sennsitive dependence on initial conditions is not a new discovery. It is exhibited in the following problem from classical physics. Solve

$$\frac{\partial^2 f}{\partial x^2} + \frac{\partial^2 f}{\partial y^2} = 0$$

(this is Laplace's equation) subject to the boundary condition

$$f(x, y) = \varepsilon \cos(x) \text{ at } y = 0, \qquad \frac{\partial f}{\partial y} = 0 \text{ at } y = 0.$$

Here ε is assumed to be small. It is best to think of the term $\varepsilon \cos(x)$ as representing our error in the measurement of x on the boundary. It is easy to check that the solution is

$$f(x, y) = \varepsilon \cos(x) \cosh(y).$$

Even though ε is small as y increases, this will become very large indeed. Thus any error, however small, in measuring the value of the function on the boundary will have a major effect on the value of the solution in the interior of the domain. The behaviour of this system is essentially impossible to predict.[9]

The results of dynamic systems theory have a fine structure which is hard to reconcile with observed economic behaviour. In the theory of the logistic map in Section 2, as the parameter r is varied in the interval [3, 4] an infinite number of stable orbits can be found. There are also several other features of the behaviour occurring in infinitely minute detail which we have not discussed. (An important example of this is Feigenbaum's universal scaling theory: see Feigenbaum 1980 and Citanovic 1984a.) In the chaotic region the probability distributions describing the motion can be extremely complex. They can contain a large number of point masses. Typically, they will not be continuous; that is, the distribution cannot be represented by a density function.

---

[8] This point is due to Richard Day of the University of Southern California.
[9] I heard about this example through Hermann Bondi.

The inclusion of random errors changes this quite dramatically. The theoretical dynamics becomes a much more plausible description of actual economic data. All but a finite number of periodic orbits disappear. Usually the number of such orbits is very low, say around 4, so they do not need to be closely packed. Similarly, the probability distributions become much smoother. Thus, in the presence of noise it is much easier to believe that chaotic dynamics provides a good description of economic behaviour.

For those interested in further reading, two good mathematical references are Collet and Eckman (1980) and Preston (1983).

PART VI

19

Some Micro and Macro Implications of Inventories

J. P. THOMAS

1. Introduction

There has been considerable interest recently in the theory of inventories, from both a microeconomic and a macroeconomic point of view. Unfortunately, there appears to be a large number of different models with an almost equally large number of results to be had. In this chapter we shall concentrate on a single aspect of the literature, namely, the influence of the level of inventories on output. This is of interest at both micro and macro levels. We shall argue that at the microeconomic level a negative influence comes through uniformly, despite all the differences in the models, while at the macroeconomic level there is good reason to doubt that any such relationship exists in equilibrium models.

Broadly speaking, there are two main types of models, depending on production technology. When costs are non-convex, it pays to produce in a large lump not very often so as to take advantage of increasing returns. Under certain conditions this leads to the '(S, s) production rule', which we shall investigate below. With convex costs, the opposite incentive exists: inventories can be used to smooth production even when sales vary from period to period. The nature of production smoothing has been examined recently by Abel (1985) and Ashley and Orr (1985). Roughly speaking, we can think of production smoothing as a situation in which the variation of sales is greater than the variance of output. Blinder (1981) has argued that empirically the variance of output tends to be greater than that of sales, so production smoothing models may not be appropriate for many sectors of the economy. He suggests that the (S, s) model should be used, although it has not received much attention from economists since the 1950s. When demand is uncertain, the model with convex costs is also sometimes referred to as a 'buffer-stock' model, in that it is desirable to hold inventories against the possibility of high demand. While this motive undoubtedly exists in such models, it is probably misleading terminology since the same effect can also operate in models with non-convex costs.

Assumptions about production costs are not the only reasons why models can differ radically in their predictions: prices may be fixed or variable, before or after the demand curve becomes known; it may or may not be possible to backlog unsatisfied demand; there may be lags in production; and so on. All these assumptions can be very important. I shall argue, however, that in a broad class of models the relationship between the level of inventories and that of output is always negative; that is, higher stocks inherited from the past depress current output.

Turning to macroeconomic considerations, there appear to have been three broad strands in the literature. The first, stressed by Blinder (1982), is that the existence of inventories can lead to 'sticky' prices, a phenomenon that is obviously of great importance to macroeconomics. The second relates to the aggregate implications of (S, s) behaviour. (See Blinder 1981, and also Caplin 1985, who shows in an aggregate model that if retailers follow (S, s) policies the variance of orders they place exceeds the variance of their sales.) The third area, and the one we are interested in here, is the idea that aggregate inventories exert a negative influence on equilibrium output, so that a mechanism is provided to explain serially correlated aggregate output. (See for example Blinder and Fischer 1981; Koenig and Nerlove 1986.) The argument is roughly as follows. An unanticipated demand shock, say a positive one, leads to a depletion of inventories below some 'natural level' as firms take advantage of prices that they believe to be abnormally high. In future periods low levels of inventories lead to higher output as firms try to restore stocks to their original levels. The adjustment is spread over a number of periods, so output remains high (and this simultaneously rationalizes pro-cyclical real wages).

I shall argue that it is not at all clear that the hypothesized aggregate relationship between inventories and output follows from the microeconomic stories.

2. Microeconomic Models

We shall consider a general infinite-horizon model of inventory control which will encompass both production smoothing and (S, s)-type models. We assume that a firm faces a random demand function each period $t = 0, 1, 2, \ldots$, given by $g(p_t, \varepsilon_t)$ where ε_t is an independently and identically distributed random variable with finite support and p_t is the price charged. We assume that $g_p \leq 0$, and that $pg(p, \varepsilon)$ is bounded above.

At the beginning of any period t, before ε_t is known, the firm must choose an output level y_t. This is available for sale in period t. The output costs $c(y_t)$ to produce, and various assumptions concerning the form of c will be considered below.

Inventory at the beginning of period $t + 1$ is denoted x_{t+1} and satisfies

$$x_{t+1} = \max[x_t + y_t - g(p_t, \varepsilon_t), a] \tag{1}$$

where $a \leq 0$. The case $a = 0$ corresponds to the assumption of no backlogging of unsatisfied demand and $a = -\infty$ corresponds to arbitrary backlogging, although we shall assume that a is finite.

We assume that there is a holding cost associated with each level of inventory, $h(x_t)$, being incurred in period $t - 1$. If backlogging is permitted, then h is defined for negative values of x_t and in such cases is interpreted as the cost of backlogging. Finally, we assume that g, c, and h are continuous.

Profits per period are thus

$$\Pi_t \equiv p_t \min[g(p_t, \varepsilon_t), x_t + y_t - a] - c(y_t) - h(x_{t+1})$$

on the assumption that, if backlogging is allowed, payment is made when orders are placed.

The firm is assumed to be risk-neutral and it maximizes expected discounted profits, where β is the discount factor, $0 < \beta < 1$. A policy from time t onwards, P_t, is a sequence of contingent choices (y_t, p_t), (y_{t+1}, p_{t+1}), $(y_{t+2}, p_{t+2}) \ldots$, choices that depend upon the history (from t onwards) of realizations of the random terms known when the decision is made. For any level of stocks at the start of t, x_t, and for a given policy P_t, expected profits discounted to t are

$$V(P_t, x_t) = E_t \sum_{\tau=t}^{\infty} \beta^{\tau-t} \Pi_t$$

where E_t represents expectations taken at the beginning of t (before ε_t is known). (Since Π_t is uniformly bounded above, this expression is well defined.) The problem facing the firm is therefore to maximize by choice of P_0 the value of $V(P_0, x_0)$, assuming the initial level of inventories, x_0, is given.

I have been deliberately vague about which variables p_t is allowed to depend upon, although we shall assume throughout that y_t may depend on each shock up to time $t - 1$: $\varepsilon_0, \varepsilon_1, \ldots, \varepsilon_{t-1}$. In the original development of the literature $\{p_t\}_{t=0}^{\infty}$ was assumed exogenous, so the problem facing the firm was to produce to meet random demands in such a way as to minimize the various ordering (or production) costs and holding (backlogging) costs (see Arrow, Karlin, and Scarf 1958). More recently, models with endogenous price setting have become popular. In these models firms have some control over demand through price. For example, in Reagan (1982) it is assumed that p_t is chosen after ε_t is observed. In this case, although the price is still positively related to demand, its variance is reduced by the existence of inventories. This assumption about price setting goes naturally with the assumption of no backlogging. On the other hand, in Abel (1985) it is assumed that p_t is set before ε_t is observed, and this would probably be a more appropriate model for many retail outlets. The same assumption is made in Amihud and Mendelson (1983), who relate price smoothing properties to the shape of $h(x)$ for positive and negative values of x.

For the moment, all we shall assume about the determination of p_t is that the choice set and current information is the same each period, so the problem is stationary.

By far the most useful technique in this context is dynamic programming, and we define the value function

$$V(x_t) = \sup_{P_t} V(P_t, x_t),$$

which gives the maximum value that can be achieved from t onwards when inventories at the beginning of period t are x_t. It will also turn out to be extremely useful to define another function representing the maximum value given inventory x_t *and* output y_t. Clearly, it will depend only on their sum $(x_t + y_t)$, and we denote it $G(x_t + y_t)$. In fact, formally we shall define G in terms of V:

$$G(x_t + y_t) = \sup_{P_t} E\{P_t \min[g(p_t, \varepsilon_t), x_t + y_t - a] - h(x_{t+1}) + \beta V(x_{t+1})\} \quad (2)$$

where x_{t+1} satisfies (1). Depending on the price formulation, p_t may be fixed at a constant level; it may be chosen before ε_t is known, or allowed to depend on ε_t.

The optimality equation for this problem then allows us to express V in terms of G (and hence in terms of itself):

$$V(x_t) = \sup_{y_t}[G(x_t + y_t) - c(y_t)]. \quad (3)$$

Assuming that values of y_t and p_t exist which achieve the suprema in (2) and (3), these choices also form part of an optimal policy; in particular, the optimal choice of y_t, given x_t, must maximize $G(x_t + y_t) - c(y_t)$, if an optimal choice exists (see Bertsekas 1976: Ch. 6). The latter will be assumed for the time being. Given that we are concerned mainly with output in this chapter, this is a convenient formulation as it does not involve explicit consideration of p_t, and it will allow us to derive general conclusions about the output rule.

We shall see that, if the value function G turns out to be concave, then the effect of higher x_t is to reduce y_t. I shall then illustrate conditions under which G is indeed concave, and shall investigate what happens when the concavity condition might fail.

While my main interest is to show that $dy_t/dx_t \le 0$, I shall also make reference to a stronger condition, which is a particular definition of 'production smoothing' found in Abel (1985), namely, $-1 < dy_t/dx_t < 0$. This condition states that an increase in inventories x_t reduces output y_t, but by less than the increase in x_t. Since the dependence of y_t on x_t may not be differentiable, we use more general definitions in the statement of the proposition.

PROPOSITION 1. (i) If G is strictly concave, then when x_t is increased from x to x', y_t does not increase; i.e., $y' \le y$.

(ii) If in addition c is strictly convex, then $x' - x \ge y - y'$ (i.e. 'production smoothing').

Proof. Since y maximizes $G(x + y) - c(y)$, we have

$$G(x + y) - c(y) \ge G(x + y') - c(y'), \tag{4}$$

and similarly,

$$G(x' + y') - c(y') \ge G(x' + y) - c(y). \tag{5}$$

Suppose that $y' > y$. Then by strict concavity of G, $G(x + y') - G(x + y) > G(x' + y') - G(x' + y)$. Hence, using (4) and (5),

$$c(y') - c(y) > c(y') - c(y),$$

a contradiction. So we conclude that $y' \le y$.

(ii) Suppose, contrary to assertion, that $x' - x < y - y'$. Equation (4) must still hold, with y' replaced by $(x' + y' - x)$:

$$G(x + y) - c(y) \ge G(x' + y') - c(x' + y' - x). \tag{6}$$

and similarly, equation (5) holds with y replaced by $(x + y - x')$:

$$G(x' + y') - c(y') \ge G(x + y) - c(x + y - x'). \tag{7}$$

Combining (6) and (7),

$$c(x + y - x') - c(y') \ge c(y) - c(x' + y' - x), \tag{8}$$

which, since $x + y - x' < y$, is impossible by the strict convexity of c. Hence $x' - x \ge y - y'$. Q.E.D

Note that the qualification 'strict' can be removed from the statement of the proposition, provided optimal choices are unique. Also, the proof of part (ii) does not require the concavity of G, although we are more interested here in the conditions under which (i) holds.

Thus, provided the various functions have the economist's preferred shape, there is no problem in showing that output responds in the expected way to inventories. Under what conditions will G be concave? In general, we require the maximization problem each period itself to be concave.

For example, consider the case in which p_t is chosen 'ex post', that is after ε_t is known. We can regard the firm's problem each period as a two-step one, with y_t being determined first, using G as before, and then the best p_t being chosen, given $(x_t + y_t)$ and ε_t. As remarked earlier, this assumption about price determination goes naturally with the assumption of no backlogging, so we will take the case $a = 0$. We may think of revenue as a function of sales for a given value of ε, say $R(q, \varepsilon)$, where R is revenue and q sales; so $R(q, \varepsilon) \equiv pq$ where p satisfies $q = g(p, \varepsilon)$. We are ignoring the possibility of excess demand, as it would clearly be suboptimal to set p at such a level (given $a = 0$). A sufficient condition for the concavity of G then is that $R(q, \varepsilon)$ is concave in q for each ε, and $c(y)$ and $h(x)$ are both convex.

To see why these fairly standard assumptions imply concavity of $G(z)$, suppose first that $V(x)$ is concave. Part of the optimality equation for this problem is, using (2),

$$G(z) = \sup_{p(\varepsilon)} E \langle p(\varepsilon) g[p(\varepsilon), \varepsilon]$$

$$- h\{z - g[p(\varepsilon), \varepsilon]\} + \beta V\{z - g[p(\varepsilon), \varepsilon]\} \rangle. \quad (9)$$

Consider two possible values z and z', and a number λ, $0 < \lambda < 1$. We can find a least value for $G[\lambda z + (1 - \lambda)z']$ in the following way. For each ε choose $p(\varepsilon)$ so that sales $q^\lambda = \lambda q + (1 - \lambda)q'$ where q and q' are, respectively, optimal sales for z and z' when ε occurs. Then unsold stock will amount to

$$\lambda z + (1 - \lambda)z' - q^\lambda = \lambda(z - q) + (1 - \lambda)(z' - q').$$

By the concavity and convexity assumptions, profits from this strategy are at least the weighted average of the profits under z and z' for the given value of ε. Take expectations, and the concavity of G follows. The concavity of G in turn straightforwardly implies the concavity of V from (3), the other part of the optimality equation. This argument implies that, if we start with an arbitrary bounded value function V^1 which is concave and iterate using (2) and (3), the new function V^2 will also be concave. Under discounted dynamic programming, the limit of this process is the function V,[1] which is therefore itself concave (since a sequence of concave functions must converge to a concave function). If R is strictly concave for some ε, and h is strictly concave, then so is V.

At the other extreme, when the price is exogenous throughout, similar assumptions guarantee the concavity of G (see e.g. Bertsekas 1976: Ch. 3).

To summarize, under fairly standard conditions it is possible to prove the concavity of G and consequently to deduce a negative relationship between beginning-of-period inventories and production. In the retail

---

[1] Per-period profits π are bounded above but not below. (This is a 'negative' programming problem.) Nevertheless $V(x)$ is clearly finite. If $a > -\infty$, then since V is increasing it is bounded. Standard arguments then imply that, starting with an arbitrary bounded value function and iterating, the sequence converges uniformly to V.

context, however, convexity of c is a rather bad assumption, as c would typically represent ordering (as opposed to production) costs and these normally have a large fixed cost element. Unfortunately, results are much more difficult to derive when costs are not convex. In particular, it is no longer possible to prove the concavity of G. Nevertheless, with a positive fixed cost and constant marginal cost, we will show that the negative relationship always holds, although production smoothing breaks down.

We shall demonstrate the optimality of (S, s) policies in such circumstances. These are policies that specify two numbers, S and s, and a production rule that says increase total stocks (beginning-of-period inventories plus current production) up to S if $x < s$ and do not produce if $x \geq s$. That is,

$$y_t = \begin{cases} S - x_t & \text{if } x_t < s \\ 0 & \text{if } x_t \geq s. \end{cases}$$

Note that these policies imply a negative relationship between y_t and x_t.

The proof of the optimality of (S, s) policies under constant marginal costs with positive fixed cost requires the notion of K-concavity, which is weaker than concavity. The idea is due to Scarf (1960). This has traditionally been done in the case of a fixed price where the firm has control only over production. I shall argue that an (S, s) policy is optimal under certain conditions even when the firm has control over price. The argument is a generalization of the usual approach, although I am not aware of its having been made elsewhere. (See the comments in Blinder 1981: 455.)

First, we give the definition of K-concavity. A function $f: R \rightarrow R$ is K-concave, where $K \geq 0$, if, for any x, x' with $x < x'$ and λ, $0 < \lambda < 1$,

$$\lambda f(x) + (1 - \lambda)f(x') - (1 - \lambda)K \leq f[\lambda x + (1 - \lambda)x'].$$

For a concave function, a chord joining any two points on the function when extended forward (i.e. for higher values of x) never lies below the function. For a K-concave function, such a chord never lies more than K below the function, so K-concavity is weaker and $K = 0$ corresponds to normal concavity.

The particular value of K we are interested in here is the amount of the fixed cost that has to be incurred before any production can take place, so define K to be this cost. The constant marginal cost will be denoted by C. So

$$c(y) = \begin{cases} 0 & \text{for } y = 0 \\ K + Cy & \text{for } y > 0. \end{cases}$$

To see why the K-concavity and continuity of G implies the optimality of an (S, s) rule, consider the function

$$f(z) \equiv G(z) - Cz.$$

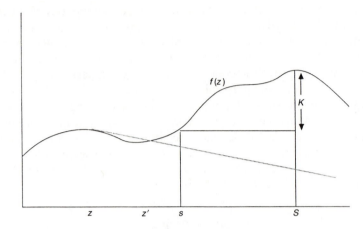

Fig. 19.1

Notice that the condition $f(x + y) - K \geqslant f(x)$ is equivalent to $G(x + y) - Cy - K \geqslant G(x)$, which, when $y > 0$, says that production of y is better than no production at all. So production is profitable when a $y > 0$ can be found such that f increases by at least K, thus covering fixed costs; and indeed, once this condition is satisfied, the best $y > 0$ is simply the one that maximizes $f(x + y)$. Let S belong to $\arg\max f(z)$,[2] so if $x < S$ and production takes place, it will be such that $x + y = S$. Finally, let s be the nearest value below S such that $f(S) - K = f(s)$, that is, so that it is just profitable to produce, if such a value exists.

We note that K-concavity of G trivially implies K-concavity of f. Between s and S production is not desirable by definition of s. Also, f must be an increasing function below s, otherwise we must have a z, z' with $z < z' \leqslant s$, $f(z) > f(z')$, so a chord through $f(z)$ and $f(z')$ projected forward must have a negative slope and hence must lie more than K below $f(S)$ at S, contradicting K-concavity. Hence production up to S is desirable for all $x \leqslant s$; see Figure 19.1. Lastly, we investigate whether production might be profitable for some $x \geqslant S$. If this were so, then $f(x) < f(S)$ since $f(S)$ is the largest value of f and there must be a y such that $f(x + y) - K \geqslant f(x)$. A chord joining $f(S)$ and $f(x)$ must have a negative slope and $f(x + y)$ must by K-concavity be no more than K above the chord at $(x + y)$, so less than K above $f(x)$, contradicting the profitability of y. Hence we have shown that an (S, s) rule is optimal. If no s, as defined, exists, then no production ever takes place.

To prove the K-concavity of G, we proceed as before. That is, we first assume that V is K-concave and show that this implies from the

---

[2] This exists because $\lim_{z \to \infty} f(z) = -\infty$.

optimality equation (2) that G is K-concave, and then show that the latter implies by the optimality equation (3) that V is K-concave.

We shall sketch the argument for the case considered earlier: price determined after ε_t is observed, no backlogging, and concave revenue function $R(q, \varepsilon)$.

Take two values of inventory plus production, z and z', with $z < z'$, and let q, q' and x, x' be the respective optimal choices of sales and end-of-period inventory for a particular realization of ε. We need first to establish that $x \leq x'$. Suppose otherwise. Then, for q, x to be optimal for z,

$$R(q + x - x', \varepsilon) - R(q, \varepsilon) \leq \beta[V(x) - V(x')];$$

that is, it must not be profitable to switch $(x - x')$ units from inventory to sales. The opposite is true for z'; thus,

$$R(q', \varepsilon) - R(q' - x + x', \varepsilon) \geq \beta[V(x) - V(x')],$$

which, by the concavity of R and the fact that $q' > r + x - x'$, is impossible if either of the above inequalities is strict. If they are not, we assume that the choice $x = x'$ is taken; this involves no loss of generality, as it is the value of profits that matters, so $x \leq x'$. The rest of the argument is more or less as before. For any λ, $0 < \lambda < 1$, with initial stock $\lambda z + (1 - \lambda)z'$, choose sales of $\lambda q + (1 - \lambda)q'$ so end-of-period stock is $\lambda x + (1 - \lambda)x'$. The concavity of R and the K-concavity of V thus imply that this strategy yields at least $\lambda[R(q, \varepsilon) + \beta V(x)] + (1 - \lambda)[R(q', \varepsilon) + \beta V(x')] - \beta(1 - \lambda)K$, and consequently that G itself is K-concave. (We needed to have $x \leq x'$, otherwise the last term would have been $\beta\lambda K$ whenever $x > x'$.)

We have established that K-concavity of V implies the K-concavity of G in this particular case. Proving the opposite causality is standard; see Bertsekas (1976: 86–8). The major technicality we are omitting is the proof of continuity of G.[3]

Thus, the (S, s) production rule can be optimal even when prices may be varied by the firm after ε_t is known. A similar argument should be possible when the price is chosen before ε_t is observed: the principles are exactly the same. From our point of view, the important thing is that the negative relationship between x_t and y_t holds for an (S, s) rule. For values of x_t above s, y_t is always zero. When x_t is below s, y_t increases one to one with reductions in x_t. (There is a discontinuity at $x_t = s$, and for any two values of x_t on either side of s, production smoothing is violated.) Abel (1985), however, has shown in a particular model that, if a one-period

[3] To prove continuity, start with an arbitrary bounded K-concave and continuous value function V^1. Using (2) to derive G^1, it is easy to see that G^1 is also continuous. Since an (S, s) policy achieves the supremum in (3), it is clear from the proof of its optimality that V^2 will be continuous, and we know that it will be K-concave. Continuing to iterate, the sequence converges uniformly to V so V must itself be continuous.

time lag in production is assumed, then with constant marginal cost and no fixed cost, $0 > dy_t/dx_t > -1$.

3. Macroeconomic Implications

We have seen that, while inventory models differ in a number of respects, the negative relationship between stocks and output seems to be quite pervasive. Hopefully, then, we can conclude that aggregation should cause no major problem to the basic message. As remarked in the introduction, a negative macroeconomic relationship between stocks and output has become widely accepted as a cause for serially correlated output levels. In this section we want to suggest that the microeconomic relationship does not necessarily have the usually assumed macroeconomic implications. The reason is quite simple: in the microeconomic analysis a number of things are assumed to be given which are not in general invariant to changes in the aggregate levels of inventory—in particular, cost and demand functions. From the point of view of the traditional equilibrium macroeconomic model, does the aggregate level of inventories affect the demand curve for labour? If it does not, then we would not expect employment and aggregate output to change.

To extend the results of the previous section to the macroeconomic context, we shall take the simplest possible model. Suppose that firms' prices are flexible after the state of the world is known, and demand functions are perfectly elastic. (It is probably not sensible to have rigid prices *and* perfectly elastic demand curves.) To make the point as simply as possible, in fact, let us assume that there is no uncertainty. In this case we will show that the equilibrium will involve each firm setting marginal cost equal to price as usual. That is to say, the existence of storage possibilities does not affect price–cost relationships, and it is these that determine the demand for labour.

Consider an economy with N competitive markets. Let p^i be the price in market i, and assume there is a price index $\pi(p^1, p^2, \ldots, p^N)$ which is used to deflate nominal magnitudes (valid under homothetic preferences). Labour is the only input into production, and there is an economy-wide labour market, the nominal wage being w. The aggregate supply of labour depends only on the real wage, written $L(w/\pi)$. The model is assumed to be symmetric in the sense that π is a symmetric function, all firms have the same production function, and there is an equal number of firms in each market.

Our purpose is to determine the relationship between inventories and output. The distribution of inventories may be asymmetric across firms within a market and also across markets. We shall find that the first form of asymmetry causes few problems, and the second can be handled for small deviations from symmetry.

Consider a typical firm in a representative market. Let $c(y)$ be labour requirement where y is output, and assume $c' \geq 0$, $c'' > 0$, $c(0) = c'(0) = 0$. Let h be the fixed per-unit cost of storage, and again let β be the factor with which profits are discounted. Let p_t be the price in the market at t (there is perfect foresight), q_t the quantity sold at t, and x_t the level of inventory at the start of t. Thus, assuming no backlogging, the firm maximizes, given x_0,

$$\sum_{t=0}^{\infty} \beta^t [p_t q_t - w_t c(y_t) - hx_{t+1}]$$

$$\text{s.t. } x_t \geq 0, \qquad x_{t+1} = x_t + y_t - q_t.$$

While the problem appears complicated, the optimal production policy turns out to be very simple. In fact, it is no different to the optimal policy in the absence of inventories: the firm should set marginal cost equal to price; that is, $w_t c'(y_t) = p_t$. The formal argument is given in the Appendix, but the intuition is fairly straightforward. It can never pay to have marginal cost less than price, since profits can be increased by producing more and selling immediately. If marginal cost is greater than price, then the firm must be taking capital gains since current sales could not be optimal. It is possible to show that if one firms hoards all its output then all others will do likewise, but zero aggregate supply cannot occur in equilibrium, so this case can also be ruled out.

The important conclusion is that the existence of inventories does not affect marginal cost pricing. This allows the usual aggregation theorem to be invoked, whereby the entire industry can be treated as if it were a single competitive firm, and it is not the distribution of inventories across firms that matters, but only their aggregate. While under perfect competition higher inherited stocks have no effect on output at the level of the firm, this will not be true at the level of the industry, where the negative effect identified in the last section will reappear. If the industry inherits higher stocks from the previous period, then its aggregate supply will be higher—indeed, at prices at which it does not pay to carry over stocks, the supply function is increased by the entire amount of the increase in inventory. This will tend to depress the relative price and, by the equality of price and marginal cost, to depress output. Is this partial equilibrium argument valid once we take account of repercussions elsewhere? Certainly, the fall in the price in one market is likely to reduce output in other markets. To see what happens overall, consider the conditions for labour market equilibrium where f is the production function of each industry and l_t^j is employment in industry j:

$$w_t f'(l_t^j) = p_t^j \tag{10}$$

for all j, and

$$\sum_j l_t^j = L[w_t / \pi(p_t^1, \ldots, p_t^N)]. \tag{11}$$

Product market equilibrium will be of the form

$$y_t^j + x_t^j = g^j(p_t^1, \ldots, p_j^N; W) + x_{t+1}^j \qquad (12)$$

for each j, where g^j is the demand function for good j, assumed symmetric, and it depends upon prices and the aggregate value of expenditure W (which itself may vary according to real balance effects, interest rates, or whatever: it doesn't matter to the argument). The point is that the labour market conditions tie down output irrespective of the existence of inventories. Substitute (10) into (11):

$$L\{1/\pi[1/f'(l_t^1), 1/f'(l_t^2), \ldots, 1/f'(l_t^N)]\} = \sum_j l_t^j \qquad (13)$$

after using the homogeneity of degree 1 of π to eliminate w. Taking the differential of this expression, we get

$$(-L'/\pi^2) \sum [\pi_j' f''(l_t^j)/f'(l_t^j)] \, dl_t^j = \sum dl_t^j.$$

Provided we start from a symmetric situation, $l_i = l_j$, all i and j, this requires that $\Sigma dl_t^j = 0$. (The Jacobian condition is satisfied provided the labour supply curve is upward-sloping.) So locally about symmetry the equilibrium labour supply is constant—this is just a generalization of the standard natural rate argument.

From out point of view, the importance of this result is that, provided the equilibrium conditions have a continuity property (in particular, provided g^j is continuous), then the effect on employment of a movement away from symmetry owing to a small increase in x^j is (generically) zero. It also follows from (13) that an across-the-board increase in inventories of any magnitude that preserves symmetry will have no effect on employment. The partial equilibrium analysis of the previous section breaks down in the latter case for a simple reason. It is true that, if inventories are increased and wages and other prices are held constant, then each industry will increase supply and cut output as its price falls relative to its cost; however, the simultaneous attempt to cut prices will lead to a fall in wages and hence in costs, so prices relative to costs will be unaltered, and it is this that determines output. (The aggregate price level will fall until demand plus desired future inventories have increased by the same amount as initial inventories, so satisfying (12).)

It has been recognized for some time that, at the level of the firm in a competitive industry, the production and inventory decisions 'decompose' in the sense that production is independent of the particular firm's inventories (Blinder 1978; Blinder and Fischer 1981). Eichenbaum (1983) has investigated the conditions under which this decomposition can be true at the industry level. He finds that a necessary and sufficient condition for decomposition is a perfectly elastic industry demand curve. This is not surprising, for an increase in industry inventories would mean that industry supply is in some sense higher. Sooner or later, with downward-sloping demand curves price must be depressed (in principle, this need not be immediate since the extra inventories would be carried forward), and under rational expectations it is shown that in fact the current price will fall and with input prices given this depresses current output. So, although inventories have no effect on output at the firm level, they do have an effect at the industry level under normal competitive conditions. The point being argued here is that the effect goes away again at the economy level, because input prices are now endogenous and will fall along with output prices under usual assumptions (that input supply depends only on *current* relative prices). The introduction of imperfect competition does not substantially alter this story, the main difference being that the individual imperfectly competitive firm now behaves in a fashion similar to the competitive *industry*. In other words, an increase in the individual firm's inventories will depress its relative price and hence its output. But at the macro level, there is no convincing reason to suggest that price–cost margins will be reduced when aggregate inventories increase.

What I have said above ignores possible intertemporal effects owing to labour supply along the Lucas–Rapping lines combined with the possible wealth effects of higher inventory levels (see Blinder and Fischer 1981). It seems unlikely however that such effects would be of great empirical significance.

An equivalent way of thinking about the possible macroeconomic implications of inventories is to consider whether the relationship between marginal cost and marginal revenue is affected by their existence. This is the relationship that normally governs the demand for labour, and in broad terms, if it is unaffected then the determination of labour market equilibrium will be as before and independent of the aggregate level of inventories. When prices are variable *ex post* (as in Blinder and Fischer 1981, for example), marginal cost is set equal to expected marginal revenue, and so the relationship has not been seriously disrupted, and the demand curve for labour should be independent of inventory levels.

When price is determined before the demand shock is known, the relationship between marginal costs and marginal revenue is not so clear. Abel (1985) shows that, if (costless) backlogging is allowed and if demand shocks have an additive form, marginal cost still equals expected marginal revenue, but for general demand shocks equality breaks down. On the other hand, if backlogging is not permitted, then even for additive demand shocks there is no equality (see also Sengupta 1985). This result suggests that inventories may exert an aggregate influence on output in 'buffer-stock' models when backlogging is not permitted, although a coherent model of this has not been developed yet, as far as I know. In Maccini (1976) an aggregate model is developed, but only for a fixed money wage, and I have argued that it is labour market equilibrium that is crucial. An interesting aggregate model with prices chosen in advance and no backlogging is developed in Brunner, Cukierman, and Meltzer (1983). However, an assumption that demand curves are kinked means that prices are not in essence variable, and this allows inventories to have a negative one-for-one effect on desired output at a given real wage.

In conclusion, the message of the microeconomic models that inventories have a powerful negative effect on output does not carry over easily to the macroeconomic realm. In so far as a negative effect exists in reality, it is an indication that the world may be Keynesian rather than classical, since this is a natural feature of Keynesian models with inventories.

APPENDIX: PROOF THAT $p_t = w_t c'(y_t)$

As before, dynamic programming may be used, and if $V_t(x_t)$ is the value discounted to t of the firm when inventories at t are x_t, the optimal policy must attain the supremum in the optimality equation:

$$V_t(x_t) = \sup_{q_t, y_t} [p_t q_t - w_t c(y_t) - hx_{t+1} + \beta V_{t+1}(x_{t+1})]$$

$$\text{s.t. } q_t \geqslant 0, \qquad x_{t+1} \geqslant 0, \qquad x_{t+1} = x_t + y_t - q_t.$$

Necessary conditions for this are

$$y_t > 0 \tag{A1}$$

$$p_t \leqslant w_t c'(y_t); \qquad q_t \geqslant 0 \tag{A2}$$

$$\beta V'_{t+1}(x_{t+1}) \leqslant w_t c'(y_t) + h; \qquad x_{t+1} \geqslant 0 \tag{A3}$$

and

$$V'_t(x_t) = w_t c'(y_t) \tag{A4}$$

where both (A2) and (A3) hold with complementary slackness. Now we claim that in equilibrium we must in fact have $p_t = w_t c'(y_t)$. If this were not so, then by (A2), $p_t < w_t c(y_t)$ and $q_t = 0$. There must be some future date T at which $q_T > 0$ (this follows from strict discounting—it cannot pay to take capital gains indefinitely), and we assume that T is the first date. From (A2) and (A4), we have $V'_T(x_T) = p_T$. By assumption, $q_{T-1} = 0$, so from (A1) $q_T > 0$, and by (A3) $\beta V'_T(x_T) = w_t c'(y_{T-1}) + h$. Hence $\beta p_T = w_t c(y_{T-1}) + h$, and by (A1),

$$p_{T-1} = w_t c'(y_{T-1}) \geqslant \beta V'_T(x_T) - h = \beta w_t c'(y_T) - h \geqslant \beta p_T - h,$$

which is the reverse inequality. While $q^j_{T-1} = 0$ for firm j, there must be at least one firm i for which $q^i_{T-1} > 0$, otherwise sales would be zero. Hence $\beta p_T - h = p_{T-1}$. Going back to firm j, since $x_T > 0$,

$$V'_{T-1}(x_{T-1}) = w_t c'(y_{T-1}) = \beta V'_T(x_T) - h = \beta p_T - h = p_{T-1}.$$

Because the marginal value of inventory at T was just the price at T, we have been able to show that the marginal value of inventory of $T-1$ is also the price at $T-1$, even though sales at $T-1$ are assumed to be zero. Continuing this process backwards unitl we reach t, we have $V'_t(x_t) = p_t$, so by (A4) $p_t = w_t c'(y_t)$, as was to be established.

NB: The argument is still valid if cost functions vary between firms and if the discount factor varies over time, although h may not vary between firms.

20

Business Cycles in Equilibrium: An Example

SALVATORE MODICA

1. Introduction

A driving force of business cycles may lie in the dynamics of preferences, if one assumes that the latter undergo changes at random times and then tend to stabilize; that unchanging preferences call for specialization of factors of production; and that specialized factors cannot be 'reconverted' instantaneously from one use to another.

Loosely speaking, the idea is as follows. Preferences tend to stabilize over time, owing to the influence of the status quo, social habits, and so on. As this process goes on, firms (rationally) become confident that preferences will in fact remain unchanged, which makes it profitable for them to specialize factors of production to some extent with a gain in productivity (and a loss in flexibility). However, at some random time preferences do change, and they take some time to stabilize again, while the change finds the (by then rigid) productive structure unable to meet current (changing) preferences—which causes a fall in output, and possibly a tendency towards de-specialization. But as preferences begin to assume their new form, firms again start to adapt the productive structure to it; preferences tend again to remain unchanged, and the process repeats itself, with periods of unchanging preferences corresponding to high levels of output, periods of change to low levels. Thus, output varies through time with the 'degree of matching' between preferences and productive structure, in a cyclical way, owing to the described evolution of preferences over time.

And as far as this cause–effect mechanism is concerned, cycles are not due to 'mistakes'. A slow rise, however, is due to lack of information (here about preferences) and can be made quicker by increasing it.

The following is a competitive equilibrium model which tries to capture the essence of this story; it is meant to be just an example, and as such is made simple by strong assumptions. It has the following characteristics. Time is divided into periods of equal length, so henceforth 'period' will have this precise meaning. In any one period, preferences over the goods of that period either may have a given structure (form) or may be

Research in connection with this chapter was supported by CNR, 'Modelli Probabilistici' 40 per cent 1985.

changing, their evolution over time being Markovian. For simplicity, the new, fixed structure that preferences may assume after a period of change is taken to be always equal to the old. In any period, factors of production have to be specialized (if at all) *before* the state of the world (i.e. the state of preferences) is known, on the basis of available information on the past. Confidence in the occurrence of a given structure of preferences would *per se* call for factor specialization, the more so the higher the productivity differential between specialized and non-specialized factors. But if factors are specialized (if the more productive structure is to some extent 'rigid'), occurrence of a state of change in preferences makes for a low level of output, for only a fraction of existing resources can be profitably used in such states: While non-specialized factors are less productive, but may suit a wider range of preferences, so (on average) they do better in states of changing, 'less known' preferences. Then, intuitively, the higher the probability that preferences have the given form (that preferences are 'structured', to abbreviate), and/or the higher the productivity differential, the stronger is the incentive for specialization. In fact, as will be seen in the following sections, in equilibrium, the higher these two parameters are, the larger is the extent of factor specialization. In turn, the greater the latter is, the wider is the possible fluctuation of output across states, because more intense specialization will make for higher levels of output in good states (when preferences are structured) and for lower levels in bad ones (when they are changing). If the productive structure is totally flexible (no factor specialization), output is always constant.

Turning to output autocorrelation, let—to anticipate notation—$\bar{q}$ and q be probabilities of transitions, respectively, from a period of 'structured' preferences to another and from a period of change to a period of structured preference. Positive autocorrelation in output (when this fluctuates) emerges iff $\bar{q} > q$, that is iff, loosely speaking, current stability in preferences makes the probability of future stability increase. The inequality $\bar{q} > q$ formalizes the assumption, stated in the first paragraph, that 'preferences tend to stabilize'. Finally, the model displays abrupt falls and slower rises of output over time.

Specifically, the economy considered in the following is a competitive Arrow–Debreu economy, standard in all except that some contingent markets for factors of production are missing. So it is assumed that firms cannot buy different combinations of inputs for all the different states of the world for all future periods; they can choose at time 1 the combinations of inputs for time $t \geq 1$, but these must be invariant through some subsets of states. The interpretation is that the chosen future combinations of inputs cannot be 'reconverted' instantaneously.

The complete description of the economy is given in the following sections, together with the analysis of its equilibrium. Conclusions follow.

2. The Economy

There are T periods, $t = 1, 2, \ldots, T$, two physically different consumption goods, $i = 1, 2$, and labour.

The terms 'state of the world' and 'event' are used so that a state of the world in period t is a history of events from period 1 to period t.

In any one period, one event is that preferences over the goods of that period have the given form; otherwise they are changing. Now this may be thought of as a situation in which there is uncertainty as to what preferences are over the two goods. The simple, extreme assumption made here is that in this case consumers' utility (consumers will be assumed to be identical) may depend on either only the first or only the second good,[1] with equal probabilities. This tries also to model the fact that when preferences change some of the 'old' goods are no longer liked. Thus, in any period there are three possible events: that consumers like only good 1; that they like only good 2; and that preferences over the two goods have the given form. These events will be numbered respectively as events 1, 2, and 3, the first two 'composing' the event of changing preferences.

The sequence of events is assumed to be a homogeneous Markov process in stationary state. From what has been said here and in the Introduction, the transition matrix of this process is

$$E \equiv \begin{pmatrix} p & p & q \\ p & p & q \\ \bar{p} & \bar{p} & \bar{q} \end{pmatrix}$$

with $p = (1 - q)/2$, $\bar{p} = (1 - \bar{q})/2$. In fact, letting henceforth the symbol e denote events, one has for example that E_{33} is the probability of a transition from e_3 to e_3, i.e., from one period when preferences have the given form to another. I have said in the Introduction that this occurs with probability $\bar{q}$. With probability $1 - \bar{q}$, from e_3 the system passes to e_1 or e_2, with equal probability: $(1 - \bar{q})/2 = \bar{p}$. These are E_{31} and E_{32}. The other elements are derived similarly.

Letting $p_t = \Pr(e_t = 1) = \Pr(e_t = 2)$, $q_t = \Pr(e_t = 3)$, it is easily checked that the stationary distribution (p^s, q^s) is given by $p^s = (1 - q^s)/2$, $q^s = q/(q + 1 - \bar{q})$. It will be assumed that $(p_0, q_0) = (p^s, q^s)$, so that for any $t = 1, 2, \ldots, T$ one has $(p_t, q_t) = (p^s, q^s)$, and for the sake of symmetry e_0 is known after time 1 (at which tradking takes place). Also, it is taken that $q, \bar{q} \in (0, 1)$.

With this particular Markovian structure, the only information about the past that may influence choices for period t is whether $e_{t-1} = 3$ or

[1] My results will depend on this assumption significantly, for it ensures that in some states one good is not produced and so output is low. To dispense with it, the model should be modified by explicitly introducing, for instance, leisure.

$e_{t-1} = 1$ or $2 \equiv 3^c$ (3^c for the complement of 3, abusing notation a bit), because the probabilities of events $e_t = 1, 2$, or 3 are independent of $e_0, e_1, \ldots, e_{t-2}$. Hence there are effectively six states of the world in period t (for $t = 1, 2, \ldots, T$): three corresponding to $e_{t-1} = 3$ and $e_t = 1, 2, 3$, and three corresponding to $e_{t-1} = 3^c$ and $e_t = 1, 2, 3$. These states will be denoted by $j_t = 1, 2, \ldots, 6$ and numbered as follows, with (e_{t-1}, e_t) denoting the relevant partial history:

$$j_t = 1, 2, 3 \text{ if } (e_{t-1}, e_t) = (3, 1), (3, 2), (3, 3), \text{ respectively,}$$

$$j_t = 4, 5, 6 \text{ if } (e_{t-1}, e_t) = (3^c, 1), (3^c, 2), (3^c, 3), \text{ respectively.}$$

One may compute, for example, $\Pr(j_t = 1) = q^s \bar{p}$, $\Pr(j_t = 6) = (1 - q^s)q$; etc.

Then there is a total of $T \times 2 \times 6$ (contingent) consumption goods; subscripts (t, i, j) will denote good i in period t in state j.

Markets for all these goods are assumed to exist at time 1. The other goods markets, like that for good i at time t in state (e_{t-2}, e_{t-1}, e_t) and so on, are neglected because in this model they are irrelevant, in the sense that the resulting allocations at time t with or without them would be the same.

The labour market is organized as follows. In each period t ($t = 1, 2, \ldots, T$), consumers are endowed with homogeneous labour. Firms buy this at time 1, and at time t they internally divide it between specialized and non-specialized labour, at no cost. Non-specialized (specialized) labour cannot be used as specialized (non-specialized) labour once the subdivision has been made. Non-specialized labour can produce both goods, and there are two types of specialized labour, the first (second) being capable of producing only the first (second) physical good. Labour is more productive when specialized than when not specialized, but it is being assumed—forgive the repetition—that, say, specialized labour of type 1 (producing the first good) cannot be used as non-specialized labour to produce good 2 within the period.

The crucial assumption is that in any period the decision by firms on specialization must be taken before the state of the world is known—which in fact means before e_t is known. The interpretation is that specialization 'takes time'.

Hence the present value of homogeneous labour at t depends, via contingent goods' prices, on the probabilities of the events $e_t = 1, 2, 3$. Since these in turn depend on e_{t-1} being 3 or 3^c (but not on e_{t-2}, etc.), homogenous labour in period t must be regarded as different goods according to whether e_{t-1} is 3 or 3^c (but e_{t-2} (etc.) are irrelevant), that is, as different goods in the subsets of states $A \equiv \{1, 2, 3\}$ and $B \equiv \{4, 5, 6\}$ in period t.

The two markets for homogeneous labour in period t contingent on the

subsets of states *A* and *B* are assumed to exist at time 1, for each
$t = 1, 2, \ldots, T$.

To sum up, the above assumptions imply that the extent of specialization (the 'chosen combinations of inputs' of the penultimate paragraph of
the Introduction) may vary from *A* to *B*, but it must be constant within
each of them. The interpretation is that the impossibility of instantaneous
reconversion of input combinations prevents them from varying freely
across states; on the other hand, existing markets allow for 'revision of
plans' for period *t* on the basis of information on period $t - 1$.

With this specification of goods and markets, given the evolution of
states, no agent has any incentive to recontract after time 1. So all market
activity (contracts in all goods and labour) is carried out at that time.

The specification of the production side is completed as follows.
Technologies, invariant through time, are all linear, so it will be assumed
that there is only one firm, making zero profits in equilibrium. Homogeneous labour L_t (resp. M_t) in period *t* in the subset *A* (resp. *B*) of states
may be bought—at time 1—at the wage v_t (resp. w_t) and then divided
between specialized and non-specialized labour L_{ts}, L_{tn} (resp. M_{ts}, M_{tn}),
where $L_{ts} + L_{tn} = L_t$ (resp. $M_{ts} + M_{tn} = M_t$). Specialized labour of type
$i = 1, 2$, denoted by L_{ts}^i (resp. M_{ts}^i), can produce only good *i* in period *t*,
and $L_{ts}^1 + L_{ts}^2 = L_{ts}$ (resp. $M_{ts}^1 + M_{ts}^2 = M_{ts}$); non-specialized labour can
produce both goods in each state.

More specifically, all specialized labour has productivity λ, non-
specialized labour has productivity μ, with $\lambda > \mu$. For example, let y_{tij} be
output of good (t, i, j): if $j \in \{1, 2, 3\}$ and L_{ts}^i, L_{tn} units are used, output
will be $y_{tij} = \lambda L_{ts}^i + \mu L_{tn}$, $i = 1, 2$ and $t = 1, 2, \ldots, T$. Similarly with *M*
replacing *L* if $j \in \{4, 5, 6\}$.

Thus, λ/μ is a direct measure of the productivity differential, higher
values of it indicating greater advantage from specialization and vice
versa.

Letting π_{tij} be the price (at time 1) of good (t, i, j), the problem the
firm must solve is then

$$\max \sum_{t=1}^{T} \left\{ \left[\sum_{i=1}^{2} \sum_{j=1}^{3} \pi_{tij} y_{tij} - v_t(L_{ts}^1 + L_{ts}^2 + L_{tn}) \right] \right.$$

$$\left. + \left[\sum_{i=1}^{2} \sum_{j=4}^{6} \pi_{tij} y_{tij} - w_t(M_{ts}^1 + M_{ts}^2 + M_{tn}) \right] \right\}$$

subject to the technological constraints. As already anticipated, it will be
assumed that in states 1 and 4 (resp. 2 and 5) consumers like only good 1
(resp. 2) in each period, so for each *t* in equilibrium, $y_{t21} = y_{t12} = y_{t24} = y_{t15} = 0$. To ease exposition, this is taken into account in the above

problem. Then the constraints are, for $t = 1, 2, \ldots, T$,

$$y_{t11} = \lambda L_{ts}^1 + \mu L_{tn}$$

$$y_{t22} = \lambda L_{ts}^2 + \mu L_{tn}$$

$$y_{t13} = \lambda L_{ts}^1 + \mu L_{tn}^1$$

$$y_{t23} = \lambda L_{ts}^2 + \mu(L_{tn} - L_{tn}^1)$$

$$y_{t14} = \lambda M_{ts}^1 + \mu M_{tn}$$

$$y_{t25} = \lambda M_{ts}^2 + \mu M_{tn}$$

$$y_{t16} = \lambda M_{ts}^1 + \mu M_{tn}^1$$

$$y_{t26} = \lambda M_{ts}^2 + \mu(M_{tn} - M_{tn}^1).$$

Here L_{tn}^1 is the amount of non-specialized labour used in period t in state 3 to produce good 1; similarly for M_{tn}^1. So in state 1 the firm can use the fraction L_{ts}^1 of specialized labour L_{ts} and all non-specialized labour L_{tn}; in state 3 the latter can be used to produce both goods; and so on.

That profits must be zero in equilibrium may be seen by substituting the constraints in the objective function and factoring out labour of the various kinds. This implies that it is immaterial to specify who owns the firm.

Turning to consumers, there are H identical individuals endowed with a constant amount l of homogeneous labour at each date, and no consumption goods. As anticipated, they are assumed to derive no utility from good 2 in event 1 (i.e. in states 1 and 4) and from good 1 in event 2 (states 2 and 5), at each date. The utility from good 1 (resp. 2) in event 1 (resp. 2) will be represented by the function $u: R_+ \rightarrow R$. The given, fixed structure of preferences they have in event 3 (states 3 and 6) over the two periods will be represented by the function $z: R_+^2 \rightarrow R$. In addition, they are assumed to derive no disutility from work. This implies that total labour supply is fixed and equal to Hl in each period, in each state.

Specifically, it is assumed that all have the same utility function $U(x)$ over bundles $x = (x_{tij}) \in R_+^{T \times 2 \times 6}$, and that $U(x)$ is an expected utility, of the form

$$U(x) = \sum_{t=1}^{T} \{q^s[\bar{p}u(x_{t11}) + \bar{p}u(x_{t22}) + \bar{q}z(x_{t13}, x_{t23})]$$
$$+ (1 - q^s)[pu(x_{t14}) + pu(x_{t25}) + qz(x_{t16}, x_{t26})]\}$$

with u, z concave, strictly increasing in their arguments. For simplicity, it will be assumed that, for any $(x, y) \in R_+^2$, one has $z(x, y) = z(y, x)$. Also, it is assumed that for any $x \in R_+$, one has $z(x/2, x/2) = u(x)$.

Consumer h's problem is then, for $h = 1, 2, \ldots, H$,

$$\max U(x)$$

$$\text{s.t.} \sum_{t=1}^{T} \sum_{i=1}^{2} \sum_{j=1}^{6} \pi_{tij} x_{tij}^{h} = l \sum_{t=1}^{T} (v_t + w_t)$$

where superscript h refers to consumer h.

3. Equilibrium and Output Fluctuations

In this section it is shown how the amplitude of equilibrium output fluctuations depends on the parameters given by the probabilities of states and the productivity differential.

Notice first that invariance of input combinations within some subset of states is necessary for the possibility of equilibrium output fluctuations in this model: if input combinations could freely vary across states (complete markets), it is not difficult to see that all labour would be specialized in each state and output would be always constant. This is clear, for in this case the decision on specialization can be effectively taken after the state of the world is known.

The economy described in the previous section behaves as a standard Arrow–Debreu economy as far as existence of equilibrium is concerned, so this is guaranteed.

In equilibrium supply equals demand; that is,

$$\sum_{h=1}^{H} x_{tij}^{h^*} = y_{tij}^{*}, \qquad t = 1, 2, \ldots, T: \quad i = 1, 2; \quad j = 1, 2, \ldots, 6$$

$$Hl = L_t^* = M_t^*, \qquad t = 1, 2, \ldots, T,$$

where starred optimal choices correspond to equilibrium prices $\pi_{tij}^*, v_t^*, w_t^*$.

Since all consumers are identical, $x_{tij}^{h^*} = x_{tij}^*$, for all h is an equilibrium. In most of what follows, strict concavity of $U(x)$ is assumed, so this is the only equilibrium. And only this case will be considered in the sequel. Furthermore, it is straightforward to show that equilibrium prices must be time-invariant, in the sense that $\pi_{tij}^* = \pi_{ij}^*, v_t^* = v^*, w_t^* = w^*$. This follows (by contradiction arguments) from the fact that the system is in stationary state and from the time-invariance of technologies, preferences, and endowments. Hence it will be taken that $x_{tij}^* = x_{ij}^*$, so that equilibrium allocations $(x_{tij}^{h^*})_{h=1,2,\ldots,H}$ will be time-invariant too; that is,

$$(x_{tij}^{h^*})_{h=1,2,\ldots,H} = (x_{ij}^*) \in R_+^{H \times T \times 2 \times 6}.$$

Recall that, by our assumptions, one has $x_{21}^* = x_{12}^* = x_{24}^* = x_{15}^* = 0$. Time-invariance of $L_{tm}^*, L_{ts}^{i^*}, M_{tm}^*, M_{ts}^{i^*}(i = 1, 2)$ follows from that of prices and allocations; they will be denoted by L_n^*, etc.

Now one can see that the equilibrium allocation (x_{ij}^*) must be Pareto-optimal relatively to the existing markets. The proof of this is like the standard proof for complete markets. Then from the above remarks one deduces that, by symmetry, the problem that must be solved by $x_{ij}^* \in R_+^{2 \times 6}$ is the following:

$$\max \{q^s[\bar{p}u(x_{11}) + \bar{p}u(x_{22}) + \bar{q}z(x_{13}, x_{23})]$$
$$+ (1 - q^s)[pu(x_{14}) + pu(x_{25}) + qz(x_{16}, x_{26})]\}$$

$$\text{s.t.} \quad x_{11} = \lambda l_s^1 + \mu l_n$$

$$x_{22} = \lambda l_s^2 + \mu l_n$$

$$x_{13} = \lambda l_s^1 + \mu l_n^1$$

$$x_{23} = \lambda l_s^2 + \mu(l_n - l_n^1)$$

$$x_{14} = \lambda m_s^1 + \mu m_n$$

$$x_{25} = \lambda m_s^2 + \mu m_n$$

$$x_{16} = \lambda m_s^1 + \mu m_n^1$$

$$x_{26} = \lambda m_s^2 + \mu(m_n - m_n^1)$$

$$l_s^1 + l_s^2 + l_n = l$$

$$m_s^1 + m_s^2 + m_n = l.$$

Then, if l_s^{1*}, m_s^{1*} (etc.) solve this problem, $Hl_s^{1*} = L_s^{1*}$, $Hm_s^{1*} = M_s^{1*}$ (etc), where starred capital letters are equilibrium values. And equilibrium allocacation is given by $x_{11}^* = \lambda l_s^{1*} + \mu l_n^*$ (etc.).

This problem separates into two exactly analogous problems, one corresponding to the subset A of states, the other to B. In fact, they differ only if $\bar{q} \neq q$. So considering the first will suffice. This—and so the equilibrium for subset A—is parametrized by $\bar{q}$ (and $\bar{p}$, but $\bar{p} = (1 - \bar{q})/2$), λ, and μ.

To have an idea about how the solution depends on them, consider first the particular case in which $z(x, y) = u(x + y)$ and u is linear. In Appendix 1 it is shown that, with $l_s^* = l_s^{1*} + l_s^{2*}$, one has

$$l_s^* = 0 \quad \text{if} \quad \bar{q} < q^* \equiv 2\mu/\lambda - 1,$$

$$l_s^* = l \quad \text{if} \quad \bar{q} > q^* \equiv 2\mu/\lambda - 1,$$

the choice of l_s^{1*}, l_s^{2*} being arbitrary. (If $\lambda < 2\mu$, then $0 < q^* < 1$; if $\lambda > 2\mu$, $q^* < 0$, so always $l_s^* = l$.) We shall take to fix ideas $l_s^{1*} = l_s^{2*} = l_s^*/2$. Thus, high values of $\bar{q}$ and/or λ/μ bring about complete specialization, and the opposite occurs for low values.

Total output is defined to be the total number of units of all goods produced; for example, in state 3 it is $H(x_{13}^* + x_{23}^*)$.[2]

Thus, if $l_s^* = 0$, that is if $L_s^* = 0$, then total equilibrium output is constant across states in A and equal to $\mu H l$. If on the contrary specialization prevails, then output fluctuates, being $\lambda H l$ in state 3 and $\lambda H l/2$ in states 1 and 2.

Turning to the general case, and assuming from now on strict concavity of u and z for uniqueness, observe first that, by symmetry of z, if $l_s^* > 0$, then $l_s^{1*} = l_s^{2*} = l_s^*/2$ (because symmetry and strict concavity of z imply that for any $a \neq 0$ it is $z(x, x) > z(x + a, x - a)$; then add strict concavity of u). This implies that output is the same in states 1 and 2. Of course no sharp formulas can be obtained, but the sense of the result remains unaltered. Output fluctuations within subset A are wider when more labour is specialized, for this makes for higher output in state 3 and lower output in states 1 and 2, when half of the specialized labour is left idle; and there are none if and only if $l_n^* = l$. If $\lambda/\mu > 2$, then $l_n^* = 0$; and for interior solutions, by substituting the constraints as in Appendix 1 and then differentiating totally the first-order conditions with respect to $\bar{q}$, λ, μ, one obtains

$$\frac{\partial l_s^*}{\partial \bar{q}} > 0, \qquad \frac{\partial l_s^*}{\partial \lambda} > 0, \qquad \frac{\partial l_s^*}{\partial \mu} < 0,$$

all signs changed for the derivatives of l_n^*. (Recall that $l_n^* + l_n^* = l$, constant.)

In turn, assuming that $\lambda < 2\mu$ (for otherwise the choice would be independent of $\bar{q}$, with all labour specialized), greater specialization implies higher output in state 3 and lower output in states 1 and 2, that is, wider output fluctuations. This becomes clear if one thinks of replacing two units of non-specialized labour by two units of specialized labour (one of each type): in state 3 one would have two units of specialized labour working in place of two units of non-specialized labour, producing more; in states 1 and 2, one would have one unit of specialized labour in place of two units of non-specialized labour, producing less (for $\lambda < 2\mu$).

This makes precise what was said in the Introduction: the higher the confidence in unchanging preferences ($\bar{q}$) and/or in the productivity differential, the greater the labour specialization and so the wider the output fluctuations.

For the second problem, the derivatives have the same signs, with l replaced by m and $\bar{q}$ by q.

---

[2] Thus we shall have to say for instance that three units of the first good plus three of the second is more than four units of the first good, which is questionable. However, when this happens the resources used to produce the $3 + 3$ combination could produce four units of the first good plus some of the second.

Notice that if $\bar{q} > q$, the foregoing implies that $l_s^* \geq m_s^*$, inequality being strict if $l_s^* > 0$ and $m_s^* < l$. If the latter occurs, then output fluctuations are wider in subset A than in B, for in this case it must be $\lambda < 2\mu$.

4. Cycles and Output Autocorrelation

This section is devoted to showing that, as anticipated in the Introduction, $\bar{q} > q$ is a necessary and sufficient condition for positive autocorrelation in equilibrium output and so for cyclical behaviour.

The argument showing that $\bar{q} > q$ (resp. $\bar{q} = q$) implies that positive (resp. null) autocorrelation in output will be given in full. (A parallel argument may be used to show that $\bar{q} < q$ implies negative autocorrelation; this argument is omitted.) The two together prove the assertion.

Suppose $\bar{q} > q$—the case $\bar{q} = q$ will be dealt with in the course of the argument. Then from Section 3, one has $L_s^* \geq M_s^*$, so if $L_s^* = 0$ output is always constant, which is not the case of interest here. Assume then that $L_s^* > 0$. Hence, from Section 3 again, M_s^* equal to (smaller than) Hl implies L_s^* equal to (greater than) M_s^*, so in subset A specialization is never lower than in B. That is, if preferences are not changing in period t, specialization in period $t + 1$ will not be lower than it would be if they were. We have seen in Section 3 that equilibrium total output (there defined) in state 1 is equal to that in state 2. Analogously, total output in state 4 is equal to that in state 5. Recall that states 1 and 2 (resp. 4 and 5) representing changing preferences in subset A (resp. B).

Let Q^1 (resp. Q^2) denote total output in states 1 and 2 (resp. 4 and 5), and Q^4 (resp. Q^3), total output in state 3 (resp. 6). For example, $Q^1 = Hx_{11}^* = Hx_{22}^*$, $Q^4 = H(x_{13}^* + x_{23}^*)$. Then one has $Q^4 > Q^1$, for $L_s^* > 0$ (from Section 3), and $Q^1 \leq Q^2 \leq Q^3 \leq Q^4$, because in subset B specialization is not greater than in A, so that in B output fluctuations are not wider than in A. The sequence of outputs Q_t, $t = 1, 2, \ldots, T$ is a homogeneous Markov process, in stationary state (since the event process is), with transition matrix given by

$$\begin{bmatrix} 0 & 1-q & q & 0 \\ 0 & 1-q & q & 0 \\ 1-\bar{q} & 0 & 0 & \bar{q} \\ 1-\bar{q} & 0 & 0 & \bar{q} \end{bmatrix}$$

if $L_s^* > M_s^*$, and by

$$\begin{bmatrix} 1-q & q \\ 1-\bar{q} & \bar{q} \end{bmatrix}$$

if $L_s^* = M_s^*$ (see Appendix 2).

Let $a_n = Q^n - EQ$ for $n = 1, 2, 3, 4$, E being the expectation operator.

A bit of calculation gives

$$\text{cov}(Q_t, Q_{t+1}) = [a_4 q^s \bar{q} + a_3(1 - q^s)q][a_4 \bar{q} + a_1(1 - \bar{q})]$$
$$+ [a_2(1 - q^s)(1 - q) + a_1 q^s(1 - \bar{q})][a_3 q + a_2(1 - q)]$$
$$\equiv (1)\cdot(2) + (3)\cdot(4).$$

From

$$0 = E(Q - EQ)$$
$$= a_4 q^s \bar{q} + a_1 q^s(1 - \bar{q}) + a_3(a - q^s)q + a_2(1 - q^s)(1 - q),$$

one deduces

$$(1) + (3) = 0$$
$$q^s \cdot (2) + (1 - q^s) \cdot (4) = 0.$$

Consider at this point the case $\bar{q} = q$. This implies $L_s^* = M_s^*$; that is, $Q^1 = Q^2$, $Q^3 = Q^4$, and so $a_1 = a_2$, $a_3 = a_4$. Hence $(2) = (4)$ so both must be zero, and therefore $\text{cov}(Q_t, Q_{t+1}) = 0$.

Going back to the case $\bar{q} > q$, it is easy to see that $(1) > 0$ and $(3) < 0$ (using the facts that $a_1 \leqslant a_2 \leqslant a_3 \leqslant a_4$ and $a_1 < a_4$, and $(1) + (3) = 0$). The argument provided in Appendix 3 shows that $\bar{q} > q$ also implies that $(2) > 0$, $(4) < 0$ and so that $\text{cov}(Q_t, Q_{t+1}) > 0$.

Since the same line of argument can be used to show that $\bar{q} < q$ implies $\text{cov}(Q_t, Q_{t+1}) < 0$, the conclusion is that $\text{cov}(Q_t, Q_{t+1}) > 0$ if and only if $\bar{q} > q$. Thus in this model it is the fact that 'stability in preferences increases confidence in stability' which determines output positive autocorrelation.

Finally, from the output transition matrix (when $L_s^* > M_s^*$) one deduces that this economy displays expansions longer than contractions, in the sense that it takes at least two periods to reach Q^4 from Q^1 and Q^2, while output falls from Q^4 and Q^3 to Q^1 always in one period. This is because Q^1 and Q^2 occur in periods of changing preferences, followed by periods in which the productive structure is relatively flexible and for this reason relatively less 'productive' in good states (structured preferences), while on the contrary Q^4 and Q^3 occur in periods of structured preferences, followed by periods in which the productive structure is relatively more rigid and so less productive in bad states (when preferences are changing).

5. Interpretation and Conclusions

Unlike in the model presented, there exist in the real world many different factors of production, in particular capital goods. Now these goods by their nature last relatively long—so that generally decisions concerning then must be taken before the demand is known—and cannot be reconverted instantaneously from one use to another. But these are facts, it is thought, which the assumption of missing contingent markets for labour reflects in the context of the model. (With this interpretation of labour of various kinds in terms of capital goods, the fact that in periods of changing preferences some specialized labour—although paid for—is left idle in the model would correspond to the shut-down of unprofitable plants of the real world.)

In the model, the assumptions stated in the first paragraph of the Introduction and their implication of missing contingent markets for factors of production generally imply, in equilibrium, some specialization of factors and hence (via $\bar{q} > q$) cyclical fluctuations of output over time.

Moreover, the (equilibrium) evolution of this model economy would display abrupt falls in output and the shut-down of 'plants' which, to the external observer, might seem due to mistakes on the part of the agents and 'misdirected investment'.

But in fact, the equilibrium is a perfect-foresight equilibrium, in that all trade occurs in the first period and no one has any incentive to recontract after then; and, given the constraint that combinations of input cannot be reconverted instantaneously from one use to another, it is also Pareto-efficient.

There remains the informational issue mentioned in the Introduction—that slow rises may be speeded up by increasing information. The model presented is too simple to deal with this explicitly, but, as far as the cyclical fluctuations that have been described are concerned, this seems to be the chief direction in which policy may be effective.

APPENDIX 1

The problem we are considering is problem (P) of Appendix 3 below, with $z(x_{13}, x_{23}) = u(x_{13} + x_{23})$, u linear, and $q = \bar{q}$.

By first substituting in the objective function the constraints on x and then writing $l_s^1 = l - l_s^2 - l_n$, this problem may be written as

$$\max M \equiv \max\{\bar{p}u[\lambda(l - l_s^2 - l_n) + \mu l_n] + \bar{p}u(\lambda l_s^2 + \mu l_n) + \bar{q}u[\lambda(l - l_n) + \mu l_n]\}.$$

By hypothesis, $u'(\cdot) = \text{const.}$ Also, $2\bar{p} + \bar{q} = 1$ so $\bar{p} + \bar{q} = (1 + \bar{q})/2$. Then

$$\frac{\partial M}{\partial l_n} = \bar{p}u'(\cdot)(\mu - \lambda) + \bar{p}u'(\cdot)\mu + \bar{q}u'(\cdot)(\mu - \lambda)$$

$$= u'(\cdot)[\mu - (\bar{p} + \bar{q})\lambda] = u'(\cdot)[\mu - \lambda(1 + \bar{q})/2] = 0$$

iff $\mu - \lambda(1 + \bar{q})/2 = 0$, i.e. iff q^*q^*.

Recalling that $l_s^* = l - l_n^*$, one obtains l_s^* as in the text. Also,

$$\frac{\partial M}{\partial l_s^2} = -p\bar{u}'(\cdot)\lambda + \bar{p}u'(\cdot)\lambda \equiv 0$$

so the choice of l_s^1, l_s^2 is arbitrary.

APPENDIX 2

Take for instance the last element of the last row, i.e. the probability of a transition from Q^4 to Q^4. If $L_s^* > M_s^*$, then $Q_t = Q^4$ only if $j_t = 3$. Thus,

$$\Pr(Q_{t+1} = Q^4 \mid Q_t = Q^4) = \Pr(j_{t+1} = 3 \mid j_t = 3)$$
$$= \Pr(e_{t+1} = 3 \mid e_t = 3) = \bar{q}$$

(the last equality from the transition matrix E in Section 2).

If $L_s^* = M_s^*$ then $Q_t = Q^4$ in $j_t = 3$ or $j_t = 6$. (Recall that in this case there are only two distinct values of output: $Q^1 = Q^2 < Q^3 = Q^4$.) Since

$$\Pr(j_t = 3 \mid e_t = 3) = \frac{\Pr(\{j_t = 3\} \cap \{e_t = 3\})}{\Pr(e_t = 3)}$$

$$= \frac{\Pr(j_t = 3)}{\Pr(e_t = 3)} = \frac{q^s \bar{q}}{q^s} = \bar{q}$$

and similarly,

$$\Pr(j_t = 6 \mid e_t = 3) = \frac{1 - q^s}{q^s} q,$$

in this case one has

$$\Pr(Q_{t+1} = Q^4 \mid Q_t = Q^4) = \Pr(j_t = 3 \mid e_t = 3)[\Pr(j_{t+1} = 3 \mid j_t = 3)$$
$$+ \Pr(j_{t+1} = 6 \mid j_t = 3)] + \Pr(j_t = 6 \mid e_t = 3)[\Pr(j_{t+1} = 3 \mid j_t = 6)$$
$$+ \Pr(j_{t+1} = 6 \mid j_t = 6)]$$
$$= \bar{q}(\bar{q} + 0) + [(1 - q^s)/q^s]\bar{q}(\bar{q} + 0) = \bar{q}[q^s \bar{q} + (1 - q^s)q]/q^s = \bar{q},$$

the last equality by stationarity of q^s. Check:

$$q^s \bar{q} + (1 - q^s)q = \bar{q} \frac{q}{q + 1 - \bar{q}} + q\left(1 - \frac{q}{q + 1 - \bar{q}}\right)$$

$$= \frac{1}{q + 1 - \bar{q}}[\bar{q}q + q(1 - \bar{q})] = \frac{q}{q + 1 - \bar{q}} = q^s.$$

Actually, when $L_s^* = M_s^*$, the states $j_t = 3$ and $j_t = 6$ are essentially the same—the only thing that counts is $e_t = 3$. So we might have written directly

$$\Pr(Q_{t+1} = Q^4 \mid Q_t = Q^4) = \Pr(e_{t+1} = 3 \mid e_t = 3) = \bar{q}.$$

Take as another example the first element of the first row when $L_s^* > M_s^*$, which is equal to zero. This denotes the probability of a transition from Q^1 to Q^1. When $L_s^* > M_s^*$, it is $Q^2 > Q^1$ because in the event 'changing preferences'—states 4 and 5—more is produced, for more resources can be used. Now Q^1 occurs in states 1 and 2, when $e_t = 3^c$. So it must be $j_{t+1} \in B$. And in B output is either $Q^2 > Q^1$ or $Q^3 \geq Q^2 > Q^1$. So the probability in question is zero. The other elements are derived in an analogous way.

When $L_s^* = M_s^*$ there are only two possible values of total output: the lower in states 1, 2, 4, 5, and the higher in states 3 and 6. In this case, as far as output is concerned, there are only three states in any period t, corresponding to $e_t = 1$, 2, or 3. Output is lower in $e_t = 1$ and 2, higher in $e_t = 3$. So the transition probabilities are derived directly from the event transition matrix E of Section 2, by the same arguments.

APPENDIX 3

It is to be shown that, if $\bar{q} > q$, then

$$(2) \equiv a_4\bar{q} + a_1(1 - \bar{q}) > 0$$

$$(4) \equiv a_3q + a_2(1 - q) < 0.$$

Since $q^s \cdot (2) + (1 - q^s) \cdot (4) = 0$, it suffices to show $(2) > (4)$, which is equivalent to showing

$$\bar{q}Q^4 + (1 - \bar{q})Q^1 > qQ^3 + (1 - q)Q^2,$$

where Q^n, $n = 1, 2, 3, 4$ are equilibrium total outputs. Now these are just H times individual equilibrium consumptions (in the various states). And the latter solve the constrained Pareto optimum problem of Section 3. Denoting, with no change of notation, individual consumptions by the same symbols, Q^n, $n = 1, 2, 3, 4$, one has that $\bar{q}Q^4 + (1 - \bar{q})Q^1$ (resp. $qQ^3 + (1 - q)Q^2$) is just optimal expected consumption for the sub-problem of subset A (resp. B) of states. Thus, the assertion is proved if one can show that, in the following problem (with $p = (1 - q)/2$),

$$
\left.
\begin{aligned}
&\max[pu(x_{11}) + pu(x_{22}) + qz(x_{13}, x_{23})] \\
&\text{s.t. } x_{11} = \lambda l_s^1 + \mu l_n \\
&\qquad x_{22} = \lambda l_s^2 + \mu l_n \\
&\qquad x_{13} = \lambda l_s^1 + \mu l_n^1 \\
&\qquad x_{23} = \lambda l_s^2 + \mu(l_n - l_n^1) \\
&\qquad l_s^1 + l_s^2 + l_n = l,
\end{aligned}
\right\} \quad \text{(P)}
$$

parameterized by q, optimal expected consumption—henceforth denoted by $Q_E(q)$—strictly increased in q. In fact, since we have assumed that $L_s^* > 0$, we can restrict attention to pairs $q^1 < q^2$ such that optimal $l_n^*(q^2) < l$.

Denote by $Q^L(q) \leqslant Q^H(q)$ optimal consumptions for the q-problem (L, H for low, high); that is, $Q^L(q) = x_{11}^*(q) = x_{22}^*(q)$, $Q^H(q) = x_{13}^*(q) + x_{23}^*(q)$.

By definition,

$$Q_E(q) = qQ^H(q) + (1 - q)Q^L(q).$$

Take two arbitrary values, $q^1 < q^2$, of q such that $Q^L(q^2) < Q^H(q^2)$. If $l_n^*(q^1) = 0$, then also $l_n^*(q^2) = 0$, whence $Q^H(q^1) = Q^H(q^2)$, $Q^L(q^1) = Q^L(q^2)$, so obviously $Q_E(q^1) < Q_E(q^2)$.

Suppose then that $l_n^*(q^1) > 0$. This implies that $l_n^*(q^2) < l_n^*(q^1)$ so

$$Q^L(q^2) < q^L(q^1) \leqslant Q^H(q^1) < Q^H(q^2).$$

Also (as in Section 3), strict concavity of u and z plus symmetry of z and the technology with respect to the two physical goods imply that $x_{13}^*(q) = x_{23}^*(q) = Q^H(q)/2$; therefore

$$z[x_{13}^*(q), x_{23}^*(q)] = z[Q^H(q)/2, Q^H(q)/2]$$
$$= u[Q^H(q)],$$

the last equality by assumption (Section 2).

Consider the optimal value function of the q-problem,

$$V(q) \equiv pu[x_{11}^*(q)] + pu[x_{22}^*(q)] + qz[x_{13}^*(q), x_{23}^*(q)]$$
$$= (1-q)u[Q^L(q)] + qu[Q^H(q)].$$

It will be shown that

(i) $V(q)$ increases with q
(ii) (i) implies that $Q_E(q^1) < Q_E(q^2)$,

completing the proof.

To show (i), observe that, since, for any q,

$$u[Q^H(q)] \geq u[Q^L(q)],$$

one has

$$V(q^2) = (1-q^2)u[Q^1(q^2)] + q^2u[Q^H(q^2)]$$
$$\geq (1-q^2)u[Q^L(q^1)] + q^2u[Q^H(q^1)]$$
$$\geq (1-q^1)u[Q^L(q^1)] + q^1u[Q^H(q^1)]$$
$$= V(q^1).$$

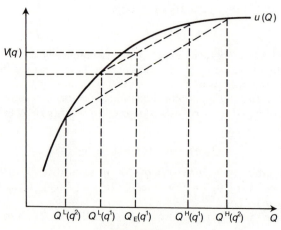

Fig. 20.1

The proof of the last claim will be clear from the following graphical argument, so is omitted.

In Figure 20.1, $Q^L(q^1) < Q^H(q^1)$, without loss of generality.

By concavity, and from $Q^L(q^2) < Q^L(q^1) \leq Q^H(q^1) < Q^H(q^2)$, the chord from $u[Q^L(q^1)]$ to $u[Q^H(q^1)]$ lies always above the other (see the figure). Hence if $Q_E(q^2) \leq Q_E(q^1)$, one would have $V(q^2) \leq V < V(q^1)$, contradicting (i). Therefore $Q_E(q^2) > Q_E(q^1)$, as was to be shown.

21

Keynes's Liquidity Preference Theory: A Suggested Reinterpretation

LOUIS MAKOWSKI

1. Introduction

In his second lecture in *The Crisis in Keynesian Economics,* Hicks (1974) challenges economists to try to achieve a deeper, more integrated, view of the relationship between investment and money than he was able to achieve in his original statement of the *IS–LM* model. He notes that Keynes's concept of money demand as reflecting a preference for *liquidity* is not explicitly incorporated in his original statement.

In particular, Hicks suggests a reworking of the standard portfolio choice model to incorporate the possibility of learning and of deferring decisions until one has learned more. In this reworking, money demand is viewed as a demand for liquidity: a demand for staying *flexible,* for keeping one's options open until one has learned more about one's situation.

By contrast, the standard portfolio choice model does not incorporate the possibility of learning and of deferring decisions. For example, the idea of money as liquidity does not appear in Tobin's (1958) 'Liquidity Preference as Behaviour towards Risk', which has become the standard interpretation of Keynes's theory of the speculative demand for money. In this interpretation, the speculative demand for money is rationalized—unlike in Keynes—by risk aversion on the part of savers.

In this chapter I shall respond to Hicks's challenge. In particular, I shall show how to incorporate into his *IS–LM* framework Keynes's idea that money—as opposed to irreversible physical investment—is liquid. This will involve a reinterpretation of Keynes's liquidity preference theory of money demand, more in the spirit of Keynes than Tobin's interpretation.

In the process of meeting Hicks's challenge, I shall also find a response to Tobin's challenge of Keynes. Tobin, in his classic 1958 article,

This paper has profited from many enjoyable conversations with Joe Ostroy. Indeed, the idea of contrasting liquidity preference as behaviour towards risk with liquidity preference as behaviour towards uncertainty comes from Jones and Ostroy (1984). I have also benefited from conversations with Steve Sheffrin, Tom Mayer, and John Boyce. None of these friends, however, is culpable for the ideas expressed here.

motivates his approach to liquidity preference as overcoming a basic difficulty in Keynes's theory. The latter depends crucially on most savers believing that the long-term rate of interest will go up substantially in the future. Consequently, savers want to stay liquid today in order to avoid expected capital losses from going long today. Tobin argues that there is no reason for savers systematically to expect the long rate to go up; so Keynes's theory lacks empirical relevance. This argument supported Tobin in dropping Keynes's assumption that savers have point expectations (hence are certain) about the future long-term rate of interest, and in building a theory of the speculative demand for money based solely on risk aversion. In my reinterpretation, I shall use the concept of uncertainty to answer Tobin squarely, to rationalize why savers may sometimes *systematically* expect the long rate to go up.

2. The Concept of Uncertainty

As in Keynes, the key concept in my rationalization of liquidity preference is that of *uncertainty*. By 'uncertain situations' (e.g. uncertain investment opportunities) I shall mean situations involving risk *plus* the possibility of learning and utilizing new information if one postpones one's decisions. (For example, uncertain investment opportunities involve the possibility of learning more about which of one's possible investment projects to pursue and which to discard, if one postpones one's investment decisions.) Summarizing schematically,

Uncertainty = risk + the possibility of learning.

Notice that it is the possibility and profitability of deferring decisions—waiting—until one has learned more about one's situation that is the key to distinguishing uncertain situations from merely risky ones.

If investment decisions were not costly to reverse, then there would be no reason to defer such decisions: investment would be just as liquid as money. But realistically, investments tend to be durable and costly to reverse. Hence we shall see that, when investors' uncertainty increases, liquidity preference (i.e. money demand) also increases. By contrast, Tobin's theory of money demand concerns situations involving risk *without* the possibility of learning, hence without the possibility of a proper liquidity preference.

The concept of uncertainty was never formalized by Keynes, although it can easily be read into his *General Theory*. We all know that Keynes was very fond of characterizing the future as dark and uncertain, and of characterizing investment as a current irreversible decision whose fruits would materialize only in the future.

The particular formalization of 'uncertainty' that I shall build on was first developed by Marschak (1938, 1949), Tintner (1942), and especially Hart (1942), around the time Keynes's *General Theory* first appeared. I am not sure how much the *General Theory* influenced these authors. Although their formalization did not catch on, it is currently being resurrected by several economists, including Hicks (1974), Jones and Ostroy (1984), and Bernanke (1983).

It is interesting to observe that Bernanke builds upon the literature dealing with the optimal depletion of a non-renewable natural resource; for example, when (if ever) to cut down a sequoia forest. This is sometimes referred to as the 'option value' literature (Weisbrod 1964; Arrow and Fisher 1974, Henry 1974a, 1974b). Recalling Hicks's suggestion, this literature may be suggestively viewed as dealing with optimal portfolio choice when there is the possibility of learning. For example, what is the best mix to hold one's portfolio of wealth between sequoia forest land and cut redwood timber when, if one waits before cutting down the forest, one will learn more about its best use—timber or parkland? In this analogy, to hold more forest land is to be more liquid—it leaves more future options open—while to hold more cut timber is to be more illiquid—one cannot recreate the forest in any near future.

Notice that, unlike Knight, I do not view uncertain situations as amorphous. Rather, I am completely sympathetic with the traditional theory of uncertainty that expresses degrees of belief by probabilities and that models learning as updating these probabilities. Thus, I am *not* proposing a new theory of uncertainty, in the sense of disputing Savage's axioms or Bayes's theory of learning. Indeed, my concept of uncertainty can be captured in an intertemporal model of decision-making under uncertainty consistent with this traditional theory of uncertainty.

The approach to integrating money and investment that I propose requires one to distinguish carefully between *savers*—whose portfolio choice problem (as in Keynes and Tobin) involves a choice between money and long-term bonds—and *investors*—who sell bonds to savers in order to finance new physical investment. We shall see that, when uncertainty increases among *investors,* it causes increased liquidity preference among *savers*. The key innovation of this paper is systematically to analyse this link between investors and savers, and to incorporate it into Hicks's *IS–LM* model.

Other authors only treat investor uncertainty, without noticing its implications for savers' liquidity preference (e.g. Bernanke 1983); or they integrate the role of savers and investors rather than separating out the two roles (e.g. Hicks 1974; Jones and Ostroy 1984). The current contribution, however, is very much influenced by all three of these papers. It is interesting to notice that Keynes also seems to have confounded the roles of savers and investors during the early years of the development of his ideas on liquidity preference:

Whilst liquidity-preference due to the speculative-motive corresponds to what in my *Treatise on Money* I called the 'state of bearishness', it is by no means the same thing. For 'bearishness' is there defined as the functional relationship not between the rate of interest (or price of debts) and the quantity of money, but between the price of assets and debts, taken together, and the quantity of money. This treatment, however, involved a confusion between results due to a change in the rate of interest [hence the saving decision] and those due to a change in the schedule of the marginal efficiency of capital [hence the investment decision] . . . (Keynes 1973: 173–4; words in brackets added for emphasis)

3. An Example of Investor Uncertainty

Before specifying the interaction between savers and investors further, it is perhaps useful to give an example of investor uncertainty, to help fix the concept of uncertainty in readers' minds. A lovely example is given by Bernanke (1983); I present it, in only slightly modified form.

Imagine that it is 1974. The OPEC oil cartel has just formed and has quadrupled the price of oil. Investors, however, are unsure whether the cartel will last. If it does, it is more economical for firms to switch to energy-saving heavy capital equipment; if it doesn't, it is more economical to continue using oil-intensive durable capital, since oil prices will fall again.

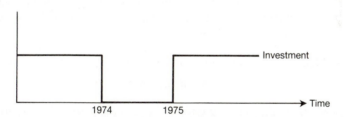

Fig. 21.1 *When uncertainty increases, desired investment drops temporarily.*

Suppose investors believe that if the cartel lasts one year it is highly probable it will last a long time; but if it collapses within a year it will not appear again. So, they rationally wait to see if the cartel lasts, deferring new capital equipment orders for the present. They do not want to be stuck with the wrong kind of capital equipment.

To complete the story, suppose the cartel does last the year. Then the economy's pattern of aggregate investment may look like that in Figure 21.1.[1] In 1975 investors begin to buy energy-saving capital equipment.

---

[1] A similar figure appears in Bernanke (1983). In his telling, investment temporarily rises to a higher level in 1975 as firms replenish depreciated capital and renovate their old capital. So there is a complete investment cycle. He also introduces a lag between the cartel's formation and the drop in investment.

But while uncertainty is high (1974–5), they just wait to see if the cartel lasts, deferring irreversible investment commitments until they learn more about the cartel's staying power.

4. The Interaction between Investors and Savers

I am now prepared to complete the circle, and specify the interaction between savers' and investors' decisions in the presence of uncertainty, in other words, to complete my interpretation of Keynes's liquidity preference theory.

The example above illustrates the principle formally derived in Jones and Ostroy (1984) that, *when uncertainty is high, then the desire for flexibility is high,* where one situation is defined as more flexible than another if the former leaves more options open. The intuition behind the principle should be plain: if one expects to learn in the *future,* then one wants to remain flexible *today* in order to be in a position to utilize one's learning; that is, one wants to keep one's options open today.

The example also illustrates the main consequence of the principle stressed by Jones and Ostroy: since investment decisions are typically durable and irreversible, they typically involve a loss of flexibility. Hence, *when uncertainty is high, then the desire for investment is temporarily low.* As the example illustrates, it is important that readers realistically think of investment decisions as involving production choices among heterogeneous capital goods; otherwise the rationale for waiting will be lost. Summarizing schematically,

$$\text{Uncertainty} \uparrow \Rightarrow \text{desire for flexibility} \uparrow \Rightarrow$$
$$\text{desire for investment} \downarrow \text{temporarily.}$$

But recall that *uncertain* situations—as opposed to risky situations—have built-in dynamics. Uncertainty does not stay high forever. Indeed, by the definition of uncertainty, economic agents *expect* uncertainty to be resolved in the future. Thus, when uncertainty is high, desired investment is low only *temporarily*—until uncertainty gets resolved. Let us trace out the implications of these dynamics for the level of long-term interest rates, *r.*

Assume temporaily that the supply of loanable funds is interest-inelastic, and focus on the demand for such funds. When uncertainty is high, we have seen that investors will rationally defer investment decisions until the future, when they expect their uncertainty to be resolved. Thus, when uncertainty is high, investors' demand for loanable funds to finance new investment projects will be relatively low, and consequently, *r* will be relatively low. Then, when investors' uncertainty is resolved their desire for investment will revive; consequently, their demand for loanable funds will revive and the level of r will increase again.

But now we must relax our assumption that the supply of loanable funds is interest-inelastic, because there is a minimum level of r below which no saver will be willing to lend. Why? Savers, realizing the above pattern of r induced by uncertainty's waxing and waning, will rationally expect r to increase in the future if the present is marked by a lot of investor uncertainty. This induces, by the familiar textbook argument, a liquidity trap level of r—an $r_{critical}$, as Tobin (1958) calls it—below which savers will not be willing to lend, preferring instead to stay liquid today. This closes the circle!

Summarizing, investor uncertainty rationalizes Keynes's dynamics of speculation by *savers*: when uncertainty is high, savers will be rationally liquid, expecting r to increase in the future (into money); and when uncertainty is relatively low, savers will be rationally committed and illiquid (into long-term bonds).

5. The Analysis of Uncertainty Incorporated into the *IS–LM* Model

Analytically, the most interesting feature of my interpretation of Keynes's liquidity preference theory is that it explicitly analyses the interaction between the real—investment—and financial—money—sides of an economy. The interaction sketched above may be rephrased in terms of *IS–LM* analysis: if uncertainty increases then desired investment decreases; so the *IS* curve moves leftward and r falls. But savers expect r to increase again in the future, when uncertainty is resolved and desired investment increases again. This rational expectation by savers leads to the emergence of a floor on the current long-term interest rate r at which savers are willing to lend, that is, to a liquidity trap in the *LM* curve. Thus, the *IS* (real) and *LM* (financial) curves move simultaneously when uncertainty increases.

The process is illustrated in Figure 21.2. Suppose that before uncertainty increases there is full employment at (r^*, Q^*), at the intersection of IS_1 and LM_1. (We follow Keynes in assuming that the velocity of *active* balances is not interest-sensitive, and that people have point expectations about the future level of r, so they hold no speculative balances in the sense of Tobin. Hence, the *LM* curve is initially vertical.) Now when uncertainty strikes, the *IS* curve decreases to IS_2. Nevertheless, full employment could be maintained if r were to fall to r_2. It does *not* fall this much because, *simultaneous* with the drop in *IS*, the *LM* curve rotates around $r_{critical}$ to the liquidity-trap-shaped LM_2. In particular, if we assume that all savers expect the *IS* curve to return to IS_1 and hence expect r to return to r^* after uncertainty clears—as in the OPEC oil cartel example above—then $r_{critical} = r^*/(1 + r^*)$, assuming that the long-

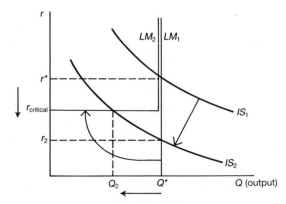

Fig. 21.2 *An increase in uncertainty has both real (IS) and financial (LM) consequences.*

term bond is a consol. (For the formula, see the summary of Keynes's theory in Tobin 1958, the concept of $r_{critical}$ is taken from the same source.) To complete the story, notice that when uncertainty is resolved the economy returns to IS_1 and the vertical LM_1, hence to the full employment position (r^*, Q^*). (The *LM* is again vertical, since in the absence of uncertainty, under Keynes's stylized assumptions, money demand would not be interest-sensitive.)

To contrast the above theory of 'liquidity preference as behavior towards uncertainty' with Tobin's 'Liquidity Preference as Behavior toward Risk', I have purposely constructed the example under the assumption that savers hold point expectations about the future level of r. Hence savers *never* demand money purely for diversifying against risk, as in Tobin—neither when uncertainty is low nor when it is high. It is also fundamentally important to notice that, under the uncertainty interpretation of Keynes's liquidity preference theory, there can be a liquidity trap *only* in bad times when uncertainty is high: when uncertainty is resolved, savers again lend to investors—they are into bonds rather than money. By contrast, Tobin assumes a steady state, where everyone always expects r to remain unchanged. In such a state, the *LM* curve would always be vertical under the assumptions in the example, reflecting (1) the absence of a Tobin speculative demand for money (owing to risk aversion), (2) the absence of interest sensitivity in the transaction and precautionary demands for money, and (3) the *absence of uncertainty*.

6. Concluding Remarks

When A. G. Hart first struck on the idea of uncertainty, he recognized its powerful predictive potential for economics. Written long *before* Tobin's

'Liquidity Preference as Behavior toward Risk', the following quote from Hart summarizes my view of the sorry historical consequences resulting from the success of Tobin's interpretation of Keynes:

It is the position of this paper that 'risk' [without learning] has comparatively little importance in economic analysis in view of the characteristics of the time relations in which we are interested . . . In consequence, the writer urges that theorists concentrate their attention on uncertainty rather than on risk. (Hart 1942: 110; words in brackets added for clarification)

A second quote, one from Hicks's *The Crisis in Keynesian Economics* (1974), summarizes the positive objective of this essay: to show how one can achieve a deeper, more integrated, view of the relationship between the real and financial sides of Hicks's *IS–LM* model, based on a different interpretation of Keynes's liquidity preference theory. Written more than three decades after his invention of the *IS–LM* apparatus, this extract emphasizes Hicks's regret for not having sought such an integration in his first exposition of Keynes. After discussing Keynes's multiplier theory, Hicks writes:

I pass to consider the other main parts of the Keynes theory—the marginal efficiency of capital and the theory of money. *I shall take them together, for I think I can show that they belong together.* In the multiplier theory, which I have been discussing, Keynes is dealing with the effects of changes in investment on income (and so on employment); he then turns to examine the possibility of controlling investment by monetary means. Both the marginal efficiency of capital and the theory of money belong to this second subject. (In my 'Mr. Keynes and the Classics', *Econometrica*, 1937, I similarly reduced Keynes's three relations to two, taking the multiplier with the marginal efficiency of capital to form the *SI* curve. I have come to feel that the alternative grouping, which I am following here, is more revealing.) *So much of his book is concerned with this second subject that Keynes must have attached great importance to it* . . . (Hicks 1974: 31; italics added for emphasis)

Bibliography

Abel, B. A. (1985). 'Inventories, Stock-Outs and Production Smoothing'. *Review of Economic Studies*, 52, 283–93.

Abreu, D. (1983). 'Repeated Games with Discounting'. Ph.D. dissertation, Princeton University.

——, Pearce, D., and Stacchetti, E. (1986a). 'Optimal Cartel Equilibria with Imperfect Monitoring'. *Journal of Economic Theory*, 39, 251–69.

——, Pearce, D., and Stacchetti, E. (1986b). 'Toward a Theory of Discounted Repeated Games with Imperfect Monitoring'. IMSSS Technical Report no. 487, Stanford University.

—— and Rubinstein, A. (1986). 'The Structure of Nash Equilibrium in Repeated Games with Finite Automata'. ICERD Theoretical Economics no. 86/141, London School of Economics.

Admati, A. and Perry, M. (1987). 'Strategic Delay in Bargaining'. *Review of Economic Studies*, 54, 345–64.

Akerlof, G. (1970). 'The Market for Lemons: Quality Uncertainty and the Market Mechanism'. *Quarterly Journal of Economics*, 89, 488–500.

—— and Miyazaki, H. (1980). 'The Implicit Contract Theory meets the Wage Bill Argument'. *Review of Economic Studies*, 47, 321–38.

Alger, D. and Huang, P. (1986). 'On the Notion of an Equilibrium'. US Federal Trade Commission working paper.

Allais, M. (1953). 'Le Comportement de l'homme rationnel devant le risque, critique des postulats et axiomes de l'Ecole Americaine'. *Econometrica*, 21, 503–46.

—— (1979). 'The Foundations of a Positive Theory of Choice Involving Risk and a Criticism of the Postulates and Axioms of the American School', and 'The So-called Allais Paradox and Rational Decisions under Uncertainty'. In Allais and Hagen (1979).

—— and Hagen, O. (eds.) (1979). *Expected Utility Hypotheses and the Allais Paradox*. Dordrecht, Holland: D. Reidel.

Allen, B. (1982). 'Strict Rational Expectations Equilibria with Diffuseness'. *Journal of Economic Theory*, 27, 20–46.

—— (1983). 'Expectations Equilibria with Dispersed Information: Existence with Approximate Rationality in a Model with a Continuum of Agents and Finitely Many States of the World'. *Review of Economic Studies*, 50, 267–85.

—— (1987). 'Smooth Preferences and the Local Expected Utility Hypothesis'. *Journal of Economic Theory*, 41, 340–55.

Amihud, Y. and Mendelson, H. (1983). 'Price Smoothing and Inventory'. *Review of Economic Studies*, 50, 87–98.

Anderlini, L. (1986a). 'Competitive Banking in a Simple Model'. In J. Edwards *et al.* (eds.), *Recent Developments in Corporate Finance*. Cambridge University Press.

—— (1986b). 'Correctly Anticipated Bank Runs'. Economic Theory Discussion Paper no. 95, Cambridge.

—— (1986c). 'Central Banks and Moral Hazard'. Economic Theory Discussion Paper no. 103, Cambridge.

Anderson, R. (1985). 'Quick-response Equilibria'. Mimeo.

—— and Sonnenschein, H. (1985). 'Rational Expectations Equilibrium with Econometric Models'. *Review of Economic Studies*, 52, 359–69.

Anderson, T. W. (1958). *An Introduction to Multivariate Statistical Analysis*. New York: John Wiley.

Arrow, K. J. (1953). 'Le Role des Valeurs Boursieres pour la Repartition la Meilleure des Risques'. *Econometrie*, Colloques Internationaux du CNRS 11, 41–47.

—— (1958). 'Toward a Theory of Price Adjustment'. In M. Abramovitz *et al.* (eds.), *The Allocation of Economic Resources: Essays in Honour of B. F. Haley*. Stanford University Press.

—— (1964). 'The Role of Securities in the Optimal Allocation of Risk-bearing'. *Review of Economic Studies*, 31, 91–6.

—— (1973). 'Higher Education as a Filter'. *Journal of Public Economics*, 2, 193–216.

—— (1974). *Essays in the Theory of Risk-Bearing*. Amsterdam: North-Holland.

—— and Fisher, A. C. (1974). 'Environmental Preservation, Uncertainty, and Irreversibility'. *Quarterly Journal of Economics*, 88, 312–9.

——, Karlin, S., and Scarf, H. (1958). *Studies in the Mathematical Theory of Inventory and Production*. Stanford University Press.

Ashley, R. A. and Orr, D. (1985). 'Further Results on Inventories and Price Stickiness'. *American Economic Review*, 75, 964–75.

Atkinson, A. B. and Stiglitz, J. E. (1980). *Lectures on Public Economics*. Maidenhead: McGraw-Hill.

Auerbach, A. J., Kotlikoff, L. J., and Skinner, J. (1983). 'The Efficiency Gains from Dynamic Tax Reform'. *International Economic Review*, 24, 81–100.

Aumann, R. J. (1959). 'Acceptable Points in General Cooperative n-person Games'. In *Contribution to the Theory of Games IV*. Princeton University Press.

—— (1974). 'Subjectivity and Correlation in Randomized Strategies'. *Journal of Mathematical Economics*, 1, 67–96.

—— (1975). 'Subjectivity and Correlation in Randomized Strategies'. *Journal of Mathematical Economics*, 1, 67–96.

—— (1976). 'Agreeing to Disagree'. *Annals of Statistics*, 4, 1236–9.

—— (1981). 'Survey of Repeated Games'. In *Essays in Game Theory and Mathematical Economics in Honor of Oskar Morgenstern*. Mannheim: Bibliographisches Institut, 11–42.

—— (1987). 'Correlated Equilibrium as an Expression of Bayesian Rationality'. *Econometrica*, 55, 1–18.

—— and Shapley, L. (1976). 'Long-term Competition: A Game-Theoretic Analysis'. Mimeo.

—— and Sorin, S. (1987). 'Cooperation and Bounded Rationality'. Mimeo, Stanford University.

Axelrod, R. (1984). *The Evolution of Cooperation*. New York: Basic Books.

Azariadis, C. (1975). 'Implicit Contracts and Underemployment Equilibria'. *Journal of Political Economy*, 83, 1183–1202.

—— (1981). 'Self-Fulfilling prophecies'. *Journal of Economic Theory*, 25, 380–96.

—— and Guesnerie, R. (1986). 'Sunspots and Cycles'. *Review of Economic Studies*, 53, 725–36.

Bacharach, M. (1985). 'Some Extensions of a Claim of Aumann in an Axiomatic Model of Knowledge'. *Journal of Economic Theory*, 37, 167–90.

Baily, M. N. (1974). 'Wages and Employment under Uncertain Demand'. *Review of Economic Studies*, 41, 37–50.

Balasko, Y., Cass, D., and Shell, K. (1980). 'Existence of Competitive Equilibrium in a General Overlapping-Generations Model'. *Journal of Economic Theory*, 23, 307–22.

Balasko, Y. and Shell, K. (1980). 'The Overlapping-Generations Model I: The Case of Pure Exchange Without Money'. *Journal of Economic Theory*, 23, 281–306.

—— (1981), 'The Overlapping-Generations Model III: The Case of Log-linear Utility Functions'. *Journal of Economic Theory*, 24, 143–52.

Balassa, B. (1967). *Trade Liberalization Among Industrial Countries*. New York: McGraw-Hill.

Banks, J. S., and Sobel, J. (1987). 'Equilibrium Selection in Signaling Games'. *Econometrica*, 55, 647–61.

Barnett, W. and Chen, P. (1986). 'Deterministic Chaos and Fractal Attractors as Tools for Non-parametric Dynamical Econometric Inference with an Application to the Divisia Monetary Aggregates'. Technical Report no. 33, Center for Statistical Studies, University of Texas, Austin.

Barro, R. (1974). 'Are Government Bonds Net Wealth?' *Journal of Political Economy*, 82, 1095–1117.

—— (1977). 'Long-term Contracting, Sticky Prices, and Monetary Policy'. *Journal of Monetary Economics*, 3, 305–16.

Bartle, R. (1976). *The Elements of Real Analysis* (2nd edn.). New York: John Wiley.

Basar, T. and Oldser, G. J. (1982). *Dynamic Noncooperative Game Theory*. London: Academic Press.

Battalio, R., Kagel, J., and Macdonald, D. (1985). 'Animals' Choices over Uncertain Outcomes'. *American Economic Review*, 75, 597–613.

Baumol, W. and Oates, W. E. (1975). *The Theory of Environmental Policy: Externalities, Public Outlays, and the Quality of Life*. Englewood Cliffs, NJ: Prentice-Hall.

Baumol, W., Panzer, J. C. and Willig, R. D. (1982). *Contestable Markets and the Theory of Industry Structure*. San Diego: Harcourt, Brace and Jovanovich.

Begg, D. K. H. (1982a). *The Rational Expectations Revolution in Macroeconomics: Theories and Evidence*. Oxford: Philip Allan.

—— (1982b). 'Rational Expectations, Wage Rigidity and Involuntary Unemployment: A Particular Theory'. *Oxford Economic Papers*, 34, 23–47.

Beja, A. (1976). 'The Limited Information Efficiency of Market Processes'. Research Program in Finance Working Paper no. 43, University of California, Berkeley.

Bell, D. (1982). 'Regret in Decision Making Under Uncertainty'. *Operations Research*, 30, 961–81.

Ben-Porath, E. (1986). 'Repeated Games with Bounded Complexity'. Mimeo.

Benhabib, J. and Day, R. H. (1982). 'A Characterization of Erratic Dynamics in the Overlapping Generations Model'. *Journal of Economic Dynamics and Control*, 4, 37–55.

Benhabib, J. and Nishimura, K. (1985). 'Competitive Equilibrium Cycles'. *Journal of Economic Theory*, 35, 284–306.

Benoit, J. P. and Krishna, V. (1985). 'Finitely Repeated Games'. *Econometrica*, 53, 905–22.

—— (1987). 'Dynamic Duopoly: Prices and Quantities'. *Review of Economic Studies*, 54, 23-35.

Bergin, J. (1986). 'A Characterization of Sequential Equilibrium Strategies in Infinitely Repeated Incomplete Information Games'. Northwestern University Discussion Paper no. 686.

Bernanke, B. S. (1983). 'Irreversibility, Uncertainty, and Cyclical Investment'. *Quarterly Journal of Economics*, 98, 85–106.

Bernheim, B. D. (1984). Rationalizable Strategic Behavior. *Econometrica*, 52, 1007–28.

—— (1985). 'Axiomatic Characterizations of Rational Choice in Strategic Environments'. Unpublished paper, Department of Economics, Stanford University.

——, Peleg, B., and Whinston, M. (1987a). 'Coalition-proof Nash Equilibria. I: Concepts'. *Journal of Economic Theory*, 42, 1–12.

—— (1987b). 'Coalition-proof Nash Equilibria. II: Applications'. *Journal of Economic Theory*, 42, 13–29.

Bernoulli, D. (1738). 'Specimen Theoriae Novae de Mensura Sortis'. *Commentariii Academiae Scientiarum Imperialis Petropolitianae* (Papers of the Imperial Academy of Sciences in Petersburg), V, 175–92. English translation' 'Exposition of a New Theory on the Measurement of Risk'. *Econometrica*, 22 (1954), 23–36.

Bertle, R. (1976). *Elements of Real Analysis*. New York: John Wiley.

Bertrand, J. (1883). 'Theorie mathematique de la Richesse Sociale'. *Journal des Savants*, 48, 499–508.

Bertsekas, D. P. (1976). *Dynamic Programming and Stochastic Control*. New York: Academic Press.

Bewley, T. (1980). 'The Optimum Quantity of Money', In J. Kareken and N. Wallace (eds.), *Models of Monetary Economies*, pp. 169–210. Minneapolis: Federal Reserve Bank of Minneapolis.

—— (1982). 'An Integration of Equilibrium Theory and Turnpike Theory'. *Journal of Mathematical Economics*, 10, 233–67.

—— (1983). 'A Difficulty with the Optimum Quantity of Money'. *Econometrica*, 51, 1485–1504.

—— (1986, 1987). 'Knightian Decision Theory, I and II. Cowles Foundation Discussion Papers, nos. 807 and 835, Yale University.

Billingsley, P. (1968). *Convergence of Probability Measures*. New York: John Wiley.

Bils, M. J. (1985). 'Real Wages over the Business Cycle: Evidence from Panel Data'. *Journal of Political Economy*, 93, 666–89.

Binmore, K. (1980). 'Nash Bargaining Theory II'. International Centre for Economics and Related Disciplines Discussion Paper 80/14, London School of Economics.

—— (1985). 'Bargaining and Coalitions'. In A. Roth (ed.), *Game-Theoretic Models of Bargaining*. Cambridge University Press.

—— (1987a). 'Modelling Rational Players I and II'. Mimeo.

—— (1987b). 'Remodeled Rational Players'. ICERD Discussion Paper 87/149, London School of Economics.

—— and Dasgupta, P. (1986a). 'Game Theory: A Survey'. In Binmore and Dasgupta (1986b).

—— and Dasgupta, P. (eds.) (1986b). *Economic Organizations as Games*. Oxford: Basil Blackwell.

——, Shaked, A., and Sutton, J. (1985). 'An Outside Option Experiment'. International Centre for Economics and Related Disciplines Discussion Paper 85/124, London School of Economics.

Binswanger, H. P. (1981). 'Attitudes toward Risk: Theoretical Implications of an Experiment in Rural India'. *Economic Journal*, 91, 867–90.

Black, F. and Scholes, M. (1973). 'The Pricing of Options and Corporate Liabilities'. *Journal of Political Economy*, 81, 637–54.

Blinder, A. S. (1978). 'Inventories and the Demand for Labour'. Unpublished paper, Princeton University.

—— (1981). 'Retail Inventory Behavior and Business Fluctuations'. *Brookings Paper on Economic Activity*, 2, 443–505.

—— (1982). 'Inventories and Sticky Prices: More on the Microfoundations of Macroeconomics'. *American Economic Review*, 72, 334–48.

—— and Fischer, S. (1981). 'Inventories, Rational Expectations, and the Business Cycle'. *Journal of Monetary Economics*, 8, 277–304.

Blume, L. (1986). 'Lexicographic Refinements of Nash Equilibrium'. Unpublished paper, University of Michigan.

——, Bray, M. M. and Easley, E. (1982). 'Introduction to the Stability of Rational Expectations Equilibrium'. *Journal of Economic Theory*, 26, 313–17.

Bodkin, R. G. (1969). 'Real Wages and Cyclical Variations in Employment: A Re-examination of the Evidence'. *Canadian Journal of Economics*, 2, 353–74.

Böge, W. and Eisele, Th. (1979). 'On Solutions of Bayesian Games'. *International Journal of Game Theory*, 8, 318–39.

Boldrin, M. and Montrucchio, L. (1985). 'The Emergence of Dynamic Complexities in Models of Optimal Growth: The Role of Impatience'. Working paper no. 7, Rochester Center for Economic Research, New York.

—— (1986). 'On the Indeterminacy of Capital Accumulation Paths'. *Journal of Economic Theory*, 40, 26–39.

Borch, K. and Mossin, J. (1968). *Risk and Uncertainty: Proceedings of a Conference held by the International Economic Association*. London: Macmillan.

Bowen, H. R. (1943). 'The Interpretation of Voting in the Allocation of Economic Resources'. *Quarterly Journal of Economics*, 58, 27–48.

Brandenburger, A. (1986). 'Hierarchies of Beliefs in Decision Theory'. Ph.D. dissertation, Cambridge University.

—— and Dekel, E. (1985). 'Hierarchies of Beliefs and Common Knowledge'. Research Paper no. 841, Graduate School of Business, Stanford University.

—— (1986). 'On an Axiomatic Approach to Refinements of Nash Equilibrium'. Unpublished paper, University of California, Berkeley.

—— (1987). 'Rationalizability and Correlated Equilibria'. *Econometrica*, 55, 1391–1402.

Brander, J. A. (1981). 'Intra-industry Trade in Identical Commodities'. *Journal of International Economics*, 11, 1–14.

—— and Krugman, P. (1983). 'A Reciprocal Dumping Model of International Trade'. *Journal of International Economics*, 15, 313–21.

—— and Spencer, B. J. (1981). 'Tariffs and the Extraction of Foreign Monopoly Rents under Potential Entry'. *Canadian Journal of Economics*, 14, 371–89.

—— (1984a). 'Tariff Protection and Imperfect Competition'. In H. Kierzkowski (ed.), *Monopolistic Competition and International Trade*. Oxford University Press.

—— (1984b). 'Trade Warfare: Tariffs and Cartels'. *Journal of International Economics*, 16, 227–42.

—— (1985). 'Export Subsidies and International Market Share Rivalry'. *Journal of International Economics*, 18, 83–100.

Braun, E. and Macdonald, S. (1982). *Revolution in Miniature: The History and Impact of Semiconductor Electronics* (2nd edn.). Cambridge University Press.

Bray, M. M. (1981). 'Futures Trading, Rational Expectations, and the Efficient Markets Hypothesis'. *Econometrica*, 49, 575–96.

—— (1982). 'Learning, Estimation, and the Stability of Rational Expectations'. *Journal of Economic Theory*, 26, 318–39.

—— (1983). 'Convergence to Rational Expectations Equilibrium'. In R. Frydman and E. S. Phelps (eds.), *Individual Forecasting and Aggregate Outcomes*. Cambridge University Press.

—— and Kreps, D. (1986). 'Rational Learning and Rational Expectations'. In W. Heller, D. Starett, and R. Starr (eds.), *Essays in Honour of K. J. Arrow*. Cambridge University Press.

—— and Savin, N. E. (1984). 'Rational Expectations Equilibria, Learning and Model Specification'. Economic Theory Discussion Paper no. 79, Department of Applied Economics, Cambridge.

Brealey, R. (1983). *An Introduction to Risk and Return from Common Stocks* (2nd edn.). Oxford: Basil Blackwell.

Bromze, I. M. (1986). 'Non-cooperative Two-person Games in Biology: A Classification'. *International Journal of Game Theory*, 15, 31–57.

Brunner, K., Cukierman, A., and Meltzer, A. (1983). 'Money and Economic Activity, Inventories and Business Cycles'. *Journal of Monetary Economics*, 11, 281–319.

Bulow, J. I., Geanakoplos, J. D., and Kemperer, P. D. (1985). 'Multimarket Oligopoly: Strategic Substitutes and Complements'. *Journal of Political Economy*, 93, 488–511.

Burke, J. L. (1986). 'On the Existence of Equilibria in Dynamic Production Economies." Unpublished paper.

—— (1987). 'Inactive Transfer Policies and Efficiency in General Overlapping-Generations Economies'. *Journal of Mathematical Economics*, 16, 201–22.

—— (1988). 'On the Existence of Equilibria in Dynamic Economies.' *Journal of Economic Theory*, 44, 281–300.

Calvo, G. and Phelps, E. (1977). 'Employment Contingent Wage Contracts'. *Journal of Monetary Economics*, 2 (Supplement), 160–8.

Canning, D. (1982). 'The Theory of Wage Bargaining'. Ph.D. thesis, Cambridge University.

Caplin, A. S. (1985). 'The Variability of Aggregate Demand with (S, s) Inventory Policies'. *Econometrica*, 53, 1395–1409.

Cass, D., Okuno, M., and Zilcha, I. (1979). 'The Role of Money in Supporting the Pareto Optimality of Competitive Equilibrium in Consumption-Loan Type Models'. *Journal of Economic Theory*, 20, 41–80.

Cass, D. and Shell, K. (1983). 'Do Sunspots Matter?' *Journal of Political Economy*, 91, 193–227.

Cass, D. and Yaari, M. (1966). 'A Re-examination of the Pure Consumption Loans Model'. *Journal of Political Economy*, 74, 353–67.

Chacholiades, M. (1970). 'Increasing Returns and Comparative Advantage'. *Southern Economic Journal*, 37, 157–62.

—— (1978). *International Trade Theory and Policy*. Tokyo, McGraw-Hill.

Chatterjee, K. and Samuelson, L. (1987). 'Bargaining with Two-Sided Incomplete Information: An Infinite Horizon Model with Alternating Offers'. *Review of Economic Studies*, 54, 175–92.

Chew, S. (1983). 'A Generalization of the Quasilinear Mean with Applications to the Measurement of Income Inequality and Decision Theory Resolving the Allais Paradox'. *Econometrica*, 51, 1065–92.

—— and Waller, W. (1986). 'Empirical Tests of Weighted Utility Theory'. *Journal of Mathematical Psychology*, 30, 55–72.

Cho, In-koo (1987). 'A Refinement of Sequential Equilibrium'. *Econometrica*, 55, 1367–89.

—— (1986). 'Refinement of Sequential Equilibrium: Theory and Application'. Ph.D. dissertation, Princeton University.

—— and Kreps, D. M. (1987). 'Signaling Games and Stable Equilibria'. *Quarterly Journal of Economics*, 102, 179–221.

Coase, R. H. (1960). 'The Problem of Social Cost'. *Journal of Law and Economics*, 3, 1–44.

Collet, P. and Eckmann, J.-P. (1980). *Iterated Maps on the Interval as Dynamical Systems*. Boston: Birkhausers.

Cournot, A. A. (1838). *Recherches sur les Principes Mathematiques de la Theorie des Richesses*. Paris: Hachette.

Crawford, V. and Sobel, J. (1982). 'Strategic Information Transmission'. *Econometrica*, 50, 1431–51.

Cremer, J. (1986). 'Cooperation in Ongoing Organizations'. *Quarterly Journal of Economics*, 101, 33–49.

—— and McLean, R. (1985). 'Optimal Selling Strategies under Uncertainty for a Discriminating Monopolist when Demands are Interdependent'. *Econometrica*, 53, 345–61.

Crutchfield, J. P., Farmer, J. D., and Huberman, B. A. (1982). 'Fluctuations and Simple Chaotic Dynamics'. *Physics Reports*, 92, 45–82.

Cvitanovic, P. (1984a). 'Universality in Chaos (or Feigenbaum for Cyclists)'. *Acta Physica Polonica*, A65, 203–39.

—— (1984b). Universality in Chaos. Bristol: Adam Hilger.

Dalkey, N. (1953). 'Equivalence of Information Patterns and Essentially Determinate Games'. In H. Kuhn and A. Tucker (eds.), *Contributions to the Theory of Games,* II (Annals of Mathematics Studies, 28). Princeton University Press.

Danthine, J. P. (1978). 'Information, Futures Prices and Stabilizing Speculation'. *Journal of Economic Theory,* 17, 79–98.

Dasgupta, P. (1986). 'The Theory of Technological Competition'. In J. E. Stiglitz and J. F. Mathewson (eds.), *New Developments in the Analysis of Market Structure.* London: Macmillan.

—— (1988a). 'The Welfare Economics of Knowledge Production'. *Oxford Review of Economic Policy,* forthcoming.

—— (1988b). 'Patents, Priority and Imitation; or, The Economics of Races and Waiting Games'. *Economic Journal,* 98, 66–80.

—— and David, P. (1987). 'Information Disclosure and the Economics of Science and Technology'. In G. Feiwel. (ed.), *Arrow and the Ascent of Modern Economic Theory.* London: Macmillan.

—— and Maskin, E. (1986a). 'The Existence of Equilibrium in Discontinuous Economic Games, 1: Theory'. *Review of Economic Studies* 53, 1–26.

—— and Maskin, E. (1986b). 'The Existence of Equilibrium in Discontinuous Economic Games, 2: Applications'. *Review of Economic Studies,* 53, 27–41.

—— and Maskin, E. (1987). 'The Simple Economics of Research Portfolios'. *Economic Journal,* 97, 581–95.

—— and Stiglitz, J. E. (1980a). 'Industrial Structure and the Nature of Innovative Activity'. *Economic Journal,* 90, 266–93.

—— (1980b). 'Uncertainty, Industrial Structure and the Speed of R&D'. *Bell Journal of Economics,* 11, 1–28.

—— (1985). 'Learning-by-Doing, Market Structure and Industrial and Trade Policies'. Economic Theory Discussion Paper no. 84, Cambridge University.

—— (1988a). 'Potential Competition, Actual Competition and Economic Welfare'. *European Economic Review,* 32, 569–77.

—— (1988b). 'Economic Organization and Technological Change'. Mimeo, University of Cambridge.

Day, R. H. (1982). 'Irregular Growth Cycles'. *American Economic Review,* 72, 406–14.

—— (1983). 'The Emergence of Chaos from Classical Economic Growth'. *Quarterly Journal of Economics,* 98, 201–13.

—— (1986). 'Unscrambling the Concept of Chaos Through Thick and Thin: Reply'. *Quarterly Journal of Economics,* 101, 425–6.

Deaton, A. and Muellbauer, J. (1980). *Economics and Consumer Behavior.* Cambridge University Press.

DeBraal, J. P. and Wunderlich, G. (1983). *Rents and Rental Practices in US Agriculture.* Washington, DC: US Department of Agriculture.

Debreu, G. (1954). 'Valuation Equilibrium and Pareto Optimum'. *Proceedings of the National Academy of Sciences,* 40, 588–92.

—— (1970). 'Economies with a Finite Set of Equilibria'. *Econometrica,* 38, 387–92.

De Groot, M. (1970). *Optimal Statistical Decisions.* New York: McGraw-Hill.

Dekel, E. (1986). 'An Axiomatic Characterization of Preferences under Uncertainty: Weakening the Independence Axiom'. *Journal of Economic Theory*, 40, 304–18.

Deneckere, R. and Pelikan, S. (1986). 'Competitive Chaos'. *Journal of Economic Theory*, 40, 13–25.

Diamond, D. W. (1984). 'Financial Intermediation and Delegated Monitoring'. *Review of Economic Studies*, 51, 393–414.

—— and Dybvig, P. H. (1983). 'Bank Runs, Deposit Insurance and Liquidity'. *Journal of Political Economy*, 91, 401–19.

Diamond, P. A. (1967). 'The Role of a Stock Market in a General Equilibrium Model with Technological Uncertainty'. *American Economic Review*, 57, 759–76.

—— and Mirrlees, J. A. (1971), 'Optimal Taxation and Public Production, I: Production Efficiency'. *American Economic Review*, 61, 8–27.

—— and Rothschild, M. (eds.) (1978). *Uncertainty in Economics*. New York: Academic Press.

Dixit, A. K. (1976). *The Theory of Equilibrium Growth*. Oxford University Press.

—— (1984). 'International Trade Policy and Oligopolistic Industries'. *Economic Journal*, 94 (Supplement), 1–16.

—— and Norman, V. (1980). *Theory of International Trade*. Cambridge University Press.

—— and Stiglitz, J. (1977). 'Monopolistic Competition and Optimum Product Diversity'. *American Economic Review*, 67, 297–308.

Doyle, C. (1986). 'Intertemporal Price Discrimination, Uncertainty and Introductory Offers'. *Economic Journal*, 96, Supplement, 71–82.

—— (1987a). 'Price Matching Strategies and Oligopoly'. Unpublished paper, Department of Applied Economics, University of Cambridge. Revised version of Economic Theory Discussion Paper no. 83, Cambridge University.

—— (1987b). 'Refund Promises and Trial Periods as Quality Signals'. Economic Theory Discussion Paper no. 115, Cambridge University.

Dreze, J. (1975). 'Existence of an Exchange Equilibrium under Price Rigidities'. *International Economic Review*, 16, 301–20.

Dubey, P. (1978). 'Finiteness and Inefficiency of Nash Equilibria'. Cowles Foundation Discussion Paper no. 508.

Dunlop, J. T. (1938). 'The Movement of Real and Money Wage Rates'. *Economic Journal*, 48, 413–34.

Dutta, J. and Polemarchakis, H. M. (1985). 'Assets, Shocks and Memory'. First Boston Working Paper no. FB-85-34, Graduate School of Business, Columbia University.

Eaton, J. and Grossman, G. M. (1986). 'Optimal Trade and Industrial Policy Under Oligopoly'. *Quarterly Journal of Economics*, 101, 383–406.

Edgeworth, F. Y. (1881). *Mathematical Psychics*. London: C. Kegan Paul.

Edwards, W. (1955). 'The Prediction of Decisions among Bets'. *Journal of Experimental Psychology*, 50, 201–14.

Eichenbaum, M. (1983). 'A Rational Expectations Equilibrium Model of Inventories of Finished Goods and Employment'. *Journal of Monetary Economics*, 12, 259–77.

Ells, E. (1982). *Rational Decision and Causality*. Cambridge: University Press.

Ellsberg, D. (1961). 'Risk, Ambiguity, and the Savage Axioms'. *Quarterly Journal of Economics*, 75, 643–69.

Elmes, S. and Reny, P. (1987). 'The Equivalence of Games with Perfect Recall'. Unpublished paper, Department of Economics, Princeton University.

Engers, M. (1987). 'Signalling with Many Signals'. *Econometrica*, 55, 663–74.

Epstein, L. (1985). 'Decreasing Risk Aversion and Mean–Variance Analysis'. *Econometrica* 53, 945–61.

Ethier, W. (1982). 'National and International Returns to Scale in the Modern Theory of International Trade'. *American Economic Review*, 72, 389–405.

Evans, G. (1987). 'The Fragility of Sunspots and Bubbles'.

Farmer, R. (1984). 'A New Theory of Aggregate Supply'. *American Economic Review*, 74, 920–30.

—— and Woodford, M. (1984). 'Self-fulfilling Prophecies and the Business Cycle'. Unpublished paper.

Farrell, J. (1985). 'Credible Neologisms in Games of Communication'. Mimeo, Massachusetts Institute of Technology.

—— and Maskin, E. (1987). 'Renegotiation in Repeated Games'. Mimeo.

Feigenbaum, M. J. (1980). 'Universal Behavior in Non-linear systems'. *Los Alamos Science*, 1, 4–27. Reprinted in Citanovic (1984b).

Feller, W. (1971). *An Introduction to Probability Theory and its Applications* (2nd edn.). New York: John Wiley.

Ferguson, T. (1967). *Mathematical Statistics*. New York: Academic Press.

Fischhoff, B. (1983). 'Predicting Frames'. *Journal of Experimental Psychology*: *Learning, Memory and Cognition*, 9, 103–16.

Fishburn, P. (1982), 'Nontransitive Measurable Utility'. *Journal of Mathematical Psychology*, 26, 31–67.

—— (1983). 'Transitive Measurable Utility'. *Journal of Economic Theory*, 31, 293–317.

—— (1984). 'SSB Utility Theory: An Economic Perspective'. *Mathematical Social Sciences*, 8, 63–94.

Fisher, F. M. (1983). *Disequilibrium Foundations of Equilibrium Economics*. Cambridge University Press.

Forges, F. (1986). 'An Approach to Communication Equilibria'. *Econometrica*, 54, 1375–85.

Fraysse, J. and Moreaux, M. (1985). 'Collusive Equilibria in Oligopolies with Finite Lives'. *European Economic Review*, 27, 45–55.

Friedman, J. (1971). 'A Noncooperative Equilibrium for Supergames'. *Review of Economic Studies*, 38, 1–12.

—— (1985). 'Equilibria in Finite Horizon Cooperative Noncooperative Supergames'. *Journal of Economic Theory*, 35, 390–8.

Friedman, M. (1953). 'The Methodology of Positive Economics'. In *Essays in Positive Economics*. University of Chicago Press.

—— (1960). *A Program for Monetary Stability*. New York: Fordham University Press.

—— (1968). 'The Role of Monetary Policy'. *American Economic Review*, 58, 1–17.

Fudenberg, D., Kreps, D. M., and Levine, D. K. (1988). 'On the Robustness of Equilibrium Refinements'. *Journal of Economic Theory*, 44, 354–80.

Fudenberg, D. and Levine, D. (1983). 'Subgame-Perfect Equilibria of Finite- and Infinite-Horizon Games'. *Journal of Economic Theory*, 31, 251–68.

—— (1986). 'Limit Games and Limit Equilibria'. *Journal of Economic Theory*, 38, 261–79.

Fudenberg, D., Levine, D., and Tirole, J. (1985). 'Infinite Horizon Models of Bargaining with One-sided Incomplete Information'. In A. Roth (ed.), *Game-theoretic Models of Bargaining*. Cambridge University Press.

Fudenberg, D. and Maskin, E. (1987a). 'Discounted Repeated Games with Unobservable Actions, I: One-sided Moral Hazard'. Mimeo.

—— (1987b). 'Discounted Repeated Games with Unobservable Actions, II: Two-sided Moral Hazard'. Mimeo.

Fudenberg, D. and Tirole, J. (1983a). 'Dynamic Models of Oligopoly'. Mimeo.

—— (1983b). 'Sequential Bargaining with Incomplete Information'. *Review of Economic Studies*, 50, 221–47.

—— (1984a). 'The Fat-Cat Effect, the Puppy-dog Ploy, and the Lean and Hungry Look'. *American Economic Review*, 74 (Papers and Proceedings), 361–6.

—— (1984b). 'Learning-by-Doing and Market Performance'. *Bell Journal of Economics*, 14, 522–30.

Gaertner, W. (1984). 'Periodic and Aperiodic Consumer Behaviour'. Unpublished paper.

—— (1986). 'Zyklische Konsummuster'. *Jahrbucher fur Nationalokonomie und Statistik*, 201, 54–65.

Gale, D. (1973). 'Pure Exchange Equilibrium of Dynamic Economic Models'. *Journal of Economic Theory*, 6, 12–36.

—— (1986a). 'Bargaining and Competition, I: Characterization'. *Econometrica*, 54, 785–806.

—— (1986b). 'Bargaining and Competition, II: Existence'. *Econometrica*, 54, 807–18.

—— and Hellwig, M. (1985). 'Incentive-Compatible Debt Contracts: The One-Period Problem'. *Review of Economic Studies*, 52, 647–63.

Gatsios, K. (1985). 'International Trade Under Increasing Returns, Product Differentiation and Monopolistic Competition'. Economic Theory Discussion Paper no. 118, University of Cambridge.

—— (1986). 'Learning-by-doing and International Trade Policy'. Unpublished paper, Cambridge University.

Geanakoplos, J. D. and Brown, D. J. (1985). 'Comparative Statics and Local Determinacy in OLG Economies: An Application of the Multiplicative Ergotic Theorem'. Cowles Foundation Discussion Paper no. 773.

Geanakoplos, J. D. and Polemarchakis, H. M. (1984). 'Intertemporally Separable, Overlapping-Generations Economies'. *Journal of Economic Theory*, 34, 207–15.

—— (1985). 'Existence, Regularity, and Constrained Suboptimality of Competitive Allocations when the Asset Market is Incomplete'. CORE Discussion Paper no. 8537, Louvain.

—— (1986). 'Walrasian Indeterminacy and Keynesian Macroeconomics'. *Review of Economic Studies*, 53, 755–79.

Gilboa, I. (1986). 'Information and Meta-information'. Working Paper no. 30-86, Foerder Institute for Economic Research, Tel-Aviv University.

Gordon, D. F. (1974). 'A Neo-classical Theory of Keynesian Unemployment'. *Economic Inquiry*, 12, 431–59.

Grandmont, J. M. (1983). 'Periodic and Aperiodic Behaviour in Discrete Onedimensional Dynamic Systems'. CEPREMAP D.P. no. 8317. Also available as a Technical Report of IMSSS, Economics, Stanford University, and as a Technical Report of EHEC, University of Lausanne.

—— (1985). 'On Endogenous Competitive Business Cycles'. *Econometrica*, 53, 995–1045.

—— (1986). 'Local Bifurcations and Stationary Sunspots'. Mimeo.

—— and Laroque, G. (1987). 'Stability, Expectations, and Predetermined Variables'. CEPREMAP, Mimeo no. 8714.

Green, E. J. (1980). 'Noncooperative Price Taking in Large Dynamic Markets'. *Journal of Economic Theory*, 22, 155–82.

—— and Porter, R. (1984). 'Noncooperative Collusion Under Imperfect Price Information'. *Econometrica*, 52, 87–100.

Grether, D. and Plott, C. (1979). 'Economic Theory of Choice and the Preference Reversal Phenomenon'. *American Economic Review*, 69, 623–38.

Grossman, S. J. (1976). 'On the Efficiency of Competitive Stock Markets Where Trades Have Diverse Information'. *Journal of Finance*, 31, 573–85.

—— (1977). 'The Existence of Futures Markets, Noisy Rational Expectations and Informational Externalities'. *Review of Economic Studies*, 44, 431–49.

—— (1978). 'Further Results on the Informational Efficiency of Competitive Stock Markets'. *Journal of Economic Theory*, 18, 81–101.

—— (1981a). 'An Introduction to the Theory of Rational Expectations Under Asymmetric Information'. *Review of Economic Studies*, 48, 541–59.

—— (1981b). The Informational Role of Warranties and Private Disclosure about Product Quality'. *Journal of Law and Economics*, 24, 461–83.

—— and Hart, O. D. (1981). 'Implicit Contracts, Moral Hazard and Unemployment'. *American Economic Review*, 71 (Papers and Proceedings), 301–7.

—— and Hart, O. D. (1983). 'Implicit Contracts Under Asymmetric Information'. *Quarterly Journal of Economics*, 98 (Supplement), 123–56.

——, Hart, O., and Maskin, E. (1983). 'Unemployment with Observable Aggregate Shocks'. *Journal of Political Economy*, 91, 907–28.

—— and Perry, M. (1986a). 'Perfect Sequential Equilibrium'. *Journal of Economic Theory*, 39, 97–119.

—— and Perry, M. (1986b). 'Sequential Bargaining under Asymmetric Information'. *Journal of Economic Theory*, 39, 120–54.

—— and Stiglitz, J. E. (1980). 'On the Impossibility of Informationally Efficient Markets'. *American Economic Review*, 70, 393–408.

Grubel, H. and Lloyd, R. (1975). *Intra-industry Trade: The Theory and Measurement of International Trade in Differentiated Products.* London: Macmillan.

Guckenheimer, J. and Holmes, P. (1983). *Nonlinear Oscillations, Dynamical Systems, and Bifurcations of Vector Fields.* New York/Heidelberg/Berlin: Springer-Verlag.

Guesnerie, R. (1986). 'Stationary Sunspot Equilibria in an *N* Commodity World'. *Journal of Economic Theory*, 40, 103–27.

Gul, F., Sonnenschein, H., and Wilson, R. (1986). 'Foundations of Dynamic Monopoly and the Coase Conjecture'. *Journal of Economic Theory*, 39, 155–90.

Haberler, G. (1936). *The Theory of International Trade with its Application to Commercial Policy*. London: William Hodges.

Hagen, O. (1979). 'Towards a Positive Theory of Preferences under Risk'. In Allais and Hagen (1979).

Hahn, F. H. (1962). 'The Stability of the Cournot Oligopoly Solution'. *Review of Economic Studies*, 29, 329–31.

—— (1977). 'Exercises in Conjectural Equilibrium Analysis'. *Scandinavian Journal of Economics*, 79, 210–26.

—— (1978). 'On Non-Walrasian Equilibria'. *Review of Economic Studies*, 45, 1–17.

—— (1984). 'Implicit Contracts and Involuntary Unemployment'. Economic Theory Discussion Paper no. 71, Cambridge University.

Halpern, J. (ed.) (1986). *Theoretical Aspects of Reasoning About Knowledge*. Los Altos: Morgan Kaufmann.

Harely, C. B. (1981). 'Learning the Evolutionary Stable Strategy'. *Journal of Theoretical Biology*, 89, 611–33.

Harris, C. (1985). 'A Characterisation of the Perfect Equilibria of Infinite Horizon Games'. *Journal of Economic Theory*, 37, 99–125.

—— and Vickers, J. (1985a). 'Perfect Equilibrium in a Model of a Race'. *Review of Economic Studies*, 52, 193–209.

—— (1985b). 'Patent Races and the Persistence of Monopoly'. *Journal of Industrial Economics*, 33, 461–81.

Harris, M. and Raviv, A. (1981). 'A Theory of Monopoly Pricing Schemes with Demand Uncertainty'. *American Economic Review*, 71, 347–65.

Harsanyi, J. C. (1959). 'A Bargaining Model for the Cooperative *n*-Person Game'. In Tucker and Luce (eds.), *Contributions to the Theory of Games*, Vol. 4. Princeton University Press.

—— (1967–8). 'Games with Incomplete Information Played by Bayesian Players, I, II, and III'. *Management Science*, 14, 159–82, 320–34, 486–503.

—— (1973a). 'Games with Randomly Disturbed Payoffs: A New Rationale for Mixed-strategy Equilibrium Points'. *International Journal of Game Theory*, 2, 1–23.

—— (1973b). 'Oddness of the Number of Equilibrium Points: A New Proof'. *International Journal of Game Theory*, 2, 235–50.

—— and Selten, R. (1972). 'A Generalized Nash Bargaining Solution for Two-Person Games with Incomplete Information'. *Management Science*, 18, 80–106.

Hart, A. G. (1942). 'Risk, Uncertainty, and the Unprofitability of Compounding Probabilities'. In O. Lange, F. McIntyre, and T. Yntema (eds.), *Studies in Mathematical Economics and Econometrics*. Chicago University Press.

Hart, O. D. (1983). 'Optimal Labour Contracts under Asymmetric Information: An Introduction'. *Review of Economic Studies*, 50, 3–35.

—— and Holmstrom, B. (1986). 'The Theory of Contracts'. In T. Bewley (ed.),

490 *Bibliography*

Advances in Economic Theory: Fifth World Congress, 1985. Cambridge University Press.

—— and Moore, J. (1985). 'Incomplete Contracts and Renegotiation'. Massachusetts Institute of Technology, Department of Economics Working Paper no. 367.

Hayek, F. A. (1945). 'The Use of Knowledge in Society'. *American Economic Review*, 35, 519–30.

Helpman, E. (1981). 'International Trade in the Presence of Product Differentiation, Economies of Scale and Monopolistic Competition'. *Journal of International Economics*, 11, 305–40.

—— (1984). 'A Simple Theory of International Trade with Multinational Corporations'. *Journal of Political Economy*, 92, 451–71.

—— (1985). 'International Trade in Differentiated Middle Products'. In K. Junkenfelt and D. Hague (eds.), *Structural Adjustment in Developed Open Economies*. London: International Economic Association/Macmillan.

—— and Krugman, P. (1985). *Market Structure and Foreign Trade*. Cambridge, Mass.: MIT Press.

Henon, M. (1976). 'A Two-dimensional Mapping with a Strange Attractor'. *Communications in Mathematical Physics*, 50, 69–77.

Henry, C. (1974a). 'Investment Decisions under Uncertainty: the Irreversibility Effect'. *American Economic Review*, 64, 1006–12.

—— (1974b). 'Option Values in the Economics of Irreplaceable Assets'. *Review of Economic Studies*, Symposium, 89–104.

Hershey, J., Kunreuther, H., and Schoemaker, P. (1982). 'Sources of Bias in Assessment Procedures for Utility Functions'. *Management Science*, 28, 936–54.

—— and Schoemaker, P. (1980). 'Risk-taking and Problem Context in the Domain of Losses—An Expected Utility Analysis'. *Journal of Risk and Insurance*, 47, 111–32.

Hey, J. (1979). *Uncertainty in Microeconomics*. Oxford: Martin Robertson.

Hicks, J. R. (1932). *The Theory of Wages*. London: Macmillan.

—— (1974). *The Crisis in Keynesian Economics*. Oxford: Basil Blackwell.

Hillas, J. (1986). 'Sequential Equilibrium and Stable Sets of Beliefs'. Mimeo, Stanford University.

Hillier, F. and Lieberman, G. (1986). *Introduction to Operations Research* (4th edn.). Oakland, Cal.: Holden-Day.

Hirsch, M. W. and Smale, S. (1974). *Differential Equations, Dynamical Systems and Linear Algebra*. New York: Academic Press.

Hoel, M. (1986). 'Perfect Equilibria in Sequential Bargaining Games with Non-linear Utility Functions'. *Scandinavian Journal of Economics*, 88, 383–400.

Holmstrom, B. (1983). 'Equilibrium Long-term Labour Contracts'. *Quarterly Journal of Economics*, 98 (Supplement), 23–54.

Holt, C. (1980). 'Competitive Bidding for Contracts under Alternative Auction Procedures'. *Journal of Political Economy*, 88, 433–45.

Hopcroft, J. E. and Ullman, J. D. (1979). *Introduction to Automata Theory, Languages, and Computation*. Reading, Mass.: Addison-Wesley.

Hurwicz, L. (1972). 'On Informationally Decentralized Systems'. Ch. 14 in C. B.

McGuire and R. Radner (eds.), *Decision and Organization*. Amsterdam: North-Holland.

Irwin, M. C. (1980). *Smooth Dynamical Systems*. New York: Academic Press.

Jaffee, D. and Russell, T. (1976). 'Imperfect Information, Uncertainty, and Credit Rationing'. *Quarterly Journal of Economics*, 90, 651–66.

Jakobson, M. V. (1981). 'Absolutely Continuous Invariant Measures for One-parameter Families of One-dimensional Maps'. *Communications in Mathematical Physics*, 81, 39–88.

Jevons, W. S. (1884). *Investigations in Currency and Finance*. London: Macmillan.

Jones, R. and Ostroy, J. M. (1984). 'Flexibility and Uncertainty'. *Review of Economic Studies*, 51, 13–32.

Jordan, J. S. (1982a). 'Admissable Market Data Structures' A Complete Characterization. *Journal of Economic Theory*, 28, 19–31.

—— (1982b). 'A Dynamic Model of Expectations Equilibrium'. *Journal of Economic Theory*, 28, 235–54.

—— (1983). 'On the Efficient Markets Hypothesis'. *Econometrica*, 51, 1325–43.

—— and Radner, R. (1982). 'Rational Expectations in Microeconomic Models: An Overview'. *Journal of Economic Theory*, 26, 201–23.

Joskow, P. L. (1985). 'Vertical Integration and Long-term Contracts: The Case of Coal-burning Power Plants'. *Journal of Law Economics and Organisation*, 1, 33–80.

Kahneman, D. and A. Tversky (1979). 'Prospect Theory: An Analysis of Decision Under Risk'. *Econometrica*, 47, 263–91.

—— (1982). 'The Psychology of Preferences'. *Scientific American*, no. 246, 160–173.

—— (1984). 'Choices, Values and Frames'. *American Psychologist*, 39, 341–50.

Kalai, E. (1977). 'Proportional Solutions to Bargaining Situations: Interpersonal Utility Comparisons'. *Econometrica*, 45, 1623–37.

—— and Samet, D. (1985). 'Monotonic Solutions to General Cooperative Games'. *Econometrica*, 53, 307–27.

—— and Stanford, W. (1986). 'Finite Rationality and Interpersonal Complexity in Repeated Games'. Northwestern University Discussion Paper.

Kaldor, N. (1934). 'A Classificatory Note on the Determinateness of Equilibrium'. *Review of Economic Studies*, 1, 122–36.

Kaneko, J. (1982). 'Some Remarks on the Folk Theorem in Game Theory'. *Mathematical Social Sciences*, 3, 281–90.

—— (1987). 'Structural Common Knowledge and Factual Common Knowledge'. RUEE Working Paper no. 87-27, Department of Economics, Hitotsubashi University.

Kareken, J. H. and Wallace, N. (1978). 'Deposit Insurance and Bank Regulation: A Partial-Equilibrium Exposition'. *Journal of Business*, 51, 413–38.

Karmarkar, U. (1974). 'The Effect of Probabilities on the Subjective Evaluation of Lotteries'. Sloan School of Business Working Paper no. 698-74, Massachusetts Institute of Technology.

—— (1978). 'Subjectively Weighted Utility: A Descriptive Extension of the Expected Utility Model'. *Organizational Behavior and Human Performance*, 21, 61–72.

Karni, E. and Safra, Z. (1987). '"Preference Reversal" and the Observability of Preferences by Experimental Methods'. *Econometrica,* 55, 675–85.

Katz, M. and Shapiro, C. (1987). 'R&D Rivalry with Licensing or Imitation'. *American Economic Review,* 77, 402–20.

Kawasaki, S. and McMillan, J. (1985). 'The Design of Contracts: Evidence from Japanese Subcontracting'. Mimeo, University of Western Ontario.

Kehoe, T. J. (1986). 'General Equilibrium Models with Infinite Numbers of Consumers and Goods'. Unpublished paper.

—— and Levine, D. K. (1984a). 'Intertemporal Separability in Overlapping-Generations Models'. *Journal of Economic Theory,* 34, 216–26.

—— and Levine, D. K. (1984b). 'Regularity in Overlapping Generations Exchange Economies'. *Journal of Mathematical Economics,* 13, 69–93.

—— and Levine, D. K. (1985a). 'Comparative Statics and Perfect Foresight in Infinite Horizon Economies'. *Econometrica,* 53, 433–53.

—— and Levine, D. K. (1985b). 'Empirical Implications of Complete Contingent Claims'. Unpublished paper.

—— and Levine, D. K. (1986). 'The Economics of Indeterminacy in Overlapping Generations Models'. Unpublished paper.

——, Levine, D. K., Mas-Colell, A., and Woodford, M. (1986a). 'Gross Substitutability in Large-square Economies'. Unpublished paper.

——, Levine, D. K., Mas-Colell, A., and Zame, W. R. (1986b). 'Determinacy of Equilibrium in Large-square Economies'. *Journal of Mathematical Economics,* forthcoming.

——, Levine, D. K., and Romer, P. M. (1988). 'Determinacy of Equilibrium in Dynamic Models with Infinitely Lived Consumers'. *Journal of Economic Theory,* forthcoming.

Kelsey, D. (1988). 'The Economics of Chaos'. *Oxford Economic Papers,* 40, 1, 1–31.

—— and Ng, Y. K. (1984). 'Non-inflationary Expansion and Recurring Business Cycles: Practical Relevance and Implications of a Non-traditional Result'. Working Paper, Monash University, Melbourne.

Kemp, M. (1969). *The Pure Theory of International Trade and Investment.* Englewood Cliffs, NJ: Prentice-Hall.

Keynes, J. M. (1973). *The General Theory of Employment, Interest and Money.* London: Macmillan (first published 1936).

Knight, F. H. (1921). *Risk, Uncertainty and Profit.* New York: Houghton Mifflin.

Koenig, H. and Nerlove, M. (1986). 'Price Flexibility, Inventory Behaviour and Production Responses'. In W. P. Heller, D. A. Starrett, and R. M. Starr (eds.), *Essays in Honour of Kenneth J. Arrow,* Vol. II. Cambridge University Press.

Kohlberg, E. and Mertens, J.-F. (1986). 'On the Strategic Stability of Equilibria'. *Econometrica,* 54, 1003–37.

Kohlleppel, L. (1983). 'Multidimensional Market Signaling', Discussion Paper no. 125, Institut fur Gesellschafts und Wirtschaftswissenschaften, University of Bonn.

Koopmans, T. C. (1957). *Three Essays on the State of Economic Science.* New York: McGraw-Hill.

Kravis, I. (1971). 'The Current Case for Import Limitations'. In *United States Economic Policy in an Independent World.* Washington, DC: Commission on International Trade and Investment Policy.

Kreps, D. (1977). 'A Note on Fulfilled Expectations Equilibria'. *Journal of Economic Theory*, 14, 32–43.

—— (1987). 'Nash Equilibrium'. In J. Eatwell, M. Milgate, and P. Newman (eds.), *The New Palgrave*, pp. 584–8. London: Macmillan.

—— and Ramey, G. (1987). 'Structural Consistency, Consistency, and Sequential Rationality'. *Econometrica*, 55, 1331–48.

—— and Scheinkman, J. (1983). 'Quantity Precommitment and Bertrand Competition Yield Cournot Outcomes'. *Bell Journal of Economics*, 14, 326–37.

—— and Spence, A. M. (1985). 'Industrial Organization and Competition'. In G. R. Feiwel (ed.), *Issues in Contemporary Microeconomics and Welfare*. London: Macmillan.

—— and Wilson, R. (1982). 'Sequential Equilibria'. *Econometrica*, 50, 863–94.

—— *et al.* (1982). 'Rational Cooperation in the Finitely Repeated Prisoners' Dilemma'. *Journal of Economic Theory*, 27, 245–52.

Krugman, P. (1979). 'Increasing Returns, Monopolistic Competition and international Trade'. *Journal of International Economics*, 1, 469–79.

—— (1980). 'Scale Economies, Product Differentiation and the Pattern of Trade'. *American Economic Review*, 70, 950–9.

—— (1982). 'Trade in Differentiated Products and the Political Economy of Trade Liberalization'. In J. N. Bhagwati (ed.), *Import Competition and Response*. University of Chicago Press.

—— (1984). 'Import Protection as Export Promotion: International Competition in the Presence of Oligopoly and Economies of Scale'. In H. Kierzkowski (ed.), *Monopolistic Competition and International Trade*. Oxford University Press.

Kruz, M. (1985). 'Reconsideration of Duopoly Theory: A Co-operative Perspective'. In G. R. Feiwel (ed.), *Issues in Contemporary Microeconomics and Welfare*. London: Macmillan.

Kuh, E. (1966). 'Unemployment, Production Functions, and Effective Demand'. *Journal of Political Economy*, 74, 238–49.

Kuznets, S. (1962). 'Inventive Activity: Problems of Definition and Measurement'. In R. R. Nelson (ed.), *The Rate and Direction of Inventive Activity: Economic and Social Factors*. Princeton University Press.

Kydland, F. E. and Prescott, E. C. (1982). 'Time to Build and Aggregate Fluctuations'. *Econometrica*, 50, 1345–70.

Lambson, V. E. (1984). 'Self-Enforcing Collusion in Large Dynamic Markets'. *Journal of Economic Theory*, 34, 282–91.

Lancaster, K. (1979). *Variety, Equity, and Efficiency*. New York: Columbia University Press.

—— (1980). 'Intra-industry Trade under Perfect Monopolistic Competition'. *Journal of International Economics*, 10, 151–75.

Leland, H. E. and Pyle, D. H. (1977). 'Informational Asymmetries, Financial Structure, and Financial Intermediation'. *Journal of Finance*, 32, 371–87.

Levine, D. K. (1986). 'Infinite Horizon Equilibrium with Incomplete Markets'. Unpublished paper.

Lewis, D. (1969). *Convention; a Philosophical Study*. Cambridge, Mass.: Harvard University Press.

Li, T. and Yorke, J. A. (1975). 'Period Three Implies Chaos'. *American Mathematical Monthly*, 82, 985–92.

Lichtenstein, S. and Slovic, P. (1971). 'Reversals of Preferences between Bids and Choices in Gambling Decisions'. *Journal of Experimental Psychology*, 89, 46–55.

—— (1973). 'Response-induced Reversals of Preference in Gambling: An Extended Replication in Las Vegas'. *Journal of Experimental Psychology*, 101, 16–20.

Lindman, H. (1971). 'Inconsistent Preferences among Gambles'. *Journal of Experimental Psychology*, 89, 390–7.

Lockwood, B. (1986). 'The Folk Theorem for Dynamic Games without Discounting'. Mimeo.

Loomes, G. and Sugden, R. (1982). 'Regret Theory: An Alternative Theory of Rational Choice Under Uncertainty', *Economic Journal* 92, 805–824.

Loury, G. (1979). 'Market Structure and Innovation'. *Quarterly Journal of Economics*, 93, 395–410.

Lucas, R. E., Jr. (1975). 'An Equilibrium Model of the Business Cycle'. *Journal of Political Economy*, 83, 1113–44.

—— (1981). *Studies in Business Cycle Theory*. Oxford: Basil Blackwell.

Luce, R. and Raiffa, H. (1957). *Games and Decisions*. New York: John Wiley.

Mabro, R., Bacon, R., Chadwick, M., Halliwell, M., and Long, D. (1986). *The Market for North Sea Crude Oil*. Oxford University Press.

Maccini, L. J. (1976). 'An Aggregate Dynamic Model of Short-Run Price and Output Behaviour'. *Quarterly Journal of Economics*, 90, 177–96.

MacCrimmon, K. (1965). 'An Experimental Study of the Decision Making Behavior of Business Executives'. Ph.D. dissertation, University of California, Los Angeles.

—— (1968). 'Descriptive and Normative Implications of the Decision–Theory Postulates'. In Borch K. and Mossin J. (1968).

—— and Larsson, S. (1979). 'Utility Theory: Axioms versus 'Paradoxes''. In Allais and Hagen (1979).

Machina, M. (1982). '"Expected Utility" Analysis Without the Independence Axiom'. *Econometrica*, 50, 277–323.

—— (1983). 'Generalized Expected Utility Analysis and the Nature of Observed Violations of the Independence Axiom'. In Stigum and Wenstøp (1983).

—— (1984). 'Temporal Risk and the Nature of Induced Preferences'. *Journal of Economic Theory*, 33, 199–231.

—— (1987). 'Choice under Uncertainty: Problems Solved and Unsolved'. *Journal of Economic Perspectives*, 1, 121–54.

Makowski, L. (1983). 'Rational Conjectures' Aren't Rational: 'Reasonable Conjectures' Aren't Reasonable'. Economic Theory Discussion Paper, Cambridge.

Malcolmson, J. M. (1985). 'Incomplete Contracts and Involuntary Unemployment'. *Oxford Economic Papers*, 37, 196–209.

Marcet, A. and Sargent, T. (1986). 'The Convergence of Least Square Learning Mechanisms in Self-referential Linear Stochastic Models'.

Marschak, J. (1938). 'Money and the Theory of Assets'. *Econometrica*, 6, 311–325.

—— (1949). 'Role of Liquidity Under Complete and Incomplete Information'. *American Economic Review*, 39, 182–95.

—— (1950). 'Rational Behavior, Uncertain Prospects, and Measurable Utility'. *Econometrica*, 18, 111–41 ('Errata', *Econometrica*, 18, 312).

—— and Selten, R. (1974). *General Equilibrium with Price Making Firms: Lecture Notes in Mathematical Systems*. Berlin: Springer-Verlag.

Marschak, T. (1978). 'Restabilizing Responses, Inertia Supergames and Oligopolistic Equilibria'. *Quarterly Journal of Economics*, 92, 71–93.

Marshall, A. (1879). *The Pure Theory of Foreign Trade*. London: London School of Economics, 1930.

Maskin, E. S. and Riley, J. G. (1980). 'Auctioning an Indivisible Object', Kennedy School of Government Working Paper no. 87D, Harvard University.

—— (1981). 'Auction Design with Correlated Reservation Values'. Mimeo.

—— (1982). 'On the Uniqueness of Equilibrium in Sealed High Bid Auctions', Mimeo.

—— (1984a). 'Monopoly with Incomplete Information'. *Rand Journal of Economics*, 15, 171–96.

—— (1984b). 'Optimal Auctions with Risk Averse Buyers'. *Econometrica*, 52, 1473–1518.

—— (1986). 'Asymmetric Auctions'. UCLA Discussion Paper.

Maskin, E. and Tirole, J. (1988). 'A Theory of Dynamic Oligopolies, I and II'. *Econometrica*, 56, 549–69.

Matthews, R. C. O. (1949–50). 'Reciprocal Demand and Increasing Returns'. *Review of Economic Studies*, 17, 149–58.

Matthews, S. (1983). 'Selling to Risk Averse Buyers with Unobservable Tastes', *Journal of Economic Theory*, 30, 370–400.

Maxwell, C. (1982). 'Monopolistic Marketing of a Divisible Commodity for which Demand is Unknown: The Symmetric Deterministic Case'. Unpublished doctoral dissertation, Harvard University.

Maynard Smith, J. (1982). *Evolution and the Theory of Games*. Cambridge University Press.

McAfee, R. and McMillan, J. (1987). 'Auctions and Bidding'. *Journal of Economic Literature*, 25, 699–738.

McCord, M. and de Neufville, R. (1983). 'Empirical Demonstration that Expected Utility Analysis Is Not Operational'. In Stigum and Wenstøp (1983).

—— (1984). 'Utility Dependence on Probability: An Empirical Demonstration'. *Large Scale Systems*, 6, 91–103.

McLennan, A. (1985). 'Justifiable Beliefs in Sequential Equilibrium'. *Econometrica*, 53, 889–904.

Megiddo, N. and Widgerson, A. (1985). 'On Play by Means of Computing Machines'. Mimeo.

Melese, F. and Transue, W. (1986). 'Unscrambling Chaos Through Thick and Thin'. *Quarterly Journal of Economics*, 101, 419–23.

Melvin, J. (1969). 'Increasing Returns to Scale as a Determinant of Trade'. *Canadian Journal of Economics*, 2, 389–402.

Mertens, J.-F. (1986). 'Repeated Games'. CORE Discussion Paper no. 8624.

—— and Zamir, S. (1985). 'Formulation of Bayesian Analysis for Games with Incomplete Information'. *International Journal of Game Theory*, 10, 619–32.

Merton, R. C. (1973). 'An Intertemporal Capital Asset Pricing Model'. *Econometrica*, 41. 867–88.

Merton, R. K. (1973). *The Sociology of Science: Theoretical and Empirical Investigations*, ed. N. W. Storer. University of Chicago Press.

Meyer, P. L. (1970). *Introductory Probability and Statistical Applications* (2nd edn.). Reading, Mass.: Addison Wesley.

Milgrom, P. (1986). 'Auction Theory'. In T. Bewley (ed.), *Advances in Economic Theory: Fifth World Conference, 1985.* Cambridge University Press.

—— and Roberts, J. (1982). 'Limit Pricing and Entry under Incomplete Information: An Equilibrium Analysis'. *Econometrica*, 50, 443–59.

—— and Roberts, J. (1986). 'Price and Advertising Signals of Product Quality'. *Journal of Political Economy*, 94, 796–821.

—— and Weber, R. J. (1982). 'A Theory of Auctions and Competitive Bidding'. *Econometrica*, 50, 1089–1122.

Millan, T. (1981). 'On the Existence of Optimal Competitive Equilibria in the Overlapping Generations Model'. Ph.D. dissertation, University of Minnesota.

Mirowski, P. (1984). 'Macroeconomic Instability and the 'Natural' Processes in Early Neoclassical Economics'. *Journal of Economic History*, 44, 345–54.

Montague, R. (1974). *Formal Philosophy*. New Haven, Conn.: Yale University Press.

Montrucchio, L. (1984). 'Optimal Decisions Over Time and Strange Attractors'. Unpublished paper, Politecnico di Torino.

Moore, J. (1984). 'Global Incentive Constraints in Auction Design'. *Econometrica*, 52, 1523–36.

Morrison, D. (1967). 'On the Consistency of Preferences in Allais' Paradox'. *Behavioral Science*, 12, 373–83.

Moskowitz, H. (1974). 'Effects of Problem Representation and Feedback on Rational Behavior in Allais and Morlat-Type Problems'. *Decision Sciences*, 5, 225–42.

Mowen, J. and Gentry, J. (1980). 'Investigation of the Preference-reversal Phenomenon in a New Product Introduction Task'. *Journal of Applied Psychology*, 65, 715–22.

Mueller, D. C. (1976). 'Public Choice: A Survey'. *Journal of Economic Literature*, 14, 395–433.

Muller, W. J., III, and Woodford, M. (1985). 'Determinacy of Equilibrium in Stationary Economies with Both Finite and Infinite Lived Consumers'. *Journal of Economic Theory*.

Musgrave, R. A. and Peacock, A. T. (eds). (1958). *Classics in the Theory of Public Finance*. London: Macmillan.

Mussa, M. and Rosen, S. (1978). 'Monopoly and Product Quality'. *Journal of Economic Theory*, 18, 301–17.

Muth, J. F. (1961). 'Rational Expectations and the Theory of Price Movements'. *Econometrica*, 29, 315–35.

Myerson, R. (1978). 'Refinements of the Nash Equilibrium Concept'. *International Journal of Game Theory*, 7, 73–80.

—— (1981). 'Optimal Auction Design'. *Mathematics of Operations Research*, 6, 58–73.

—— (1984). 'Two-Person Bargaining Problems with Incomplete Information'. *Econometrica*, 52, 461–88.

—— (1985). 'Bayesian Equilibrium and Incentive-Compatibility: An Introduction'. In *Social Goals and Social Organization*, eds. L. Hurwicz, D. Schmeidler, and H. Sonnenschein. New York: Cambridge University Press.

—— (1986). 'Multistage Games with Communication'. *Econometrica*, 54, 323–58.

—— and Satterthwaite, M. (1983). 'Efficient Mechanisms for Bilateral Trading'. *Journal of Economic Theory*, 29, 265–81.

Nash, J. F. (1950). 'The Bargaining Problem'. *Econometrica*, 18, 155–62.

—— (1951). 'Non-cooperative Games'. *Annals of Mathematics*, 54, 286–95.

Neftci, S. N. (1978). 'A Time-series Analysis of the Real Wages–Employment Relationship'. *Journal of Political Economy*, 86, 281–91.

Negishi, T. (1960a). 'Monopolistic Competition and General Equilibrium'. *Review of Economic Studies*, 28, 196–201.

—— (1960b). 'Welfare Economics and Existence of an Equilibrium for a Competitive Economy'. *Metroeconomica*, 12, 92–7.

—— (1969). 'Marshallian External Economies and Gains from Trade between Similar Countries'. *Review of Economic Studies*, 36, 131–5.

Nelson, P. (1970). 'Information and Consumer Behavior'. *Journal of Political Economy*, 78, 311–29.

Newbery, D. M. G. (1980). 'Externalities: The Theory of Environmental Policy'. Ch. 4 in G. A. Hughes and G. M. Heal (eds.), *Public Policy and the Tax System*. London: George Allen and Unwin.

—— (1983). 'Commodity Price Stabilization in Imperfectly Competitive Markets'. Ch. 11 in G. G. Storey, A. Schmitz, and A. H. Sarris (eds.), *International Agricultural Trade*. Boulder, Colo.: Westview Press.

—— (1984). 'Commodity Price Stabilization in Imperfect or Cartelized Markets'. *Econometrica*, 52, 563–78.

—— and Stiglitz, J. E. (1981). *The Theory of Commodity Price Stabilization*. Oxford University Press.

—— (1982a). 'Optimal Commodity Stock-piling Rules'. *Oxford Economic Papers*, 34, 403–27.

—— (1982b). 'The Choice of Techniques and the Optimality of Market Equilibrium with Rational Expectations'. *Journal of Political Economy*, 90, 223–46.

—— (1984). 'Pareto Inferior Trade'. *Review of Economic Studies*, 51, 1–12.

—— (1985). 'Wage Rigidity, Implicit Contracts, Unemployment and Economic Efficiency'. CEPR Discussion Paper no. 67, Centre for Economic Policy Research, London.

Neyman, A. (1985). 'Bounded Complexity Justifies Cooperation in the Finitely Repeated Prisoners' Dilemma'. *Economic Letters*, 19, 227–9.

—— (1985). 'Bounded Rationality Justifies Cooperation in the Finitely Repeated Prisoner's Dilemma'. Unpublished paper, Department of Mathematics, Hebrew University.

Nordhaus, W. (1969). *Invention, Growth, and Welfare*. Cambridge, Mass.: MIT Press.

Novshek, W. (1980). 'Cournot Equilibrium with Free Entry'. *Review of Economic Studies*, 47, 473–86.

Ogburn, W. P. and Thomas, D. S. (1922). 'Are Inventions Inevitable?'. *Political Science Quarterly*, 37.

Ohlin, B. (1933). *Interregional and International Trade*. Cambridge, Mass.: Harvard University Press.

Oswald, A. J. and Turnbull, P. J. (1985). 'Pay and Employment Determination in Britain: What are Labour Contracts Really Like?' *Oxford Review of Economic Policy*, 1, 80–97.

Payne, J. and Braunstein, M. (1971). "Preferences Among Gambles with Equal Underlying Distributions", *Journal of Experimental Psychology*, 87, 13–18.

Pearce, D. (1984). 'Rationalizable Strategic Behavior and the Problem of Perfection'. *Econometrica*, 52, 1029–50.

Phelps, E. S. (1967). 'Phillips Curves, Expectations of Inflation and Optimal Unemployment over Time'. *Economica*, 34, 254–81.

Pigou, A. C. (1938). *The Economics of Welfare*. London: Macmillan.

Plott, C. R. and Sunder, S. (1982). 'Efficiency of Experimental Security Markets With Insider Information: An Application of Rational-Expectations Models'. *Journal of Political Economy*, 90, 663–98.

Png, I. and Hirshleifer, D. (1987). 'Price Discrimination Through Offers to Match Price'. *Journal of Business*, 60, 365–83.

Polemarhakis, H. and Weiss, L. (1978). 'Fixed Wages, Layoffs, Unemployment Compensation and Welfare'. *American Economic Review*, 68, 909–17.

Pommerehne, W., Schneider, F., and Zweifel, P. (1982). 'Economic Theory of Choice and the Preference Reversal Phenomenon: A Reexamination'. *American Economic Review*, 72, 569–74.

Porter, R. (1983). 'Optimal Cartel Trigger Price Strategies'. *Journal of Economic Theory*, 29, 313–38.

Postelwaite, A. and Vives, X. (1987). 'Bank Runs as an Equilibrium Phenomenon'. *Journal of Political Economy*, 95, 485–91.

Pratt, J. (1964). 'Risk Aversion in the Small and in the Large'. *Econometrica*, 32, 122–36.

Preston, C. (1983). *Iterates of Maps on an Interval*. Berlin: Springer-Verlag.

Quiggin, J. (1982). 'A Theory of Anticipated Utility'. *Journal of Economic Behavior and Organization*, 3, 323–43.

Quinzii, M. and Rochet, J-C. (1984). 'Multidimensional Signaling'. Discussion Paper, Ecole Polytechnique.

Quizon, J. B., Binswanger, H. P., and Machina, M. J. (1984). 'Attitudes Towards Risk: Further Remarks'. *Economic Journal*, 94, 144–8.

Radner, R. (1979). 'Rational Expectations Equilibrium: Generic Existence and the Information Revealed by Prices'. *Econometrica*, 47, 655–78.

—— (1980). 'Collusive Behaviour in Noncooperative Epsilon—Equilibria of Oligopolies with Long but Finite Lives'. *Journal of Economic Theory*, 22, 136–54.

—— (1982). 'Equilibrium under Uncertainty'. In K. J. Arrow and M. D.

Intriligator (eds.), *Handbook of Mathematical Economics*, Vol. II. Amsterdam: North–Holland.

—— (1985). 'Repeated Principle–Agent Games with Discounting'. *Econometrica*, 53, 1173–98.

—— (1986). 'Repeated Partnership Games with Imperfect Monitoring and No Discounting'. *Review of Economic Studies*, 53, 43–57.

Raiffa, H. (1968). *Decision Analysis: Introductory Lectures on Choice under Uncertainty.* Reading, Mass.: Addison-Wesley.

Ramakrishnan, R. T. S. and Thakor, A. V. (1984). 'Information Reliability and a Theory of Financial Intermediation'. *Review of Economic Studies*, 51, 415–32.

Ramey, G. (1987). 'Product Quality Signaling and Market Performance'. Institute for Mathematical Studies in the Social Sciences, Technical Report no. 504, Stanford University.

Ramsey, F. (1926). 'Truth and Probability'. In Ramsey (1931); reprinted in Ramsey (1978).

—— (1931). *The Foundations of Mathematics and other Logical Essays.* New York: Harcourt Brace/London: K. Paul, Trench, Trubner.

—— (1978). *Foundations: Essays in Philosophy, Logic, Mathematics and Economics.* Atlantic Highlands, NJ: Humanities Press.

Rand, D. (1978). 'Exotic Phenomena in Games and Duopoly Models'. *Journal of Mathematical Economics*, 5, 173–84.

Reagan, P. B. (1982). 'Inventory and Price Behaviour'. *Review of Economic Studies*, 49, 137–42.

Reilly, R. (1982). 'Preference Reversal: Further Evidence and Some Suggested Modifications in Experimental Design'. *American Economic Review*, 72, 576–84.

Reinganum, J. (1981). 'On the Diffusion of New Technology: A Game-theoretic Approach'. *Review of Economic Studies*, 48, 395–405.

—— (1984a). 'Uncertain Innovation and the Persistence of Monopoly'. *American Economic Review*, 73, 741–8.

—— (1984b). 'Uncertain Innovation and the Persistence of Monopoly: Reply'. *American Economic Review*, 74, 243–6.

—— and Wilde, L. (1986). 'Settlement, Litigation and the Allocation of Litigation Costs'. *Rand Journal of Economics*, 17, 557–66.

Ricardo, D. (1951). *On the Principles of Political Economy, and Taxation*, ed. P. Sraffa (The Works and Correspondence of David Ricardo, vol. I). Cambridge University Press.

Riley, J. G. and Samuelson, W. F. (1981). 'Optimal Auctions'. *American Economic Review*, 71, 381–92.

Roberts, K. (1982). 'Long-term Contracts'. Mimeo, University of Warwick.

Roberts, J. and Sonnenschein, H. (1977). 'On the Foundations of the Theory of Monopolistic Competition'. *Econometrica*, 45, 101–13.

Rosenberg, N. (1986). 'The Impact of Technological Innovation: A Historical View'. In R. Landau and N. Rosenberg (eds.), *The Positive Sum Strategy.* Washington, DC: National Academy Press.

Ross, S. (1977). 'The Determination of Financial Structure: The Incentive-Signalling Approach'. *Bell Journal of Economics*, 8, 23–40.

Roth, A. (1979). *Axiomatic Models of Bargaining* (Lecture Notes in Economics and Mathematical Systems, 170). Berlin: Springer-Verlag.

—— and Schoumaker, F. (1983). 'Expectations and Reputations in Bargaining: An Experimental Study', *American Economic Review*, 73, 362–72.

Rothschild, M. (1974). 'A Two-armed Bandit Theory of Market Pricing. *Journal of Economic Theory*, 9, 185–212.

—— and Stiglitz, J. (1970). 'Increasing Risk: 1. A Definition'. *Journal of Economic Theory*, 2, 225–43.

—— and Stiglitz, J. (1976). 'Equilibrium in Competitive Insurance Markets: An Essay on the Economics of Imperfect Information'. *Quarterly Journal of Economics*, 90, 629–49.

Rubinstein, A. (1976). 'Equilibrium in Super-games'. Centre for Mathematical Economics and Game Theory, Hebrew University of Jerusalem.

—— (1979). 'Equilibrium in Supergames with the Overtaking Criterion'. *Journal of Economic Theory*, 21, 1–9.

—— (1980). 'Strong Perfect Equilibrium in Supergames'. *International Journal of Game Theory*, 37, 99–125.

—— (1982). 'Perfect Equilibrium in a Bargaining Model'. *Econometrica*, 50, 97–109.

—— (1985a). 'A Bargaining Model with Incomplete Information About Time Preferences'. *Econometrica*, 53, 1151–72.

—— (1985b). 'Choice of Conjectures in a Bargaining Game with Incomplete Information'. In A. Roth (ed.), *Game-theoretic Models of Bargaining*. Cambridge University Press.

—— (1986). 'Finite Automata Play the Repeated Prisoner's Dilemma'. *Journal of Economic Theory*, 39, 83–96.

—— and Wolinsky, A. (1986). 'Decenteralized Trading, Strategic Behaviour and the Walrasian Outcome'. Mimeo, Hebrew University of Jerusalem.

Sabourian, H. (1984a). 'Rational Conjectural Equilibrium in a Game Theoretic Framework, I and II'. Mimeo.

—— (1984b). 'An Imperfect Competition Model with Increasing Returns to Scale in a General Equilibrium Framework'. Mimeo.

—— (1984c). 'Anonymous Repeated Games with Large Number of Players Part I'. Mimeo.

—— (1986a). 'The Folk Theorem in Repeated Games with Bounded Memory', Mimeo.

—— (1986b). 'Refinements of Nash Equilibria in Repeated Games'. Mimeo.

—— (1987). 'Essays on Non-Walrasian Economics', Ph.D. thesis, Cambridge University.

—— (1988). 'Wage Norms and Involuntary Unemployment'. *Economic Journal*, 98 (Conference Papers), 177–88.

Salant, S. (1984). 'Preemptive Patenting and the Persistence of Monopoly: Comment'. *American Economic Review*, 74, 247–50.

Samet, D. (1987). 'Ignoring Ignorance and Agreeing to Disagree'. Discussion Paper no. 749, J. L. Kellogg Graduate School of Management, Northwestern University.

Samuelson, P. A. (1939). 'Interaction between the Multiplier Analysis and the Principle of Acceleration'. *Review of Economic Statistics*, 21, 75–8.

—— (1947). *Foundations of Economic Analysis*. Cambridge, Mass.: Harvard University Press.

—— (1952). 'Probability, Utility, and the Independence Axiom'. *Econometrica*, 20, 670–8.

—— (1954). 'The Pure Theory of Public Expenditure'. *Review of Economics and Statistics*, 36, 387–9.

—— (1958). 'An Exact Consumption–Loan Model of Interest with or without the Social Contrivance of Money'. *Journal of Political Economy*, 66, 467–82.

—— (1977). 'St Petersburg Paradoxes: Defanged, Dissected, and Historically Described'. *Journal of Economic Literature*, 15, 24–55.

Sanghari, A. P. and Sobel, M. J. (1976). 'Bayesian Games as a Stochastic Process'. *International Journal of Game Theory*, 5, 1–22.

Santos, M. S. and Bona, J. L. (1986). 'On the Structure of the Equilibrium Price Set of Overlapping Generations Economies'. *Journal of Mathematical Economics*, forthcoming.

Sargent, T. J. (1978). 'Estimation of Dynamic Labour Demand Schedules under Rational Expectations'. *Journal of Political Economy*, 86, 1009–44.

—— (1979). *Macroeconomic Theory*. New York: Academic Press.

—— (1987). *Dynamic Macroeconomic Theory*. Cambridge, Mass.: Harvard University Press.

Savage, L. J. (1954). *The Foundations of Statistics*. New York: John Wiley. Rev. and enlarged edn., New York: Dover Publications, 1972.

Scarf, H. (1960). 'The Optimality of (S, s) Policies in the Dynamic Inventory Problem'. In K. J. Arrow, S. Karlin and P. Suppes (eds.), *Mathematical Methods in the Social Sciences 1959*. Stanford University Press.

Scheinkman, J. and Weiss, L. (1986). 'Borrowing Constraints and Aggregate Economic Activity'. *Econometrica*, 54, 23–45.

Schelling, T. (1960). *The Strategy of Conflict*. Cambridge, Mass.: Harvard University Press.

Schmeidler, D. (1986). 'Subjective Probability and Expected Probability without Additivity'. *Econometrica*, 57, 571–87.

Schoemaker, P. J. H. (1982). 'The Expected Utility Model: Its Variants, Purposes, Evidence and Limitations'. *Journal of Economic Literature*, 20, 529–63.

—— and Kunreuther, H. (1979). 'An Experimental Study of Insurance Decisions'. *Journal of Risk and Insurance*, 46, 603–18.

Schwartzman, D. (1976). *Innovation in the Pharmaceutical Industry*. Baltimore: Johns Hopkins University Press.

Selten, R. (1965). 'Spieltheoretische Behandlung eines Oligopolmodels mit Nachfragetragheit'. *Zeitschrift fur die Gesamte Staatswissen Schaft*, 121.

—— (1975). 'A Re-examination of the Perfectness Concept for Equilibrium Points in Extensive Games'. *International Journal of Game Theory*, 4, 25–55.

—— (1978). 'The Chainstore Paradox'. *Theory and Decision*, 9, 127–59.

Sen, A. K. (1979). 'The Welfare Basis of Real Income Comparisons: A Survey'. *Journal of Economic Literature*, 17, 1–45.

Sengupta, J. K. (1985). *Optimal Decisions under Uncertainty*. Berlin: Springer-Verlag.

Shaked, A. and Sutton, J. (1984). 'Involuntary Unemployment as a Perfect Equilibrium in a Bargaining Model'. *Econometrica*, 52, 1351–64.

Shapley, L. S. (1953). 'Quota Solutions of *n*-person Games'. In H. Kuhn and A. Tucker (eds.), *Contributions to the Theory of Games*, Vol. II (Annals of Mathematical Studies, 28). Princeton University Press.

—— and Shubik, M. (1977). 'An Example of a Trading Economy with Three Competitive Equilibria'. *Journal of Political Economy*, 85, 873–5.

Shell, K. (1971). 'Notes on the Economics of Infinity'. *Journal of Political Economy*, 79, 1002–11.

Shin, H. (1987). 'Logical Structure of Common Knowledge, I. A Framework for the Analysis of Differential Information'. Unpublished paper, Nuffield College, Oxford.

Simon, H. A. (1976). 'From Substantive to Procedural Rationality'. In S. J. Latsis (ed.), *Method and Appraisal in Economics*. Cambridge University Press.

—— (1979). 'Rational Decision Making in Business Organizations'. *American Economic Review*, 69, 493–513.

Simon, L. and Stinchombe, M. (1986). 'Extensive Form Games in Continuous Time: Part I: Pure Strategies'. Mimeo.

Singer, D. (1978). 'Stable Orbits and Bifurcations of Maps of the Interval'. *SIAM Journal of Applied Mathematics*, 35, 260.

Slovic, P. (1969). 'Manipulating the Attractiveness of a Gamble without Changing its Expected Value'. *Journal of Experimental Psychology*, 79, 139–45.

—— and Tversky, A. (1974). 'Who Accepts Savage's Axiom?' *Behavioral Science*, 19, 368–73.

Smale, S. (1980). 'The Prisoner's Dilemma and Dynamical Systems Associated to Non-cooperative Games'. *Econometrica*, 48, 1617–34.

Smith, B. D. (1984). 'Private Information, Deposit Interest Rates, and the "Stability" of the Banking System'. *Journal of Monetary Economics*, 14, 293–317.

Snower, D. (1984). 'Rational Expectations, Non-linearities, and the Effectiveness of Monetary Policy'. *Oxford Economic Papers*, 36, 177–99.

Sobel, J. and Takahashi, I. (1983). 'A Multistage Model of Bargaining'. *Review of Economic Studies*, 50, 411–26.

Solow, R. M. (1982). 'On the Lender of Last Resort'. Ch. 10 in C. P. Kindleberger and J. P. Laffargue (eds.), *Financial Crises: Theory, History, and Policy*. Cambridge University Press.

Sparrow, C. (1982). *The Lorenz Equations: Bifurcations, Chaos, and Strange Attractors*. New York: Springer-Verlag.

Spear, S. E. (1984). 'Sufficient Conditions for the Existence of Sunspot Equilibria'. *Journal of Economic Theory*, 34, 360–70.

—— (1985). 'Rational Expectations in the Overlapping Generations Model'. *Journal of Economic Theory*, 35, 251–75.

Spence, A. M. (1974). *Market Signaling*. Cambridge, Mass.: Harvard University Press.

—— (1981). 'The Learning Curve and Competition'. *Bell Journal of Economics*, 12, 49–70.

Stahl, I. (1972). 'Bargaining Theory'. Stockholm School of Economics.

Stanford, W. (1986a). 'On Continuous Reaction Function Equilibria in Duopoly Supergames with Mean Payoffs'. *Journal of Economic Theory*, 39, 233–50.

—— (1986b), 'Subgame Perfect Reaction Function Equilibria in Discounted Duopoly Supergames are Trivial'. *Journal of Economic Theory*, 39, 226–32.

Starr, R. and Ho, Y. C. (1967a). 'Nonzero-Sum Differential Games'. *Journal of Optimization Theory and Applications*, 3, 184.

—— (1967b). 'Further Properties of Nonzero-Sum Games'. *Journal of Optimization Theory and Applications*, 3, 184.

Stigler, G. (1961). 'The Economics of Information'. *Journal of Political Economy*, 69, 213–25.

Stiglitz, J. E. (1982). 'Information and Capital Markets'. In W. F. Sharpe and C. M. Cootner (eds.), *Financial Economics: Essays in Honor of Paul Cootner*. Englewood Cliffs, NJ: Prentice-Hall.

—— and Mathewson, G. (eds.) (1986). *New Developments in the Analysis of Market Structure*. Basingstoke: Macmillan.

—— and Weiss, A. (1981). 'Credit Rationing in Markets with Imperfect Information'. *American Economic Review*, 71, 393–410.

—— and Weiss, A. (1985). 'Sorting Out the Differences Between Screening and Signaling Models'. Mimeo, Princeton University.

Stigum, B. and Wenstøp, F. (1983). *Foundations of Utility and Risk Theory with Applications*. Dordrecht, Holland: D. Reidel.

Sutton, J. (1986). 'Non-cooperative Bargaining Theory: An Introduction'. *Review of Economic Studies*, 53, 709–24.

——, Shaked, A., and Binmore, K. (1985). 'An Outside Option Experiment'. International Centre for Economics and Related Disciplines, London School of Economics, Discussion Paper no. 85/124.

Tan, T. and Werlang, S. (1985). 'On Aumann's Notion of Common Knowledge—An Alternative Approach'. Unpublished paper, Department of Economics, Princeton University.

—— (1988). 'The Bayesian Foundations of Solution Concepts of Games'. *Journal of Economic Theory*.

Tarshis, L. (1939). 'Changes in Real and Money Wages'. *Economic Journal*, 49, 150–4.

Thomas, J. and Worrall, T. (1984). 'Self-enforcing Wage Contracts'. Economic Theory Discussion Paper no. 74, Cambridge University.

—— (1985). 'Income Fluctuation and Asymmetric Information'. Mimeo, University of Western Ontario.

Thompson, F. (1952). 'Equivalence of Games in Extensive Form'. Research Memorandum RM-759, RAND Corporation, Santa Monica.

Thornton, H. (1802). *An Enquiry into the Nature and Effects of the Paper Credit of Great Britain*. Reprinted in 1939 by George Allen & Unwin, London.

Tiebout, C. M. (1956). 'A Pure Theory of Local Expenditures'. *Journal of Political Economy*, 64, 416–24.

Tintner, G. (1942). 'A Contribution to the Nonstatic Theory of Production'. In O. Lange, F. McIntyre, and T. Yntema (eds.), *Studies in Mathematical Economics and Econometrics*. Chicago University Press.

Tobin, J. (1958). 'Liquidity Preference as Behavior Towards Risk'. *Review of Economic Studies*, 25, 65–86.

Todhunter, I. (1865). *A History of the Mathematical Theory of Probability*.

Cambridge: University Press. Reprinted edn.: New York: Chelsea Publishing Co., 1949.

Turvey, R. (1963). 'On Divergences between Social Cost and Private Cost'. *Economica,* 31, 309–13.

Tversky, A. (1975). 'A Critique of Expected Utility Theory: Descriptive and Normative Considerations'. *Erkenntnis,* 9, 163–73.

—— and Kahneman, D. (1981). 'The Framing of Decisions and the Psychology of Choice'. *Science,* no. 211, 453–8.

—— (1986). 'Rational Choice and the Framing of Decisions'. *Journal of Business,* 59, S251–S278.

van Damme, E. (1984). 'A Relation between Perfect Equilibria in Extensive Form Games and Proper Equilibria in Normal Form Games'. *International Journal of Game Theory,* 13, 1–13.

Venables, A. J. (1984). International Trade in Identical Commodities: Cournot Equilibrium with Free Entry. Discussion Paper no. 9, Centre for Economic Policy Research, London.

Vickers, J. (1986). 'Pre-emptive Patenting, Joint Venture, and the Persistence of Oligopoly'. *International Journal of Industrial Organization,* 3.

Vickrey, W. (1961a). 'Auction and Bidding Games'. Mimeo.

—— (1961b). 'Counterspeculation, Auctions, and Competitive Sealed Tenders'. *Journal of Finance,* 16, 8–47.

von Neumann, J. and Morgenstern, O. (1944). *Theory of Games and Economic Behavior.* Princeton University Press (2nd edn. 1947; 3rd edn. 1953).

Weisbrod, B. A. (1964). 'Collective-Consumption Services of Individual-Consumption Goods'. *Quarterly Journal of Economics,* 78, 471–7.

Weiss, N. O. (1985). 'Chaotic Behavior in Stellar Dynamics'. *Journal of Statistical Physics,* 39, 477–91.

White, M. (1981). *Payment Systems in Britain.* Aldershot: Gower Press.

Wicksell, K. (1896). 'A New Principle of Just Taxation'. Translated in Musgrave and Peacock (1958).

Williamson, O. E., Wachter, M. L., and Harris, J. E. (1975). 'Understanding the Employment Relation: The Analysis of Idiosyncratic Exchange'. *Bell Journal of Economics,* 6, 250–78.

Wilson, C. A. (1981). 'Equilibrium in Dynamic Models with an Infinity of Agents'. *Journal of Economic Theory,* 24, 95–111.

Wilson, R. (1971). 'Computing Equilibria in *N*-person Games'. *SIAM Journal,* 21, 80–7.

Wilson, R. (1979). 'Auctions of Shares'. *Quarterly Journal of Economics,* 93, 675–90.

—— (1985a). 'Multi-dimensional Signaling'. Unpublished paper, Stanford University.

—— (1985b). 'Reputations in Games and Markets'. In A. E. Roth (ed.), *Game-Theoretic Models of Bargaining.* Cambridge University Press.

—— (1986). 'Efficient and Competitive Rationing via Priority Service'. Fisher–Schultz Lecture, European Meeting of the Econometric Society, Budapest, September? Mimeo, Stanford University.

—— (1987). 'Auction Theory'. In J. Eatwell, M. Milgate, and P. Newman (eds.), *The New Palgrave.* London: Macmillan.

Woodford, M. (1984). 'Indeterminacy of Equilibrium in the Overlapping Generations Model: A Survey'. Mimeo.

—— (1986a). 'Expectations, Finance Constraints, and the Instability of Investments'. *Journal of Economic Theory*, 40, 128–37.

—— (1986b). 'Learning to Believe in Sunspots'. Unpublished paper.

—— (1986a). 'Stationary Sunspot Equilibria: The Case of Small Fluctuations Around a Deterministic Steady State'. Mimeo.

—— (1987). 'Learning to Live with Sunspots'. Mimeo.

Worrall, T. (1983). 'Implicit Contracts and Asymmetric Information'. Economic Discussion Paper, no. 46, University of Liverpool.

Wright, B. D., and Williams, J. C. (1984). 'The Welfare Effects of the Introduction of Storage'. *Quarterly Journal of Economics*, 99, 169–92.

Yaari, M. (1987). 'The Dual Theory of Choice Under Risk'. *Econometrica*, 55, 95–115.

Younes, Yves (1984). 'Implementation of Plans or Contracts and Equilibria with Rationing'. CARESS Working Paper, no. 83-19, University of Pennsylvania.

Zarnowitz, V. (1985). 'Recent Work on Business Cycles in Historical Perspective'. *Journal of Economic Literature*, 23, 523–80.

Zemel, E. (1986). 'On Communication, Bounded Complexity and Cooperation'. Northwestern University Discussion Paper.

Index